WILLIE

Also by Robert Calder

W. Somerset Maugham and the Quest for Freedom

WILLIE

THE LIFE OF
W. SOMERSET MAUGHAM

Robert Calder

St. Martin's Press
New York

Library of Congress Cataloging-in-Publication Data

Calder, Robert.
    Willie : the life of W. Somerset Maugham / Robert Calder.
        p.   cm.
    ISBN 0-312-03954-9
    1. Maugham, W. Somerset (William Somerset), 1874–1965—Biography.
2. Authors, English—20th century—Biography. I. Title.
PR6025.A86Z5594 1990
823'.912—dc20
    [B]

89-27127
CIP

First published in Great Britain by William Heinemann Limited.

First U.S. Edition
10 9 8 7 6 5 4 3 2 1

For Lynda

CONTENTS

ILLUSTRATIONS

ACKNOWLEDGMENTS

I am deeply indebted to the late Alan Searle for his encouragement and generous assistance in the preparation of this book. Though I had been told by many people that I would receive no co-operation from him in the writing of a biography of Maugham, he immediately responded to my enquiry with an invitation to visit him in Monte Carlo. He had kept his promise to Maugham not to write about their life together, he said, and indeed he had not extensively assisted potential biographers. Having nevertheless grown increasingly concerned about the portrait of his friend emerging in a number of memoirs, and apprehensive of a full-scale biography which would further sensationalize and distort that picture, he was thus not opposed to a book which would be scholarly, accurate, and objective.

Over a period of five days in March 1977, and another in August 1981, I was able to interview Searle for about twenty-five hours. As one might expect, his memory of details was not always reliable, and there were areas about which he remained guarded. Nevertheless, he provided a great many insights into Maugham and the life they shared for thirty-five years. The excerpts from Searle's letters, published here for the first time, are printed with his permission.

Many other people generously assisted my research. Among those who agreed to be interviewed, I am especially grateful to Arthur Marshall, Ethel Mannin, Dame Rebecca West, Cynthia Harrison and Roderick Cameron, but in various ways all of the following contributed to my understanding of Maugham: Francis King, Raymond Mortimer, Georges Rosanoff, George Rylands, Lionel Hale, Peter Quennell,

Graham Sutherland, Ann Fleming, Raymond Marriott, J. C. Trewin, André David, Peter Burton, Grenville Cook, Richard Shulman, and Thorold Dickinson. Wallace Harvey, historian of Whitstable, and Paul Pollak, archivist of King's School, provided invaluable information about Maugham's early years.

The following people corresponded with me, some at considerable length and over a number of years: Joseph Dobrinsky, J. P. P. Newell, Lord Boothby, David Daiches, Patrick Back, Quentin Bell, Eric Ambler, Lovat Dickson, Lord Clark, Richard Cordell, Ludovic Kennedy, K. C. Harrison, H. Montgomery Hyde, Michael Holroyd, Cathleen Nesbitt, Raymond Toole Stott, J. B. Priestley, Norman Sherry, Frank Swinnerton, John Whitehead, Leopold Bellak, and Shirley Charters. Among others whose advice has been useful are: Peter Millard, Maryna Komolova, Wayne Schmalz, Neil Richards, and Len Conolly.

While I am grateful for the information and insights offered by all of these contributors, the responsibility for the judgements and conclusions in this book is mine.

It would be impossible to write a scholarly biography without consulting archival material, and I am indebted to the following institutions which not only made their holdings available to me but treated my enquiries with patience and generosity: the Fales Library, New York University; the Department of Special Collections, Stanford University Libraries; the Lilly Library, Indiana University; the Harry Ransom Humanities Research Center, University of Texas at Austin; the Bodleian Library, Oxford University; the National Register of Archives; the Imperial War Museum; the Theatre Museum; the University of London Library; the Beinicke Rare Book and Manuscript Library, the Yale University Library; the Berg Collection of English and American Literature, New York Public Library; the Central Registry Office, Somerset House; the British Library; the Public Records Office; the BBC Written Archives Centre; King's College Library, Cambridge University; St Thomas's Hospital; the Royal Literary Fund; the Murray Library, the University of Saskatchewan. The following provided copies of documents held in their collections: the Huntington Library; the University Library, University of Illinois at Urbana-Champaign; Princeton University Library; Columbia University Library; University of Arkansas Library; Northwestern University Library; University of Iowa Library; Metropolitan Toronto Library; and the Canadian Broadcasting Corporation.

I am indebted to several people who assisted in the preparation of the typescript. My friend Claud Thompson provided not only a wealth of shrewd advice but a judicious and sensitive reading of the manuscript. Kathy Swann meticulously transformed it into a typescript, and Lisa Glass patiently and carefully saw it through its copy-editing. I am especially grateful to Roger Smith, of Heinemann, for his enthusiastic support, judgement, and personal kindnesses. Throughout, my research has been generously sustained by grants from the Dean's Discretionary Fund, the President's Research Fund for the Social Sciences and Humanities, and the Publications Fund, of the University of Saskatchewan. Much of the book was completed on two sabbatical leaves. I was also assisted by a grant from the Social Sciences and Humanities Research Council of Canada.

As always, I have received the unqualified encouragement of my parents, and my children – Alison, Kevin, Lorin, and Dani – have come to understand my lengthy absences in pursuit of someone else's life. My greatest debt, however, is to Lynda Haverstock. Her fierce conviction and support were so much a part of a decade's work that this book is as much hers as mine.

PREFACE

I began working on this book fourteen years ago, when, following the completion of my critical study *W. Somerset Maugham and the Quest for Freedom*, I concluded that there was a need for a thorough, scholarly and objective biography of Maugham. Those who had known him had already begun to write fragmentary recollections – affectionate in Garson Kanin's *Remembering Mr Maugham* (1966) and caustic in Beverley Nichols's *A Case of Human Bondage* (1966) – but they did not examine his life as a whole.

Robin Maugham's *Somerset and All the Maughams* (1966), already in typescript on the day of Maugham's death, provided valuable genealogical material and some shrewd analysis of Maugham's character. Its scholarly element was contributed by the research assistant, Derek Peel, and when Robin went on to rework his Willie Maugham material in *Escape From the Shadows* (1972) and *Conversations With Willie* (1978), it became progressively less accurate and increasingly fabricated, heightening the melodramatic, sensational aspects with each rewriting. In fact, as Robin's friend and secretary Peter Burton has recently revealed, much of *Conversations With Willie* came from Robin's imagination and Burton's pen:

'I'm afraid we don't have enough conversations,' Robin complained one day. 'Do you think you can make some up?'
This was a task I didn't find at all difficult – and I must say that I'm still proud of my efforts. If Willie Maugham didn't actually say the words I put into his mouth, at least he could have done. I think I caught his tone of voice rather well.'[1]

Both Anthony Curtis's *Somerset Maugham* (1977) and Frederic Raphael's *Somerset Maugham and His World* (1974) are intelligent, objective, and balanced portraits, but neither can be considered a full biography. Similarly, Joseph Dobrinsky's shrewd *La Jeunesse de Somerset Maugham (1874–1903)* (1976), unavailable in English translation, deals with only the first thirty years of Maugham's life.

The first truly full-scale biography to use the wealth of archival material available in various institutions throughout the world was Ted Morgan's *Maugham* (1980). Having persuaded Maugham's first literary executor, Spencer Curtis Brown, to remove the ban on publication of previously unpublished material, he was able to draw extensively on Maugham's correspondence, especially the letters to Bertram Alanson, previously inaccessible at Stanford University. As well, Maugham's daughter, Lady Glendevon, was persuaded to end her silence about her father, and she and her husband provided Morgan with their version of Maugham's senile final years.

Alan Searle, on the other hand, remained apprehensive about the kind of biography that Morgan proposed to write, and he refused to co-operate. As a result, all of the information attributed to him in *Maugham* came to its author by way of Patrick O'Higgins, at one time secretary to Helena Rubinstein. O'Higgins had visited Maugham's villa several times, hoping apparently to replace Searle as the author's companion, and once planned to write his own biography of Maugham. It was the same O'Higgins who published a fictional account of a weekend at Cecil Beaton's Reddish House, including a spurious description of a visit by the Queen Mother. Its appearance in *Town and Country*, where it was presented as true, so embarrassed and infuriated Beaton that he accused O'Higgins of being 'a cheap gossip writer'.[2] It is thus hardly surprising that, since the appearance of *Maugham*, a number of people have written to various publications to dissociate themselves from comments attributed to them.

There is no doubt that *Maugham* contains more facts about the author's life than any previous book, and that it provides numerous excerpts from Maugham's correspondence, previously available only to those who could read it in various archives. The heart of any biography, however, is the selection and interpretation of this raw material, and it is here that Morgan's work is open to question.

Quite simply, *Maugham* reveals an essential distaste for its subject, which casts almost everything in the darkest light. Thus, while properly suspicious of the motives and veracity of Robin Maugham, Beverley Nichols, and many others, Morgan nevertheless perpetuates many of their often-told anecdotes which portray Maugham as malicious and vindictive. Maugham's correspondence, witty, playful, and often affectionate when read in context, has been carefully excerpted and frequently paraphrased to present his most caustic and cynical side, missing its light ironic touch. Similarly, Morgan always places the most pejorative interpretation on Maugham's attitudes and behaviour – arguing, for example, that he was anti-semitic, hated women, often quoted verbatim in his fiction, was always willing to compromise in order to be published, and was so thin-skinned that the slightest criticism would upset his writing for a week.

It is in the area of Maugham's sexual life and his relationships, however, that Morgan's antipathy to the man is most damaging. Though his treatment of Maugham's homosexuality is more explicit than anything previously published, it always emphasizes the nasty, procuring side of his homosexual life. At no time is there a recognition that a homosexual relationship might be supportive, sensitive, compassionate, and loving. As a result, all the melodramatic stories about Gerald Haxton are trotted out again, and Alan Searle, whose unselfish devotion to the ageing author in the difficult last years has been praised by all those who knew Maugham, is grossly misrepresented as a self-seeking sycophant.

My own interpretation of Maugham is obviously very different from Ted Morgan's. I am convinced that the longstanding and inaccurate perception of him as a malicious, bitter, and spiteful misanthrope must be replaced by a portrait which recognizes his sensitivity, wit, loyalty, and numerous kindnesses to many people. The story of his homosexuality and what his guilt about it did to him as a man and as a writer also needs to be explored in depth – in part because it may help explain how a generation of homosexual writers were forever scarred by the trial of Oscar Wilde and the vicious laws regarding homosexual conduct in Britain in effect until recently.

Whether my view of Willie Maugham is any more accurate than Ted Morgan's is, of course, for readers to decide. Unlike Morgan I had the opportunity to talk at length with Alan Searle, and I came away with a strong impression of a sensitive and caring man who had loved Maugham deeply. I was not able to meet Lady Glendevon – though I twice sought her assistance – but I do not think that this has coloured my treatment of their respective roles in the final, calamitous years of Maugham's life.

Regrettably, I am not permitted to quote from Maugham's correspondence. The present literary executor, the Royal Literary Fund, has decided that since it benefits from Maugham's will it should adhere to his wishes that none of his unpublished writing be published after his death. Understandable as this is, it prevents readers seeing the wit, warmth, and generosity revealed when he wrote as 'Willie' rather than 'W. Somerset Maugham'.

Extracts from Maugham's published works are reproduced with the permission of William Heinemann Ltd.

1

ORPHAN: 1874–1889

IT IS APPROPRIATE that William Somerset Maugham, the most widely travelled writer of his time, came into the world carrying a passport. His birth in France to English parents on 25 January 1874 was not on French soil but on a tiny island of British territory in Paris. Because the recent Franco-Prussian War had severely depleted the numbers of French troops, the French government was considering legislation that would require military service from all boys born in France. Since the British Embassy was legally foreign land, those born there would be exempt from French law, and so Willie Maugham became one of three children delivered within its walls.

In light of the events of the succeeding ninety-one years of his life, there is an aptness in the ambiguity of Maugham's birthplace and an irony in the attempt to free him from future military service. He would, after all, spend his first ten years in France, an alien whose first language was nevertheless French. Later, he would return to settle along the Côte d'Azur, which would be his residence for thirty-one years, though he would remain essentially English and deeply loyal to Britain. And, ironically, in both wars, he would offer himself to his country with an unusual alacrity and serve in a remarkable variety of ways, and often at considerable personal risk.

The privilege of Willie Maugham's birth in the Embassy came from his father's professional connections with the British delegation. Robert Ormond Maugham, following his own father's footsteps in the legal profession, had moved to France about 1848 to manage the Paris office of the firm he had established with Albert Dixon. Several years later he was appointed semi-officially to the position of solicitor to the British Embassy, which was located across the street from the offices of Maugham *et* Dixon, located at 54 rue du Faubourg Saint Honoré.

As Robin Maugham reveals in *Somerset and All the Maughams*, Robert's family was middle-class, having like Galsworthy's Forsytes risen from the land to the law in three generations. Until the eighteenth century the Maughams were farming stock when William Maugham's son Robert (born 1732) became a glazier. All but one of Robert's eight children joined the common migration to the cities, and the oldest, William (born 1759), moved to London. Little is known of William's occupation, but Robin Maugham is probably right when he suggests that he was in some way involved with the legal profession, perhaps as a clerk for one of the Chancery Lane stationers or booksellers.

Whatever the nature of William's connection with the law, his son Robert (born 1788) must have absorbed the atmosphere of Chancery Lane and the Inns of Court because he became an attorney in 1817. Before long Robert had achieved an affluence and stature far beyond that of even his immediate ancestors, and he went on to a distinguished legal career. One of the founders in 1825 and first secretary to what later became known as the Law Society, he edited the *Legal Observer*, which he created in 1830, for twenty-six years. As well, Robert was the first writer in what was to become a prolific literary family, producing a number of books on the law and one collection of essays.

A portrait of Robert Maugham hangs in the Chancery Lane building of the Law Society, and in *The Summing Up* Willie describes how he was impelled to view it when told by an old solicitor that his grandfather was 'the ugliest little man he ever saw'. The picture, however, conveyed a very different impression:

> If what my old gentleman said was true the painter must have grossly flattered my grandfather; he has given him very fine dark eyes under black eyebrows, and there is a faintly ironic twinkle in them; a firm jaw, a straight nose and pouting red lips. His dark hair is windswept as becomingly as that of Miss Anita Loos. He is holding a quill, and there is a pile of books, doubtless his own, by his side. Notwithstanding his black coat, he does not look so respectable as I should have expected, but slightly mischievous.[1]

Though this portrait persuaded Willie that his grandfather's lack of attractiveness had been exaggerated, he remained convinced that his own father was 'a very ugly man', who with his wife was known in

2

Paris as 'Beauty and the Beast'.[2] In this case, no photograph exists by which to judge the aptness of this title, though Robin Maugham uncovered a terracotta statuette of him in the office of a Paris law firm. When he gave his uncle a photograph of this piece, the older man was both curious and touched, not having been able to remember so many years later what his father looked like. As Robin pointed out, the small plump figure had crossed his legs in exactly the same manner as Willie did throughout his life.

Willie Maugham always believed that the greater part of a person's physical and psychological being was genetically determined and that there was little that one could do to alter certain essential traits. He had, for example, met a distantly related Maugham in New York in 1910, and was astonished to see a young man with dark hair, brown eyes, and sallow complexion – all his own features. Moreover his visitor was sensitive, Bohemian, and highly strung; and he spoke with an emphatic stammer. In him Willie saw essential familial characteristics which he felt were inescapable:

> We're the product of our genes and chromosomes. And there's nothing whatever we can do about it . . . No one can. Because we can't change the essential natures we're born with. We can't alter the essential product that we are. All we can do is try to supplement our own deficiencies.[3]

His father's short stature and manner of crossing his legs no doubt simply confirmed Willie's belief in family traits. The reputed ugliness of both father and paternal grandfather, however, may well have had a more destructive and lasting effect on him in adolescence and young manhood. It is hard to imagine that a sensitive, self-conscious young man with a strong belief in genetic determinism would not wonder if he had inherited unattractive features. It is perhaps here that one can find a source of the self-consciousness and feeling of inferiority which marked the writer throughout his adult life. It may explain Alfred Lunt's intriguing comment that Maugham was the exception to the rule that men always stare in mirrors more than women. 'Men', he said, 'are more vain of their appearance than women. They seem almost to pirouette with their reflections. I've known only one man who didn't look in mirrors. Somerset Maugham. He never looks in a mirror.'[4]

Notwithstanding his appearance, Robert Ormond Maugham was a good and loving father. One of the few recorded impressions of him is contained in Violet Hammersley's essay 'A Childhood in Paris', which is amplified by Robin Maugham's account of a conversation with her. The daughter of one of Maugham's mother's closest friends, Isabella Williams-Freeman, Violet was another of the children born in the Embassy in 1874 and she saw a good deal of the Maughams in her early childhood. She writes that Robert Maugham had 'a large, very sallow face one timidly explored, but when he took me on his knee to blow his watch open, I remember stealing over me a sense of complete safety and happiness.'⁵ To Robin, she confided that he was a loving parent and 'wonderfully kind to children'. 'Somehow', she said, 'there used to come out of him an intense sweetness which transformed him. You know he was a man of great virtue – a man one could tremendously respect. And he adored his wife.'⁶

Robert's wife, Edith, was indeed a woman worthy of adoration. In *The Summing Up*, Maugham describes her as 'very small, with large brown eyes and hair of a rich reddish gold, exquisite features, and a lovely skin. She was very much admired.'⁷ Violet Hammersley wrote that 'she was lovely, with russet hair, brown eyes and creamy complexion, and there was an air of romance and tragedy about her.'⁸ In his autobiography, *Stranger Within*,⁹ Sir Francis Oppenheimer recalls that Mrs Maugham was considered the beauty in the British community in Paris and delighted in arranging theatrical shows for her sons while they were on holiday from school in England.

Like the Maughams Edith's family were middle-class with roots in Cornwall. When her father, Major Charles Snell, died at the age of fifty in 1841, her mother returned to Europe with her two daughters to settle in Paris. There Mrs Snell and her younger daughter, Rose, earned a living writing novels and children's books in French – Mrs Snell produced twelve and Rose six. Edith, meanwhile, met and fell in love with Robert Maugham and they were married at the British Embassy on 1 October 1863. She was twenty-three; he was thirty-nine.

For seven years, the Maughams prospered. The well-established firm of Maugham *et* Dixon thrived, and Robert Maugham grew more affluent. According to Willie's brother, Frederic Herbert, their mother 'knew almost everyone worth knowing in Paris'.¹⁰ The Maughams lived on the third floor of 25 avenue d'Antin, a beautiful and spacious street near the Rond Point on the Champs-Élysées. The apartment was large, with a good-sized drawing-room and a billiard room, and they kept a large staff of servants. From here they entertained and were entertained by the British community connected with the Embassy.

Soon after their marriage the Maughams began a family, and in a period of less than four years in the mid-sixties, they produced three sons. Charles Ormond was born on 14 November 1865; Frederic Herbert on 20 October 1866; and Henry Neville on 12 June 1868. It was to be almost six years before the next child – William Somerset – was born, a passage of time which became a gulf between Willie and his brothers.

By the time that Willie was four, and before there was any likelihood of a bond developing with the older boys, they were sent to boarding-school at Dover College in England. Thus, as Frederic Raphael observes,[11] Willie had the illusion of being an only child, an impression which accounts for the absence of brothers in the autobiographical *Of Human Bondage*. As he grew older he must have been conscious not only of a distance from his siblings but that he was somehow different. They would all go to Dover College; he would attend King's School. They would all follow the family profession of law; he would become a writer. Though he would maintain contact with them for the remainder of their lives, at times even an affectionate link, there was never the deep loyalty and trust which comes from shared experiences and which often sustains sibling relationships. Indeed Charles's wife, Mabel, once told Robin that, though Willie used to visit them in Paris, 'he never really cared for any of us'.[12] And it is significant that he was closer to Frederic's wife, Helen, than he was to his own brother. All the first editions of his books sent to their home were inscribed, not to Frederic, but to her.

One reason for the break in the growth of the Maugham family must have been the Franco-Prussian War of 1870–71, which forced most British residents out of Paris. Robert took his family to London for the duration of the war and the bloody civil strife which swept the French capital, returning in August 1871 to rebuild his shattered practice. From then until his death thirteen years later, he worked very hard to regain the professional stature and affluence which he and his wife had previously enjoyed. According to Robin, Robert spent long days away from home and was rarely able to share the lives of his wife and children. It is not surprising, therefore, that in a memoir written at the end of his life Willie would refer to him in a single sentence: 'My father was a stranger to me.'[13]

With his mother, however, things were very different. The departure of his brothers to school, which made them distant figures, meant that the young Willie had her exclusive attention and love. His life then was one of emotional warmth, comfort, and security. With his nurse he shared a bedroom next door to his nursery, and twice a day he was taken out to play with French friends in the Champs-Élysées. Following the custom of the day and of his class, Willie saw his mother in a semi-formal manner, being allowed to go into her bedroom for a few minutes after she had taken her morning bath and was resting in bed. Later he would occasionally be brought in to tea and asked to recite for her friends the La Fontaine fable which he had memorized.

These contacts with his mother's social life gave the young boy an impression of the world of elegance and culture. At the time of her death, *Le Gaulois* wrote that she was a woman 'dont la beauté éblouissante rayonnait naguère dans nos plus élégants salons', and *Gil Blas* referred to her as 'une femme charmante, qui ne comptait que des amis dans la haute société parisienne, où elle occupait une des premières places.'[14] There was also, of course, the social life of the British community connected with the Embassy.

In the summer months the Maughams would rent a house at Deauville so that they could enjoy the seaside, and Maugham recalled his mother sitting on the beach, occupied with her embroidery and conversation and watching the three older boys playing along the shore. Too young to take part in the bathing, Willie was looked after by his nurse.

What we know of Willie Maugham's early years in Paris comes almost entirely from his own recollections and the research of his nephew. There is, however, one valuable outside view, the comments of Violet Hammersley, which, though brief, suggest a great deal. Recalling her mother's Sunday afternoon At Homes, she tells how her sister often invited Willie Maugham, who 'being considered highly imaginative'[15] was allowed to invent the games they would play. In the park, 'we kept to ourselves and Willie Maugham sometimes joined us, and fascinated us by distributing false *sous* at the *Kiosques* where paper windmills and coloured balloons and pieces of flat gingerbread pricked out in patterns were sold; or to the itinerant old woman with a tin strapped to her, out of which *gaufrettes* were produced, powdered with icing sugar. These we ate as we sat on benches watching Guignol.'[16]

This portrait, though brief, is of an imaginative, creative young boy who was considered an entertaining companion. It suggests that he also possessed a self-assuredness and sociability of a sort that is such a sharp contrast to the shy and self-conscious young man he was to become. He would go on to become one of the most popular entertainers in twentieth-century literature, but then from the seclusion of his study and at the distance provided by his pen. Most significantly,

Hammersley mentions nothing about a stammer, and when pressed about this by Robin she replied: 'No. I wasn't aware of whether he stammered or not as a child. But I remember that he told us wonderful stories.'[17] This is perhaps an ambiguous answer, but it is hard to believe that such a perceptive observer as Violet Hammersley would forget a stammer in a wonderful storyteller, an affliction which was to prevent Maugham from giving speeches or making radio broadcasts for much of his adult life.

As Anthony Curtis aptly remarks, 'What childhood could be more blissful, more privileged, more "normal"?'[18] For the young boy, the world was one of comfort, privilege, elegance, and security. With a father who, though distant, was a stable provider and a mother both beautiful and supportive, he thrived in what he was to call in *Of Human Bondage* 'the only love in the world that is quite unselfish'.[19] It was, unfortunately, to be the last time that Maugham ever believed that he was so cherished.

The seeds of destruction of Willie's world of love and security were probably sown before his birth. For some time, Edith Maugham had suffered from tuberculosis, the disease from which her sister Rose had died in 1869 at the age of twenty-seven. Her illness deepened, and one of Willie's childhood memories was of the string of donkeys which stopped at the building to provide her with the asses' milk which was reputed to inhibit the disease. As well, he and his nurse would spend part of each winter with Edith at Pau, a health resort near the Spanish border, so that the fresh air and warm climate might alleviate her suffering.

In the summer of 1881 Edith Maugham again became pregnant, likely on the advice of doctors who believed that having a child was beneficial to women with tuberculosis. Then, realizing that she was dying, she dressed in a white satin evening gown and had herself photographed. In *Of Human Bondage*, the episode is described at greater length than in *The Summing Up*, with an emphasis on the mother's desperate wish that she should not be extinguished entirely, even from the memory of her son:

> She could not bear to think that he would grow up and forget, forget her utterly; and she had loved him so passionately, because he was weakly and deformed, and because he was her child . . . She wanted her son to know what she looked like at the end. He could not forget her then, not forget utterly.[20]

Willie's mother gave birth to her sixth son – an earlier one had been stillborn – Alan Edward, on 24 January 1882, and he survived only twenty-four hours. Then on 31 January, six days after Willie's eighth birthday, Edith Maugham died at the age of forty-one.

The death of his mother was the most traumatic experience of Maugham's life. It was a devastation from which he would never recover, and it would profoundly shape his personality and the direction of his life. Characteristically, he would not – or could not – write about it at length in his autobiographical non-fiction, but the early pages of *Of Human Bondage* poignantly convey the deep sense of loss. There, in the experience of Philip Carey, he describes the happiness of 'the large warm bed, with those soft arms about him',[21] and then the shocked disbelief when he is told that he will never see his mother again. The most moving evocation of his sense of loss is the passage in which Philip is told to choose something from the drawing-room with which to remember his parents:

> Philip opened a large cupboard filled with dresses and, stepping in, took as many of them as he could in his arms and buried his face in them. They smelt of the scent his mother used. Then he pulled open the drawers, filled with his mother's things, and looked at them: there were lavender bags among the linen, and the scent was fresh and pleasant. The strangeness of the room left it, and it seemed to him that his mother had just gone out for a walk. She would be in presently and would come upstairs to have nursery tea with him. And he seemed to feel her kiss on his lips.
>
> It was not true that he would never see her again. It was not true simply because it was impossible. He climbed up on the bed and put his head on the pillow. He lay there quite still.[22]

Edith Maugham was not only remembered by her son; she haunted the remainder of his life. *Of Human Bondage* was written to free him from the pain of her loss and in *The Summing Up*, published twenty-three years later, Maugham noted with dispassionate brevity that 'after my mother's death, her maid became my nurse'.[23] When in the nineteen-forties, however, he was asked to make a recording of excerpts from the novel, he broke down when he had read only ten or twelve lines of the passage about the death of Philip's mother and he was unable to continue.

In Maugham's final years when his self-control collapsed he became periodically racked with pain over a loss which had occurred over eighty years earlier. Robin Maugham reports, for example, that once at the dinner table his uncle suddenly exclaimed: 'I shall never get over it.'[24] It is hardly surprising then that on his last visit to the Villa Mauresque the English journalist Godfrey Winn found Maugham standing in front of his mother's picture in tears.[25] And Alan Searle once told writer Lionel Hale that the old man's periodic bouts of weeping over his mother occurred in the last twenty years of his life.[26] He kept three photographs of her on his bedside table for eighty-three years, and they were there on the day he died.

One of the effects of this life-long wound was a particular sensitivity to the pain of others who had lost their mother. Hugh Walpole was among those who received a sympathetic letter from Maugham when he suffered such a loss in 1925. Much later Noël Coward fled England in anguish over the death of Violet Coward and found solace in the Villa Mauresque in July 1954. 'Willie,' he noted in his diary, was 'merry as a grig and mellow and sweet.'[27] Rather than being jealous of someone who had his mother's love until he was fifty-four, or cynical about the other's grief, Maugham was obviously touched and sympathetic.

But Edith Maugham's death shaped her son's life in much more profound ways, and he truly never did get over it. In 1896 the young writer observed in his notebook that 'few misfortunes can befall a boy which bring worse consequences than to have a really affectionate mother.'[28] This bitter comment may refer to the domestic problems of a friend, but it is more likely confessional. What, we might ask, did Maugham at the age of twenty-two recognize as the 'worse consequences' of the loss of his mother's affection?

Any discussion of the effect of the death of Edith Maugham on her youngest son must acknowledge the compounding of the trauma by the death from cancer of Robert Maugham two and a half years later. It is surely no accident that Philip Carey is nine years old at the time of his mother's death, the median between Willie's ages when he lost each parent. At ten, he no longer had the love of mother or father, and he no longer had a home.

There can be no doubt, however, that Willie's strongest attachment was to his mother, and that she represented – or in recollection came to represent – security and love. Robin Maugham is surely right when he states: 'Her love, her protection, her physical beauty, her comfortable apartment, and her elegant pattern of living – all were suddenly torn away from him and replaced soon after by an environment so alien and bleak and lacking in affection that it scarred his mind forever.'[29]

One of the more apparent scars may well be Maugham's stutter, often incorrectly referred to as a 'stammer'. A stammer is the involuntary repetition of syllables or words, whereas a stutter is the spasmodic repetition of sounds, usually the initial letters of words. From the many attempts to capture Maugham's speech in print – for example, Arthur Marshall's 'I felt I h-h-h-had to tell him the t-t-truth'[30] – there can be no doubt that Maugham's impediment was a stutter. Though stuttering may be caused by damage to the speech centre of the brain or to the nerves involved in speech, general medical opinion argues that it has its origins in the psychology of the individual. Many specialists attribute it to a disturbed home life or to a severe emotional shock.

There is no way of being certain that Maugham's stutter began with the death of his mother. There is, though, no evidence that he suffered from it prior to 1882, and Maugham's own first reference to it belongs to the Whitstable period. The shock of leaving his Paris home to live in England with his aunt and uncle, in a country where he spoke the language imperfectly, may of course have been important causes. But for a young boy the loss of a comforting and secure home, and dependable and loving parents, likely robbed him of the self-assurance that made him such an amusing companion for his young Paris friends.

It is significant that a number of those who knew Maugham attribute his worst bouts of stuttering to nervousness or self-consciousness. Both Arthur Marshall and his personal physician for the last twenty years of his life, Dr Georges Rosanoff, have told me that the impediment was most pronounced when Maugham was nervous. Similarly, the Canadian poet Ralph Gustafson, who knew Maugham during the Second World War, places the blame on his homosexuality and also 'misapprehension of him'.[31] Lord Boothby, one of the most loyal friends of the last half of his life, has written that 'he was very fond of me. When we were alone together the stammer practically disappeared: and, perhaps more important, he knew that I was very fond of him.'[32]

Another acquaintance of the later years, the writer Frederic Prokosch, agrees with the idea of a psychological basis for the stutter, but he sees it as a more calculated defence mechanism. 'At times', he writes, 'I suspected that Maugham's stammer was really a stratagem. I noticed that he stammered over commonplace words which in their very banality seemed to present some emotional barrier. He seemed to stammer in order to give his words a reluctant emphasis, to set them in perspective, to give them an air of struggle. But also perhaps to set up obstacles against an uninhibited sincerity. Thus his stammer (or so it seemed) provided him with a vocal shield.'[33]

Maugham's stutter was probably the result of a severe loss of confidence induced by a cluster of circumstances, including the death of his father, the loss of his home, the sudden demand to speak in a second language, and the cheerless milieu of the vicarage in Whitstable and the hostile environment of King's School. The death of Edith Maugham, however, must surely have been a primary cause, just as it must have helped shape Maugham's homosexual temperament.

In the past thirty years there has been an increasing amount of literature about homosexuality. This ranges from the early theories that it is an abnormality, a neurosis marked by flight from heterosexual relations, to the contemporary gay liberation position that homosexuality is simply an alternative sexual orientation. In general, earlier belief in constitutional, hereditary, or endocrine causes has been replaced by an emphasis on psychological, cultural, and social factors. Throughout there is a strong consensus that the dominant influences which create the homosexual can be found in childhood.

The most common theory of the origin of the homosexual temperament argues that children are not born with a sexual instinct exclusively directed to one sex. In Freud's words, 'Freedom to range equally over male and female objects – as is found in childhood, in primitive states of society, and early periods of history, is the original basis from which, as a result of restriction in one direction or another, both the normal and inverted types develop.'[34] More recently, a 1987 study by Johns Hopkins University psychiatrist John Money suggests that, though a prenatal release of certain hormones may give a child a sexual predisposition, the most significant factors are introduced after birth: 'Sexual orientation is not under the direct governance of chromosomes and genes, and . . . whereas it is not foreordained by prenatal brain hormonalization, it is influenced thereby, and is also *strongly dependent on postnatal socialization*.'[35] In much of the world, but by no means all of it, the socialization, together with the recognition of biological responsibilities, sanctions heterosexuality and condemns homosexuality.

In the Freudian interpretation, most children develop an Oedipal attraction to the parent of the other sex, but this normally disappears with maturity. In some, however, the development is arrested, and the individual becomes emotionally frozen at a childish level. Some respond by attempting to reject all sexual feelings, while others become unresponsive to all members of the opposite sex and can function sexually only with their own kind.

In an overwhelming number of cases this arrested development is

11

caused by severe social, physical, or emotional deprivation. In discussing male homosexuality Daniel Cappon writes:

> Severe social, physical, and emotional deprivation . . . is probably the single most powerful group of factors in the genesis of neurosis. Variants on this theme are: the death of the mother or her loss early in life, a broken home early in life, the prolonged hospitalization of the infant, physical and mental rejection and neglect of the child, or the child's many physical illnesses, deformity, or ugliness.
>
> In the operation of this theme, there is an arrest at a primary or early secondary narcissistic level. When all is lost to the infant or to the young child, or when love is felt to be absent or lost, there is, as a last resort, only one object that cannot be taken away without taking life itself – the child's own body. The body then becomes the object invested (i.e. cathected) with love or with a concentration of interest, attention and care. Later, there is an attempt to shift this object from one's own body to the body of another person of the same sex. The nearer to birth the child's psychological burn occurs, the more deep-rooted the pathological effect.[36]

Cappon's identification of the relationship with the mother as a primary factor in the formation of a homosexual is a theory held by many psychologists. Kenneth Jones, Louis Shainberg, and Curtis Byer, for example, point out that the homosexual male is often found to have had an unusually strong attachment to his mother or sister, a fixation often accompanied by a failure to identify with the parent of the same sex.[37] D. J. West is even more emphatic: 'One point stands out above all others – their unusual attachment to mother.'[38]

In this brief, and admittedly selective, summary of the theory of the development of homosexuality, it is easy to recognize a number of parallels to Maugham's childhood experience. There is the death of a beloved mother, the broken home, and the inability to identify with a vaguely known father (who, in any case, died when the boy was ten). Combined with the emotionally bleak life at the vicarage, and the exclusively male environment of King's School, this is almost a text-book formula for the creation of a homosexual.

In so many ways, the death of Edith Maugham was a blow which was profoundly to shape Maugham's life and work. In Leon Edel's words, Maugham 'had lived in a fool's paradise', and his frustration, rage, deception, despair, and guilt over its loss would be manifested over and over again in his writing. This accounts for the positive treatment of maternal women in his fiction: Norah Nesbit and Sally Athelny in *Of Human Bondage*, and Rosie in *Cakes and Ale*. Moreover, the sense of betrayal would underlie many of his reactions to other losses. 'When Maugham wept publicly at Haxton's funeral,' argues Edel, 'we may be sure he was also weeping for that long-lost mother who had unknowingly created his lost paradise.'[39]

Here too may lie the source of Maugham's distress over an incident which he recounted to Godfrey Winn. Very late in his life, he was trying to find the grave of Goethe's beloved in a cemetery near Strasburg. 'Instead,' writes Winn, 'he found a mound with a simple wooden cross, giving the names of a British bomber crew shot down in the war. One of the bodies was unidentifiable, so someone had added: "And here too, a young Englishman known only to God." Tears streamed down his cheeks as he spoke.'[40] There is a particular pathos in the idea of the person whose identity is lost to this world, his soul known only to God. Maugham, who always had a special sympathy for orphans, must have seen himself as a kind of unknown soldier, cast out from the love of his parents to wander in a world of strangers. A confirmed agnostic, however, he could hold no hope that he would ever again be known to the mother whose picture he kept with him, and there was not a God to whom he could look for recognition.

Edith Maugham's death created an essential loneliness and aloofness in her youngest son. For the next two and a half years, with his brothers away at school, his family consisted only of his sixty-year-old father. He was taken away from the French school he had always attended and was tutored by an English clergyman whose method of teaching English was, curiously, to have the young boy read aloud the accounts of police court cases reported in the *Standard*. This, it has been suggested, may have contributed to the emphasis on crime, especially murder, found in so much of his work.

In *The Summing Up*, Maugham recounts how he would accompany his father every Sunday to Suresnes to view the building of a summer house. Like his son after him, Robert enjoyed travelling, and he had brought back a sign against the evil eye from Morocco, a logo which Maugham would make famous the world over on the covers of his books. When the house was nearly complete, Maugham later wrote with deceptive brevity, 'my father died'.[41]

Robert Maugham's death on 24 June 1884 left a legacy to each of his sons of only £150 a year. Charles was eighteen and at Cambridge, while the seventeen-year-old Frederic and sixteen-year-old Henry were still at Dover College; and under the guardianship of their father's partner, Albert Dixon, all three went on to pursue careers in law. They seem, in Robin Maugham's words, to have been 'hearty, normal and robust'.[42] Willie, however, did not attend the family school. He was sent to King's School, Canterbury, and given over to the guardianship of an uncle, the Reverend Henry MacDonald Maugham, the vicar of All Saints' Church, Whitstable. He would see his brothers periodically for the rest of their lives, but they would be no closer to him than distant cousins.

When Willie crossed the English Channel in the company of his nurse, he was entering another kind of alien territory. Writing of his childhood in France, Rebecca West argues that 'even then he must have looked about him with the detached air of one who knows that there are other societies than the one around him, other standards than those with which it presents him.'[43] Maugham came to recognize this cultural detachment in himself, as his introduction to *A Traveller's Library* reveals. 'The accident of my birth,' he writes, 'which . . . instilled into me two modes of life, two liberties, two points of view, has prevented me from ever identifying myself completely with the instincts and prejudices of one people or the other, and it is in instinct and prejudice that sympathy is most deeply rooted.'[44]

The young Maugham then must surely have felt culturally adrift when he arrived in England as a stranger who could not properly speak the language. He has described, for example, the humiliation of shouting 'Porteur, Cabriolet!' on the Dover quayside and of mispronouncing 'unstable as water' in preparatory school. He was an outsider, and he knew that he was different from the boys who had grown up on English soil.

The trauma of moving from the comfortable and familiar apartment in the avenue d'Antin to the vicarage was exacerbated by the vicar's dismissal of Willie's nurse. As he related to his nephew many years later, he was told of this decision on the night of his arrival in Whitstable:

> As soon as we arrived that night at the vicarage . . . my uncle broke the news to me that my nurse was to be sent away because they couldn't afford to keep her on. After both my mother and my father had died my nurse was the only person in the world I loved. She was my one link with all the happiness and affection I'd known in the Avenue d'Antin. She was the only real friend I had. You see, my brothers were older than I was. But my nurse had been with me constantly since my mother died. She'd been my mother's maid, you know. And I think

she was as fond of me as I was of her. She was my last link with my mother and all that she had meant to me. And they took her away from me that very night.[45]

'I shall never forget', he would say, 'the misery of those next few years.'[46] So seared in his memory was the pain of his early life that for much of the remainder of his days he sought to bury it. 'He never', wrote Hamilton Basso in 1945, 'talks about his childhood if he can help it.'[47]

Maugham has provided portraits of the vicar and his wife in two of his novels – caustically in *Of Human Bondage* and more sympathetically in *Cakes and Ale*. From all accounts the Revd Mr Maugham was narrow-minded, unintelligent, pedantic, lazy, snobbish, and severe. His German-born wife, Sophie, was affectionate but prim and strait-laced. When Willie arrived from France the couple were in their fifties and childless, and certainly ill-suited to raise a sensitive young boy who had just lost both parents. The well-ordered life of the vicarage revolved around the personality and habits of the vicar, and in a multitude of ways Willie was made to feel that he was an intruder on its serenity.

As the young boy settled into their lives, the vicar and his wife became attached to him, and he developed an affection for his aunt. Even his uncle, whom he largely detested, offered Willie some emotional support, as the following comment from *Of Human Bondage* suggests: 'At first he was shy with his uncle, but little by little grew used to him, and he would slip his hand in his uncle's and would walk more easily for the feeling of protection.'[48]

Whatever else it might be, the guardianship of Henry and Sophie Maugham did at least provide some form of security for the young orphan. Even here, though, Willie's world was not certain. As the pages of the *Whitstable Times* newspaper reveal, the health of both the vicar and his wife was far from sound. Less than two years after Willie's arrival, his guardians were forced to go to the Continent for the health of Mrs Maugham (who was to die in August 1892). In July 1887 the vicar spent six weeks in Vichy 'to recruit his health',[49] and in 1888 he clearly suffered a major breakdown. In March the *Times* reported that the Revd Maugham 'who is suffering from a very serious illness, is somewhat better, and that he is pronounced to be out of danger.'[50] On 13 October the paper carried the following letter from the vicar:

To the Editor.

Sir,

Being about to leave home to winter in a more southern climate, I trust you will allow me, through the medium of your valuable paper, to return my sincere thanks to the many kind neighbours and friends who have enquired after me, and shown much sympathy during my severe and protracted illness.

I am, Sir, your obedient servant.

H. M. Maugham.

The Vicarage,
Whitstable.[51]

Maugham's uncle spent eight months on the Continent before being able to resume his duties in June 1889. He died eight years later just as Maugham's first novel was published.

In *Of Human Bondage* Philip longs for the death of his uncle, but this takes place when he is much older than Willie was during his uncle's illnesses. Maugham does not mention the vicar's poor health in any of his memoirs, and it is impossible to know what, at the age of fourteen, were his reactions to it. Having seen both parents succumb to terminal illnesses, however, he must have been especially sensitive to the possibility of losing his aunt and uncle and once again finding himself homeless. His remaining guardian would be Albert Dixon, his father's law partner, and there was no telling where he might be placed.

While the vicarage provided some sort of security for the young boy, Maugham experienced the alienation of a child who is suddenly put in the care, not of loving and forgiving parents, but of virtual strangers. Quite simply, his childhood was a period of emotional starvation, and there can be no more powerful evidence of this than a confessional remark which, at the age of sixty-three, he recorded in his notebook: 'He had had so little love when he was small that later it embarrassed him to be loved. It made him feel shy and awkward when someone told him that his nose was good and his eyes mysterious. He did not know what to say when someone paid him a compliment, and a manifestation of affection made him feel a fool.'[52]

The vicarage was a large yellow brick building located away from the centre of town on the road to Canterbury, and more than a mile from All Saints' Church. Overlooking the fields which were the vicar's tithes, it had a spacious garden, stables, and a coach house. As parsimonious as the Maughams were, they were able to keep a gardener and two maids. The front of the house, built like a church porch and used only by persons of importance, looked out on a drive. Directly above the doorway was a tiny room which became Willie's bedchamber, 'a small room for a small boy'[53] as Philip's aunt says in *Of Human Bondage*. Here was where he would come to terms with his loneliness and dream of a time when he would be master of his own life; and when Maugham climbed the stairs to revisit it in later years he was overcome with nostalgia.[54]

Whitstable in the 1880s was a fishing port dependent upon its famous oyster industry and the 300 merchant vessels which carried on their trade from there. It was built around a long winding street which led from the Thames Estuary harbour to the Kentish countryside to the south. Around the harbour was a honeycomb of narrow alleys, and along the beach were boats for hire, tea booths, bathing machines, and public houses. One such tea booth was owned by Mark Kemp who, according to Whitstable historian Wallace Harvey, used to make model yachts for the local boys, one of whom was Willie Maugham. These would be sailed in the 'backwater', a reservoir behind the harbour.

Though Whitstable might be parochial and sedate compared to Paris, there was much to excite the imagination of a young child. And Maugham's use of it in *Of Human Bondage, Cakes and Ale, Mrs Craddock*, and several short stories, indicates that it did indeed make an impression on him. He took the name of the promiscuous heroine of *Cakes and Ale*, 'Rosie Gann', from one of two Whitstable women – either a sensual young woman of his age or the respectable wife of a prominent townsman. 'Driffield' came from the town's grocer, 'Kear' from a nearby farming family, and 'Lord Scallion' from Henry Gann, whose sexual proclivities had given him the nickname of 'Lord Stallion'.

Even when Maugham had begun boarding-school in Canterbury he continued to be aware of Whitstable life, and one event in the spring of 1886 clearly made such an impression on the twelve-year-old boy that he remembered it vividly four decades later when he wrote *Cakes and Ale*. It has always been assumed that the flamboyant rogue Lord George Kemp, who suddenly absconds from Blackstable with £1500, leaving numerous debts and a penniless wife, to join Rosie in New York, was largely a fictional creation. The truth is that Maugham was retelling one of Whitstable's most sensational scandals.

As the pages of the *Whitstable Times* indicate, the Kemp family was prominent in the town, and George Kemp, who captained the Whitstable United Cricket Club, was the Registrar of Births and Deaths for the district as well as treasurer of the Whitstable Oyster Company. On 10 April 1886, the *Times* carried a seemingly unimportant announcement that George Kemp had unexpectedly resigned the office of Registrar, but a week later the news was dramatic. Under a headline reading THE DISAPPEARANCE OF MR G. KEMP, the paper reported that this respected citizen had vanished several weeks earlier and was last seen in London. A meeting of the Whitstable Oyster Company revealed that the sum of £2664 was missing from its accounts, and a warrant for Kemp's arrest was issued.

A measure of the excitement which the affair injected into the normally uneventful life of Whitstable can be found in the *Times's* comment that 'the disappearance of Mr Geo. Kemp and his defalcations as Treasurer to the Whitstable Oyster Company continue to be the all-absorbing topic of conversation in the town, fresh zest having been imparted to it this week by the holding of a special meeting of the company.'[55] It was decided to offer a reward of £100 for Kemp's apprehension, but he remained elusive, having escaped to France and then, like Maugham's rogue, to America. Since the Kemp family were prominent shareholders in the Oyster Company, making it to some degree a closed shop, it was decided to abandon the pursuit. In such a parochial community as Whitstable it was more diplomatic simply to forget.

Though the Kemp scandal obviously fascinated the young boy, his recollections were primarily of a way of life that was dull, narrow, and snobbish. Whitstable social interaction was largely determined by class distinctions and by religious belief, and within these lines the Maughams were particularly restrictive. The vicar, for example, did not approve of the London holidaymakers who would come to Kent each summer, and he preferred to spend July and August abroad so as to avoid dealing with them. Once when a wealthy banker rented a nearby house, Mrs Maugham refused to call on his wife because her husband was in trade. There was, of course, no question of anything but the briefest contact with local tradesmen, fishermen, servants, or other working-class people. Furthermore, the vicar refused to have anything to do with the chapel people – even to the point of not talking to them – and his wife would cross the street to avoid meeting a dissenting minister.

Geographically, too, the Maughams kept within narrow limits.

Kentish writer Robert Goodsall has astutely pointed out that 'those with a knowledge of the district at the turn of the century cannot but be aware of the smallness of the circles in which the Maughams moved, restricted to the main street and the western end of the town.'[56] Nowhere in Maugham's writing, argues Goodsall, is there any reference to the one important house in the area, Tankerton Tower, nor is there any indication that he ever wandered along the beach or along the cliffs to the east of Whitstable Harbour. His knowledge of the town was restricted to what he could see when he accompanied his aunt as she shopped on the High Street, though *Mrs Craddock* shows that as he grew older he must have explored the beach to the west of the town.

To the young Willie, his guardian's life was not only narrow but pretentious. 'My uncle toadied to the local squire,' he told his nephew, 'and the man was just a vulgar lout. He'd *never* have been tolerated in my mother's drawing-room. My uncle was a cracking snob.'[57] Judging by the autobiographical portraits in *Of Human Bondage* and *Cakes and Ale*, however, it is clear that Willie too became a snob. His sense of the difference between the *habitués* of his mother's salon and those people respected by the vicar suggests a well-formed sense of class distinctions. In Whitstable this soon took on the coloration of local structures. In *Cakes and Ale* Maugham refers to Ashenden's attitude of superiority and to sharing the disdain for the 'rag-tag and bobtail' of summer visitors from London, though their presence might be good for the tradespeople. When he is invited to play with Lord George Kemp's children, he refuses on the grounds that he cannot possibly have anything to do with them because they attend grammar school. His sense of his own social status is vividly conveyed when he encounters his uncle's curate in the company of a man wearing a knickerbocker suit:

> Knickerbockers were uncommon then, at least in Blackstable, and being young and fresh from school I immediately set the fellow down as a cad . . . I felt that for two pins he would have joined in the conversation and I assumed a haughty demeanour. I was not going to run the risk of being spoken to by a chap who wore knickerbockers like a game-keeper and I resented the familiarity of his good-humoured expression. I was myself faultlessly dressed in white flannel trousers, a blue blazer with the arms of my school on the breast pocket, and a black-and-white straw hat with a very wide brim.[58]

Within the narrow world of Whitstable society Willie's life was especially circumscribed. In *Of Human Bondage* when a house across from the vicarage is rented for six weeks by a man with two boys, Philip is not allowed to accept an invitation to join them in their play. In *Cakes and Ale* Willie Ashenden is able to bring a banker's son to the vicarage but he is not permitted to go to the other's house. An indication of the restrictions on young Willie can be found in his fear of being seen with people of whom his guardians did not approve, and in his certainty that if he asked permission to go brass-rubbing with the Driffields it would automatically be denied. It is hardly surprising then that James Robert Smith, who was two years younger than Maugham and delivered the *Times* to the vicarage, could tell Robin Maugham that he had never met Willie, though he had seen him from a distance a number of times.[59]

Maugham's contact with Whitstable life was obviously monitored, and he passed his years in the town almost unnoticed. The *Whitstable Times* was a weekly newspaper devoted to local news: articles about the freezing of the oyster beds, the threat of the North American competition, or the success of the latest harvest; shipping news; accounts of minor accidents to children and adults; notices of meetings of the Order of Foresters and other societies; descriptions of entertainments where local people sang or played instruments; and gossip about visitors, departing holidaymakers, or scholarship winners who were bringing glory to the community. Little of any note went on in the town which did not find its way into the columns of the *Times*. Yet in all its pages from 1884 to 1894 there is not a single mention of Willie Maugham. Though he might be the nephew of the vicar (who is mentioned on a number of occasions), a King's School scholarship student, and a traveller to the Continent, he seems to have been nearly invisible to the people of Whitstable.

The little contact Maugham did have with other children appears to have been unpleasant and certainly not the kind of thing to allay the fears of a shy boy in a new milieu. During the year before he went away to school he was tutored at Ivy House, the home of a local doctor called Etheridge, whose daughter Charlotte recalled that Willie was then an object of ridicule. He wore a velvet knickerbocker suit with a white lace collar, which led the children to laugh at him and call him 'Little Lord Fauntleroy'.[60] No longer a sought-after companion, he had become a figure of fun.

Charlotte Etheridge remembered also that Willie had an acute stutter, and years later he described how it led to at least one embarrassing incident which was forever burned in his memory. On a day trip to London with his uncle, he was sent to the railway station to purchase his ticket and return home alone. After waiting in a long queue, he found that he could not get the word 'Whitstable' out when his turn came. After a few agonizing moments which seemed like an eternity, two men sharply pushed him aside and he was forced to go back to the end of the line. 'I'll never forget', he said, 'the humiliation of that moment – with everyone staring at me.'[61]

At the heart of this anecdote is more than simply the embarrassment of the stutter. There is an acute self-consciousness, a painful shyness which was to remain with Maugham for all his days, however much he would disguise it with a mask of gentility. For the shy person, whose deepest fear is the ridicule of others, the greatest anguish is to appear foolish or even merely different. And Maugham never risked looking foolish.

In his early thirties, for example, Maugham told St John Adcock that he was dreadfully afraid of being ridiculous, and late in life he refused a number of people the use of his comments as publicity blurbs for their books on the grounds that he would make himself look as silly as Hugh Walpole. Once when a broker had misappropriated his stock, losing him a large sum of money, Maugham confessed to a friend that he would have suffered more if it looked as if he had himself been foolish. And he turned down Julian Hall's invitation to broadcast on radio because he feared that his listeners would be disappointed and he would be humiliated. Similarly, he emphatically vetoed Karl Pfeiffer's proposal to do an article on the kinds of food the writer ate because such a piece would make him look absurd.

The fear of appearing ridiculous – of being a 'Little Lord Fauntleroy' – shaped Maugham's character in a number of ways. It made him unwilling to expose himself, to take the risks that come with a spontaneous response to people and events. In *The Summing Up*, he argues that he has a 'shrinking from my fellow men that has made it difficult for me to enter into any familiarity with them'.[62] He calls this reticence 'instinctive', but a few pages later he points out that 'reserve is an artificial quality that is developed in most of us as the result of innumerable rebuffs.'[63] Maugham therefore withdrew behind a protective façade of reserve, a shell overlaid by his cultivated Victorian–Edwardian manners. Only a few people would ever really know the vulnerable and sensitive man behind the mask, and many would mistake his shyness for snobbery or disdain.

The effect on Maugham's writing can hardly be overestimated. The detachment of his first-person narrators and the sense in all but a few of his works that one is viewing life from a distance surely has its source in this reticence. Thematically the fear of ridicule runs throughout many of his social comedies and fiction, where the greatest threat is the public exposure of one's follies. More significant, however, is the apparent effect on Maugham's treatment of love. In his shrewd introduction to *Mrs Craddock*, Michael Wood writes: 'The ground for most . . . revenge in Maugham is humiliation, and Maugham's sourest and most famous contribution to the moral life of our century is probably his diagnosis of love itself as, above all, humiliation.'[64]

There are many examples to support Wood's thesis, the most striking being the tortured relationship between Philip and the waitress Mildred in *Of Human Bondage*. Here love is grounded in masochism for the young man, and he remains bound for much of the novel to someone who is vulgar, stupid, and cruel. Significantly, the relationship begins when Philip imagines that Mildred has snubbed him, in other words publicly humiliated him.

In *Cakes and Ale* Willie Ashenden describes himself as a dull little boy, who was not very talkative. This is undoubtedly an apt description of the young Maugham, and in *The Summing Up* he adds that he had a number of disabilities. He was, he said, small, shy, having endurance but little physical strength, poor health, and no facility for games. Even long walks tired him, though he went on them rather than admit his weakness. His childhood therefore was largely a solitary one, but it had one consolation which, as Anthony Curtis notes, was an unintended gift of the vicar. A great collector of books, he had acquired a considerable library to which Willie had access, and soon he began his lifelong habit of reading. By the age of ten, he had gone through E. W. Lane's three-volume translation of *The Book of the Thousand Nights and One Night*, Scott's Waverley novels, Carroll's *Alice in Wonderland* and *Through the Looking Glass*, the adventure stories of Captain Marryat, everything of Harrison Ainsworth, and other, now forgotten, works.

It was natural that this lonely boy who felt that he was trapped in a drab world should fall under the spell of romantic and fantastic literature. If *Of Human Bondage* accurately reflects Maugham's discovery of the joy of reading, there is one book there which is especially interesting. About Constantinople, it describes a vast Byzantine cistern called 'The Hall of the Thousand Columns' where a boat is always ready at the entrance to lure a traveller into the darkness from which no one ever returns. His imagination 'peculiarly stirred' by this legend, Philip wonders whether the boat goes on forever through the pillared alleys or finally arrives at some strange mansion. Did Willie, we might wonder, look out from Whitstable Harbour over the North Sea and similarly dream of the day when he would explore the pillared alleys of the world? Did the lure of the unknown, even with its terrors, seem preferable to the conventional tedium of Whitstable?

Books, in any case, became Maugham's escape from life's humiliations, a form of social interaction which did not require his stuttering attempt at conversation and which did not invite a rebuff. In *Of Human Bondage*, he shrewdly reveals how Philip is introduced to literature as a compensation for his failure to meet the expectations of others. Unable to memorize the collect as required by the vicar, the wretched boy is comforted by his aunt when she reads from a picture book illustrating travel in the Middle East. Soon he forgets about the unhappiness of life around him, forming what Maugham calls 'the most delightful habit in the world'. Thus he is providing himself with 'a refuge from all the distress of life'.[65]

Until his sight failed him in his last years, Maugham was an omnivorous reader, turning, as he said in 'The Book Bag', to the printed page as an opium addict turns to his pipe. From Greek tragedies to modern mysteries, Shakespeare to Sinclair Lewis, Schopenhauer to the Upanishads, he ranged over an enormous variety of subjects and in a number of languages: English, French, German, Italian, and Spanish. Few authors read as widely as Maugham, and his works are peppered with references to other literature. It was, as he confessed in *The Summing Up*, 'a relief to me when I can get away [from social intercourse] and read a book'.[66]

After a year of private lessons in Whitstable, it was decided that Willie would attend King's School six miles away in Canterbury. In May 1885 he thus became a boarding student of the Junior Department. To the shy eleven-year-old, the high brick wall with a little door looked like a prison, and for the next five years he felt caught in a trap.

Maugham's school years have been graphically portrayed in *Of Human Bondage*, and though there are factual differences, the development of Philip Carey's personality during that period closely reflects that of his author. Willie studied classics, mathematics, English, and French, and he won prizes in each of his two years in the Junior Department. In July 1887 he moved to the senior school and was elected a King's Scholar, which meant that he could wear a short black academic gown and was provided with a grant. The latter benefit no doubt pleased the parsimonious vicar, who had written several times to request – unsuccessfully – that his nephew be absolved from paying fees. In his first year in the senior school, Willie won a prize in music, which is interesting in light of his later love of opera, and in 1888 he won prizes in divinity, history, and French. He also developed some skill in drawing, and when the vicarage was unfortunately demolished in the 1970s a Greek school exercise book containing two doodles on the back page was found. There can be little doubt that the sketches – one seemingly a self-portrait – were Maugham's.

Notwithstanding this academic success, Maugham claimed that his two years in the Junior Department were especially wretched, though Anthony Curtis is probably right to argue that he was not as badly treated as numerous other English public school boys have been. But he suffered at the hands of bullies and endured a series of sarcastic and overbearing teachers. On his arrival, he begged his uncle, 'Tell him I stammer,' but his impediment made him an object of derision for the boys and an easy target for insensitive masters.

The misery of Willie's years at King's School made him intellectually aware of what he had intuitively begun to realize: that he was different from the others and that he had his own unique identity. This process of discovery is skilfully conveyed in *Of Human Bondage* where Philip grows intensely self-conscious. This feeling of separateness, says Maugham, is a normal occurrence at puberty, though the fortunate people are those who remain only vaguely aware that they are any different from their fellows. They are the ones who can lose themselves in the shared pleasures of social animals and therefore have the best chance for happiness. In Philip, however, the ridicule of his club foot, like that of Willie's stammer, accelerates his understanding of his uniqueness, and together with a growing imagination shapes his personality. By the end of Willie's schooldays, that personality would be ready to fight for its independence.

It is likely also that his years at King's provided Maugham with his first homosexual experience. Indeed, given the English public school environment, the segregation of adolescent boys from female students at a time of their developing sexuality, it would be surprising if he did not have some sort of homosexual encounter. In *Homosexuality and Literature: 1890–1930*, Jeffrey Meyers observes that virtually all public school boys had homosexual experiences, and he notes that after the conviction of Oscar Wilde in 1895, the English journalist W. T. Stead wrote: 'If all persons guilty of Oscar Wilde's offences were to be clapped in gaol, there would be a surprising exodus from Eton and Harrow, Rugby and Winchester to Pentonville and Holloway.'[67]

As we have seen, the events of Maugham's early life – the loss of a beloved mother, the lack of a father with whom to identify, the breakup of a home, and his generally frail constitution – follow a common pattern in the development of homosexuality. Added to these factors are the emotional starvation and isolation of the vicarage. If Willie's contacts with other boys in Whitstable were minimal, he seems to have had almost none with girls. It is significant that in *Of Human Bondage* Philip 'had never known any girls' and though at King's School other boys knew several young women, 'Philip had always concealed under a lofty contempt the terror with which they filled him.'[68] Neither does *Cakes and Ale* show Willie Ashenden having any association with girls, and the recollections of Maugham and others suggest that these accounts accurately reflect Willie's own childhood. His only experience with the opposite sex seems to have been the humiliating lessons at Ivy House described by Charlotte Etheridge.

At school Maugham's social interaction was entirely with males, and though much of it was unpleasant he must have formed attachments to some of his fellows. In *Of Human Bondage* Philip falls into an emotional relationship with a young man which, though not physically consummated, may be homosexual in nature. The boy is called 'Rose', and though there were no students at King's with that surname, it occupies a curious place in Maugham's writing. In 'The Artistic Temperament of Stephen Carey', the unpublished embryonic version of *Of Human Bondage*, the young woman who is the Mildred figure is called 'Rose Cameron', and of course the engaging heroine of *Cakes and Ale* is called 'Rosie'. These may simply be coincidences, but it does seem that Maugham attached the name to a number of important love objects.

Like many adolescent friendships the attachment between Philip and Rose begins with proximity, when they share a study, and it develops out of common interests. In personality Rose is everything that Philip is not – charming, gregarious, popular, and good at games – and, just as Maugham's later relationships would always be with those who complemented his own character, Philip becomes passionately attached to him. This liaison thrives for some time, but soon Philip is gripped by a jealous possessiveness and is tortured by his friend's contacts with others. The association ends painfully for Philip when, returning from an extended absence caused by illness, he discovers that Rose has formed other attachments and now treats him with amiable casualness. Characteristically he feels humiliated and seeks revenge.

On the surface this experience is not uncommon. There is hardly a child who has not suffered such jealous pangs in the normal shifting of youthful allegiances. The manner and intensity of Philip's emotional investment in his friendship, however, suggests something more profound. One of the steps in Cappon's theory of the formation of the homosexual is the shifting of attention from one's own body to that of another person of the same sex. Thus it is important to note that the passages developing the relationship with Rose are immediately preceded by a description of Philip's desire to change places with 'the dullest boy in the school who was whole of limb':

> He took to a singular habit. He would imagine that he was some boy whom he had a particular fancy for; he would throw his soul, as it were, into the other's body, talk with his voice and laugh with his laugh; he would imagine himself doing all the things the other did. It was so vivid that he seemed for a moment really to be no longer himself. In this way he enjoyed many intervals of fantastic happiness.[69]

Rose thus becomes the object of adoration who will take the shy and unpopular Philip out of himself and connect him with the world from which he feels excluded.

Maugham would never, of course, have risked giving the Philip–Rose relationship a physical side, and one can only speculate about the nature of its real-life original. Alan Searle, however, has suggested that Maugham did experience some homosexual liaison at school. According to Searle, he was dining with Maugham one day at the Garrick Club when an old man passing their table saw Maugham, stopped and exclaimed: 'Good God!' Maugham responded with a similar note of surprise and the two men talked for a while. When the other man had departed, Searle asked about his identity and Maugham replied: 'Oh, he's someone I went to bed with at King's.'

In *Of Human Bondage*, Philip's studies at King's School end prematurely because of what seems to be anger over Rose's perceived betrayal. Maugham himself left Canterbury before finishing his studies, but if an unrequited friendship was responsible, there were additional reasons. The school records for 1889 indicate that he was absent for part of the time, and in 'Looking Back' he claims that a severe attack of pleurisy persuaded his guardians that, with the family history of tuberculosis and his own recurring lung trouble, he should not remain at school. He was sent instead to Hyères, on the French Riviera, where he was given lessons by an English tutor.

When he returned to King's School Maugham's academic performance deteriorated. Through the unhappiness of the first four years he had at least maintained a position near the top of his class, and he seemed likely to win a scholarship to Cambridge. There are, however, indications that his studies did not always hold his interest. On three occasions his name appeared in the School Black Book, in which the boys' misdeeds were recorded, twice for 'inattention' and once for 'gross inattention'. These all occurred during his senior years, corroborating Maugham's claim to have wanted to be away from the routine of the school and the regime of dull teachers. Many years later James Robert Smith remembered how unhappy the fifteen-year-old Willie appeared on his visits home in Whitstable: 'I don't think he liked school much, and he probably wanted to be free and living at home as I was . . . I'll never forget how sad he looked.'[70]

If anything could have kept him at school, it might have been one master whose enlightened attitude and sensitivity held an enormous appeal for Maugham. The dashing, black-bearded Thomas Field was a former King's student, Captain of the School for three years, an Oxford graduate, a master at Harrow, and in 1886 the Headmaster at King's. In *Of Human Bondage* he is portrayed at length as Tom Perkins, the liberal, compassionate, and generous headmaster whose appointment shocks the school staff. Philip reveres Perkins, just as Willie Maugham adored Field. When the aged writer once revisited Canterbury he was asked to identify himself in a group photograph and he replied that if he were in the picture he would be sure to be close to Field. On inspection he was found to be tucked up against the headmaster's legs.[71]

It was Maugham's misfortune, however, to be placed on his return from Hyères in the fifth form, whose master was a particularly irascible Scot called E. J. Campbell (portrayed as B. B. Gordon in *Of Human Bondage*). On the first day of term Willie was asked to construe a simple passage in Latin but an attack of nerves caused him to stutter. As the hapless boy struggled with the words, the class began screaming with laughter and finally Campbell pounded the desk and shouted: 'Sit down you fool, I don't know why they put you in this form.'[72] So vivid was Maugham's memory of the embarrassment that, though the stutter is translated to a club foot elsewhere in *Of Human Bondage*, Philip's agony is here presented as one of inarticulation. 'Why don't you speak?' roars Gordon. 'Speak you blockhead, speak!'[73]

In 'Looking Back', Maugham describes his response to this humiliation. 'I was enraged,' he writes, 'I could have killed the man. I was helpless, I could do nothing, but I made up my mind, then and there, that I would never spend another term with that beast of a master. I knew exactly what to do. I was small for my age and frail but cunning.'[74]

As this passage suggests, Willie Maugham was no longer a helpless little boy clutching his uncle's hand for protection, nor was he content to be a prisoner of King's School. He had adopted some defence mechanisms, knew how to counter-attack, and had developed a forceful will which he was ready to test against the determination of others. Above all he yearned to be master of his own life.

Though the adult Maugham presented to the world a façade of detachment and cynicism, he was in fact deeply emotional, a trait reflected in Philip Carey. Maugham tells us that the young man was easily moved by the sentiment of others and very emotional himself, though he hid it behind a 'placid exterior'. His face, 'partly by nature, but also from the habit of all these years at school, seldom except by a quick flushing showed what he felt.'[75] He had learned, Maugham says, 'not to express his emotions by outward signs, and shyness still tormented him, but he had often very high spirits; and then, though he limped about demurely, silent and reserved, it seemed to be hallooing in his heart.'[76] Here one can see part of the Maugham mask of reserve being put in place, a shell that was protective but also isolating.

During his school years, Maugham had also begun to sharpen the wit for which he later became famous. 'He was developing', Maugham writes of Philip, 'a sense of humour, and found that he had a knack of saying bitter things, which caught people on the raw; he said them because they amused him, hardly realizing how much they hurt, and was much offended when he found that his victims regarded him with active dislike.'[77] Frederic Raphael is certainly right to argue that the young Maugham's increasing familiarity and facility with words had armed him with a new and devastating weapon. Into his fertile imagination the phrases would come, and though he might struggle to articulate them they could be lethal blows. He would later discover, like Arnold Bennett, that while language might betray him in speech, it would flow with ease on the printed page.

In the four years that Maugham had spent in Canterbury he had grown from eleven to fifteen, and this period saw the formation of a determined will that became nearly intractable as he matured. From this point on his life was always the working out of a pattern which he had conceived, and which he would see to completion. He would manipulate those around him to let him spend a year or two in Germany, he would arrange to study medicine in order to live in London, and he would make himself into a successful author by sheer determined effort.

As the title indicates, *Of Human Bondage* is about enslavement and liberation, primarily emotional bondage but also a variety of forms of physical, economic, intellectual, and philosophical constraints. In his final years the author confessed to an interviewer that 'the main thing I've always asked from life is freedom. Outer and inner freedom, both in my way of living and my way of writing.'[78] The course of his long life was indeed a succession of attempts to find complete freedom – not merely physical liberty, but true independence of spirit. This freedom meant more than mere escape from duties and obligations, financial dependence, or the restraints of time and place. These were only the surface of a search for a deeper liberation – intellectual freedom and emotional detachment. In one way or another almost everything Maugham willingly did was motivated by this vision.

Maugham's concern with freedom is apparent in the numerous manifestations of human bondage and independence in his fiction. Although the situations may differ and the forms may vary the essential theme which runs throughout his writing is that of autonomy and enslavement. It is most profoundly explored in *Of Human Bondage*, but many of his other novels pursue variations of the theme. Often the titles – *The Merry-Go-Round*, *The Painted Veil*, *The Narrow Corner*, *Cakes and Ale*, *The Razor's Edge* – carry the connotation that man is in some way faced with narrowness and restrictions on all sides. Maugham's writing treats many ideas – man's paradoxical nature, the importance of rhythm in people's lives, the colonial ethos; the central issue, however, is freedom and bondage, whether it is Liza trapped in the slum, Bertha Craddock stifled among the landed gentry, Philip Carey tormented by Mildred Rogers, Charles Strickland enthralled by the urge to paint, Rosie Driffield defying puritanical convention, Dr Saunders on his voyage of liberation, or Larry Darrell seeking to escape the grip of American materialism.

When Willie Maugham decided that he would not spend another term at Canterbury he was claiming his independence and beginning a battle for control of his own life. He managed to persuade the vicar that for health reasons he should spend another winter in Hyères, and following that he was permitted to study in Heidelberg. In *The Summing Up* Maugham attributes this success to a weakness in his uncle and a lack of real concern about the boy's future. In 'Looking Back', he suggests that his poor health probably led the vicar to assume that it was unlikely that Willie would live long.

In *Of Human Bondage*, however, Philip's bid for freedom is described as a power struggle, with his will emerging dominant over that of the Careys and the headmaster. When he is first refused permission to leave school his reaction is characteristic: 'He felt almost sick with humiliation, the humiliation of having to ask and the humiliation of the curt refusal . . . Philip writhed under that despotism which never vouchsafed a reason for the most tyrannous act.'[79] Through unfaltering persistence and careful manipulation, however, he persuades his aunt and uncle to let him leave for Germany, but his most difficult struggle is with the admired Mr Perkins. The headmaster shrewdly assesses his student's discontent and agrees to let him go at the end of the next term if he so wishes. Philip senses victory, and he feels a 'thrill of pride' in his triumph. 'He had got his own way, and he was satisfied. His will had gained a victory over the wills of others.'[80]

When the term is over, however, Mr Perkins almost convinces Philip to stay, and the boy is prevented from doing so only because of the embarrassment he will feel if he changes his mind. Thus Philip gains his freedom, but his victory lacks the joy he thought it would possess. 'He asked himself dully', writes Maugham, 'whether whenever you got your way you wished afterwards that you hadn't.'[81] For the author of *Of Human Bondage*, life would hold many such triumphs of will, and so often he would discover that the prize was not worth the price of victory.

At the age of fifteen, however, Willie Maugham was anxious to get out into the world. His childhood, full of uncertainty and pain, was essentially over, though he would carry its scars with him until his death. He would have a long way to go before he would have complete mastery of his own affairs, but he left for Germany with a sense of self and a determination to find his own way in the world.

2

APPRENTICE: 1889–1897

WILLIE MAUGHAM LEFT King's School forever in the summer of 1889. As he later said, he was 'impatient for life', but it was a life 'which he saw not in the present of his adolescence but only in the future of his manhood'.[1] After a second winter in Hyères, it was arranged, at the suggestion of his aunt, that he should spend a year or two in Heidelberg in order to learn German. With an allowance of £15 a month, he lived in a small pension kept by the wife of a professor at the university who taught him German.

Although Maugham was not officially registered at the university the months at Heidelberg were a period of intense intellectual awakening. In addition to his German studies he attended lectures, used the library, and generally absorbed the ferment of ideas in the university milieu. Most memorable were the lectures on Schopenhauer given by Kuno Fischer, whose reputation was such that Maugham had to fight to get into the theatre. Fischer's brilliance fired the young man with an interest in metaphysical speculation which would remain with him for the rest of his life, and soon he was reading Schopenhauer, Spinoza, and a host of other philosophers.

Like many European universities in the last years of the nineteenth century, Heidelberg was being challenged by the avant-garde, and it undoubtedly gave Maugham a taste of the experimental in art before many of his contemporaries back in insular Britain. In drama, for example, he discovered the new realism of Ibsen (whom he once saw in a Munich café) and Henry Becque; and Sudermann's *Die Ehre* made a particular impression on him. More generally his first taste of

31

theatre (he had not been allowed to see touring productions in Whitstable) excited his imagination and planted the seeds of his later career as a dramatist. Though Philip in *Of Human Bondage* does not become a playwright, his first experience in theatre surely reflects the awakening enthusiasm of Maugham himself: 'The passion of the stage seized him. He felt a thrill the moment he got into the little, shabby, ill-lit theatre . . . To him it was real life . . . Philip was carried away by the sordid intensity of it all. He seemed to see the world again in another fashion, and this world too he was anxious to know.'[2]

In music, Heidelberg introduced Maugham to Wagner, whose operas were as revolutionary as Ibsen's plays. In the twenties, Maugham once replied to a questionnaire from Compton Mackenzie by identifying his favourite composer as Wagner, his favourite music as The Fire Music, and his favourite singer as the great Wagnerian interpreter Lotte Lehmann. From the twenties on, he regularly attended the Bayreuth Festival, and frequently went to Munich for the opera. His tastes were nevertheless catholic, and he enjoyed instrumental music as well as opera. The last composition that he was able to enjoy before deafness robbed him of that pleasure was Debussy's *Prélude à l'Après-midi d'un Faune*, the premiere of which he could remember attending.[3]

By the time that Maugham was sixteen, he was a voracious reader, but he lacked discrimination or direction. His choice of books had been limited to those which might fall into his hands in Whitstable or Canterbury, the most challenging being the occasional classic from the eighteenth or early nineteenth centuries. In Heidelberg, however, Maugham discovered many of the great European authors and much of the contemporary literature which was *au courant* at the end of the century.

It was inevitable that in Germany Maugham would come to know the works of Goethe, and he once claimed that the most thrilling moment of his life was when he first read *Faust*. Beyond this he became familiar with a wide range of other writers, and this he owed to his association with an idiosyncratic Englishman, John Ellingham Brooks.

Brooks, whom Maugham calls 'Brown' in *The Summing Up*, had studied law at Cambridge, but after a year of living in London had moved to Heidelberg to learn German. Although short in stature, he was considered unusually handsome, with good features, curly hair, pale blue eyes and a wistful expression some called poetic. In *The Summing Up* Maugham describes him as vain, sentimental, and completely lacking in willpower, a judgement which no one has disputed. He came to Germany with a small income, which he had decided was sufficient for him to lead a life of indolence and aestheticism – though he ended up surviving on the generosity of friends and on a financial settlement from his wife, the painter Romaine Brooks. One of the many homosexuals who fled London in 1895 in the wake of the Wilde trial, he spent the next forty years in Capri, pursuing his lifelong ambition of publishing his translation of the Hérédia sonnets, playing Beethoven sonatas on his piano, and smoking his pipe. He died in May 1929 of cancer of the liver, and was probably the model for Thomas Wilson, the idler of Maugham's 'The Lotus Eater'. He is graphically portrayed in *Of Human Bondage* in the character of Hayward.

Though Brooks never created anything of note he was a great appreciator of art with a finely honed sense of excellence. He had a genuine passion for good literature and Maugham later acknowledged that Brooks taught him a great deal. When they first met, Maugham was reading Fielding's *Tom Jones*, but soon the older man had introduced him to Meredith's *Diana of the Crossways* and *Richard Feverel*, Swinburne's *Poems and Ballads*, Shelley's translation of the *Symposium*, and the work of Verlaine, Walter Pater, Cardinal Newman, Matthew Arnold, and Dante. Brooks had written out the verses of Fitzgerald's translation of *The Rubáiyát of Omar Khayyám* in longhand and Maugham thrilled to hear his friend's reading of them.

One of the authors Brooks discussed with Maugham was Renan, whose *Vie de Jésus* became the catalyst for Maugham's loss of religious faith – or, more accurately, for his realization of his lack of faith. What belief he possessed had been inculcated into him as an impressionable youth by the vicar and the twice-daily attendance at church on Sundays. Even then his faith was seriously undermined on one occasion when he put God to a dramatic test. Having been assured by his uncle that the Bible correctly states that faith can move mountains, he prayed to God one night to remove his stutter. Convinced of the miracle he awoke next day full of exultation and was shocked to discover that his impediment was as severe as ever.

This episode is used in *Of Human Bondage* with a certain force, but Maugham confessed that his own reactions were emotional rather than intellectual. A few years later in Germany, though, he began more rationally to question the basis of his faith. He saw people in that country who believed in their particular religion as intensely as his uncle's congregation, and he concluded that faith is largely a matter of environment and conditioning. This discovery, together with his discussions with Brooks and reading of Renan, revealed the lack of intellectual foundation to Maugham's belief, and he became an agnostic.

In *The Summing Up* and *Of Human Bondage* Maugham character-istically associated his loss of faith with intellectual independence: 'I felt the exhilaration of a new freedom.'[4] This gain in openness of outlook was, however, accompanied by a loss, one which probably affected Maugham's life far more than has generally been understood. For a young intellectual at the end of the nineteenth century, loss of faith was hardly uncommon, but it left Maugham with a split between his emotional attraction to belief and his intellectual rejection of it.

In *Of Human Bondage* the autobiographical Philip does not have a 'religious temperament',[5] but Maugham did in fact have a religious mind, and he retained it to the end of his life. Always an avid scholar of the religions of the world, he found those of the Far East especially attractive, though incredible, and this interest is reflected in the mysticism of *The Razor's Edge*, written in his late sixties. In many of his works of non-fiction – notably *The Summing Up* and 'Looking Back' – he devotes considerable space to a discussion of faith and the importance of Jesus and other Biblical figures. Scattered throughout his writing are indications that he was not only curious but widely knowledgeable about various saints, clerics, and questions of dogma.

Alan Searle has told me that Maugham very much wanted to believe but he could not. Whenever they were in Italy they attended Mass during which the old man often wept openly. It is not surprising, therefore, that in 'Looking Back' Maugham affirmed the powerful emotional appeal of the Catholic service:

> However confirmed a skeptic you are, when you attend Mass, even low Mass, and watch the priest, served by an acolyte, in his heavily embroidered vestments reading rapidly and inaudibly, the prescribed prayers of the liturgy, you can hardly fail to be impressed; and when, as the acolyte tinkles his bell to herald the elevation and the congregation fall to their knees; when for the faithful the miracle of transubstantiation takes place and the celebrant raises successively the Host and the Chalice for all to worship and adore, unbeliever though you be you cannot fail to be deeply awed. How bleak is the Protestant service compared with the awe-inspiring celebration of the Mass![6]

Searle is convinced that, had Maugham lived a few more years, he would have been converted. In this regard it is worth noting that the final lines of Maugham's last published work tell a strange story of the aged writer believing that he saw Christ turn his head to him in a painting in a Venice gallery in April 1958. Though this was likely a trick of his failing eyesight, this episode and the importance Maugham attached to it suggest that his mind was at least occupied with matters of faith.

Maugham's Heidelberg sojourn gave him more than just an intellectual awakening. For the first time in his life, he came into close contact with a variety of people who were not members of his family or schoolmates, and though he was essentially a detached observer his understanding of people was significantly increased. In the pension were the owner's two daughters and a son, a French and a Chinese student, and a New Englander who had taught Greek at Harvard. The original of Weeks in *Of Human Bondage*, this American became interested in the young man, taking him for walks, to see the ruined Schloss, and on a fortnight's trip to Switzerland. Though *Of Human Bondage* shows Weeks and Hayward together in the pension, giving Philip contrasting intellectual and philosophical arguments, the American had actually left before Brooks arrived.

Maugham has acknowledged an intellectual debt to both men, but in 'Looking Back' he claims that it was not until much later that he realized that their interest in him was homosexual. He was then so innocent, he argues, that it never occurred to him that they wanted anything more from him than his company, and that they must have been puzzled by his lack of response to their advances.

This may well be an accurate account of Maugham's relationships with the two men. It needs to be remembered, though, that Maugham was always exceptionally guarded, even disingenuous, about his sexual orientation, and so such stories cannot necessarily be accepted at face value. Against this version, for example, is the claim made by Glenway Wescott that the old man once confided to him that his first sexual experience was with Brooks.[7]

The answer is that Maugham was probably not as innocent when he left school as Wescott's story implies, but that a liaison with an older, experienced man was a different matter from a brief homosexual contact with a fellow schoolboy. Brooks was handsome, intelligent, and literate, and it would be surprising if his sympathetic interest and skills in persuasion did not lead the young Maugham into some sort of relationship. And it was with Brooks that Maugham and E. F. Benson later shared a villa among the expatriate homosexuals on Capri.

When Maugham left Heidelberg in the spring of 1892, he was no longer the schoolboy vaguely aware of a larger world of life and literature. In addition to French and English he now knew German and some Italian. He had begun to explore the world of art and, caught up in the excitement of creativity, he had written a biography of Meyer-beer, which, though never published, confirmed his growing conviction that he would become an author. Finally, he had broadened his understanding of people, their complexities and proclivities, both through his studies and his observations of those whom he had come to know.

Maugham returned to England still painfully shy but with a stronger sense of self, of what he could and could not do, of what he was and was not prepared to do. 'I had', he would write in *The Summing Up*, 'very decided views about my own future. I had been happier than ever before. I had for the first time tasted freedom, and I could not bear the thought of going to Cambridge and being subjected once more to restraint. I felt myself a man, and I had a great eagerness to enter at once upon life.'[8] It is understandable that when Philip returns from Heidelberg he is surprised to see how old and insignificant his aunt and uncle have become. Willie had taken control of his life.

The eighteen-year-old Maugham, however, faced the immediate problem of choosing a profession, writing for money being considered not only precarious but disreputable by his family. The vicar therefore made enquiries of an old friend in the Civil Service but was advised that it was no longer the place for a gentleman to make his career. Willie's other guardian, Albert Dixon, then arranged for him to work in a chartered accountant's office in Chancery Lane, but he hated the relentless drudgery of adding account to account, and returned to Whitstable.

After some indecisive weeks, Maugham accepted the suggestion of a local doctor that he study medicine. He was not especially interested in the profession, but since his studies would require his living in London he agreed with alacrity and his guardians approved. Thus, after some weeks of intense preparation at a crammer's, he passed the entrance examinations, and in the autumn of 1892 became a medical student at St Thomas's Hospital.

Founded in the thirteenth century, St Thomas's is located along the south bank of the Thames directly opposite the Houses of Parliament. A long corridor connects eight blocks of Gothic buildings, one of which houses the medical school. From there generations of students have looked across the river at the stunning spectacle of British history, tradition, and privilege: Parliament, Big Ben, Westminster Abbey, and beyond them St James's Park and Buckingham Palace. To their backs, however, have been some of the worst slums in London – in the boroughs of Lambeth, Battersea, Camberwell, Southwark, and Wandsworth – and it was from this misery that the hospital drew its patients.

Maugham lived across the Thames in Westminster in a boarding house at 11 Vincent Square. Supported by his £150-a-year legacy, he paid eighteen shillings a week for his two rooms on the ground floor and twelve shillings for breakfast and evening meals. Looking back at the age of eighty, he claimed that as a student he could live comfortably, pay his school fees, buy his instruments, clothe himself, and have a good deal of fun on £14 a month. Proud of his first really independent lodgings, he furnished them in the Pre-Raphaelite style of the period, as *Cakes and Ale* suggests, covering one wall with a Moorish rug and hanging reproductions of works by Perugino, Van Dyck, and Hobbema.

Like those of medical students everywhere, Maugham's days were almost fully absorbed by the hospital. After the breakfast prepared by his landlady, Mrs Foreman, he would walk along Horseferry Road, across Lambeth Bridge, and along the embankment to arrive at St Thomas's by nine o'clock. He lunched at the hospital for threepence on a scone, butter, and glass of milk. Around six o'clock, he would make the return journey in time to have high tea at Mrs Foreman's, after which he occupied the evening reading and writing.

Though Maugham spent his days at St Thomas's, he was never really part of the place. In *The Summing Up*, he recalls that 'I entered little into the life of the hospital and made few friends there,'[9] and he passed five years almost unnoticed by the medical community. When Joseph Lurie was later completing his own studies at St Thomas's he made a number of attempts to discover what traces the famous writer had left. There was, he learned, 'nothing more than a few crumbs that Maugham was a shy, retiring, aloof, and almost forbidding individual who had but one friend in whose company he was always to be seen.'[10]

The one friend may have been Adney Walter Payne, whom Maugham had come to know in Heidelberg, and with whom he was later to live for more than a decade. Payne was a man of wide interests who had been born and educated in London before studying in Germany. He began his professional life as an accountant in London, but turned to law in 1899, building up an impressive practice in the next ten years. In 1910 he nevertheless abandoned his legal work in order to manage various music hall and theatre interests bequeathed to him by his father. From this point until his death in 1949 Payne was prominent in the theatrical life of London in such roles as managing director of the London Pavilion, director of the Victoria Palace, and chairman of Variety Theatres. In 1924 he became President of the Society of West

End Theatre Managers and was instrumental in the formation of the London Theatre Council, a conciliatory body for managers and artists.

Walter Payne's obituary in *The Times* refers to his 'steely precision of mind and an unalterable determination to obtain his objectives' but notes that 'he was one of the most likeable of men and in manner suggested the country gentleman rather than the theatre manager.'[11] Maugham found him attractive and intelligent, and the friendship begun in Heidelberg deepened during the years at St Thomas's so that the actress Marie Lohr, who came to know the young dramatist in the first decade of this century, described the two men as 'inseparable'.[12] It was to Payne that Maugham dedicated his first book, *Liza of Lambeth*, and when he wrote years later that it was with pride that in the first copy of the novel 'I put the name of a friend who had been the dear companion of my lonely youth',[13] he was probably paying tribute to this relationship.

This comment may, however, refer to Wentworth Huyshe, a friend of this period to whom the young author also sent one of his six presentation copies of *Liza*. Maugham had met Huyshe through Henry Maugham, who, having graduated from university, was then living in London and dabbling in literature. Henry was part of a group of young homosexuals of whom Huyshe was one, and when Maugham refers in *The Summing Up* to knowing 'a group of young men who had by nature [artistic] gifts that seemed to me much superior to mine'[14] he is likely referring to the young aesthetes he came to know through his brother.

Little is known of Huyshe's relationship with Maugham, but the letter which Maugham sent along with the copy of *Liza* suggests that, like Brooks, Huyshe was a kind of mentor. In it the young author talks of being taken about and shown things, of being exposed to all kinds of new ideas, and he offers him his first book to show that Huyshe's cultivation has borne fruit.[15]

Maugham also maintained contact with Brooks, who was then living in Italy. In 1894 he used the six weeks of Easter vacation and twenty pounds of his income to visit Italy for the first time. With the writings of Walter Pater, John Ruskin, and John Addington Symonds as guides, he toured Genoa and Pisa, and spent most of a month in Florence. There he took a room in the Via Laura, from which he could see the dome of the Cathedral, lived on three shillings a day, and took Italian lessons from his landlady's daughter. On the way back he went to Venice, Verona, and Milan.

Maugham ventured further in 1895, travelling down to Naples and

Capri, then relatively unknown to tourists. Living was cheap and comfortable and the atmosphere was romantically Bohemian. Brooks was now a permanent resident, and there were a composer, several painters, a sculptor, and a colonel who had fought for the south in the American Civil War. Their conversations about art, literature, and history were so lively and argumentative that Maugham, thinking Capri the most enchanting place he had ever seen, spent his entire holiday there. For the next thirty years, he would return frequently, and in 1901 he wrote in a review of George Gissing's *By the Ionian Sea* that the natives of Capri were 'the most charming and companionable creatures in the world. Nowhere do I find myself more at home than in that enchanting island of Capri, among the peasants and fishermen, whom I know so well, and now, alas! have not seen for so long.'[16] At the age of ninety he told a reporter: 'I want to go to Capri because I started life there.'[17]

In some respects it is not surprising that Maugham discovered the pleasures of Capri in 1895, a profoundly significant date in the history of homosexuality in Britain. It was the year of the notorious Oscar Wilde trial, the judgment and public reaction to which drove thousands of homosexuals out of the country. Many, like Brooks, went to Capri, whose greater tolerance of unconventional sexual behaviour would for decades provide a haven for such expatriates as E. F. Benson, Norman Douglas, and other homosexuals.

The story of the downfall of Oscar Wilde is complicated, and millions of words have been written about it. In brief, the Irish playwright, born in 1856, had by the 1890s achieved both popularity and critical acclaim with a number of charming children's fables, *The Picture of Dorian Gray*, and several dramatic comedies. *Lady Windermere's Fan* was highly successful, but *The Importance of Being Earnest* brought Wilde to the peak of his fame when it was produced in London in 1895.

Though he had married in 1884 and produced two children, Wilde formed a homosexual liaison with Lord Alfred Douglas, the younger son of the Marquis of Queensberry. When the father attacked Wilde by leaving a card at the playwright's club referring to his 'posing as a somdomite', Wilde ill-advisedly sued for libel. When he lost his case, he was himself tried and given a sentence of two years' hard labour in prison. Disowned by his family, he went through Bankruptcy Court and Divorce Court, and died at the age of forty-four, three years after he left Reading Gaol. Within a year he had plummeted from a position of social, artistic, and professional eminence to one of vilification and ruin. After leaving prison he published nothing.

The effects of the Wilde trial on British public attitudes were deep and long-lasting. No longer could homosexuals count on general ignorance or tolerance to ensure an environment in which their opinions, tastes, and practices, however discreetly they might be expressed, would be accepted. As a result, for the next seventy years, there was enormous damage to the careers, lives, and artistic achievements of thousands of Britons. The historian A. L. Rowse has written of this black moment in British social history:

> It is impossible to assess the appalling consequences of this historic case . . . In Britain it led to an accumulation of barbarous inhumanity and suffering that was incalculable. We need not attach much importance to the number of people who fled abroad, or thought it better to live abroad – some of them people of distinction who were a loss to the country. Within the country, during the next century, there were thousands of people whose lives were ruined – many of them valuable lives, doctors, medical officers of health, schoolmasters, soldiers and seamen, men of service to the nation. The matter does not bear argument: the loss was unforgivable.[18]

Until the Sexual Offences Act of 1967 homosexual conduct between consenting adults in private was a criminal offence, and men of any class and position could be, and frequently were, imprisoned. Many more spent their lives in public disguise, forever careful to ensure that the façade was intact, and that their conversation, gestures and personal style would not betray them. Others felt compelled to live abroad. As late as June 1931, for example, Earl Beauchamp, Knight of the Garter, Lord Warden of the Cinque Ports, and leader of the Liberal Party suddenly resigned all his positions and left the country. Unknown to the public, he was a practising homosexual, a fact which his brother-in-law the Duke of Westminster had threatened to reveal. To avoid the scandal Beauchamp became an exile, returning for his son's funeral five years later only after official assurances that he would not be arrested. George V commented: 'I thought they shot themselves.'

Of course many did shoot themselves. In a famous such case, which Maugham certainly would have known about, Sir Hector Macdonald, whose knighthood had been awarded for distinguished military service, was recalled from his post of general in command of Ceylon in 1903. A complaint of homosexual misconduct had been made against him and the War Office ordered a court of inquiry. Rather than face it, he shot himself in a Paris hotel. Fifty-seven years later, in 1961, a Paris hotel was the site of a similar tragedy when Arthur Jeffress, the son of the head of a tobacco company, killed himself after homosexual charges were made against him in Venice.

In 1895 the immediate effect of Wilde's conviction was a wave of paranoia rippling through the British homosexual community. Maugham was twenty-one and living in London at the time, and it is hard to believe that he was not deeply affected by the trial and its aftermath. For a shy young man who, aside from his sexual orientation, felt that he was different from other people, and who may have had several homosexual encounters, the demonstration of the crushing force of orthodox public opinion would have made a lasting impression. If by then he was a more active member of a coterie of young homosexuals – that of his brother, Wentworth Huyshe, and others – the effect would have been much more traumatic.

In any case the young and impressionable Maugham must have been deeply affected by the trial. As a neophyte writer with dreams of literary eminence, he would have been struck by the spectacle of the destruction of an author at the peak of his fame. No one, he must have concluded, could defy public standards regarding sexual orientation and expect to maintain his position. Thus, for the remainder of his life, he was scrupulously careful never to let his homosexuality become known to the general public. And, like E. M. Forster and many other homosexual writers of the period, Maugham took great pains not to reveal his sexual orientation in his writing. When homosexual themes or incidents do appear, they are subtly presented and carefully camouflaged.

While Oscar Wilde's life was disintegrating, Maugham continued to study medicine and dream of becoming a writer; and almost inevitably the two worlds came together. Medicine was always a means to an end for him, a reason to live in London and an insurance should he fail as a professional writer. Thus he was bored by the first two years of his training and worked only as hard as was necessary to pass. When he became a clerk and a dresser in the outpatients department, however, his interest grew, so much so that he once grew restive when illness kept him from the wards. Attending confinements in the Lambeth slums, where he delivered sixty-three babies, protected from the inherent violence only by the symbol of his black medical bag, left him exhausted but exhilarated.

In *The Summing Up* Maugham wrote that he knew of no better training for an author than some years in the medical profession, and he often claimed that he could have been a better writer if he had gone into private practice for three or four years. The value of medicine, argued Maugham, was that it enabled one to see human nature in the raw, stripped of the protective façades people normally present to the world. As well, medical studies gave him an elementary knowledge of science and the scientific method, a discipline and a method often ignored by artists.

However much knowledge Maugham gained from his five years at St Thomas's, it was their effects on his character and outlook that were most significant. As a child, he had absorbed some of the Maugham family traits – industry, ambition, moderation, and a legal turn of mind. He would, after all, call his autobiography *The Summing Up*, and Joseph Lurie has suggested that 'especially in the travel books and essays, Maugham reveals by his clear and lucid writing, his logical sequences and systematic orderliness, his mental absorption of the legal atmosphere which must inevitably have pervaded his childhood.'[19] He had, however, grown shy and detached, more comfortable as an observer of life, though desperately wanting to be in the thick of it. The medical mode provided a professional confirmation of his natural reticence, the detachment of the diagnostician matching Maugham's own isolation from others.

As Frederic Raphael has pointed out, medicine has an advantage for the shy man in sanctioning 'a certain methodical curiosity ("Now tell me all about it") and a certain self-assertion ("Doctor's orders")'.[20] Moreover, in order not to be emotionally exhausted by the sufferings of his patients, the doctor must set himself apart in cool objectivity. Thus, the doctor becomes a 'therapeutic inquisitor', paying a price in that, just as the clergy are required to be celibate, the man of medicine must adopt an emotional neutrality. With Maugham, the objective clinical eye became his way of seeing the human race, both in his writing and in real life.

Over the years Maugham's diagnostic approach frequently created an unintended emotional distance between himself and others, and on more than one occasion it unnerved those who met him. In 1931 Louise Morgan saw him as a 'devoted specimen hunter. One is rather dashed to realize that he is "collecting" one, tabulating one with this or that group of the *genus humanum*.'[21] Similarly, Hazel Lavery once confessed that, though she admired Maugham, he always frightened her. 'Perhaps', she said, 'it's because he was a doctor once. For when I'm with him, I always feel that I've been placed like a butterfly on an operating table for dissection.'[22] Patrick Back, the son of one of Maugham's closest friends, had the distinct impression that the author was 'an iguana sunning itself on a rock and watching with tired but quick eyes for some passing fly that might unwittingly come within striking distance of his tongue'.[23]

Even late in Maugham's life, Michael Wardell found him charming and gentle, but 'behind the peaceful front there lurks a critical and somewhat malicious demon watching and evaluating and mentally picturing his subject, and putting him away in camphor until he, or some part of him can be used in print.'[24] When Lionel Hale interviewed Maugham in the Villa Mauresque on his ninetieth birthday, the old man was lucid only for ten-minute intervals, but at one point he suddenly got up from his chair and sat next to Hale on a sofa. 'Forgive me,' he said, 'I wanted to see you a little better.' While Maugham fixed him with a long, intense gaze, as if unable to break a deeply ingrained habit, Hale had the feeling of cold fingers going up his spine. As he later told me, 'It scared the piss out of me.'

The training in the scientific method to which Maugham refers in *The Summing Up* clearly influenced his writing, though in more ways than he and many critics have realized. In his discussion of three writer/doctors – John O'Hara, Sinclair Lewis, and Maugham – Raphael identifies some common characteristics, arguing that 'they were free, or seemed to be free, of literary affectation. Their mode was literal rather than metaphorical. They were impatient of the metaphysical and of humbug. They were unshockable, and so they could afford to be accurate. The medical mode led them to observe and to listen – hence the importance they gave to dialogue.'[25]

Raphael's thesis is borne out over Maugham's lengthy career, but his medical training at St Thomas's had a particular immediate advantage which played a major role in launching him as a professional writer. Because of its proximity to the Lambeth slums the young intern had an access to a way of life which would otherwise have remained unknown to him, and which he was to see little of thereafter. Few other writers of his class and background at the turn of the century had first-hand experience of life at the subsistence level among the down and out in London. Maugham had the sense to recognize this, and to use it with great effect in his first novel.

Maugham had begun to write plays in Germany, no doubt in the excitement of his first encounter with serious theatre. These were Ibsen-esque one-acters, full of harrowing naturalism, a mode which was reinforced by the suffering and pain he observed at the hospital. He knew that he was serving a sort of apprenticeship, and on his trip to Florence in 1894 he translated Ibsen's *Ghosts* from German in order to learn the noted dramatist's technique. In London, though his days might be spent at St Thomas's, all evenings were devoted to making himself into a writer. He read widely in the literature of England, France, Germany, and Italy, ranging through philosophy, history, and science. At this time he began his habit of keeping a notebook which he filled with plots for plays and stories, bits of dialogue, brief character sketches, and various observations and reflections.

Maugham's self-education in professional authorship involved weekly field trips to the London theatres, observing what worked on stage and what held audiences. Among the great performers he saw were Henry Irving, Ellen Terry, Mrs Patrick Campbell, and George Alexander, acting in such noted plays as *The Second Mrs Tanqueray* and *The Importance of Being Earnest*. Sometimes there was more drama surrounding the stage action, as it was on 5 January 1895, when Maugham attended the first night of Henry James's *Guy Domville* and saw the author retreat from the stage to a chorus of boos. He never forgot James's mortification, and throughout his career as a dramatist he attended his own opening nights tormented by apprehension.

The young Maugham did not, however, confine his theatre-going to the serious drama of the West End. 'My greatest pleasure', he recalled on his eightieth birthday, 'was to go to the Tivoli of a Saturday afternoon. The music hall, now alas, obsolete, was at the height of its glory. Dear Marie Lloyd, Bessie Bellwood, Vesta Tilley, Albert Chevalier, Dan Leno were at the top of their form. Each of them, alone on the stage, was able to hold an audience entranced for twenty minutes at a time.'[26]

About 1894 or so Maugham completed several curtain-raiser plays and sent them to various theatre managers. When no one showed any interest in producing them, he turned to writing short stories, two of which – 'Daisy' and 'A Bad Example' – showed promise. The plot of 'A Bad Example' is one to which Maugham was to return in *Sheppey* forty years later: the good man whose Christ-like behaviour causes his relatives to see him as mentally unbalanced. James Clinton is a respectable city clerk who, after serving on a coroner's jury on the deaths of three poverty-stricken people, begins to read the Bible. He then offers his home to indigents, contemplates selling his stock to help the poor, and loses his job, causing his wife to have him committed. The strengths of the story are an emphasis on external details and some vivid descriptions of the poor which were probably based on the author's experiences in the Lambeth slums. On the other hand the ironic comments about Victorian attitudes, respectability, and the middle classes are heavy-handed, and the prose is occasionally turgid.

'Daisy' is a much more effective story and of more interest from an autobiographical point of view. It recounts how a young Blackstable girl, Daisy Griffiths, elopes with a married officer. Her father is devastated but her brother and mother are secretly pleased because they have always been jealous of her education and skills in singing and dancing. When Daisy is eventually abandoned by her lover and writes in desperation to her father, his indecision prevents him from going to her aid, and a year later she is discovered living as a prostitute in London. The young woman nevertheless escapes this life, becomes a theatrical star, and marries an aristocrat. After a number of rebuffs, she is finally allowed to visit her father, who remains rigidly unforgiving. In spite of this rejection she settles £15 a week on her struggling family, and departs to walk nostalgically through Blackstable.

'Daisy' is Maugham's first use of his Kentish background, and much of it anticipates *Mrs Craddock*, *Of Human Bondage*, and *Cakes and Ale*, though his attitude toward his childhood environment changed as he became more mature and detached from it. In *Mrs Craddock*, the milieu is still the narrow world of 'Daisy', but presented less heavy-handedly. The Blackstable life in *Of Human Bondage* is much more detailed and complex, and Maugham is not so judgmental. Finally in *Cakes and Ale* the town is recreated with warmth and affection, though its life remains parochial and inhibiting.

In 'Daisy', however, Blackstable is portrayed with the contempt and bitterness of a man of twenty who sees himself as part of a world far beyond its narrow boundaries. The townspeople are shown to be full of pretension, hypocrisy, and love of gossip. There are many references to religious hypocrisy and to petty vindictiveness, and the text is dotted with ironic comments about 'Christian', 'Christian way', and 'Providence'. Daisy's weak and indecisive father is especially contemptible, initially concerned about her but then becoming the narrow voice of Victorian morality, prepared to forgive her when she is suffering for her sins but loathing her when she surmounts them to achieve success and happiness.

After Daisy's departing gift to her family of an allowance, her brother comments to Mrs Griffiths: 'If you'd asked for it, I believe she'd have gone up to six quid a week.'[27] The story really ends here, and the mature Maugham would have left his readers on this delicious note of hypocrisy and greed. There are none the less another forty lines which are a kind of coda, coming from more deeply within the author. On leaving her family the young woman walks through the town:

Daisy walked down the High Street slowly, looking at the houses she remembered, and her lips quivered a little; at every step smells blew across to her full of memories – the smell of a tannery, the blood smell of a butcher's shop, the sea-odour from a shop of fishermen's clothes . . . At last she came on to the beach, and in the darkening November day she looked at the booths she knew so well, the boats drawn up for the winter, whose names she knew, whose owners she had known from her childhood; she noticed the new villas built in her absence. And she looked at the grey sea; a sob burst from her; but she was very strong, and at once she recovered herself. She turned back and slowly walked up the High Street again to the station. The lamps were lighted now, and the street looked as it had looked in her memory through the years; between the Green Dragon and the Duke of Kent were the same groups of men – farmers, townsfolk, fishermen – talking in the glare of the rival inns, and they stared at her curiously as she passed, a tall figure, closely veiled. She looked at the well-remembered shops, the stationery shop with its old-fashioned, fly-blown knick-knacks, the milliner's with cheap, gaudy hats, the little tailor's with his antiquated fashion plates. At last she came to the station, and sat in the waiting-room, her heart full of infinite sadness – the terrible sadness of the past.[28]

On the simplest level, Daisy's walk is Maugham's own nostalgic farewell to the Whitstable which essentially he had left some years earlier when he had gone to Canterbury as a boarding student. Though his life there was unhappy – 'the terrible sadness of the past'? – the town had become part of his consciousness and still had the power to evoke memories. On another level, Daisy's rebellion, success, and triumphant return to the priggish and narrow people who had rejected her may have represented the author's own feelings toward those he had left behind in Whitstable. He had, after all, eloped in a fashion to Heidelberg, and he attributed his success in resisting the pressures to go to Cambridge to his uncle's having given up on him. Professional authorship, within the Maugham family as well as Victorian society at large, was considered nearly as disreputable an occupation as Daisy's being an actress.

It may be that 'Daisy' was an expression of Maugham's dream of achieving fame and position, and some day returning triumphantly to the scene of his earliest humiliations. That his heroine receives no forgiveness from her father may suggest that Maugham did not expect – or masochistically did not want – a good word from the vicar. For someone who felt that he had had so little love when he was young, Daisy's final desperate plea to her husband articulates the price one pays for a childhood lacking in affection. 'You do love me, Herbert, don't you?' she cries, 'I want your love so badly.'[29]

In March 1896 Maugham sent two long short stories, 'A Bad Example' and possibly 'Daisy', to Fisher Unwin in the hope that the publisher might include them in his series of short books called the Pseudonym Library. There is no evidence that Unwin's readers even looked at both stories – Edward Garnett did not see 'Daisy' until December 1898 – but Garnett did report on 'A Bad Example' in June 1896. 'There is some ability in this,' he wrote, 'but not *very* much. Mr Maugham has imagination, and he can write prettily but his satire against society is not deep enough or humorous enough, and his fairy tale is not *striking* enough to command attention. He should be advised to try the humbler magazines for a time, and if he tries anything more important to send it on to us.'[30]

Garnett was one of Unwin's most shrewd and experienced readers, and on the basis of this advice the publisher returned Maugham's stories, saying that they were interesting but not long enough for inclusion in his series. If the young writer, however, had a novel handy, he would be glad to consider it. Having sent a diplomatic rejection letter, Unwin probably did not expect to hear from Maugham again, but he could not know that he was dealing with a young man with a powerful inner direction. And so, what many people would have accepted as a terminal decision, Maugham saw as a reason for exultation. Unwin wanted a novel and he would provide it. Maugham wrote the publisher to tell him of his intention, and ten minutes after mailing the letter he began *Liza of Lambeth*.

Maugham not only knew that he could give Unwin a novel; he had a clear idea of the kind of novel he was best suited to write. Throughout his career his awareness of the literary fashions of any particular age was keen, and, chameleon-like, he was able to adapt to the colours of the time. When the *Bildungsroman* was at the height of its vogue in Britain, with the publication of such novels as Lawrence's *Sons and Lovers* and Joyce's *A Portrait of the Artist as a Young Man*, he produced *Of Human Bondage*. When the artist-outcast became a figure of romance for those disillusioned by the routine of twentieth-century life, he wrote *The Moon and Sixpence*. And when Aldous Huxley, Gerald Heard, and Christopher Isherwood began to create an interest in Indian mysticism, the seventy-year-old Maugham responded with *The Razor's Edge*. This is not to say that he lacked originality or that he gave the reading public only what it wanted. His achievement was to adapt his own themes – especially that of freedom and bondage – to the literary fashions as they changed over the years and within each framework to develop an individual and personal expression.

This pattern began with *Liza of Lambeth*, which was modelled on the realistic slum novels in vogue in the last twenty years of the nineteenth century. Under the influence of the French naturalistic school of Flaubert, Zola, Huysmans, the Goncourts, English writers such as George Gissing, George Moore, Arthur Morrison, Hubert Crackanthorpe, Rudyard Kipling, and Edwin Pugh had produced harrowing studies of English slum life. Adopting a form of the scientific method, the writers examined social conditions in a detached and objective manner, emphasizing the powerful forces of heredity and environment. Their protagonists were shown to be trapped by their milieu and by economic circumstances, oppressed by the violence inherent in subsistence living, and degraded by the cheapness of life in slum ghettos. In most cases, characters were defeated by circumstances, and the stories ended with their deaths.

Whether or not he fully realized it, the young Maugham was admirably suited in two important ways to write a realistic slum novel. First, his duties as a medical student provided him with a first-hand knowledge of material normally ignored or unknown to other writers. In the preface to the collected edition of *Liza of Lambeth*, he describes the kind of environment to which he was exposed:

> The messenger led you through the dark and silent streets of Lambeth, up stinking alleys and into sinister courts where the police hesitated to penetrate, but where your black bag protected you from harm. You were taken to grim houses, on each floor of which a couple of families lived, and shown into a stuffy room, ill-lit with a paraffin lamp, in which two or three women, the midwife, the mother, the 'lady as lives on the floor below', were standing round the bed on which the patient lay.[31]

A second, and perhaps more important, circumstance which benefited Maugham was the objective, detached nature of his medical studies. This diagnostic stance admirably suited the mode of the realistic novelist, whose aim was to present his material as graphically as possible without intruding himself into his story. Thus Maugham's approach made him a much more effective slum novelist than Gissing, for example, whose moralizing and personal intrusion undercut the force of his work.

In the preface to *Liza*, Maugham wrote that he modelled his first novel after the French master of the short story, Guy de Maupassant, for whom he had a great admiration. Maugham was indeed deeply influenced by Maupassant and other nineteenth-century French writers, and his writing always bore the mark of his early use of the French language. With *Liza of Lambeth*, however, it was the English writer Arthur Morrison who exerted the strongest influence both in subject matter and approach, a debt Maugham acknowledged in *The Summing Up*. Now little known, Morrison had built a reputation among serious readers with two excellent books: *Tales of Mean Streets* (1894) and *A Child of the Jago* (1896). Having carefully weighed the problems of illustrating the miseries of slum life, he used a technique which would expose the reader to the facts without giving him the protection of an emotional catharsis. Writing with austerity and frankness, he refused to express sympathy on behalf of his readers so that they could then avoid coming to terms with the implications of social and economic inequality. Maugham adopted this point of view in his first novel, and was therefore, like Morrison, accused of a lack of conviction.

Liza of Lambeth is the story of a vital, high-spirited girl who is brutalized and eventually destroyed by the slum environment. The darling of the street, she has a pleasant and conventional beau, but she becomes attracted to the more powerful sexuality of a married man. For a while the affair is a joyous stolen pleasure, but when it becomes known to the Lambeth community its tribal sanctions make Liza an outcast. The jokes and bantering of the street life become moralistic and cruel, and finally the young girl is forced publicly to fight her lover's wife in a communal trial by combat. Now pregnant, she miscarries from the savage beating she endures and the novel ends with her death.

Although *Liza of Lambeth* closely follows the pattern of many slum novels, it presents a number of themes and devices which are typical of Maugham's later work. The characters for the most part are paradoxical mixtures of good and evil, of nobility and vulgarity. Adultery is the catalyst which introduces conflict and action, and, as in Maugham's mature work, he does not expressly condemn it. The theme of unrequited love, close to Maugham's own experience and so common in his writing, is presented in the plight of Liza's jilted young man.

At the heart of the novel, however, is the concern for freedom which was the driving force behind the young author and which would run throughout his career. Liza's revolt against the pattern which Lambeth is imposing on her life is really a form of the rebellion which can be found in the artists, seekers, adulterers, and criminals of Maugham's later work. As much as Rosie in *Cakes and Ale* or Larry Darrell in *The Razor's Edge* she is rejecting dull conventionality and attempting to embrace her own pattern. The novel is thus really about rebellion against tribal pressures, an individual's desperate bid to be free from the pressures to conform to the rules of a particular society. Maugham would later develop this theme in other settings – fashionable Mayfair houses, stockbrokers' offices, Parisian artist colonies, and Chicago suburbs; in 1896, however, circumstances meant that he would see it in the slums of London.

Maugham delivered the typescript of what he provisionally called 'A Lambeth Idyll' to Fisher Unwin on 14 January 1897, and the publisher immediately sent it to three readers. The first report, by Vaughan Nash, could hardly have been more damning. 'The novel', it said, 'reveals the author's familiarity with the speech and customs of the London poor, but there is no indication that he knows how to use this knowledge effectively. Some details are revolting and unpublishable; there is no romance, sense of character, or atmosphere; and the incidents are unconvincing.' It would not, the reader concluded, rank with any of the sketches of slum life which had recently appeared.

Fortunately for the young author, Nash's report was not the only one given to Unwin. The influential Edward Garnett saw the novel quite differently, and he praised the authenticity of its portrayal of the speech, intemperance, roughness, violence, and kindheartedness of the Lambeth characters. 'The temper and the tone of the book', wrote Garnett, 'is wholesome and by no means morbid. The work is *objective* and both the atmosphere and the environment of the mean district are unexaggerated.' Since Arthur Morrison's *A Child of the Jago* was well received by 'the intelligent section of the public', if Unwin does not publish 'A Lambeth Idyll' someone else will. 'Mr Maugham', said Garnett prophetically, 'has insight and humour and will probably be heard of again.'

The third reader, W. H. Chesson, reported on 2 February that the novel was 'interesting, impressive and truthful', with 'a cleanness and sense of proportion' which softened the grimness of the story. He recommended publication on the grounds both of artistic merit and moral force, and Unwin accepted this advice.[32] Understandably elated, Maugham signed a contract with alacrity in April 1897. Because of the celebrations associated with Queen Victoria's Diamond Jubilee, Unwin delayed releasing the novel until the autumn, but on 2 September Maugham became a professional writer.

Sometime before its publication, 'A Lambeth Idyll' became *Liza of Lambeth*, and the young writer abandoned his intention of publishing under the name of 'William Somerset'. His original decision to use his first two names may have been in keeping with the idea of Unwin's Pseudonym Library, which kept the author's real name from the public. It may also indicate Maugham's desire to deflect the criticism of his family, which wholly disapproved of his entering the world of professional authorship.

It is curious that Maugham should have chosen to be known as William Somerset and then throughout his career as W. Somerset Maugham. In fact, he heartily disliked both his names (in *Cakes and Ale*, the young Willie Ashenden prefers 'Roderic Ravensworth' and 'Ludovic Montgomery' to his given names). 'Somerset' had come from a remote military ancestor on his mother's side, General Sir Henry Somerset (1794–1862), and no one who knew the writer ever called him that. Once at a seance in the late twenties, Maugham found the 'spirits' of his parents addressing him as 'Somerset', to which he quietly but firmly replied that his mother and father would never have called him by what they regarded as part of his surname.

Maugham's antipathy to 'William', which he once called 'a silly name' he had 'a great misfortune to own',[33] may have its source in the vicarage. Since it is likely the name by which he was called there, it may have forever carried connotations of that life he was trying to leave far behind. In any case, to his closest friends he was always known as 'Willie', though occasionally someone would call him 'Bill'. Thus, when he replaced 'William' by 'W.' in 1909 and considered 'Somerset' as part of the surname, he was making his professional name more formal than it might first appear.

In *A Writer's Notebook* Maugham claims that his publisher warned him that his novel would be violently attacked, and the firm's trade manager reported that the office 'was in a state of nervous apprehension on the day of publication'.[34] Unwin's instincts were sound, and *Liza of Lambeth* attracted considerable attention, both positive and negative, for a first novel. To the *Spectator*, 'the squalor of the little book is often positively nauseating',[35] while *The Academy* felt that it had 'taken a mud-bath in all the filth of a London street'.[36] The *Bookman* thought the novel 'all very hopeless and unrelieved by any sense of strong feeling working in the writer'. 'And yet', it added, 'he is clever and should be heard of again.'[37] This positive note was echoed by the *Athenaeum*, which praised the 'uncompromising fidelity and care'[38] of Maugham's depiction of slum life, and by Augustin Filon, who wrote in the French

Le Journal des Débats that the well-crafted book gave an accurate and vivid picture of the London poor.

The reviews in the popular press were generally unfavourable, but *Liza* attracted admirers – for example, the distinguished Victorian man of letters Edmund Gosse – from among literary people. It also gained a certain prominence through its use by Basil Wilberforce, later Archdeacon of Westminster, in a Sunday night sermon at Westminster Abbey. Frederic Maugham's wife, Helen, might note in her diary that 'Willie's book came out ... a most unpleasant story',[39] but other members of the public responded to it, and within a month a second edition was being printed.

It would be interesting to know the reaction of Henry MacDonald Maugham to *Liza* and the kind of attention his nephew was attracting. Willie had inscribed one of his presentation copies 'To the Vicar and Aunt Ellen [his second wife] with the Author's love. Sep. 2nd, 1897,' suggesting that though he addressed his guardian with the formal 'the Vicar' rather than 'Uncle Henry', he cared enough to send a copy with his 'love'. It is unlikely that the vicar ever read the book, though, since he died sixteen days later. The funeral was held on 21 September in Whitstable, with the chief mourners being Willie and his brother Harry. The funeral procession left from the vicarage, and, as it retraced the familiar route to All Saints' Church, Willie could not have helped but recall the many times that as a shy little boy he had accompanied his uncle on that journey. He had long since become free of the vicar's guardianship, though it would be years before he would be emotionally detached from the unhappiness associated with it, but he must have sat in the church that day with conflicting feelings of relief and nostalgia.

However mixed the reception accorded *Liza of Lambeth*, it was a considerable achievement. Maugham revealed a deft hand at dialogue, a skill that led the playwright Henry Arthur Jones to predict that the young writer had a future in the theatre. He also demonstrated an ability to convey a vivid scene with a minimum of carefully selected details. Some of the characters are memorable and the account of brutality and death is told without lapses into sentimentality. It was a good first novel, and Maugham ought to have been very pleased.

Judging from his own comments, however, the young author seems to have been unable fully to enjoy his success. In the preface to *Liza of Lambeth*, he writes that 'such is the perverseness of authors, I was much more distressed by the unfavourable criticism than pleased by the favourable ones.'[40] He was indeed stung by the negative reaction to his novel, and his response to one suggestion in *The Academy*'s review showed a particular sensitivity. 'The success of one season', it said, 'may be known by the imitations of the next, and Mr Arthur Morrison may afford a smile at the sincere flatteries of *Liza of Lambeth*. The mimicry, indeed, is deliberate and unashamed.'[41]

For a fledgling writer trying to make his literary reputation by writing about his own experiences in the south London slums, any suggestion of imitation would be galling. The type of comment, however, is a common one among critics wanting to place authors in schools, and a year earlier *The Academy* had in fact suggested that Morrison should throw off the traces of Kipling, Daudet, Dickens, and Zola and develop *his* own originality.

For Maugham, though, the charge seemed more serious, and in a letter to *The Academy*, written only two days later, he raised it to a more damning level. 'It is perhaps a little amazing', he wrote, 'to be charged with plagiarism, when my book was finished three months before *The Child of the Jago* appeared.'[42] As Morgan has pointed out, Maugham's response was not entirely forthright. First, it was *Tales of Mean Streets*, published in 1894, which had been the real influence, not *A Child of the Jago*, which appeared in October 1896. Second, *Liza of Lambeth* was almost certainly finished after the appearance of *A Child of the Jago*, though in Maugham's defence his novel must have been far enough along that it would have been little influenced by any other work. Finally, Maugham claimed not to have read Morrison's books, and, though he never subsequently admitted otherwise, he did acknowledge in *The Summing Up* that he had benefited from the interest Morrison had aroused in slum literature. No one who reads Morrison carefully can doubt that Maugham had indeed known his work when he wrote *Liza*, and when he came to assemble his short story anthology *Tellers of Tales* forty-two years later, he thought enough of this minor Victorian writer's fiction to include one of the stories from *Tales of Mean Streets*.

In his maturity Maugham always maintained that he never paid any attention to bad reviews, but in fact he was sensitive to critical remarks. In 1897 he was of course concerned to make an impression on the literary world, and any suggestion that he was merely an imitator was certain to rankle. Though he rarely thereafter ever wrote to the public press, he seems to have felt compelled to defend his artistic integrity on one occasion a decade later. According to Mrs Belloc Lowndes,[43] someone claimed to have rewritten *Lady Frederick* in order to make it acceptable after its numerous rejections. Maugham, she said, was so enraged that he wrote to the *Daily Mail* asserting that the play was being performed exactly as he wrote it, without a single comma being changed.

Maugham's sensitivity to the more general negative reactions to *Liza of Lambeth* found its way into print in another way. In his second novel, *The Making of a Saint*, written while *Liza* was in the bookshops, he used part of his introduction to attack the English for what he saw as their unwillingness to face unpalatable truths:

> I have a friend who lately wrote a story of the London poor, and his critics were properly disgusted because his characters dropped their aitches, and often used bad language, and did not behave as elegantly as might be expected from the example they were continually receiving from their betters; while some of his readers were shocked to find that people existed in this world who did not possess the delicacy and refinement which they felt palpitating in their bosoms. The author forgot that Truth is a naked lady, and that nudity is always shameful, unless it points a moral. If Truth has taken up her abode at the bottom of a well, it is clearly because she is conscious that she is no fit companion for decent people.[44]

There was another disappointment attached to the publication of *Liza of Lambeth*, one which was connected to his sense of accomplishment and to his plans for a career in writing: money. Maugham's contract with Unwin stipulated that he receive no advance or royalties on the first 750 copies. Thereafter, he was to receive ten per cent up to 2000, twelve and a half for the next 2000, fifteen for the next 2000, and twenty per cent for everything beyond that. The books sold for three shillings and sixpence, and though sales were brisk the royalty cheque, received a year later, was for only £20. Maugham was disappointed at the meagre return for his work, and he came eventually to believe that his publisher had taken advantage of his youthful inexperience. Twelve years later, he claimed to his agent, J. B. Pinker, that Unwin did him thoroughly in the eye over *Liza*.[45]

For a young man who had just seen his first novel published by a major house and who could now join, however tentatively, London's literary world, Maugham does not seem to have been swept by exhilaration. Undoubtedly, he did experience feelings of satisfaction and excitement, but in his qualified, perhaps muted, response can be found one of the tragic elements of his life. In *The Summing Up*, he writes that 'it is one of the faults of my nature that I have suffered more from the pains, than I have enjoyed the pleasures of my life.'[46] This comment is obviously a more inclusive and profound version of his remark that he was more distressed by negative criticism than pleased by favourable responses. It is related, as well, to his suggestion that he had so often lived in the hope of future pleasure, that anticipated happiness when realized often fell short of expectation. Even in his ninety-first year, he confessed that 'I have always lived so much in the future now, though the future is so short, I cannot get out of the habit.'[47]

Happiness, of course, is a relative sensation, depending largely on the individual's capacity to feel happy or to experience pleasure. Like love, happiness is more a function of the person feeling the emotion than the object of that emotion. Thus one person will take great pleasure in a humble meal while another apathetically leaves a banquet. The joy of a morning walk can for one individual far surpass that of another who faces an ocean cruise with ennui.

The process by which a person develops a capacity to respond to life with pleasure is no doubt complex, probably having its roots in childhood. Moreover, it seems to have less to do with the rational mind than with one's intuitive self. Though preachers, philosophers, and psychologists claim that one can alter one's outlook on events so as to achieve a greater degree of happiness, the capacity for pleasure seems more deeply rooted. In Maugham's case, the trauma, pain, and insecurity of his childhood certainly helped create in him a melancholia. Perhaps he had grown suspicious of happiness, distrustful of its transitoriness, and fearful of its being snatched away as his mother had been taken from him. Whatever the case, Maugham was robbed of the capacity for real joy and, though he would pursue it throughout the world for the rest of his life, he would find it only occasionally.

In the autumn of 1897 Maugham had good reason to be happy. Not only was he a published author, he had just completed his medical studies and was awarded the Conjoint Diploma of Member of the Royal College of Surgeons and a Licentiate of the Royal College of Physicians. He was now a qualified doctor, giving him the security of a profession he had sought, and indeed he was offered a minor appointment at St Thomas's by the Senior Obstetric Physician. Maugham, however, never practised medicine. As he wrote in *Don Fernando* in 1935, 'I had spent five years in a London hospital and for the first time in my life was my own master.'[48] So, confident that he could easily earn his living through his pen, he left for Spain three days after passing his final examinations.

3

STRUGGLES: 1897–1907

MAUGHAM'S DEPARTURE FOR Southern Spain in the autumn of 1897 was, he recalled fifty-seven years later, for the purpose of learning Spanish and writing another book. During his eight months in Andalusia, he made sure that he did both, but the impetus to leave England once more came from deep within him. In *The Land of the Blessed Virgin*, his travel book written shortly after his Spanish sojourn, Maugham explained why Seville meant 'ten times more' than it possibly could to anyone else. 'I came to it after weary years in London,' he writes, 'heartsick with much hoping, my mind dull with drudgery; and it seemed a land of freedom. There I became at last conscious of my youth, and it seemed a *belvedere* upon a new life. How can I forget the delight of wandering in the Sierpes, released at length from all the imprisoning ties, watching the various movements as though it were a stage-play, yet half afraid that the falling curtain would bring back reality!'[1] So vivid was this sense of escape that four decades later he wrote in *Don Fernando* that 'I have been back in Spain a dozen times since then; it has never ceased to possess for me the glamour of those first few months of heavenly freedom. I had no ties and no responsibilities. I had no care in the world but to write well.'[2]

After five years of balancing intensive medical studies with his relentless pursuit of authorship, it is hardly surprising that Maugham should relish a period of relative lack of pressure. But London, it must be remembered, had originally meant freedom, just as Heidelberg before it had meant an escape from the constraints of King's School. Maugham, in fact, had not lived in one place for more than five years since the age of fifteen. He had arrived at Whitstable in 1884 and, after five years of alternating between Whitstable and Canterbury, left for Hyères and Heidelberg in 1889. He began his studies in London in 1892 and now in 1897 was on the move again. He would return to London in the summer of 1898, but in another six years would be impelled to move to Paris for a year. After another nine years in London, he would welcome the chance to spend the four years of the First World War abroad, and for the remainder of his life he would be one of the most itinerant of modern writers.

Maugham's ambivalence to London, which remained with him throughout his life, is perhaps best illustrated by two letters to Ada Leverson. On 23 April 1909 he wrote that he could not understand why anyone ever left London, because it was the most agreeable place in the world, but less than a year later he told her that he had been in London for four months and he ached to get away.[3] London was the centre of his literary world, and he enjoyed its cosmopolitan pleasures and the society of his friends there. It always, however, represented professional duties, and much more important, personal entanglements from which eventually he wished to be free.

Maugham's urge to travel, though, was more complex than simply a desire to avoid the obligations of London. No matter where he set up residence, even at the Villa Mauresque where he spent thirty years, he was always gripped by wanderlust. According to Alan Searle, Maugham was perpetually restless to the end of his life, always wanting to start out on a journey.[4] In part, of course, he travelled for professional reasons – to collect material and specimens for his writing, to see people in unusual settings which often exposed their characters more nakedly than would be visible in their native settings.

Maugham's travel was also, of course, a defence mechanism, a form of flight from situations which he could not, or would not, face. So long as he was on the move he could avoid the commitments which inevitably develop when one remains in one place for very long. In his fascinating article 'Somerset Maugham: A Thematic Analysis of Ten Short Stories',[5] psychiatrist Leopold Bellak comes to an interesting conclusion about Maugham's travel based on his thematic analysis of a random selection of thirty of his short stories. 'There seems to be', he suggests, 'a conflict between active participation in the demands of the world, especially those of the bourgeois culture and the giving in to passive desires, to the call of simpler living under more primitive circumstances. From the attempted resolution of this conflict arises the beachcomber, the wanderer, albeit in this case a highly sophisticated one.'[6]

Maugham's many travels were largely a romantic quest for something better than he was experiencing at the moment, a search that seems never to have been fully satisfied. For someone who had lost his home at the age of ten, his comment in 'The Alien Corn' (1931) may be significant. When his first-person narrator is asked, 'Do *you* feel at home in England?' he replies: 'No . . . but then I don't feel at home anywhere else.'[7]

Judging by Maugham's account, his eight months in Andalusia were a period of delicious freedom and romance, and it may have been the most carefree time of his life. With some vision before him of what a young adventurer-writer should look like, he grew a moustache, began smoking Filipino cigars, learned to play the guitar, and wore a broad-rimmed flat hat. Living with generous friends in Seville, he rode through the countryside on horseback. As was his habit, Maugham went armed with literary guides, notably Lane-Poole's *The Moors in Spain*, George Borrow's *The Bible in Spain*, Théophile Gautier's *Wanderings in Spain*, Richard Ford's *Handbook for Travellers in Spain*, and a book by Prosper Mérimée. As he later admitted, he saw the country through their eyes. He was enchanted by the landscape and the people, and the warmth of his enthusiasm radiates through *The Land of the Blessed Virgin*.

In that book also can be found a number of references to a young woman called 'Rosarito' (another variant of the 'Rose' pattern), with whom he claimed to have fallen 'very pleasantly in love'.[8] If this seems like a casual remark, the description in *The Land of the Blessed Virgin* is almost flippant: 'It was not love I felt for you, Rosarito; I wish it had been; but now far away, in the rain, I fancy (oh no, not that I am at last in love), but perhaps that I am just faintly enamoured – of your recollection.'[9]

It is difficult to say whether Rosarito ever existed or was a fictional addition needed to complete a romantic travel book. There is just a touch of protesting too much about her presence, and a two-page description of her physical features – eyes, hair, teeth, skin, hands – is androgynous enough to allow for the possibility that Maugham was actually writing about a Rosario.

More persuasive are the accounts of the author riding through the cobble-stoned streets exchanging discreet glances with beautiful young women on balconies. Or the story of his brief stop for shelter at a farmhouse where a pretty Spanish girl gave him a bunch of violets before he continued on his journey. More indicative yet of the young Maugham's sexual experiences in Spain is an episode which he did not choose to include in *The Land of the Blessed Virgin*. At the age of sixty, however, he could be more detached about his youth, and he wrote in *Don Fernando*:

> There was a young man who went to Granada. It was his first visit. On the night of his arrival, after dinner, too excited to stay in, he went down to the town. Here, because he was twenty-four and also perhaps a little because he thought the gesture suited to the occasion he had himself directed to a brothel. He picked out a girl of whom he could remember nothing afterwards but that she had large green eyes in a pallid face. He was struck by their colour, for it was that which the old Spanish poets and story-tellers were always giving to their heroines, and since it is a colour very seldom seen in Spain the commentators have opined that when the writers talked of green they meant something else. But here it was. When the girl stripped the young man was taken aback to see that she was still a child.
> 'You look very young to be in a place like this,' he said. 'How old are you?'
> 'Thirteen.'
> 'What made you come here?'
> 'Hambre,' she answered. 'Hunger.'
> The young man suffered from a sensibility that was doubtless excessive. The tragic word stabbed him. Giving her money (he was poor and could not afford much) he told the girl to dress up again, and, all passion spent, slowly climbed the hill and went to bed.[10]

When Maugham wrote *The Land of the Blessed Virgin*, however, he saw a passionate, romantic Spain. He describes the songs, the dances, the carefree hours in the orange gardens, and the colour, life and exuberance of Seville at night. He tells of bullfights, wine-making, and cathedrals. In contrast, London is a monotonous greyness, leaden and cold in the ceaseless rain. While the Spaniards, poor as they may be, possess a joy of life, the English 'walk with a dull, heavy tramp, with the gait of strong men who are very tired'.[11] For Maugham, while England meant obligations and duties, in Seville he 'seized life eagerly, with both hands, forgetting everything but that time was short and existence full of joy'.[12]

There can be no doubt that the young Maugham found the life of the Mediterranean countries immensely appealing, and it was an attraction which remained with him for the rest of his life. By the time that he discovered Spain he was already familiar with Capri, and his love of that island sprang from the same sources. In his 1901 review of Gissing's *By the Ionian Sea*, Maugham's attitude towards southern Italy is remarkably similar to his treatment of Spain. As Anthony Curtis points out, it is not so much a review as a public affirmation of fellow-feeling for someone who has also basked in the warm Mediterranean sun.

In his review of Gissing, Maugham expresses doubt about the author's respect for certain wines and offers his own unabashed endorsement of an almost inaccessible peasant variety. Though the southern Italians, he says, will cheat you shamefully, they have so much grace and charming friendliness that they are irresistible. When he lands at the marina at Capri, there is always a little crowd which bursts into a shout of joyous surprise when it recognizes him, and the people crowd round to tell him their names and remind him that they are old friends. 'In Italy, in the sunshine,' he concludes, 'life is freer and more worth living. One has an impression that in the South it is possible to seize more vigorously all that existence has to offer; every minute there seems so much fuller; every experience, every pleasure and pain, seems so much more intense.'[13]

Maugham was, of course, only one of countless northern Europeans who fell under the spell of warmth, sun, olive trees and wine. In his case, though, the Mediterranean ambience stood in such marked contrast to his own shyness, control, and restraint. At the end of *The Land of the Blessed Virgin*, he writes of the Spanish 'insouciance' – the same word which D. H. Lawrence would later use to describe the spiritual and emotional spontaneity with which one should confront life. But, while Lawrence could – perhaps at his own cost – adopt an insouciant attitude, Maugham was never able to throw off his self-consciousness, embrace his fellows, and lose himself in a bottle of wine or a song. Lawrence may have detected this in Maugham when he referred to him as 'a narrow-gutted "artist"'[14] after their meeting in Mexico, another country with the Mediterranean temperament, in 1924.

Maugham was attracted to southern Europe for the same reason that he was drawn into various relationships in his life. That is, unable to be spontaneous and outgoing himself, he looked to those who could provide the vitality and gregariousness he lacked. Thus, though he would remain essentially an onlooker, the natural exuberance of those on the marina at Capri or in the villages of Spain might break through his reserve and warm him with the illusion of a shared humanity.

Even in the midst of Maugham's panegyrics about the south, there is a suggestion that the reality was something less than fully satisfying. At the end of *The Land of the Blessed Virgin*, for example, he argues that it is much better to read books of travel than actually to go abroad, that the man who stays at home preserving his illusions is better off than the one who learns that 'the reality is full of disappointment'.[15] And in 'The Ionian Sea', he writes that 'after all it is in reminiscences that people and places have their greatest charm. I swear that in real fact the sight of Vesuvius at night with its glow, or the *pergolas* of Capri, never gave me such exquisite sensations as when I dream of them in the dreariness of London. Alas, I never enjoy the sunshine of Naples and the cool azure of the sea so intensely as when the rain pours down in the English winter, and I look, rather sadly, at the desolation without.'[16]

However much Maugham revelled in the freedom and vitality of Andalusia, he had gone there to write a book, and by the end of his stay he had produced a novel called first 'An Artistic Temperament' and then 'The Artistic Temperament of Stephen Carey'. An early version of *Of Human Bondage*, this autobiographical novel of adolescence is an immature piece of writing. Loosely constructed and sloppily written, it lacks the little touches and details which give authenticity to *Of Human Bondage*. Flabby with superfluous passages and characters, it is written in an inflated and romantic style so at odds with *Liza of Lambeth* and the later Maugham. As the title implies, the young author was writing under the influence of the turn-of-the-century aesthetes, and his protagonist, rather than a candid self-portrait, is a picture of what Maugham thought a young man should be. Indicative of this is the absence of Hayward, who in *Of Human Bondage* is given many of Stephen's aesthetic pretensions. Made to be excessively Byronic, Stephen imagines that he has a 'Byronic soul', believes that he is Childe Harold, and plays Wagner – especially *Tannhäuser* – on the piano.

When Maugham took the manuscript of 'The Artistic Temperament of Stephen Carey' back to London in the late summer of 1898, he told his agent that since it was 'a little strong' he wanted to publish something milder first so that he would not become known as a writer as grimly serious as George Moore.[17] His worries about its effect on his reputation were groundless since Fisher Unwin refused to pay even £100 for it and no other publishers were interested at any price. Thus the novel never appeared, a stroke of good fortune which he later acknowledged, because it preserved his material for a time when he could explore it with maturity and relative detachment. More importantly, he was denied a cathartic release from a number of obsessions and memories which were weighing on him and which he had not been able to resolve. It is the exposure of these wounds in such painfully honest detail that gives *Of Human Bondage* the force of personal commitment that is unusual in Maugham's work.

The author donated the manuscript of 'The Artistic Temperament of Stephen Carey' to the Library of Congress in 1950 with the stipulation that no portion of it ever be published, a provision that has not denied the reading public any literary gem. It remains, however, a valuable source of biographical clues such as the absence of a club foot or any other handicap in the protagonist. Maugham, it would seem, was not yet ready to deal with his stutter and its effect on his life and personality.

The other important component of the novel is the young man's painful infatuation with a waitress, Rose Cameron, the counterpart of Mildred in *Of Human Bondage*. Though Rose is more physically attractive and emotionally warmer than Mildred, she is also a betrayer and destroyer, and she holds Stephen in a painful thrall until he finally breaks free to marry a wholesome young woman.

The strength of Mildred's hold on Philip has always puzzled readers of *Of Human Bondage* because, unlike the destructive females in all other novels of adolescence, she does not bind the young man to her with feminine beauty. She is in fact described androgynously, with a pale, almost green, complexion, flat chest, and thin, anaemic figure. Philip's attraction to her essentially has nothing to do with her being female; it is a complex reaction to her initial humiliation of him in a tea-shop and its continuing basis is masochism.

Because of the androgynous nature of Mildred, there are a growing number of people who believe that here Maugham was describing some painful homosexual liaison from his medical student days. The original of the waitress, the theory runs, could just as easily have been some vulgar cockney homosexual for whom Maugham developed the kind of adulation that Philip has for the schoolboy Rose in the early part of *Of Human Bondage*. The strongest evidence for this argument is the comment of one of Maugham's close friends of this period, Harry Philips, to Joseph Dobrinsky that 'the real Mildred was a youth'.[18] When he wrote 'The Artistic Temperament of Stephen Carey' three years after the Wilde trial, he may have felt compelled to translate this young man into Rose Cameron, but by the time he reworked the material he felt secure and skilled enough to make Mildred much closer – that is, less feminine – to the original. If Maugham did in fact reverse the sex of the antagonist of his novel, he would simply be joining a long list of authors who until recently felt it necessary to disguise the homosexual elements of their fiction.

Against this hypothesis is Maugham's own presentation of Mildred as a female, and Alan Searle has told the present writer that he is convinced that she was indeed a waitress in a tea-shop near Victoria Station. According to Searle, she taunted the young medical student about his stutter in a particularly derisive manner and like many people with a sensitive temperament, he was fascinated by her vulgarity. She taught him, he added, a number of things about sex that he had not known before.

Unless some hitherto unknown correspondence comes to light, the sex of the original of Mildred will never be known, and readers of *Of Human Bondage* must decide for themselves what lies at the heart of her creation. The important thing is that Maugham obviously did have a very painful and formative relationship with someone. It was so traumatic that it would be the foundation for his very long autobiographical novel written when he was nearly forty, and variations of its unrequited and tortured emotion would recur in other works. If the original of Mildred was a woman after all, the liaison may even have played a major part in confirming Maugham's predominantly homosexual temperament. He had gone to London, after all, with virtually no experience of women, and if this shy, insecure young stutterer's first heterosexual affair was that described in *Of Human Bondage*, the effect may well have been a devastating and permanent distrust of female love.

The importance of the Stephen–Rose Cameron material in 'The Artistic Temperament of Stephen Carey' is that it definitely places this difficult liaison in Maugham's medical student days. This is corroborated by his next published work, a novel called *The Making of a Saint*, which was released on 31 May 1898, though actually written in Maugham's last year at St Thomas's.

Following the acceptance of *Liza of Lambeth*, Fisher Unwin had asked for another slum novel, but Maugham was wary of becoming stereotyped and moved in the opposite direction. Some time before, he had read several articles by the Victorian critic Andrew Lang which argued that the only worthwhile novel that a young writer could produce was an historical one. Misguided by this advice, Maugham recalled the eighth book of Machiavelli's *History of Florence*, which tells the bloody story of Caterina Sforza and the siege of Forli. In the hours he could spend away from St Thomas's, he read whatever he could on the subject in the reading-room of the British Museum. During the summer vacation in 1897 he went to Capri and wrote strenuously until he completed the novel.

The Making of a Saint is tedious reading, and the author was right not to include it in the collected edition of his works. It is an imaginative fabrication, lacking the immediacy, simplicity and sincerity of *Liza of Lambeth*, possessing neither romantic historical flair nor real insight into the period. In the midst of this historical invention, however, an account of a passionate and painful affair with a woman stands out so vividly that it seems to have come more directly from the author's own experience. The narrator falls in love with the beautiful Giulia, whose betrayal of him with another throws him into an agony of rejection. He talks of his essential loneliness before meeting her, of walking through the country as an exile, of killing himself in his solitude. Finding Giulia, he was 'like the ship that arrives in the harbour, and reefs her sails and clears her deck, settling down in the quietness of the waters'.[19] After her betrayal, however, he becomes heartsick, resentful, and humiliated. Eventually they are reconciled and marry, but when she deceives him again he allows her family to murder her to redeem its honour.

In one sense, this episode is in the best tradition of Italian history and romance, with its passion, adultery, and killings of honour. Beyond that, however, the emotions of Maugham's first-person narrator – the first time he was to write from this point of view – seem to be the author's own. Though it cannot be proven, the essential similarity between this story and that of Stephen–Rose and Philip–Mildred suggests that they all came from the same painful affair.

In writing his Italian novel during that summer in Capri, Maugham established a work schedule which he was rigidly to follow until he could no longer put pen to paper in the senile last years. *Liza of Lambeth* had necessarily been written during the evenings away from the hospital, but with *The Making of a Saint*, he started working at six o'clock in the morning and continued until he was tired. He then bathed and enjoyed the Capri sunshine for the remainder of the day.

Maugham discovered that his creative mind seemed to work better in the morning than later in the day. 'My brain is dead by one o'clock,' he would say,[20] and he once claimed that, when he learned that Darwin never worked more than three hours a day and revolutionized biological science, he decided that he could accomplish his goals by the same amount of labour.[21] And so, with only slight adaptations to time and place, he thereafter adhered to this daily routine. During the years at the Villa Mauresque, visitors, no matter how intimate their friendship, knew that they would not see their host until noon. He would write through the entire morning but appear punctually at twelve o'clock for cocktails and lunch, and in the afternoon he would take a nap.

Even on his travels throughout the world, his schedule varied only a little. In 1922, for example, Dwight Taylor met the famous author on board the *Aquitania* sailing from New York to Europe. 'I am a man', Maugham told him, 'of very rigid habits. In the morning I remain in my cabin going over letters and business correspondence with my secretary. At precisely twelve o'clock I appear at the Dutch door in the smoking room, where I have one Martini cocktail. I then walk around the deck until a quarter to one, at which time I descend to the dining salon for my lunch. After lunch I retire to my cabin again and remain incommunicado for the remainder of the day.'[22]

Not even the worst conditions could interfere with Maugham's regimen, as composer and conductor Eugene Goossens observed during an Atlantic crossing in 1923. 'The *Aquitania*, a notorious "pitcher", put on a terrific exhibition during a heavy three-day blow,' he recalled. 'This effectively reduced a racehorse on board called Papyrus to such a state of exhaustion that after landing in New York it was quite unable to beat an American contestant named Zev, and was later returned ignominiously in the same padded cabin to its country of origin. William Somerset Maugham kept to his cabin for most of the trip, but emerged in the end with a completed short story.'[23]

Maugham's routine, maintained day after day, at home and abroad, in peacetime and war, through personal crises or times of calm, is one of the reasons that he could point to volumes of his books on the shelves. It is another aspect of his remarkable self-discipline, but one which is at odds with the patterns of many creative people, There can be no doubt that writing was one of the real satisfactions of his life. He told Kenneth Allsop that the three morning hours of intense writing remained his time of greatest pleasure: 'After they are over, everything else is invariably anti-climax.'[24] And at the end of his life he wrote: 'I have never been so happy or so much at my ease as when, seated at my table, from my pen word followed word till the luncheon gong forced me to put an end to the day's work.'[25]

From this account, one would think that the gong was a prison bell summoning inmates back to their cells after a few hours in the open air. But it was a self-imposed restriction, a signal that Maugham himself was sending that, no matter how pleasurable was his creation, it must cease for the day. Did he never, one wonders, long to burst the boundaries and write passionately through the day, to capture an emotion or idea that might prove elusive if allowed the time to escape? Why, if writing brought such joy, should he have parcelled it out in prescribed daily doses? Maugham's schedule brought him enduring success as a professional author, but it is interesting that he should approach his greatest joy with an iron will and self-discipline that was almost imprisoning in its rigidity.

When Maugham returned to London from his Spanish idyll in 1898, he was brought sharply back to the harsh world of professional authorship. It was then that he learned that *Liza of Lambeth* had earned him only £20, and he soon discovered that 'The Artistic Temperament of Stephen Carey' would attract no buyers. *The Making of a Saint* was a critical and commercial failure. A short story from his Spanish experience, 'The Punctiliousness of Don Sebastian', was published by *Cosmopolis* in October 1898, but because of the dishonesty of the editor Maugham was never paid for it. With the poor response to *The Making of a Saint* and the rejections of *The Land of the Blessed Virgin*, the young writer soon realized that the relative success of *Liza of Lambeth* had been a lucky accident. To become a successful writer, he would have to apply himself intensely to his profession.

Over the next nine years Maugham worked very hard indeed. He sustained his dream of becoming a marketable dramatist by continuing to write plays, though only two were accepted for only very limited runs. He produced six more novels, each different from the others, in an attempt to discover his *métier*. *The Making of a Saint* had been the result of his belief that a neophyte author should attempt only historical novels, and *The Hero* (1901) was intended to capitalize on interest in the Boer War. *Mrs Craddock* (1902) was Maugham's version of *Madame Bovary*, with touches of *Hedda Gabler*, though of all his novels of this period it has the most substance and interest. *The Merry-Go-Round* (1904) was an experiment in structure inspired by the aesthetes, and *The Bishop's Apron* (1906) was a comic play turned into a novel. Another converted play, *The Explorer* (1907), was a poor imitation of Kipling's imperialistic fiction, and *The Magician* (1908) was a straightforward attempt to tap the considerable interest in magic and the occult. All these novels were the experiments of an immature writer, and if they accomplished anything it was to show Maugham his limitations.

As his correspondence from 1898 to 1907 demonstrates, Maugham pursued his profession with considerable tenacity. This effort began with the engagement of his first literary agent, William Maurice Colles. Walter Payne had been acting on his friend's behalf while Maugham was in Spain, and he continued to handle his financial affairs for a number of years. In April 1898, though, Payne handed over three short stories to Colles, who was operating a literary and dramatic advisory office under the name of The Author's Syndicate. For the next seven years, until Maugham grew dissatisfied with Colles's handling of his scripts, the author bombarded his agent with suggestions, questions, urgings, and complaints. Not for Maugham was the role of the sequestered writer working away on his stories, letting his agent handle all the business end of authorship.

Colles's first success was the acceptance by Unwin of six short stories which were published under the title of *Orientations*. These included 'A Bad Example', 'Daisy', and 'The Punctiliousness of Don Sebastian', as well as three other stories from the Andalusian period. Edward Garnett reported favourably on 'Daisy' in December 1898, but the following month told Unwin that none of the other five stories was nearly as good. Despite this advice, *Orientations* was published in June 1899.

With *The Land of the Blessed Virgin* Colles was less successful. In June 1899 Maugham wrote to ask whether he was arranging to have it published serially, a matter he took up again in August. By December he was reporting that his friend Augustus Hare had recently declined an invitation to write travel sketches for the *Daily News*, and did Colles not think that the paper therefore needed *The Land of the Blessed Virgin*? Nothing came of these efforts, nor did Murray and Macmillan show any interest in 1901. In the end a version which Maugham rewrote and improved in 1902 was accepted by William Heinemann in February 1903, though to the author's chagrin Heinemann was then bringing out a similar book and so wished to avoid duplication. It was therefore not published for another two years, and Maugham had to argue for an advance on it.

Though Colles was Maugham's literary agent, Walter Payne continued to handle some of his manuscripts, suggesting that the author did not entirely trust Colles. On his return to London, Maugham had moved into Payne's flat in Albany Chambers, near St James's Park, and in the autumn of 1899 the two men moved into a small flat at 27 Carlisle Mansions, just off the Vauxhall Bridge Road near Victoria Station. The arrangement suited Maugham well: Payne was an agreeable companion whose absence at his law practice during the day gave Maugham the solitude he needed to write. A maid came in each day to cook and keep the flat tidy.

In 'Looking Back' Maugham revealed another advantage of his domestic arrangement with Payne. The young lawyer, he said, was very handsome and had no trouble getting girls to sleep with him, and when he was through with these minor actresses, shopgirls and clerks, he passed them over to his friend. Once a week, Payne would arrange to be absent, and then Maugham was able to indulge in 'sexual congress' as he called it – an unromantic and unemotional satisfaction of appetite.

This practice was far from admirable and in confessing it in 'Looking Back' Maugham seemed to be revealing himself, warts and all. As we know, however, that memoir though sincere in most ways is dishonest in sexual matters. Thus one is entitled to question whether the procession of young women was not in fact a procession of young men. The exact nature of the relationship with Walter Payne has never been explained, but the likelihood is that at some point it was homosexual. Payne was later twice married, and according to Ted Morgan's sources,[26] when he died Maugham pressed his widow for the return of his letters. This is probably the source of the story that went around London that after a former lover had died Maugham employed a moving company to help him retrieve a cabinet full of incriminating letters.

If, on the other hand, Maugham's version of the story is true, it is at least further evidence of sexual relationships with women which were empty of emotion. Here it is worth noting that some psychologists argue that the sexual sharing of women among men is indicative of latent homosexuality, the common object representing the real desire for sexual contact with the other male. In any case these encounters were as cynical as those with the Piccadilly prostitutes Maugham claimed to engage, despite an attack of gonorrhoea, whenever he could afford it.

Late in his life Maugham told his nephew that his greatest mistake was that 'I tried to persuade myself that I was three-quarters normal and that only a quarter of me was queer – whereas really it was the other way round.'[27] This remarkable confession identifies one of the most fundamental and damaging conflicts in Maugham's life: that between his natural inclinations and how he wanted to be seen. He had, after all, grown up in a period and a society which considered homosexuality abnormal and unacceptable.

There is reason to suspect that even Maugham's three-quarters 'queer' is misleading. The English author and critic Francis King, who knew Maugham in his later years, has told this writer that he believes that the ratio was more like seven-eighths homosexual and one-eighth heterosexual. The stories Maugham related of a succession of women were, according to King, his way of avoiding the truth about his own nature. And in a review, King offers a fascinating suggestion about Philip's club foot in *Of Human Bondage*, arguing that it was 'a metaphor for a graver disability than the stammer that most critics have assumed it to have been'.[28] Moreover, in his recent study of Maugham's work, John Whitehead shrewdly suggests that the unexplained power of El Greco, 'the secret which [Philip] felt the mysterious painter held for him', was revealed twenty years later in *Don Fernando* when Maugham uncharacteristically discussed the artist's homosexuality.[29]

Whatever the degree of Maugham's homosexuality, his confessional remark is significant for its admission that he fought against acceptance of his own nature. This fight, we now know, took place from about 1898 to the end of the First World War, a period in which he pursued heterosexual relationships but found homosexual ones less difficult and binding. Even if his own accounts are exaggerated, there can be no doubt that he did have several important sexual relationships with women. His claim to have had a brief but pleasant affair with Sasha Kropotkin, the daughter of Prince Kropotkin living in exile in London, has been corroborated by Rebecca West. According to West, Kropotkin was the original of the woman in Maugham's short story 'The Luncheon'.[30] She certainly appears in 'Mr Harrington's Washing' (*Ashenden*) as Anastasia Leonidov, to whom Ashenden once proposed marriage. Maugham also had a lengthy affair with Ethelwyn Arthur Jones between about 1906 and 1913, and of course there was the relationship begun in 1913 with Syrie Wellcome, whom he married four years later. As well, Rebecca West told Ted Morgan that Maugham's friendship with the writer Violet Hunt, which developed about January 1903, initially had a sexual base.[31]

There may have been other heterosexual liaisons – Maugham claimed there were – but there is no firm evidence of them. Having reached his mid-twenties with very little experience of the opposite sex, Maugham seems in these few relationships to have been trying to prove that he was not 'queer', to use his own pejorative term. His admission to his nephew implies that it was a futile struggle, and indeed from 1920 onwards he was entirely homosexual. But even during the earlier period, he was more actively homosexual than otherwise.

The publication of *Liza of Lambeth* had given Maugham a certain status in London's literary society, and he was frequently invited to literary parties and to weekends in the country. One of the first men of letters of note whom Maugham came to know was Augustus Hare (1834–1903), a writer of travel books and a lover of good conversation and good society. Impressed by Maugham's first novel, Hare contrived to meets its young author, and before long Maugham was a frequent weekend guest at Hare's country house, Holmhurst. Here, as he has described in detail in *The Vagrant Mood*, the routine of such visits was formal and Victorian.

In the early days of his writing career, Maugham felt a certain discomfort on such weekends. He was embarrassed by the modest quality of his luggage and toiletries, which were always unpacked by a footman, and his financial constraints made the necessary tips to footmen and butlers awkward. After 1908, when he suddenly became affluent, these parties became easier, though the valet whom he would take along from his London residence often complained of his lack of status as an author's man. Before then, however, youth and modest finances had their advantages. According to Raymond Mortimer, Maugham once told him that on such weekends in the country he was occasionally asked to share a bed with some other young man. More often than not this led to a sexual encounter which, in Maugham's words, 'turned out to be very pleasant'.[32]

Similarly, Peter Quennell told this writer that Maugham once described how as a young man he always went to the Chelsea Arts Ball, usually dressed in El Greco Spanish style, and he boasted of never returning home alone at the end of the evening. The implication was that the author's companions were young women, but Quennell got the distinct feeling that they were in fact men. Gerald Kelly, who first met Maugham in the summer of 1904 and became one of his most trusted and loyal friends, claimed that since Maugham was homosexual while he was heterosexual there was never a basis for sexual jealousies or quarrels between them (though this may not have been true with Ethelwyn Jones). Maugham, said Kelly, was no threat to Kelly's women, nor Kelly to Maugham's young men; thus their friendship was never jeopardized.[33]

Maugham continued to see Wentworth Huyshe for a while after 1897, but many of his male friendships in the early years of this century were connected with the two traditional universities, Oxford and Cambridge. He had come to regret giving up the chance to go to Cambridge and had been self-conscious in the presence of the many fellow students at St Thomas's who had spent several years at one of the universities. Perhaps this underlying feeling of insecurity led him to seek out those who were at Oxford or Cambridge and by association compensate for what he came to see as a lack in his education.

Maugham was fond of staying in Oxford, and by 1903 had a good number of friends there. The writer Douglas Goldring was then in his first term there and very much enthralled by a prefect he would identify only by the title of 'The Influence', a man 'to whom the term "friend" in its accepted connotation scarcely applies'.[34] 'The Influence' was surrounded by 'god-like figures', one of whom Goldring identifies only as 'H. V. P.' – undoubtedly Harry V. Philips – whom he describes as 'quite the most dazzling figure for charm, good looks, and brilliant wit that I had ever encountered'.[35] Through this coterie, Goldring came to know Maugham, who had just returned from his second lengthy stay in Spain. 'I looked on him', says Goldring, 'with a good deal of awe as an established literary figure, and ordered myself much more lowly and reverently towards him than a literary youth of the 1935 vintage would dream of doing to anyone.'[36]

If Maugham seemed to Goldring to be 'an established literary figure', he nevertheless treated the young student with a kindly and sincere interest. He read Goldring's attempts at poetry, and gave him copies of Hérédia's *Les Trophées* and Henri de Régnier's *La Sandale Ailée*. On the fly-leaf of *Les Trophées*, Maugham inscribed two lines which Goldring found had a profound significance for the rest of his life: 'Qu'importe sa vie à qui peut par son rêve / Disposer de l'espace et disposer du temps.'[37]

Maugham's friendships extended also to Cambridge. The writer Louis Wilkinson recalled being introduced to him by a fellow undergraduate, Ralph Straus, in about February 1904, when Maugham came to Cambridge with a production of *A Man of Honour*. He struck the young student as 'an unobtrusive, rather wary, unusually good-looking man'.[38] His reputation at that time, remembered Wilkinson, rested almost entirely on *Liza of Lambeth*, though he had by then published three more novels.

The Making of a Saint had excited neither critics nor the reading public, and in 1900 all he had been able to get into print were two short stories, 'Cupid and the Vicar of Swale' and 'Lady Habart', which appeared in *Punch*. In July 1901 Hutchinson published *The Hero*, a novel suggested by the Boer War and written very much under the influence of Flaubert. Only 1500 copies were printed, and Maugham later claimed that though the critics liked it the public did not, and that he made no more than the £75 advance.

It is understandable why *The Hero* did not appeal to the turn-of-the-century reading public. On one level it deals with the conflict created by the loss of religious faith of one member of an engaged couple. Essentially, however, it explores a young man's struggle to free himself from the smothering effect of ignorance, prejudice, and illusion, as represented by the demands of his parents and the pressures of public opinion. In the course of the story, Maugham attacks patriotism, home, family, church, and honour, and the novel ends with a suicidal expression of despair and loneliness.

The Hero is one of Maugham's strongest expressions of determinism, and his protagonist's dilemmas may have been a fictional representation of some of the author's own unresolved conflicts. The young man's years abroad bring him an intellectual awareness which makes the narrowness of his parents and his village intolerable. On the other hand, his cosmopolitanism has not brought him emotional security, and thus, though he has nothing but contempt for his background, he needs the solidity of his roots. He is thus essentially homeless, a displaced person wherever he is in the world, not unlike his author, who had lost his home and had no roots in Whitstable.

One part of Maugham's early home life which became attached to *The Hero* was the sign against the evil eye, which thereafter appeared on the covers of all his books. His father had discovered the symbol on a trip to Morocco, and the author remembered it being engraved on a large amount of glass at the country house in Suresnes. That he would adopt it as a personal logo seventeen years later indicates a longing to connect himself to a lost home. 'My father was a stranger to me when he was alive,' he told his nephew, 'yet somehow that sign against the evil eye seems to have bound us together, for as you know I've used it a great deal.'[39] And use it he did – on stationery, matchbooks, and the gates to the Villa Mauresque.

If *The Hero* was not the sort of book to capture a reading public, his next novel, *Mrs Craddock*, was likely to shock it. Written in 1900, it was considered far too daring by a succession of publishers until Robertson Nicoll, though rejecting it on behalf of Hodder & Stoughton, recommended it to William Heinemann. According to Maugham, Heinemann agreed to publish it only if some sexually direct passages were excised, and it appeared in November 1902. With this publication began a relationship with the Heinemann company which, though occasionally strained, continued for the remainder of Maugham's career.

Mrs Craddock made publishers uneasy because its protagonist is a woman with a passionate sexual attraction for a man whom she pursues and marries. Bertha Ley is intellectual, imaginative, and sensitive, while her husband has little education, less understanding of women, and a generally narrow, insular outlook. Moreover, in a complete reversal of the standard Victorian sex roles, Maugham portrays the woman as passionate and sensual, while the man is cold and inhibited. Once the physical attraction wears off, Bertha finds herself trapped in an oppressive marriage, from which she is freed only by her husband's accidental death. The novel ends with her departure for Italy, where she will retire into herself, building her world within and living with a few intimate relationships. 'Now', writes Maugham, 'she had no ties on earth, and at last, at last she was free.'[40]

Mrs Craddock is the best novel that Maugham produced between *Liza of Lambeth* and *Of Human Bondage*, and it remains one of the most readable of his early works. Critical reaction was generally favourable and, more than a decade ahead of D. H. Lawrence's explorations of sexuality, it was a minor sensation for many readers. Douglas Goldring counted himself among the young Edwardians who were 'so thrilled' – while their elders were so shocked – by Maugham's work because it introduced 'a note of nastiness in English fiction'.[41]

Mrs Craddock gave Maugham a reputation for pushing the limits of what was acceptable in fiction, and for the next few years he repeatedly assured his agent and publishers that his next works would offend no one. Over the length of his career, however, he continued to present problems for editors, censors, and other arbiters of propriety. During his years as a dramatist, the Lord Chamberlain's Office frequently requested deletions of sexual references and religious comments. One of the most notable examples was the requirement that the young woman in *Our Betters*, produced in England in 1923, should not be the one to discover a pair of illicit lovers together in a summer house. Even so, the exclamation 'The slut!' sent ripples of shock through the theatre. Similarly, in *The Unknown* (1920), when a widow whose only son has been killed in the war is driven to exclaim 'And who will forgive God?' audiences were stunned.

Maugham's writing frequently created even greater apprehension when it was adapted for the more popular media: film, radio, and television. From 1917 to the present there have been dozens of cinema and television adaptations of his work, but until the BBC series of short stories in 1969, his plots and themes were consistently altered or diluted in order not to offend censors or audiences. When 'Rain', for example, was put on the screen, the Hollywood Hayes Office required that the minister who becomes sexually attracted to the prostitute be transformed into some sort of professional reformer. With 'The Letter', the Hollywood code demanded that Mrs Crosbie should not get away with murder as Maugham had written the story, and so she is killed by the Chinese mistress at the end of the film.

Similarly, though Maugham's stories have been dramatized countless times on BBC radio over the years, they have often proved to be too strong for the network's tastes. In 1935, for example, a production of *The Breadwinner* deleted a lengthy scene from Act III involving a discussion between the middle-aged Charles Battle and the eighteen-year-old daughter of a friend. The offensive elements were talk of her love for him, her possibly becoming his mistress, and her virginity. *The Circle* was broadcast the same year only after considerable discussion and on condition that certain passages be cut, that it carry a warning that it might be distasteful to certain listeners, and that it be aired very late in the evening. In 1941, 'The Closed Shop' was deemed unacceptable because it dealt with a brothel, and *Up at the Villa* was rejected because it was considered too explicit. As late as 1948, 'Rain' was considered 'rather a ticklish (moral) job',[42] and *East of Suez* was judged unsuitable in 1953 because of concerns about the Eurasian question and the treatment of mixed marriage.

These problems of publication and production of his work refute the charge that Maugham merely reflected public tastes. It is true that he was almost entirely conventional in matters of literary form, offering very little in the way of experimentation and thus being ignored in literary histories of the period. In content, however, he was much more daring, and he deserves more credit than he is usually given for extending the boundaries of what could be explored in print.

With *Mrs Craddock*, however, the shock came not because of its examination of sexual matters but because its frankly sexual protagonist is a woman. Maugham had contradicted Victorian attitudes by showing that a woman could be just as sensual as a man without, like Hardy's Tess or Pinero's Paula Tanqueray and so many others, being forever damned by it. In doing so, he had revealed a particular sensitivity toward his heroine which made her a very believable woman.

The protagonist of Maugham's first novel had been a woman, and throughout his career many of his most fully drawn characters would be women: Mildred in *Of Human Bondage*, Kitty Fane in *The Painted Veil*, Rosie in *Cakes and Ale*, Julia Lambert in *Theatre*, Isabel in *The Razor's Edge*, Leslie Crosbie in 'The Letter', and Betty Welldon-Burns in 'The Human Element'. Even more than his fiction, Maugham's plays are filled with a succession of female roles which provided memorable parts for many of this century's greatest actresses: Lady Frederick, Mrs Dot, Penelope, Grace, Smith, and Caroline, who gave their names to the title of the plays; and Norah in *The Land of Promise*, Constance in *The Constant Wife*, Lady Kitty and Elizabeth in *The Circle*, and Victoria in *Home and Beauty*.

Maugham is often accused of being a misogynist, and there is no doubt that he disliked, and felt threatened by, certain types of women. He nevertheless had many friendships with women throughout his life, and more often than not he developed a greater closeness with the female half of a married couple. He was, for example, especially attracted to Alfred Sutro's wife, Esther; to Ivor Back's Barbara; and to Garson Kanin's Ruth Gordon. Though he knew both the Eugene O'Neills well, it was to Carlotta that he wrote, and he preferred Nellie Maugham to his own brother Frederic. In his later years, his fondness for Ann Fleming led her husband, Ian, to joke that 'our friendship is largely based on the fact that he also wishes to be married to my wife, and he is always pleased to see me if only to hear news of her.'[43]

Maugham's writing also reveals a surprising empathy with the opposite sex. This sensitivity may have been an aspect of his homosexual temperament, but in any case Anthony Curtis is right to argue that Maugham was among the innovators in portraying twentieth-century women: 'Maugham understood women much better than any other playwright of this period whether it was women of the political and social aristocracy, the wives of the professional middle-class or the common prostitute. He understood them much better than Shaw, for example, who merely created new stereotypes of his own by giving women many of the qualities of leadership and resourcefulness traditionally ascribed to men.'[44]

When *Mrs Craddock* was released, Maugham was in what he came ironically to call his intellectual period – '*Et ego in Arcadia vixit*: I too have been a highbrow', he would write in the preface to his *Collected Plays*. Four months after the publication of the novel, Maugham had his first play produced in London, *A Man of Honour*, by the experimental Stage Society. He had written this Ibsenesque drama in 1898 after his return from Spain, but its harrowing realism had led to a number of rejections, notably by Forbes-Robertson and Charles Frohman. In the meantime, he had one of his short curtain-raisers, *Marriages Are Made in Heaven*, produced in Berlin in January 1902, in Max Reinhardt's Schall und Rauch theatre. Written about 1896, it was given eight performances as *Schiffbruechig (Shipwrecked)*, with Maugham doing the translation himself.

Maugham's first two productions were thus associated with experimental theatre in both Germany and England. The Stage Society had been formed in 1899 in order to provide exposure for worthwhile plays which were not likely to be produced by the usual commercial theatres. Its practice was to offer performances on Sunday evenings and Monday afternoons, and though a play might last only a brief time it would necessarily come to the attention of critics. Maugham's play impressed the Stage Society's selection committee, and thus on 22 February 1903 he saw his work on an English stage for the first time. The occasion was important enough to him that he invited his brothers Harry and Frederic, and the latter's wife, who noted in her diary: 'Very enthusiastic audience, and it was quite well acted. Willie was pale with terror!'[45] So convinced was the young dramatist that the production was a pivotal point in his career that he threw a lavish party for the cast and others at the Westminster Palace Hotel. Among the guests were Walter Payne, the composer Herbert Bunning and his wife Marguerite, and the playwright's brother Harry, who arrived late in a very shabby blue suit and declared: 'I'm glad to hear that my little brother has had some success at last.'[46]

A Man of Honour was indeed 'some success', but its author soon learned that it had gained him little beyond a reputation among those interested in experimental theatre. The play lasted for its two days, receiving mixed reviews, and a revival by the actress Muriel Wylford in London's Avenue Theatre in February 1904 ended after twenty-eight performances. Accompanying this second production was another curtain-raiser, *Mademoiselle Zampa*, which was dropped in the final week because of unfavourable reviews. *A Man of Honour*, however, seems to have fared better, as one of the actors, Hylton Allen, later remembered: 'I recall vividly the thunder of applause at the fall of the curtain on *A Man of Honour* at the Avenue. I was near the pass door, and I can see now the shy young author, quite shaken by the cheers and prolonged applause, coming through to the stage but quite unwilling to take a call.'[47]

Maugham had waived his royalties on the second run of *A Man of Honour* because he felt it was an investment in his future as a dramatist. His reputation had been somewhat enhanced in March 1903 when the script of the play was published by the prestigious *Fortnightly Review*, which had a circulation of more than 5000. Its editor, W. L. Courtney, had been impressed by *A Man of Honour* when he read it as a member of the Stage Society committee, but since it was too long for the *Review* he asked its author for a one-act play. When Maugham baulked at the idea, Courtney showed his respect for the work by bringing it out in a special supplementary issue.

Another of Maugham's esoteric forays at this time was his co-editorship with Laurence Housman of a periodical called *The Venture: An Annual of Art and Literature*. Housman, nine years older than Maugham, was also a homosexual and like Maugham had been unable to follow his brother to university. *The Venture* was an annual of short stories, essays, poems, and art work in the fashion of *The Yellow Book*. Though it survived for only two issues, in 1903 and 1905, its contributors make impressive company: John Masefield, G. K. Chesterton, Thomas Hardy, Richard Garnett, Havelock Ellis, Edmund Gosse, Alfred Noyes, Arthur Symons, and James Joyce. Included in the 1903 issue was the text of Maugham's *Marriages Are Made in Heaven*.

Despite whatever reputation these activities brought Maugham among the intelligentsia, they did nothing to make him a self-supporting author. His only other published work in 1903 was a short story, 'Pro Patria', which appeared in *Pall Mall*. Late in 1902, he had given his agent the typescript of a novel called 'Loaves and Fishes' and a play called 'The Explorer'. When by June 1903 no publisher could be found for the former, Maugham rewrote it as a play, and it began an unsuccessful tour of theatre managers' offices. Colles found 'The Explorer' distasteful because, he said, it was based too closely on the recent story of H. M. Stanley and there were living people who would be affected by the publicity. However, he sent it to Frank Curzon and then Charles Wyndham, both of whom rejected it. In July the prominent actor Lewis Waller saw possibilities if Maugham were prepared to collaborate with an experienced dramatist to revise and improve it. Maugham found the idea of collaboration abhorrent, and so it went on to Forbes-Robertson and Lilian Braithwaite and elicited no interest.

Long before this, in January 1903, Maugham had given Colles the typescript of yet another play, 'The Fortune Hunters', which Colles later testified was written by Maugham and his brother Harry. Though possible, it seems unlikely that Maugham would collaborate with his brother and there is now no way of knowing whether Harry had a hand in this work. By the time that it was produced as *Mrs Dot* in 1908, Harry was dead and it was credited solely to W. S. Maugham.

It was not until September 1904 that Maugham next saw his work in print, when *The Strand Magazine* ran two short stories: 'A Point of Law' and 'An Irish Gentleman'. Much more important that month was Heinemann's publication of another novel, *The Merry-Go-Round*. Maugham had completed it the previous January, and he repeatedly nagged Colles to ensure that it would be promoted vigorously. There was no use in Heinemann accepting it, he said, if he did not intend to push it, and after *Mrs Craddock* he should be able to generate considerable interest. Three weeks after publication, the author reminded Colles to convey to Heinemann the importance of advertising well. In the end, the book did not go well, selling only several thousand copies, and in early December Maugham complained sarcastically to his agent that Heinemann was doing little to put it before the public.[48]

The Merry-Go-Round is interesting, though immature, because it is one of the author's rare attempts at experimentation with form. In presenting a trio of stories linked by the presence of a few central characters, he tried to portray a wide spectrum of life and thus illustrate the complexity of social interaction. 'I saw my novel', he wrote in the preface to *Liza of Lambeth*, 'like one of those huge frescoes in an Italian cloister in which all manner of people are engaged in all manner of activities, but which the eye embraces in a single look.'[49]

One of the stories concerns the love of the daughter of the Dean of Tercanbury for a young poet. Though they learn that he is dying, she marries him and enjoys a brief but happy relationship. In the second story a woman becomes a prisoner of her passion for a young rogue, commits adultery, but later redeems herself by becoming a more sympathetic and sensitive wife. The third, and most interesting, tale is a novelization of *A Man of Honour*, which deals with one of Maugham's favourite ideas: that any virtue taken to an extreme will become a vice.

This theme is developed in the story of Basil Kent, a young solicitor and aspiring author who, though in love with a beautiful widow, becomes sexually attracted to a cockney barmaid, Jenny Bush. When she becomes pregnant, his keen social conscience tells him that he must sacrifice himself to do the honourable thing, and so he marries her in the belief that he is saving her from pain. It soon becomes apparent, however, that they are entirely unsuited for one another, and life becomes intolerable for them both. The marriage continues to deteriorate until Jenny commits suicide.

The Basil–Jenny section of *The Merry-Go-Round* is a bleak expression of determinism, of the power of social convention as it was portrayed in *The Hero*. Public opinion is once again shown to be able to exert a great and damaging pressure on the individual, who has seemingly little control over his own life. 'Society', argues one character, 'is a grim monster, somnolent apparently, so that you think you can take every kind of liberty; but all the time he watches you, he watches slily, and when you least expect it puts out an iron hand to crush you . . . Society has made its own decalogue, a code just fit for middling people, who are neither very good nor very bad; but the odd thing is that it punishes you just as severely if you act above its code as if you act below.'[50]

This theme, presented very forcefully in *The Hero* and *The Merry-Go-Round*, was a preoccupation of Maugham in the early years of his career. Basil Kent speaks so emphatically of his imprisonment to his own conscience, of the futility of his marriage, and of the freedom he discovers at the end, that it invites speculation about what happened to the author to cause him to write with such passion. It may be that Maugham, having seen how public opinion crushed Wilde for flouting its rules, was expressing a growing tension between his own inclinations and the norms of society. 'For God's sake,' says Basil, 'let us be free. Let us do this and that because we want to and because we must, not because other people think we ought.'[51]

Basil is one of the author's voices in *The Merry-Go-Round*, and Maugham put much more of himself into him than has generally been recognized. He is a young solicitor, estranged from his dominant mother by her scandalous behaviour, who spends his free time working to become an author. He has published a novel set in sixteenth-century Italy, which he has studied for months in the British Museum. Finally, after Jenny's death, he seeks relief in travel and near the end of a winter in Spain he writes to a friend:

> You must have known what effect it would have on my mind, tortured and sick. It is a land of freedom, and at last I have become conscious of my youth. How can I forget the delight of wandering in the Sierpes, released from all imprisoning ties, watching the various movement as though it were a stage-play, yet half afraid that a falling curtain would bring back the unendurable reality?[52]

This passage will be recognizable as an almost word-for-word repetition of Maugham's description of his own response to Seville in *The Land of the Blessed Virgin*. Only the root of the despair is changed: the memoir refers to being 'heartsick with hoping' and 'dull with drudgery'; the novel describes a mind 'tortured and sick'.

Maugham may of course be simply cannibalizing one of his works in order to provide material for another, a practice common to his early career, and it would not be surprising to find him using some of his own experiences and traits for a character. Basil is nevertheless more autobiographical than many of his figures and he represents some aspects of Maugham in 1904. Interestingly enough two more strikingly different characters represent other sides of the author.

To provide some common links between the novel's three stories, Maugham has created two people who stand outside the action as observers and *raisonneurs*: Frank Hurrell and Miss Ley. Hurrell is thirty (the author's age at the time he wrote *The Merry-Go-Round*), an assistant

79

physician at 'St Luke's Hospital' (a position similar to that offered Maugham at St Thomas's) who is about to set up practice in Harley Street. Extremely reserved, Hurrell is often silent with strangers and disconcerts them with 'an unwilling frigidity of manner' which they frequently mistake for superciliousness. 'Few knew', writes Maugham, 'that Frank Hurrell's deliberate placidity of expression masked a very emotional temperament. In this he recognized a weakness and had schooled his face carefully to betray no feeling; but the feeling all the same was there, turbulent and overwhelming, and he profoundly mistrusted his judgement which could be drawn so easily from the narrow path of reason. He kept over himself unceasing watch, as though a dangerous prisoner were in his heart ever on the alert to break his chains.'[53]

Schooling the face to avoid the betrayal of feeling is of course the trait adopted by the autobiographical Philip in *Of Human Bondage*, and Hurrell's search for truth and certainty 'with an eagerness which other men reserve for love or fame or opulence'[54] parallels Maugham's own youthful pursuit. 'For years', complains Hurrell, 'I've toiled night and day to distinguish truth from falsehood; I want to be clear about my actions, I want to walk with sure feet; but I find myself in a labyrinth of quicksands. I can see no meaning in the world and sometimes I despair; it seems as senseless as a madman's dream.'[55] A few years earlier, in Capri, Maugham had written in his notebook:

> I wander about alone, forever asking myself the same questions: what is the meaning of life? Has it any object or end? Is there such a thing as morality? How ought one to conduct oneself in life? What guide is there? Is there one road better than another? And a hundred more of the same sort . . . I could make nothing out of it all; it seemed to me one big tangle. In desperation, I cried out: I can't understand it. I don't know. I don't know.[56]

In creating Basil Kent and Frank Hurrell, Maugham was portraying opposing sides of his own character. Basil is the artist, whose law studies are only a means to pursuing a career as a writer. He is also the emotional element in Maugham which, if left to act impetuously, will bring pain and humiliation. Frank is the intellectual medical student, the searcher after truth, whose rational mind is able to keep a strong emotional side in safe check. Seeing no meaning in life, he can be flippant though compassionate about human affairs. And at the end of *The Merry-Go-Round*, the two men go in the different directions which were open to Maugham with the publication of *Liza of Lambeth* and the earning of his medical degree. Basil has gone to Seville and will return to pursue authorship. Frank, though aware that he has missed his youth through the drudgery of medical studies, will pursue a distinguished medical career to satisfy the expectations of his family.

The other character of particular interest in *The Merry-Go-Round* is Miss Ley, the first in a long series of Maugham figures who watch the world with a calm but compassionate detachment. She initially appeared in *Mrs Craddock* as the maiden aunt of Bertha Craddock, and her cool objectivity served as a perfect foil for her niece's unrestrained passion. Maugham did not include her in *A Man of Honour*, but she perfectly suited the role of confidante and *raisonneur* required by the structure of *The Merry-Go-Round*.

Miss Ley is a delightful creation, fully independent, intelligent, witty and free of humbug. She serves to undercut the pretensions of the other characters, though not without a certain sensitivity. As well, Maugham employs her as another voice in his debate with himself about how one should live one's life. To Frank's expression of despair at not finding absolute truth, Miss Ley replies that man is a chess player having to accept the unique moves of each piece but able still to make his own good game – a metaphor that Maugham repeated thirty-four years later in *The Summing Up*. Like that of Philip in *Of Human Bondage*, any meaning in her life will be that given to it by intelligence, and to her eyes at least it will form 'a graceful pattern on the dark inane'. And, like her author, she pursues a form of hedonism: 'I aimed at happiness, and I think, on the whole, I've found it. I lived according to my instincts, and sought every emotion that my senses offered.'[57] Miss Ley is given the final comment of the novel, that the compensation for all the misery and disappointment of life's merry-go-round is beauty. As Anthony Curtis has pointed out, Maugham came to reject beauty as the most important value in the world, but Miss Ley's remark in 1904 was then certainly his own.

Miss Ley is a rarity among fictional characters in having a novel dedicated to her. In an Epistle Dedicatory to *Mrs Craddock*, Maugham describes meeting her in Naples at the Gallery of Masterpieces while looking at a statue of Agrippina, and in a later edition he claimed to have based the character on this work of art. It has been suggested that the real model for Miss Ley was Maugham's Aunt Julia, to whom he had dedicated *The Hero*, and who had a close friendship with a very much younger man. On her death in 1910 she left her house on Westbourne Street, near Hyde Park, to Maugham.

Miss Ley may resemble Julia Maugham, but for the most part she was based on Mrs George W. Steevens, whom Maugham had come to know shortly after publishing *Liza of Lambeth*. Like a stage heroine of the period she was a woman with a past, having suffered social exile because of her role in the divorce of Sir Charles Dilke. She then married the very much younger George Steevens, a classical scholar and journalist who was killed while covering the Boer War for the *Daily Mail*. Having an independent income, she continued to entertain, and both her flat in Coleherne Court and her home at Merton Abbey became meeting places for intellectual and Bohemian London. She knew a great many people, and among the painters, actors, and writers who might be found there were Henry Arthur Jones, Max Beerbohm, George Street, William Pett Ridge, Reginald Turner, and Willie Maugham.

Maugham once asked a society hostess what it was that made her include him in her parties, and she replied: 'You were different from the other young men. Though quiet and silent, you had a sort of restless vitality that was intriguing.'[58] This mysterious reserve attracted a number of lion hunters, one of the most famous being Emerald Cunard. He was frequently a guest at her country home, Neville Holt, and remained her friend until her death fifty years later. So illustrious were many of her gatherings that Dorothy Peel recalled that one party failed because 'the celebrities were too many and the audience so few.'[59] According to Mrs Belloc Lowndes, Maugham was also one of those whose work attracted 'the brilliantly intelligent hostess' Mrs Crackanthorpe, who from her home at Rutland Gate cut a considerable figure in the literary social world of the late nineties and early part of this century.[60] Then, too, there were the Sunday afternoon luncheons given by Max Beerbohm's mother at her home in Upper Berkeley Street, where Maugham would join other writers as well as theatrical figures such as Viola, Felicity, and Iris Tree. During the First World War, he might be seen at Lady Sackville's Hill Street home along with Robert Graves, Augustus John, Arnold Bennett, or Sacha Guitry.

Mrs Steevens, however, was the most colourful of them all, and Maugham so appreciated her wit and iconoclastic good sense that he put her in his fiction as Miss Ley and dedicated his novel *The Explorer* to 'My Dear Mrs G. W. Steevens' in 1907. She was considerably older than him, and he seems to have looked to her as a kind of confidante and mentor. Like Miss Ley she lived apart from the pressures of his professional career and the difficulties of his emotional life, and could therefore serve as a constant and trusted friend. Because she was much older, there was no sexual tension between them, and thus they developed the close relationship so common between homosexual men and older women.

Another friendship which follows this pattern was Maugham's association with Violet Hunt. A contributor to the first issue of *The Venture*, she was a suffragette, edited a periodical called *The Freewoman*, and wrote novels. She was far more sexually experienced than Maugham, who was eleven years her junior, and, according to Morgan, she took the role of the older woman seducing the younger man.[61] Whatever sexual basis there was to the relationship lasted only briefly, soon giving way to a lasting and supportive friendship. Rebecca West told this writer: 'I do not think Violet meant very much to Maugham, but he was fond of her, and indeed she was, in spite of being very difficult as she grew older, a lovable character. He was always very kind to her.'

Maugham and Hunt continued to see each other for several decades after 1903, exchanged advice and encouragement about their writing, and maintained a kind of loyalty. Hunt dedicated *White Rose of Weary Leaf* to her young friend, and he dedicated *The Land of the Blessed Virgin* to her. Thirty years after that Maugham joked to Edward Marsh that Hunt had been annoyed because the dedication had appeared without her permission and she could not see why she would be in a country called *The Land of the Blessed Virgin*.[62]

Like Mrs Steevens, Violet Hunt endured a period of ostracism for having broken certain of society's rules. In 1908 she began an affair with Ford Hermann Hueffer (later Ford Madox Ford), who in 1911 left his wife to live with Hunt. A number of friends – notably Henry James – abandoned her after this, and more did so a few years later when Hueffer's wife sued for restitution of conjugal rights. Ford eventually left Hunt in 1919, by which time she was no longer an important literary or social figure.

Throughout her difficulties, Hunt could nevertheless count on Maugham's loyalty. Alec Waugh recalled a luncheon at the St Pancras Station Hotel organized for the contributors to a volume called *Georgian Stories*. Maugham sat next to Hunt, conversed with her throughout the meal, and as they were leaving picked up both bills, saying: 'I think I can stand you a lunch, Violet.' Coming at a very low point in her fortunes, suggested Waugh, 'Maugham's gesture re-established her as regards that gathering. He seemed to be saying to us all that she was not only an old friend, but the one person in the room of any consequence to himself.'[63]

Maugham developed yet another friendship with an older woman when he met Netta Syrett shortly after the Stage Society production of *A Man of Honour*. Now forgotten, Syrett contributed to *The Yellow Book* in 1894 and wrote more than thirty novels, a number of children's fantasies, and an autobiography during a career that stretched from the 1890s until her death in 1943. 'Her work', said her obituary in *The Times*, 'always bore the stamp of a woman of education and intelligence.'[64]

The relationship which began in 1903 continued in Paris two years later when both Maugham and Syrett were living there, and it lasted in some form until the Second World War. When Maugham suddenly achieved success as a dramatist in 1908 Syrett was invited to the supper parties he threw for cast and friends at the Bath Club. These celebrations were, she recalled, 'very gay and great fun'.[65] For her part Syrett dedicated her autobiographical novel *Rose Cottingham* to Maugham in 1915. Maugham may have had her partly in mind when creating the character of Norah Nesbit in *Of Human Bondage*, the older woman who offers a maternal and supportive friendship to Philip.

In 1909 Maugham wrote to his agent to see if he could get some work for Syrett adapting his play *Penelope* for serial publication, and as late as 1939 he was helping her deal with the affairs of another writer. In 1911 he also assisted her younger brother, Jerrard, who had just published a novel called *A Household Saint*. Maugham wrote the author a generous and encouraging note, what Netta Syrett called 'a wonderful letter for a young man to receive from such an authoritative critic'.[66] Maugham did even more. He wrote to Robert Ross, then reviewing for *The Bystander*, to tout the novel's virtues, albeit in a somewhat disingenuous fashion. 'It seems to me', he said, 'a very extraordinary study of a certain type. I am wondering who the author is. He must be quite young, but his work suggests a very original talent. Although I recognise that the book is in parts badly constructed and careless in writing, those defects seem to me unimportant beside the merits of its novelty.'[67] So enthusiastic was Maugham's praise that Ross reviewed *A Household Saint* and quoted the remarks without – to Maugham's relief – identifying their author.

Throughout his life Maugham had a special sympathy for young writers attempting to build a career and he was generous in his efforts to help them. In Jerrard Syrett's case he went further than usual, perhaps because he recognized unusual qualities in the young man. Maugham referred to 'a very extraordinary study of a certain type', and it is interesting to note that an earlier novel by Syrett had been accepted, put in proof, but never released. The publisher, according to

Netta Syrett, 'imagined he had found in it a horrible suggestion which is simply not there, [Jerrard] himself being astonished and overwhelmed by having attributed to him something he had never imagined, much less written!'[68]

The disturbing element in this novel, intended or not, must have been homosexual, and there is a good chance that the root of Syrett's problems was sexual tension. According to his sister, he was abnormally nervous and highly strung, a disorder that wrecked the later years of his life. Unable to write steadily, he spent long periods in idleness, and finally in 1926 he died of pneumonia. Once, when Netta Syrett lamented the wasted life of her gifted brother, Maugham observed: 'He is paying for his talents.'[69]

This enigmatic comment may be an expression of a romantic belief in the wasting powers of creativity, but it may also refer more specifically to the conflict arising in Jerrard Syrett from his homosexual nature. It echoes a remark attributed to Maugham when describing the suicide of his brother Harry. For whatever reasons, Harry swallowed nitric acid, and it was Willie who called on him on 27 July 1904 at his home in fashionable Cadogan Square to find his brother dying. He had lain in anguish for three days and, though Willie rushed him to St Thomas's, he died within a few hours. The coroner's verdict was 'suicide while of unsound mind'.

Harry had followed his two older brothers into law, but he hated being a solicitor, preferring like his younger brother to write. Though Harry was much more of a dilettante, he wanted to be a successful author, and his literary output has always been underestimated by those writing about the Maughams. *Beatrix*, his play adapted from Thackeray's *The History of Henry Esmond*, was privately printed early in his career, and he went on to produce *The Fall of the Queen, A Drama of Ancient Egypt* (1896), *The Husband of Poverty, A Drama of the Life of Francis of Assisi* (1896), *Sir Paul Pindar, and Other Plays* (1899), and *The Book of Italian Travel* (1903). As well, in 1901 he wrote a series of sixteen articles on various topics of the day under the heading 'The Amiable Egoist', in *Black and White Magazine*. Harry's work was far too esoteric for the general public and, since he refused to compromise for the commercial theatre, his plays remained unproduced. Having developed a nervous disorder some years earlier, he must have reached a point of despair when even corrosive acid was preferable to living.

When Willie had shown him the typescript of *Liza of Lambeth*, Harry had advised him to give up any ideas of authorship, and his remark at the opening of *A Man of Honour* must have rankled.

According to Charles's wife, however, Harry was the sweetest of the Maugham boys, someone who needed a lot of understanding of the sort that few people could give. It is hard to believe that Willie did not care about his closest brother, and years later he admitted that Harry was a charming and gifted man who cared deeply about his writing. The manner of his death must have been deeply shocking, and perhaps the reasons for it raised more questions about his own nature than have generally been recognized. Willie once remarked to his nephew that 'I'm sure it wasn't only failure that made him kill himself. It was the life he led.'[70] Frederic Raphael may be right when he suggests that Harry's pathetic self-destruction reinforced Willie's fear of being branded a homosexual. It may, moreover, have reinforced a feeling of guilt and fear in him for *being* a homosexual.

A week after Harry's death, Willie left for France, where Charles and his family were renting a summer house in Meudon. There he met a friend of Charles, a twenty-five-year-old Anglo-Irish painter named Gerald Kelly, who had been studying art in Paris since 1901. Kelly was short, slender, with a mass of black untidy hair, good features, and a great vitality which shone in his eyes. To Kelly, Maugham was also striking: 'his whole face was just one colour – very pale – and . . . his eyes were little pieces of brown velvet – like monkey's eyes. I thought he looked very distinguished.'[71]

The two young men struck up a deep friendship which was to last six decades, a relationship based only partly on an attraction of similarities. Both were small, energetic, and determined to succeed, and both, having been raised by parsons, were attempting to live as professional artists. Both had travelled widely, had cosmopolitan tastes, and had an integrity about what they admired in art and literature.

In many ways, however, it was the dissimilarities which attracted the two men to each other. Kelly was impetuous, outgoing, and gregarious; Maugham was reserved and shy. Kelly was loquacious, whereas Maugham chose every word carefully – as Kelly said, 'I am a great chatterbox and he is a reflective, silent man.'[72] Moreover, though they accepted each other as promising young artists, it was a good many years before Kelly was able to match his friend in public or critical acclaim. Three years before his death in 1972, Sir Gerald told me that this difference in their professional success might have destroyed their friendship were it not for Maugham's loyalty. Willie, he said, never implied that they were anything but equals, and he used his own success to throw parties and luncheons so that Kelly could be introduced to people who would help his career.

As Kelly's biographer, Derek Hudson, has said, Maugham's earliest letters to his friend 'set the tone for many that followed during the next sixty years – namely a lively practical interest in Kelly's work and a consistent wish to advise, admonish, and encourage him in his career'.[73] Maugham always visited the exhibitions of Kelly's work, and in the privacy of their correspondence analysed his paintings in detail and provided constant encouragement. On one occasion, he advised Kelly to take a long trip to Burma – even providing some financial aid – which became a critical turning point in the artist's career. Maugham later urged his friend to open a studio in London's West End, promising to underwrite the expenses if necessary. When Kelly eventually became President of the Royal Academy, no one was more pleased than Maugham. As Kelly said after his friend's death, 'Willie was a duck, an absolute duck. A bit rum towards the end, mind you.'[74]

Back in that first summer of 1904, Kelly's talk was of the artist's life in Paris, and it touched a responsive chord in Maugham. It had been five years since his months in Seville, and though he had travelled frequently to France and Italy, he was feeling the urge for a complete change of milieu and companions. This restlessness was deeply rooted and it was to remain with him throughout his life. A measure of its strength can be found in *The Merry-Go-Round*, where Frank Hurrell talks to Miss Ley of seeing his youth slip away in the tedium of London, where people are narrow and self-satisfied. In a passage which not only reveals Maugham's state in 1904 but presents a remarkably accurate blueprint for his later wanderings, Frank describes his attitude to travel:

I want to sail in ships, and battle with hurricane and storm; I want to go far away among men who actually do things – to new countries, Canada and Australia, where they fight hand to hand with primitive nature; I desire the seething scum of great cities, where there's no confounded policeman to keep you virtuous. My soul aches for the East, for Egypt and India and Japan; I want to know the corrupt, eager life of the Malays and the violent adventures of South Seas Islands. I may not get an answer to the riddle of life out in the open world, but I shall get nearer to it than here; I can get nothing more out of books and civilization. I want to see life and death, and the passions, the virtues and vices, of men face to face, uncovered.[75]

Maugham was himself thirty when he wrote the novel, and despite enjoying his social life he seemed to be getting no closer to his goal of professional success. Thinking that a dramatic change might be catalytic, he discussed the matter with Payne, who agreed that they should sell their furniture and give up their flat. Thus, in February 1905, Maugham left for Paris, where with Kelly's help he found an apartment near the Lion de Belfort in Montparnasse on the fifth floor of a house at 3 rue Victor Considérant. For £28 a year, he got two rooms and a kitchen and a spacious view of the cemetery of Montparnasse. He made the flat comfortable with second-hand furniture, and arranged for a woman to come in for a half day to cook breakfast and lunch.

Though Maugham's memoirs are silent on the matter, he did not go to Paris alone. His companion was one of the Oxford undergraduates he had come to know several years earlier, the handsome Harry Philips, with whom he had developed an intimate relationship. Philips had invited the author to stay at his family home in Staffordshire, where Maugham was viewed as clever but iconoclastic about religion. As Philips later hinted to Joseph Dobrinsky, his relationship with Maugham was homosexual. 'I cannot say', he wrote, 'that I was his secretary although we used that *nom de plume*. I was his companion and wrote a few notes – social and otherwise – for him.'[76] Their relationship lasted throughout most of 1905, through the summer in Capri, until Philips grew concerned about his lack of security. If Maugham tired of him, he would have nothing to fall back on, and being one who always acted on impulse he had become distressed by Maugham's cynical belief that no one ever did anything without a motive. Philips returned to England late in the year, the two men remained friends, and Maugham dedicated *The Bishop's Apron* to him the following year.

Philips recalled that in the Paris months Maugham maintained his disciplined writing schedule, working hard from breakfast until half past twelve, and that during this time he rewrote *Loaves and Fishes* back into a novel (*The Bishop's Apron*). Always a moderate drinker, he took an aperitif only on Sundays, when they went to the Café de la Paix and sat sipping a grenadine before having an inexpensive lunch. Maugham loved to frequent the Louvre, and in the afternoon they often went to see the work of his favourite painter, Velázquez, and others. His tastes then did not include the more contemporary art which later became the basis of his collection of paintings.

The pair went frequently to the theatre, where Maugham astounded his friend with his knowledge of French, German, and Italian – 'a born linguist', according to Philips. He especially enjoyed the kind of Grand Guignol drama he had come to know as a child in Paris, and he was very attracted to the noted French actress Dorziat. On some of these theatrical outings, Maugham was accompanied by Kelly and Netta Syrett, who was living in Paris and enjoying the company of the two fascinating young men.

Maugham and Philips also made frequent outings to Versailles, which Maugham adored. They occasionally saw Charles Maugham, but Philips noted that there was little mutual affection between the brothers. Willie, he recalled, was always very reticent about talking of his childhood and family, and it is interesting that he never spoke to his companion about Harry, who had died only months earlier. If this seems incredible, Gerald Kelly told me that he had never heard of Harry Maugham, though Kelly's first acquaintance with Willie occurred several weeks after Harry's suicide. One might conclude that his brother's death meant little to Willie, but it is more likely that it meant too much for him to be able to talk about it.

By far the most interesting part of Maugham's Paris experience were the evenings he spent at a restaurant in the rue d'Odessa called the 'Chat Blanc'. Situated near the Gare Montparnasse, this cheap and flourishing café had a ground floor for regular trade, but an upstairs room reserved for a varied group of artists, companions, models, and lovers. One could get a good dinner for next to nothing, after which the evening would be spent in vigorous debates about philosophy, politics, literature, and art. At the heart of the arguments, of course, was the debate about Impressionism, questions of how to use language, paint, or clay to convey reality.

Clive Bell, who was to become a member of the 'Bloomsbury Group' and a respected art critic, sharpened his critical thinking at the Chat Blanc. The unofficial club, however, was primarily an artists' circle, and Maugham has drawn portraits of many of them in *Of Human Bondage* and *The Magician*, where the Chat Blanc is described in detail as the 'Chien Noir'. Gabriel Thompson, a Welsh painter, and the American artist Alexander Harrison were regulars, as well as the American sculptor Paul Bartlett, who became 'Clayson' in *The Magician*. Penryhn Stanlaws, a young and successful American illustrator, is described as 'Flanagan', an amiable poseur, in *Of Human Bondage*, and in the same novel Kelly appears as Lawson, the hot-headed painter. Kelly, who liked to joke that all of Maugham's bad painters were portraits of him, was also the original of Lionel Hillier in *Cakes and Ale* and O'Malley in 'His Excellency'.

More interesting was the Canadian artist James Wilson Morrice, whose age and experience had given him a thoughtful yet lively outlook on life. His charm, wit, knowledge, and association with the glamorous Paris of the nineties impressed the young habitués of the café, and he became its philosopher. Maugham enjoyed Morrice and portrayed him with affection twice, first as a painter called 'Warren' in *The Magician* – 'the only man in the room of whom you'll never hear a word of evil'.[77] In *Of Human Bondage*, some of Morrice's qualities appear in Cronshaw, the drunken but sympathetic and wise café philosopher who teaches Philip about freedom, society, and the individual.

Not all the patrons of the Chat Blanc were sympathetic to the reticent English author who sat quietly observing their boisterous arguments. One figure whom Maugham found both intimidating and fascinating was the Irish painter Roderick O'Conor. Considered the most formidable man in the Latin Quarter, he was forty years old, experienced, highly intelligent, and very knowledgeable about art. He was also sullen, sharp-tongued, and iconoclastic. For some reason he took an immediate dislike to Maugham, who later recalled that his presence at the table seemed to irritate the Irishman and he had only to venture a remark to have O'Conor attack it. In Aleister Crowley's words, Maugham struck O'Conor as 'a bed-bug, on which a sensitive man refuses to stamp because of the smell and the squashiness'.[78]

From all accounts, Maugham suffered from the vitriolic attacks of O'Conor and Crowley, and, never verbally adept in groups, he must have endured much humiliation in silence. He had discovered his strongest weapons long before, however, and thus in *The Magician* O'Conor appears as a painter called 'O'Brien'. He is a failure whose bitterness has warped his soul so that, unforgiving of the success of others, he lashes out at any artist of talent. In *Of Human Bondage*, the Irishman appears as 'Clutton', a sardonic painter who is most cheerful when he can find a victim for his sarcasm. Here, though, Maugham uses his original to create a more complex character who ultimately has a profound effect on the direction of Philip's life. O'Conor, too, influenced Maugham's career. A disciple of Gauguin from the time he had met the painter in Brittany, O'Conor became an exponent of Gauguin's aesthetic theories and an apologist for his anti-social attitude. Maugham was intrigued by the stories of this strange figure, and they became the germ of *The Moon and Sixpence* fourteen years later.

Of all the people who frequented the Chat Blanc, no one was more bizarre nor as interesting to Maugham as Aleister Crowley. An eccentric English poet and Satanist, Crowley had inherited £40,000, which he soon exhausted on travel, mountain-climbing, dabbling in occult rituals, and financing the publication of luxurious editions of his own poetry. Kelly had met Crowley in 1898, when both were Cambridge undergraduates, and Crowley later made an unfortunate marriage with Kelly's sister, Rose, within two weeks of first meeting her. Rose eventually became an alcoholic and developed mental disorders, and Kelly never lost his hatred of the man.

In later years Crowley's eccentric dress, drug-taking, frankly erotic poetry, and conducting of black-magic rituals led the British press to call him 'the wickedest man in the world'. Much of his behaviour was pure charlatanism, but there was something in his character which was frightening. For example, Edward Marsh recalled a dinner in Soho when Crowley arrived as a kind of apparition in a conjurer's outfit, with a large diamond in the middle of his shirt-front. In the company of such attractive figures as Rupert Brooke and Wilfrid Gibson, Crowley seemed like a monstrous bird of prey. While the others cowered nervously, he talked wittily, cruelly, diabolically. 'For once in my life', said Marsh, 'I felt I had been in the presence of Evil with a capital E.'[79]

For some of the Chat Blanc regulars in 1905, Crowley's personality must have elicited the same reaction of anxiety and discomfort. Maugham confessed that he immediately disliked the man, no doubt because Crowley baited him mercilessly, but he remembered the aura of evil several years later when he wrote *The Magician*. While the central figure, Oliver Haddo, has elements of Svengali and Dr Moreau, he is a caricature of Crowley. Haddo has Crowley's skill as a mountaineer, his ostentation and verbosity, and the occult powers that Crowley at least pretended to possess. Haddo is also a skilled hypnotist, and the story of his psychic domination of a young English woman is based on Crowley's strange hold over Rose Kelly.

Through Gerald Kelly Maugham met another visitor to the Chat Blanc who was destined to make his mark on the literary world: Arnold Bennett. Older than most of the others at the café, he had yet to write his best work and was therefore treated with condescension. At the beginning, recalled Kelly, there was a mutual jealousy and tension between the uncouth and bumptious Bennett and the dapper and urbane Maugham. During their first meeting, Bennett unfortunately corrected his fellow author on his French, and Maugham, who prided himself on his use of his first language, boiled with rage. Despite this gaffe, as Maugham later admitted, Bennett was lovable, and a friendship developed between them that lasted until Bennett's death in 1931. Maugham was among the first people to pronounce *The Old Wives' Tale* a work of genius.

Like Maugham, Bennett was a careful observer, and a journal entry in

March 1905 provides one of the most interesting sketches of Maugham during this period. 'He had', wrote Bennett, 'a very calm almost lethargic demeanour. He took two cups of tea with pleasure and absolutely refused a third: one knew instantly from his tone that nothing would induce him to take a third. He ate biscuits and *gaufrettes* very quickly, almost greedily, one after the other without a pause, and then suddenly stopped. He smoked two cigarettes furiously, in less time than I smoked one, and solidly declined a third. I liked him.'[80] As Anthony Curtis has pointed out, the impression of Maugham here is of absolute self-control, of a strength of will which allows so much pleasure and then no more.

Over tea that day, Maugham told Bennett that he had recently sold a play, *Lady Frederick*, for an advance of £300 plus £100 for every quarter until it was produced. An actor named Fred Kerr had told the American theatre manager George C. Tyler about a young writer in Paris who had written a very clever comedy. Everyone in London had rejected it, but it was worth Tyler having a look. As a result, the manager invited Maugham for cocktails, liked the play, and took a year's option on it with the intention of putting the American actress Ellis Jeffreys in the lead part. In the end, Tyler could not persuade Jeffreys or any other actress to do it, and his option expired.

Another professional matter which Bennett and Maugham discussed was the problem of literary agents. Several years earlier, Bennett, like George Gissing, had become disenchanted with W. M. Colles's work, and had left him for J. B. Pinker. Maugham had been disappointed with what he saw as Colles's lack of effort in urging Heinemann to promote *The Merry-Go-Round*, and he was unhappy with his agent's rate of success in placing his work. In seven years, Colles had been sent eight plays and only *A Man of Honour* had been sold. Eight novels had fared better, with five of them being published, but of twenty-five short stories and articles, only eleven had been placed. Maugham was working very hard to establish a reputation, and he believed that Colles was failing him.

In June 1905 Bennett wrote to Pinker to introduce Maugham, whom he said he had got to know well. 'He seems to me', he said, 'to be a man who will make his way.'[81] At the end of June, Maugham himself wrote to Pinker to ask him to handle his fiction and to place the newly-rewritten *The Bishop's Apron*. He assured the agent that the novel was quite moral, but expressed dissatisfaction with Heinemann, who seemed to him to have grown complacent and did not advertise well. In early June, Maugham wrote from Capri, where he was spending the summer, to suggest that Pinker try Methuen and then Chapman and Hall. He did not believe that literary agents were capable of selling plays, and he wished to keep this part of his work to himself.

A week later Maugham wrote to Colles to say that, because of the failure of *The Merry-Go-Round*, he wished to make other arrangements for the sale of future work. He thanked Colles for his efforts and asked him to send his manuscripts to Walter Payne. When Colles objected to Maugham's version of his handling of *The Merry-Go-Round*, the author replied that 'we must agree to differ. I do not wish to enter into recriminations; but I cannot help thinking that what is obvious to me now, your experience might have suggested to you then, namely that when a publisher does not like a book and has made up his mind that it will not sell, one might just as well throw it into the Thames as let him publish it.'[82]

Colles thus ceased to be his agent, but following Maugham's sudden dramatic success in 1908, Colles sued for his commission on *The Explorer*, produced finally by Lewis Waller. The agent argued that since he had sent the play to Waller four years earlier he was responsible for its acceptance. Maugham's position was that, following Colles's unsuccessful efforts, the work had been sent to two other agents and then rewritten. Colles won his case and was awarded £21.10s.

Under his new agent Maugham continued to struggle to make a living with his pen, and Pinker soon found himself the recipient of the same instructions and urgings as had Colles. In August the author wrote to assure him that *The Bishop's Apron* had nothing 'that would bring a blush to the cheek of an American matron'.[83] and to ask that he get commissions for stories because he can be trusted to be suitably moral. He wrote to complain that the *Lady's Field* was delinquent in paying for a sketch it had published; and he wanted to know when Fisher Unwin would pay for the sixpenny edition of *Liza of Lambeth* and how many copies of *The Land of the Blessed Virgin* were sold. In the autumn of 1905 he was infuriated when *The Bystander* rejected a story which he had promised would be about well-dressed and rich people, and he sat down to write another.

There is a distinct note of desperation in Maugham's correspondence in the years from 1905 to 1907. His annuity of £150 a year was running out and, though his income of about £100 a year from his writing meant that he was not impoverished, he was finding an increasing gap between his financial situation and that of his friends. This accounts for his concern that he not be viewed as a writer whose work might offend a large number of readers. As well, it is the reason that he attempted to get as much as he could out of what he had already written. Thus he urged Pinker to promote a sixpenny edition of *The Bishop's Apron* a year after the first edition, and failing that to offer it to the *Daily Mail* for its sixpenny series. He suggested to Heinemann that *Mrs Craddock* be offered to the *Daily Mail* as well, and he hoped that *The Strand Magazine* would reprint one of the stories from *Orientations*.

Few of these suggestions came to fruition, and Maugham met with only a little more success with new short stories. One was published in *The Sketch* in December 1905, another in the *Daily Mail* in February 1906, and a third in *The Bystander* in March of the same year. For the first, and really only, time in his career, he attempted journalism and got nowhere. He moved out of his Paris flat at the end of November 1905, and after a few weeks in England left for a lengthy journey through Europe to Greece and Egypt. Before departing he suggested to Pinker that he should arrange for the writer to do a series of travel articles for some ladies' magazines. They would be similar to his sketches of Spain, and would, he thought, be of interest to the *Westminster*, *Pall Mall*, *Chronicle*, or *The World*.

Maugham left for the Middle East early in January 1906, travelling through Switzerland to Venice, where he took a boat to Port Said. There he stayed with a friend in the Sanitary Department, Dr Ross, who provided a room where he could write, and he took jaunts to Alexandria, Cairo, and up the Nile. Finding himself for the first time in a country where he knew nothing of the language, he attempted to learn Arabic. He spent three months in Egypt, much of it in Cairo, and wrote enthusiastically to Violet Hunt that the warm climate, blue sky, and fresh air made him feel eighteen.[84] During this time, he continued to send his impressions of the country to Pinker, but none were ever accepted for publication.

When Maugham returned to London in early May 1906 Walter Payne had moved into rooms at 56 Pall Mall, a more fashionable address befitting his stature as a successful lawyer. Maugham was able to share in this by renting a bedroom in the same building and using Payne's sitting room as a study. From here he continued to write and to reacquaint himself with the literary-social life of London, and during this period he developed one of the most important relationships of his life.

One summer day, possibly in 1904 but probably after his return from Paris in 1906, Maugham met a young actress at one of Mrs Steevens's afternoon parties at Merton Abbey. She had blue eyes and pale golden hair, and, except that she was not as buxom and heavy, she resembled a Renoir figure. It is almost certainly she who is described in his notebook as a woman with 'blonde radiancy, with eyes blue as the sea at midsummer and hair like corn under the August sun . . . She was a woman of ripe and abundant charms, rosy of cheek and fair of hair, with eyes blue as the summer sea, with rounded lines and full breasts.'[85] Though her figure was attractive, her greatest charm was her vicacity, which gave her the most beautiful smile Maugham had ever seen.

The young woman was Ethelwyn Sylvia Jones, the second daughter of the playwright Henry Arthur Jones. Always called 'Sue', Ethelwyn was born in New Hampton in 1883, and began an acting career at the age of fourteen in her father's *The Manoeuvres of Jane*. After an apprenticeship in the provinces, where she was noticed by George Bernard Shaw, she returned to London where she appeared in a number of productions. Most notably, she played under Sir Herbert Beerbohm Tree as Calpurnia in *Julius Caesar*, Charmian in *Antony and Cleopatra*, and Patience in *Henry VIII*. When she appeared in Bergstrom's *The Head of the Firm* in 1909, Max Beerbohm wrote that she 'radiates a natural vivacity that well suits the part'.[86] Offstage, Sue Jones had the same infectious vitality and, according to her sister Doris, 'a most amusing direct way of talking'.[87]

In 1902, at the age of nineteen, Sue married a theatrical manager, Montague Vivian Leveaux, in a lavish wedding ceremony. She was not in love, but wished to keep up with one of her sisters who was engaged, and her marriage soon deteriorated. She divorced Leveaux in the summer of 1909 on grounds of cruelty and desertion, but the marriage had been dissolved in all but name by the time she had met Maugham.

The quiet, reserved, tightly controlled Maugham was enchanted by the vivacious and outgoing young actress, and one night after dinner he took her to his room in Pall Mall, where they became lovers. Maugham thought the affair would last six weeks. In fact, it went on for eight years and gave Maugham his most delightful female character: Rosie, in *Cakes and Ale*.

Some time after this liaison began Maugham visited Kelly in Paris and told him that he was in love with a woman who was not strikingly beautiful but whom he would like painted. Kelly did at least two portraits, one of which – 'Mrs Leveaux in White 1907' – became the painting of Rosie by 'Lionel Hillier' (Gerald Kelly) described in detail in Chapter Twenty-Four of *Cakes and Ale*. Sue is, as Maugham describes, in the white silky dress, with the black velvet bow in her hair.

Her position and stance correspond exactly; she is in the middle of the canvas, with her head thrown back 'like an actress taking a call'. The only disparity is that, in Kelly's picture, Sue has her palms facing behind her, rather than forward as in Maugham's description. Maugham may have forgotten some of the details, or he decided that his version better emphasized the gesture of giving of herself which he saw in Rosie. In any case, as Kelly said, the portrait enchanted Maugham: 'She posed beautifully for the picture, so patiently, and both of us did our best, and I think Willie loved the portrait. I did several portraits of her – all, I felt, quite good. The picture was painted when I myself was very much under the influence of the great Whistler: but it really was like dear Sue.'[88]

Though Rosie is a disguised portrait of Sue Jones – the name of 'Rosie Gann', for example, was taken from a Whitstable woman the same age as Maugham – it is as accurate a picture of her character and qualities as Hillier's painting is Kelly's portrait. Thus the autobiographical *Cakes and Ale* may provide some clue to Sue Jones's appeal for Maugham. She was, after all, significantly different from the other women whom he knew – younger, less intellectual, and less cosmopolitan.

Sue's beauty was of course what first captivated Maugham. As he knew her better, her vivacity as represented in her smile and in the glow that he described in Rosie attracted the reticent author as did so many others who had the vitality and gregariousness that he lacked. Beyond this, however, may lie more complex reasons. Like Rosie, Sue Jones was warm, generous, and tender, qualities to which Maugham was especially susceptible. It is interesting that, while Sue was nine years younger than Maugham, Rosie is presented as being older than Willie Ashenden. This suggests that Rosie's wonderful fusion of hetaera and mother figure, of frank sexuality and maternal loving kindness, is at the heart of what Maugham saw in Sue. And there is an excellent chance that the description of Ashenden's first lovemaking with Rosie, one of the most moving passages in all of Maugham's writing, came from the author's own experience with Sue Jones:

> Rosie raised her hand and softly stroked my face. I do not know why I should have behaved as I then did: it was not at all how I had seen myself behaving on such an occasion. A sob broke from my tight throat. I do not know whether it was because I was shy and lonely (not lonely in the body, for I spent all day at the hospital with all kinds of people, but lonely in spirit) or because my desire was so great, but I

began to cry. I felt terribly ashamed of myself; I tried to control myself, I couldn't; the tears welled up in my eyes and poured down my cheeks. Rosie saw them and gave a little gasp.

'Oh, honey, what is it? What's the matter? Don't. Don't!'

She put her arms round my neck and began to cry too, and she kissed my lips and eyes and my wet cheeks. She undid her bodice and lowered my head till it rested on her bosom. She stroked my smooth face. She rocked me back and forth as though I were a child in her arms. I kissed her breasts and I kissed the white column of her neck; and she slipped out of her bodice and out of her skirt and her petticoats and I held her for a moment by her corseted waist; then she undid it, holding her breath for an instant to enable her to do so, and stood before me in her shift. When I put my hands on her sides I could feel the ribbing of the skin from the pressure of the corsets.

'Blow out the candle,' she whispered.[89]

There is no proof outside the novel that this passage is anything more than a fictional creation. There is about it, however, a very strong ring of authenticity, partly because of its unconventionality, and partly because it is such a persuasive and powerful outburst of emotion in an otherwise controlled, detached narrative. Moreover, Maugham presents the episode apologetically, prefacing it with a long digression on the use of the first-person narrator, as if he is embarrassed to reveal such a personal intimacy. It may well be, therefore, that Maugham was emotionally less experienced than Sue and that she provided a form of maternal love he had lost. As much as he loved her, though, she was married – perhaps for him safely married – until the summer of 1909.

Professionally, meanwhile, Maugham's only successes continued to be with novels, and they were modest at best. He had gone to Chapman and Hall with *The Bishop's Apron* because, not having another writer of note, they might promote him more vigorously than did Heinemann, whose major author was the immensely popular Hall Caine. *The Bishop's Apron* was the first of three novels written simply for financial reasons. His earlier works had been done with integrity, and though they attracted a certain intellectual following they gave their author no economic security. Thus he turned to satisfying popular tastes, and rarely in *The Bishop's Apron*, *The Explorer*, or *The Magician* is there a serious attempt to deal with an important idea.

The Bishop's Apron relates the attempts of Canon Spratte to get a bishopric, and his diplomatic manoeuvring is treated with light humour and the slightest touch of satire. There is some exploration of the Canon's love of power, but this is prevented from becoming a serious theme by the consistent epigrammatic and farcical tone. Years later Maugham claimed that *The Bishop's Apron* made him a good deal of money, but the truth is that though the popular press reviewed it fairly well it was not until Newnes brought out a sixpenny edition after Maugham's dramatic success in 1908 that it paid off for him.

Like *The Bishop's Apron*, *The Explorer* was a novelization of an unproduced play, and it was equally superficial. Maugham converted it in a month of tedious work and later confessed that 'it irked my conscience like the recollection of a discreditable action'.[90] Imperialistic fiction had become very popular at the end of the nineteenth century, and *The Explorer* was an attempt to reach the readers who wanted to escape from the problems of British life into the Kiplingesque world of imperialism, jingoism, and racial superiority. Maugham had used these qualities to make Edward Craddock a figure of scorn, but only five years later he was prepared to give them to his rugged caricature of a hero. If *The Explorer* has any element of the real Maugham, it is the emphasis on personal freedom that the protagonist gains in Africa away from the restrictions and narrowness of England.

With *The Explorer* Maugham returned to William Heinemann, though he had intended to go to another publisher with a different novel. Before converting *The Explorer* into fiction, he had signed a contract with Methuen for three books and received an advance for *The Magician* in October 1906. One of the partners of the firm was shocked on reading the proofs, however, and Methuen decided against publication. Returning the advance meant a financial squeeze for the author, so Maugham revised *The Explorer* in several weeks of hack work and sent it to Heinemann, who also eventually brought out *The Magician* in November 1908. By 1911 Methuen were casting envious glances at the by then popular dramatist, and wrote to him to claim that their contract was still binding. Maugham firmly pointed out that Methuen's refusal to publish *The Magician* had cancelled the agreement, a fact confirmed by their silence when Heinemann had subsequently brought out *The Explorer*. His threat to take the matter to court ended the Methuen challenge.

When Maugham delivered the typescript of *The Magician* to Pinker on 1 October 1906 he wrote: 'I have come to the conclusion that it is very dull and stupid; and I wish I was an outside broker, or Hall Caine, or something equally despicable.'[91] Years later, he professed to wonder how he could have accumulated all the occult material which he used to give his story a feeling of authenticity, and he suggested that he must have spent long hours in the British Museum.

The truth of the matter is that Maugham gathered his material from books given him by Gerald Kelly, who had learned a good deal about mysticism from Aleister Crowley, then a member of the Order of the Golden Dawn. When Crowley read *The Magician* in 1908 he could not help recognizing so many aspects of his life and character in Oliver Haddo, and the many passages of mystical theory were all too familiar. Reviewing the novel in *Vanity Fair* in December 1908, under the name of 'Oliver Haddo', Crowley proved conclusively that large segments were little more than transcripts of material from books on the occult that Maugham had borrowed from Kelly. He had plagiarized, among others, the introduction to MacGregor Mathers's *Kabbalah Unveiled*, Franz Hartmann's *The Life of Paracelsus*, Eliphas Levi's *Rituel et Dogme de la Haute Magie*, Mabel Collins's *The Blossom and the Fruit*, Dumas's *Memoirs of a Physician*, and Wells's *The Island of Dr Moreau*. 'Maugham took my riposte in good part,' Crowley wrote later. 'We met by chance a few weeks later, and he merely remarked that there were many thefts beside those which I pointed out.'[92]

Because of the circumstances in which it was written, *The Magician* lacked sincerity and honesty. It was devoid of any serious purpose and failed even to create the atmosphere of horror necessary for success in that genre. 'To me', Maugham confessed later, 'it was all moonshine. I did not believe a word of it. It was a game I was playing. A book written under these conditions can have no life in it.'[93]

From a biographical point of view, however, there are several aspects of *The Magician* worth noting. First, such thematic interest as there is comes from the idea of bondage, cast this time in the form of hypnotic slavery, though this is eventually obscured by the occult hocus pocus. More significant, perhaps, is a repetition of the pattern established in *A Man of Honour* of a young man having to extricate himself from a destructive relationship with a young woman in order to find a more tranquil happiness with an older one. Arthur Burdon is a young doctor at St Luke's who is engaged to the beautiful young Margaret Dauncey. Though Arthur knows little of cultural matters, he shares many other of his author's characteristics. Like Maugham, he 'was sufficiently conscious of his limitations not to talk of what he did not understand, and sincere enough not to express admiration for what he did not like.'[94] His two traits which strike others, however, are 'an imposing strength of purpose and a singular capacity for suffering. This was a man who knew his mind and was determined to achieve his desire . . . but those quick dark eyes were able to express an anguish that was hardly tolerable, and the mobile mouth had a nervous intensity which suggested that he might easily suffer the very agonies of woe.'[95]

Margaret's friend Susie Boyd observes this capacity for suffering in Arthur, and warns his fiancée that she has the power to 'make him more unhappy than any human being should be'.[96] Nevertheless, as the story progresses, the young woman falls under the spell of Haddo and betrays Arthur. Through all his anguish, Susie, an older and less attractive woman, is a loyal friend, and he comes to value her dependable virtues. Though there is no explicit suggestion that Arthur will turn to Susie when Margaret dies at the end, all of the emotional development has tended in that direction.

The Magician is pretty much a fabrication, and it would be a mistake to argue that Arthur Burdon is strongly autobiographical. It is nevertheless interesting that even here Maugham seems to set up a dichotomy between the betrayal of the young, sensual woman and the loyalty of the older, maternal one. He had done it in *A Man of Honour* and *The Merry-Go-Round*, and he would do it again in *Of Human Bondage*.

Before the publication of *The Magician* in 1908, Maugham's career took its most important turn. After rewriting *The Explorer*, he left in September 1907 to visit Sicily for the first time. He had been in Messina only a few days when a letter reached him from Golding Bright, who was now his dramatic agent: A play at London's Court Theatre had unexpectedly failed, and its manager, looking for a piece to fill a six-week hiatus, decided to produce the much rejected *Lady Frederick*. On 16 September Maugham sent Bright an excited reply, but his exhilaration did not blunt his characteristic anxiety about his work being done right, and from southern Italy he expressed concern about casting since, as he told Bright, all managers were born idiots.[97] He did not want the part of the rich Jewish Captain Montgomerie to go to an insensitive actor since if the role were exaggerated it would become grotesque. He was delighted that the illustrious Ethel Irving had been chosen for the lead, and he hoped that Fred Kerr would play Paradine Fouldes since the character had been created with him in mind. Maugham had not had much experience in seeing his plays through production, but his years of writing for the stage and of studying works of others had given him a shrewd sense of theatre.

In later years Maugham enjoyed telling of his mad race back to London in order to attend rehearsals. In fact, after he replied to Bright's letter, he moved further along the island, and it was at Girgenti one

Sunday that he received news that *Lady Frederick* would go into production the following Thursday. Short of funds to pay for the return trip and unable to wait for some expected money to arrive, he took a boat from Palermo to Naples, persuaded a steamship company to cash a cheque and sailed to Marseilles, from where he took the train to Paris and on to the Channel and England. At eleven o'clock on Thursday morning, claimed Maugham, he walked into the Court Theatre, feeling like Phileas Fogg after his eighty-day trip around the world.

Maugham had written *Lady Frederick* with the idea that a colourful central female part might attract a major actress. Thus he created the middle-aged adventuress, Lady Frederick, who can rid herself of heavy debts by marrying the rich young Lord Mereston, who is enthralled by her. In the end, though, she rejects this solution, and in the play's famous scene disillusions the young man by letting him see her in her boudoir in the morning light, without her makeup and with her hair in disarray. This final scene is a brilliant piece of satire worthy of Jonathan Swift, but it is also the reason why *Lady Frederick* remained unproduced for so many years. In an age when actresses strived to project glamour, the idea of appearing on stage without any makeup was unthinkable, and one by one the famous names of the day had refused the part.

When *Lady Frederick* finally opened on 26 October 1907 Maugham sat in the back of his box with Frederic and his wife, very pale and silent. Opening nights were always torture for him, but this was the most important one of his career. Tired of turning out novels which brought only a modest return and clearly unsuited for journalism, he still saw the stage as the only chance for financial security. The failure of his first full West End production after so many years of rejections would be deadly. He later wrote that, should that have happened, he would have returned to medicine and secured a position as a ship's surgeon. With his determination, it is more likely that he would have persevered with his writing, but a poor response to *Lady Frederick* might have condemned him to a career of hack work.

Lady Frederick, however, was an enormous success, and when the author went to his supper party for cast and friends at the Bath Club after the performance, it was with a sense of elation which would rarely be matched in the rest of his life. Though planned as a stopgap, *Lady Frederick* continued for 422 performances at the Court, the Garrick, the Criterion, the New, and the Haymarket Theatres. The American impresario Charles Frohman bought the rights at twice the price he would have paid a year earlier, and Ethel Barrymore made it a hit in

New York and on the cinema screen. After more than a decade of struggle and disappointment, Maugham had finally broken into the theatre.

4

SYRIE AND GERALD:
1908–1918

THE SPECTACLE OF full houses nightly leaving *Lady Frederick* soon made theatrical managers take another look at Somerset Maugham. Within eight months, they produced three more of the plays which they had been rejecting for years. At the Vaudeville Theatre on 26 March 1908 the Gattis presented *Jack Straw*, a farcical comedy of snobbery and mistaken identity written in 1905 from a story which Harry Philips had told Maugham about a family living near his home in North Staffordshire. Carried by the performances of the great comic actor Charles Hawtrey and the talent of Lottie Venne, *Jack Straw* ran for 321 performances.

One month later, Arthur Chudleigh produced *Mrs Dot* at the Comedy Theatre. Finished in 1904 as 'Worthley's Entire', it is a light comedy about another of Maugham's colourful adventuresses. Unlike *Lady Frederick*, however, Mrs Dot is a wealthy widow, and her manipulation is designed to capture in marriage an attractive young aristocrat. Once again, Maugham was favoured with two of England's best actors, Fred Kerr and Marie Tempest, and *Mrs Dot* continued for 272 performances.

Much less successful was *The Explorer*, which was produced by Lewis Waller at the Lyric Theatre on 13 June and ran for only forty-eight nights. Written nearly a decade earlier and having undergone translation into a novel and back to a play, its fundamental insincerity was apparent to audiences. Forced to end the run earlier than he had expected, Waller opened again in May 1909 with a third act revised and strengthened by the author, but this run lasted only a week.

Despite the lukewarm reaction to *The Explorer*, Maugham had in only eight months become London's most popular dramatist. In June 1908 he had four plays running simultaneously in London, a feat never accomplished before and matched since only by Alan Ayckbourne seventy years later. In its 24 June issue, *Punch* saluted this achievement with its now famous cartoon showing Shakespeare biting his thumb and glancing enviously at posters of the four plays.

A clue to Maugham's reaction to his sudden emergence as a popular and affluent playwright can be found in an entry in his notebook for 1908:

Success. I don't believe it has had any effect on me. For one thing I always expected it, and when it came I accepted it as so natural that I didn't see anything to make a fuss about. Its only net value to me is that it has freed me from financial uncertainties that were never quite absent from my thoughts. I hated poverty. I hated having to scrape and save so as to make both ends meet.[1]

This self-analysis may have been made in all sincerity, but its calm detachment – like that of *The Summing Up* – hides a lot. *Lady Frederick* had been a pivotal point of his career as a dramatist – he told Ward Morehouse in 1940 that his most exciting experience in the theatre had been its opening night – and the series of triumphs could not have left him unaffected.[2] He had always had faith in his abilities and a determination to succeed, and thus he may well have seen his acclaim as inevitable. But he was also acutely aware of the narrow line between success and failure, between the doors that were open in 1908 and those that had been firmly closed only a year earlier.

Maugham refers in this notebook entry, as he often did elsewhere, to the 'poverty' that he endured during his years of struggle. In fact, though he was not free of financial worries until 1908, he was never poor in the accepted sense of the word. Until his early thirties he had his legacy of £150 a year, and this was at a time when one could live comfortably, though not luxuriously, on £100. It should be remembered, for example, that Maugham was able to rent his comfortable Paris flat for £28 per annum. In addition, he had his income from his writing, and he later confessed to Godfrey Smith that 'for my first ten years as a writer I earned £100 a year, but one could live on it easily!'[3]

Maugham had not endured poverty at the vicarage or at King's School or in Heidelberg. His rooms at 11 Vincent Square were modest but comfortable, and the flats he shared with Walter Payne in Carlisle Mansions and Pall Mall were hardly the garrets of destitute artists. Moreover, his trips to Spain, France, and Italy, though managed with careful economies, were not the jaunts of the impoverished.

What Maugham meant by poverty was the humiliation of being unable to live in the style of some of his friends and most of his acquaintances. As he had become drawn into the London literary-social scene following the publication of *Liza of Lambeth*, he moved in increasingly affluent circles, to dinners and weekends in the country with the well-to-do and with young men from wealthy families. Temperamentally self-conscious, and already suffering some feelings of inferiority, he must have been acutely embarrassed by little unavoidable signs of his financial state. As Frederic Raphael says, 'His lack of affluence did not leave him hungry; it left him ashamed.'[4]

More important to Maugham in 1908 than a more luxurious way of life – and this remained true until his death many years later – was the freedom that money gave him. At the vicarage and during the King's School years, his uncle had reminded him that everything was circumscribed by his £150 per annum, and until young adulthood Willie did not control even that sum. As a medical student and in the following decade, he felt constricted by what he called the degrading and constant anxiety about means of livelihood and by having to arrange his life within the limits of a modest income. With success in the theatre, however, and the guarantee of future royalties, came much more control over his own life. 'I was glad to earn a great deal of money as a dramatist,' he wrote in *The Summing Up*. 'It gave me liberty. I was careful with it because I did not want ever again to be in a position when for want of it I could not do anything I had really a mind to.'[5]

Much later Maugham argued that his affluence had given him the power to tell any publisher or theatre manager to go to hell, and this freedom was indeed used to preserve his artistic integrity more often than his critics like to admit. His economic independence enabled him to resist the pleas of Charles Frohman to lighten the second act of *The Land of Promise* in order to make the play more commercially viable. When he was invited to Hollywood in 1920 – along with other writers such as Maurice Maeterlinck, Edward Knoblock, Gertrude Atherton, and Sir Gilbert Parker – effectively to be window dressing for film studios, he was able to turn his back on the charade and head for the South Seas for new material. Similarly, Maugham once wrote to his American literary agent, Charles Hanson Towne, to protect his artistic independence: 'I will not conceal from you that I am extremely vexed at your having signed an agreement with Doran which gives me nothing that I wanted but on the contrary takes away what I value most dearly, my freedom of action.'[6] George Doran, his American publisher for many years, himself testified to Maugham's artistic integrity:

I have been with him on two occasions when he gave emphatic evidence of his freedom. One was when he returned a cheque for $25,000 offered to him if he would write a brief scenario for one of the earliest talking picture producers. The other was when he returned a contract which involved the payment within twelve months of not less a sum than $150,000 if he would write talking picture scenarios. He was totally unwilling to risk the hazard of any misrepresentation of his art.[7]

It is important that Maugham used his financial independence to gain artistic control of his career. It is equally significant that after 1908 he almost never let his affluence interfere with his writing. For several decades he was the highest paid author in the world, and it would have been easy for him to follow many other writers – for example, Max Beerbohm and E. M. Forster – into an early and comfortable retirement. To his credit, he continued to write daily for another fifty-five years, and to study philosophy, religion and human nature as avidly as he did as a struggling writer.

In 1908 and after, Maugham maintained that money was a means to an end for him. 'Money', he was fond of saying, 'is like a sixth sense without which one cannot make a complete use of the other five. Without an adequate income half the possibilities of the world are cut off.'[8] His wealth enabled him to buy a succession of beautiful houses in London's fashionable Mayfair, and then a luxurious villa in one of the most beautiful parts of the Côte d'Azur. It permitted him to decorate them with Picassos, Gauguins, Matisses, Renoirs, Pissarros, Utrillos, and others, and to visit regularly the great galleries of Florence, Venice, Paris, and London. He was able to become the most widely travelled writer of the twentieth century – traversing the globe from Istanbul to Angkor Wat, from Stockholm to Tahiti – staying when he wished at the Raffles Hotel in Singapore, the Gritti Palace in Venice, or the Dorchester in London. And his affluence gave him the means to help others: relatives, friends, and young writers struggling as he had done to find their place.

Though money was undoubtedly a means to an end for Maugham, it came to represent much more than mere luxury or independence. If, as he said, life was a chess game, money became the most powerful and versatile piece on the board. For someone who is prevented by his reserve and speech impediment from being openly assertive, yet possessing a very strong sense of self and of the pattern he wishes to create out of his life and environment, wealth is the most effective weapon both for protection and manipulation of circumstances. It is the ideal means for the individual who characteristically wishes to assert his will quietly and from a distance, without the potential embarrassment of direct confrontation. As Malcolm Muggeridge said, 'Like all timid, lonely people, money seemed to him a protection. It set up a buffer between him and a largely alien and hostile world. To this end he sought it, first diligently and ardently, and finally as an addiction.'[9] Maugham's affluence thus allowed him to withdraw from the world into various homes, insulated from others by a number of butlers, maids, cooks, and chauffeurs. It bought the seclusion of first-class passage on ships and in the best hotels, and it bought the time to write and to read omnivorously.

Francis King has suggested to me that Maugham came to view his extensive earnings as a form of protective coloration for his homosexuality. If he had been homosexual and of only modest means, he would have been more vulnerable and open to ridicule. Great wealth, however, let him feel that he could say to potential detractors: 'But, look what I have accomplished.' It also, argues King, gave him the power to cut people out of his life by paying them off so that they would leave quietly. His affluence attracted a number of people to him and to the Villa Mauresque, but it also allowed him to sever relations with more discretion than is often possible.

With his roots in nineteenth-century naturalism, Maugham had a great respect for the way in which economics shapes lives, and this is a recurring theme in his writing. In his preface to Louis Wilkinson's novel *Two Made Their Bed*, he referred to 'the great, the insinuating, and the overwhelming significance of money in the affairs of life. It is the string with which a sardonic destiny directs the motions of its puppets.'[10] Poverty is, of course, the real antagonist of *Liza of Lambeth*, and the decisions of the heroines of *Penelope* and *The Constant Wife* are tempered by economic considerations. In *A Writer's Notebook* and 'A Man With a Conscience', Maugham claimed that almost all crimes, even murder, are motivated by financial hardship, and in *Of Human Bondage* a casualty ward nurse tells Philip: 'People don't commit suicide for love, as you'd expect, that's just a fancy of novelists, they commit suicide because they haven't any money.' In *The Merry-Go-Round*,

Miss Ley had claimed that 'poverty is a more exacting master than all the conventions of society put together', and *Up at the Villa*, written in 1941, tells of a struggling young Austrian for whom poverty has destroyed the pleasures of youth. 'I live in a prison,' he explains, 'and there's no escape from it.'

For much of his life, Maugham's respect for money was healthy and realistic, but Muggeridge is quite right to point out that ultimately it became an addiction. Late in his life, it was far more than a means to an end, as it became an obsessive symbol of security and power. Most of the terrible mistakes of his final years can be traced to his inability to separate money from his image of himself and from the basic human concerns of loyalty and love.

When people cite Maugham's statement that 'money is like a sixth sense without which one cannot make a complete use of the other five', they rarely include his important qualification: 'The only thing to be careful of is that one does not pay more than twenty shillings for the pound one earns.'[11] For the most part, Maugham adhered to his own injunction, but in 1908 there were those who believed that he had paid too dearly for his successes with the general public. Even in the wake of the triumph of *Lady Frederick*, an argument began to develop that Maugham had sold out to the commercial theatre, and in November he wrote to George Egerton to complain that with his recent prominence people were saying that he had degenerated.

Maugham unintentionally contributed to this cooling of the intelligentsia toward him by observing to an interviewer that there was a great deal of nonsense talked about serious drama. 'All that high-falutin' chatter about ideals,' he said. 'A playwright's and a missionary's appear to me to be two distinct and quite separate callings which should not be permitted to overlap. I cannot understand why a serious play should be held to be pre-eminently greater or more important than a humorous play, a comedy for instance.'[12] The primary task of the playwright, he argued, was to amuse – an unfortunate choice of words, as he later admitted.

According to Maugham, a Kensington debating society devoted an evening to discussing his decline, and in August 1908 *Current Literature* contributed to the argument with an article called 'The Tragedy of Mr Maugham's Dramatic Success'. The playwright, it reasoned, had offered managers and audiences plays of substance and quality but they had been consistently rejected; now that he was writing plays that were merely amusing, theatrical London was at his feet. There was a tragedy in his adopting this kind of writing but, the article shrewdly pointed out, it was as much a tragedy of the London theatre scene as of the playwright himself. What St John Hankin had recently said of Oscar Wilde applied equally to Maugham, that is, 'had the National Theatre or any theatre of dignity and influence existed in his time to which a dramatist might look to produce plays for their artistic value, not solely for their box office, Wilde might have done really fine work for it.'[13] The dilemma for Wilde and Maugham was the lack of a firm middle ground between uncommercial serious theatre and profitable popular theatre, and both opted for the latter.

Maugham was stung by the suggestion that he had sold his soul to Mammon, and he knew that he could write better plays. In May 1908 he told St John Adcock that he had achieved his purpose in these plays and did not think that he would write anything like them again.[14] Thus, when he wrote his next two plays, *Penelope* and *Smith*, it was with the intention of consolidating his place in London theatre, but with more boldness than he had shown in the previous four plays. As Anthony Curtis has pointed out, *Penelope* is very much set in the twentieth century, focusing on the middle class rather than the aristocracy and using a more realistic dialogue. It introduces a theme which Maugham was to explore repeatedly in much of his work: the marriage contract. The story is one of marital infidelity, and Penelope's response to her husband's betrayal is to feign unpossessiveness, a quality which Maugham frequently praised in women. Marie Tempest played the lead, and the production ran for 246 performances from 9 January 1909.

Like Barrie's *The Admirable Crichton*, *Smith* satirized a frivolous middle class through the device of a more capable servant, and, like Alfred Sutro's *The Walls of Jericho* (1904), used the eyes of a returning colonial to focus sharply on the follies of that class. In *The Hero* and *The Explorer*, Maugham had drawn a contrast between the freedom of the colonial life and that in England, and he would return to it four years later in *The Land of Promise*. In *Smith*, a character appropriately named Freeman returns from a period in Rhodesia, is offended by the shallow cynicism of his family and its circle, and eventually proposes to their maid. In the play's most shocking scene, a bridge foursome refuses to abandon its game, even when it is learned that the baby of one of the players is dying. The part of the maid was taken by another of the noted actresses of the English stage, Marie Lohr (later Irene Vanbrugh), and Robert Loraine was excellent as Freeman. It opened at the Comedy Theatre on 30 September 1909 and ran for 168 nights.

Between the productions of *Penelope* and *Smith* Maugham translated and adapted Grenet-Dancourt's *The Noble Spaniard* for Charles Hawtrey, and this light farce ran for fifty-five performances at the Royalty Theatre. Much less successful was his adaptation of Molière's *Le Bourgeois Gentilhomme*, which lasted only eight nights when produced by Sir Herbert Beerbohm Tree at His Majesty's in 1913. Of his own original work, Maugham penned two plays in 1910 which he considered to be more serious than any he had written since *A Man of Honour*. He wanted to experiment with form and to see how far he could go with his audience.

The first of these, *The Tenth Man*, was a grim story of political and financial intrigue among the landed gentry, ending with a suicide. Produced and performed by Arthur Bourchier at the Globe in February 1910, it did not appeal to audiences and closed after several months. *Grace* was a reworking of the section of *The Merry-Go-Round* in which a middle-class woman commits adultery but is impelled to redeem herself when the daughter of the gamekeeper on her estate kills herself over her seduction and pregnancy. The cast was illustrious – Irene Vanbrugh, Lady Tree, Lillah McCarthy, and Dennis Eadie – but the story was too strong for most tastes, and *Grace* ran for seventy-two performances.

With *The Tenth Man* and *Grace*, Maugham clearly was attempting to return to the kind of serious drama with which his career had begun. Five days after the opening of *Grace*, however, a correspondent signing himself only 'P. J.' wrote to *The Saturday Review* to state a thesis about Maugham's play-writing career that was to haunt him for decades. Maugham, argued the correspondent, had earlier written a good play that failed commercially and so wrote superficial comedies that succeeded. Writing poor plays in order to cultivate an audience is a bad habit that is hard to throw off. *Grace* thus reveals that its author has lost the ability to create real people and so it fails to be persuasive.[15]

Throughout his life Maugham professed to be indifferent to criticism, but in fact he was acutely sensitive to the judgements of others. He once advised his young nephew that the way to face the potential failure of his play was to hide his mortification and go on as though nothing embarrassing had happened to him.[16] This mask of indifference was Maugham's own protective means of coping with adverse criticism, and in *The Summing Up* and numerous prefaces and autobiographical fragments it hid a longing for the respect of serious readers and fellow writers.

Maugham had worked to earn that respect early in his career with *Liza of Lambeth*, *A Man of Honour*, *Mrs Craddock*, *The Merry-Go-Round*

1. One of the three photographs of his mother which Maugham kept at his bedside until he died.
(*Courtesy The Estate of Robin Maugham*)

2. The Reverend Henry Macdonald Maugham, vicar of Whitstable, who became Maugham's guardian upon the death of his father.
(*Courtesy The Estate of Robin Maugham*)

3. Young Willie Maugham with his uncle, the Reverend Henry Macdonald Maugham, behind the vicarage, Whitstable.
(*Humanities Research Center Library, The University of Texas at Austin*)

4. Maugham as a ten-year-old schoolboy.
(*Humanities Research Center Library, The
University of Texas at Austin*)

5. The eighteen-year-old medical student
at St Thomas's Hospital.
(*Humanities Research Center Library, The
University of Texas at Austin*)

6. Maugham, third from the left in the front row of this King's School picture, seems
already to be looking at distant points.
(*Humanities Research Center Library, The University of Texas at Austin*)

7. (*top left*) Gerald Kelly, one of
Maugham's oldest friends, had been
encouraged by him to go to Burma.
(*The Bettmann Archive/BBC Hulton*)

8. (*top right*) Violet Hunt, one of a
number of older women writers who
became loyal friends of the young
Maugham.
(*The Mansell Collection*)

9. (*left*) The black magician, Aleister
Crowley, who tormented Maugham in
Paris and became 'Oliver Haddo' in *The
Magician*.
(*The Mansell Collection*)

10. Syrie Barnardo Wellcome, aged 21, about ten years before she met Maugham.
(*The Wellcome Trustees*)

W·SOMERSET·MAUGHAM·
AD 1911.

11. The successful playwright and novelist in 1911.
(*The Mansell Collection*)

12. (*left*) 'Mrs L[eveaux] in white', the C
Kelly portrait of Sue Jones, which Mau
recreated in words in Chapter XIV of *Ca
Ale*.
(*Estate of Lady Lilian Kelly*)

13. (*below*) Godfrey Winn, a protégé w
writing for women's magazines earn
Maugham's contempt.
(*The Bettmann Archive/BBC Hulton*)

14. Beverley Nichols, whose friendship with Maugham, begun in the twenties, was shattered by the attack on Syrie in 'Looking Back'.
(*The Bettmann Archive/BBC Hulton*)

15. Hugh Walpole at his home near Keswick just before Maugham savagely caricatured him in *Cakes and Ale*.
(*The Mansell Collection*)

16. Maugham and Syrie just before their divorce in 1929.
(*Syndication International*)

and other works. But he had come from the upper-middle class and he was determined also to make writing an affluent career, and so he turned to *The Bishop's Apron*, *The Explorer*, and *The Magician*, as well as the commercial plays of 1907–1908, in order to achieve economic security. Unfortunately, the intelligentsia never forgave him his commercial success, and for the rest of his life he was accused of writing down to the public. He might give them *Of Human Bondage*, *The Moon and Sixpence*, or *Cakes and Ale*, or the serious plays of the early thirties, but he could not escape the label of 'middle-brow writer'. He had wanted both critical and commercial success of a high order, and after 1908 he became embittered by what at least for him seemed to be their incompatibility.

Maugham might have impressed serious theatre-goers when Charles Frohman mounted a repertory season at the Duke of York's beginning in February 1910, and announced that Maugham had been invited to contribute a play. The season eventually offered a list of impressive plays: James's *The Outcry*, Shaw's *Misalliance*, Galsworthy's *Justice*, Granville-Barker's *The Madras House*, and Barrie's *The Twelve-Pound Look*, but for reasons that are now obscure Maugham was never represented.

In other ways, however, Maugham had become part of the fraternity of dramatists. On 29 October 1907 he joined seventy-one other writers in signing a letter to *The Times* protesting the censorship of plays by Edward Garnett and Harley Granville-Barker. Then, in March 1909, he met with Barrie, Pinero, Sutro, H. M. Paull, W. J. Locke, Cecil Raleigh, and R. C. Carlton at the Criterion Restaurant to found the Dramatists' Club. Two months earlier he had been elected to the Garrick Club, frequented by actors and playwrights, his nomination being made by Arthur Bourchier and his candidature being endorsed by such literary figures as A. B. Walkley, J. Forbes-Robertson, William Pett Ridge, Nigel Playfair, W. W. Jacobs, and Edward Terry.

On 1 December 1908 Maugham had attended one of the more notable literary evenings of the Edwardian period, a testimonial dinner for Robert Ross. A Canadian journalist, writer and art dealer, Ross had remained one of Oscar Wilde's most loyal friends after his conviction, and as administrator of his estate had brought it out of bankruptcy. As well, he had edited the first collected edition of Wilde's works. In recognition of this service, two hundred writers and critics, notably H. G. Wells, William Rothenstein, Frank Harris, William Archer, and More Adey, gathered to pay tribute. A day later, Maugham wrote Ross warmly to congratulate him on his speech, which he found moving, while Wells's 'might have been entitled First and Last Things that one would rather have left unsaid'.[17]

Maugham had not met Wilde, but he developed friendships with a number of what Louis Wilkinson called 'the Oscarian magic circle'. He had collaborated with Laurence Housman on *The Venture*, and came to know Robert Hichens and Mabel Beardsley, the sister of Aubrey Beardsley. The member of this coterie whom Maugham most enjoyed, however, was the journalist and drama critic Reginald Turner, once labelled by Maugham 'the most amusing man I have known'. 'He would take a theme,' said Maugham, 'and embroider upon it with such drollery that at last you had to beg him to stop.'[18] Maugham recalled that when Wilde was dying in a cheap hotel in Paris, Turner visited him every day. When the exiled dramatist one morning was distraught because he had had a terrible dream that he was supping with the dead, Turner brought him to a roar of laughter by replying: 'Well, I'm sure you were the life and soul of the party, Oscar.' 'It was not only witty,' wrote Maugham admiringly, 'but kind.'[19]

In the years before the First World War, Maugham frequently visited Turner at his flat near Berkeley Square, and they spent several holidays together in Italy. On one such trip to Florence in the spring of 1909 they were joined by Louis Wilkinson and a friend, and Wilkinson recalled the vivid impression Maugham made:

> It was the special quality of the young dramatist's personal appearance that arrested me and that I valued ... What has stayed clear in my memory is the look of that unbelieving and guarded face that seemed so beautifully and smoothly, so strongly worked, as in rare ivory: that look of an ancient civilization, Orientally luxurious and wise. The dark brown eyes, congruous with his lustrous dark hair, suggested the eyes of some painted portrait. They gave the same effect of rich pigmentation in sudden contrast with skin pallor ... If I had never read a book or seen a play of his, I should be none the less convinced, remembering his looks and especially his eyes, that when he seems to be harsh and 'cynical' he is really a romantic *à rebours*.[20]

Another of the Wilde circle with whom Maugham developed a close friendship was the writer Ada Leverson. Several years older than Maugham, she had published a number of novels and was an established figure in the London literary milieu. Their friendship began in 1908, flourished most strongly until the First World War, and continued until her death in 1933, when Maugham's photograph finally came down off her mantelpiece. An indication of the warmth of their relationship is Leverson's gift to Maugham in 1909 of her first edition of Wilde's *The Sphinx*. In it, she had written a poem beginning, 'Oh dark tormenting face of beauty, loved.'[21]

Maugham appreciated Leverson's intelligence and especially her quick wit, and in his letters he attempted to match her kind of cleverness. Writing from a sickbed in 1909, he claimed that fifteen vases of flowers in the room made him feel like a prima donna. Another letter, he claimed, was becoming so dull that he would leave a space for Leverson to insert a few sparkling epigrams and ascribe them to him.

Like Violet Hunt, Leverson was an unthreatening and warmly supportive friend. She offered advice about his writing and her praise – which his basic insecurity would not let him accept without suspicion – gave him great pleasure. He was, he explained to her in 1908, so much inclined to believe the disagreeable things people said to him and to distrust the agreeable. Whenever people complimented him, he said, he was always tortured by the fear that they were laughing at him.[22] For his part, Maugham offered detailed encouragement on Leverson's novels and suggested that she could write excellent plays.

As one who moved in London literary circles, Leverson helped Maugham meet a number of interesting figures. Early in 1909 he asked her to arrange a meeting with Wilde's friend Lord Alfred Douglas. On another occasion, however, he wrote to Leverson to explain that he would not accept an invitation because it had been extended to him indirectly through her by one of her friends. There were conventional ways of making acquaintances, and Maugham felt that these were being neglected simply because he was a writer, who could be treated like a court jester.[23] This comment is interesting both for what it reveals about Maugham's Edwardian sense of proper social conduct and his insistence that the profession of writing deserved the respect granted others.

Leverson has provided a useful sketch of Maugham in her 1911 novel *The Limit*, in which he appears as 'Gilbert Hereford Vaughan', known to a few intimate friends as 'Gillie'. Thirty-four, quiet, reserved and modest in spite of his success as a dramatist, Vaughan is 'rather secretive and mysterious than blatant or dashing', and this makes him more intriguing to women. His bachelorhood has led to much speculation that he is secretly married or has had a tragic love affair, and Leverson teases Maugham by giving the character an unrequited love affair with a publican's daughter. Alluding to Maugham's theory that the unattainable is always the most desired, she adds: 'This ungratified wish was, in all his full life with its brilliant success, perhaps his greatest real pleasure.' Her description of Vaughan at a party is a revealing portrait of Maugham's manner at this period of his life:

> Hereford Vaughan, who was an object of considerable curiosity to several of the guests on account of his phenomenal success in having eleven plays at the same time being performed in London, New York, Berlin, Paris, and every other European city, was, to those who did not know him before, an agreeable surprise. Heaven knows what exactly people expected of him; perhaps the men feared 'side' and the women that he would be overpowering after so many triumphs, but he was merely a rather pale, dark, and rather handsome young man. He behaved like anybody else, except that perhaps his manner was a little quieter than the average. Unless one was very observant (which one isn't), or unless one listened to what he said, he did not at first appear to be alarmingly clever. He had one or two characteristics which must have at times led to misunderstandings. One was that whatever or whoever he looked at, his dark opaque eyes were so full of vivid expression that women often mistook for admiration what was often merely observation.[24]

This emphasis on Maugham's reserve and seeming passivity, however, tells only part of the story. He was in these years, as he remained until his late eighties, physically active, golfing frequently and playing squash once a week at the Bath Club with fellow author Francis Toye. Toye's relationship with Maugham was typical of that of many who knew him, 'a thirty-five year acquaintance . . . that has never, on either side, shown any sign of ripening into intimacy'.[25] A more unlikely partnership was that with the American social hostess Elsa Maxwell, who recalled meeting him in 1912. 'He was young, handsome and solvent, one of London's wittiest bachelors and most indefatigable dancers. One night . . . Willie and I locked horns in an endurance contest. I pounded the piano and Willie danced for three hours, without a break. What an evening! It ended only when both of us dropped from sheer exhaustion.' When reminded of this marathon many years later, Maugham characteristically replied, 'I should have joined the ballet, instead of the marriage-go-round.'[26]

This picture of Maugham as the handsome and lively partygoer, so at odds with the clichéd view of him as a saturnine grumbler, is corroborated by the memoirs of several eminent actresses who appeared in many of his plays. Marie Lohr, who was taken to her first dance in 1906 at the age of sixteen by Maugham (then thirty-two), later recalled, 'I was very fond of him and we used to have great fun.'[27] Irene Vanbrugh wrote that 'he was a gay dancing partner and I have memories of a barn dance with him about midnight on the polished floor of Covent Garden Theatre at a gala charity ball.'[28] When the beautiful American actress Billie Burke met him for the first time in 1910, she said, 'He was Parisian instead of Bond Street in elegance: always with his swallowtails and striped trousers, piping on his coat, smart gloves, a stick, beautifully made shoes, a grey top hat with a black band, and his briskly clipped moustache. And he had great smouldering brown eyes.'[29] He enjoyed dancing, at which he was adept, said Burke, and she often accompanied him to parties with the actress Maxine Elliott and the Forbes-Robertsons. It was with Maugham that she went to a costume ball at the Hotel Astor in New York on New Year's Eve in 1913, where Burke met and fell in love with Florenz Ziegfeld.

The portrait which best captures the Willie Maugham of this period is Gerald Kelly's *The Jester*, painted in the summer of 1911. The writer had dropped into Kelly's studio in William Street one morning full of delight at having purchased a new grey top hat. Kelly was struck by his look of self-satisfaction and persuaded his friend to sit for a picture.[30] The result was, in Derek Hudson's words, 'one of the most attractive and spontaneous [portraits] Kelly ever painted, capturing with a touch of affectionate mockery a morning call from the fashionable playwright at the height of his career'.[31]

Maugham's financial success in 1908, and in the years that followed, let him move in almost any social circle with ease. In 1908 he shared a flat with Walter Payne at 23 Mount Street, near Berkeley Square in Mayfair. Three years later, when his theatrical success was assured, he bought a Georgian house a short distance away at 6 Chesterfield Street. Built in 1734, it had a leasehold of 800 years, and it cost £8000. From here he was able to write in seclusion and entertain comfortably when he wished. Hugh Walpole recalled that Maugham's home 'became for many of us, one of the happiest, most hospitable, most amusing houses in London.' The lower part was ideally sociable, and in great contrast to the isolated room on the top floor where Maugham did his work. 'That top floor remains,' said Walpole, 'after all these years, as the most ideal spot for a writing room that I have ever seen.'[32] In his home, at least, Maugham seems to have been able to reconcile the artist and the socialite.

Shortly after Maugham remodelled and moved into 6 Chesterfield

Street, he invited Charles Frohman to dinner with the words, 'Will you come and see the house that Frohman built?'[33] Though he also generously called Billie Burke the woman who had bought the house for him with her success in the 1910 American production of *Mrs Dot*, he owed the greater debt to Frohman. The American producer was one of the most influential men in theatre, controlling properties on both sides of the Atlantic and energetically mounting good plays with excellent casts. His association with Maugham began in 1908 when he produced *Lady Frederick* in New York with Ethel Barrymore, and in the same year he collaborated with Arthur Chudleigh to put on *Mrs Dot* in London. Frohman produced six more of Maugham's plays on both sides of the Atlantic and suggested the writing of *The Land of Promise*, one of the most successful of his plays of this period. On 7 May 1915 Frohman died when the *Lusitania* was sunk by a German submarine, and Maugham lost not only a friend but a dynamic and shrewd producer.

With the success of *Lady Frederick* and the immediate commissions from Frohman and others, it did not take Maugham long to conclude that he had finished writing fiction. He later remembered the feeling of freedom as he looked up at the clouds above the Comedy Theatre and realized that he would never again have to describe them in prose. Thus he wrote to Pinker on 17 November 1907 to inform him that he no longer needed an agent. He would not write any more short stories and since he intended to remain with Heinemann there would be no problem in his placing the occasional novel with them. There were four short stories in various stages of publication and *The Magician* to be dealt with, but effectively Maugham ended his relationship with Pinker.

Maugham's association with Frohman and the enthusiastic acceptance of his plays in New York made it inevitable that the playwright would soon make his first trip to the United States. He had intended to go in 1908 and was prevented by circumstances, but in October 1910 he crossed the Atlantic for the first of what was to be many voyages. In New York, he attended productions of his plays, and studied those of others, and he visited the Pierpont Morgan Library, where he was touched with emotion to be able to hold the manuscript of Keats's *Endymion*.

Maugham spent a week in Boston, whose cultivated pretensions he found a little stifling. Charles Eliot Norton had provided him with a letter of introduction to his sister, Grace, who gave him the opportunity of meeting Henry James again. James was back in the United States of his brother's death, having once promised that he would wait in Cambridge for six months in case William was able to communicate from beyond the grave. Not surprisingly Maugham found him forlorn and bewildered in America, and longing to return to the less boisterous atmosphere of Europe.

On the way back to New York Maugham visited Washington where he met his distant relative Ralph Maugham and his son John. In New York he called on Mary Cadwalader Jones, the sister-in-law of Edith Wharton and whose house on Eleventh Street was one of the most lively literary centres in the city. It may have been here that Maugham met a twenty-four-year-old playwright, Edward Sheldon, with whom he was to develop a close friendship. They shared a love of the theatre and similar temperaments, and for a number of years whenever Maugham was in New York he stayed with Sheldon at his apartment on Gramercy Park. The American dramatist had achieved a Broadway reputation with *Salvation Nell* and *The Nigger*, and his *Romance* became one of the most successful plays of its time. Tragically, Sheldon developed a disease which progressively left him more paralysed so that at his death in 1946 he could not see, hear, or speak.

Maugham's American trip was cut short by the need to return to England for rehearsals of *Loaves and Fishes*, the last of the earlier plays. Irene Vanbrugh was to appear in it but when illness interfered Maugham was able to get Ellis Jeffreys, the actress who had once turned down the chance to play Lady Frederick. *Loaves and Fishes* opened at the Duke of York's on 24 February 1911, and though it had an excellent cast, audiences were uncomfortable at seeing a clergyman being satirized and it ran for only fifty-eight performances.

Loaves and Fishes, however, was a play from the past, and by the time that it was in production Maugham had already decided to stop writing plays for a while. His reputation as a popular playwright was now secure, he was financially comfortable, and he was enjoying a varied social life. Without worries about his immediate future, he was free to think more deeply about the events of his earlier life, traumatic experiences which he had attempted to forget without ever coming to terms with them. Increasingly, he later realized, he had become obsessed with the wretched memories of his childhood and coming of age:

> I was but just firmly established as a popular playwright when I began to be obsessed by the teeming memories of my past life. The loss of my mother and then the break-up of my home, the wretchedness of my first years at school for which my French childhood had so ill-prepared

me and which my stammering made so difficult, the delight of those easy, monotonous and exciting days in Heidelberg, when I first entered upon the intellectual life, the irksomeness of my few years at the hospital and the thrill of London; it all came back to me so pressingly, in my sleep, on my walks, when I was rehearsing plays, when I was at a party, it became such a burden to me that I made up my mind that I could only regain my peace by writing it all down in the form of a novel.[34]

The actual idea of writing an autobiographical novel to resolve the traumas of the past may have come from Edward Sheldon on the New York visit. According to both Eric Barnes and Van Wyck Brooks,[35] friends of the two writers were convinced that Sheldon suggested that Maugham write such a cathartic work in order to overcome a disturbing sense of inferiority caused by his stutter. 'It occurred to Ned,' explains Barnes, 'that he might conquer the defect, or at least change his attitude towards it, if he wrote it out of his system.'[36]

Whether from Sheldon's advice or his own compulsion, Maugham began what would become *Of Human Bondage* early in 1911, and by late July he was able to tell C. F. Cazenove that he was in the process of writing a realistic novel which would not be completed for another six to nine months.[37] On 28 February 1912 Maugham observed to Frohman that fashioning the adaptation of *Le Bourgeois Gentilhomme* was just the sort of work he wanted after many months on his novel. An indication that he had by then completed the first draft is his comment to Frohman that he hoped, after returning from a trip to Spain, to get back to playwriting after his long holiday from it.[38]

Of Human Bondage was not published, though, until August 1915, and after a surprising number of changes in title. As the manuscript now in the Library of Congress indicates, the author's first choice was 'Beauty for Ashes' (which Maugham mistakenly recalled as 'Beauty from Ashes' in *The Summing Up*), a phrase from Isaiah 61:23. When he discovered that Lady Henry Somerset had used the title in 1913, however, Maugham suggested a series of alternatives. His contract with Heinemann, signed on 6 October 1914, has three successive titles: 'Of Fleeting Things', 'The Pride of Life', and finally, and clearly added later, 'Of Human Bondage'. Before the last choice, there was 'Life's Thoroughfare', as the novel was provisionally entitled in the American rights contract signed by Heinemann and George Doran on 9 December 1914.[39]

Given the aptness of *Of Human Bondage* for a novel about emotional enslavement, it seems astonishing that the other possibilities were even considered. It may be, though, that titles did not come easily to Maugham. In his library at King's School, there is a 1909 edition of Bartlett's *Familiar Quotations* in which the flyfleaf page is filled with potential titles he had gleaned from within. Among them are two that he finally used: 'The Sacred Flame' and 'The Narrow Corner'.

The Heinemann contract for *Of Human Bondage* reveals that there were concerns about more than just the title. In addition to the standard clauses, the following qualification has been typed in: 'An advance of £500 (five hundred pounds) shall be made on account of royalties, any unearned portion of which shall be returnable by the Author if the free circulation of the book is impeded at the Libraries, by either its being placed in the class "B" or objection being raised and free access to it is not given to subscribers on account of its contents.'[40] This unusual clause, rarely seen in contracts of the period, clearly indicates a fear that something in the novel might offend the private lending libraries, an influential and powerful source of income for publishers. It is impossible to know what the questionable passages were, but the safest assumption is that they involved the sexual activities of the waitress, Mildred Rogers.

Frohman, chafing at the inactivity of his most popular dramatist, suggested that Maugham adapt the central idea of Shakespeare's *The Taming of the Shrew* to a new setting. Thus, in the autumn of 1912, Maugham set out for North America to gather material for what became *The Land of Promise*, a journey he is unlikely to have undertaken if *Of Human Bondage* had not been largely completed. Though he would have preferred to have had an American background to his story, he did not have enough confidence that he could recreate it to the satisfaction of New York audiences, and so he went to the Western Canadian prairies. He remembered that his Aunt Julia once had a companion who left to live with a brother on a farm in Canada, where she married one of the hired men. Maugham spent some time on a farm in Manitoba at the end of 1912, fascinated by the intensity of frontier life and absorbing material for *The Land of Promise* and another play which he never wrote.

Maugham used the raw pioneer setting primarily as background for the *Shrew* story, but *The Land of Promise* is more interesting because of the contrast drawn between the narrow claustrophobia of England and the opportunity and freedom of the colonial life. The home country is especially stifling for the heroine, a lady's companion who, following the death of her mistress, has been left with no income and no means of earning a living. She is thus forced to move to her brother's farm in Canada, marries a hired hand, and then has to cope with a powerful and seemingly insensitive male in a setting of isolation and struggle against the elements. By the end of the play, she has abandoned her English detachment and class consciousness and has learned respect for her husband's honest strengths.

The Land of Promise reveals Maugham's ability to absorb subtle details about a particular milieu in only a brief period, and it presents a fairly accurate picture of life in Western Canada in the early decades of this century. Though the author's sympathies are with the new land as opposed to England, his picture of the land of promise disturbed Canadian government officials, who were then conducting an extensive campaign to encourage British immigration to Canada. A superintendent of the immigration service felt impelled to issue a refutation of the implications of the play, and an officer of the Canadian emigration department in London stated: 'No Canadian man would dream of ordering his wife about . . . If there is one thing Canadian men do well, it is the way they treat their wives.'[41]

In New York and London, though, The Land of Promise was a triumph. Billie Burke played the lead in the American production, which opened on 26 November 1913, and ran for seventy-six performances, and three years later she starred in the first of two silent film adaptations. Across the Atlantic, Irene Vanbrugh, Charles V. France, and Godfrey Tearle were part of an excellent cast in a production which played 185 nights at the Duke of York's Theatre, and in 1917 Vanbrugh and France repeated their roles for another sixty performances.

When The Land of Promise went into production in November 1913 Maugham was in the United States ostensibly to attend rehearsals and to see the opening night. Unknown to anybody, however, he was on a much more important, private mission. Sue Jones, now divorced and with whom Maugham had maintained some kind of affair, was appearing in Sheldon's Romance in Chicago. She had continued to pursue a career as an actress without ever going beyond supporting roles. Indeed, Maugham had secured a minor part for her in Penelope in 1909, in which she drew praise from the Times critic for 'the stoic and impeccable maid of Miss Ethelwyn Arthur Jones, who "buttled" as well as the most time-honoured butler'.[42] Maugham's purpose in travelling to Chicago was, however, as dramatic as anything she played on stage: he came to ask her to marry him.

Part of the reason why, after an intermittent relationship of eight years, Maugham decided to propose can be found in *Of Human Bondage*, completed not many months earlier. Though most of the novel deals with his life up to about 1897, providing a fairly accurate representation in fiction of his experiences, the final chapters are a complete fabrication which none the less reflects his state of mind when he completed the work about 1912–13. This section describes Philip's decision to marry Sally, a warm, maternal young woman, not intellectual but radiating loving-kindness. In choosing a domestic life with her and the modest profession of a country doctor, Philip abandons his dreams of travel and discovery. This was not Maugham's own choice in 1897, but it represented his feeling fifteen years later that he might like to be married. Over the years, readers have sensed the dichotomy between the final chapters and the realism of the rest of the novel, and they find them unpersuasive.

In 'Looking Back', Maugham wrote that after moving into 6 Chesterfield Street he realized that his friendship with Walter Payne was no longer intimate, and so he began to think of marriage. In *The Summing Up*, he explained that he was then close to forty and that if he were going to marry and have children he would soon have to do so:

> For some time I had amused my imagination with pictures of myself in the married state. There was no one I particularly wanted to marry. It was the condition that attracted me. It seemed a necessary motif in the pattern of life that I had designed, and to my ingenuous fancy . . . it offered peace; peace from the disturbance of love affairs, casual it might be in the beginning, but bringing in their train such troublesome complications . . . peace that would enable me to write all I wanted to write without the loss of precious time or disturbance of mind; peace and a settled and dignified way of life. I sought freedom and thought I could find it in marriage.[43]

Like much of *The Summing Up*, the apparent calm and control of this passage hides a great deal. There is, of course, no hint of sexual tension, of concern about his homosexual inclinations, but it is likely that much of the impetus for this interest in marriage came from a desire, before it was too late, to follow what Maugham believed was a pattern of normality. In the last chapter of *Of Human Bondage*, after all, he had written that 'the simplest pattern, that in which a man was born, worked, married, had children, and died, was likewise the most perfect.'[44]

Maugham was thus looking for a marriageable woman, and though not in love with Sue Jones he was, he said, 'fond' of her. She had taken most of his friends as lovers, but he decided that there was no one whom he liked better, and so he bought a ring and planned to join Sue in Chicago. He wrote Frohman on 28 October to say that he would arrive in New York on 15 November and go directly to Chicago for three days. Contrary to the version in 'Looking Back', Sue had already joined the company, and when they met for dinner he asked her to marry him. To his astonishment, she rejected him, and no amount of persuasion could change her mind.

Maugham returned to New York, and after attending to *The Land of Promise* sailed for England sooner than planned, seen off by Sheldon and Harrison Rhodes and accompanied by American playwright Avery Hopwood. According to Maugham, he was later walking down Piccadilly when a newspaper hoarding told him that Sue had married an earl's son. In fact, she married Angus McDonnell, the second son of the Earl of Antrim, on 13 December. A handsome and congenial young man, he had gone to North America a few years earlier and was managing a Canadian construction company. He had won a large contract to work on the harbour at Victoria, British Columbia, but he was part of the social scene in Ottawa. He was awarded the CB and CMG for service during the First World War and from 1924 to 1929 he held the parliamentary seat of Dartford for the Conservative Party. In the Second World War, he served in Washington as an honorary attaché, helping the ambassador present the British cause to the American public, and he was respected for his wit and amiability. Back in England, the McDonnells lived at Five Ashes, a village south of Tunbridge Wells, and it was here on 3 April 1948 that Sue Jones died.

In writing about the end of his affair with Sue, Maugham speculated that at the time of his proposal she was pregnant, and elsewhere he claimed that she eventually miscarried. 'I often wonder', he told Garson Kanin, 'what course my life might have taken had it not been for that . . . freakish happenstance.'[45] It is highly unlikely that a marriage to Sue Jones or any other woman would have lasted, but Maugham was more in love with her than his version in 'Looking Back' suggests. Kanin claims that Maugham once told him that she was the only woman to whom he had ever proposed, and that there were tears in Maugham's eyes at the end of the story. Similarly, Alan Searle has told me that his rejection was a wound that Maugham would recall with emotion years later.

Sally Athelny is not a portrait of Sue Jones, though Maugham may have had her vitality and warmth in mind when he created his heroine.

Sue's appeal was nevertheless similar to that of the young woman in the novel, and Maugham either invented his wish fulfilment character and then viewed Sue as the closest to it or he gave Sally some of the qualities he valued in the young actress. In any case, there would be no real-life counterpart to the idyllic marriage at the end of his autobiographical novel. Back in England in the early part of 1914, Maugham none the less remained interested in the possibility of marriage and he became deeply involved with a woman quite unlike Sally or Sue: Syrie Barnardo Wellcome.

Born in 1879, Gwendolyn Maud Syrie Barnardo was the daughter of Dr Thomas John Barnardo, famous for his establishment of the Barnardo homes for orphans. A beautiful young woman, with black hair, brown eyes, a lovely complexion that she would retain all her life, and a wonderful figure, she attracted many men. In 1901, at the age of twenty-one, she married the forty-seven-year-old Henry Wellcome, who together with Silas M. Burroughs had created the pharmaceutical firm of Burroughs, Wellcome and Company. The company was developing into the hugely successful international firm, and the Wellcomes had the luxury of beautiful homes and glamorous international travel. A son was born in 1903, but the marriage had already begun to collapse. The difference in ages, as well as a sexual incompatibility, soon estranged husband and wife, and in the summer of 1910 they quarrelled and parted forever. In September 1910 a deed of separation was signed, which gave Syrie an allowance of £2400 a year and custody of her child for part of each year.

According to Maugham, he first met Syrie one evening late in 1913, when the wife of a London representative of the art firm of Knoedler asked him to complete a foursome for dinner and a play. A man had backed out and they needed a replacement. Maugham went and was introduced to a beautiful woman with lovely brown eyes and marvellous skin. She was fashionably dressed, and the author was flattered when she said that she would prefer listening to him all evening rather than go to the theatre.

Ted Morgan places this initial meeting in 1911 on the strength of the inscription 'Xmas 1911 – much love Syrie' in a volume of Shaw plays contained in the Maugham Library at King's School. It may indeed be that Maugham's account missed by two years – he was frequently wrong about early dates in his life, and such a volume is certainly the kind of gift one might give a playwright, even if only to let him know the work of his competitors. One needs, however, to be cautious about seeing the inscription as irrefutable evidence. Maugham is not specifically identified as the recipient of the book, something one might expect in light of the warmth of the words. Maugham's library contains a number of books which had originally belonged to others – Walter Payne, his father George Adney Payne, Frederick Bishop, Henry Bishop, and Syrie – and the Shaw volume may have been brought to their marriage by Syrie.

Furthermore, if Maugham and Syrie first met late in 1911, it is unlikely that by Christmas their relationship would have developed to the point where she would write 'much love from Syrie'. And if such an intimacy had grown, would Maugham have bought a ring and proposed to Sue Jones a year or so later? In 'Looking Back', Maugham claimed that his second meeting with Syrie was at the opera, where she explained that she had recently bought a house in Regent's Park and that she would soon invite him to a housewarming party. Syrie in fact bought her house late in 1913, and had her party on 26 February 1914.

Another reason for accepting Maugham's date is that after the separation in the fall of 1910, Syrie had several important affairs, one with the wealthy storeowner Gordon Selfridge. Another was her liaison with Desmond Percy Fitzgerald, the failure of which Rebecca West has called 'the great tragedy of her life'.[46] According to her biographer, Gerald McKnight,[47] Syrie wanted to marry Fitzgerald, but he ended the relationship when Wellcome refused to grant her a divorce.

Maugham was attracted to Syrie's beauty and style, her liveliness and gaiety. As he later admitted, he was flattered to be the lover of one of London's most interesting women. If, of course, he were trying to persuade himself – and the world at large – that he was in fact heterosexual, he could do little better than form a liaison with a beautiful woman known to have been the lover of several prominent men. Moreover, Syrie moved in many of London's highest social circles, and she provided an entry otherwise denied Maugham. She had a vitality and gregariousness which Maugham lacked, and like those who came before and after her, she complemented his own shy and reserved temperament.

Syrie was a remarkable woman, something Maugham must have sensed in 1914, though he would deny it later. Rebecca West recalled being 'deeply attached to Syrie Maugham, who showed me great kindness, as she did to many young people. She was a woman of great talent, and remarkable courage.'[48] For Lord Birkenhead, she was 'a woman of unusual ability and strength of character',[49] a view corroborated by a large number of her friends who rose in her defence when Maugham maligned her in 'Looking Back'. She was also intelligent and interested in art, and this undoubtedly played a part in her attraction to Maugham. That she was anything but frivolous is indicated by her books which were still in Maugham's possession when he gave his library to King's School: Turgenev's *Virgin Soil*, A. E. Taylor's *Aristotle*, Bishop Berkeley's *Theory of Vision and Other Writings*, Rudolf Eucken's *A Philosophy of Life*, John Stuart Mill's *Utilitarianism, Liberty, and Representative Government*, and R. C. Punnett's *Mendelism*

Part of the attraction of Maugham was his talent and stature as a writer. He was at the peak of his reputation as a dramatist, and his conversation was cultured, witty, and intelligent. Syrie enjoyed the company of a successful writer, and even long after their divorce, when Maugham had little to do with her, she continued to follow his career and become excited about his latest publication.

Maugham was, as the sketches by Leverson, Maxwell, and Burke show, affluent, handsome and cosmopolitan. He may, as well, have been a welcome relief from the sort of sexual relationship she had experienced with Wellcome and her lovers. According to McKnight, Syrie had been disgusted with her husband's insensitive sexual demands, and had rejected him entirely in the final years of their marriage. 'Syrie', he argues, 'was never, thereafter, to be capable of easy stimulation: erotically, she had been wounded to the point of extinction.'[50] In this, perhaps, can be found the reason why so many of her male friendships thereafter were with homosexuals.

One can only guess at how much Syrie was aware of Maugham's homosexual nature at the time of their affair. According to her sister-in-law, Syrie knew nothing of it and was deeply shocked when her brother, Cyril, enlightened her some years after her marriage.[51] Syrie, though, was hardly an innocent in 1913. She was a woman of the world who had travelled widely and in sophisticated London circles for a dozen years. She was unlikely to be ignorant of the homosexual temperament and to be oblivious to its elements in Maugham. Their liaison was his last effort at a heterosexual relationship, and, though he may have worked hard at playing the lover, it would have been difficult for Maugham to have disguised his bisexuality over the years of their affair. Indeed, it may well have been that Maugham's love-making – never very aggressive at any time – was muted enough to seem sensitive after the dominant heterosexuality of Syrie's other men.

According to Maugham he became Syrie's lover early in 1914, following the housewarming party, and after a few months she suggested that they have a child. Her brother and his wife could take it and after a few years she would adopt it and no one would see that she was the mother. Syrie had a nonchalant attitude about public opinion, but Maugham was always conscious of its power, and it is surprising that he agreed to her plan. Always careful about guarding his freedom, and having written frequently about those who had lost it, he must have accepted Syrie's assurances that her separation agreement left her free in every way.

Several years later Maugham learned to his regret that Syrie had not been given complete freedom of action. There is, moreover, a strong possibility that she was well aware of the limitations of the agreement and that her desire to have a child by the writer was deliberately provocative. According to McKnight Syrie was convinced that she had lost Desmond Fitzgerald because of her marriage tie, and that she needed to create a situation where neither her husband nor her lover could back out of a divorce and remarriage. 'She may have reached the bitter conclusion', argues McKnight, 'that nothing short of practical necessity, or the threat of scandal, could alter her husband's iron-willed opposition to a public divorce. When Syrie persuaded Somerset Maugham into marriage it was as a result of two things: her pregnancy by him, and the fact that Wellcome could not refuse the divorce once she was carrying another man's child.'[52]

At the time of Syrie's proposal, Maugham wanted to be a father, though his comment in 'Looking Back' that 'the *idea* of being the father of a child amused me'[53] (my italics) and Syrie's remark that 'Willie is really terribly proud of being a father at all'[54] are more accurate. Rebecca West, for example, recalled arriving at the Maugham home with a friend one evening some years later to collect them for an outing to the cinema. Syrie had just received a telephone call from the country to say that their daughter, Liza, to whom she was devoted, was seriously ill. Overwrought, she threw the telephone on the floor. When Maugham quietly picked up the telephone, calmly replaced it, and chided Syrie for her outburst of temper, she exclaimed: 'You always wanted to be a father; you never wanted a child!' Years later, Maugham forgot that West had been present and repeated the remark, remembering it, he said, because it was so 'nicely balanced'.[55]

Syrie's comment was also apt. Though Maugham always had a compassion for children – he once said that no one could believe in God who had seen a child die of meningitis – he was not comfortable around them. His reserve and self-consciousness prevented him from losing himself in a child's world, from having that sense of abandon which is so important to creating a rapport. In his own household, of course, a child and later grandchildren brought noise and playful disorganization into a life which he intended to be patterned and disciplined.

Thus, though Maugham obviously cared about his offspring, his affection was restrained. During the Second World War, Hamilton Basso reported that 'Maugham saw his grandchildren frequently when they were in New York and, while he could not squeeze himself into the mold of the doting grandfather, he occasionally read to them.'[56] Similarly, E. M. Korry noted twenty years later that though the aged writer strove to fulfil the role of the affectionate grandfather, 'he obviously finds it difficult to forget himself; he remains the outsider looking in.'[57] In fact, Maugham found it easier to deal with his grandchildren when they were young; as they grew older and more sophisticated, he was less able to relax with them.

Maugham agreed to Syrie's idea of having a baby, and in April 1914, after a few days with Sibyl Colefax and her husband at their country home near Tunbridge Wells, he joined her in Biarritz. Following a motor trip through northern Spain, they went to Paris before returning to London. Syrie became pregnant during this holiday but miscarried back in England. In a state of depression, she suggested to Maugham that they should part, but he declined to end their affair.

In the summer of 1914 Syrie and Maugham did temporarily go their separate ways – she to the country with her son and her mother, and he to Capri for July and August with Gerald Kelly. After an idyllic month of bathing, playing tennis, and exploring the island, they learned on 4 August of the outbreak of war. A few days later Syrie arrived, against Maugham's wishes, and within a week they returned to London.

Maugham immediately wrote to Winston Churchill, whose acquaintance he had made five years earlier, to offer his services to the war effort. He was multilingual and familiar with a number of European countries, and so he could usefully serve in a London intelligence or propaganda office, a common wartime occupation of writers. While awaiting a posting, and anxious to serve more actively, Maugham learned that the Red Cross had formed the American Volunteer Motor Ambulance Corps for use in France. Chaired by Henry James, the Corps was an innovation in the care of the wounded in that for the first time casualties could be quickly moved away from the front to the hospitals. It comprised all kinds of automobiles from Fords to Rolls Royces and the volunteer drivers were made up of ordinary Americans and millionaires as well as such unlikely candidates as the pianist Melville Gideon, the writer Shane Leslie, and Maugham.

In many ways, Maugham's haste to get into active service is surprising. He was, after all, forty years of age and neither physically imposing nor strong. In early 1909 his tuberculosis had put him into Miss Dora Isaac's Nursing Home in Hinde Street for a month, and he was hardly likely to stand up to the rigours of field work. Furthermore, in *The Hero*, *Mrs Craddock*, and other works, he had attacked patriotism, as he would do again in *The Unknown* (1920) and *For Services Rendered* (1932). For many, Maugham's cynicism and detachment made him an unlikely candidate for the varied and extensive contribution he would make in both world wars.

Maugham was none the less a product of the Victorian period, a man whose early adult years were shaped by the Edwardian era, and his reaction to the outbreak of war was what he thought would be that of an Edwardian gentleman: service. However much he might have criticized jingoism in peacetime, his respect for the concept of honour meant that in war he would not watch from the wings – the position from which he viewed many of life's other conflicts. He was, moreover, genuinely proud of being English and deeply loyal to his country, though he might criticize particular British follies and vices. Patriotism, he ventured in *Ashenden*, was 'in peacetime an attitude best left to politicians, publicists and fools, but in the dark days of war an emotion that can wring the heart-strings.'[58]

Maugham's anxiety to serve was, however, more complex, surely fuelled by his sense of inferiority. In *A Writer's Notebook*, he argued that if he had been four or five inches taller, the attitudes of others toward him and his own response to them would have been different. Beverley Nichols has described how Maugham, hating his littleness, would pull himself up, bracing his shoulders, or edge himself to a higher level so that he might appear taller in group photographs.[59] Because of his stature, and the other sources of his inferiority complex, Maugham had a lifelong need to prove himself. In part, his desire to earn more money than any other writer in history came from this drive, as did his pride as an octogenarian in climbing over the hills of Cap Ferrat or in diving into his pool. Suffering from the classic 'little man' syndrome, Maugham saw the outbreak of war as an opportunity to prove himself the equal of any man, not merely by translating reports in a Whitehall office but by risking his life in the field.

Finally, and most importantly, the war gave Maugham a reason for making another of his psychological and physical uprootings. The years from 1908 to 1914 had been ones of theatrical and financial success as well as immersion in London's social and cultural life and the purchase of a beautiful house. Maugham had achieved almost everything he had pursued for a decade – the critical acclaim had been withheld – but he found the prizes less glittering than he had envisaged. He was tired of the people he knew and the life he was leading. He had enjoyed the fame, the luxury, the dinners, balls, and week-end parties, and the company of brilliant writers, artists, and theatre people. But, he wrote, 'it was stifling me and I hankered after a different mode of existence and new experiences.'[60] He thought of his old panacea of travel and contemplated a trip to Russia to learn the language. He considered marriage as a means of breaking the routine of his life, but this had proved impossible with Sue Jones, and Syrie Wellcome was still married.

In addition, by the time that war was declared Syrie's pursuit of Maugham suddenly intensified when she informed him that she was again pregnant. His enthusiasm about having a child had waned over the months and he attempted to dissuade her from going through with the birth, but Syrie was adamant. Confronted with her determination, he promised to take her abroad when her condition could no longer be disguised.

For various reasons, therefore, the war came as a godsend. In the autumn of 1914 Maugham crossed the Channel as an interpreter with the ambulance corps and for a number of weeks saw action in northern France in Doullens, Montdidier, and Amiens. Stationed within fifteen miles of the front, he got to see the horrors and absurdities of war. He worked in an improvised hospital where 300 wounded were attended to by two doctors and a couple of dressers. Pressed into using medical skills he had not practised for seventeen years, he treated hideous wounds – shattered bones and gaping holes where shells had blown away the flesh. After one disastrous battle, Maugham's unit was faced with 300 dead and 1600 wounded to evacuate from the front. He witnessed men dying, some stoically and some in despair. At Amiens he was amused to hear of one volunteer lady who managed to kill a man by ignoring the doctor's advice and feeding him soup though he had been shot through the gullet. When the luckless soldier drowned from her ministrations she promptly blamed the doctor.

Fascinated by the reactions of people to the battlefield and death, he recorded his observations in his notebooks until his duties prevented his writing. The work was exhausting and his schedule was dictated by others, but he found the life exciting and curiously liberating. Others were responsible for imposing discipline on those in the corps, and once Maugham had done his day's work he felt free to waste his time.

Before this, he had always suffered from a conscience which said that, since any hour can be used to write, one should be creating at all hours.

Maugham's unit eventually moved across the French border with Belgium to Steenvoorde and Poperinghe. At Ypres he visited the thirteenth-century Cloth Hall, and shortly after he walked away from one of its walls a shell burst where he had been standing. He was intrigued by the element of pure chance that stood between himself and sure death.

Some time in this period from October 1914 to January 1915, Maugham met the young man who was to have a profound effect on the direction of his life: Frederick Gerald Haxton. Born on 6 October 1892 in San Francisco, Haxton had grown up in England with his mother after his parents' separation. Eighteen years younger than Maugham, he was attractive, of medium height, with a moustache and brown hair. He was athletic and masculine, and Peter Quennell recalled being surprised on first meeting Maugham and Haxton that the two lovers resembled tough colonial officials.[61] More important, Haxton radiated the vitality to which Maugham was always so drawn. Enormously high-spirited, courageous in his own fashion, and adventurous, Haxton was outgoing and gregarious – in Harold Acton's words 'as gay and irresponsible a companion as a careworn man could wish for'.[62]

Haxton has been the subject of a great deal of speculation, much of it verging on melodrama, and he has usually been painted in dark colours. He was clearly a cad – 'louche' is the word used by many who knew him – who gambled and drank far too heavily and who was familiar with the tougher parts of the homosexual underworld. He was also immensely charming, and among those who found him good company were Arthur Marshall, André David, George Rylands, Cyril Connolly, Harold Acton, and Rebecca West. Raymond Mortimer has argued that the Villa Mauresque was never so lively as during the thirties when Haxton presided over activities as Maugham's companion-secretary and lover. And Alec Waugh has written that 'nearly everyone liked Gerald Haxton, right away. And I have heard more than one man say that his best times with Maugham were in a trio with Gerald Haxton.'[63]

The rigours and dangers of the Flanders war zone undoubtedly highlighted Haxton's best qualities, and Maugham fell deeply for what many have called 'the love of his life'. Alan Searle stated that Maugham initially had an intense infatuation,[64] and George Rylands has called it a 'rapturous' affair.[65] Maugham's friend of later years Glenway Wescott is surely right when he argues that the liaison with Haxton was 'the first completely beautiful, completely appropriate love affair he had ever had'.[66] Maugham once wrote that his tragedy was that he had never loved anyone who had been in love with him, and he had had a series of affairs which for various reasons had been unsatisfactory. In the particular permissiveness of the battlefield situation, he may, if only briefly, have experienced the one passionate, truly requited love of his life.

The liaison with Haxton must have shown Maugham beyond any doubt that, no matter what he had tried to persuade himself, he was a homosexual. With Haxton, love was as yet uncomplicated, and the physical consummation more complete and satisfying than that which he had experienced with women, and he must have recognized its more authentic answering of his sexual drive. For some years, he had tried to convince himself that he was a 'normal' heterosexual man and to play the part, but it was a role that was superimposed on his real self. Thus, in a sexual sense at least, Frederic Raphael is right when he argues that, after meeting Haxton, 'the old persona was sloughed forever'.[67] From this point on, Maugham's orientation was entirely homosexual, though he maintained a façade which suggested otherwise.

Syrie's pregnancy, however, meant that Maugham's life was still bound up with hers. He had no intention of reneging on his promise to help her, and when she wrote in January to say that she could no longer stay in London he took a leave and returned to England. After attending to some business matters, he met Syrie at Dover and took her to Rome where she could be delivered in relative anonymity. After staying at the Hotel de Russie in the via Babino and another hotel in the via Lombardia, they took an apartment near the Pincio.

Syrie was expecting the baby in May (in his biography Morgan claims that the birth took place on 1 September but in fact it occurred, as Maugham has written, in May). For nearly three months Maugham and Syrie lived in seclusion in Rome, with Maugham golfing several times a week and writing a new and very satiric play, *Our Betters*. Syrie had entertained the dramatist at length with descriptions of her lover Gordon Selfridge, and this became the basis of the character of the vulgar and wealthy Arthur Fenwick. The play was a caustic satire about the American expatriates living in London, especially the rich women who went there to marry into the British aristocracy, and Maugham drew upon his shrewd observation of a number of other people to create acid portraits of social climbers.

Maugham completed *Our Betters* in April and had it typed while on a visit to Capri in May. Charles Frohman had been lost on the *Lusitania* in early May but his partner Al Hayman still intended to produce it at the Duke of York's in London in the autumn. In July Maugham sent a melody to be used in the first act and discussed casting with Hayman, but the production was eventually scrapped. The British Foreign Office, never happy about the playwright's public cynicism about the military ethos, had become concerned about what it perceived as anti-American sentiment in *Our Betters*. With the United States not yet in the war but an important ally nevertheless, the British wanted to avoid anything which might turn American public opinion against them. Thus, according to Rhodri Jeffreys-Jones,[68] the Foreign Office classified Maugham's play as undesirable, and it was not performed in Britain until 1923.

When *Our Betters* was finally produced at London's Globe Theatre, with Margaret Bannerman, Constance Collier, Ronald Squire, and Reginald Owen, it was a great success, running for 548 performances. In order to satisfy the Lord Chamberlain's Office, the ending of the second act had to be changed so that Lord Bleane, not the young Elizabeth, was the one who discovered the couple in their love-making in the garden house. Critics noted that the thematic purpose would have been much better served had the innocent woman made the discovery, and one correspondent attacked a form of censorship where stage innocents must be prevented from receiving imaginary shocks in imaginary summer houses. As well, the play had long been rumoured to contain caricatures of well-known London society people, and the programme therefore carried a disclaimer in which the author stated that the characters were entirely fictitious.

As the date of Syrie's delivery approached, her mother joined them in their Rome apartment. According to Maugham, Syrie had had an operation which made a normal delivery impossible, and so as labour began she was rushed in the middle of the night to the Royal Clinic, in the Via G. M. Lancisi. On 6 May, a daughter was born by Caesarean section, and named Elizabeth Mary, though always called Liza after the protagonist of Maugham's first novel. Syrie was told several days later that she would never be able to have another child.

As soon as Syrie had recovered Maugham went to Capri, where he visited John Ellingham Brooks. Compton Mackenzie and his wife were living on the island, and Maugham frequently dined with them, though Faith Mackenzie suggests that friends sometimes seemed to come second to news from Britain. 'The bundle of papers that arrived by every post from England attracted him, and he did not pretend otherwise. I did a drawing of him, showing nothing but a chair, an open newspaper and a pair of crossed legs, and called it *Somerset Maugham dines with friends*.'[69]

After a few weeks, Maugham rejoined Syrie and their daughter. They returned to England in early June, with Maugham going to his house and Syrie to a hotel in Curzon Street. Unknown to them both, Henry Wellcome had employed detectives to observe their movements, and on his return to England from America in July the reports of his wife's affair and the birth of the child persuaded him to sue for divorce. Maugham was aghast at being named co-respondent, but he recognized that there was no way of fighting the action. On the advice of his solicitor, he employed Sir George Lewis, one of Britain's most distinguished divorce lawyers.

Maugham learned that Wellcome had given Syrie not the £5000 a year that she had said she received, but £2400, and that she had not been completely free under the terms of the separation agreement. Wellcome now proposed to give her £1000 a year if Maugham did not marry her, but she had considerable debts and would have found it very difficult to manage on the reduced allowance. Lewis suggested that Maugham should settle twenty or thirty thousand pounds on her, and thus buy his way out of the entanglement.

This was the age, however, when it was expected that the co-respondent in a divorce action would marry the woman, and Maugham was always acutely conscious of how he would appear in the eyes of London social circles. He had, moreover, a deeper concern. When Lewis asked if he wanted to marry Syrie, Maugham claims to have responded: 'No, but if I don't I shall regret it all my life.' He did not, he said, tell his lawyer that his motivation was the baby, that he could not bear to think what its future would be if he did not marry Syrie.[70]

We have only Maugham's word that his main thought was for the well-being of the child, but such a concern is consistent with his personality. His bleak childhood as an orphan had left him with a particular sensitivity to children who were alone or who had lost parents, and it is likely that he was reluctant to create such a life for another person. That his daughter might have suffered materially under the care of her spendthrift mother was also a consideration.

In 'Looking Back', Maugham argues that he was very anxious that there be no mention of the child in court, so that Syrie would be spared some humiliation, and Wellcome's lawyers acceded to the request. They had evidence collected from the doctor and nurses in Rome, and this formed part of the documentation though it was not read out in court. When the case was argued on 14 February 1916 the charges of adultery pertained to the various residences in Rome, the Castle Hotel in Windsor in July 1915, and the same hotel in September of that year.

The last-mentioned incident appears to have been a deliberate planting of evidence, a common practice in a period when divorce laws were less liberal than those of the present. According to the testimony of the hotel manager, a man called up, identified himself as W. S. Maugham, and reserved a double bedroom and sitting-room. Following this a man and woman came for the weekend and took all but one of their meals in their rooms. Since Wellcome had served notice two months earlier that he was filing for divorce, such a carefully documented weekend was hardly discreet, and certainly more like the kind of thing Maugham and Syrie might have done a year earlier rather than when they had a four-month-old baby back in London. Thus it is likely that, in order to keep the case as brief and uncontroversial as possible, they agreed to provide this clear proof of their adultery.

Syrie did not contest the suit, and in the face of the evidence Justice Bargrave Deane granted a decree nisi, with costs, and gave Henry Wellcome custody of his son. For several days the case was given prominence in the English papers – on the crime page of the *Daily Chronicle* and under the title of 'Playwright as Co-respondent: *Wellcome* v. *Wellcome and Maugham*' in *The Times*. The *News of the World* provided the most fulsome details with the heading 'Author Co-respondent: Mr Somerset Maugham in Divorce Case', and the moralizing subtitle 'Erring Wife A Daughter of Great Philanthropist'.

Always reticent about exposing his personal life to the public, Maugham was mortified by the publicity, and undoubtedly hated the discussions with lawyers, the negotiations, and the decisions which would affect the direction of his life. The press coverage and public gossip must also have embarrassed the Maugham family, which, like Galsworthy's Forsytes, was always careful not to invite public disapproval. In an act that belies Willie's and Robin's portrayals of him, Frederic wrote his brother shortly after the hearing to express his support.

If Maugham was embarrassed by Wellcome's suit, he did not let the public see his discomfort. He was in London during the week preceding the hearing, and gave a dinner party at his home to celebrate the opening of *Caroline* on 8 February. If his account in 'Looking Back' is true, he none the less took Syrie to Switzerland immediately thereafter to escape the barrage of publicity. He had spent much of the winter of 1915–16 there, having gone in the autumn to work for the British

Intelligence Service. On his return from Rome, he had decided not to go back to the ambulance unit, and through Syrie's social connections, he met an important figure in intelligence whom he identifies only as 'R', almost certainly Sir John Wallinger, responsible for espionage in France and Switzerland. Because he was multilingual and had the perfect cover of a writer living in a neutral country to complete a play, Maugham was despatched to Lucerne to replace an agent who had suffered a nervous breakdown under the pressure. On 26 October he was met in Boulogne by Major Walter Kirke, in charge of secret service activities in Switzerland, along with two other recruits, one of whom was a fat Dutchman who kept two mistresses in addition to his wife.[71]

Maugham's role in Switzerland was essentially one of liaison, conveying information to and from agents in Frankfurt, Koblenz, Trier, and Mainz, passing on orders, collecting and sending data, and paying the spies. Kirke's diaries, now in the Imperial War Museum, reveal that one of Maugham's contacts was an old butter-woman who sold butter, eggs, and vegetables across the border in Switzerland. Another was a Swiss-German with the codename 'Bernard', who, it was discovered, had been fabricating his espionage trips to Germany.[72] Both are accurately recreated in *Ashenden*.

In *The Summing Up* Maugham claimed that the assignment appealed both to his sense of romance and of the ridiculous, the methods he was instructed to employ seeming to be very much out of melodramatic spy novels. In *Ashenden* he dramatized both the romance and absurdity of espionage, as well as its ruthlessness and brutality. At one point, for example, he describes 'Count von Holzminden', the German agent in Vevey, whom Ashenden had known in London a few years earlier. Now, however, in war the two men pretend that they do not know each other, though both know what secret service work the other is doing.

Like much of *Ashenden*, this brief vignette probably comes from the author's actual experiences, in this case his encounter with the German author Karl Gustav Vollmoeller (1878–1948). A writer of poems and plays, his best-known work was the massive pantomime *The Miracle*, staged first by Max Reinhardt in Vienna in 1911. During the First World War, it has been alleged, Vollmoeller was a German spy operating under the cover of recovering from tuberculosis in Davos, near Zurich, and writing a play. According to the British theatre impresario C. B. Cochran, Maugham later revealed that Vollmoeller had been filing intelligence reports in code and that he (Maugham) had been assigned to watch him.[73] If so, Maugham could hardly have failed to be amused by the situation of one dramatist-spy watching another dramatist-spy and both knowing what each other was doing.

Maugham was officially a member of the British Intelligence Service from October until February 1916, but when he returned to Switzerland with Syrie his spying was conducted more informally. On 8 February, Kirke recorded in his diary: '*Somerset Maugham* discharged but will examine the Swiss frontier on his own for John [Wallinger], but no expense to us to be incurred. Has been writing a play during his time in Switzerland and got into the Divorce Court. John is sending a new man.'[74] The implication of this entry is that the publicity surrounding Syrie's divorce had cost Maugham his status as an official British agent.

Maugham's play, called *The Unattainable* and produced as *Caroline*, was completed in the final months of 1915. It is a comedy about a woman whose husband dies in Africa, causing her young lover to find her less interesting when she is no longer an unattainable prize. An older suitor also backs away from marriage, arguing that their love would be destroyed by the wear and tear of everyday domestic life. In Act III, this passion is restored by the fabrication that Caroline's husband is not really dead. Years later, Maugham confessed that the play is really over by the end of the first act, but when it was produced in 1916 with Irene Vanbrugh and Lillah McCarthy it enjoyed a run of 141 performances.

The success of *Caroline* was one of the few bright spots in one of the most difficult years of Maugham's life. Syrie stayed in Geneva for some weeks following the divorce hearing, and with Maugham's commitment to his work and her boredom relations became strained. Her eventual departure for England was a relief to him, but his intelligence work had become too routine to sustain his interest, and he took an extended leave. He returned to England some time in the summer of 1916 with plans for a more exotic journey than any he had yet made.

Our Betters was due to be produced in New York, and the playwright proposed to go there first to make the necessary arrangements. His sights, though, were set on the South Seas, which had intrigued him since his youth, when he read Herman Melville, Pierre Loti, and Robert Louis Stevenson's *The Ebb-Tide* and *The Wrecker*. In Paris, Roderick O'Conor had sharpened his interest in Tahiti with his descriptions of Paul Gauguin's life and art. Maugham had become increasingly absorbed by the story of the painter who had turned his back on Europe – as indicated by the passage in *Of Human Bondage* – and wanted to write a novel about this artist-rebel.

Maugham's interest in the South Seas and Gauguin's flight was far more than merely professional. Behind it lay a deep dissatisfaction with the life he had been leading in London and which had been only temporarily interrupted by his war service. As early as 1904 he had articulated his boredom with the London cultural and social life in *The Merry-Go-Round* through Frank Hurrell, who desperately wanted to travel to exotic places. Though Maugham undeniably enjoyed the London milieu, he came to feel that he was somehow missing real life, that in London he was experiencing it at second-hand – at the theatre, in the concert hall, or in the pages of the newspaper or the latest book. Looking back on the period in *The Summing Up*, he observed that 'ever since I left St Thomas's Hospital I had lived with people who attached value to culture. I had come to think that there was nothing in the world more important than art. I looked for a meaning in the universe, and the only one I could find was the beauty that men here and there produced. On the surface my life was varied and exciting; but beneath it was narrow.'[75]

Added to this restlessness was the more immediate personal crisis coming with Syrie's divorce. In *The Summing Up*, he guardedly refers to their relationship when he writes: 'I wanted to recover my peace of mind shattered through my own foolishness and vanity by occurrences upon which I need not dwell . . . I went, looking for beauty and romance and glad to put a great ocean between me and the trouble that harassed me.'[76]

The facts are more mundane, and it can hardly have been coincidental that Maugham embarked for New York shortly before Syrie's divorce decree became absolute on 30 August, making her free to marry. In 'Looking Back' he claims that he had not been in America for more than a few weeks before Syrie followed with Liza and her nurse. When Maugham told her of his plans to travel to Tahiti, he says, she made one of her scenes and became resigned to his leaving only when confronted with his determination and promise to marry her on his return.

This account is interesting for several reasons. First, if Maugham had left England for Tahiti without informing Syrie of his plans, so that she had to sail across the Atlantic to get the truth, their relationship at this time could hardly have been intimate. Second, if she was so upset by his travelling to the South Pacific, it may well have been that she knew that he was not going alone. Maugham had invited Gerald Haxton, whom he had seen occasionally since their days in the ambulance corps, and who was then living in Chicago, to accompany him as his 'secretary'. It is likely that by this time Syrie knew of the nature of Maugham's attraction to the young American, and felt compelled to go to New York in an attempt to prevent the relationship from becoming any more intimate or committed.

Haxton was back in the United States because he had run afoul of the law in London in the autumn of 1915. On 13 November, he and a man called John Lindsell were arrested in a Covent Garden hotel, and on 7 December they were charged at the Old Bailey on six counts of gross indecency – in other words, homosexual conduct – under Section 11 of the Criminal Law Amendment of 1885. Both pleaded not guilty, and with the assistance of skilled lawyers were acquitted of all charges on 10 December. Shortly after the trial Haxton left England and returned to America rather than to the ambulance corps.

Whether Maugham was involved with Haxton's defence will never be known, but it is hard to believe that he was unaware of the arrest. He had maintained contact with the young man and, though he was in Switzerland in November and December, kept in close touch with England. Ted Morgan, whose research has uncovered the most specific details known about the trial, quotes a departmental records officer at the Home Office as saying that the file on Haxton indicates that 'he had money behind him and got off on a technicality'.[77] That money could have come discreetly from Maugham.

Maugham picked up Haxton in Chicago and they sailed from San Francisco in early November 1916 on the *Great Northern*, arriving in Honolulu on 14 November. They spent three weeks there, touring the red-light district of Iwelei and visiting the Kilauea volcano on the island of Hilo. On 4 December, the pair left Honolulu on the *Sonoma*, a ship sailing to Pago Pago, the capital of Eastern Samoa, as part of its run to Sydney. As Wilmon Menard has discovered, the passenger list of the *Sonoma* included: 'Somerset Maugham, Mr Haxton, W. H. Collins, Miss Thompson, Mr and Mrs J. J. Mulqueen'.[78]

Miss Thompson was a prostitute who had left Honolulu after a raid on Iwelei, and was on her way to Apia, in Western Samoa, where she hoped to work in a hotel bar. Another passenger was a missionary with, as Maugham recorded in his notebook, 'a look of suppressed fire'.[79] From his observations of these two people, and his impression of the stifling heat and monotonous rain in Pago Pago, Maugham later created his most famous short story, 'Rain' – or 'Miss Thompson', as it was first called. Incredibly, he used the actual name of the colourful prostitute but was never sued.

The South Pacific enchanted Maugham, opening his eyes to an

environment and people quite unlike anything he had known before, and he filled his notebook with descriptions of the ocean, the trees, plants, and idiosyncratic characters. In addition to the essential elements of 'Rain', he found rich material which he would later use in 'Red', 'Honolulu', 'The Pool', *The Moon and Sixpence*, and *The Narrow Corner*. As he said in *The Summing Up*, he was like a naturalist who had gone into a country where the fauna were of an unimaginable variety.

To Maugham the characters of the people in the South Seas were revealed with an explicitness rarely seen in Europe, where culture and breeding masked personalities. Away from the civilization which rubbed smooth the individual's rough edges, people were free to develop their idiosyncrasies, and they seemed to Maugham to be closer to the fundamental elements of human nature than the people he had known for years in Europe. His imagination sparked by the various impressions, he began to invent stories around these unique characters, and, though the war would delay the process, this South Seas voyage reawakened his interest in writing short stories. It was a form that best suited the varied and often disparate material he found in the South Pacific and later the Far East, and his most memorable tales are those which came from the many trips he made there in the twenties.

Maugham and Haxton spent several weeks in Pago Pago, probably delayed by the quarantine inspection described in 'Rain', and left for Apia in mid-December on the *Manua*, a 70-ton schooner whose skipper once cheerfully said: 'One day, she'll turn turtle and we shall all go to the bottom of the Pacific.'[80] During the month's stay, Maugham visited the grave of Robert Louis Stevenson, and toured the island of Savii and the extinct volcanic island of Apolima. On 13 January he and his secretary left Samoa on the *Atua* and arrived at Suva, Fiji, several days later. After a week they sailed on the *Talune*, arriving in Auckland, New Zealand, on 28 January, after a brief stop at Tonga and a delay because of fiercely rough seas.

Maugham spent about ten days in New Zealand, travelling from Auckland to Wellington, and he found the country a surprising oasis of Britishness in the Pacific. 'I was expecting', he wrote to a friend, 'to find Wellington like a city in the Western States, but it is much more like Bristol or Plymouth ... I confess it makes me just a little homesick.'[81] Not surprisingly, *A Writer's Notebook* contains no passages about New Zealand.

Maugham and Haxton sailed from Wellington to Tahiti on the *Manoa* and arrived in Papeete on 11 February. It had been the main destination on his trip, and he spent nearly two months there, staying at the Hotel Tiare. Its manager was a massive half-caste woman, Louvaina Chapman, whose ready smile, hearty laugh, and generous good nature appealed to the English writer. She died of influenza in 1918, and in *The Moon and Sixpence* he paid tribute by portraying her as 'Tiare Johnson'.

Aided by Gerald's gregariousness, Maugham tracked down as much Gauguin material as he could, meeting Emile Levy, a pearl merchant who had known the painter, and Captain 'Winny' Brander, who had discovered his body shortly after his death in 1903. Hearing that there were still a few Gauguin pictures in an old hut in the bush, Maugham went there in a hired car and discovered a painting on the glass panel of a door. Gauguin had painted three such panels while recovering from an illness, but children had scratched away the other two. Before long, the third one would be destroyed, and the native owner readily agreed to sell it for two hundred francs, the price of a new door. Maugham and Haxton carefully unscrewed it and drove back to Papeete, where they paid a further £200 to another native who claimed part ownership. With great excitement and apprehension, Maugham transported the Gauguin-on-glass back to the United States, and twelve years later it was mounted in the Villa Mauresque. When he sold his collection in 1962 it brought £37,400.

Maugham collected enough material about Gauguin and the Tahitian milieu for his novel, but he also did considerable exploring of the countryside and surrounding islands. On one occasion he went to Murea, where he was moved by the singing of hymns by a raucous choir led by a blind girl. Another time Emile Levy took him to the island of Tetioroa, which was owned by a Canadian dentist, Dr Johnstone Williams. In a short article called 'My South Sea Island', published in the *Daily Mail* in 1922, Maugham has described how, accompanied by only a Chinese cook, he camped on this deserted island – deserted, that is, except for a shadowy figure who the author later discovered was a resident leper.

Maugham and Haxton sailed from Tahiti on the *Moana* on 8 April, arriving in San Francisco a week later. Their South Sea sojourn had lasted five months, and for one of the rare occasions in his life the reality had matched his expectations. It had given him fresh new material, which would in the next two decades be the source of some of his best, and certainly his most characteristic, work. It had also provided him with an escape from the responsibilities awaiting him in New York and London, and he delighted in wandering from place to place, absorbing the local character and life without having any demands put upon him.

The ambience of the Pacific appealed to Maugham as did that of few other places. He had grown up next to the sea and was attracted to its vastness, mystery, and solitude. But, while the North Sea off Whitstable Harbour was grey and cold, the Pacific was colourful and warm, at times teeming with life and at others serenely quiet. Thus, Maugham's descriptions of the South Pacific are unusually lyrical in a writer whose mature style is spare and economical. On one of the last nights before he sailed from Tahiti, he wrote of the tranquil beauty he was leaving: 'The night is wonderfully silent. The stars shine with a fierce brilliancy, the Southern Cross and Canopus; there is not a breath of wind, but a wonderful balminess in the air. The coconut trees, silhouetted against the sky, seem to be listening. Now and then a sea bird gives a mournful cry.'[82]

Back in San Francisco, their South Seas idyll ended, Maugham and Haxton again faced the world of obligations and ties. The United States had entered the war only two weeks earlier and Haxton received a cable from his mother urging him to enlist. He was subsequently sent to train in South Africa, but when his ship was captured and sunk by the Germans, the passengers and crew were taken aboard the *Sea Wolf* to Germany. Haxton spent the remainder of the hostilities in a prisoner-of-war camp in Gustrow in north-east Germany.[83]

Maugham, meanwhile, returned to New York at the end of April, where the question of his relationship with Syrie had to be resolved. The divorce decree had become absolute and so there was no longer any legal impediment to their marrying. Within a month they were man and wife, and the recollection of the English actress Cathleen Nesbitt, a friend of both, suggests that the decision was made quickly. Syrie was staying with a mutual friend – probably the Countess of Colebrook – who telephoned Nesbitt one morning to say: 'Well they have decided! It happens this week, they are going to Atlantic City for the honeymoon! There is a doomed entanglement if ever there was one.'[84]

They were married on 26 May in Jersey City, with Ned Sheldon and the Countess of Colebrook as witnesses. The ceremony was performed by a judge, and years later Maugham characterized the wedding as lacking both sentiment and glamour. 'My memory of it', he told Leonard Lyons, 'is of standing with my bride-to-be before a justice-of-the-peace – who first sentenced the drunk in front of us, then married us, then sentenced the drunk behind us.'[85] After a reception at the Brevoort Hotel, attended by some of Maugham's theatrical friends such as Ethel Barrymore, the couple spent a month in New York before having a belated honeymoon in July at the Maidstone Inn, at East Hampton, on Long Island. If the wedding had indeed lacked 'sentiment', Nesbitt remembers that Maugham and Syrie 'looked very contented with each other when they returned to New York'.[86]

Despite this appearance of happiness, Syrie's and Maugham's marriage was indeed a doomed entanglement, and there has been considerable speculation about why Maugham agreed to it. He was, after all, forty-three years old and, though perhaps emotionally less mature than might be expected, had seen enough of life to know the dangers of marriage without love. Fifteen years earlier he had written passionately in *A Man of Honour* of the destruction caused by a man doing what society called 'the honourable thing'.

It is important to remember, however, that Maugham's decision to marry Syrie was not made exclusively in New York in 1917. Like most significant changes in one's life, it occurred in stages, and he had already committed himself to a large degree at the time of the divorce. He had been able to avoid the final step because for a number of months Syrie was not free and thereafter he was travelling in the South Pacific. When she awaited him in New York, however, he was forced either to go back on his earlier promise or to marry her, and he was someone who kept his word. It has been suggested that Ned Sheldon persuaded his reluctant friend that he had to marry the woman to whom he had given a child, but Maugham had a strong enough sense of propriety that he did not need any such prompting.

Thus, two of the reasons Maugham had earlier rejected a financial settlement for Syrie – the expectations of society and his concern for Liza – were still telling factors in 1917. Moreover, marriage to an attractive and socially well-connected woman would be useful both professionally and as a façade of respectability behind which he would continue to lead his own life as a homosexual. According to Glenway Wescott, it was 'a marriage of convenience on both sides. They knew all about each other. They didn't have to apologize. Willie knew all about her past and her lovers, and Syrie knew about his homosexuality. She wanted a father for her child and a man who was at the height of his fame as a playwright. He wanted a hostess, who knew the *tout-Londres* and would give him as much rope as he needed.'[87]

There is, however, a darker possibility that cannot be discounted: that Syrie used an overt form of blackmail, or perhaps an implied threat. Alan Searle has told me that in her pursuit of Maugham in the United States in 1917 she threatened to make public his relationship with Haxton and several other men, and this corroborates the theory of a number of others who knew Maugham. Syrie had many connections in English society, and she could not only damn him in its eyes but also put in a word with those in authority who could make life difficult for a homosexual author.

Whether or not Syrie actually used blackmail, Maugham could not have helped thinking that, were she scorned, she might well do him considerable damage. 'In his mind', writes Frederic Raphael, 'it must have seemed certain that Syrie would betray his secret and render him ridiculous, even odious in the eyes of his fellow countrymen. London was not necessarily his love, but it was his great market. He split his bets and his personality. He married Syrie and divorced himself. Only his cynicism endured as a reconciling factor.'[88]

Maugham may nearly have divided his essential self some years earlier when he tried to believe that he was heterosexual and that he genuinely wanted to be married. By the time of the wedding, however, he was surely beyond divorcing himself from his homosexual temperament. He had always been ambivalent about London – and his discovery of the pleasures of exotic travel with Haxton must have allowed him to envisage a marriage of convenience that would satisfy Syrie and permit him the freedom to live a divided life. He would be husband and father, with Syrie as the beautiful and lively hostess, and his literary career in London would flourish. Haxton, meanwhile, would be discreetly in the wings in London, and they would continue to travel the world for material and for escape.

In this sense, Maugham's cynicism was the factor which reconciled his real self to the role of husband. The problem was that Syrie was sincerely and deeply in love with him, and remained so for a great many years. As such, she was unable to accept the conditions that Maugham thought he was laying down, and she fought his involvement with Haxton. Alan Searle, for example, has reported that Maugham once said that while Sue Jones was aware of the writer's bisexuality and was tolerant, Syrie learned of it and was unaccepting.[89] Had the marriage really been one of convenience for both parties, she would have been invulnerable to the sense of betrayal and insult in Maugham's liaison with Haxton, but she wanted a true marriage.

Syrie's love for Maugham meant also that sex would inevitably become an area of destructive tension. By the time of their wedding, Maugham was no longer bisexual, but almost completely homosexual, and he could not respond to her femininity. Glenway Wescott has said that 'Willie told me himself that her physical demands were intolerable, inexcusable,'[90] and Gerald Kelly has said that the sex life between

Maugham and Syrie had deteriorated badly from the beginning of their affair. Whether her demands were unreasonable is not important – it is unlikely that they were, but Maugham saw them as oppressive and was unable to satisfy them. According to Searle, Maugham once admitted that sex with Syrie had become an effort in which he had to use all the resources of his imagination.[91] In Rebecca West's words, 'You can't be a homosexual and then go and marry a very feminine woman; it is not likely to work out very well! And Willie was, well, he'd got a *desire* to be heterosexual.'[92]

Maugham's marriage was the most serious mistake of his life. It is true that Syrie was in love with him, pursuing him with tenacity, and that he did it in part in the belief that it was the right thing to do. None the less, like Basil Kent in *A Man of Honour*, he was unwilling to inflict a measure of immediate pain in order to avoid much deeper and more lasting misery in the future. He had always had great difficulty in making anyone unhappy in a face-to-face situation, and he was vulnerable to Syrie's appeals. As well, it can be argued that he also lacked the courage to fly in the face of public opinion, to emulate the protagonist of his next novel – *The Moon and Sixpence* – and thumb his nose at its demands.

However one judges Maugham's motivation in marrying Syrie, it was a disastrous mistake which would haunt them both, as well as their daughter, for the rest of their lives. In *Forewords and Afterwords*, another respected homosexual writer of the twentieth century, W. H. Auden, has described the marriage of Oscar Wilde in terms which are equally applicable to that of Maugham and Syrie:

This was certainly the most immoral and perhaps the only really heartless act of Wilde's life. It can happen that a homosexual does not recognize his condition for a number of years and marries in good faith, but one cannot believe that Wilde was such an innocent. Most homosexuals enjoy the company of women and, since they are not tempted to treat them as sexual objects, can be most sympathetic and understanding friends to them: like normal men, many of them long for the comfort and security of a home and the joy of having children, but to marry for such reasons is heartless. I have never seen a marriage of this kind – at least if the partners were under fifty – in which the wife, even when she knew all about her husband's tastes, did not suffer acutely.[93]

Before Maugham had much of a chance to test married life, he was travelling again, this time on an espionage mission far more important than anything he had done in Switzerland. Some time in early June, only a few days after the wedding, he was approached by an old family friend, Sir William Wiseman, who was head of MI1C (now known as MI6) in the United States. A banker before the war, Wiseman had served in Flanders but was invalided out and sent to the United States officially as head of the British Purchasing Commission but in fact in charge of British intelligence there. He worked well with Colonel E. M. House, the American president's foreign policy adviser, and had become the key liaison figure between British and American intelligence.

Wiseman made a proposal that staggered Maugham: he would be sent to Russia to support whatever forces were committed to keeping that country in the war. He was admirably suited because he had the natural cover of appearing to be there to write a series of articles for an English paper, and his performance in Switzerland had shown that he had the nerves and the organizational skill to carry out a delicate propaganda/espionage mission. He would work from the United States because it would be easier to get into Petrograd anonymously and with less bureaucratic difficulty by leaving from the American west coast and going by the trans-Siberian railway. As well, there were a number of members of Middle European national groups who would work with him, the price of co-operation being eventual independence for Czechs, Slovaks, and Poles.

Those who have written about Maugham's intelligence activities in Russia in 1917 have always accepted the writer's own estimation that his assignment was important but ultimately a failure. In his recent study *American Espionage: From Secret Service to CIA*, however, Rhodri Jeffreys-Jones argues persuasively that the English writer's role was far more significant, that in fact he was the chief agent in Russia for the British and American intelligence services. Providing the most detailed analysis to date of Maugham's activities, Jeffreys-Jones concludes that his mission was not a failure.

Maugham was indeed sent to keep the Russians in the war, but he was not to intervene in the internal political situation unless it was to further that cause. He was to collect information on developments within the country but also unofficially to sound out the commitment of various factions to the defeat of Germany. Any involvement in the internal affairs of Russia was to be only in the form of disseminating propaganda. The Allies were clearly supporting the Menshevik government of Alexander Kerensky, but it was a socialist party, and the

Maugham mission was to determine whether there was a more acceptable element which could be encouraged. No overt support was to be given to any reactionary group, but the direction of political events might be subtly influenced. If there were to be a sudden upheaval, it would be very important for someone to have the confidence of the new regime, and thus Maugham's assignment included identifying the new leaders and working with them as an intermediary.

Because of the extremely sensitive nature of Maugham's mission, he was given a code name – 'S' or 'Somerville' (which he later gave his narrator in *Ashenden*) – and only a few of the most senior intelligence figures knew his identity. At the request of Wiseman, for example, Sir Eric Drummond, private secretary to the Secretary of State for the Foreign Office, sent the vaguest sort of description of his assignment to the British Embassy at Petrograd. 'Mr Somerset Maugham', he cabled, 'is in Russia on a confidential mission with a view to putting certain phases of the Russian situation before the public in the United States.'[94] In this way, the diplomatic staffs of the United States and Great Britain could be spared any embarrassment and Maugham was more free to operate independently of the bureaucracy. In addition, of course, it meant that if he got into any difficulty he would be disavowed by the Allies and left to suffer the fate of a captured spy.

In preparation for his Russian trip, Maugham was briefed by Professor Richard Gottheil of Columbia University, the former president of the Federation of American Zionists, and Rabbi Wise of New York, about co-operation he might receive from Jews in Petrograd. As well, he met Emanuel Voska, Secretary of the Bohemian National Alliance and Director of the Slav Press Bureau in New York. Voska represented one of the many national groups which wanted to free their homeland – in this case the area that became Czechoslovakia – and thus were willing to work with the Allies. Voska was also going to Petrograd, to help rally the Czechs and Slovaks in Russia to counter German propaganda.

Maugham was given $21,000 to fund his Russian venture. In addition, he asked Wiseman whether he would be paid a salary, his concern being not so much about money as a fear of humiliation. 'I will not pretend', he said, 'that I actually need one, but in Switzerland I refused to accept anything and found afterwards that I was the only man working for the organization for nothing and that I was regarded not as patriotic or generous but merely as damned foolish. If the job carries a salary I think it would be more satisfactory to have one; but if not I am not unwilling to go without.'[95]

According to Maugham, Syrie made no objection to this trip, and on 28 July he sailed from San Francisco to Tokyo, and from there to Vladivostok. After a day's wait, he took the trans-Siberian railway and arrived in Petrograd in early September. Voska and three Czech compatriots travelled on the same ship and train, but their instructions were to communicate with each other only with extreme caution. To three Americans going to join the United States Embassy the small quiet man who shared their dinner table was merely an author going to write articles for the *Daily Telegraph*.

In Petrograd Maugham settled into the Hotel Europa, and diligently and efficiently went about his work. He was helped in this by Sasha Kropotkin, back in Russia after her period of exile in England, who served as his interpreter. He had taken Russian lessons a decade earlier and could understand some of the language, but he could not move easily through Russian society without assistance. Sasha's connections also facilitated Maugham's meeting a number of powerful figures.

Maugham also saw something of his friend Hugh Walpole, who had been in Petrograd for some time, having earlier served as a Red Cross orderly attached to the Russian Ninth Army. Several years later Walpole remembered that 'the secret service job that fell to [Maugham] was made for him, made for his knowledge of languages, his knowledge of human nature, his knowledge of when to speak and when to keep silent . . . his refusal to be hurried into sentimental assumptions, his cynical pretence that "all was anyway for the worst" (he did not himself believe that for a single moment) gave him a poise and calm that some others of us badly needed. He watched Russia as we would watch a play, finding the theme, and then intent on observing how the master artist would develop it.'[96]

During his time in Russia, Maugham absorbed as much as he could of its society and culture, both to know the people's attitudes to the political situation but also to increase his own understanding as a writer. He visited the grave of Dostoevsky, and found the look on the face of the bust more terrifying than any of the great novelist's works. He went to the ballet and the theatre, and he often studied the crowds in the streets. Particularly intriguing was a misshapen dwarf who perched above the crowd on a seat at the top of a pole 'like the spirit of irony watching the human race'.[97] On one occasion he and the American Consul were taken by Louise Bryant, the wife of journalist John Reed, to the Alexander Market ('the Thieves Market') where Maugham bought several beautiful bead purses.[98]

As well as getting a feeling for Russian public life, Maugham made numerous contacts with powerful political figures. He met Thomas Masaryk, who had gone to Russia in 1917 to organize a legion of Czechs, and Maugham was impressed by the common sense and determination of the future president of Czechoslovakia. Maugham would later claim that the most remarkable man he met in Russia was Boris Savinkov, the Minister of War in the Menshevik cabinet. A long-time revolutionary, he had assassinated the Grand Duke Sergius and the chief of police under the Tsar, Dmitri Trepov. This colourful past, as well as his deliberate speech, restraint, and determined will, gave the English writer the feeling that nothing could stand in his way.

Much less impressive was Kerensky, whom he met at Sasha Kropotkin's apartment and heard address the Democratic Convention. Though the Menshevik leader had the ability to excite others to do things for him, and had a certain quiet oratorical skill, Maugham recognized an essential lack of strength and personal magnetism. As early as 24 September Maugham warned his superiors that Kerensky was losing popularity and was unlikely to survive.

Three weeks after this message, Maugham cabled a detailed proposal to Wiseman, who presented it to those in charge of American intelligence. The plan called for the distribution of propaganda in the form of popular literature and speakers sent to political meetings, church services and the army. The societies of Poles, Czechs, and Cossacks would be encouraged to counter German subversion, and the Mensheviks would be only one of the anti-German forces which would be supported. Each group would operate without knowledge of the activities of the others or even that they were working under one direction. Only Maugham would know that they had a common goal, and even he would be unaware of who was underwriting their costs. The plan, Maugham estimated, would cost about $500,000, a price that Wiseman thought worth paying.

On 7 November, before Maugham's proposal could be put into effect, the Bolsheviks seized power. At the beginning of his mission in Petrograd, Maugham's cover had been persuasive, but as time went by the Bolsheviks inevitably became aware that he was a spy. Since he had consistently stressed the connection with the Mensheviks and the national groups, rather than with the Bolsheviks, he was, in Jeffreys-Jones's words, 'a marked man, the secret agent of reactionary imperialism'.[99] As the Bolsheviks grew in power, Maugham's position became more precarious, and forty-eight hours before the fall of Kerensky's government, Wiseman had him recalled. Though fond of returning to places he had visited and known, at no time in the last forty-eight years of his life did Maugham go back to the Soviet Union.

Before Maugham left Petrograd, he had an interview with Kerensky, who asked him to convey a message to the British Prime Minister, Lloyd George. Shortly after Maugham's return to London by way of Scandinavia and Scotland, he delivered the Russian leader's message, writing it out because he feared that his stammer would ruin his presentation. Kerensky emphasized that he needed something to boost the morale of the soldiers, that the Allies must send more guns and ammunition, that the newspapers in Britain and the United States needed to treat Russia more sympathetically, and that there needed to be a more sensitive British ambassador in Petrograd.

According to Maugham Lloyd George hastily read the transcript of the interview and replied that he could do nothing. In any case, as Maugham had already privately reported to Wiseman, the situation in Petrograd was out of control and it would be impossible to halt the growth of the Bolsheviks. Very shortly after the meeting with Lloyd George, Kerensky was overthrown, and on 18 November Sir Eric Drummond wrote on Maugham's report: 'I fear this of only historical interest now.'[100]

Maugham's espionage duties, however, were not yet ended. According to Jeffreys-Jones, he attended a meeting called by Wiseman on 20 November in the office of the editor of The Times, Edward Carson. Also present were Lord Hardinge, from the Foreign Office, Auchincloss, secretary to the general war command, Sir George Macdonogh, Rufus Isaacs, and Wladislaw H. F. Horodyski, a librarian and historian who was very active in the cause of Polish nationalism. Part of Horodyski's proposal was that Maugham be sent back to Russia to provide support not to the Mensheviks but the Cossacks, who were led by General A. M. Kaledin. If Kaledin agreed to fight the Bolsheviks and the Germans, Maugham was to guarantee 100,000 Allied troops, money, and ammunition. Auchincloss thought that the idea had merit, but that the best results would come through Romania.

In the end, Auchincloss was unable to implement the plan, and even if he had been able to put it into effect, Maugham was by this time in no condition to carry it out. The tuberculosis which had bothered him in Switzerland and New York had been aggravated by the harsh climate and poor heating in Petrograd, and operating as an independent agent had meant that he had to survive on the meagre rations available to the general Russian population. As a result, he was now coughing and had a fever. An examination at St Thomas's confirmed that he needed rest in a sanatorium, and when it became apparent to those in charge of intelligence that he was an agent who might collapse on them, they agreed that he should take a leave. Even so, Wiseman remembered Maugham's skilled service, and, in early February 1918, when he was looking for a suitable man to act as a go-between for Polish groups in Paris and London he recommended Maugham. By this time, however, the writer had gone to a sanatorium in Scotland, and his war work was finished.

When Maugham looked back on his Russian mission, he concluded that it had been a failure and that if he had been sent six months earlier he might have been able to prevent the Bolsheviks from seizing power. As the history of Russia reveals, however, it is highly unlikely that anyone could have countered the impetus for social and political change which lay behind the revolution. Furthermore, as Jeffreys-Jones points out, Maugham was wrong in interpreting his assignment as the prevention of a Bolshevik takeover, and thus was unnecessarily harsh in his judgement of his own performance.

According to Jeffreys-Jones Maugham succeeded remarkably well in carrying out the mandate given him by Wiseman. His reports were more accurate than those of other agents and embassy officials, giving earlier warning of Kerensky's weakness, the strength of the Bolsheviks, and the potential of Polish and Czech movements. As well, Maugham provided a shrewd analysis of political and economic methods which would help the Allies to influence developments in East Central Europe. The essential elements of this analysis were later adopted by Western European countries and the United States in their responses to the invasions of Czechoslovakia and Poland in the late 1930s.[101] As an intelligence agent, rather than an *agent provocateur*, Maugham's contribution was therefore one of the major sources of information on Russia and Central Europe in the last half of 1917.

Because of the secrecy and sensitivity of his intelligence work – and perhaps because of the publicity attached to Syrie's divorce – Maugham received no official public recognition for his wartime service. Hugh Walpole, on the other hand, was awarded the CBE in 1917, and when Maugham wrote warmly to congratulate him in January 1918 he must have had to overcome a certain feeling of cynicism.

5

WANDERER: 1918–1929

BECAUSE THE WAR made it difficult for Maugham to go to one of the fashionable sanatoria in Davos or St Moritz, he was sent to one at Nordrach-on-Dee, near Banchory in northern Scotland. For the first six weeks he remained in bed, seeing no one but a doctor, some nurses, and the woman who brought his meals. For one who cherished his independence and had found it in travel, such a confinement should have been intolerable. In fact, Maugham adjusted to it, and after the intensity and rigours of his intelligence work, he enjoyed the womb-like seclusion of the invalid's quarters. 'I delighted in the privacy of my room', he wrote in *The Summing Up*, 'with the immense window wide open to the starry winter night. It gave me a delicious sense of security, aloofness, and freedom. The silence was enchanting. Infinite space seemed to enter it, and my spirit, alone with the stars, seemed capable of any adventure. My imagination was never more nimble.'[1]

When he became well enough to mingle with other patients, Maugham found ample material for his writer's imagination. He was intrigued by the love affairs, quarrels, scandals, and tears which went on in the shadow of the disease every bit as much as they did in the restaurants of London and the cafés of Paris. He discovered that the unshakeable illness and the sheltered, claustrophobic life of the invalid warped and accentuated character; as he had done during his months with the ambulance corps, he saw how people reacted to the prospect of death. All of these elements are represented in his short story based on his Scottish experience, 'Sanatorium'.

Maugham's confinement marked the beginning of an extremely

151

productive period in his career. Though he had done some writing during the previous four years, it was as if the seclusion of the sanatorium released a creative flow blocked by the turmoil of the war. Within twenty months he wrote four plays – *Home and Beauty*, *Caesar's Wife*, *The Unknown* and *The Circle* – and a major novel, *The Moon and Sixpence*. Beyond this burst of activity would lie two decades of enormous output and success, not only in drama but in the novel and short story, a period in which Maugham's own disillusionment and longing for escape struck a responsive chord with a great many audiences and readers.

Before the appearance of these new works, however, there was a production of a wartime play written in the early part of 1917, *Love in a Cottage*. Maugham's good friend, playwright Edward Knoblock, had revised it in the author's absence in Russia in October, to make it acceptable to the Lord Chamberlain's office, and it opened on 26 January 1918 at the Globe Theatre while Maugham was convalescing in Nordrach-on-Dee. With Marie Lohr and Haidee Wright in the cast, it ran for 127 nights.

Though Maugham never considered *Love in a Cottage* worthy of publication, it is interesting for several reasons: its concern for individual freedom, its disillusionment with materialism and its negative treatment of marriage. The protagonist, a young woman who married at eighteen and now sees herself chained to a man who hates her, is only one of a number of unhappily married characters. Another is a man who, married to a rich woman, has discovered that 'the whip of conscience has nothing like so keen a sting as the bank balance of a rich wife'. Even an affair is viewed as an imprisoning trap, and the author here may be remembering how his liaison with Syrie eventually became inextricable. One young woman refers to the light hearts with which people begin an intrigue and the heavy hearts with which they end it. The lying, the secrecy, the subterfuge, the jealousy, the misery that follow the short delight are heavy chains.

The question of materialism is presented largely in Owen Butterfield, a man married to an invalid and whose only purpose in life is to amass a large fortune. Now in late middle age, he realizes that he has missed much of the gaiety and joy of his youth by working so hard – a conclusion that Maugham had come to about his own early life. In the end, Butterfield cannot stand the feeling that his wealth is suffocating him and he shoots himself.

The heroine, who in the course of the play has inherited a fortune after the suicide of her husband and then has discovered the emptiness of the lives of the affluent, rejects her wealth to marry a doctor. A foil for the unhappy rich, Dr Bell speaks for the author when he says that he is an 'artist in life' because admirable living is surely a work of art. To use all of one's faculties to the utmost, he argues, to live fully, is no less useful than amassing a fortune. When asked for his definition of treasure in heaven he replies: 'To some it is art which is unending as time and to others it is a sacrifice which is as illimitable as space. Owen Butterfield aimed at the possible and the achievement left him desolate but the only thing worth aiming at is the unattainable.'[2] Ironically, Maugham's own career and life was aimed at the possible, and in the end, when he had achieved it, he came to recognize its emptiness.

The bondage of marriage is a theme which runs through all of Maugham's writing in 1918 and 1919 and recurs through his work of the next decade. *Home and Beauty*, composed in the sanatorium in 1918, is a farce created only to amuse war-weary audiences. Superbly performed in London by Gladys Cooper, Lottie Venne, and Charles Hawtrey, it did provide a welcome diversion, enjoying a run of 265 performances (in America, however, it folded after a fortnight), and a revival in 1968 by Britain's National Theatre was a sparkling triumph. Underlying the style and wit of the play, however, is a certain bitterness not perhaps far from the author's own situation. *Home and Beauty* is about a woman who, having remarried after the death of her husband during the war, discovers that he is in fact alive. Though it appears that the humour will arise from a battle to see which man will win the right to remain with her, Maugham reverses the situation by having each vying to be the one who will gracefully bow out. Marriage, they have discovered, is restrictive and irritating – as one says: 'I did sometimes wish I could call my soul my own.'[3] The play ends happily for both men when their wife decides to marry someone else, and they joyfully toast him and their new-found liberty.

In *Caesar's Wife*, written in 1918 and very successfully produced in London the following year, Maugham presents a far more serious and high-minded treatment of the constraints of marriage. It is the story of the union of a middle-aged British consul in Egypt and his young wife, and the dilemma that is created by her love for a dashing young man. The tragedy of her meeting and forming a passionate attachment to her lover only months after a kind of marriage of convenience parallels Maugham's own discovery of Haxton, a few months after Syrie's pregnancy began the process which bound him to her. In 1918 he almost certainly wrote from personal experience when he gave the consul the line: 'You didn't know what marriage was and how insane it must be unless love make its constraints sweeter than freedom.'[4]

153

Caesar's Wife was based on Madame de La Fayette's *La Princesse de Clèves*, and Maugham has described its theme as 'the triumph of will over passion'.[5] As such, it is a variation of the thesis of *Of Human Bondage*, and one of its author's firmest tenets. Thus, when the consul resolutely places his integrity as a government official over his own emotions as a husband, and when the young wife surrenders her lover in order to honour her marriage vows, Maugham may subconsciously have been reminding himself of the necessity of maintaining the proper façade of his imperfect marriage. He never had any intention of giving up Haxton, but he undoubtedly found himself caught in a situation where he was forced to do the noble thing by marrying Syrie.

Maugham, however, did not have any extended experience of marriage until the summer of 1918. He had gone to Scotland soon after his return from Russia, while Syrie remained in London, and it was not until May that he was considered well enough to leave the sanatorium. Syrie had found a suitable summer house, Charles Hill Court, near Farnham in Surrey, and while Liza enjoyed the large gardens Maugham found the study perfect for his work. The poet Robert Hichens was then living nearby at Highmead, near the Frensham Ponds, and he remembered a sunny summer spent with Maugham. They played croquet and frequently rode, stopping for teas at the Frensham Ponds Hotel. Maugham, said Hichens, never complained and was always good company. On one occasion, the singer Maude Valerie White was staying with Hichens, and Maugham spent much of an evening with her at the piano as she played music for him which might be suitable for the Egyptian background for *Caesar's Wife*.[6]

Maugham lived at Charles Hill Court from May until August, during which time he produced the first fruits of his South Seas trip, *The Moon and Sixpence* (which, as his contract with Heinemann shows, he first called 'Sixpence and the Moon'). His interest in writing a novel about an artist had begun in Paris in 1905 and his Tahitian voyage in 1916 had given him the exotic material he needed to balance the English social setting he knew all too well. By 1918 his own dissatisfaction with the direction of his life made *The Moon and Sixpence* almost as much a personal statement as *Of Human Bondage* had been.

Maugham's artist-hero, Charles Strickland, is loosely based on Paul Gauguin, but is more fictional than biographical, a character whose revolt against society, duty, and convention resembles that of Stephen Dedalus in Joyce's *A Portrait of the Artist as a Young Man* and Paul Morel in Lawrence's *Sons and Lovers*. These creative figures, like those in Richardson's *Maurice Guest*, Shaw's *The Doctor's Dilemma*, Dreiser's

The Genius, Cannan's *Mendel*, Lewis's *Tarr*, and dozens of other early twentieth-century works, had a romantic appeal to the readers who felt caught in the complexities of modern society. For those disillusioned by the First World War and seeing that increased mechanization and industrialization were destroying a more passionate, instinctual life, the artist-heroes seemed able to preserve their individuality and creativity. 'The artist', Maugham wrote, 'can within certain limits make what he likes of his life. In other callings, in medicine for instance, in the law, you are free to choose whether you will adopt them or not, but having chosen, you are free no longer. You are bound by the rules of your profession; a standard conduct is imposed on you. The pattern is pre-determined. It is only the artist, and maybe the criminal, who can make his own.'[7]

The Moon and Sixpence is about a conventional middle-class English stockbroker who suddenly abandons his wife and children to go to Paris to learn to paint. In a foretaste of what was to come in *Cakes and Ale*, Maugham uses the early part of the novel to paint a wickedly satiric picture of the Edwardian social and literary scene – caricaturing such writers as Violet Hunt and George Street in his sketches of Rose Waterford and George Road. More important, in the social set of the Strickland family he presents a portrait of dull, pretentious and stifling conformity, which is later contrasted vividly with the vitality and energy of the painter's life in Paris and with the meaningfulness of his final years in Tahiti.

Strickland's flight from this mediocre conventionality involves a complete denial of family, duty, honour, and orthodox morality. More-over, apart from any effect they may have on his art, surroundings and material comfort mean nothing to him and he has no desire for recognition or fame. Since he no longer has a social conscience – which Maugham calls 'the policeman in our hearts, set there to watch so that we do not break its laws . . . the spy seated in the central stronghold of the ego'[8] – he has almost complete freedom. In the Paris section Strickland reveals his amorality when he destroys the lives of the Stroeves, driving Blanche Stroeve to a grisly suicide and ruining her decent husband. In the process, however, Strickland has created a great painting and Maugham seems to suggest that, given the choice between the happiness of a good but ordinary man and woman and the creation of a masterpiece through their destruction, the painting is more important.

One of the key elements of *The Moon and Sixpence* is the relationship between the artistic temperament and love or sex. Strickland is involved with three women, but none is allowed to interfere with his creative life. His wife, like the second Mrs Driffield (*Cakes and Ale*), Isabel Longstaffe ('The Fall of Edward Barnard'), and Isabel Bradley (*The Razor's Edge*), is a threat to a man's freedom, a trap by which he can be dragged into a conventional social posture which destroys his individuality. Blanche Stroeve is the instinctual woman who binds her men to her through her sexual attraction, and Strickland resents her appeal. 'I can't overcome my desire,' he laments, 'but I hate it; it imprisons my spirit; I look forward to the time when I shall be free from all desire and can give myself without hindrance to my work.'[9] Ata, the native girl living with the painter in Tahiti, is presented as the ideal woman for an artist. Warm, generous, and open, she is both sensual and maternal, but above all she makes few demands. Life with her entails no intense commitment or spiritual involvement, and so the man can dedicate himself fully to his art.

Like nearly all of Maugham's work, *The Moon and Sixpence* is essentially about freedom, and though Strickland is shown in a successful rebellion against orthodoxy he is in fact slave to a far more powerful bondage: his artistic urge. 'A tormented spirit striving for the release of expression,' he finally achieves liberation in his last monumental paintings on the walls of his house in Tahiti. Passionate, sensual, primeval, and mystical, they are his soul in paint, a vision at the end, like Kurz's in Conrad's *Heart of Darkness*, of man's basic nature. To underline that this creation is an extremely personal act of catharsis, Maugham adds that the paintings were destroyed on the painter's orders. As M. C. Kuner noted, his destruction is 'a supreme gesture of contempt for the world's opinion. Here is a study of revolt and ultimate freedom rivalling even the Gidean ideal.'[10]

In *The Moon and Sixpence* Maugham presented his views of creative genius, which he was to discuss again in *The Summing Up*, and much of his identification is with his artist-rebel protagonist. Like *Of Human Bondage*, it is about freedom, but though only five years separated the writing of the two novels they reveal significantly different attitudes. The title of the later work indicates their fundamental connection, coming as it does from the *Times Literary Supplement* review of *Of Human Bondage* in which it observed that 'like so many young men he [Philip] was so busy yearning for the moon that he never saw the sixpence at his feet.'[11] Maugham was so clearly struck by this summation of his autobiographical protagonist that he adopted the phrase. In a note which was intended to precede the text, he explained that 'in his childhood he [the author] was urged to make merry over the man who, looking for the moon, missed the sixpence at his feet, but having reached years of maturity he is not so sure that this was so great an absurdity as he was bidden to believe. Let him who will pick up the sixpence, to pursue the moon seems the most amusing diversion.'[12]

Of Human Bondage, however, had ended with Philip abandoning his search for the moon – i.e. travel and adventure – in order to claim the sixpence, a quiet domestic life as a country doctor with Sally. Though this conclusion was an exercise in wish fulfilment, it did represent the author's state of mind in 1913, which was to adopt the pattern of birth, marriage, work, children and death. At that point of his life Maugham thought he was ready to accept a relatively conventional life. In 1918, however, he was arguing that pursuing the moon is the most desirable goal just as Dr Bell in *Love in a Cottage* had stated that 'the only thing worth aiming at is the unattainable.'

By the time that he wrote *The Moon and Sixpence*, Maugham had come to realize that his flirtation with domesticity, which had found a fictional expression in *Of Human Bondage*, was a mistake, that indeed he was sexually unorthodox and temperamentally a loner. His awareness of the artificiality of his London life, which he had felt as early as 1904, was confirmed by his travels to the South Pacific and his experiences as a British agent. As well, his contact with death on the battlefields of northern France undoubtedly influenced his outlook on life, giving him a kind of philosophical change which found expression in John Wharton in *The Unknown* and Larry Darrell in *The Razor's Edge*.

It is, however, one thing to write about rebellion and artistic iconoclasm and another to do it, and in 1918 Maugham was forty-four years old, married, and comfortably established as a prominent author. Always torn between contempt for the conventional social life and a desire to be successful within it, he was not prepared to turn his back on affluence and the approval of his peers. He could nevertheless admire, approve, and enjoy those who did search for the unattainable, and thus it is no accident that *The Moon and Sixpence* is written in the first-person singular.

Only once before had Maugham used a first-person narrator for a novel – in 1898 in *The Making of a Saint* – but after *The Moon and Sixpence* it was the point of view which became increasingly comfortable for him. Whereas the traditional omniscient voice in *Of Human Bondage* had brought the reader closer to the protagonist, the narrative persona of *The Moon and Sixpence* created a distance between the reader and the artist-hero. The result is an endorsement of Strickland while the author and reader remain detached from him, seeing his actions through the eyes of one who prefers the safer path of moderation and compromise. In effect, Strickland and the narrator represent the two sides of Maugham's character, and the discussions about art, morality and social obligation are a debate within Maugham himself.

That debate, however, is weighted on the side of caution through Maugham's choosing to describe the action from the point of view of a detached witness, and his increasing use of that voice suggests that he had concluded that the time had passed when he might himself rebel. The narrator of *The Moon and Sixpence* is not named, but in *Cakes and Ale* he becomes 'Willie Ashenden', admiring observer of the free-spirited Rosie, Lord George Kemp, and Edward Driffield. Between that novel and *The Moon and Sixpence* lie dozens of short stories in which the action is seen at a distance through the vision of a first-person narrator or a character within the story.

These forms of detached narrative reflect the author's feeling as he approached his fiftieth year that his life as an emotionally active participant had largely run its course. In 1923, for example, he announced what was the first of many farewells which would stretch over the next forty years when he confided to Burton Rascoe that he had reached the period in his life when he wanted to write essays. 'That means', he said, 'that I am beginning to think about life rather than to feel it. It is a sign of age to wish to write essays. It means that the emotions are no longer so capable of stimulation as they once were. It means that I am withdrawing to the sidelines of life and taking up the point of view of a spectator.'[13]

Maugham may have been right that his emotions had lost some of their intensity over the years, but as we know it would be decades before they were truly extinguished. Though *On a Chinese Screen* (1922) and *The Gentleman in the Parlour* (1930) are evidence of a shifting interest to commentary, he did not abandon drama or fiction for many years. When he continued to write fiction, it was thus increasingly from the point of view of uninvolved commentator, and the effect was to bring the reader closer to the narrative voice than to the action of the story or the emotions of the characters.

At the end of August 1918 the Maughams returned to 6 Chesterfield Street, from which Walter Payne had moved at the end of the summer. Syrie had preferred them to live in her house in Regent's Park, but Maugham objected to inhabiting a residence which he considered to have been bought for her by Gordon Selfridge. While 6 Chesterfield Street had been a perfect writer's house, it did not suit a family and Maugham had to give up his writing room to his wife as a bedroom, working in a small first-floor room overlooking the street. Thus in the spring of 1919 Maugham bought 2 Wyndham Place, a large four-storey Georgian house just off Bryanston Square in Marylebone, and after several months in a rented house in Hans Place they were able to move into their new home. Within a week, however, Maugham was off on another extended trip through the Far East.

Maugham had returned to Nordrach-on-Dee in October 1918, and over the winter months wrote *The Unknown*, a play based on his early novel *The Hero*. Once again he used the device of a soldier's traumatic experience as a catalyst for his dissatisfaction with his former way of life. The dramatic tension was intended to lie in the conflict between the soldier's agnosticism and the faith of his fiancée, a division that destroys their relationship. For audiences, however, the interest lay in the debates about faith, not in the emotions of the characters, and the most dramatic moment was the mother's angry cry: 'And who will forgive God?'

Home and Beauty had been written to provide light entertainment for war-weary audiences, but *The Unknown* forced them to confront a disturbing reality. It was Maugham in a serious vein, and he confided to Eddie Marsh, who had praised *Caesar's Wife*, that *The Unkown*, his unpleasant play, would be much more important.[14] Produced in London on 9 August 1920 with a strong cast which included C. V. France, Haidee Wright, Lady Tree, and Basil Rathbone, it ran for a modest seventy-seven performances. Within a fortnight of its opening, the newspapers were full of comment about its 'unpleasantness', and the author was receiving fifty letters a day. Though it did not capture a large audience, Maugham thought highly enough of it to include it in his *Collected Plays*.

The last of Maugham's plays of this early post-war period, *The Circle*, is the most skilfully crafted thing he ever wrote for the stage. Its first production in March 1921 with such stage luminaries as Allan Aynesworth, Ernest Thesiger, Leon Quartermaine, Lottie Venne, and Fay Compton, played for 181 nights, and it was successfully revived in 1931, 1944, and in a glittering version at the Chichester Festival in 1976. It is the story of the past elopement of two lovers, Lord Porteous and Lady Kitty, and the present re-creation of that act by Lady Kitty's daughter-in-law, Elizabeth, and Teddy, a young man on leave from Malaya. The plot revolves around the younger woman's decision to bolt and the efforts of her husband, Arnold Champion-Cheney, and his father, Clive – Lady Kitty's former husband – to prevent her departure.

Much of the craftsmanship of *The Circle* lies in its balancing of two heroines and their discussions about the advantages and disadvantages of eloping. One has in the past been involved in a marriage which was conventional and respectable, and the other is presently enduring the same tedium. To leave, however, means surrendering comfort and economic security as well as a position in society. Recognizing Elizabeth's romantic view of her earlier flight, Lady Kitty enlightens her about the miseries of social outcasts wandering from one European city to another – a life of dissolution, questionable companions, lack of children, and without even the guarantee that love will endure. 'The tragedy of love', observes Lady Kitty in one of Maugham's most famous lines, 'isn't death or separation. One gets over them. The tragedy of love is indifference.'[15] Despite the vision of the underside of the romantic escape, Elizabeth prefers the youthful exuberance of Teddy to the stifling luxuries of the Champion-Cheney house, and they leave for the Far East.

In common with so much of Maugham's writing in the period after the First World War, *The Circle* presents marriage as a social contract that entails both the advantages of social acceptance – stature, security, comfort – and the disadvantages: loss of freedom, boredom and the absence of passion. Like *The Moon and Sixpence*, the play does not recognize passion or creativity within marriage or in a conventional social setting. The choice confronting Lady Kitty and Elizabeth is comfortable stagnation in England or a much less secure but more passionate life in exile. In both the novel and the play freedom is equated with escape to distant places.

At least two of Maugham's short stories of this period also portray the desirability of flight and exile. 'The Fall of Edward Barnard', first published in September 1921, is an early working of the plot of *The Razor's Edge*, describing the transformation of a young Chicago businessman into a beachcomber who prefers the easy and leisurely life of Tahiti to financial success and marriage. Looking back on Chicago's schedules and responsibilities as a prison, he sees material comforts as impediments to self-knowledge and self-expression. 'I tremble with fear when I think of the danger I have escaped,' he tells a friend. 'I never knew I had a soul till I found it here. If I had remained a rich man I might have lost it for good and all.'[16]

Similarly, 'Mayhew' (1923) describes a successful and wealthy Detroit lawyer who, at the age of thirty-five, suddenly abandons a life which, says Maugham, had given him 'all it had to offer'. He buys a house in Capri and for the next fourteen years devotes himself to gathering material for a history of the second century of the Roman Empire. Just as he is about to begin writing, however, he dies.

Mayhew is obviously another of the Maugham characters of the early twenties who escape entrapment in convention and find freedom – in this case, in the author's own beloved Capri. Maugham admires his protagonist because he is one of the few men who successfully take life in their own hands and mould it to their own vision, and although he fails to complete his project his life is good and complete. In a concluding observation that reveals Maugham's own sense of disillusionment with attained goals, he writes: 'He did what he wanted, and he died when his goal was in sight and never knew the bitterness of an end achieved.'[17]

The Circle had been completed in November 1920 and by that time Maugham had good reason to be preoccupied with the question of marriage and the freedom to pursue one's passions – both emotional and creative. Early in 1919 he had discovered that an essential component of the marriage of convenience he had envisaged with Syrie had been made impossible. Gerald Haxton, released from the prisoner-of-war camp at the end of the war, returned to England from Copenhagen and was deported as an alien.

Access to Haxton's Home Office file is restricted until 2019, but Ted Morgan was told by a departmental records officer that the deportation was not the result of the earlier morals charge. There were, it appears, several other matters which concerned British officials, and it was determined that he should not be allowed to enter the country again. Over the succeeding years, said the records officer, applications were made on Haxton's behalf – and influence used through club connections – but the decision was never reversed.[18]

Until the Haxton file is opened, the real reasons for his deportation and exclusion will remain a matter of speculation. If, as has been suggested, he was acquitted of the morals charge only on a technicality, and if other of his sexual escapades were known to the authorities, they may have concluded that he was an undesirable alien. There is also the possibility that some of his wartime activities had made him a risk to British security. In the absence of firm evidence, however, there does seem to have been an extraordinary effort to keep Haxton out of Britain, lending some credence to the suggestion that Syrie had used her influence with highly-placed government officials. She was battling the young man for the possession of her husband's loyalty, and may well have seen his deportation as a major triumph and impediment to the men's relationship. If so, it would explain the virulence of Maugham's dislike of her after their divorce, and the claims of more than one of his friends that her manipulation was the cause of much of his unhappiness.

Whether or not Syrie was instrumental in Haxton's deportation, it significantly changed the basis on which Maugham had married. From 1919 onwards if he was to enjoy the young man's company it would have to be on his travels or in Paris, where Maugham kept an apartment. Thus, for the next two decades Maugham increased the time spent abroad, and Haxton's banishment ultimately led to Maugham's buying a villa in France and spending only a few months of each year in England. Life once again imitated art, and like the heroine of *The Circle*, Maugham chose exile with his lover over the attractions of London.

Maugham had not even settled into 2 Wyndham Place at the beginning of August 1919 when he sailed on the *Orduna* from Liverpool for an extended journey to China. After a few days in New York watching rehearsals of *Home and Beauty* (called *Too Many Husbands* in the United States), he took the train to Chicago to fetch Haxton. Together they spent about four months in China in the winter of 1919–20, travelling 1500 miles up the Yangtze by sampan. Maugham made extensive notes along the way, and in 1922 he published fifty-eight sketches as *On a Chinese Screen*. These word-pictures, almost prose-poems, are polished and precise, many no more than a few paragraphs in length, and they vividly evoke a sense of place. In China Maugham discovered a culture and civilization in which his own sensitive and philosophical nature was very much at home, though he admitted that he could never fully understand any of the Chinese people he encountered.

Maugham was always more interested in people than places, preferring revealing conversation with a chance acquaintance to a tour of a famous site, and he was intrigued by the behaviour of westerners living in the midst of Chinese civilization. *On a Chinese Screen* presents a number of shrewd and gently critical portraits of missionaries, consuls, company managers and army officers who are generally narrow, intolerant, and insensitive to the culture and customs of the Chinese. One Englishwoman, oblivious to the art around her, delights in making her living-room a replica of thousands of English parlours. Similarly, the endless spectacle of Chinese life goes unnoticed by a tobacco company official who can find excitement only in American adventure magazines. In such sketches Maugham began his explorations of the attitudes and behaviour of westerners in the colonial milieu, a subject with which he became almost uniquely associated. More specifically, *On a Chinese Screen* provides a revealing picture of the tensions created by the colonizing of pre-revolutionary China.

Maugham returned to England in April 1920 while Gerald went back to Chicago. After three months in London, and following the opening of the controversial *The Unknown*, Maugham, Syrie and Liza holidayed in August on the Isle of Wight. There they shared a house at Totland Bay with the Lehmann family, and Liza played with John, Rosamund, and their two sisters. On 17 September, however, the writer sailed for New York to begin another journey, one which would last for more than a year.

As before, Maugham went to Chicago to meet Haxton, and he spent some weeks there visiting, among others, Ned Sheldon. Fanny Butcher, who owned a bookshop there at the time, recalled how Maugham 'evaded the allurement of social life, living with three (or was it four?) young men in a handsome brownstone. One of them was a popular extra man on the social circuit, and Chicago hostesses angled for Willie Maugham (as close friends always called him) but never landed him.' Maugham, she said, seemed to be avoiding the glare of publicity from the success of *The Moon and Sixpence* and so 'went into the silences'. On the other hand, he enjoyed the seclusion of the book-shop, becoming absorbed in reading if a customer came in. 'But if there were a few quiet moments he would sit on one of the uncushioned kitchen chairs . . . and we would talk, and we plainly "got on".'[19]

In the more pretentious surroundings of Hollywood, however, Maugham got on much less well. On the way to the Far East he and Haxton stopped in California, in part at the invitation of Jesse Lasky, who was then hiring a number of famous European authors to write screenplays for his company, Famous Players-Lasky. On a trip to Europe in 1920 he had signed Henry Arthur Jones, Edward Knoblock, Arnold Bennett, Sir Gilbert Parker, and Elinor Glyn. He also in-terested Maugham, who realized that films represented an op-portunity to make a great deal of money, and he hoped thereby to earn enough to make himself financially independent for the rest of his life.

Maugham's attitude towards film, as he expressed in an article in 1921, was that the writer was the key figure and the director's role is that of an interpreter. Filmmakers, he believed, would discover that it is ultimately futile to adapt stories for the screen from plays and novels and that the only advance in the art of the cinema would come from original screenplays. He was, of course, wrong about the efficacy of using material from other media but right to emphasize the importance of the script written uniquely for the screen. In Hollywood, however, he discovered – long before a succession of other writers left in disillusionment – that the studios really only wanted noted authors for window-dressing, that it was their names that were being bought.

Maugham therefore spent only several weeks in Hollywood, discussing possibilities with studio officials, before deciding that he would move on to the Far East and send screenplays from there. He managed to sell one script for $25,000, a rewriting of *Love in a Cottage* which was released as *The Ordeal* in May 1922. However, a slump in the American film market cut off the possibility of more, and by August 1921 he wrote to Knoblock that he had parted from the film world with relief.[20] In fact, Maugham continued to produce screenplays, though he admitted years later that he lacked the particular sense needed to write for films. Instead, and ironically, he had to content himself with seeing his plays, novels, and short stories presented in cinemas and on television in hundreds of popular adaptations.

Maugham's Hollywood visit did pay off in a most unexpected way. One of the other guests at his hotel was the playwright John Colton, also in California to write screenplays, and unable to sleep one night he borrowed the galley proofs of Maugham's story 'Miss Thompson' which had arrived in the mail that day. Joining its author for breakfast next morning, Colton confided that he had lain awake thinking what a marvellous play it would make, and could he adapt it? Maugham was sceptical, believing that it could not be translated, but agreed to let him try. When the story was published in *The Smart Set* in April and as 'Rain' in *The Trembling of a Leaf* in the following September, one of a number of dramatists wanting the rights offered Maugham's agent, Elizabeth Marbury, $7000. Colton did not have that kind of money, and had only the author's handshake, but when Miss Marbury's cable caught up with Maugham in the South Seas, he replied: 'The handshake with Colton still stands.'

Colton's adaptation, written with Clemence Randolph, opened in New York in November 1922 and was a smashing triumph. With a superb Jeanne Eagels as Sadie Thompson, the play ran for an astonishing 648 performances, was seen by several million people, and grossed three million dollars. Twice produced in London, revived in America in the thirties, produced as a musical in New York in the forties, and filmed three times (successively with Gloria Swanson, Joan Crawford, and Rita Hayworth), it not only brought Maugham a great deal of money but made 'Rain' his most famous story.

Maugham's California sojourn was not entirely preoccupied with business. He enjoyed seeing Knoblock in Hollywood and he tried unsuccessfully to persuade his friend to accompany him on a jaunt to

Mexico. Together they saw something of Hugh Walpole, who was touring the United States, and on New Year's Eve 1920 Knoblock, Maugham, and Haxton went to Dreamland, a rundown dance hall that boasted an outstanding Negro band. With the country in the grip of prohibition, they drank thirty-dollar whisky out of teacups.

Even more important to Maugham than his friendship with Knoblock was that with Bertram Alanson, whom he and Haxton visited in San Francisco before they embarked for the Far East. They had first met Alanson while sailing to Hawaii in 1916, and Maugham not only maintained contact but visited him on the way to Russia in 1917 and China in 1920. A deep friendship and loyalty developed between the two men which lasted until Alanson's death in 1958. Born in San Francisco in 1877, Alanson went into partnership with his brother and proved to be a shrewd investment broker, eventually becoming president of the San Francisco Stock Exchange. Tall and well dressed, he was intelligent, well read, and cultured, and he enjoyed the company of his urbane English friend. Alanson seemed to have little interest in women, and like Maugham married relatively late in his life – at forty-six to an attractive divorcée. As the wedding drew near, Maugham teased his friend by writing that he and Haxton were secretly hoping to find him still a single gentleman,[21] but afterwards he wrote warmly to congratulate both Bert and Mabel and he always enjoyed their company and their beautiful home on Russian Hill.

As the large volume of correspondence from Maugham to Alanson now held by Stanford University reveals, Maugham had a special affection for, and trust in, his friend, and he was more distraught over the decline of Alanson's health in the final years than he was over the deaths of anyone except his mother and Haxton. The appeal of Alanson was that, while intelligent and cultivated, he was remote from the literary–social milieu of London and New York, and far from the world in which Maugham's personal life was entangled, and so he offered no complications. Moreover, though Alanson obviously liked playing host to a famous writer, he had nothing else to gain from the relationship, and this put Maugham, who increasingly felt himself exploited by others, at ease. Thus Alanson was someone whose judgement he trusted, to whom he could confide some of his most private concerns and seek advice, without fear that his confidence would be betrayed.

In addition to his friendship, Alanson became Maugham's financial adviser, and in nearly four decades his skill as a broker built the writer's investments into a very considerable sum. As well, Maugham had

Alanson establish trust funds for Haxton, Searle, Robin Maugham, and Liza and her children. The writer was fond of telling how he had given his friend $15,000 to invest, forgot about it for years, and then discovered that it had grown to a million dollars. Even allowing for the storyteller's hyperbole, Alanson made his friend much wealthier, and Maugham was deeply grateful.

Following their visit with Alanson, Maugham and Haxton sailed on the *Wolverine State* to Honolulu in February 1921, and after another eighteen days at sea reached Manila. From there they went to Singapore and then on an expedition to Sarawak, on the island of Borneo. Using a succession of launches, paddle boats, and pole boats, they worked upriver into the jungle, seeing monkeys along the shore and watching for crocodiles while they bathed in the evening. They slept in Dayak houses on piles, among head-hunters who were polite and generous, though Maugham found their hospitality exhausting when each village insisted on honouring its guests with a feast and a dance lasting until dawn.

It was on this trip that Maugham, having observed the deaths of others many times, came very close to it himself. Travelling upriver, their boat was overtaken by a bore, a tidal wave which as it moves into estuaries and up narrowing rivers develops height and force. Maugham saw two or three waves coming which by the time they struck were twelve feet high, capsizing the craft and hurling its occupants into the water. As they clung to the boat, they were swept along by the surge, and Maugham, now exhausted and swallowing water, would have perished had Haxton not kept a grip on him. Eventually, with a rolled-up mattress serving as a life-preserver, they made it to the shore where they climbed through knee-deep black mud onto the bank.

According to Maugham, Haxton then suffered a heart attack brought on by the intense effort, and as they lay on the bank the writer was sure that his companion would die. After an hour, though, they were rescued by others in the party, and Haxton recovered. When they resumed this journey the next day, much bruised and cut, Maugham felt an intensified pleasure in the sky and sunshine and green trees. Back in the coastal town of Kuching, their survival was viewed with astonishment by those familiar with the treachery of the bore.

The mishap drove Maugham and Haxton back to Singapore to refit and rest. While there they experimented with opium, an interesting though finally painful experience for Maugham. He first enjoyed a feeling of physical well-being, followed by an opium dream of a long road, a quick ride through long rows of trees down to the grey calm sea of a harbour. The next morning, however, brought a throbbing headache and he vomited for most of the day, dubious about the pleasures of the drug.

Maugham's reaction to opium was much the same as the effect on him of an evening of drinking alcohol. As he observed, he seemed to have a constitution which meant that if he became drunk he suffered a painful hangover, and thus he always drank in disciplined moderation. He could recall being inebriated several times during his Heidelberg days, and Alan Searle can remember only two occasions when he ever saw his friend less than sober.[22] As in so many other aspects of his life, Maugham exercised rigid control over his drinking: always the one dry martini before lunch and dinner, a glass of wine with the meal, and perhaps a brandy with his cigar. There was never, however, a binge, never a cathartic blowout when, though narcotically induced, he might let go of himself, temporarily at least losing his vigilant self-control and perhaps giving expression to his deepest resentments and wounds.

While in Singapore, Maugham also learned of one of the most famous scandals in the Federated Malay States, the essentials of which became the basis of one of his most famous short stories, 'The Letter'. Staying at the home of Mr Courtenay Dickinson, a lawyer in the firm of Dickinson, Manson and Company, he listened in fascination to the story of Ethel Proudlock, who in 1911 had killed a man on the veranda of the house. After a sensational trial, Mrs Proudlock was found guilty of murder and sentenced to be hanged, though the considerable efforts of the European community in Malaya eventually secured her pardon.

Maugham, who had first learned English by reading criminal court reports in newspapers, realized that he had stumbled onto the material for a wonderful tale. With some changes and an imaginative exploration of motive and attitudes, it became a story which ranks with his best and which subsequently was made into a popular play and a film. For some of the characteristics of Mr Joyce, the defence lawyer, and his wife whose 'million-dollar cocktail' was famous in the Federated Malay States, the author used his host and hostess in Singapore. Though much borrowing from real life gave him a certain notoriety in the Far East, he sent a copy of 'The Letter' to Mrs Dickinson – remembering, apparently, her hospitality more than that of her husband – acknowledging its debt to her.[23]

After Maugham and Haxton had recovered their strength and had been reoutfitted in Singapore, they set off again through the Federated Malay States, staying with various local people and colonial administrators to whom they had letters of introduction. They worked their way down to Australia, where, in Sydney and up the east coast, Maugham was much interviewed, photographed, and lionized. From there they sailed on a fifty-five-foot ketch with its white master and four Torres Straits blacks to Thursday Island, but after two days of fierce storms were forced to take shelter on one of the small islands in the Arafura Sea. For nearly a week they slept on the boat, living on canned meat and fish and swearing that they would never again trust anything but steamships.

Maugham and his companion continued to explore the Malay Archipelago, stopping at the Hotel Sanatorium Tosari on Java in August to rest and enjoy the coolness of the heights. They had intended to return to Singapore in several weeks, but when Haxton suffered a severe attack of typhoid and Maugham was beset by colitis they were obliged to remain in Java until mid-November, and Maugham did not get back to England until some time in January 1922.

Before leaving the Far East, Maugham was deeply disturbed to learn that Trippe and Company, a firm with which he had entrusted all his savings for the previous four years, had collapsed. Even though as a class A creditor he got back almost two-thirds of his investment, he was dismayed by the thought that his dream of financial independence now seemed even further away. With the triumphant *The Circle* grossing $20,000 a week, he would nevertheless earn a good deal, and at Alanson's suggestion Maugham let his friend become his broker.

Back in England after a year of wandering in the jungles of Malaya, Maugham was amused to discover that old friends believed his joke that he had been away at Brighton for the weekend. To Alanson he wrote that he was enjoying the comforts of home and even the lionizing. *The Trembling of a Leaf*, the first of his collections of Far East stories, had appeared in September and was quickly sold out. Not having written a short story for a decade, and having published only fifteen of them in the earlier formative stage of his career, these were in effect a fresh attempt in the genre. As such, they are an impressive achievement: 'Rain', 'Mackintosh', 'The Fall of Edward Barnard', 'Red', 'The Pool', and 'Honolulu'. Maugham had happily discovered that the fragments of experience he encountered on his travels could be easily transformed into well-crafted short stories, and with this volume he began an enormously fruitful period. From 1922 until the beginning of the Second World War, he would publish seventy-five more tales, in such periodicals as *Cosmopolitan*, *Nash's Magazine*, *International Magazine*, *Good Housekeeping*, and *Harper's Bazaar*. In an age not dominated by radio or television, the general magazine flourished, providing a large market for the writer of short fiction, and a new Maugham story was a heralded event. By the late twenties, he was able to command a dollar a word.

Maugham spent nearly eight months of 1922 in London, the longest period he had lived at home as a married man. A glimpse of the kind of life he then led can be found in *On a Chinese Screen*, published in September of that year. In it he reminisces about a typical day in London, smoking his pipe by the fire and reading *The Times*. Liza, for whom he bought a white squirrel coat from China and a pair of moccasins from the Malay States, comes in and he plays trains with her before she is sent outdoors. After some hours of work, he may go to the Garrick for a few rubbers of bridge, and when he gets home for dinner before going to a first night he reads a bedtime story to his daughter. Like any affectionate father he thinks that she looks sweet in her pyjamas with her hair done up in two plaits.

Maugham's relations with Syrie were undoubtedly much less serene, though outwardly of course they maintained the appearance of marital felicity. In February, for example, the Maughams threw a dinner party for Knoblock, Osbert Sitwell, Eddie Marsh, Charles McEvoy, Sinclair Lewis, and Christopher Nevinson. This kind of small, informal dinner party was relatively new, replacing the larger Edwardian formal dinner, and Osbert Sitwell remembered evenings at the Maughams' with fondness. 'They were always', he said, 'particularly kind to the young and the gifted. There in Wyndham Place in the large beige-painted, barrel-vaulted drawing room of this eighteenth-century mansion, their friends were privileged to meet all the most interesting figures connected with the world of art, literature, and the theatre in both England and America.'[24] Similarly, Fay Compton, who performed so sensitively in *Caesar's Wife*, remembered that 'he and Syrie took a personal interest in one. They came to choose all the clothes with me. I didn't have a voice in it at all. Syrie took over and that was that. Maugham had perfect faith in her taste in dress, and he was quite right.'[25]

That Maugham dedicated *On a Chinese Screen*, published in October 1922, to Syrie suggests a warm regard. It seems less so, however, when it is remembered that this public gesture came only after he had dedicated *The Trembling of a Leaf* to Bertram Alanson and *The Unknown* to Viola Tree. Neither the more important *The Moon and Sixpence* nor *The Circle* carried any name, and given the contents of either it would have been ironic to attach Syrie's to them. On the other hand, an entry in Maugham's notebook for 1922 almost certainly refers to her, enumerating her virtues and defects, the latter of which were echoed years later in 'Looking Back'. Referring to the woman only as 'X' (*A Writer's Notebook* was published while Syrie was still alive), he confesses that she is a mixture of paradoxical qualities:

Take X for instance. She is not only a liar, she is a mythomaniac who will invent malicious stories that have no foundation in fact and will tell them so convincingly, with such circumstantial detail, that you are almost persuaded she believes them herself. She is grasping and will hesitate at no dishonesty to get what she wants. She is a snob and will impudently force her acquaintance on persons who she knows wish to avoid it. She is a climber, but with the paltriness of her mind is satisfied with the second rate; the secretaries of great men are her prey, not the great men themselves. She is vindictive, jealous and envious. She is a quarrelsome bully. She is vain, vulgar and ostentatious. There is real badness in her.

She is clever. She has charm. She has exquisite taste. She is generous and will spend her own money, to the last penny, as freely as she will spend other people's. She is hospitable and takes pleasure in the pleasure she gives her guests. Her emotion is easily aroused by a tale of love and she will go out of her way to relieve the distress of persons who mean nothing to her. In sickness she will show herself an admirable and devoted nurse. She is a gay and pleasant talker. Her greatest gift is her capacity for sympathy. She will listen to your troubles with genuine consideration and with unfeigned friendliness will do anything she can to relieve them or to help you bear them. She will interest herself in all that concerns you, rejoice with you in your success and take part in the mortifications of your failure. There is real goodness in her.

She is hateful and lovable, covetous and open-handed, cruel and kind, malicious and generous of spirit, egotistic and unselfish. How on earth is a novelist so to combine these incompatible traits as to make the plausible harmony that renders a character credible?[26]

Another work written in 1922 is obviously an expression of Maugham's personal dilemma. One of 200 authors asked to contribute a handwritten miniature book for Queen Mary's Dolls House Library, he wrote – surprisingly for a man reported to be a cynic – a fairy tale called 'The Princess and the Nightingale'. Published as well in periodical form in 1922 and later in *The Gentleman in the Parlour*, it is Maugham's conception of the ideal relationship between love and art.

The story recounts how Princess September is befriended by a nightingale which comes to sing for her each day. When her jealous sisters suggest that the bird might leave her some day she is persuaded to put him in a golden cage. Now, however, the nightingale cannot sing: denied the freedom to fly outdoors and gather inspiration from the outside world, his artistic sense is inhibited. When the princess protests that she loves him and will take him out every day, he replies that it is not the same thing, that the rice fields and lake and the willow trees look quite different when you see them through the bars of the cage. When the nightingale claims that 'I cannot sing unless I'm free, and if I cannot sing I die,' the princess reluctantly gives him his liberty. The story ends with the nightingale free to come and go, returning to sing for the princess when he is so inclined. With no restraints, his artistic temperament thrives.

Maugham exercised his own freedom again in September 1922 when he left for another Far East trip, following the opening of a play based on his Chinese journey of 1920: *East of Suez*. The theme is the difficulty of inter-racial marriage, but the plot is an old-fashioned morality tale about a *déclassée* woman who is married to a decent man and in love with another. Though the play reveals a few of the sort of insights into oriental culture and customs found in *On a Chinese Screen*, its treatment of the theme is surprisingly melodramatic, and critics were justifiably severe in their reactions.

While the text of the play did not impress reviewers or audiences, its staging did. To create the illusion of the bustling mass of humanity Maugham had observed in Peking, he uncharacteristically resorted to spectacle and mime. The opening scene had about forty Chinese actors and actresses as well as a number of Caucasians, playing coolies, water carriers, rickshaw boys, and even a Mongolian caravan. A Chinese orchestra played atmospheric music, the authenticity of which was dubious at best, coming as it did from a visit the composer, Eugene Goossens, made to a pub in Chinatown.

East of Suez was produced and directed by Basil Dean, who soon became aware of the playwright's concern for authenticity. During a rehearsal, a stage manager asked Dean what sort of sandwiches should be offered the Eurasian heroine, to which the director casually replied: 'Oh, I don't know. Cucumber, I should think.' Sitting beside him, Maugham suddenly spluttered: 'It's the l-l-last th-th-thing they'd have.' Throughout rehearsals, said Dean, Maugham remained 'withdrawn, neither helpful nor instructive, never offering advice unless it was asked for. I think he found the whole business tiresome and the actors' arguments rather petty. Yet, when appealed to, he was always ready with the unconvincing response: "Oh, ex-excellent." Once I asked him whether I might cut certain lines: "wh-wh-why not?" he spluttered. "The st-st-stage is a w-w-workshop." The significance of his attitude was that Maugham lacked genuine enthusiasm for the theatre.'[27]

Though Maugham's feeling for the theatre had perhaps begun to wane in the twenties, his excitement about the stage had been real. His imagination was fired by the plays he had seen in Germany in 1892, and *The Summing Up* and *Theatre* are persuasive testimonies to his enthusiasm. He was in fact always deeply concerned about the productions of his works, both from the point of view of a professional and that of an artist, and he kept a close proprietary eye on their progress. Irene Vanbrugh, for example, remembered Maugham's constant presence at rehearsals, where, immaculate and direct, he would often surprise her with an unexpected word of appreciation. He was especially particular about dialogue and once in *The Land of Promise*, when Vanbrugh was required to converse while ironing, he complained that, though she was an excellent laundress, the language was being sacrificed to gesture and the theme was being forgotten.[28] Similarly, Fay Compton found the dialogue of *Caesar's Wife* difficult to learn and to speak, and Maugham, though charming, would stop her by saying: 'We must have the correct words. I can't pass anything.'[29]

Maugham always had firm ideas about the productions of his plays – from casting to direction – and he was forthright about them in writing to agents and managers. Temperamentally, however, he was never a dramatist who became intensely and actively involved in the day-to-day mounting of a play. Even if his stutter had not made it nearly impossible for him to engage in vigorous give-and-take discussions, he would never have been comfortable arguing with actors, directors and other theatre professionals. He preferred to leave the immediate orchestration of rehearsals to the participants, offering his suggestions and demands at the end of the day. When satisfied, he said little, though he was generous in praise of successful performers. Thus, when John Gielgud directed *Sheppey* in 1933 he received suggestions from the playwright in matters of detail but not in interpretation, and so was unaware of what he thought about the production until a luncheon party at Claridge's after the play's opening. There, at the end of the meal, Maugham took Gielgud aside to the cloakroom and quietly gave him a signed copy of *Sheppey* dedicated to the actor-director.

In part, Dean's impression of Maugham's disinterest in the theatre comes from the playwright's willingness to let skilled theatre professionals adapt his works as they saw fit. Gladys Cooper, for whom he had great respect, remembered that she and the director, Gerald du Maurier, decided that a blackout in *The Letter* lacked dramatic value. Maugham's reaction was that they should change it. 'Somerset Maugham', she said, 'is almost too accommodating; he even comes down to a rehearsal with a sharpened blue pencil to cut out anything that is felt to be wrong ... "I have had so many of my lines blue-pencilled that I think I shall collect them together and make a whole play out of them some day," he said to me.'[30]

Long before the opening of *East of Suez* on 2 September 1922, Maugham was restless, impatient to be wandering again. He explained to Alanson that London was congenial but ultimately boring. Not very real, it seemed like an artificial comedy, amusing for a while, but tedious over time. It was time, he said, for the curtain to fall.[31]

Carrying a letter of introduction from Winston Churchill, Maugham left for Burma on 5 September. With Haxton, he sailed on the French ship *Porthos* to Colombo, Ceylon, by way of the Suez Canal, and from there boarded a ship which took them first to Rangoon and then up the Irrawaddy River. After touring the palace at Mandalay and a Buddhist convent at Mengon, the travellers took a train south to Thazi and then a car to Taunggyi in the Shan states.

Between there and the railroad in Siam, which was their route to Bangkok, lay 500 miles of jungle, inhabited by less friendly headhunters than they had encountered in Sarawak, as well as tigers and snakes. Maugham and Haxton made the trek across Burma with a caravan of mules and ponies, frequently covering no more than ten or fifteen miles a day. Living primarily on a diet of eggs, bananas, and rice, they slept in huts provided by the local villagers. The days were monotonous, but Maugham enjoyed the isolation and, if his account in *The Gentleman in the Parlour* is accurate, his mind was free to meditate. After they crossed the great Salween River, their road became a trail through dense jungle, and finally they arrived at Keng Tung, very near the Chinese border. After a week, Maugham and Haxton moved leisurely south in Siam, where they eventually were able to hire a Ford car, the first that had ever travelled along their route, and then reached Bangkok by train. There in the intense heat Maugham succumbed to a severe attack of malaria, undoubtedly contracted on the trip from Keng Tung. With a temperature of 105°F, he endured several feverish days, during which the manager of the Imperial Hotel wanted to evict him because she thought he was dying. When he could breathe easily once more, he was allowed to recuperate while lying on the hotel terrace watching the bustling traffic on the river.

When Maugham had recovered, they took a run-down, cockroach-ridden boat to Kep, along the Cambodian coast and then to Phnom Penh by car. To reach the awesome ruins of Angkor Wat, which he thereafter would always consider the most astonishing spectacle he had ever seen, Maugham and his companion made another exhausting inland journey. After working up a tributary of the Mekong River in a steamer, they crossed the wide and shallow Tonle Sab lake by flat bottomed boat, and then were rowed through mangrove swamps in sampans.

Returning by much the same water routes, Maugham and Haxton went back south to Saigon, now changed by history from the 'blithe and smiling little place'[32] which then charmed them. Taking a ship, they moved up the coast to Hue to see the Chinese New Year celebrations at the court of the Emperor. After attending a party at the Emperor's palace, and in the presence of the Resident Superior, they drove to Hanoi, then to the port city of Haiphong to take a boat to Hong Kong.

During the months in Burma, Siam, and Indo-China, Maugham dictated 70,000 words of description and character study to his secretary, and four years later he fashioned this material into *The Gentleman in the Parlour: A Record of a Journey from Rangoon to Haiphong*. Unlike *On a Chinese Screen*, which was a series of unconnected, though skilfully crafted sketches, *The Gentleman in the Parlour* is a chronological account of the author's travels together with other material woven into the narrative. Included, for example, is 'The Princess and the Nightingale', and another episode is a reworking of his short story 'A Marriage of Convenience', first published in 1906. Though the revised version is essentially the same as its forerunner, it is significant that Maugham had added a disquisition on the idea of a successful marriage of convenience, a statement which in 1927 may well have been directed at Syrie:

The fact is that in a marriage of convenience you expect less and so you are less likely to be disappointed. As you do not make senseless claims on one another there is not reason for exasperation. You do not look for perfection, and so you are tolerant to one another's faults. Passion is all very well, but it is not a proper foundation for marriage. *Voyez-vous*, for two people to be happy in marriage they must be able to respect one another, they must be of the same condition and their interest must be alike; then, if they are decent people and are willing to give and take, to live and let live, there is no reason why their union should not be as happy as ours.[33]

Providing little practical travel information, *The Gentleman in the Parlour* is an impressionistic portrait by a sensitive and sensible traveller who enjoys a quiet hour on a lazy river as much as a tour through a temple. It is suffused with a warmth and gentle humour that is reflected in the lucid and relaxed prose, and Maugham subtly interweaves his own meditations with his descriptions of people and places so that his metaphysical conclusions seem to have been evoked naturally from the milieu of the travels.

The Gentleman in the Parlour, like *On a Chinese Screen* written five years earlier, reveals a growing and surprising nostalgia in its author, a development which began as Maugham approached his fiftieth year. Amid the bamboos of China, for example, he was suddenly struck by the resemblance to the Kentish hop fields of his youth: 'Do you remember the sweet smelling hop-fields and the fat green meadows, the railway line that runs along the sea and the long shining beach and the desolate greyness of the English Channel? The seagull flies over the wintry coldness and the melancholy of its cry is almost unbearable.'[34] Later, a broad Chinese plain brought back a flood of memories of Heidelberg, where he first discovered beauty and knowledge. Approaching Angkor Wat on a shallow river, he was reminded of a country stream near Whitstable where he used to catch minnows on a Sunday afternoon. And a yellow primrose in northern Burma sparked a memory of England and a woman much like Sue Jones. 'It is', he wrote, 'a small yellow flower, ever so faintly scented with the rain and grey balmy mornings in February where you have a funny little flutter in your heart, and the smell of the rich wet Kentish earth, and kind dead faces, and the statue of Lord Beaconsfield in his bronze robes in Parliament Square, and the yellow hair of a girl with a sweet smile, hair now grey and shingled.'[35]

It is hardly unusual that in his fifties Maugham should begin to think about the past, even if there is an irony in his nostalgia for a wretched childhood. What makes his reminiscences notable is their revelation of a deep-seated regret and disillusionment, best illustrated in this passage from *On a Chinese Screen*:

The woodland odours are the same as those which steal up from the fat Kentish soil when you pass through the woods of Bleane; and nostalgia seizes you. Your thoughts travel through time and more, far from the Here and Now, and you remember your vanished youth with its high hopes, its passionate love, and its ambition. Then if you are a cynic, as they say, and therefore a sentimentalist, tears come to your unwilling

175

eyes. And when you have regained your self-control the night has fallen.[36]

Like his fictional counterpart Philip Carey, Maugham had gone through childhood and adolescence living, as he said in 'The Traitor', not for the present but for imagined future happiness. He came to believe that he had missed many of the pleasures of youth through the intense efforts needed to complete his medical training and to become a professional author. Now in middle age, having materially achieved much of what he had pursued and having found its reality much less satisfying than the illusion, he came to regret and sentimentalize a past which he saw as wasted. He went on, as he admitted late in life, living in the future, but increasingly he looked back to the distant past. In the present, meanwhile, he continued to find it difficult to embrace life joyfully.

One of Maugham's real pleasures, however, was travel, and the source of the title of *The Gentleman in the Parlour* provides the most explicit statement of its attraction. In *On a Chinese Screen*, he had written that he travelled for 'the sensation it gives you of freedom from all responsibility' and so that he could meet 'people I shall never see again'.[37] By the time that he came to his next travel book, he had read William Hazlitt's essay 'On Going a Journey' and found a passage which perfectly described how he wished to pass through the world:

> Oh! it is great to shake off the trammels of the world and of public opinion – to lose our importunate, tormenting, everlasting personal identity in the elements of nature, and become the creature of the moment, clear of all ties – to hold to the universe only by a dish of sweet-breads, and to owe nothing but the score of the evening – no longer seeking for applause and meeting with contempt, to be known by no other title than *The Gentleman in the Parlour*.[38]

For someone as intensely self-conscious as Maugham, the idea of losing an 'importunate, tormenting, everlasting personal identity' was infinitely seductive. From his childhood on, he was imprisoned by an awareness that he was different from others and by a feeling of inferiority. He recognized that those who could lose themselves in common activity or approach life with a natural insouciance were happier than he, but he was temperamentally unable to escape his inhibitions.

One of Maugham's ways of dealing with his self-conscious lack of spontaneity was to adopt a pose of flippancy. Writing about him in 1926, the young Beverley Nichols recounted a discussion about love, where Maugham suddenly exclaimed: 'I don't see why one shouldn't love people flippantly.'[39] In 'The Fall of Edward Barnard', flippancy had been one of the first signs that the young American businessman was throwing off his commitment to the American Dream, and it was the tone of many of Maugham's popular dramatic comedies. It also became one of the more notorious characteristics of Maugham's public pronouncements since it was easily misinterpreted as disdain or disinterest. In fact, it was meant to shield an overly sensitive temperament from a painfully direct involvement with life. Calculated flippancy was none the less a poor substitute for natural and easy insouciance.

Another of Maugham's ways of coping with his 'tormenting personal identity' was to create an ideal one, and increasingly the narrative voice of his writing was, as Anthony Curtis has argued, an idealized self-portrait. If he could not be the wise, sensitive, objective, and warm man in person, he could be that in the seclusion of his study. Thus, the warmth of the narration in *The Gentleman in the Parlour* carried the persona of *The Moon and Sixpence* a step further, and the process would continue through the character of the middle-aged spy in *Ashenden*, the mocking self-portrayal of 'Willie Ashenden' in *Cakes and Ale*, the thoughtful and apparently serene memoirist in *The Summing Up*, to the compassionate observer, 'Mr Maugham', in *The Razor's Edge*.

But the matter is more complex. While Maugham was continuing this ideal literary mask of the gentleman in the study, he was also less consciously creating another public persona: the 'W. Somerset Maugham' who became nearly as much a character as any of his inventions. Just as Shaw and Coward, for example, became self-created public figures who were expected to behave in certain ways, Maugham became a personage. Interviewed at every dockside arrival or departure, at every opening night, on the annual autumn visits to London in his late years, and on each birthday that made him increasingly a Grand Old Man of English Literature, he was expected to be the urbane, cosmopolitan, and witty author. Moreover, he was reputed to be a sharp-tongued and world-weary cynic, and in part his responses were calculated to satisfy the expectations of his public.

At the end of the journey described in *The Gentleman in the Parlour*, Maugham and Haxton sailed from Hong Kong to Shanghai and from there to Yokohama on the *Porthos*. In Japan they caught the *Empress of Canada* and arrived in Vancouver on 23 April. A fellow traveller, American journalist Jack Hines, was fascinated by Maugham's skill at poker, a pastime he enjoyed immensely for ten successful evenings. Still pale and thin from his bout of malaria, the author sat nightly at the green and beige card table with a 'deeply melancholic soul', shrewdly studying his opposition. 'His briar going valiantly', wrote Hines, 'takes the curse off the rigid jacket and boiled linen; his cards racked in a spatulated set of fingers; his glance piercing the brains of each of the six opponents watching intently the individual play of each set of features.'[40]

From Vancouver, Maugham and Haxton took a train to San Francisco and after visiting Alanson moved on to Hollywood, where Maugham spent a busy few days attempting to sell several screenplays. He was pleased to learn that a studio was willing to pay $150,000 for the rights to 'Rain', even if his share would be only a quarter of that amount. After a brief stopover in Chicago Maugham continued to New York, where he completed arrangements for a play he had written while on his travels, *The Camel's Back*. A superficial farce about a priggish English barrister and his wife's battle against tyranny, it was badly received and played only fifteen nights in the United States and seventy-six in England. It has never been published.

While in New York, Maugham was interviewed by journalist Beatrice Wilson who saw in him 'a face of disillusionment', though he looked a decade younger than his forty-nine years.[41] At her apartment, Maugham met H. L. Mencken, who found most celebrated writers boring but was fascinated by the Englishman. Though both had engagements for the evening – Maugham's agent was giving a party for him – they became so deeply involved in conversation that they did not part until after midnight. 'Maugham', wrote Carl Bode, 'was so intent that his stutter grew pronounced and Mencken often tried to help him out. Yet the ideas went back and forth swiftly; the conversation was brilliant. The men ate the crackers she served and finished her small store of liquor before they left. Listening to them made it one of the best evenings of her life.'[42]

Maugham and Haxton sailed for England (Haxton as usual disembarking at Cherbourg) on 22 May on the *Aquitania*. Like Jack Hines, Dwight Taylor, the son of Maugham's friend the actress Laurette Taylor, was able to observe the famous author and his companion, but his record of the voyage presents a somewhat more ominous picture of Haxton. With his blond hair standing up like a brush, and careless, almost slovenly dress, he conveyed a 'devil-may-care' attitude. After an evening of cards, where the young Taylor had lost a considerable sum, Maugham's secretary insisted on joining the next night's play. When Haxton came to deal, Taylor discovered that he had been given three aces, to which he drew the fourth. At Haxton's instigation the pot increased, and Taylor won more than enough to cover the previous night's losses. Maugham, the young man later realized, had sent his companion to give him an advantage, and as Haxton had flung the cards so casually around the table his experienced gambler's hand had been dealing from the bottom of the deck.[43]

Back in London in the summer of 1923 the Maughams moved house again. Syrie, he said later, felt that 2 Wyndham Place was no longer satisfactory and persuaded him to sell it and buy a much larger house nearby at 43 Bryanston Square. The success of 'Rain' in so many places made the purchase feasible, and Maugham soon relished the feeling of spaciousness in the new house. When Arnold Bennett first visited it two years later, he called it 'simply magnif.' Maugham's study, he judged, was larger than his own drawing-room. On this occasion Bennett had 'a great evening there',[44] though another visitor, Basil Dean, noted that Syrie had done the interior in her famous all-white decor and Maugham, uncomfortable and irritable, did not seem to fit into the design.[45]

In July and August Maugham was busy on a number of projects. *Our Betters*, finally to be produced in England, was in rehearsal, and he was correcting proofs for the publication of several earlier plays. As well, there were stories to be written for *Cosmopolitan*. Then, too, he discovered that he was needed for rehearsals of *The Camel's Back* in America, but this was an unexpected pleasure since it meant being with Haxton again.

In the middle of September, Maugham sailed on the *Aquitania* to New York, where he and his secretary rented a comfortable apartment on 59th Street in the same building as Edward Knoblock, whose company he always enjoyed. One night he went to the theatre with Charlie Chaplin and was impressed by, and somewhat envious of, the public acclaim for the actor. Maugham also delivered three stories to Ray Long at *Cosmopolitan*, and was delighted to be offered a contract for eight more at $2500 each. Rehearsals of *The Camel's Back*, however, proved to be a much less happy experience, and though he rewrote it extensively it moved inevitably to failure.

After his first visit to Washington since 1910, Maugham sailed to England on the *Majestic* on 24 November. One of his fellow passengers was the English playwright Frederick Lonsdale, who liked Maugham and his wit very much, even if it was occasionally gently directed toward himself. On one such Atlantic crossing, for example, Lonsdale fended off an obnoxious theatre manager by suggesting that he would do much better to talk to Maugham, the diminutive figure across the room in an armchair, surrounded by books and paper. After about ten minutes, Lonsdale became aware of Maugham standing beside him. 'As this voyage is going to last six days,' he said, 'don't you think it would be fairer if we were to share our responsibilities?'[46]

Back in London Maugham began work on his first novel in nearly six years, *The Painted Veil*, and he confessed to beginning with apprehension. By late January however, after a party-filled five days with Haxton in Paris at the New Year, he found the novel progressing well. Following the unhappy experience with *The Camel's Back* in New York, and in the middle of rehearsals of the same play in London, he enjoyed the sequestered writing of fiction. Though he might look at the empty white pages with misgivings, once they were filled he was free from having to see them brought to life by other people with varying skills and sensibilities.

Though Maugham had gone to Paris again for four days at the beginning of February, the first draft of *The Painted Veil* was completed on 2 April 1924. He then celebrated with a jaunt through Spain with Haxton, a trip that was in part intended to improve their Spanish for a South American expedition the following year, which would be, he told Alanson, an exciting excursion into new territory.[47]

Maugham began this exploration by sailing to New York on the *Majestic* with Haxton on 17 September. Also on board were Eugene Goossens, on his way to become conductor of the Eastman Orchestra, Basil Dean, and Noël Coward. This was the voyage, Goossens recalled, where he over-ate and over-laughed so much at the dinner table that he arrived in the United States with indigestion.[48] Dean, though he burdened Maugham with two bad plays to read on the way over, found him congenial but 'steered clear of Haxton as much as possible'.[49]

On arriving at New York, Maugham was disappointed to hear that the health of Alanson's new bride prevented them from accompanying him to Central America. New York was as interesting as ever, but each passing year had made Maugham more and more lionized, and after an exhausting week or so of lunches, dinners, parties, business meetings, and press interviews – as well as ten plays in ten days – he was glad to head to New Orleans.

Maugham came away from New York with a copy of *The Tattooed Countess*, a gift which delighted him, from its author, Carl Van Vechten, whom he had just met and with whom he was to share a friendship for many years. Van Vechten, a noted New York figure for several decades, was a prolific novelist, essayist, critic, and photographer, and his fascination with black culture made him one of the earliest intellectual champions of its music, literature and art. He had an intimate knowledge of Harlem, whose jazz clubs were particularly intriguing to whites, who on their forays into the black section were able vicariously to experience an exuberance and raw animal vitality absent in their own culture and denied them by their own inhibitions.

For the same reason, Maugham was attracted to the relaxed vitality of the Italians and Spaniards and the more primitive feelings of the South Seas natives. Only a year earlier his New York visit had led a journalist to observe that 'one gets the impression that Maugham is wearied of the careful, cultivated, bloodless artificialities of super-civilization. There is a caveman pawing about inside of him somewhere and Maugham himself is too cultivated to let it out.'[50] Thus he welcomed Van Vechten's introduction to Harlem life. In addition to some of the famous nightclubs, Van Vechten took Maugham, Haxton, and John Colton on a field-trip to a Harlem brothel.[51]

In Mexico in early November Maugham met another writer who believed in letting the 'caveman' out and who was temperamentally much more capable of doing so: D. H. Lawrence. The two men had little in common – though the lives of both had been dominated by their mothers and Lawrence's latent homosexuality might perhaps have made him sympathetic to Maugham – and their encounter was unrewarding for them both. Lawrence was first annoyed when he and Frieda arrived in Mexico City to discover that Maugham had moved south to Cuernavaca that day to work. 'But apparently', he wrote to Mabel Dodge Luhan, 'he too is no loss: a bit sour and full of nerves and fidgets lest he shouldn't produce a Maughnum opus with a Mexican background before Christmas. As if he could fail!!'[52]

Before Maugham left Mexico, he did meet the Lawrences at lunch in the home of Zelia Nuttall, an English widow who was an archaeologist and social figure in Mexico City. When Maugham learned that the Lawrences were also invited to Mrs Nuttall's suburban house in Coyoacan, he had Haxton telephone to suggest sharing a taxi. Unaware that Maugham stuttered much more than usual on the telephone and thus avoided using it, Lawrence was offended and refused to travel together. At lunch Mrs Nuttall took an aversion to Haxton, and to Frieda's question about his reaction to Mexico, Maugham replied: 'Do you want me to admire men in big hats?' The lunch was then, in her words, 'drowned in acidity all round'.

Maugham was hardly unique in drawing the wrath of D. H. Lawrence, but Frieda, more balanced than her husband, shrewdly saw Maugham as an object of pity. 'An unhappy and acid man,' she observed, 'who got no fun out of living. He seemed to me to have fallen between two stools as so many writers do. He wanted to have his cake and eat it. He could not accept the narrow social world and yet he didn't believe in a wider human one. Commentators and critics of life and nothing more.'[53]

Maugham and Lawrence were unlikely to have enjoyed each other's company under the best conditions, and by the time that they met, Maugham was depressed by the realization that Mexico was not providing the kind of material for his writing that he had anticipated. The only elements of the country which interested him were those connected with Spanish culture and for that, he reasoned, he would be better off in Spain itself. Lawrence might have been confident that Maugham could turn out another book on schedule, but Maugham found little inspiration and produced nothing from the trip.

Maugham's failure to find useful material in Mexico or even in the rest of Central America is interesting. It may be that he needed the special ambience of a British colonial setting with the subtle tensions and conflicts which arose from the imposition of British culture on a native environment. Though he knew something of the Spanish mentality, he understood it much less clearly than he did that of the British, and the imperial hold on Mexico was a much different thing in 1925. It may also be that the ambience of Mexico was too vivid – brightly coloured, passionate, violent – for Maugham's ironic, subtle approach. In any case, it was left to Lawrence in *The Plumed Serpent*, Malcolm Lowry in *Under the Volcano*, and Graham Greene in *The Power and the Glory* to capture some of that country's extravagantly brutal life.

Maugham and Haxton left Mexico City in early November and travelled to the Yucatan Peninsula, from where they sailed to Havana. For the next few weeks, in Cuba and surrounding islands, Maugham worked on a dramatization of 'The Letter'. Six months earlier, he had been intrigued by a suggestion from his American agent, Charles Hanson Towne, that Towne and writer Oliver Herford adapt the story, but they did not follow through. When Gladys Cooper and Margaret Bannerman both thought that it would make a wonderful play, Maugham remembered 'Rain' and decided to do it himself. By mid-December he was able to send a typescript to his American dramatic agent, John W. Rumsey.

From Cuba Maugham and Haxton went to Jamaica, and then to

Belize, in the British Honduras, where they spent a month and made an expedition by boat and mule into the jungle. By late January they were in Guatemala, and after two weeks they worked their way back to New York, arriving in early March.

In New York Maugham met with Basil Dean, who had secured the English rights to the dramatic version of *Rain* and wished to consult the author about the lead. Since the triumphant Jeanne Eagels had decided not to repeat the role, Maugham very much wanted Gladys Cooper, though when she became unavailable he thought Fay Compton would be satisfactory. Dean, however, preferred the young American actress with the whisky voice, Tallulah Bankhead, who was one of many desperately seeking the part. A few days after Maugham's discussion with Dean, Bankhead arrived back from England and made the mistake of following the playwright to Washington, where he had gone for a short visit, to plead her case. Though she did not realize it, few things made him more angry and unyielding than the feeling of being harassed or exploited.

Maugham and Dean sailed for England on the *Aquitania* on 14 March to put the English production into rehearsal with Bankhead reading the part of Sadie. After two days, however, Maugham concluded that she was unsuitable for the role, and Dean was forced to replace her with Olga Lindo. Humiliated and disappointed, Bankhead left Dean's office and went home to make, in Brendan Gill's words, 'the smallest possible attempt at suicide'. Putting on her Sadie Thompson costume, she took a modest number of aspirins, and left a suicide note reading: 'It ain't goin' to rain no mo.'[54] Referring to Maugham's recently published story 'The Man Who Wouldn't Hurt a Fly', she wired to her manager: 'The Man Who Wouldn't Hurt a Fly is crucifying me.'[55]

Within days of her rejection, Bankhead was asked by Noël Coward to replace someone in a good part in his new play *Fallen Angels*, for which she earned critical acclaim. Even then she could not resist an opportunity to exercise her wit, and on opening night when she came to Coward's line 'Oh dear, rain,' she changed it to 'My God, RAIN!' Delivered with an icy shudder, the reference was not lost on an audience aware of her recent difficulty, and it brought the house down.[56] Some time after the opening, Maugham took her to lunch and praised her performance in glowing terms, but Bankhead never forgave him. When she finally played Sadie to excellent reviews in an American revival of *Rain* in 1935, she made sure that the best notices were sent to the playwright.

Maugham's troubles with Tallulah Bankhead were nothing compared to the difficulties he encountered over the mounting of *The Letter*. Anthony Prinsep, the manager of the Globe Theatre, had secured the rights to Maugham's dramatization and was determined to have Margaret Bannerman, of whom he was then enamoured, to play the lead. Maugham, however, thought she had been dreadful in *The Grand Duchess* and refused to have her play Leslie Crosbie, so much preferring Gladys Cooper that he was prepared to give her an option on his next five plays. When Prinsep remained obdurate, a stalemate developed, and production of the play was delayed for three years. Eventually Cooper put £400 in her own company, played for 338 performances at London's Playhouse, and got back her investment a hundredfold.

Even the much simpler and less politically complicated world of fiction had its problems for Maugham. The English edition of *The Painted Veil* was published on 23 April and within weeks Heinemann and Maugham received a letter of complaint from the Assistant Secretary of the Hong Kong Government objecting to the story being set in that colony. This was not the first of such problems with the novel, since when *Nash's Magazine* began serializing it in November 1924, a couple with the same name as the protagonists – 'Lane' – threatened to sue for libel. That matter was resolved when the magazine settled for £240 and the names were changed to 'Fane' for the remainder of the issues. In book form, 'Walter and Kitty Lane' became 'Walter and Kitty Fane'.

The colonial official's suit, however, was far more serious, and in the face of potentially heavy damages Heinemann recalled its edition. 'Hong Kong' was changed to 'Tching-Yen' (though the editors missed at least two references), allusions to 'Canton' and 'Happy Valley' were removed, and an author's note claimed that no existing colony was described in the novel. No alterations were made in the American edition, and years later Tching-Yen was changed back to Hong Kong, but a lawsuit had been avoided. As well, Maugham had received invaluable publicity, and on both sides of the Atlantic the novel quickly became a best-seller.

The background of *The Painted Veil* had come from Maugham's travels through China, but the fundamental idea had been with him for forty years, from the time that he first read Dante's *Purgatorio* in Italy in 1894. Starting from the Italian's story of a gentle woman whose husband suspected her of adultery and took her to a place where he believed the noxious vapours would kill her, he created a tale of adultery and redemption in an English woman in the Far East. Walter

Fane, a biologist in Hong Kong, discovers that his wife has been unfaithful, and takes her inland with him to fight a cholera epidemic. Ironically, it is he who contracts the disease and dies, and Kitty eventually returns to England. In the course of her experience in the plague-ridden city, she meets one of Maugham's mildly eccentric *raisonneurs*, the deputy commissioner Waddington, and a group of nuns who have sacrificed almost everything to work in an alien country. As a result, she goes back to Britain with a new freedom and set of values.

In 1959 Maugham wrote R. F. V. Heuston to say that he used his brother Frederic as a model for Walter Fane. That may be partially true, but there are a number of more striking similarities between the character and the author himself. Walter's shyness, for example, 'was a disease', and he never makes a speech if he can avoid it (three years after the appearance of *The Painted Veil*, for example, Maugham wrote to Paul Dottin firmly declining to give a speech as that was one thing he felt he could not possibly do).[57] Like Maugham, Walter never thinks himself very lovable and his wife comes to know his 'extreme sensitiveness, for which his acid irony was a protection, and how quickly he could lose his heart if his feeling were hurt'.[58] A 'moody, cold and shy man', Walter has 'a natural affection for very little babies',[59] and his characterization of himself as 'a very good [bridge] player of the second class'[60] is identical to Maugham's assessment of his own game.

While Walter Fane embodies a number of Maugham's traits, it has never been recognized that his wife in many ways bears a striking resemblance to Syrie. The physical portrait of the young Kitty, for example, is unmistakably that of Syrie in her youth:

> Kitty was a beauty. She gave promise of being so when she was still a child, for she had large, dark eyes, liquid and vivacious, brown, curling hair in which there was a reddish tint, exquisite teeth and a lovely skin. Her features would never be very good, for her chin was too square and her nose, though not as long as Doris's, too big. Her beauty depended a good deal on her youth, and Mrs Garstin realized that she must marry in the first flush of her maidenhood. When she came out she was dazzling: her skin was still her greatest beauty, but her eyes with their long lashes were so starry and yet so melting that it gave you a catch at the heart to look into them. She had a charming gaiety and the desire to please.[61]

Here are Syrie's dark eyes, beautiful brown hair, and above all the gorgeous skin which was her best-known feature – 'if you had laid the petal of a magnolia on her cheek it would have melted into the background,' wrote Beverley Nichols.[62] As well, of course, there is Syrie's vivacity. Moreover, as a photograph of her taken about the age of twenty-one reveals, if there are any flaws in her face they are a slightly prominent nose and jaw.

As a young woman, Kitty's beauty, like that of Syrie, attracts a lot of men, and her mother's worries about the number of suitors over forty years is interesting in light of Syrie's early marriage to a man who was forty-seven. Syrie, too, married on the rebound from an engagement broken by her parents, and it was an unhappy union; Kitty married Walter in haste because a younger sister had become engaged before her, and their marriage failed.

The emotional failure of the relationship between the vivacious, outgoing and sociable Kitty and the shy, moody, undemonstrative Walter may well reflect the distance between Syrie and Maugham. In any case, Walter's attitude to Kitty – except that he claims to love her deeply – is that of the author to his wife. One speech, for example, describes the woman in the same disdainful terms that Maugham used of Syrie in 'Looking Back':

> I had no illusions about you . . . I knew you were silly and frivolous and empty-headed. But I loved you. I knew that your aims and ideas were vulgar and commonplace. But I loved you. I knew that you were second-rate. But I loved you. It's comic to think how hard I tried to be amused by the things that amused you and how anxious I was to hide from you that I wasn't ignorant and vulgar and scandal-mongering and stupid. I know how frightened you were of intelligence and I did everything I could to make you think of me as as big a fool as the rest of the men you know. I knew that you'd only married me for convenience.[63]

The plot of *The Painted Veil* – the woman's adultery, the death of the husband, and the woman's redemption through the knowledge she gains in China – has few parallels to Syrie's and Willie's lives. It has been claimed that Maugham learned of affairs that Syrie had during their marriage, but there is no real evidence for them, and if she had sought emotional or sexual release elsewhere her itinerant husband was hardly justified in complaining. Kitty's adultery is a fictional device, a dramatic catalyst which sets off the chain of events which takes the Fanes to the cholera city and forces Kitty to examine the principles of her life. It does not preclude the possibility, however, that in a more subtle allegorical way Maugham was using the novel as a self-justification and as implied condemnation of Syrie and her values as he saw them.

Maugham seems to have been saying that if one were to take a woman like Syrie, raised in affluence and living in the shelter of English middle-class values, and expose her to the cultural and philosophical shock of life in, say, the Far East, she might experience a kind of spiritual rebirth. In this regard, it is important to examine the novel's last chapter, in which Kitty not only sloughs off much of her past triviality but foresees a more useful and independent life for her unborn daughter.

The Painted Veil concludes with Kitty's return to her family home in England, following Walter's death and a brief final sexual encounter with her lover in Hong Kong. She goes back a changed woman, and to underline the possibility of regeneration Maugham juxtaposes the death of her snobbish and superficial mother with Kitty's promise of raising her daughter more sensitively. In the early chapters, he painted a withering portrait of the mother, giving her some of the harassing qualities which in later years he ascribed to Syrie. 'She nagged him [her husband] without mercy,' he wrote. 'She discovered that if she wanted him to do something which his sensitiveness revolted against she had only to give him no peace and eventually, exhausted, he would yield. On her side she set herself to cultivate the people who might be useful. She flattered the solicitors who would send her husband briefs and was familiar with their wives. She was obsequious to the judges and their ladies. She made much of promising politicians.'[64]

When Kitty returns to live with her father, she suddenly realizes that her mother's death has meant freedom for him for the first time in many years. Wishing to be with him, she nevertheless respects his independence and is determined not to 'batten' on him any longer. Thus the death of the mother is the burial of a certain kind of worthless, trivial life, and Kitty, hoping that she has learned compassion and charity, looks to find a peace that had eluded her previously.

There is of course another incarnation of womanhood, the anticipated daughter of the third generation, and Kitty intends to make her into something that she never was: a free woman who will be more than an ornament and a burden. 'I'm going to bring up my daughter', she says, 'so that she's free and can stand on her own feet. I'm not going to bring a child into the world, and love her and bring her up, just so that some man may want to sleep with her so much that he's willing to provide her with board and lodging for the rest of her life

... I want her to be fearless and frank. I want her to be a person, independent of others because she is possessed of herself, and I want her to take life like a free man and make a better job of it than I have.'[65]

In 1924 Maugham of course had more than a passing interest in how a daughter should be raised. Liza was nine years old, and Maugham, having written so many novels and plays about women so often trapped in meaningless social roles, hoped that she might grow into a woman of character and independence. Not surprisingly, one of his complaints about Syrie in later years was his feeling that she raised their daughter to believe that the only important goal in life was a good marriage. And increasingly he had come to resent having to provide 'board and lodging' for Syrie for the rest of her life because of his earlier infatuation.

However much one disagrees with Maugham's judgements of Syrie – and there is ample evidence that she was more intellectual and self-sufficient than he gave her credit for – The Painted Veil is a cleverly disguised sermon for her. It is a fictional indictment of her present life and an illustration of how it would be different if she encountered some meaningful experience away from the London social set which Maugham despised. As well, it is an expression of hope that she would raise Liza to be a woman of strength and character. That Walter had died and was thus no longer there to see his child raised may at least reflect a feeling in Maugham that, so far as his marriage and relationship with Syrie was concerned, he was as if dead, and that the major influence on Liza over the years would be her mother.

By 1925 relations between Syrie and Maugham had deteriorated, though they continued to preserve the façade of marriage. By then, she had begun her career as an interior decorator, which over the next decade would give her an international reputation. With capital of £400 and furniture from her Regent Street house, she opened a shop first in Baker Street and then in Grosvenor Square, and became famous for her all-white interiors. Syrie, however, had a propensity to use their home to display various pieces, and this led to an incident that Raymond Mortimer has said was the act that finally convinced Maugham that he could not live with Syrie.[66] A witness was Cathleen Nesbitt, who was staying with the Maughams for a week and who later remembered 'him coming back one day and finding his writing desk – which I feel must be sacred to any writer – had been sold by Syrie and replaced by another of a different shape and size. He appeared to take it calmly but I sensed a rage of fury coldly controlled.'[67]

When Maugham later bought a house in Chelsea for Syrie, the same sort of uncertainty prevailed. Olive Cruikshank, Syrie's personal secretary from the twenties until the Second World War, recalled that 'the trouble was that he might go out in the morning and come back to find that the room had been entirely refurnished. Mrs Maugham might have taken it into her head that she needed just the piece of furniture he was using for somewhere else she was working on. Naturally Mr Maugham objected to this because he always wrote at certain set hours of the day. And such changes went against the grain with him.'[68] Maugham's disposition was not helped either by Syrie's placing a mat outside the front door with 'Wellcome' printed on it.

In 'Looking Back', Maugham complains that Syrie's business dealings were ethically questionable, that she made him 'scenes' that lasted until two or three in the morning, and generally plagued him with complaints and nagging. Lacking any resources of her own, she leaned on him, and without a real interest in art and ideas she remained outside his world. For his part, he says, he was bored by the sort of parties Syrie insisted on attending and he often left early while she remained until the early hours of the morning.

Those who knew Maugham well heard him tell this version of his life with Syrie years before he put it in print in 'Looking Back', and there is a good deal of exaggeration in all of it. Syrie was far more intelligent and more interested in the arts than Maugham gave her credit for – witness the loyalty of creative people like Rebecca West, Noël Coward, Olive Reed, Osbert Sitwell, and Beverley Nichols. Furthermore, though some of her business dealings bordered on the unethical, she proved to be a capable and shrewd interior designer. Above all, she was a devoted mother.

Though Maugham may have overstated Syrie's faults, there were nevertheless serious fundamental problems in their relationship aside from the major impediment created by the author's attachment to Haxton. Syrie spent large sums of money and Maugham, so disciplined himself about financial matters, became increasingly irritated by her profligacy. Then, too, his long-established work schedule and need for quiet seclusion made it difficult to coexist happily under the same roof. Whether Syrie really harassed and nagged her husband to the extent he later claimed is questionable, though Bruce Lockhart's *Diaries* note an occasion when the author, having tea with a friend, was so unnerved by Syrie's voice downstairs that he hid behind a sofa and remained there until she left.[69]

Clearly the Maughams' marriage was collapsing by 1925. Having returned from the United States in March, he spent a week in Paris with Haxton following the opening of *Rain* and another week or two with him at a spa in Brides-les-Bains in early July. There they took the waters, golfed, and played tennis and bridge. By October the pair departed again for another seven-month journey through south-east Asia.

Syrie, meanwhile, was using the money she had earned as a decorator to build a house at Le Touquet, a fashionable seaside resort on the north coast of France. Called the Villa Eliza, it was tastefully decorated and became the subject of fashion magazine articles. Conveniently close to the Calais–Dover ferry, Le Touquet had golf links, tennis courts, bathing and a casino, which Syrie seems to have hoped might attract her husband enough for them to live there where Haxton could be close at hand.

Years later Maugham claimed that he always felt like a guest at the Villa Eliza, a complaint corroborated by a weekend described by Beverley Nichols first in *The Sweet and Twenties*[70] and then more dramatically in *A Case of Human Bondage*. Even if Nichols has magnified the events so as to defend Syrie, it is clear that there could be no coexistence of Maugham, Syrie and Haxton at Le Touquet. Maugham, says Nichols, seemed faintly bored by the company – Noël Coward, Lord and Lady Plunket, Gertie Millar, Doris de la Vigne, and Nichols – who were his wife's friends, not his. Haxton won a large sum of money at the casino, became drunk and offensive, and ended up naked on the bedroom floor covered with thousand-franc notes. Maugham, moreover, was at best distant with Syrie and at worst deliberately insulting, so that the party ended when Syrie and Nichols impulsively left and returned to England.

In a letter to Knoblock in October 1925 Maugham referred to a stay at the Villa Eliza, which perhaps is another perspective on these events. Syrie, he confessed, worked hard to be accommodating, but he clearly was already prepared to break with her. He could not change, and if she would not accept him as he was he was quite willing to be divorced.[71] Maugham, moreover, spent two weeks in Capri that summer and found it so delightful that he asked his old friend John Ellingham Brooks to look out for a house for him, with the idea that he would have his own place there permanently.

In that summer of 1925 Maugham was not yet free from problems in the theatre. A fierce heat wave in June kept audiences away from London performances, and the returns from *Rain* plummeted. Concerned that Dean's company might not be able to continue, Maugham suggested to Colton and Randolph that they join him in waiving royalties should the production begin operating at a loss. He reasoned that if they survived the heat the autumn might be successful and closing in England might adversely affect the tours of the play in the United States.

Maugham had also become involved in a dramatization of *The Moon and Sixpence*, produced in London on 24 September. It had been adapted by Edith Ellis the previous year and, while liking the scenario, Maugham thought the dialogue was appalling. After some discussion, he agreed to work on the script, and in the end rewrote it far more than Miss Ellis realized. She arrived in London just before dress rehearsals, and so could do little to object to his revisions. The play opened to good reviews but the run ended after only seventy-five performances.

In another of his professional arenas, Maugham had grown dissatisfied with his American publisher, George Doran. The writer's complaint was virtually the same as his grievance about Heinemann had been twenty years earlier: the publisher had not properly promoted his book. *The Painted Veil* had been highly successful in England and had sold well in the United States, but Maugham was convinced that the American sales would have been even larger if Doran had pushed it well. The publisher, he told Towne, had promised to bring out a booklet about his work before the novel was released, but there was nothing but perfunctory advertising. Doran seemed to view him as a guaranteed money-maker and had grown complacent, and Maugham argued that the only way to force a publisher to guarantee success is to extract such a large advance that he must work hard to get his money back.[72]

Eugene Saxton had recently left Doran for Harper's and, anxious to attract Maugham to his company, he was prepared to guarantee the success that the author thought he deserved. Towne, however, counselled Maugham to remain with Doran, and Maugham agreed providing that there was a guarantee of an American sale of two-and-a-half times the British figures. This was preferable to a larger advance because, he argued, he was not anxious to make a large sum of money out of a book but to have it as widely read as possible.[73] He had always liked Doran as a person, and he was persuaded by his agent that there were special factors which inhibited the sales of *The Painted Veil*.

When Towne eventually signed an agreement with Doran on Maugham's behalf in April 1926 however, Maugham was angered. Doran had not guaranteed the two-and-one-half formula, but Maugham's greater concern was the long-term conditions of the contract. With the departure of the capable Saxton and Grant Overton from the Doran firm, Maugham was convinced that the company would collapse if its head should retire or die, and in such a case he wanted to be free to move. Because of his friendship with Doran, Maugham wanted Towne to keep his dissatisfaction from the publisher so as to maintain cordial relations.

The matter was ultimately resolved in July 1926 when the Doran company signed an agreement recognizing that the writer's contract was directly with George Doran. Should the latter lose control of the company for any reason, Maugham would be entitled to reimburse the company for half the cost of such materials as plates, dyes, and illustrations, and then be free to go to another publisher.[74] With this resolution, Maugham remained with Doran and in fact continued with the firm when it became Doubleday Doran for the remainder of his career. In November 1930 Nelson Doubleday made a further concession when he agreed to pay Maugham a royalty of 20 per cent on all books sold, rather than 15 on the first 5000 and 20 thereafter.

On 6 October Maugham left England for Singapore so thrilled at getting off, he told a friend, that he could think of nothing else. Sailing by way of the Suez Canal, he was returning to the Malay Archipelago to collect more material for a novel (*The Narrow Corner*) he had already plotted. Maugham had always believed in imposing a pattern on life, and early in his career he had devised a list of novels, plays, and essays which he intended to write. To Burton Rascoe he confided that he had worked out the plots of two novels, one of them a 'picaresque' tale of modern London, a book of travel – 'not the ordinary sort written either by people who do not know how to observe or by people who describe their impressions when they have no personality' – and two plays.[75]

By 1927 Maugham was able to give French scholar Paul Dottin a more specific agenda which he proposed for the remainder of his career. When he had completed *The Gentleman in the Parlour*, he would write: three more stories to go with those already done to make up a volume (*Six Stories Written in the First Person Singular*), a novel set in the Malay Archipelago (*The Narrow Corner*), another volume of English stories, a book about Spain (*Don Fernando*), a collection of Malay stories (*Ah King*), a picaresque novel set in England (*Cakes and Ale*), and a volume of essays assessing his activities and thoughts (*The Summing Up*). That done, he said, he would be finished, though he suggested to Dottin that he had already written his major works, and that these final books would merely fill some gaps.[76]

Maugham and Haxton spent four months in Malaya and Indo-China in the winter of 1925–6, gathering background material and revising three remaining stories to be included in *The Casuarina Tree*, published in September 1926. Towne must have been impressed by their authenticity as he looked at the smudged scripts typed by Haxton in the heat and humidity of the tropical jungle. By 1 March Maugham and his companion had reached Hue, and shortly thereafter they sailed from Saigon to Marseilles on a French ship.

As much as Maugham had been thrilled to begin the expedition, he was now exhausted and suffering from a bout of malaria. He looked forward to working quietly at home, but even before landing in France he had learned that he was temporarily homeless. Syrie had gone to the United States to establish her first shop there and had let 43 Bryanston Square for a number of months. Maugham therefore went first to Gerald's flat in Paris, concluding that it was not wise to go to London until things were settled one way or another with Syrie. She had sent him a telegram to let him know that she was having a party at Le Touquet at Easter but, as Maugham indicated to Knoblock, he sensed that the end had come, that she had finally decided on a separation, though she had opposed it the previous autumn.[77] While waiting for matters to be decided, Maugham headed for the Côte d'Azur to stay at the Réserve de Beaulieu, a beautiful hotel near Nice.

By late April Syrie had persuaded the tenants of 43 Bryanston Square to surrender it for two months if they could have it back for July, August, and September. Maugham returned to London not knowing whether Syrie would be living at the house or at her shop in the King's Road and whether there would be a nasty confrontation. The result, however, was an understanding: she would have her house in London and he would have his villa on the Riviera, and they would stay with one another as guests when convenient. Maugham confided to friends that he thought this best for both of them, and that it would allow him to work in peace and without interruption. The conditions of the agreement were that 43 Bryanston Square would be sold, and the money used to buy Syrie a house and adjoining property in the King's Road. Maugham would take his bedroom furniture, books, theatrical pictures, and *objets d'art* that he had accumulated.

The arrangement marked a further deterioration of the Maughams' relationship, though it preserved a façade of sorts. They were to stay with each other as guests and, though Maugham found it disagreeable, Syrie set up a room for him on the top floor of her King's Road house. They continued to spend some time in each other's company – as in

August 1926 when Syrie joined her husband for the Salzburg Festival. On 6 April 1927 they attended the opening night of *The Constant Wife*, and the writer A. E. W. Mason entertained them for dinner at his Grosvenor Street flat in June of that year.

The façade, however, was not without cracks. Arnold Bennett, for example, had 'a great time' dining with the Maughams in June but earlier in April he reported that the Maugham party following the opening of *The Constant Wife* was 'a great success', except that 'Maugham and his wife were a bit gloomy. *He* always is.'[78] Similarly, Lytton Strachey described Maugham at one of Lady Aberconway's parties as 'a hangdog personage, I thought . . . with a wife'.[79]

An essential part of Maugham's agreement with Syrie was having his own house on the Continent. It was an idea he found increasingly attractive, and during his weeks in Beaulieu in the spring of 1926 he found the place he wanted. On twenty acres of land at almost the furthest point of Cap Ferrat, a peninsula extending into the Mediterranean between Nice and Monte Carlo, was a house lying empty because it required renovations to make it habitable. The Villa Mauresque had been built by a bishop who had served in French North Africa and it had a distinctly Moorish flavour: horseshoe windows, horseshoe colonnades, horseshoe columns, and a large cupola on the roof. Enchanted by the location, surrounded by the blue Mediterranean and in sight of Italy, Maugham saw the possibilities of the house, and bought it in the autumn of 1926. Over the next year, he employed two architects, Barry Dierks and Colonel Eric Sawyer, to remodel the house and remove the Moorish façade.

Back in May 1926 when Maugham had made his agreement with Syrie he was still in London, and he became involved with the General Strike, when about half of Britain's six million workers left their jobs in sympathy with striking miners. Like thousands of members of the middle and upper classes, Maugham volunteered to provide essential services, in his case offering his shrewdness and experience as a secret agent. According to Arnold Bennett Maugham worked at Scotland Yard as a detective, a police car picking him up and his job occupying him from eleven in the evening until half past eight in the morning. The last few hours, Maugham said, were simply terrible and an ordeal to get through.[80]

Maugham's friend and former head of Scotland Yard, Sir Ronald Howe, has said that the writer's powers of observation and deduction would have made him a good detective,[81] and there is evidence that his secret service activities did not entirely end in 1917. The world of espionage is a brotherhood which, once entered, is difficult ever to leave totally behind. Alan Searle has suggested that occasional guests at the Villa Mauresque seemed to be connected with some level of intelligence work, and during such visits Maugham would advise Searle to stay out of the discussions because the less he knew the better off he would be.[82] Furthermore, when Franklin Delano Roosevelt decided early in the Second World War to create a secret intelligence agency – which became the Office of Strategic Services and later the Central Intelligence Agency – the special assistant in charge of staffing, Harold Guinzberg, sought Maugham's advice because of his experience in the First World War.[83]

By the middle of June 1926 Maugham had returned to France, first to Paris and then with Haxton to the spa at Brides-les-Bains for a fortnight. In August he joined Syrie in Salzburg, following which he and Haxton went to Capri, and in September he was back in London, where he attended the opening night of Margaret Kennedy's and Basil Dean's *The Constant Nymph*. Here, as Dean later recalled, Maugham again displayed his generosity toward younger writers: 'Maugham wrote to me in terms of unusual enthusiasm welcoming me to "the fraternity of British dramatists."'[84]

On 28 September Maugham sailed to New York to attend rehearsals of his new play, *The Constant Wife*. After the customary rush of conferences and interviews, he went to Cleveland with the company for the opening there on 1 November. The lead was played by the brilliant Ethel Barrymore, but on that evening she could not remember her lines. The director, George Cukor, who was to become an intimate friend of the dramatist, hid in the fireplace to prompt her, and pages of script were secreted about the stage. After painfully watching Barrymore struggle through the performance, a grim-faced Maugham went backstage to be met by the actress's confident remark: 'Darling, I've ruined your play, but don't worry, it'll run for two years.'[85] Barrymore was right, and when it was transferred to the Maxine Elliott Theatre in New York, it ran for 295 performances and became her greatest triumph of the twenties.

When *The Constant Wife* was produced in London five months later, however, its reception was much different, and it closed after only seventy shows. In part, the failure was the result of a disastrous first night when one of those accidents of the theatre damaged the performance and affected the reviews. Through an error of house management, the rope barrier separating the pit from the stall seats had been misplaced and, as the curtain was about to go up, there were a large number of people sitting in stall seats for which others had reserved tickets. Because the first group had queued since eight in the morning for the pit, it would not budge, and violent arguments broke out while the house manager appealed from the stage for some to leave. The result was that the company was unnerved, the gallery was restless and rude, and when Fay Compton sharply thanked the 'civil members' of the audience at the end she was greeted by catcalls. Maugham, sitting in a box with Syrie, was aghast.

This opening night fiasco undoubtedly influenced reviewers, but, as Anthony Curtis has pointed out, the play itself may have been more than British audiences were prepared to accept in 1927. Another of Maugham's stories of a woman's fight for independence, its proposition is that as long as men pay their bills wives have no justification for claiming any liberties, but when the woman removes the economic obligation she has the right to demand freedom equal to that of her husband. As the heroine, Constance, says, a middle-class wife is nothing but a parasite:

> Have you considered what marriage is among well-to-do people? In the working classes a woman cooks her husband's dinner, works for him and darns his socks. She looks after the children and makes their clothes. She gives good value for the money she costs. But what is a wife in our class? Her house is managed by servants, nurses look after her children, if she has resigned herself to having any, and as soon as they are old enough she packs them off to school. Let us face it, she is no more than the mistress of a man of whose desire she has taken advantage to insist on a legal ceremony that will prevent him from discarding her when his desire has ceased.[86]

The Constant Wife owes some of its inspiration to its author's own marriage and his attitude toward money and Syrie's burgeoning career as an interior decorator. She was part of a new generation of middle- and upper-class women after the First World War who from boredom or economic necessity went into business for themselves, as shopkeepers, designers and managers of hotels, cinemas, and beauty parlours. In Maugham's play, Constance gains equality with her husband and her freedom by going into business with a friend and thus becoming economically independent. 'There is only one freedom that is really important,' she claims, 'and that is economic freedom, for in the long run the man who pays the piper calls the tune.'[87]

When Maugham had returned to England on 6 November 1926 on

the *France*, 43 Bryanston Square had just been sold and his possessions were in storage until the renovations to the Villa Mauresque were completed. For the next eight months he lived at various addresses: the flat in Paris, at Montague Mews just off Bryanston Square, and at Syrie's new house in Chelsea. During this period he busied himself with the stories for *Ashenden*, which was published in March 1928, rehearsals for the English production of *The Constant Wife* and for the long delayed opening of *The Letter*.

With the renovations nearly completed, Maugham and Haxton were able to move into the Villa Mauresque in August 1927. The writer was pleased with the house and large garden, and the remainder of the summer was spent bathing and lying in the sun around the large pool. Not even this sybaritic life, however, was allowed to interfere with work, and the autumn and winter were devoted to writing *The Gentleman in the Parlour*.

When he had completed his travel book at the end of February 1928, Maugham began work on a play whose central theme had occupied his thoughts for some time. His brother Charles and his wife, Beldy, had three daughters and a son, Ormond, who at the age of twelve fell out of a tree and was paralysed for life. Seventeen years old in 1927, his crippled condition troubled his uncle as did his mother's devoted care of him, and the dramatist decided to write a play about maternal devotion and euthanasia.

In *The Sacred Flame* the son is a war veteran who has been left badly paralysed. His wife is pregnant with his brother's child, and to prevent his discovering the infidelity his mother kills him with an overdose of drugs. This is an act of merciful love, and Maugham succeeds in enlisting the audience's sympathies for the mother's anguish and devotion. The voice of conventional morality, however, is heard in the protests of the young man's nurse, who threatens to expose his death as murder. At the mother's subsequent confession, she is nevertheless shattered and agrees that the doctor should sign the death certificate.

Though Maugham had written serious plays before – notably *A Man of Honour*, *Caesar's Wife*, and *The Unknown* – none had the substance and depth of *The Sacred Flame*, which was an attempt to strike out in a new direction in the final phase of his career as a dramatist. When his American producer, Messmore Kendall, announced the forthcoming play in December 1927, he characterized it as a 'theme play' and claimed that 'with it the playwright enters a new field'.[88] In the introduction to the collected edition of his plays, Maugham himself admitted that he had tried a more elaborate dialogue, a less natural but more articulate way of speaking necessary to the metaphysical arguments in the drama.

The Sacred Flame, For Services Rendered, and finally *Sheppey* were Maugham's attempt to show, before he retired from playwriting, that he was capable of serious, significant drama, and though they did not capture a large audience they are among the most powerful things he wrote. For two decades one of the most popular writers of light comic plays, he decided in the mid-thirties to round out his career with pieces of substance. It may be that Maugham, who paid more attention to critics than he liked to admit, had read and taken to heart a review article in the *New York Times Book Review* in May 1923, which surveyed his dramatic career on the occasion of the publication of a number of his plays. Calling him the best of the 'stage dramatists', the article argued that he nevertheless does not belong in the company of the greatest playwrights – Shaw, Barrie, or Granville-Barker. Maugham could still, it reasoned, raise the level of his drama, remembering that before *Of Human Bondage* and *The Moon and Sixpence*, he had written such inferior novels as *Mrs Craddock, The Explorer,* and *The Magician.* 'There is no doubt', it said, 'that he can do better and more lasting things, and there is no reason why he should not do them yet.'[89]

Evidence that Maugham was reaching for new directions for his drama can be found in a letter written to fellow playwright Edward Knoblock on 1 February 1925, in which he says that he intends to become acquainted with the work of the young dramatists in France and Germany. In all the arts, he argued, to stand still is to go back.[90] Unfortunately Maugham was always reticent about discussing his work at length, and there is no indication in his correspondence of which writers he studied. Always travelling widely in Europe, he was *au courant* with new drama, and this undoubtedly influenced the move to more serious intent in his final plays.

The Sacred Flame did not open until the autumn of 1928, and until then Maugham spent much of the year at the Villa Mauresque, with trips to London in May and Brides-les-Bains for the cure in June. After another summer in the Riviera sun, he and Haxton sailed to New York in mid-October for rehearsals. They had planned to travel on the *Mauretania,* but when Maugham learned that Syrie had booked passage on it he changed to the *Aquitania.* The pretence of marriage, however forced by this point, would hardly be maintained when she would have her cabin and Maugham would be sharing his with his secretary. According to Maugham Syrie had offered him passage on the *Olympic,* on which she had been booked until learning that he was sailing on the *Mauretania*. Both Edward Molyneux and Noël Coward had tried to dissuade her from taking the *Mauretania* but, Maugham told a friend, her professional good taste did not extend to life in general.

The rehearsals of *The Sacred Flame* exposed a serious problem. Fay Compton, cast in the key role of the invalid's wife, was acting badly. The manager, Messmore Kendall, later wrote that she was 'nearly adequate', having sufficient beauty and stature to balance the stage presence of Claire Eames as the nurse, but that she broke down at rehearsals and 'refused to go on in a part which she confessed was beyond her power'.[91] Compton may have realized her failure and withdrawn, but Maugham had diagnosed it already and had wired his agent a week earlier to say that he was making a change in the cast. Fortunately for the actors, he said, she could blame Equity rules about foreign performers and so save face.

Consultations between Maugham, the director Gilbert Miller, and Kendall led to the decision to use the understudy, Casha Pringle, who was tiny, pretty, and appealing – and totally wrong for the role. As a result, reviewers attacked the miscasting, and the production folded after only four weeks. In England, on the other hand, where Gladys Cooper played the part in February 1929, the play was a success, running for 209 nights. That *The Sacred Flame* meant more to Maugham than anything he had previously written for the stage is revealed in his comment to Kendall that the English run was a great relief and an encouragement to complete the plays with which he would end his career as a dramatist.[92]

Maugham and Haxton returned to France in December 1928 without complications, but by February he was involved in divorce proceedings. According to his account in 'Looking Back', he had invited Syrie to visit the Villa Mauresque while she was staying at Antibes with Elsie Mendl, and following the visit she wrote him a note expressing her wish to divorce him. This episode may have occurred in the summer of 1928 – though it is hard to understand why Syrie should then wish to travel on the same ship as Maugham unless out of a perverse desire to embarrass him – or it could have happened in January of 1929. In any case, Maugham agreed not to make matters difficult if the divorce took place in France, where the law was simpler and there would be less publicity.

The divorce was granted in a Nice court on 11 May 1929 on grounds of incompatibility. Maugham agreed to a lump sum payment of £12,000, £2400 a year in alimony until Syrie remarried, and £600 annual support payments for Liza. As well, Syrie was given the house in the King's Road, fully furnished, and a Rolls Royce.

The divorce went almost unnoticed by the British press, with nothing at all in *The Times*, and in the United States it received a two-sentence report in the *New York Times*. Maugham was nevertheless anxious about people's reactions, and especially concerned about what Syrie might say to their circle. Even before the divorce he complained to Barbara Back of her gossip, in this case sparked by his niece Kitty's claim that Syrie had been spreading malicious rumours about her. Back, he said, should assure Kitty that no one would believe anything said by an abandoned liar.[93]

Maugham continued to harbour a fear of Syrie spreading stories about their marriage, its collapse, and his relationship with Haxton. Some years later, the writer was even reluctant to have Alan Searle meet her because 'the less she knows about you the better it will be.'[94] Though this may have bordered on paranoia, Maugham did have some cause to be worried, as revealed in the writer Anita Loos's recollections of Syrie at the end of the twenties. 'Never known for her reticence,' wrote Loos, 'Syrie's conversation dealt with the awful things Somerset Maugham was doing to her; in fact some of his finest talent went into the invention of diabolic things to do to Syrie. He found ways to flaunt her successor, who was of the wrong sex to rationalize any woman's jealousy. Syrie's life was as packed with heady emotion as any that Maugham ever achieved on his type-writer.'[95]

Notwithstanding Maugham's claims, Syrie seems on the whole to have done little more talking about the divorce than people normally do after its emotional trauma. David Herbert, for example, recalls that 'she took immense pains to keep her difficulties to herself. Her friends knew how much she minded both the separation and the vindictiveness to which she was subjected.'[96] If on one occasion she spoke with 'heady emotion', it was because – incredible as it seems – she remained in love with Maugham and did so for many years.

Raymond Mortimer, for example, told me that Syrie adored Maugham even after their divorce, asking him how her ex-husband was and what he was doing. Similarly, Rebecca West remembered Syrie telling her of leaving a party in a car with Lord Lovat and when he suddenly kissed her she exclaimed: 'Don't speak – don't speak. Then I can pretend you're Willie!'[97] Garson Kanin recounts another occasion in New York during the Second World War when Syrie was 'flushed with excitement' about the imminent publication of *The Razor's Edge*. Struck by her pride in his accomplishment and her 'deep appreciation of his art', Kanin asked her if she had told Maugham of her pleasure. 'Of course not,' she replied frostily.[98] 'She loved Willie,' observed Beverley Nichols, 'and continued to love him till the end of her life. Of this I had the most poignant proof shortly before her death. She was ill in bed, but she had tried to make herself look pretty because she had a vain hope that he might come to see her.'[99]

If the remainder of Syrie's life was bound to Maugham by a strange sort of love, Maugham's was linked to hers by a bizarre sort of hatred. Both Alan Searle and French writer André David, who knew Maugham well in the thirties and forties, have told me that Maugham detested Syrie after their divorce. Arthur Marshall recalls being baffled by an occasion, years after the break, when Maugham suddenly launched into a long series of bitter accusations against her.[100] Similarly, H. G. Wells once told Frank Swinnerton that Syrie was incapable of realizing the depth of Maugham's distaste for her and that she always expected a reconciliation to take place.[101]

How does one account for this deep-seated resentment, this almost pathological hatred in Maugham? He grumbled about the cost of the settlement, but it was a modest amount for a wealthy author. He complained that Syrie was bringing up their daughter to be a snob, to believe that seeking a good marriage was the only important thing in life. Against this, however, he was free from a bond that he had found irksome for a decade.

Such an intense hatred must come from deep within, and in Maugham's case the end of his marriage represented a failure which he did not want to admit. He had, as he later confessed, tried to persuade himself that he was three-quarters normal and sought to prove it by embarking on a series of heterosexual relationships. He had formed a liaison with Syrie to deny his homosexuality, and when he could not sustain such a union he blamed her for *his* failure. When Syrie had bought her villa in Le Touquet, where they might live in some *ménage à trois*, she compelled her husband consciously to reject a life with her. By asking for a divorce and forcing his acquiescence, she made him admit – if only to himself – that he wanted the relationship to end.

Syrie was far from blameless in the failure of their marriage but she did not deserve his contempt. A living reminder of his own defeat, she remained an irritant even after her death. Moreover, while Maugham might voice his anger to a few intimate friends, he characteristically adopted a pose of civilized detachment in public, and thus in such autobiographical pieces as *The Summing Up* there is barely a ripple of concern. Inside, however, his hatred festered and grew until in old age he could no longer control it, and his own imagined Syrie came back to drive him to one last enormously self-destructive act.

6

THE GENTLEMAN IN THE VILLA: 1929–1932

A YEAR BEFORE Maugham's fifty-fifth birthday in 1929 he confided to Bertram Alanson that he was considering making one last journey to the Far East before he became too old. In the event, he did not make that trip, substituting a more modest tour of Greece, Egypt, and Turkey. In the winter of 1935–6, Maugham and Haxton travelled to Haiti, Colombia, Trinidad, and Martinique, and in 1938 they made a three-month tour of India. As well, of course, there were the shorter trips to Italy, Germany, Holland, Spain, Scandinavia, and the United States, but in the thirties there were few journeys to match the great wandering explorations of the previous decade. Significantly only the Spanish trips of 1932 and 1934 and the Indian sojourn resulted in literary work of any note.

Maugham may have pretended that age was diminishing his wanderlust but he was a young fifty-five, and would retain a surprising vigour until his late eighties. Part of the attraction of travel had always been its release from responsibilities and obligations, especially those in London involving Syrie, and the divorce in 1929 had freed him of these restraints. Moreover, for the first time in a decade he had his own house, which, except for his relationship with Haxton, offered another form of retreat from the pressures of the world. For the next ten years, and then again for a dozen years after the Second World War, he brought much of the world he wanted to see to be entertained and to entertain him at the Villa Mauresque.

Maugham had chosen to live in one of the most stunningly beautiful locales in Europe. Except for an infrequent snowfall and the occasional storm, the climate along the Côte d'Azur is a mixture of tropic and temperate zone. Summer temperatures average 72°F, sometimes rising to the high 80s, and the winters rarely go below 50°F. Apart from thunderstorms, most of the rain falls in the autumn when Maugham would leave for London after the four dry sunny months of summer.

According to Maugham's Riviera neighbour and friend Roderick Cameron Cap Ferrat is particularly blessed by superb weather. The mountains rising sharply along the coast are nearly free of vegetation and therefore act as reflectors to the sun, storing heat and radiating it back along the shore. Moreover, they act as a buffer for the clouds, frequently leaving clear blue sky above Beaulieu and Cap Ferrat.

Because the Mediterranean is deep, transparent, and of a higher-than-normal salinity, its famous blue is richer than that of almost any other sea. From the grounds of the Villa Mauresque, located on the highest point of Cap Ferrat, could be seen the sweep of the water from Italy on the one hand to St Tropez on the other, and towards the mainland lay the harbour of Villefranche. Beyond and above the harbour are the steep, sparsely covered mountains in which nestle the villages of Eze, Cagnes, Roquebrune, and La Turbie. 'The view', writes Cameron, 'never palls; all the time the light changes, and it is quite remarkable the clarity with which things stand out when the mistral [the vigorous and exhilarating wind deified by the Romans] is blowing; every stone and tree on the distant hills is visible, while Ventimiglia and Bordighera in Italy look almost next door . . . But this is only when the mistral is blowing, and more often than not the distances are smudged in an opaque veil of blue mist, giving the country the poetical quality of a Claude Lorraine landscape.'[1]

It is little wonder that Maugham, who had grown up fascinated by the grey and chilly North Sea, was enchanted by Cap Ferrat and decided to create a gracious retreat in its spectacular setting. With the removal of the Moorish façade the villa was left with clean lines, which were highlighted by its white walls and green trim. At the gate was the familiar sign against the evil eye, repeated above the main door, and inside was an entrance hall of black and white marble. To one side was a large thirty-nine-foot by eighteen-foot drawing-room, with a fireplace of Arles stone, impressionist paintings, and numerous works of art collected in the Far East. Along one wall were bookshelves built into recesses, running two-thirds of the way up to the fifteen-foot-high ceiling, and containing several thousand volumes. Around the fireplace were two sofas and over it was a large gilt-carved wooden eagle. French windows opened out onto three terraces bordered by orange and lemon trees.

The small round dining-room had a very high ceiling and was decorated with modern paintings. White marble steps led to the upper floor, which contained most of the house's seven bedrooms and four bathrooms. Maugham's own chamber was spacious but somewhat austere, and beside the bed stood a bookcase with his favourite works of Hazlitt, Butler, James, Yeats, Sterne, Shakespeare, Grimm's *Fairy Tales*, the *Letters of Edward Lear*, and the diaries of André Gide. Along the walls were paintings by Lepine, Renoir, Rouault, Gauguin, and Bonnard.[2]

Maugham's writing-room, designed for absolute privacy, was an oblong chamber built on the flat roof of the house and accessible only by a small wooden stairway and a walk across the white gravel. One wall was made up of french windows and another was covered with cases containing his most valuable books, but the wall facing the harbour at Villefranche was blocked up so that the view would not distract the working author. The only light came from the three-paned Gauguin window, mounted in a part of the room out of the line of vision of Maugham as he sat at the dark walnut seventeenth-century Spanish refectory table which served as his desk. In front of a sofa was a small fireplace in which he burned small amounts of the scarce olive and orange-wood sticks on the mornings when the mistral blew and reminded him of being on the deck of a ship.

Over the years the grounds of the Villa Mauresque were shaped to suit the interests and tastes of their owner. His love of tennis led to the installation of a court, on which he once played a titanic match with fellow writer Michael Arlen. As well, there were the avocado trees brought from California, of which Maugham was proud and from which he would make a pale – and to some visitors tasteless – ice-cream. There was an orangery, a covered walkway with plants trailing over trelliswork, and a garden arranged on three ascending terraces. On the highest terrace Maugham built a fifty-four-foot by eighteen-foot swimming-pool, constructed of marble with a lead sculptured pine cone in the Italian style at each corner. At the very deep end was a diving board while opposite water trickled from a faun carved in marble by Bernini. Within sight of the sea and surrounded by cacti and palms, the pool had a large old bronze gong brought from the Far East, which guests could strike to summon a steward with a cocktail.

Amidst the pleasures of climate, scenery, garden, and pool, visitors to the Villa Mauresque were entertained with grace and luxury. Guest bedrooms were furnished with desks and the latest books, Vichy water and fruit, and various kinds of expensive soaps and colognes. Maids and valets attended discreetly, and more than one new arrival was perplexed on the first morning to find any laundry not locked in his luggage gone, only to learn that evening that it had all been returned to his room impeccably laundered, starched, and pleated.

Since their host always spent the morning secluded in his writing-room, guests could take a leisurely breakfast in bed and casually amuse themselves until twelve-thirty. At precisely that time Maugham would join them on the terrace for a cocktail – either his favourite very dry and very cold dry martini or the sweeter White Lady in hot weather. Maugham's longtime cook, Annette, was famous along the Riviera for her culinary skill, and the luncheon that was served by liveried waiters would be simple but elegant. After coffee Maugham would excuse himself to take his afternoon nap, following which he might read a detective novel.

Afternoon at the Villa Mauresque could be spent lounging at the side of the pool, playing tennis, or perhaps sailing in his small yacht berthed at Villefranche Harbour. From time to time Maugham would hire a boat so that his guests could enjoy aquaplaning, and, according to their tastes, he would take them to the ballet in Monte Carlo or the boxing matches in Nice.

By six-thirty guests would be dressed for dinner and enjoying a cocktail with their host on the terrace. Here amid the oleanders, camellias, tuberoses, and sweet peas, with the scent of orange blossoms and the sounds of crickets in the trees, the party would frequently dine in moonlight. Dinner, more elaborate than luncheon, would be accompanied by champagne and served in silver dishes. Though Maugham, always careful about his diet and his weight, ate sparingly himself, he was proud of his table, consulting Annette about each day's menu the evening before. Even those who spent a fortnight under his roof were never served the same dish twice. Dinner would be followed by cigars and conversation, and often several hands of bridge. Never later than eleven o'clock Maugham would bid his guests good evening and retire.

Over the years an astonishing number of people were entertained at the Villa Mauresque, which as Anthony Curtis has observed became one of the Riviera's great literary pilgrimage points, along with Max Beerbohm's residence at Rapallo and the villas of Bernard Berenson and Harold Acton near Florence. Regular guests included the Gerald Kellys, the Alansons, the Alexander Freres, G. B. (Peter) Stern, the Kenneth Clarks, Garson Kanin and Ruth Gordon, Ian and Ann Fleming, Noël Coward, George Rylands, Beverley Nichols, Godfrey Winn, Arthur

17. Maugham in the thirties.
(*Wide World Photos*)

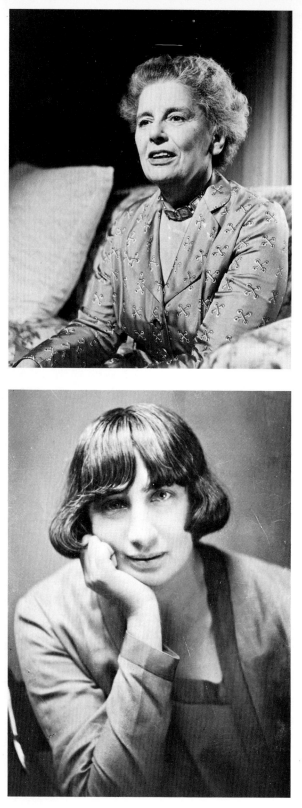

18. Rebecca West, fiercely loyal to Syr
but a friend to Maugham until the fina
years.
(*The Bettmann Archive/BBC Hulton*)

19. Author G. B. 'Peter' Stern, with
whom Maugham maintained an
affectionate and playful relationship for
many years.
(*The Mansell Collection*)

20. Maugham, Haxton and friends at Salzburg, 1934.
(*The Mansell Collection*)

21. Maugham and Liza at Yosemite Park during the Second World War with Bert and Mabel Alanson.
(*The William Somerset Maugham Collection [M013], Department of Special Collections and University Archives, The Stanford University Libraries*)

22. Gerald Haxton at the time when Maugham first met him on a First World War battlefield.
(*The Stanford University Libraries*)

23. Gerald Haxton, as gregarious and outgoing as Maugham was shy and taciturn.
(*The British Library*)

24. Alan Searle, strikingly handsome when he first met Maugham in 1928, became the devoted companion of his old age.
(*Mrs Cynthia Harrison*)

25. Willie and Frederic in
Badgastein, 1936.
(*The British Library*)

26. Maugham and Haxton :
Central Park, New York, 19
(*Humanities Research Center*
Library, The University of Te
at Austin)

Liza's wedding to Vincent Paravicini
in 1936.
(*Syndication International*)

Robin Maugham, who found Willie
re understanding than his own father.
(*The Stanford University Libraries*)

29. Maugham in the forti
when he had become 'T
Old Party'.
(*Humanities Research Cent
Library, The University of
Texas at Austin*)

30. Liza with John Hope
Lord Glendevon) and t
son Julian. (*The Stanf
University Libraries*)

Marshall, and of course Liza and her children and Robin. Occasional visitors were, among others, Churchill, Lord Beaverbrook, the Duke and Duchess of Windsor, Cecil Beaton, Jean Cocteau, Marc Chagall, C. P. Snow, Frank Swinnerton, Evelyn Waugh, Diana Cooper, Rebecca West, Rudyard Kipling, Arnold Bennett and Raymond Mortimer. In addition to the illustrious, however, there were many less affluent and influential whom Maugham invited to share his sybaritic life.

One of the most frequent and welcome guests at the villa in the thirties was Barbara Back. The wife of the well-known surgeon Ivor Back, whom the author had come to know through Gerald Kelly during the days of the Chat Blanc, she was beautiful, elegant, and vivacious – in Rebecca West's words, 'a plain Diana Cooper'.[3] Entertaining and quick-witted, she had a droll sense of humour, but what Maugham most appreciated was what he termed her 'guttersnipe humour'.[4]

Because Barbara was devoted to her husband, there was never any romantic or sexual tension in her relationship with Maugham, and both he and Gerald were relaxed in her presence. Her vitality, like that of Haxton, was warming to Maugham, and he enjoyed having her sit at the other end of the table as a kind of hostess. A sophisticate, she enjoyed the particular sensibility of the homosexual, and especially Maugham's witty and penetrating judgements of people. His lengthy correspondence with her over three decades reveals a greater trust and intimacy than he exhibited with any other person. He frequently paid for her trips to Cap Ferrat, and after the death of her husband in 1951, he gave her some financial support, a practice later continued by Alan Searle.

Whenever Maugham was in residence the villa was rarely without guests, and they often came and went in a steady stream. Preferring intimate gatherings and equipped to handle only a small number of visitors, Maugham had thus carefully to choreograph the changes. An invitation therefore was precise, with a discreet but firm limit to one's stay. For the same reason, Maugham was anxious that the house should be run with precision, and he was quick to become angry with those who lacked his own sense of punctuality. G. B. Stern recalled his irritation in the thirties when an elegant dinner party was delayed by the guest of honour's excessive lateness, an episode repeated years later when Lily Elsie arrived for luncheon twenty minutes late. Furious that his other guests had been kept waiting, Maugham muttered to Cecil Beaton: 'She always was a stupid woman.'[5]

Tardiness was no more tolerated in Maugham's own offspring. Peter

Quennell was once staying at the villa and was off bathing with Liza and two of her children when their return was delayed by about ten minutes because of traffic. Liza became increasingly anxious, and Quennell watched in amazement as she and the children bolted from the car into the Villa Mauresque, leaving the doors open rather than risk incurring Maugham's wrath.[6]

Maugham clearly wanted his home to be run with the same control and discipline that he applied so rigorously to his own life, and guests were expected to fit into that pattern. On occasion someone would be asked to leave prematurely because of a breach of manners, though the stories of such evictions have been exaggerated with retelling. For example, there is the often-told account of the writer Paddy Leigh-Fermor's unthinking description at dinner of the College of Heralds as 'all stammerers'. At the end of the evening, he was told by his host that he was saying goodbye then because 'you will have gone, of course, before I get up in the morning'. One of those present, Ann Fleming, later pointed out however that the episode was far more hilarious than it appears in cold print, that both she and Searle laughed about the blow-up. Maugham greeted her attempt to intercede with, 'He's a middle-class gigolo for a middle-aged woman', but the important thing is that Maugham relented, Leigh-Fermor returned to apologize, and stayed for the duration of his intended visit.[7]

In April 1952 Evelyn Waugh was staying at the villa with Diana Cooper, when he committed an even more horrendous gaffe. To his host's question about what a certain individual was like, Waugh replied characteristically: 'a pansy with a stammer.' 'All the Picassos on the wall blanched,' said Waugh, 'but Maugham remained calm.'[8]

Despite the occasional moments of tension, invitations to the Villa Mauresque were eagerly sought and those who later wrote disparagingly returned year after year. Maugham genuinely enjoyed entertaining his friends, and he was especially conscious during periods of British currency restriction that he could provide a kind of sojourn otherwise denied many of them. He would greet each arrival at the door, in Garson Kanin's words, 'a symbol of hospitality, all welcoming, smiling and making us feel at home'.[9] With charm, he would come forward with arms outstretched, and then the arms, said Cameron, 'would drop back again to the sides without contact, but it was meant as a welcoming gesture'.[10] G. B. Stern explained that 'at moments one can actually *see* him being French when he advances across the room to meet a guest, his arms outstretched, a gesture difficult for an out-and-out Englishman without seeming self-conscious.'[11] It was a motion not only unnatural for an Englishman, but difficult for a shy and self-conscious person, and it signified much.

Fay Compton, who had acted in a number of Maugham's plays but had failed in *The Sacred Flame*, fondly remembered being welcomed at the Villa Mauresque. Performing in Cannes with Jack Hawkins and Alec Clunes after the Second World War, she telephoned Maugham and was invited to lunch. 'We went over', she said, 'and I was greeted – now this is sweet, I always repeat it because I find it very flattering. I was greeted by Maugham on the steps of the lovely villa saying, "my beautiful Fay!" Now what could be sweeter than that?'[12]

Maugham enjoyed his guests because their visits were a way of bringing to the Côte d'Azur a taste of the London milieu he had forsaken. Many could not understand how he could tolerate and even enjoy the company of the gossipy Riviera cliques of retired rich and dispossessed European royalty talking of their money and their gardens. And he did enjoy their society, though much of his pleasure came from observing their foibles, some of which he gently satirized in 'The Three Fat Women of Antibes' and *The Razor's Edge*. Among his neighbours were the Duke of Connaught, with whom Leonie Leslie would join Maugham for dinner, and Roderick Cameron's mother, the shy and beautiful Lady Kenmare, who owned the nearby villa La Fiorentina. There was also the elegant Daisy Fellowes, who had a villa at Cap Martin, though she spent much of her time in her sizeable yacht anchored off Cap Ferrat. Among others were Lloyd Osbourne, the stepson of Robert Louis Stevenson, Violet Trefusis, the Countess Jean de Polignac, and retired actresses Denise Orme, Charlotte Boissevain, and Maxine Elliott.

Elliott was the original of one of 'The Three Fat Women of Antibes', but Maugham enjoyed the company of a number of the women he knew along the coast. Eleanor Medill 'Cissy' Patterson was entertaining because she was not a typical wealthy American tourist, and he appreciated her sensitive and earthy conversation.[13] A very different sort was Lady Bateman, a wealthy snobbish widow with whom Maugham frequently exchanged gifts and a warm correspondence whenever he was away from the Riviera.

Another expatriate American widow, Emily Borie Sherfesee, lived nearby and Maugham, like many along the Riviera, enjoyed her immense vitality. In the last two years of her life, according to Beverley Nichols, she went into a decline, suffering from a deep and unshakeable melancholy. Then, on many evenings, Maugham would walk down the road to her villa carrying a book of his short stories. Though reading aloud was a torture to him, he would face the ordeal in order to fill the void for the dying woman. 'An oddly touching picture it must have made,' comments Nichols, 'the old lady lying back on her *chaise-longue*, clutching her long black walking-stick, with Willie sitting bolt upright by her side, stuttering through his masterpieces, to the sound of crickets in the garden.'[14]

There was a part of Maugham that was a snob, and he enjoyed mingling with the titled and famous. He also loved gossip, though this interest was part of his fascination with human nature and had provided the germs of many of his best plots. Rebecca West has observed that she never saw anyone who loved to go to parties during the day as much as Maugham,[15] and the Riviera colony – especially during its last glittering heyday in the thirties – was nothing if not gossipy and sociable.

Maugham, however, missed the intimate news of the London literary world, and more than gossip he relished good conversation with the intelligent and witty. His guest list thus favoured those who could enliven his table with talk of art and literature: the erudite Raymond Mortimer, the Cambridge don George Rylands, Columbia University professor of philosophy Irwin Edman, the director of the Museum of Modern Art Monroe Wheeler, art historian Kenneth Clark, or painter Gerald Kelly. These, and a host of other writers, politicians, artists, and scholars, were there to entertain Maugham every bit as much as he was entertaining them.

One of the greatest attractions of the Villa Mauresque for its owner was that it was an arena in which to confront the world largely on his own terms. Though he moved frequently in literary and social circles on both sides of the Atlantic, his stutter and shyness prevented him ever being entirely at ease in a milieu in which the settings and rules were made by others. At Cap Ferrat, however, he was on his own territory and could create his own environment, dictate his own schedule, and subtly stage-manage the events of the day. He worked when he wanted, visited with his guests for as long as he wished, and left them when he was exhausted or bored. He was much more than merely 'the gentleman in the parlour', but here he had a freedom and control of his life matched only by that which he had known on his travels.

For some of Maugham's guests the guiding hand was a bit too obvious and therefore unnerving. Peter Quennell found him 'a severe host', as did Kenneth Clark, for whom a visit to the villa was 'rather a strain'. 'Mr Maugham was exceedingly kind to us,' he wrote, 'and we grew to have a genuine affection for him, so it sounds ungrateful to say that we always left the Villa Mauresque with feelings of relief.'[16] For the large majority, however, Maugham was a gracious and generous host who provided an island of cultivated civility in an increasingly troubled world. Ann Fleming, for example, recalled the 'haven of comfort, good food, beauty and entertaining talk'.[17] And Beverley Nichols, despite his anger over Maugham's characterization of Syrie, has referred to 'interludes of high comedy and instances of simple kindliness. And there were magic moments, in the cleansing sunlight, against the still untainted sea, when he gathered us around him and told us stories by which, when all is said and done, he is best remembered.'[18]

While Maugham saw that life at the Villa Mauresque was luxurious and civilized, much of the vitality in the early years was provided by Gerald Haxton. He mixed the cocktails and arranged the sailing parties, and he could be counted on to enliven occasions dampened by Maugham's reticence. Once in the thirties he won £1000 in the casino and treated the whole houseful of guests to a roaring party at the Plage in Monte Carlo. At times, he seemed to be a catalyst, almost a Shakespearian fool goading his master with an iconoclastic barb. Arthur Marshall, for example, recalled a luncheon attended by G. B. Stern, H. G. Wells, and the writer Elizabeth Russell. As the meal began, Maugham attempted to begin a conversation by observing genially: 'I've just had a h-h-hot bath.' Haxton, having downed a copious quantity of gin, 'gave a snort of disgust at this banality, leant forward and said loudly and clearly, "and did you masturbate?" A terrible silence fell as we scooped up our avocados. But Willie had been asked a question, and questions must be answered, if with difficulty. There were some anguished facial contortions and finger snappings, which sometimes helped, and then came, "As it h-h-happens, n-n-n-n-no." We ate on.'[19]

Though Haxton might make this kind of outrageous remark, there was never a homosexual ambience about the Villa Mauresque. Visitors were aware that Maugham and his companion were lovers, but there was no open homosexual talk and any sexual activities were conducted with discretion. Maugham strove to be respectable, and the occasional guest who attempted some sort of liaison or to bring a casual pickup to the house was immediately asked to leave. The promiscuous Gerald, who had always been much more familiar with the world of procurers and brothels, made forays into Nice for casual sexual encounters, but it was always in the face of Maugham's disapproval. Some intimate visitors like Robin or Beverley Nichols might occasionally witness Gerald's misdemeanours, but few others knew of any sexual activity.

Maugham's own liaisons were of the sort to arouse less suspicion, and some of the attractive young writers who found their way to the Mauresque became his lovers. One such individual was the handsome young journalist Godfrey Winn (1908–71), whom Maugham met in 1928 at a bridge foursome at the London home of Ned Lathom. Following the publication of his first novel, *Dreams Fade*, Winn, who had a strong feminine streak, became a journalist and was soon earning £10,000 a year writing mawkish pieces with titles like 'Do We Understand Our Parents?', 'The Girl That I Marry', and 'Have We Failed the Dead?' for *Woman* and *Woman and Home*. Though ostentatious, naïvely enthusiastic, and absurdly snobbish, Winn was an excellent tennis player, having won the South of England Championship at the age of thirteen. He was also a proficient bridge player, and these two latter qualities, together with his boyish good looks, earned him numerous invitations to the Villa Mauresque in the thirties.

Maugham eventually tired of this relationship, though it served Winn's purpose to maintain for the rest of his life that the famous writer was his mentor and teacher. In 1941, however, Maugham included a chapter in the American edition of *Strictly Personal* that described Winn as 'George Potter', a novelist who was a delightful house guest but who would slip away several hours each day to write articles for women's magazines:

> He was a colossal success. It was sentimental slush that he wrote, vulgar, snobbish, shatteringly moral and blatantly religious; but the public ate it. George Potter became the best-known journalist in England. His following among servant girls, manicurists, stenographers and shop assistants was immense. He increased its circulation, it was currently reported, by eighty thousand a day. In due course another paper with an even larger circulation lured him into its service, and he was now probably the highest paid journalist in Britain.[20]

The chapter about 'Potter' was deleted from the Heinemann edition in Britain for fear of a possible libel action, and Winn continued to increase his readership and his fortune. In 1967 he bought Maugham's antique Spanish writing table, he said, to give him encouragement and confidence.

Maugham had also developed a friendship in the twenties with another novelist-journalist, Beverley Nichols. Like Winn, Nichols wrote for the popular press and the pair became rivals of a sort for the same sort of audience, though among Nichols's sixty books are several substantial works – for example, *Cry Havoc* and *Verdict on India*. Attracted by his youthful energy, Maugham once invited Nichols to tour the world with him. Though he did not become the older man's travelling companion, Nichols frequently visited Cap Ferrat and maintained a friendship with Maugham almost until the publication of 'Looking Back' in 1962. Over the years they exchanged a warm correspondence, and Maugham would return comments on the latest book sent him by Nichols.

In 1928 Maugham began a much more meaningful relationship with Alan Frank Searle, one which would deepen and last until the day he died. The son of a London tailor, Searle had grown up in Bermondsey, and when Maugham met him he was twenty-three and strikingly handsome – with fine features, a slender physique, and dark curly hair. He had by then become a friend of Lytton Strachey, and his encounter with Maugham came about when a mutual friend called at six in the evening to invite him to an eight o'clock dinner. Immediately attracted to the shy young man, Maugham asked him what he wanted out of life. When Searle replied 'travel and adventure', the author invited him to go along to France. Searle's family, disapproving of the relationship, was horrified by the prospect of his becoming the companion of an ageing homosexual writer, but Searle went. He rarely saw his family again.

Maugham's relationship with Searle became intimate, and the young man not only frequently visited the Villa Mauresque but also accompanied Maugham on jaunts to Munich for the carnival and opera. His gentle and sensitive temperament made him apprehensive in the presence of the voluble and more aggressive Haxton, and there was always a tension between them. An indication of the closeness of Maugham's relationship with Searle is his suggestion to Barbara Back that she include her comments about Haxton in letters from Searle, because unlike his other correspondence they would be read only by himself. Haxton, however, was secure in his position at the Villa Mauresque, and Searle was left to handle Maugham's affairs in England as a quasi-secretary from about 1929 to 1945, when he joined the author in the United States.

By the late twenties, when Maugham was divorced and had moved into his villa, the passion of his relationship with Haxton had been largely extinguished. It seems that the cooling began first in the younger man, and the only lines of poetry that the author ever put into print are a rather poor verse attributed to 1929 in *A Writer's Notebook* and very likely directed to Haxton:

I could not bear the thought that I should ever lose you
Or that our lives might ever be disjoined,
But yet I knew that in your wanton heart
There was for me nor love nor tenderness.
To many another I saw you give unwanted kisses,
But when I sought to break the chain that bound me
You twined your slim soft arms about my neck
And would not let me go.
Humbly I thanked you when you feigned to love me.
I bought your grudging lips for gold.
And now the love I thought would last till death is dead.
Ah, where is that high power that you had
To make the heavens golden with a smile
Or with a careless word to cloud the summer day?
In weariness, and not in death or parting, is
The bitterness of love. Spent is my passion
Like a river dried up by the sun's fierce rays.
I look into my empty heart and shrink dismayed:
My soul is like a desert, and the wild wind blows
In its silent, barren spaces.
The night-birds build their nests amid the tombs
Of kings. My eyes rest on you sadly. I regret
My pain, my rapture, my anguish and my bliss.[21]

By 1933 Maugham confided to Arthur Marshall that, 'Gerald now likes the bottle more than he likes me.' If the passion had died, however, it was not replaced by indifference, and the pair remained loyal, if not faithful, to one another. Marshall recalled an occasion at Cap Ferrat when three of them were waiting to play tennis and Haxton arrived late. As he approached the court, Maugham exclaimed: 'Oh, here's Master Hackey.' It was said, observed Marshall, with a touching warmth and affection, as if one were talking about a child.[22]

Frederic Raphael has shrewdly pointed out that Maugham's settling along the Riviera cut him off from reality – at least so far as England was concerned. His most vivid experience of London had been the first fifteen years of the century and for the remainder of his life he remained emphatically Edwardian. According to Vane Ivanovic, who was introduced to him at the wedding of Grace Kelly and Prince Rainier in 1956, Maugham asked him what he thought of his tail-coat and trousers and then revealed the date on the tailor's label – 1906.[23]

It is thus appropriate that the first novel that Maugham wrote in the Villa Mauresque should be a retrospective look at the literary–social life he had known in London and from which he was now distancing himself. Having long wanted to write about Sue Jones, he concluded that he could work her character into a story about writers and the world of professional literature. Completed in July 1929, *Cakes and Ale* became the author's favourite book because of the ease and pleasure of its creation, though he agreed with the general opinion that *Of Human Bondage* would remain his most important work.

Maugham had also wanted to write a satiric novel about the pretensions and superficiality of London's literary–social milieu, and it was a master stroke to use the Sue Jones/Rosie figure as a foil. Employing the narrative persona of Willie Ashenden with consummate ease, he describes a childhood in Blackstable when he came to know Rosie and her husband, the novelist Edward Driffield. In the narrow provincial society of the town and in the home of Ashenden's uncle, the spontaneity and unconventionality of the Driffields and their friend Lord George Kemp is shocking. When the Driffields suddenly bolt, Ashenden loses touch until he becomes a medical student in Edwardian London. Here, under the guiding hand of the lion-hunting Mrs Barton Trafford, the novelist becomes famous, while Ashenden has an affair with the delightful but promiscuous Rosie. Driffield gradually becomes absorbed by the literary milieu and when he loses the animal high-spiritedness of his younger days, Rosie runs off to America with Lord George Kemp.

As Ashenden tells the story in the present, his help is being solicited by Driffield's second wife and a writer, Alroy Kear, to put together an expurgated biography of the famous author. Maugham's novel has a double title, and 'the skeleton in the cupboard' is Rosie, who in this authorized life must somehow be explained away as a destructive influence on Driffield's career. The spirit of the Shakespearian allusion in the other half of Maugham's title, however, applies to her equally, and the truth is that Driffield did his best work when he was part of her life-enhancing world. It is Rosie (aided by Lord George Kemp) who is the counterpart in spirit to Maria, Sir Toby Belch, and Sir Andrew Aguecheek and who is the author's way of saying, 'Dost thou think, because thou art virtuous, there shall be no more cakes and ale?' to the Malvolios of the novel: Mrs Barton Trafford, Amy Driffield, and Alroy Kear.

Rosie is one of the most delightful heroines in twentieth-century literature, and the most fully realized of a line of Maugham characters beginning with Liza, through Bertha Craddock, Sally Athelny, Betty Welldon-Burns, to Suzanne Rouvier (*The Razor's Edge*). Sharing their fullness of life, a radiant exuberance and energy, she is the most liberated of all Maugham's creations. Self-possessed and not wracked by self-consciousness, she is free from all social pressures to act in a prescribed fashion. She asks to be accepted as she is, not trapped in an illusion imposed by someone else. Even at the end, as a seventy-year-old widow she is a vibrant and lively woman.

Cakes and Ale remains both a skilfully crafted study of freedom and vitality and a delicious satire about literary poseurs. When it appeared in England on 29 September 1930, however, it immediately became the most discussed, attacked, and defended piece of contemporary fiction because of its caustic sketches of a number of fixtures of the English literary scene. Mrs Barton Trafford and her husband were thinly disguised portraits of the Sidney Colvins, and the verbose, pompous critic Allgood Newton was based on Sir Edmund Gosse. Jasper Gibbons, a poet first championed and then dropped by Mrs Barton Trafford, is Stephen Phillips, whose reputation as a poet rose and fell equally dramatically. Among the minor sketches are undoubtedly other figures recognizable to those intimately aware of Edwardian London's world of letters.

The controversy about *Cakes and Ale* in 1930, however, surrounded two of its major characters: Edward Driffield and Alroy Kear. In the ageing novelist many people were convinced that they saw Thomas Hardy, the last of the great Victorian writers, who had died just two years earlier. Maugham confessed to Paul Dottin that the veneration following Hardy's funeral had given him the idea of treating the Grand-Old-Man-of-English-Letters syndrome,[24] and there is recently disclosed evidence that he used some outward details of Hardy's life at Max Gate which he gleaned from a friend who had visited the old writer in the company of Siegfried Sassoon.[25]

Strongly criticized by a number of reviewers for attacking one of the country's greatest novelists, Maugham defended himself by arguing that he had met Hardy only once and that he could not remember much about the encounter. Indeed Driffield appears to be a composite portrait, with characteristics of Hardy, but also H. G. Wells, and Joseph Conrad, among others. Moreover, the specific traits are secondary to the effective portrayal of a creative artist who becomes trapped and stifled by being made into a social figure.

While the propriety of the possible use of Hardy was being discussed by reviewers and columnists, there was a much more intense and dramatic stir spreading through London clubs and literary gatherings. To anyone familiar with the world of English letters it was clear that the sycophantic and absurd Alroy Kear was based on Hugh Walpole. When Frank Swinnerton had read the first page, he exclaimed 'Good heavens! Hugh!' and the resemblance was equally and painfully obvious to Walpole himself, who read the book in proof as a member of the Book Society selection committee. He went to a theatre, he recorded in his journal, 'then home and, half-undressed sitting on my bed, picked up idly Maugham's *Cakes and Ale*. Read on with increasing horror. Unmistakable portrait of myself. Never slept.'[26] At four o'clock in the morning he telephoned Alexander Frere of Heinemann to demand that it not be published, and the next day at the Reform Club he was nearly hysterical when he confronted Frere, Arnold Bennett, and Frank Swinnerton. Even a month later he was still intensely agitated, as he revealed to his friend Virginia Woolf, who wrote to her sister about his being 'most cruelly maliciously at the same time unmistakably and amusingly caricatured':

He almost wept in front of Hilda Matheson, Vita and Clive, in telling us. And he couldn't stop. Whenever we changed the conversation he went back. 'There are things in it that nobody knows but Willie and myself' he said. 'There are little things that make me shudder. And that man has been my dearest friend for 20 years. And now I'm the laughing stock of London. And he writes to say he didn't mean it for me.' 'Oh but he undoubtedly did that' said Vita cheerfully. 'And he might have been jugged' said Hugh. 'You don't know the kind of life that Willie has led. I do. I could put him in a book. But then I call it a dastardly thing to do.' And so on, round and round, round and round, like a dog with a tin on its tail, till it was half past 12. Then he said it was all in the strictest confidence, and he had told no one else. But of course, Clive met Christabel next night, and Christabel had met Hugh that afternoon and had been ever so much more tactful than Vita.[27]

As soon as Walpole had begun to protest to Frere and others, a campaign was begun by J. B. Priestley, a mutual friend of Walpole and Maugham, to convince him that the portrait was really of John Drinkwater. The latter apparently did believe that he had been the target, and for a while London was amused by the story that Walpole had gone on a walking tour of the Lake District to forget *Cakes and Ale* and ran into Drinkwater who was there for the same purpose.

When Walpole confronted Maugham about the matter he received a disingenuous letter in reply, claiming that it had never occurred to Maugham that there was any resemblance between Kear and him, and that Gilbert Frankau, E. F. Benson, or Stephen McKenna could just as well recognize themselves. Kear, argued Maugham, was made up of a dozen people, and the greatest part came from Maugham himself. Walpole briefly acknowledged the letter, signing it ironically: 'Alroy Maugham Walpole'.

After Walpole's death Maugham admitted that he had indeed been the original of Alroy Kear, and that there were so many similarities that anyone in their circle would identify him. As ridiculous as Kear was painted, no one then or since has ever denied the accuracy of the portrait; any questions were about the propriety of a fellow author being so pilloried. Moreover, the two writers had been friends for two decades, a friendship which their correspondence suggests was at one time very warm. Maugham addressed him as 'My dear Hugh', variously praising his Russian book *The Secret City* and congratulating him on his successful lecture tour of the United States. In the early twenties Maugham reproached Compton Mackenzie for not taking literature as seriously as Walpole.

Walpole's diary for 20 October 1917 recorded a 'delightful lunch with Willie Maugham. He is most amusing,'[28] and the following June he noted that 'Willie at his nicest as he always is with me.'[29] Walpole was also a homosexual, and his reference to Woolf about the danger of Maugham's being 'jugged' for 'the kind of life [he] has led' suggests that he travelled in the same homosexual circles, though to what degree will never be known. What, then, lay behind Maugham's crucifixion of his friend beyond the obvious fact that Walpole was a perfect target for anyone writing a satire about self-promoting authors? Notorious for such habits as entertaining critics at lunch and making lists of the friends he liked most, he was eminently a candidate for caricature.

Maugham's antipathy to Walpole, however, was more complex and personal. There were a curious number of parallels in their lives – both had been raised by clerics (Walpole's father was a bishop, George Henry *Somerset* Walpole), were old boys of King's School, art collectors, highly successful writers, and homosexuals – but there were enough differences of a sort to arouse Maugham's jealousy and disdain. Walpole was tall and imposing, an unmistakable public presence; Maugham was always conscious of his shortness. The outgoing Walpole was a fluent speaker and made a number of successful lecture tours of the United States; the reticent Maugham had to contend with a stutter, and never gave speeches. Walpole had been in Russia during the First

World War, had got several books out of it, and had been rewarded with the OBE. Maugham, whose work had been far more important and dangerous, was constrained by the Official Secrets Act to publish only the few stories which appeared in *Ashenden*, and received no public recognition.

Though virtually unread today, Walpole had an enormous following in the twenties and was being treated as a modern Dickens or Trollope. While Maugham was also popular, most critics described him as merely a competent craftsman, though he knew that his writing was superior to that of Walpole. Compton Mackenzie, for example, wrote an article in *Vanity Fair* nominating Walpole as the likeliest among contemporary writers to become the Grand Old Man of English Letters. Its appearance in 1929, while Maugham was working on *Cakes and Ale*, must have served as a red flag.

To this contempt for Walpole as a writer must be added the possibility that Maugham had reason to dislike the man. According to Raymond Mortimer, Maugham once confided that this attack was a response to an injury Walpole once did to one of Maugham's friends, a discreditable act that he found unforgivable. Though Maugham did not disclose details, this episode may well be Walpole's graceless treatment of Maugham's friend Gerald Kelly. The painter had done portraits of Walpole from 1914 on but, as Kelly said, 'somehow, somewhere, Hugh learned that I was a photographic painter, academic in the worst sense of that word, and surely no man of sensibility could tolerate my pompous productions. So Hugh was in a fix, and, bless him, how clumsy he was!' Not only did Walpole finally let Kelly know that he no longer wanted a portrait by him, he asked Kelly to approach Augustus John to do one instead.[30] Staunchly loyal to Kelly, Maugham found this action highly offensive, perhaps accounting for the emphasis on Kear's dropping of old friends as his public reputation grows.

Surprisingly, Maugham and Walpole continued to have a friendship of sorts after *Cakes and Ale*, with Walpole forwarding his latest books and Maugham responding with warm praise. When Walpole was knighted in 1937 Maugham sent a telegram of congratulations, and in 1940 he contributed to a wartime fund-raising campaign in which Walpole was active. It took a long time for Walpole to recover from the humiliation of *Cakes and Ale*, but, as he told Hector Bolitho, 'You know, he wrote me such a kind letter afterwards – and when I felt resentful, I reminded myself of his kindness to young writers. Always kind to them, so I have tried to remember this when anyone mentions him.'[31] The closest he came to a reply in kind can be found in his novel

John Cornelius (1937), where he portrayed Maugham as Archie Bertrand, a cynical writer who professes disbelief in mankind's virtues: love, loyalty, and sincerity. The most acerbic reply to Maugham came, however, from an unexpected source.

Early in 1931 Farrar and Rinehart brought out a book called *Gin and Bitters* in the United States. Written by 'A. Riposte', the title was an unmistakable parody of *Cakes and Ale* and the protagonist, a decadent ageing writer named 'Leverson Hurle', a savage attack on Maugham. Badly written and frequently remote from the facts of Maugham's life, it was initially suspected of having been written by Walpole, though he is represented in the novel as an insignificant author called 'Polehue'.

Gin and Bitters was scheduled to be published in Great Britain as *Full Circle* by Martin Secker, but in March 1931, Walpole wrote to Maugham to protest that he was not the author, and by April he had read it and pronounced it a 'foul' attack. It would, he argued, create a nasty public uproar when it appeared in England, and he urged Maugham to take legal action. Charles Evans, of Heinemann, was also concerned about the damage that *Full Circle* might do to one of his most illustrious authors, and he sought the advice of Frederic Maugham. Though claiming to be indifferent to the attack, Maugham agreed to Evans's suggestion that British publishers be warned against it. Secker nevertheless released the book, and in early October 1931 a writ of libel and an injunction preventing distribution of further copies was issued in Maugham's name. The book was withdrawn, and copies are now collector's items.

In the midst of the *Full Circle* controversy, Walpole argued publicly and emphatically that it was 'nauseating', that Maugham had been persuaded under duress to prevent its publication, and that he was not defending Maugham merely to be seen turning the other cheek. It was subsequently revealed that the author was an American writer, Elinor Mordaunt, who had never met either Walpole or Maugham.

Mordaunt was a friend of Thomas Hardy's widow, however, and it is here that one can find the motivation for *Full Circle*. As Robert Gittings and Jo Manson have recently demonstrated so persuasively in *The Second Mrs Hardy*, Florence Hardy, ignored in the talk of her husband and Walpole, suffered as much from *Cakes and Ale* as anyone. Though her character was nothing like that of Amy Driffield, there were enough external similarities in her life and home to allow her to feel that she was being mercilessly lampooned. 'There are moments', she lamented, 'when I want to shake my fists at the sky, or shriek aloud in rage.'[32] This pain, communicated to Mordaunt, almost certainly inspired *Full Circle*.

220

With the appearance of *Cakes and Ale*, Frank Swinnerton observed: 'Maugham's reputation as a novelist had no immediate parallels. Within a few months of its publication all active novel-writers were considerably his juniors.'[33] The day after the release of his novel, Maugham enjoyed another, and much less controversial, success with his play *The Breadwinner*, his most emphatic depiction of revolt from the marriage contract. Echoing the early chapters of *The Moon and Sixpence*, it deals with a middle-aged businessman who allows his company to go bankrupt and then abandons his wife and children to escape to America. Anticipating the rejection of conventional values in *The Razor's Edge*, the protagonist is tired of the social routine, of drudgery to provide luxuries for his unloving, unfaithful wife, and his two superficial children.

Presented at London's Vaudeville Theatre, the cast of *The Breadwinner* included Ronald Squire in the lead, with Marie Lohr, Peggy Ashcroft, and Jack Hawkins, and it enjoyed a run of 158 performances. Maugham attended rehearsals in September 1930, where he was characteristically unobtrusive and, according to Hawkins, 'scrupulously polite and courteous'. One particular act of generosity remained a vivid memory, as the actor recollected years later.

Maugham had insisted on a pre-London run and on the opening night in Eastbourne the director harshly criticized the young Margaret Hood, who was playing with an experienced West End company for the first time in her career. Reduced to tears, she remained sobbing in the dressing-room while the rest of the cast went off to an opening night dinner party arranged by the author:

> While we were all sipping our aperitifs, Maugham suddenly asked in his strange stammering voice: 'Wh-where's the little girl?'
> Somebody said: 'I think she's still at the theatre.'
> 'Wh-why?'
> 'She was a little upset.'
> Maugham frowned and immediately sent his chauffeur to collect Maggie, and before she had arrived he asked the director what had upset her. The man admitted he had given her a roasting, and Maugham, putting on his most chilling, mandarin face, said that if he interfered with the cast again, the management would lose the performing rights of the play.
> Maggie arrived, red-eyed and miserable, but Willie placed her on his right at the dinner table, and spent the rest of the evening as though she was the leading lady.[34]

This act of sensitivity and kindness was a reprise of Maugham's treatment of Violet Hunt, and though rarely given the proper emphasis, they were hardly isolated occurrences in Maugham's life. His friend G. B. Stern recalled, for example, an occasion when the employee of a celebrity sat alone, shy and unhappy in a room full of glittering people who ignored her while they talked of their successes and busy social lives. After a while, a dark, quiet man joined her from across the room and they spent the evening talking about theatre, during which, encouraged by his attention, she grew animated about contemporary drama. Only at the end did she realize that she had been telling W. S. Maugham how to write plays, though his comment that 'it was most interesting; I enjoyed it very much indeed,' persuaded her that his pleasure was genuine.

Stern has also described how she and her secretary, Moira Tighe, were once staying at Cap Ferrat, and Tighe, an excellent golfer, played with a properly respectful Maugham. One day he suggested that she play with another writer who was a much better golfer but who, unknown to him, had earlier treated her with disdain. When she betrayed a wound in declining the invitation, Maugham commented gently: 'He hasn't very good manners, has he, Tiger?' It was, observed Stern, a beautiful piece of manipulative surgery, 'his tone drawing her into the circle of his real intimates who *had* good manners, and shutting [the other writer] well outside.'[35]

Cathleen Nesbitt recalled an opening night when she had gone back to the stage too soon after the birth of her first child and suddenly dried up in the middle of the first act. Having to be audibly prompted by the stage-manager, she was badly frightened and humiliated. When she got back to her dressing-room, she said, 'I found Maugham at the door – he who *never* came backstage at any first night. He had slipped through the pass door – and comforted me most tactfully, saying "that little slip in Act One only made you give a better performance all through the evening; you moved me very much," etc., etc. But I was so touched and happy at his thoughtfulness and kindness that instead of bursting into tears when my friends arrived to console me for my misfortune, I was able to laugh.'[36]

Many others could remember acts of generosity. Arthur Marshall told me about first visiting the Villa Mauresque with George Rylands and Victor Rothschild and realizing that there was no reason why Maugham should invite to luncheon three young men he really did not know well. The following Christmas, a parcel arrived containing a copy of *Altogether* inscribed: 'To Arthur Marshall from his good friend

W. Somerset Maugham.' Raymond Marriott has recounted how Maugham took him, then a young and unknown writer, to the Garrick Club and treated him as an equal in a meeting with H. G. Wells. After a visit to the Villa Mauresque, Marriott and his friend George Bullock left with 'a weighty suitcase' of books given them by their host. When the youthful David Pryce-Jones accompanied his father, Alan, a friend of Maugham, to Cap Ferrat after the Second World War, the author was particularly kind, asking about what young people thought of his books, and giving him a departing gift of an inscribed copy of *Don Fernando*.

When Frederic Raphael, then a neophyte writer, visited Maugham he was treated with congenial and unpatronizing kindness. 'What makes it memorable', he says, 'is that he behaved as if we were two fellow writers; I cannot think of a nicer or more encouraging attitude to take to a young and unpublished nobody.'[37] Similarly, Ludovic Kennedy recalled a luncheon party comprising the Kenneth Clarks, T. S. Eliot, Henry Moore, John Hayward, Alan Searle, and Maugham. As they went to the table, Maugham and Kennedy went from the drawing-room last, and Maugham observed: 'You and I are writers, and as such must go in last.' 'Including me with him', says Kennedy, 'was unexpected and nice.'[38]

Throughout his life Maugham had a special sensitivity to young writers struggling to establish themselves. When Roderick Cameron's second book, *Equator Farm*, was initially rejected by Heinemann, Maugham persuaded Alexander Frere to reconsider and it was published. The Canadian poet Ralph Gustafson was little known when he became acquainted with Maugham in the United States during the Second World War, but Maugham treated him as an equal, discussing Gustafson's work and offering warm encouragement. Among numerous other writers whose careers Maugham encouraged in some way were: Louis Wilkinson, Godfrey Winn, Beverley Nichols, Hector Bolitho, Karl Pfeiffer, Klaus Jonas, Glenway Wescott, and Alec Waugh, who commented: 'I always felt that he was the one person in the world who could completely understand me.'[39] And, of course, he always took a lively and supportive interest in the work of his nephew, as well as that of his niece Kitty, whose death cut short a promising career.

Writing of Maugham in 1927, Beverley Nichols referred to 'furtive charities' and 'shy benevolences',[40] and he did indeed frequently offer more than simply encouragement and advice to others. In the forties and fifties, when the young writer George Bullock was suffering from tuberculosis, Maugham regularly paid for necessary medical supplies and visits to a sanatorium. Throughout the Second World War he sent Edward Marsh, the shrewd editor of a number of his books, food parcels which were welcome gifts in the austerity of wartime rationing. When George Rylands was soliciting funds for the Cambridge Arts Theatre, Maugham replied, 'You know that I can refuse you nothing,' and sent a cheque for £300.

Rebecca West told of an occasion when G. B. Stern and Louis Golding were collecting money to assist Norman Douglas when he was living in Italy in straitened circumstances. Maugham observed that the group of young writers could hardly afford to contribute to such a fund, and decided to send sufficient money discreetly through a mutual friend so that Douglas would never know of the gift. The ageing writer, commented Maugham, had a tendency to attack anyone to whom he owed any sort of gratitude. This story has been questioned by some who knew of Douglas's situation, but West had written about the episode as early as 1935, when, in an article, she disguised the circumstances by referring to the central character as a great musician. There she reported that Maugham's donation absolved the others from making any contribution.[41]

John Sutro, who first met Maugham at the home of his uncle Alfred, recalled a similar act of anonymous generosity. Maugham had heard from his publisher that Richard Aldington, whose work he admired though he knew him only slightly, was living in 'lonely bitterness and near poverty' in central France. Aware that the writer's pride and obstinacy would prevent his accepting a direct gift, Maugham arranged for Heinemann to commission a book from Aldington, the advance for which Maugham would pay. He then drove a considerable distance across the country to pay his respects, but Aldington, not fooled by the plan, rejected it as charity.[42]

How can these acts of kindness and generosity, hardly rare in Maugham's life, be reconciled with his reputation as a mean and vindictive man? In part, of course, his reputation did not accurately reflect the real man, coming as it did from the apparent cynicism and detachment of his literary persona and the sharp wit of his public utterances. His breach of manners in attacking his former wife in his memoirs and his ugly public quarrel with his daughter gave him a reputation for malice which belied the behaviour of the larger other part of his very long life.

There is no doubt that Maugham could at times be very sharp-tongued, especially when angered, and over the years a number of people smarted from his sarcasm. More often than not, however, he was exercising his wit, unaware of how much he might be inflicting a wound. In *Of Human Bondage* he described how the young Philip's wit hurt people more than he realized and how surprised he was when his victims reacted with hostility. Maugham had come to maturity in an age and in a milieu which placed a high value on a quick and incisive wit, and, according to George Rylands, his remarks were no more malicious than those of Lytton Strachey and many others of the Bloomsbury Group. And, one might add, writers like Rebecca West, D. H. Lawrence, and Evelyn Waugh. 'Malice', notes Rylands, 'always seems too strong a word for what clever, amusing, and delightful writers do in conversation.'[43] As Frederic Raphael has pointed out, however, Maugham never 'quite realized that those who have no gift for clever remarks find it difficult to distinguish aesthetically between a neat phrase and a wounding one'.[44]

At times Maugham's remarks were certainly misinterpreted, often because malice makes for more delicious gossip and livelier memoirs. One of his most infamous comments, quoted repeatedly over the years, concerns his chance meeting with Syrie in the Dorchester Hotel in the summer of 1940. Syrie, the story goes, was desperately afraid of being torpedoed and asked her ex-husband what she should do if the ship went down. Maugham replied that he had only one piece of advice and that was: 'Swallow, Syrie, just sw-swallow.' The terrified woman, it is said, began to weep.

This is a marvellous story of calculated cruelty until one remembers that Maugham had just spent three weeks on a coal boat making a hazardous journey from Cannes to England. As revealed in *Strictly Personal*, published in 1941, he knew that if the ship were sunk everyone would perish, and he asked a medical friend the least painful way to drown. 'Don't struggle,' the doctor replied. 'Open your mouth, and the water pouring into your throat will bring on unconsciousness in less than a minute.'[45] Maugham was thus simply offering Syrie the same practical advice, though it was perhaps too coldly scientific for someone in a state of extreme anxiety.

Similarly, there is the frequently told story of Maugham receiving the news of Syrie's death in 1955 while at the bridge table and immediately drumming his fingers and singing: 'No more alimony. Tralala. No more alimony.' It would have been a delightfully cynical moment in one of his plays like *Smith* or *Our Betters*, but the reality is that he was informed in private one morning by a telegram from his daughter.

Whenever Maugham's wit took on a rapier's sharpness it was directed at people who were pretentious, cruel, exploitative, or abusive of a position of power and luxury. For example, Robin Maugham recounts the time that he and his uncle were awaiting their car outside a London hotel when an over-dressed, *diamanté*, heavily made-up woman, accompanied by a handsome young gigolo, suddenly rushed up to Willie to say how divine it was to see him again. Maugham first looked at her blankly, and then commented that he was awfully sorry to hear that she had lost every penny of her money. The woman reacted as if stung, saying that there must be some mistake, and the young man's face dropped. When she swept frostily away Maugham confessed to his nephew that he had no idea who the woman was but he had made his remark 'Be-because she was obviously a tiresome bitch, and she looked too pleased with herself.'[46] The point of the story is that Maugham had been offended by the pretensions of the woman, someone with affluence and power, who therefore presumed that it entitled her to greet him as an intimate friend.

While Maugham could devastate anyone who he felt had ulterior motives or who was trying to use him, he was sensitive and generous to those who were sincere and unpretentious. Karl Pfeiffer, for example, recalled dining with him in New York during the Second World War when the waiter brought a bottle of wine with a note explaining that it was from an admirer of his writing. When he was told that, rather than waiting for an invitation to join them, the individual had left, he was so touched by the act of unqualified kindness that he took great pains to discover his name and write to him.[47]

'Maugham learned', explained Hector Bolitho, 'to be gentle with people when he was first certain of their integrity, and sure they would not hurt him . . . Maugham could be spontaneously generous when he was sure of himself.'[48] In other words, when confronted with guileless honesty and warmth, he could let his own guard drop and respond with a warmth often masked when he confronted a more threatening world. In Moira Tighe's words, 'there is no denying that Maugham could sometimes be cruel to those well-insulated by wealth and position, but to many "small" people like myself with whom he came into contact he was goodness itself.'[49]

Maugham's response to people is perfectly illustrated in his relationship with Fred Bason, a little cockney bookseller whom he first met in the late twenties. Bason had grown up in the slum district of Walworth and from being a barrow-boy had opened his own small bookshop. An avid collector of autographs, Bason came to know a number of famous writers, who were amused by this chirpy cockney sparrow and his view of life from the streets of south London. Later he came to enjoy a strange kind of celebrity, writing naïvely enthusiastic articles for the annual *Saturday Book* and several volumes of diaries.

Bason came to know Maugham when he wrote to the author to say that *The Unknown* was 'lousy', and received a warm and amiable response. Maugham was amused by his honest bluntness and his love of books. As well, having long had in mind another London slum novel, Maugham thought that the young cockney would be a useful entry into the life of Walworth, and so he visited Bason in his own environs. He had tea with his parents on several occasions and in 1931 accompanied Bason to the South London Palace to see an old-fashioned London music-hall variety show. At other times Maugham asked his advice on cockney speech and on patterns of behaviour in south London.

For five years in the early thirties, Maugham visited Bason on his biannual visits to London, and sent him a number of letters and a great many postcards from various points in Europe. As well, he assisted Bason financially by ordering a number of books from him and by autographing a large number of copies of his own works, which instantly trebled their value. Once, in 1929, he signed fourteen first editions, putting in especially lengthy inscriptions, for Bason to sell. Another time, Maugham bet his young friend that he could not spend a week in Paris on less than £5, and when Bason returned with a few shillings to spare he was rewarded with an additional fiver. Bason had literary ambitions, and Maugham read and commented on one of his plays, a number of short stories, an article, and a bibliography of Maugham's writings to which he contributed a preface. On one of Maugham's visits, he brought Bason's father a pair of boots he no longer wanted, and later he sent £5 so that Bason's ailing mother could go to the country for a couple of weeks. Bason and his mother were also sent tickets for the opening nights of both the dramatization of *The Painted Veil* and *For Services Rendered*.

Bason enjoyed his friendship with what he gushingly called 'truly a great man',[50] drawing considerable benefit from it, but he did not know when to stop asking for more. As time went by, Maugham was increasingly pressed to sign piles of books – with Bason dictating what he should inscribe – which the young cockney then sold to American dealers. At one point, he seems to have suggested that he and the author do a regular business in signed Maugham copies, a practice Maugham found discreditable. Furthermore, Maugham had commissioned Bason to sell six copies of the first edition of *A Man of*

Honour and was angered to discover that the bookseller had retained the money as capital for his store rather than depositing it into Maugham's bank. When Bason did not have the money on hand, Maugham allowed him to repay it in instalments.

Finally, Bason had been permitted to explore the possibility of selling Maugham's manuscripts, the proceeds of which the author intended to use to found a literary prize for young writers. He arranged with an American dealer to sell the manuscripts for £10,000 providing Maugham would write a preface announcing the purpose of the sale and that the purchaser would be named co-founder of the prize. Appalled by the tastelessness of the proposal, Maugham told Bason that he did not believe that he was the right person to be handling his manuscripts. When Bason wrote to object to his removal, Maugham was sharply critical of his deception over *A Man of Honour* and of his assumption that he had a right to Maugham's generosity. Their friendship ended at this point in 1936, though Maugham always replied to the letters Bason sent in his attempt to continue their relationship.

Maugham's reaction to Bason was characteristic. When approached by a young, ingenuous, and struggling bookseller, he responded generously and warmly. When, however, Bason began seeing the author as a lode that could be mined endlessly, Maugham was offended. Bason's actions meant that he was no longer Willie Maugham, a man whose friendship was valued for itself, but merely a celebrity with a certain currency, and Maugham hated being used. For his part, Bason maintained a pose, writing as late as 1947 that Maugham was 'the kindest celebrity it has ever been my good fortune to meet. Put me on my feet financially when I hadn't thirty shillings in the world.'[51] A few months after Maugham's death, however, he revealed a very different side in a bitter article in which he charged that Maugham's interest in him was sexual, that he got no sympathy from him when he developed a stutter during the war, and that the writer had died owing him £1000 from the abortive manuscript deal.

Cakes and Ale was written and *The Breadwinner* blocked out in 1929, a productive year in which Maugham continued to write short stories under contract to Hearst's *International Magazine*. At the end of August, Maugham and Haxton spent a fortnight taking the cure at Brides-les-Bains, but in September Maugham had his tonsils removed in London. Because of his age, the operation was more complicated than usual, and for a fortnight he could not swallow anything without agonizing pain. When he recovered, he joined Haxton in Paris and they began a trip slowly motoring down Italy, then sailing from Brindisi to Crete and Rhodes. Much of December was spent in Egypt, and Christmas Day saw them on the *Viceroy of India* on the way back to France.

The first three months of 1930 were devoted to writing *The Breadwinner*, and in late April Maugham left for a month in London, much of it spent with Barbara Back. Returning to the villa for the summer, Maugham and Haxton were given a scare when, as Maugham related to Alanson, the younger man dived into a rock off Cap Ferrat, breaking one of the vertebrae in his neck and dislocating his spine. For years there circulated a much more dramatic version of the accident in which Haxton, in a drunken stupor, dived into a neighbour's empty swimming-pool, but this story has never been verified. In any case, Haxton suffered a good deal in a plaster-cast for months, during which he was virtually an invalid. While Maugham was in London for October and November, Haxton recuperated in Paris and by the time that they drove back down to Cap Ferrat in mid-December he was anxious to rejoin his Riviera set. For some time he carried his head a little askew and was not able to brush his hair, giving him, Maugham commented playfully, the appearance of a rough, a look fancied by some people.

Except for the controversy about *Full Circle*, 1931 was a fairly quiet year for Maugham, in which he continued to produce short stories and worked on several stage productions. In February, he went to London for rehearsals of *The Circle*, being revived by the Gattis at the Vaudeville Theatre. Though directed by Raymond Massey and starring Allan Aynesworth, Nigel Playfair, Athene Seyler, and Celia Johnson, it fell victim to the depression theatre slump and folded after a modest eighty-six performances.

During the summer, Maugham had a string of guests – Frederic and his daughters Kitty and Diana, Godfrey Winn, Barbara Back, Nelson Doubleday, and Patrick Balfour – but managed to work on a dramatization of *The Painted Veil*. An American author, Bartlett Cormack, had written a stage version, but it was so poor that it took strong encouragement from Haxton for Maugham even to attempt to put it into shape. He changed a number of scenes and extensively reworked the dialogue to make it more natural, though Cormack was given full credit for the play in the programme. *The Painted Veil* opened on 19 September and enjoyed a good run of 129 nights.

Maugham spent the autumn in England, during which he completed a new novel, *The Narrow Corner*, and back at Cap Ferrat in the spring of 1932 he wrote his penultimate play, *For Services Rendered*. In the midst of the latter work, he went to Berlin for a week in February to study the latest German plays, but found them disappointing and frequented by few paying customers. May was spent in London, where Maugham lunched with Sibyl Colefax, Harold Nicolson, David Cecil, André Maurois, Diana Cooper, and Victor Cazalet. Cazalet found the party amusing and recorded in his diary that 'it was very agreeable, and they all seemed mildly interested in the economic state of the country. How fortunate to be a creative artist, devoid of interest in what goes on in the political world! Nothing except a real crash can or could upset them.'[52] So reticent was Maugham about his own writing that Cazalet could have no idea that he had just completed an intensely political play.

Maugham returned to Germany in July, motoring with Haxton through northern Italy up to Innsbruck, Munich, and Würzburg. After a month in Spain and Portugal in September and October to collect material for his Spanish book, Maugham went to London for rehearsals of *For Services Rendered*. When the play opened at the Globe Theatre on 1 November, the audience included an unusual number of distinguished authors, among whom were H. G. Wells, Beverley Nichols, A. A. Milne, Osbert Sitwell, and J. B. Priestley. What drew them that evening was a feeling that *For Services Rendered* was a new kind of Maugham drama, a serious political statement in a decade of increasingly serious economic and social problems. At the première of Shaw's *Too True to Be Good* on 13 September he had stated that the subject of his own next play was 'the same as Mr Shaw's – this muddle of a postwar world'.[53] 'I live on the Continent,' he told a reporter, 'and every moment I see the countries of Europe arming themselves to the teeth as hard as they can go, and that is why I wrote my play . . . to try to protect the new youth of today from dying in the trenches or losing five years of their lives in a war that seems almost imminent . . . The message of my play is to the youth of the world, and to whom the men spiritually, mentally, and physically wrecked by the war are just a lot of tiresome old fogies.'[54]

Maugham had treated the question of jingoism and the betrayal of those who serve in *The Hero* and *The Unknown* and had satirized war profiteers in *Home and Beauty*, but none of these attacks were as astringent as that in *For Services Rendered*. As a catalogue of the horrors of war and their effect on an English family, the play could hardly be more harrowing. A son has been blinded in action and is reduced to spending his days playing chess and tatting. Another ex-soldier, much decorated for bravery in the service of his country, finds that his garage business is failing, and when he cannot get help he kills himself. One of the three daughters has had a fiancé killed in action, and she is reduced to a state of nervous insanity. Another daughter, having succumbed to the surface glamour of a military uniform, has married an officer during the war only to discover that in peace he is coarse and drunken. The youngest daughter, unable to face the claustrophobic life in a small town from which a generation of young men has been taken, runs off with an older man whom she does not love.

Around this human wreckage is a society that Maugham portrays as blind to the price paid by such people for an inadequate peace. Worse still are those who have benefited from the war effort. In the play's most bitter passage the blind son attacks his father's shallow patriotism:

I know how dead keen we all were when the war started. Every sacrifice was worth it. We didn't say much about it because we were rather shy, but honour did mean something to us and patriotism wasn't just a word. And then, when it was all over, we did think that those of us who'd died hadn't died in vain, and those of us who were broken and shattered and knew they wouldn't be any more good in the world were buoyed up by the thought that if they'd given everything they'd given it in a great cause.

I know [now] that we were the dupes of the incompetent fools who ruled the nations. I know that we were sacrificed to their vanity, their greed and their stupidity. And the worst of it is that as far as I can tell they haven't learnt a thing. They're just as vain, they're just as greedy, they're just as stupid as they ever were. They muddle on, muddle on, and one of these days they'll muddle us all into another war. When that happens I'll tell you what I'm going to do. I'm going out into the streets and cry: Look at me; don't be a lot of damned fools; it's all bunk what they're saying to you, about honour and patriotism and glory, bunk, bunk, bunk.[55]

For Services Rendered was acted superbly by a cast which Maugham called the finest he had ever had – C. V. France, Cedric Hardwicke, Flora Robson, and Ralph Richardson – and so convinced was he that it was one of his most important dramatic statements that when he threw a party for the cast at the Savoy in November he invited, among others, Priestley, Wells, Moura Budberg, St John Ervine, E. V. Lucas, and Hugh Walpole. Many of the reviews were glowing. James Agate wrote that the play is 'a piece of dramatic carpentry of which the English theatre may justly be proud'.[56] Calling it 'unquestionably the biggest play written since Ibsen's heyday', John Pollock argued that

For Services Rendered is a play 'that every Englishman should see with joy for its greatness, and fear as its indictment of our failure, and pride that it is by an author from among ourselves'.[57]

Despite earning the admiration of a number of reviewers and serious critics, however, *For Services Rendered* did not appeal to the general public, and its run lasted for only seventy-eight performances. Moreover, it became a matter of controversy when Cecil Roberts, a novelist and journalist, publicly accused its author of being a 'defeatist', of pronouncing doom while enjoying a life of fame and luxury. In an article entitled 'Should Maugham Get Away With It?', Roberts argued that the play is subversive:

> It is worse than a bad play. It is a play of malevolent propaganda against those who live with courage and hope, who strive to contribute something to society, to protect and strengthen the laborious evolution of a civilization that, with all its drawbacks, is the highest the world has yet seen, and which offers us the decencies of life such as were unknown to our forebears.[58]

The Roberts article reflected the dismay of a large segment of the middle- and upper-class audience, which was shocked by the play's apparent unrelenting pessimism. Two days later, however, the *Daily Express* published a lengthy response from H. W. 'Bunny' Austin, an internationally known tennis player, who, at the age of twenty-six, spoke for the generation Maugham hoped to protect. *For Services Rendered*, wrote Austin, illustrates the horror, futility, and misery of war, and if Roberts wanted to talk again of patriotism and self-sacrifice he would lead more young people to destruction:

> Does he not know that it is those who still prate of patriotism, who still wish to see their own particular nation in a position of glory and unassailable power, who are heading Europe and the whole of our civilization, not only to havoc and chaos, but to destruction and utter annihilation? We must not be deceived by heroic words. We must not be blinded into thinking that war means the blare of bugles, the sound of drums, and the tramping feet of marching men which uplift our souls so much. They are not war: they are like fumes of wine which excite us and lead us in a mad hysteria to destruction.[59]

For Services Rendered was thus a play which won the emphatic endorsement of pacifists. Its anti-war sentiments led to another London production within a year of the end of the Second World War and, when Britain's National Theatre mounted it in 1979, critics rediscovered the serious side of Maugham the playwright. Calling *For Services Rendered* 'one of the most important plays of the pre-War period', Nicholas de Jongh claimed that, by rejecting the play's message, the 1932 audiences 'were also denying the single occasion when Maugham aspired to write greatly about great issues'.[60]

A few days after the opening of *For Services Rendered*, Maugham saw the publication of *The Narrow Corner*, a novel he had planned to write for a decade. One of the characters, the rogue and outcast Captain Nichols, had appeared briefly in *The Moon and Sixpence*, and another, Dr Saunders, had already been sketched in *On a Chinese Screen*. The plot revolves around the travels in the South Pacific of Saunders, an Englishman who has been struck off the medical Register for unethical practice and has subsequently built a successful practice among the native populations.

On a lugger taking Saunders home from a distant island, he meets Captain Nichols, who is transporting a young man, Fred Blake, from Australia, where he has committed a murder. When the ship stops at the island of Kanda-Meira, this trio meets the dreamer-scholar Frith, his coolly beautiful daughter Louise, and the young Erik Christessen, who as his name suggests is the personification of idealistic goodness. The handsome Blake is attracted to Christessen and they become friends, but when Christessen discovers that Blake has gone to bed with Louise he feels betrayed and kills himself. Saunders continues his travels, and Blake is lost at sea, likely pushed overboard by the disreputable Nichols.

Overhanging this story of murder, love, jealousy, and suicide is an extensive exploration of Buddhism, elements of which Maugham had introduced into *The Painted Veil* and *The Gentleman in the Parlour* and a variant of which he would use in *The Razor's Edge*. Saunders is interested in the mystical experience from the beginning, when through opium he escapes bodily ties. At the death of a Japanese pearl diver, he considers Karma and comes to the same conclusion that Maugham did in *The Gentleman in the Parlour*: it is 'a reasonable belief but an incredible' one. Through the middle section, he listens to Frith's elucidation of Eastern faith, and by the end of the novel Saunders has come to accept some of the basic Indian beliefs. The last sentence reflects a Buddhist tenet: 'He sighed a little, for whatever it was, if the richest dreams the imagination offered came true, in the end it remained nothing but an illusion.'[61]

Dr Saunders is one of Maugham's *raisonneurs*, in company with Miss Ley and Waddington, and he shares so many of the author's own beliefs that he can nearly be considered an autobiographical sketch. He regards people dispassionately, amused by their idiosyncrasies and tolerant of their vices. Though suspicious of the value of ideals and illusions, he is none the less strongly attracted to sincere goodness, and, like Maugham, he admits to being a sentimentalist though he wears the mask of a cynic. He has rejected asceticism, hedonistically enjoying his food, drink, opium, and material comfort, and he too is searching for spiritual freedom. Having concluded long ago that life has no meaning, he is comfortable with pessimism, and his philosophy, as he explains it to Erik, is Maugham's: 'Life is short, nature is hostile, and man is ridiculous; but oddly enough most misfortunes have their compensations, and with a certain humour and a good deal of horse-sense one can make a fairly good job of what is after all a matter of very small consequence.'[62] All of these views reflect Maugham's own beliefs; that Saunders resembles his creator in being a doctor in exile from England for some ill-defined irregular behaviour is an interesting but probably unintended parallel.

Dr Saunders is also, in Frederic Raphael's view, 'a very discreet homosexual',[63] and indeed the novel, together with *The Razor's Edge*, is the closest Maugham comes to treating homosexual matters. Robin has stated that his uncle once confided that *The Narrow Corner* was his 'queer' novel, but added: 'Thank heavens nobody's seen it.' Robin, moreover, entertained ideas of making a film which would properly emphasize the bisexuality at the heart of the novel and make the 'queer' element quite clear.[64]

The homosexuality in *The Narrow Corner* lies in the relationship between Fred Blake and Erik Christessen, and perhaps subtly in the observation of their behaviour by Saunders, and his admiring glances at his slim, comely Chinese servant-boy with 'skin as smooth as a girl's'. On their first evening, Erik recites poetry from *Othello* and 'Fred Blake flushed and looked shy'.[65] After Christessen's death, Dr Saunders looks at the 'unlined boyish face' of the sleeping Blake, whose innocence gives him 'a certain beauty', and he ponders the attraction between the two men:

Who would have thought that he could be so susceptible to goodness? For, though he didn't know it, though he put what he felt in clumsy and stupid words, there was no doubt about it, what had knocked him off his feet in the Dane, what had excited his embarrassed admiration and made him feel that here was a man of a different sort, was the plain, simple goodness that shone in him with so clear and steadfast a light. You might have thought Erik a trifle absurd, you might have asked yourself uneasily whether his head were quite equal to his heart, but there was no doubt about it, he had, heaven only knew by what accident of nature, a real and simple goodness. It was specific. It was absolute. It had an aesthetic quality, and that commonplace lad, insensible to beauty in its usual forms, had been moved to ecstasy by it as a mystic might be moved by the sudden overwhelming sense of union with the Godhead. It was a queer trait that Erik possessed.[66]

No heterosexual relationship in The Narrow Corner approaches the same idealistic level. Against the noble goodness that draws Blake to Christessen is set the more pragmatic and frankly sensual behaviour of Louise. Strong-willed and sexually attracted to Blake, she seduces him – 'she put her arms around my neck and kissed me as if she wanted to eat me alive,' he explains – and then feels little remorse at bringing about Christessen's death because she had felt imprisoned by his idealistic worship of her. The only other woman in the novel, Blake's mistress in Australia, has also engineered a man's death, persuading Blake to murder her husband so that she will be free to have her lover without complication.

The homosexual interplay between Blake and Christessen is subtly woven into the story and functions at a high level. As Frederic Raphael has shrewdly pointed out, the greatest value in Maugham's view was goodness, something he believed to be so rare that any sudden natural manifestation of it was a breathtaking, almost mystical, experience. This idea of goodness, argues Raphael, likely came from the philosophy of G. E. Moore, with whose work Maugham was familiar. In Principia Ethica, especially, Moore outlined a belief in a mysterious connection between goodness and beauty, especially male beauty.[67]

Harold Acton recalled how he was once motoring along the Riviera with Maugham when his companion suddenly exclaimed: 'My God, what beauty!' He had spied a tanned young labourer driving oxen, and the youth turned 'with a warm smile on his pagan features'. It was, observed Acton, a moment of intense beauty of form and harmony, and Maugham was led to comment: 'How hideous we are in comparison!'[68] Frederic Prokosch described a later occasion when he and the author were driving back from a picnic outside Rome and were discussing death. After falling asleep, Maugham suddenly awoke and, referring to an earlier encounter with the police, exclaimed: 'I have never seen such a godlike creature . . . that blond *carabiniere*. It would comfort me to have him sitting by my bed when I'm going to d-die.'[69]

It was something of this kind of attraction to male beauty, elevating it to some form of quasi-mystical experience or embodiment of perfection, that Maugham put into a very short story, 'Salvatore', published in 1924. It tells of a fisher boy on Capri who, though not having especially good features, has 'a laughing mouth', 'carefree eyes', and a 'brown body as thin as a rail'. 'Full of grace', he has the most beautiful manners the author has ever seen, and gentle sweetness. Salvatore is to be married to a beautiful young woman, but when he returns from military service weakened by rheumatism, his fiancée rejects him. Instead, he marries a plain woman who does not have the same sexual or romantic appeal, and they have two children whom he treats with delicate care, as if they were flowers. Maugham concludes this brief vignette by saying that his purpose has been to describe the radiant quality that Salvatore so strongly and unexpectedly possesses: goodness.

More incandescent yet is the goodness of the protagonist of *The Razor's Edge*, Larry Darrell, whom Anthony Curtis calls 'a compassionate homosexual, always ready to help a lame duck, listen to the troubles and salve the wounds of his friends, but never seriously deflected from his own singleness of purpose'.[70] Maugham has said that Larry was loosely based on a young man he met at dinner in Chicago in the early twenties, an encounter that almost certainly took place on one of the author's trips to that city to collect Haxton, who was familiar with the homosexual community there.

In any case, *The Razor's Edge* contains the closest thing to a homosexual character that Maugham created: the snobbish and malicious expatriate American, Elliott Templeton. An aesthete, he collects works of art and fine furniture, and cultivates connections with the aristocracy. Though silly and superficial, Templeton is shown to be *serviable* (Maugham's term) to his women friends and relatives, and generous to others. His death is moving and, in Peter Burton's words, 'an end such as any queen of fifties fiction would have been proud of'.[71]

Even *The Circle*, which has amused audiences for decades, with its twin stories of heterosexual elopement, may contain a subtle element of homosexuality. Reviewing a revival of the play by New York's Mirror Repertory Company in 1986, Edith Oliver wrote:

Most interesting of all, though, is the implication of homosexuality, which, I suppose, could never be made overt at that time. Arnold tells his miserable Elizabeth straight out that, after three years of marriage, he doesn't want to be bothered with sex, having apparently switched his passions to period furniture. When Champion-Cheney accuses Lord Porteous of having stolen his wife, Lord P. replies, 'Why didn't you look after her?' By the time the evening is over, we know exactly why Kitty left Clive and why Elizabeth must leave Arnold.[72]

Any attempt to identify elements of homosexuality in Maugham's works must necessarily be conducted with great caution and a recognition that his main purpose was never the exploration of the homosexual consciousness. The importance of Mildred is not that she represents a male or female object of infatuation, but that she is in either case a powerful and destructive form of emotional enslavement. Fred Blake is attracted to Christessen primarily by his idealism and goodness, and the homosexual appeal is secondary. Larry Darrell's search is for spiritual liberation in Indian mysticism, not in some satisfaction of homosexual instincts. A complete re-reading and revision of Maugham will not therefore uncover a canon of homosexual works.

On the other hand, it must be acknowledged that there are more homosexual traits in Maugham's writing than has generally been recognized, that like many others of his time he adopted devices to disguise these qualities. When homosexual authors write for an audience mainly of heterosexuals, most of whom are not tolerant of unorthodox sexuality, they can do a number of things: avoid creating from their deepest instincts, write and keep the manuscripts in a drawer, have their works privately printed, or give their writing a protective colouring. The most common technique to mask the real sexual orientation is, of course, to reverse the pronouns and change the gender of the characters. Maugham probably employed the latter device in creating Mildred, the androgynous waitress who is most likely based on a young man with whom Maugham had a protracted liaison. He certainly did so when he created his short story 'The Facts of Life' from an incident in his nephew's young life. Robin had a brief affair with a sailor he met on a cruise; Maugham's fictional protagonist becomes involved with a Monte Carlo coquette.[73]

The matter is, however, even more complex. Many homosexuals writing in a predominantly hostile climate submerge the homosexual elements so subtly that they can perhaps be recognized only by other homosexuals or those especially familiar with, and sensitive to, that consciousness. There is, in other words, almost a kind of code that carries the forbidden message. More important, it is likely that most heterosexual readers simply are not able to identify the myriad of small details which are unique to a homosexual perception of the world. In 'The Homosexual Imagination: An Editorial', Louie Crew and Ricter Norton argue that 'we do not believe that heterosexuals have the best perspective from which to accurately view the gay experience – not because heterosexuals lack homosexual bedroom experience, but because they lack awareness of the non-erotic nuances of the daily, casual life of homosexuals in a hostile society, and have seldom or never been confronted with any challenges to their own heterosexual predilections and presumptions.'[74]

Maugham's work, then, may contain more traces of his homosexuality than are recognized by the average reader. Consider, for example, 'Red', the story of a young man who falls in love with a beautiful girl but who is shanghaied before they can be married. The protagonist is described as 'made like a Greek god, broad in the shoulders and thin in the flanks; he was like Apollo, with just that soft roundness which Praxiteles gave him, and that suave, feminine grace which has in it something troubling and mysterious. His skin was dazzling white, milky like satin; his skin was like a woman's . . . He had large blue eyes, very dark, so that some say they were black, and unlike most red-haired people he had dark eyebrows and long dark lashes. His features were perfectly regular and his mouth was like a scarlet wound . . . There was never anyone more beautiful. There was no more reason for him than for a wonderful blossom to flower on a wild plant. He was a happy accident of nature.'[75]

'Neil MacAdam' is the story of a young Scotsman's refusal to have an affair with the middle-aged wife of his employer, and it has always been assumed that the young man's reticence is a result of excessive priggishness. Though this may be the primary reason, it is possible to interpret his attitude as a homosexual revulsion against predatory female sexuality. The handsome MacAdam, for example, is described in feminine terms, having remarkable skin, 'very white and smooth, with a lovely patch of red on either cheek. It would have been a beautiful skin even for a woman.'[76] The wife comments that 'it's as smooth and white as a woman's. It's funny on such a manly virile figure.'[77] When she attempts to seduce him, MacAdam admits that he has never had a woman. 'He could not bring himself', writes Maugham, 'to tell her how disgusting the idea of such a thing was to him, and how vile he had thought the haphazard *amours* of his fellow students at Edinburgh. He took a mystical joy in his purity. Love was sacred. The sexual act horrified him. Its excuse was the procreation of children and its sanctification marriage.'[78] When the woman continues her pursuit, he arranges that she become lost in the jungle, where she dies.

'Lord Mountdrago' is an occult tale of a man who believes that a fellow Member of Parliament can see into his dreams, where his behaviour is described in terms which strongly echo those often used earlier in the century to describe homosexual conduct. 'The man has seen me', confides Lord Mountdrago to his analyst, 'do things that are so beastly, so horrible, so shameful, that even if my life depended on it I wouldn't tell them . . . He's seen me do things that no man with any self-respect would do, things for which men are driven out of the society of their fellows and sentenced to long terms of imprisonment.'[79]

Much more speculative is the possibility that the incest at the heart of 'The Book-Bag' is actually a representation of a homosexual liaison, which could be considered a form of gender incest. There are numerous parallels between the plight of a homosexual pair in the face of the marriage of one partner and that of the brother and sister whose intimacy is destroyed by the young man's suddenly taking a bride. Olive and Tim Hardy, for example, are not popular in the Malayan community, having a reserve and a preference for their own company. In public they must work to be sociable, while at home they are relaxed and cordial, possessing a careless elegance. Having oval faces, pale skin and soft brown eyes, they are nearly twins.

Beyond the perhaps coincidental similarities of the situations of the incestuous couple and that of a homosexual pair broken by the marriage of one, there is the manner in which Olive is portrayed. She is attractive enough to infatuate one of the men in the colony, but none of her appeal is specifically feminine. There is, rather, 'something poetic in her, a sort of lyrical quality as it were, that coloured her movements, her acts and everything about her . . . There was something so candid in her expression, so courageous and independent in her bearing that . . . made mere beauty flat and dull.'[80] 'You had a sensation of well-being when you were with her,' says one character, 'as though you could relax and be quite natural and needn't pretend to be anything you weren't.'[81] She has also, however, an aloofness, a mystery which no one can penetrate, like the forbidden chamber in Bluebeard's castle. By contrast, Tim's bride is described as much more traditionally feminine: frank, lively, and ingenuous, with a wonderful prettiness. 'The

Book Bag', first accepted for publication by the homosexual Italian bookseller Pino Orioli, may thus actually be a work in translation, incest ironically being a more acceptable subject than homosexuality.

If 'The Book Bag', 'Neil MacAdam', and possibly other of Maugham's works, describe homosexual situations in translation, they obviously approach the subject in a very circumspect and oblique way. Almost allegorical, the stories are often told at second or third hand, as if Maugham wishes to put considerable distance between himself and the subject. Thus, for example, the first chapter of *The Narrow Corner* consists only of the disclaiming sentence, 'All this happened a good many years ago', and Dr Saunders is the observing eye, the buffer between the author and the action itself. In *The Razor's Edge*, Maugham makes himself a character in the novel but strictly as an observer of Larry Darrell, careful to disassociate himself from having the ability to follow Larry's chosen path. In both 'Red' and 'The Book Bag', the story is told by a character within the story, placing the central event at a considerable distance from the author and the reader.

These novels and short stories are all specific examples of works which lend themselves to an interpretation of homosexual themes, however debatable such readings may be. More general, though, is the question of the overall effect on Maugham's writing of his being homosexual. In this regard, it is important to look at the work of Leopold Bellak, an American psychiatrist who is an authority on psycho-analysis. Believing that artistic works can be used as primary data from which inferences can be made about the personality of the artist, Bellak has psychologically analysed thirty of Maugham's short stories chosen randomly. Even allowing for the defensive layers of various narrative voices, Bellak argues that Maugham's personality emerges from such stories as 'Rain', 'P & O', 'The Fall of Edward Barnard', and 'The Kite', and his assessment of that personality is remarkable.

In Bellak's analysis, the teller of Maugham's tales reveals an anxiety about the strength of aggressive and sexual drives, the control of which is vital. Moreover, he fears being dominated, constrained, controlled, and humiliated. He has unresolved conflicts between activity and passivity, conformity and non-conformity, and identification as a man and as a woman. His main defences are reaction formation (where an unconscious impulse is consciously expressed by its behavioural opposite), emotion isolation, repression, and withdrawal to superficial relationships. The well-constructed stories, observes Bellak, reveal an ego strong enough to maintain control, though this is achieved at the expense of considerable emotional isolation, of narrowing and stereotyping of experiences, and of tangential relationships to people. Urbane, mildly compassionate, and warily expectant, he remains essentially detached from others, though there are latent hostile feelings towards women.

With regard to the treatment of women in Maugham's works, it must be noted that the latent hostility identified in the analysis is directed towards the *hetaerae*, the women as sexual objects, not all females. Bellak's random sample includes such protagonists as the prostitute Sadie Thompson, the manipulative Isabel Longstaffe in 'The Fall of Edward Barnard', the murderous native wife in 'P & O', the Lady Macbeth wife of 'Footprints in the Jungle', and the castrating, controlling spouse of 'The Kite'. It does not take into account the number of women in Maugham's writing who represent loving-kindness rather than sexuality and are therefore treated warmly: Sally Athelny, Norah Nesbit, Mrs Foreman (*Cakes and Ale*), Suzanne Rouvier, and of course Rosie Driffield. Nor does it consider the female *raisonneurs* – such as Miss Ley, Susie Boyd, or Rose Waterford – whose sharp wit and intelligence make them attractive.

With this possible qualification, Bellak's personality profile, based exclusively on an objective, scientific analysis of Maugham's writing, is astonishingly similar to the portrait which emerges from the author's life. Bellak concludes by identifying the parallels:

> When one becomes aware of some of the writer's life history, it becomes apparent that his defences indeed necessitated a certain amount of constriction of his life to a rather restless, tangential relationship to people, travelling a good deal, almost by design an onlooker who participates only vicariously via his notebook in stories in which, as seen in the sample examined, center on a relatively narrow range of themes. He was obviously able to function, nevertheless, by conforming with a character quite acceptable within the setting of the upper-crust Anglo-Saxon society – urbane, polished, knowledgeable, and, above all, not causing any difficulties by uncontrolled emotions.[82]

Behind this character analysis lies an important unspoken observation. When Bellak first published his findings in 1963, he hoped to present them to his subject and to discuss them with him, and so of necessity tactfully avoided adding the conclusion that the dynamic constellation of traits is consistent with a homosexual orientation.[83] In other words, a close psychoanalytical reading of Maugham's works reveals the attitudes, responses, and language which are characteristic of homosexuals.

At the end of his analysis, Bellak speculates about the value and possible results of having had Maugham undergo psychoanalysis. Shrewdly attributing the general critical view of him as merely a competent craftsman to his emotional constraint, Bellak argues that a successful treatment would have enhanced his greatness as a writer by increasing his emotional range and permitting a wider variety of themes and modes.

There are many who will look askance at the prospect of creative writers undergoing psychoanalysis to free them from emotional block-ages and inhibitions. In Maugham's case, however, a multitude of critics over the years who knew little of his personal life perceived a deliberate restraint in his writing, a holding back as if to protect the essential self from too much exposure. Much of this guardedness was clearly connected with his fear of exposing his homosexuality, a fear that gripped generations of homosexual writers until recently. Robin Maugham may well be right that his uncle could have written a great novel had he been free to deal openly with a homosexual subject.[84] Maugham always believed, as *The Moon and Sixpence* and *The Summing Up* reveal, that the artist creates to liberate himself from the instinctual urges within, and it can be argued that the greatest art comes from these profoundest sources. If so, what enormous damage was done to Maugham's creativity by his shutting off or disguising of his most natural and deeply felt urges – those of the homosexual?

7

CURTAIN-CALLS:
1932–1939

FOLLOWING THE OPENING of *For Services Rendered* and the publication of
The Narrow Corner in 1932, Maugham remained in London until mid-
December, when he returned to the Continent. The first three weeks
in January were enjoyably spent in Munich, where he and Haxton
rented the apartment of an aristocrat and went to the opera each night.
As well, Maugham was reading a great many volumes of history and
literature in preparation for his Spanish book and could not help noting
that during Spain's greatest period the average citizen lived almost at
the subsistence level. Looking around in 1933, he concluded that the
prosperity of the twenties had been a lucky interlude in human history.

Back at Cap Ferrat in February, Maugham began writing his final
play, *Sheppey*. In May he spent a fortnight in London attending to
various business matters and visiting Liza, who was now eighteen and
going to balls and parties. He believed that Syrie was ignoring a good
academic education for their daughter in favour of the social life and
making a good marriage, but whether he ever took any steps to
counteract this is unknown. In June Maugham and Haxton drove to
Paris to watch Davis Cup tennis, and in July they spent a fortnight at
the spa in Vichy.

On 2 September Maugham left for London for the first rehearsals of
Sheppey, which opened at Wyndham's Theatre on 14 September. A
reworking of the theme of his short story 'A Bad Example', published
in *Orientations* in 1899, the play is about a London barber who wins a
large sum of money in the sweepstakes and then decides to use it to
help the poor. His wife and daughter are horrified at this Christ-like

243

attitude and attempt to have him certified as mentally incompetent, but he dies before he can be committed.

Sheppey was directed by John Gielgud and brilliantly played by Ralph Richardson, but its amalgam of various theatrical modes confused audiences. The first act is conventional Edwardian comedy, with the second becoming social and political discussion, with some sharp satirical comments on conformity, philanthropy, and democracy. The most innovative section, however, is Act III, which experiments with a device from the medieval morality plays. The sleeping Sheppey is visited by a prostitute from Act I who becomes transformed first to the symbol of Woman and then to that of Death. To emphasize that there is no escaping death, she recounts the Arabian Nights tale of the merchant who had an appointment in Samarra, and the barber departs with her, leaving his family to grieve briefly and inherit his winnings.

Sheppey was the last of Maugham's attempts to provide serious drama after years of sparkling, though often lightly satiric, comedy. Neither audiences nor critics, however, were prepared to accept serious theatre – at least not from Somerset Maugham – and the play ran for only eighty-three performances. Though he later claimed to have retired from playwriting in response to this signal from his public, he had actually planned to cease writing for the stage for some years. Increasingly, he felt hemmed in by the restrictions of theatre – of length, unity of time, place, and character, and of actual production. He was content to take his farewell with *Sheppey*, and thereafter to devote himself to fiction and essays.

By 1933 Maugham had already taken a step toward becoming an essayist by editing an omnibus book called *The Travellers' Library* (later entitled *Fifty Modern English Writers*). An anthology of short stories, poems, and essays by British writers varying from Virginia Woolf to Michael Arlen, it included an introduction explaining the criteria for Maugham's choices. So well was the book received that Nelson Doubleday estimated a sale of half a million copies and immediately urged the author to do another. Maugham had other and more important plans, however, and though he read very widely for it over the next five years it was not until 1939 that he published *Tellers of Tales*, a collection of one hundred short stories from England, the United States, France, Russia, and Germany. His twenty-seven-page introduction, tracing the development of the short story from its nineteenth-century origins, provided one of the best surveys of the genre available at the time.

Over the next twenty years, Maugham produced other anthologies and critical essays. *Great Modern Reading* is a wide-ranging collection of American and English short stories, poems, letters, essays, and speeches compiled as part of the war effort in 1943, and it reveals the breadth of Maugham's reading. Five years later, he wrote *Great Novelists and Their Novels*, revised and published in 1943 as *Ten Novels and Their Authors*, in which he provided an introductory essay on the genre and a discussion of the lives and best work of ten great novelists. In 1952 he continued to write about the short story form in *A Choice of Kipling's Prose*, which also discussed his fellow writer with generosity and appreciation at a time when Kipling's reputation was low.

Together with his excellent introduction to his 1934 collection of his own short stories, *East and West* (*Altogether* in England), and his essays in *The Summing Up*, *The Vagrant Mood*, and *Points of View*, these pieces constitute a substantial body of literary criticism. Like much of his fiction and drama, his outlook on literature is not innovative or particularly complex, but it carries the authority of a perceptive cosmopolitan who read very widely and knew literature from the point of view of an experienced professional. As such, his judgements are sound, conventional, and readable.

Following the production of *Sheppey* and the publication of *The Travellers' Library* in 1933, Maugham was determined to complete the book about Spain that had occupied his mind for a number of years. Thus, in the middle of March 1934, he and Haxton left for six weeks in Spain on a final research trip. Motoring along the south coast, they passed through Tarragona, Valencia, Granada, Gibraltar, to Seville and north to Madrid. The weather was fine, and they encountered none of the political disturbances that were periodically making Spanish travel risky, though on their last days in Madrid there were smoke bombs and machine-gun fire in the streets. Along the way they met Alan Pryce-Jones, whom Maugham found lively and witty, and he joined them on some excursions. Most important, Maugham got the material he wanted for his study, which he completed at the end of the year.

Considered by Graham Greene to be Maugham's best work, *Don Fernando* was published in June 1935, and then re-issued with changes in 1950. More an intellectual and artistic history than a travel book, it examines the Golden Age of Spain, a period of enormous creative energy. Maugham structured his book as a search for background material for a novel he proposed to write (and did years later with *Catalina*), giving him a pretext for discussing the life of Saint Ignatius Loyola, the writings of Saint Teresa, the paintings of El Greco, and the work of such figures as Cervantes, Lope de Vega, Calderón, Velázquez,

Fray Luis de Leon, and Espinal. *Don Fernando* reflects Maugham's lifelong love and admiration for Spanish culture and civilization, and from time to time he would refer to it as his favourite book.

Following his Spanish journey in 1934, Maugham made his customary spring visit to London. As usual, he was kept busy with a round of social engagements, one of which was a dinner party at Sibyl Colefax's attended by Robert Bruce Lockhart, Geoffrey Toye, Moura Budberg, G. B. Stern, and Franz Mendelsohn, among others. He also met Alfred Lunt and Lynn Fontanne, who quickly became 'mad about him'.[1]

While in London, Maugham took his nephew Robin, then eighteen, to the Garrick Club where, he said, he would talk to him like a Dutch uncle. Robin had made his first visit to the Villa Mauresque the year before, and to a sensitive adolescent his uncle's life must have seemed glamorous and appealing. Though he was later to attest to the powerful influence of his uncle by referring to him as one of the two 'shadows' (the other being his father) dominating his life, it was Willie who offered him a sympathetic ear and supportive hand. Maugham arranged for Robin to take a trip to Vienna in the summer of 1934, promising to help with expenses if necessary, and advising his nephew that if he got into any trouble he should contact him rather than his parents, who were unlikely to be tolerant or helpful.

Maugham himself travelled through Europe considerably in 1934. In June, he and Haxton spent a few days at a comfortable old house in the French Alps about twenty kilometres from Nice. In early July they made a short jaunt into Italy, down as far as Siena, where they watched the races. Then in the last week of July they went to Salzburg for the festival, and with perfect weather they made excursions to a number of small lakes around the city, made more enjoyable by the presence of Alan Pryce-Jones, Diana Forbes-Robertson, Madeleine Carroll, Philip Astley, and other friends. From there they continued to Badgastein, where they spent three weeks taking the cure. At the end of August Maugham and Haxton made the return journey, stopping for several days at Lake Como in Northern Italy.

By 1934 relations between Maugham and Haxton had deteriorated to an uneasy coexistence. Two years earlier Maugham had confided to Barbara Back that the younger man was in the process of recovering from alcoholism and was then much changed. Though then kind, very considerate, and easy to get along with, he had not been a congenial companion for three or four years.[2] By 1934 Maugham nevertheless reported that he saw little of Haxton, who, though remaining sober, spent all his time gambling in Nice at a disreputable club. Although he was not much use to his friends, Haxton was at least avoiding serious trouble. Despite his resignation, Maugham was disenchanted enough with the situation that he put the Villa Mauresque up for sale, though he took it off the agent's list in March 1935. Haxton, however, bored by his life as companion-secretary, continued to drink and gain increasing notoriety in various sleazy bars and clubs along the Riviera.

The winter of 1934–5 was spent at Cap Ferrat, finishing *Don Fernando* and entertaining the usual series of guests. Christmas visitors were G. B. Stern, Vere Pilkington, H. G. Wells and his lover, Moura Budberg, a party that was both witty and warm. Following their departure, George Rylands and Arthur Marshall came and there was tennis and talk of writing style, language, and literature. After the Nelson Doubledays left at the end of February, Maugham and Haxton escaped for a week in Florence.

In May Maugham made his visit to England, where he attended to the final stages of *Don Fernando* and the collected edition of *The Moon and Sixpence*. Though he was by then a very much published writer, he still knew the value of a skilled proofreader, and he was delighted to have Edward Marsh read *Don Fernando*. Marsh later did *The Summing Up*, *Christmas Holiday*, and *The Mixture as Before*, and Maugham was warmly appreciative. With *Don Fernando*, however, there was an unplanned second proofreader. In January, a sixty-nine-year-old writer called Vincheles Payen-Payne wrote to Maugham to offer his services as a reader and Maugham, probably wanting to assist what he perceived to be a needy writer, agreed to send the less important and less difficult proofs of *The Moon and Sixpence*. When they came back from the press in such excellent condition that there was no need for proofing, Maugham felt that he could not go back on his word, and so sent Payen-Payne another set of proofs of *Don Fernando*.

Following a week in Venice in June 1935, Maugham and Haxton left in late July for a trip to Badgastein, Munich, Salzburg, Vienna, and Bratislava, returning to Cap Ferrat at the end of August. After spending October in London, Maugham joined Haxton and, for the first time in seven years, sailed to the United States on 2 November on the North German liner *Europa*. In New York they visited Carl Van Vechten and other friends, and in December they went south to Nelson Doubleday's estate, Bonny Hall Plantation, at Yemassee, South Carolina. From there they spent a few days at Eugene and Carlotta O'Neill's home, Casa Genotta, at Sea Island, off the coast of Georgia. The house was situated on a large isolated property facing the sea but Maugham, who jealously guarded his own privacy, was surprised when O'Neill complained that he would soon have to leave because there were too many people.

Shortly after leaving Sea Island, Maugham and Haxton began another wandering journey through the Caribbean and Central America, beginning at Port au Prince, Haiti. Island-hopping southward, they stayed for a while at Dominica, where Maugham was enchanted by the beauty of its terrain, its unspoilt charm, and its beautiful and friendly negro population. Arriving rather casually dressed and on a sloop, he caused a minor sensation when suspicious port officials refused to believe that such a shabby-looking figure could be Somerset Maugham. When they tried to prevent his landing, there was a vigorous dispute and aftermath which provided the community with a delicious minor scandal.[3]

Maugham and Haxton continued to Martinique, St Lucia, and Trinidad, and in late January 1936 sailed down to French Guyana where Maugham wished to visit the French penal settlement at St Laurent du Maroni. With letters of introduction to the governor of the prison settlements and the commandant of the camp, they were given the use of the governor's bungalow at St Laurent. Two murderers serving life sentences were assigned to act as servants, and, knowing that prison officials were occasionally found with knives in their backs, Maugham and Haxton made sure to bar the windows and lock the doors of their bedrooms at night. During the days, Maugham spent considerable time talking with a large number of convicts and was fascinated to discover that the underlying motive of all but one murder he heard of was economic hardship.

A Writer's Notebook contains a number of Maugham's observations of the penal colony, and he used the material for two short stories: 'An Official Position', and 'A Man with a Conscience'. In the second of these, he records his dismay that, though there was no cruelty at St Laurent, there was no attempt at rehabilitation. With no library, no classes to educate the mind, and nothing for the spirit, there was only a brutal existence that reduced all but a very few to apathy and despair.

From French Guyana Maugham and Haxton sailed north again to Curaçao, Cartagena in Colombia, and the Canal Zone. On 23 February they sailed from Panama City on a United Fruit Company ship and arrived in Los Angeles nine days later. After a brief stopover, they went on to San Francisco to visit the Alansons, then took the train to Chicago and New York, arriving there on 22 March. The American part of the journey was full of parties and renewing of friendships, but by the time that they sailed for Europe on the *Bremen* on 2 April an exhausted Maugham was looking forward to the relative peace of the villa.

Before returning to Cap Ferrat, however, Maugham spent several weeks in London, where he lunched at the home of Sibyl Colefax along with Winston Churchill, Victor Cazalet, Harold Nicolson, Wallis Simpson, and J. L. Garvin, the editor of the *Observer*. The conversation revolved animatedly around the increasingly ominous European political scene, with Garvin infuriating the others by arguing a strong pro-Italian position. Maugham, like Churchill and unlike his brother Frederic, was becoming concerned about the rise of fascism on the Continent, especially in Mussolini's Italy.

Maugham was back in London in the middle of July for the marriage of Liza on 20 July to Vincent Paravicini, the tall and handsome only son of the Swiss minister to the court of St James. Liza had grown into an attractive and vivacious young woman, and the wedding at St Margaret's Church in Westminster was one of the social events of the summer in London. Among the distinguished guests were Princess Marie Louise, a large number of aristocrats and members of various diplomatic corps, Syrie's friend Elsie Mendl, Osbert Sitwell, Marie Tempest, Lady Aberconway, and Jessica Mitford. Oliver Messel had designed an elegant wedding cake, which was the centrepiece of the reception held at the Swiss Legation.

Maugham was pleased with the marriage. Paravicini was not only handsome but had impeccable manners and a style shaped by his family's diplomatic circle. Beyond this, Maugham genuinely liked the young man, an affection that he never lost even when the marriage eventually failed. Maugham sat beside Syrie through the wedding ceremony, though she apparently later told her chauffeur that he had completely ignored her.[4] Their gifts were, however, more collaborative; Maugham gave the couple a house on Wilton Street and Syrie decorated it. As well, Maugham turned over a sizeable number of stock shares, and loaned the Mauresque to them for their honeymoon.

While the newlyweds were enjoying the Riviera summer, Maugham and Haxton spent August in Badgastein for the cure, and the writer was so enchanted by Austria that he considered buying a small house on one of the lakes so that he could spend the summer months there. Before returning to Cap Ferrat, the pair drove down to Budapest and relaxed in cafés by the Danube listening to tzigane music and eating good food. After a few days in Vienna, they arrived home on 6 September.

On Maugham's return the villa was soon filled once more with guests. In addition to Robin, whose way Maugham had paid, there was Osbert Sitwell and Harold Nicolson. Neither the year's travels nor the wedding, however, had prevented Maugham's working on a novel which was now at the stage of final corrections. Announced in the 'Editor's Calendar' of *Nash's* in October 1935 as 'the story of a woman's double personality', *Theatre* is a tribute of sorts to the dramatic world from which Maugham had retired.

The 'double personality' is that of Julia Lambert, a skilled actress who is a composite of the great leading ladies Maugham had known in his thirty years as a dramatist. On stage she is thoroughly professional and in complete control of her emotions; offstage, however, she succumbs to the charms of a young man and falls painfully in love. In the end, Julia finds release in the theatre, submerging her emotions in her art, making her both a greater actress and a freer woman.

Maugham left for London earlier than usual in the autumn of 1936 because he was particularly anxious to be present at the PEN Club's seventieth birthday dinner for his friend H. G. Wells at the Savoy Hotel on 13 October. G. B. Stern was there, but Maugham had ordered an extra ticket for Barbara Back, who he knew would relish the occasion. At the request of Wells, Maugham sat at the head table and listened to the guest of honour's gloomy description of the state of the world.

In the final months of 1936, however, thoughts of the future were overshadowed in Britain by the growing crisis of the King's relationship with Mrs Simpson. Maugham heard talk of it wherever he went, and it undoubtedly was the chief topic of another of Sibyl Colefax's dinners which Maugham attended on 28 October with Churchill, the Duff Coopers, the Mountbattens, the Duchess of Rutland, Desmond MacCarthy, Philip Sassoon, and Arthur Rubinstein. Several days later, Maugham went north to the Sitwell house, Renishaw Hall, in Derbyshire, where he enjoyed the seventeenth-century home, the furnishings which had been in the family since the reign of Charles II, and the charming hospitality of Osbert Sitwell.

Back in London at the end of November, Maugham invited Osbert and Clive Bell to lunch at Claridge's on 11 December, and included Robin and a friend so that they might meet the two noted men of letters. Little did Maugham know that it would be the day that Edward VIII announced his abdication, and in a corner of the public lounge at Claridge's Graham Greene, Osbert Sitwell, Edward Marsh, Maugham and others sat listening to the King's speech on a radio that Maugham had borrowed from a porter.

The period immediately following the abdication was, of course, particularly difficult for both the Duke of Windsor (as he had become) and Wallis Simpson, who had to remain apart from him along the Riviera. There was a great deal of antipathy to the woman who had brought down the King, but Maugham, who was always sympathetic to the outcast and the ostracized, invited Wallis Simpson to Christmas dinner at the Villa Mauresque, along with her friends Herman and Katherine Rogers and Sibyl Colefax. She returned for a party in the new year, and spent a weekend there in late February, and from then until the outbreak of war Maugham entertained both the Duke and the Duchess, though the Duke disliked homosexuals.

Early in 1937 Maugham's relations with Haxton went through another and more intense crisis. At the beginning of January, Haxton had gone to West Africa for a holiday, where he developed a serious illness – either a recurrence of malaria or alcoholic poisoning – and nearly died on his return to France. Thoroughly frightened, he temporarily cut out drinking and had recovered by late February, though he was advised by doctors that he could not do a cure for several months until the effects of his attack had fully disappeared. Maugham endured a month of anxiety about his companion's health and was frustrated by Haxton's inability to impose the discipline that he rigorously applied to himself. Writing to Barbara Back, he commented that if Haxton began drinking heavily again it would kill him, and rather than nurse him through a drunken slow death he would give him a pension and resume living in England. But, he added, he fervently hoped that it would not come to that.[5]

In April Maugham went to England to oversee rehearsals in Manchester and Newcastle of *The Constant Wife*, a revival that lasted only thirty-six nights at London's Globe Theatre. While in London, he sat for the painter Sir William Rothenstein, who was later asked for a copy of the portrait by Frederic Maugham. The passing years had not brought the brothers any closer together, but they had a mutually respectful relationship which was, beneath their restrained exteriors, warmer than has been portrayed. In October 1936 Frederic had sent Willie a copy of his new book *The Tichborne Case*, and received a complimentary letter praising its lucidity and noting with approval the good reviews. When Frederic became Lord Chancellor early in 1938 his brother was genuinely proud and happy, pleased especially that the appointment seemed the reward for expertise not party loyalty. It was wonderful, he confided to Alanson, that an obscure young man, without money or influence, should on professional merit achieve a position which in nine cases out of ten is a lawyer's highest reward for political services.[6]

When the new session of Parliament was opened with the traditional pomp and ceremony in the following November, Willie Maugham was, he reported to a friend, exhausted from being on his feet all morning at the House of Lords. He had waited until noon to see Frederic, resplendent in his robes of office, enact the Lord Chancellor's ritual handing of the Speech from the Throne to the King. According to one account, Willie jumped up at this point, tugged at the elbow of a companion, and cried: 'Look! It's my brother! Get up! Get up!'[7]

For his part, Frederic came to be proud of his brother's reputation as a writer, though he rarely communicated that pride to him. Nevertheless, revolted by homosexuality, he was shocked by his brother's orientation and deeply disapproving of his relationship with Haxton. That Frederic considered Willie's lover *persona non grata* is vividly illustrated by two letters written by the author on 26 June 1944 when Haxton was dying. To Robin, he gave a detailed emotional account of the younger man's condition; his letter to Frederic's wife Nellie does not even mention Haxton.

Beyond the question of public opinion and his own attitudes, Frederic was of course more aware than most people of the legal perils of practising homosexuality in England. According to Robin, his uncle General Sir Cecil Romer was told by the head of Scotland Yard in the early thirties to warn Willie to behave with more discretion in England because he was running the risk of being arrested. It was Frederic, said his son, who conveyed the message to his brother.[8] Despite this considerable barrier, the two men continued to see each other and maintain an uneasy, though not unfriendly, relationship until Frederic's death.

It may have been his brother's homosexuality which lay behind one of Frederic's witty replies to Willie. A fan letter to the author had been sent by mistake to Frederic, and when he forwarded it to Cap Ferrat, Willie responded by observing with tongue in cheek that it would be the Bacon–Shakespeare controversy all over again. Posterity would say that the Lord Chancellor had written all the books and used his brother's name as a *nom de plume*. Not to be outdone, Frederic replied that Willie might well be right to think that he wrote like Shakespeare, adding 'one word of brotherly advice. *Do not attempt the sonnets.*'[9] Perhaps the eminent lawyer knew the theory that the sonnets express a homosexual love.

In May 1937 Maugham returned to Paris for a month to collect more material for *Christmas Holiday*, a novel he had had in mind since attending the trial of Guy Davin, sentenced to life imprisonment for murder, in December 1932. From there he joined Haxton on a motor trip through Scandinavia with G. B. Stern in June, and though they enjoyed Copenhagen, Sweden was dreary and boring. At the end of the month, they rushed back to the Riviera to avoid being caught in a threatened hotel and restaurant strike.

While Maugham and Haxton were away, the Villa Mauresque was being painted so that it could again be put on the market. Following his illness in February, Haxton's behaviour improved and he spent much of his time sailing, which he always loved. In June Maugham reported to Barbara Back that Haxton had agreed to a new arrangement. If a buyer could be found for the Mauresque, for which Maugham was asking £25,000, he would sell the villa, and in the future live more in England. He would take a flat in London and spend at least five months a year there. Though Maugham was not specific, Haxton presumably would occupy the author's flat in Paris, and they would continue to see each other but much less often.

In the end there was no buyer for the villa, and the inevitable split with Haxton was prevented by the outbreak of war. Life went on as before, and in early August Maugham and Haxton went to Salzburg, where they heard Toscanini, and from there to Badgastein. At the end of the month, they went to Venice for a couple of days to see the Tintorettos and returned to Cap Ferrat in early September.

Much of 1937 had been spent reading a prodigious number of short stories for the anthology Nelson Doubleday had suggested some years earlier. As well, Maugham's autobiographical book, *The Summing Up*, was at proof stage, and once again he sought the proofreading skills of Edward Marsh for what he termed a sort of confessions of St Augustine.

The Summing Up may be confessional but, as the author indicates in its opening lines, it is neither an autobiography nor a book of memoirs. As the title suggests, the observations are a summation of ideas about professional authorship, style and craft, literature, art, drama, philosophy and religion. Most of these views had already been dramatized in his plays and fiction, given expression by various characters and in authorial digressions (as in *Cakes and Ale*), and presented in such non-fiction works as *The Gentleman in the Parlour* and *Don Fernando*. Impelled by a desire for order and coherence, however, Maugham recapitulates and amplifies a number of ideas that have occupied his thoughts for more than forty years, and concludes that 'when I have finished it I can face the future with serenity.'[10]

The Summing Up is composed of seventy-seven segments, most of which are essays on writing and philosophy. Maugham discusses his craft, explaining his view of human character and arguing for the stylistic importance of lucidity, simplicity, and euphony. He outlines the difficulties of professional authorship, the role of the writer, and the necessity of first-rate critics. Thirteen sections in the middle are a summation of his views of drama and his experience in the theatre. The final part is an examination of philosophy, ending with the conclusion that of all the great values man has cherished, neither truth nor beauty is as important as goodness. The book ends with Fray Luis de Leon's comment that 'the beauty of life is nothing but this, that each should act in conformity with his nature and his business.'[11]

In the years following its publication, *The Summing Up* has become a kind of classic, one of the most highly regarded expressions of a personal credo. Few have argued that it contains innovative or profound ideas, but a great many have enjoyed the civilized views of a cosmopolitan professional presented in lucid prose. Praised for its candour, frankness, and common sense, it almost succeeds in being the kind of valediction Maugham intended it to be. Dispassionate and unpretentious, it appears to be the work of a man who, having assessed his life and career, looks upon them with serenity.

The narrative voice of *The Summing Up*, however, was another mask, closer to the essential Willie Maugham than his fictional personae but by no means a perfect fit. Though he explains that he has 'no desire to bare my heart, and I put limits to the intimacy that I wish the reader to enter upon with me',[12] twenty-two of the sections of the book deal with autobiographical matters – from his schooldays to his medical training and his early struggles as a writer. The treatment of the material is none the less guarded and deceptively dispassionate. It can be argued that Maugham had already dealt intimately with his early life in *Of Human Bondage*, but later crises are glossed over with a laconic dismissal. His marriage is treated in very general terms in several paragraphs, and of course there is no mention of Gerald Haxton.

No writer need be compelled to make a public examination of his private life, and Maugham could easily have excluded personal references from his reflections. He nevertheless introduced a substantial autobiographical element, suggesting some sort of need for giving meaning and coherence to his life as much as to his ideas about art and philosophy. Under the circumstances, then, the book is remarkable both for the author's lack of passion about his own trials and for what it does not say.

The Summing Up was a significant part of the pattern Maugham foresaw for the conclusion of his career, not his final book but, at the age of sixty-four, a last major statement about his beliefs and his life. Life did not, however, conform to the design that Maugham attempted to impose on it, and he lived for another twenty-seven years. At the end, the restraint and self-control which marked *The Summing Up* collapsed, and all the wounds and regrets which had been so carefully submerged boiled to the surface.

Only one reviewer in 1938, V. S. Pritchett, sensed the pain below the surface of Maugham's book. Arguing that there was 'an injured and defensive heart behind the fluent mind of the impervious man of the world', he observed that '*The Summing Up* is not the book of a happy man. Under its superficial self-possession, it reveals a curious rootlessness, pathos and bewilderment, but these are kept in their place, out of sight, by Mr Maugham's warranted pride in his craft, in the accomplished planning of his career and the candid acceptance of his limitations.'[13] In light of what we now know about Maugham's life, this is a remarkable diagnosis.

Maugham took the typescript of *The Summing Up* to England in late September 1937, while Haxton sailed down the coast of Italy. In London Maugham visited Barbara Back and Peter Stern, and he sat again for Rothenstein. By far the most important meeting, however, was with his first grandchild, Nicholas Somerset, born in October. In early December he attended the christening after which, at Liza's insistence, he went to a reception at her home so that her friends could meet him. As well, he lunched at Boulestin's with Bruce Lockhart, Moura Budberg, and Harold Nicolson, who irritated him by making a facetious comment about Robin – 'the apple of his eye', noted Lockhart,[14] and about whom Maugham then felt very protective.

At this luncheon Maugham revealed plans for his first major journey in a decade: a three-month tour of southern India. He had always avoided the largest country in the Empire because friends had been disappointed by it and he was convinced that Kipling had written all the good stories to be found there. He had a low regard for the British colonial officials he met on leave from India in England, and Indian art did not sufficiently interest him to make the trip worthwhile. However, as he reported to a French journalist, he planned to write a novel set in Montparnasse but about Eastern religious beliefs, and he needed to gather material both for atmosphere and to ensure accuracy of religious beliefs. The result, though ultimately long-delayed, was *The Razor's Edge*.

Maugham left London on 10 December and eight days later he and Haxton sailed for Bombay, a voyage made enjoyable by a comfortable ship, calm seas, and excellent bridge with an Egyptian master. He had been advised that he ought to go first to Delhi to pay his respects to the Viceroy, Lord Linlithgow, but anxious to visit temples in the south he headed down the coast to the native states. Though it was hardly likely to influence Maugham's itinerary on that immense continent, Syrie was by coincidence in India as well, travelling with Elsie Mendl and Johnny McMullen. Each had his or her territory: Syrie the comfortable pleasures of the royal palaces, and Willie the ascetic life of the ashrams.[15]

From Bombay Maugham and his companion, armed with letters of introduction to various British administrators and maharajas from Rothenstein and the Aga Khan, went south to Goa. Maugham found this former capital of the Portuguese trading empire in the Far East romantic and evocative, and in its great basilica of Bom Jesus he saw the tomb of St Francis Xavier. From there the travellers went to Calicut, Travancore, and Madura, which, though possessing a magnificent temple, had no hotel, forcing them to sleep in the railway station.

Working their way slowly over to India's east coast, Maugham and his companion visited Pondicherry, Madras, and Bangalore, before heading north to Hyderabad. There he was entertained by E. M. Forster's friend Sir Akbar Hydari, the Minister of Finance, who was not only a congenial host but arranged for Maugham to meet various holy men usually inaccessible to foreigners. By late February 1938 Maugham and Haxton reached Calcutta, and after a week they headed inland to Benares, where Maugham observed that 'nothing can be more impressive than to saunter down the Ganges by boat in the evening just before the sun sets . . . It is a moving, a wonderfully thrilling spectacle; the bustle, the noise, the coming and going give a sense of seething vitality; and those still figures of the men in contemplation by contrast seem more silent, more still, more aloof from human intercourse.'[16] At Agra the beauty of the Taj Mahal literally took the writer's breath away, the artistry giving him a feeling of surprise, joy, and liberation.

By the middle of March the travellers were finally in Delhi, where Haxton's presence seems to have created a dilemma for the Viceroy. Twenty years had not lessened the British establishment's antipathy to the man, and the King's representative in India could hardly entertain someone who was still not permitted to set foot in Britain. Linlithgow decided to invite only the noted author to luncheon at the palace, but Maugham out of loyalty to his friend declined the invitation.[17]

Maugham came away from India with a renewed contempt for the British Raj. In addition to the incident in Delhi he had been told that the only difference between the Bengal Club in Calcutta and Yacht Club in Bombay was that the former did not allow dogs or Indians while the latter permitted dogs but not Indians. Moreover, he heard of a young British officer who, after four years in Agra, had never seen the Taj Mahal, and he met a general who tolerated thirty years in the country only because of the hunting. Little wonder, then, that Maugham became fond of saying that if Waterloo was won on the playing fields of Eton, future historians might say that India was lost in the public schools of England.

Had Maugham gone to India years earlier he might well have written about the Raj with the same critical eye as he described the westerners in *On a Chinese Screen* and the British colonial officials in his South Seas and Far East stories. Moreover, had he been able to make a second trip in 1939, as he planned, he might have then felt that he knew the country well enough to write a full-scale Indian novel. As it was he was overwhelmed by the vastness, colour, and variety of the country, and comprehending it in three months resembled viewing the Himalayas in one flash of lightning in a night sky.

The Indian journey was nevertheless the most satisfying and evocative trip that Maugham had made since the Malayan expedition of 1925–6. For two years he had been reading extensively in Hindu philosophy in preparation for his novel of Indian mysticism, and he was fascinated by his actual encounter with the spiritual life of the East. He met yogis, fakirs, swamis, gurus, and philosophers, and on more than one occasion succumbed to the spell of the holy sites. At the temple at Madura he felt 'a vehement overwhelming sense of the divine that sends cold shivers down your spine . . . something secret and terrible'.[18] In the mosque at the Taj Mahal one evening he experienced 'an eerie, mysterious sense of its emptiness and silence' and seemed 'to hear the noiseless footfall of the infinite'.[19]

Maugham's three months in India clearly fired his imagination in a way that it had not been sparked for more than a decade, not in Mexico, the Caribbean, or Central America. Their impact is reflected in the vivid and reverential entries in *A Writer's Notebook* and in his essay on a maharishi in *Points of View*. Though the outbreak of war prevented his return to India, his sojourn provided enough of a feeling for Indian religious belief and the mystical consciousness to allow him to write credibly about them in his last major novel. Beyond their professional value, however, Maugham found the Indian beliefs very attractive, though in the end he could not believe in them.

Maugham and Haxton sailed from Bombay to Naples on 31 March, and since the Mauresque had been loaned to a friend they worked their way slowly up Italy to arrive at home in the last week of April. In Florence they visited Maugham's old friend Reggie Turner, who was dying of cancer and had only eight months to live, and they took him to see Edith Sitwell at her father's castle in Montegufoni. At Cap Ferrat Maugham found chilly, raw weather and a multitude of letters and business matters to settle. Alan Searle was staying at the villa, and Maugham was delighted to learn that Peter Stern was living nearby.

Despite these distractions Maugham plunged into writing a new novel within a day or so of his return and found that, after several months of relative inactivity, it was exciting to work on a substantial piece of writing. This novel was not, as one might expect, the study of spiritual salvation and mysticism for which he had just gone to India. Though for two years his thoughts had been preoccupied by that work, to which he attached great importance, he put it aside in favour of a more timely and, for him, uncharacteristic novel. Since attending the sensational murder trial of Guy Davin Maugham had been interested in writing a fictional account of the murderer and his young Russian wife. By 1938, however, the political situation in Europe had deteriorated so dramatically that *Christmas Holiday* became an allegorical reflection of the ferment of that politically intense decade.

Maugham had always believed that creative writing should not treat contemporary political issues or be didactic, and for most of his career his writing was apolitical. In the twenties and thirties, however, he became increasingly aware of social and political changes which were affecting his own life. In January 1924 he commented to Bert Alanson that, while many of his acquaintances were nervous about the prospect of the Labour Party achieving power, he was not worried. It could do no worse than the others, and deserved a chance to rule. In *The Breadwinner* in 1930 his young characters referred to the 'muddle' created by the older generation, a theme developed with much greater depth and intensity two years later in *For Services Rendered*. In 1933 he accepted the invitation of H. G. Wells to become a member for England of PEN, the international society of authors whose purpose is to fight for freedom of expression throughout the world. Though he hated meetings Maugham was nominated by Marie Belloc Lowndes and Netta Syrett and subsequently elected to the Executive Committee of the London branch a year later. However, being away from London and on the road for much of the year, he was not able to be an active member, and in 1935 PEN moved him to the Council, a largely honorary body.

In September of that year Maugham joined J. M. Barrie, Hugh Walpole, John Masefield, W. B. Yeats, Sir Owen Seaman, and Ian Hay-Beith in signing a petition to the Dean of Westminster urging the consecration of a plaque in Westminster Abbey honouring Samuel Clemens. Of much more significance was a letter Maugham signed in 1937 with Virginia Woolf, H. G. Wells, Hugh Walpole, and two others appealing for signatures on a petition to establish commissions to study the economic and political causes of international tension.[20] In June 1938 he responded to a request from PEN for funds to assist Austrian Jews who had been forced to flee their country by sending a cheque for ten guineas and pointing out that, though it was not a reasonable contribution, he had anticipated PEN's campaign by helping Austrian Jews whom he knew. In October he sent a similar amount to a fund to assist Czechoslovakian writers in difficulty.

On the whole Maugham preferred to keep his participation in such efforts anonymous and to refrain from public statements about politics. A year after the opening of *For Services Rendered* he declined the invitation of his friend Raymond Marriott to be interviewed on the questions of pacifism and general strikes. In 1934, when Geoffrey West sought the opinions of a group of artists – for example, Clifford Bax, A. E. Coppard, Hugh Walpole, R. H. Mottram, William Gerhardi, and Charles Morgan – who seemed to remain detached from social and political issues, Maugham's reply was simply: 'Why should a professional writer who makes his living by his pen cry stinking fish?'[21]

Privately, however, Maugham was alarmed by the rise of fascism in Europe and the policy of appeasement in England, and this led ultimately to the end of his friendship with his French translator, Horace de Carbuccia. A Corsican politician and publisher, Carbuccia edited *Gringoire*, a journal which steadily grew more stridently anti-Semitic and pro-fascist in the years leading up to the Second World War. According to André David, a drama critic for *Gringoire*, Carbuccia began to print more and more anti-British articles, which Maugham eventually found unacceptable.[22] In *Strictly Personal* Maugham described a last meeting with the Corsican, whom he called 'Bouche', in August 1939 when Carbuccia argued that to go to war over Poland, a land of worthless people, was grotesque and that England and France should forget their promises to defend it.

With the fall of France Carbuccia's collaboration with the Germans became overt and in November 1941 he undertook to blacken Maugham in the eyes of the French. As a highly regarded author who lived in France and spoke the language, Maugham was a useful propaganda weapon for the Allies, both through his radio broadcasts and his writing, and it was necessary for the Germans to undercut this influential voice. Carbuccia accordingly wrote a vicious attack on him which was published first in *Gringoire* and later reprinted in pamphlet form. Maugham, he claimed, smoked opium, disliked Americans but went to the United States for publicity, and left England rather than live without Haxton. Maugham's story 'The Treasure', in which a man has an affair with his maid, alleged Carbuccia, was actually based on the author's liaison with one of his footmen. In the end the article did no damage to Maugham, and after the war Carbuccia was returned from Spain in disgrace, sentenced to five years' hard labour, and had his property confiscated.

Maugham's sensitivity to developments in Europe eventually found expression in *Christmas Holiday*, which became the story of an upper-middle-class English youth's discovery of the social upheavals taking place on the Continent, and a warning to the complacent, insular middle class in Britain. In his excellent essay 'Somerset Maugham and Posterity', written in 1937, Glenway Wescott argues that the novel had greater social significance than any other comparable work of fiction in 1939:

> Maugham in this slight volume, less than a hundred thousand words long, with his air of having nothing on his mind except his eight characters – how they came together and what happened and what they said and how they felt – explains more of the human basis of fascism and Nazism and communism than anyone else has done; the self-fascinated, intoxicated, insensible character of all that new leadership in Europe; the womanish passivity of the unhappy masses dependent on it and devoted to it; the Anglo-Saxon bewilderment in the matter, which still generally prevails; and the seeds of historic evil yet to come, not at all extirpated in World War II but rather multiplied and flung with greater profusion in no less receptive soil farther afield, even beyond Europe. Europe the starting point, the womb and the cradle, as it has been for millenniums.[23]

In Wescott's analysis, Charlie Mason, the young man whose Christmas jaunt to Paris reveals that the bottom has 'fallen out of his world', is a representative of the prosperous, liberal middle class, the predominant ruling caste in Europe between the wars. Robert Berger, the murderer, is a member of the 'new dictating' class which grew out of the First World War, while the embryonic revolutionary, Simon, is his intellectual apologist and propagandist. Finally, the Russian émigrée prostitute, Lydia, tortured by the need to expiate the sins of Berger, is a symbol of the mass of gullible common people.

Wescott's interpretation is persuasive, but few readers in 1939 recognized the point of *Christmas Holiday*. Though much more political than most of Maugham's work, its commentary on the ideological struggles in Europe is a subtext, an allegorical representation rather than a direct examination. Maugham might break his rule that fiction should not deal in polemics, but he could not avoid focusing on his real interest: character. Thus it is the strange psychological makeup of Berger, and the subtle quirks of Simon and Lydia, as well as the evocative Paris background against which their drama is played, that captures the reader's interest. As a result, even a shrewd reviewer like Graham Greene, who was soon to write his own study of conflicting ideologies in *The Power and the Glory*, could miss the political allegory and concentrate on what he saw as the novel's technical failings.

The typescript of *Christmas Holiday* was given to Eddie Marsh for editing in October 1938, after a summer of writing in the darkening shadows of political instability. Hitler had occupied Austria in March and in late May the world was gripped by rumours of an imminent German invasion of Czechoslovakia. Soon after returning from India Maugham arranged for Bert Alanson's German assets, which could not be removed from the country, to be deposited into his own German account. Though the writer's royalties were also frozen they were likely safer than the funds of an American Jew, and Maugham advised his friend to follow his intention of investing in a work of art which could then be shipped to the United States.

The political uncertainty also caused Maugham to forgo his annual cure at an Austrian or German spa. Since the March occupation Badgastein was out of the question, and Carlsbad was risky because the Germans might march in at any time and make matters uncomfortable for British subjects stranded there. The summer was therefore spent relatively quietly at Cap Ferrat, though the number of guests at the Villa Mauresque remained. In addition to Alan Searle and Peter Stern, there were Jacques Raindre, a Paris financier, Liza and Vincent Paravicini, Barbara Back, Sibyl Colefax, and Raymond Mortimer. Harold Nicolson's visit in early August was enlivened by the presence at dinner of the Duke and Duchess of Windsor, who had taken a villa nearby at Cap d'Antibes.

For Haxton, however, the chief excitement was the purchase of a new and larger yacht, the *Sara*, a two-masted, forty-five-ton fishing boat which, with the addition of an auxiliary diesel engine, permitted more extensive journeys. At the end of August, when it had been refitted with fresh paint, new sails, and new furnishings, he set sail along the coast to Sicily, looking happier and more excited than Maugham could remember seeing him.

On 1 September, with his companion at sea, Maugham entered a sanatorium in Clarens, Switzerland, for a fortnight's cure. With Europe even closer to war over Hitler's increasing demands that the Czechoslovakian government cede the Sudetenland to Germany, Maugham was distressed by the political uncertainty. On 17 September he left for several days in Geneva but while motoring to Paris he was very nearly killed in an automobile accident. Though his injuries – primarily a broken rib – did not require hospitalization, they were severe enough to render him unable even to turn over in bed without help for the first few days and the pain required heavy sedation. This mishap kept Maugham in Paris for ten days, though the devoted care of Alan Searle allowed him to recuperate at the Hôtel de France et Choiseul rather than a nursing home.

When Maugham was well enough to cross the Channel to England on 29 September Neville Chamberlain was flying to Munich and Britain was preparing for war. The fleet had been mobilized, gas masks issued, and air raid trenches dug in London's parks. On Chamberlain's return with 'peace in our time', however, Maugham joined the many who believed that war had been averted, perhaps for a good many years.

Maugham's London visit was the usual mixture of work and play. He delivered the typescript of *Christmas Holiday* to Eddie Marsh, along with a gift of eighteenth-century emerald sleeve buttons he had brought back from India. He dined with such friends as Frank Swinnerton, G. B. Stern, the Nelson Doubledays, and the young writer George Bullock. Bruce Lockhart gave a luncheon for Maugham, Harold Nicolson, and Jan Masaryk at Boulestin's, and Juliet Duff invited him to spend several days at Bulbridge House, near Salisbury. Stern included him in her dinner party at Quaglino's to honour her sixty-four closest friends, placing him at a table with J. B. Priestley, Rose Macaulay, H. G. Wells, and Max Beerbohm. Despite his natural inclination to relax with old friends, Maugham suggested to Stern: 'Give me a difficult table if you like, and I'll look after it for you.'[24]

Another 'grand' occasion was a luncheon in early November at Sibyl Colefax's attended by, among others, the Duke and Duchess of Devonshire, the Duchess of Rutland, Lord De La Warr, Bruce Lockhart, Max Beerbohm, and Virginia Woolf, who found Maugham 'very suspicious and tortured'. He was, she noted, 'like a dead man whose beard or moustache has grown a little grisly bristle after death. And his lips are drawn back like a dead man's. He has small ferret eyes. A look of suffering & malignity & meanness & suspicion . . . Sat like an animal in a trap: or like a steel trap.'[25]

Maugham's recent accident may have helped create this impression of grimness, but he was then in his mid sixties, when advancing age increasingly gave his features a formidable quality, so brilliantly captured in Graham Sutherland's later portrait. This aura of menace, however, was frequently belied by his behaviour, shown that day by his response to another guest, the young Christopher Isherwood, whose *Goodbye to Berlin* he greatly admired.

Though the two writers had already met, and Maugham had taken the younger man to luncheon at the Garrick Club, their acquaintance was as yet slight. Isherwood was somewhat intimidated by the grim and watchful look described by Woolf and made uncomfortable by Maugham's stuttering, but he sensed a 'shy warmth' behind the façade sufficient to make him wish to adopt the older writer as his 'Uncle Willie'. In an attempt to reach past the Maugham mask Isherwood told a comic story about the similarity of his fellow passengers on a recent voyage to some of Maugham's characters. Under the influence of too much drink, however, his narrative collapsed in embarrassing confusion and he fled the house, snapping the pen in half as he hastily signed the guest book on the way out. Rather than being offended by this behaviour, and perhaps touched by Isherwood's mortification, Maugham observed to Woolf: 'That young man holds the future of the English novel in his hands.' Maugham remained a champion of the younger writer's work for many years, and though Isherwood later observed that 'he never quite became Uncle Willie, he was a helpful, hospitable, and outspoken friend'[26] for the remainder of his life.

Within a few weeks of the Colefax party, Noël Coward's companion, Cole Lesley, was also able to observe Maugham's warmth. Together with the musical star Dorothy Dickson, Maugham spent a weekend at Coward's Kentish home, Goldenhurst, and years later Lesley recalled 'how charming he was; I had expected him to lash everyone with his tongue'.[27]

Maugham left England for Paris on a bitterly cold Christmas Day, and settled into the comfortable Hôtel de France et Choiseul. The next day, however, he headed back north to Lens, a coal-mining community near Lille on the Belgian border, where he spent two busy, but fascinating, days in the pits. It took him some time to get the coal dust out of his eyelashes and eyebrows, but he came away with the material he would use for the mining segment of *The Razor's Edge*.

Since Maugham had let the Villa Mauresque for an extended period he returned to the South of France on 3 January only to join Haxton on the *Rex* from Cannes to New York. After a hectic week of interviews, social engagements, and theatre-going, they crossed the American continent for a fortnight's holiday with Bert and Mabel Alanson in San Francisco. While on the west coast they took the opportunity to spend several days with Eugene and Carlotta O'Neill at Tao House, their pseudo-Chinese home built on the side of a mountain thirty-five miles out of San Francisco. Though O'Neill's physical deterioration and premature old age had already begun, he was still actively writing plays and was an exquisitely mannered host.

At the end of January Maugham and Haxton went by train to Chicago, where Maugham wrote to Robin to congratulate him on passing his bar exams and to encourage him to cut down on his drinking. His dismay over his nephew's intemperance, which made the young man very nervous and depressed, was the first sign of a disappointment which was to grow over the next twenty-five years. He had endured too much with alcoholics, he said in an obvious reference to Haxton, not to be dismayed by the thought of anyone else he knew becoming one.[28]

In mid-February Maugham and Haxton moved on to Washington, where the author was repeatedly interviewed, photographed, and entertained at dinner parties by ambassadors and senators. In New York in March the *New York Times* gave him a luncheon, and he was besieged with offers of commissions from all sides. For a two-minute radio talk, he was paid $500. His articles 'Books and You' and 'You and Some More Books', which appeared in the *Saturday Evening Post* in February and March, were enormously popular, and editors were anxious for more. Maugham found it exhausting to reply to the fifty letters he was daily receiving from the *Post*'s readers, but he was gratified by the response, even though his satisfaction was muted by his innate insecurity. He admitted to Alanson that he was suspicious of his success and was prepared to accept a sudden reversal philosophically.[29]

By the time that Maugham sailed from New York on 11 March he was exhausted by conferences, telephone calls, fan letters, luncheons, dinners, and, as he said, 'bright intelligent conversation'. He had planned to travel on an Italian ship, but since few Americans were booking passage on Italian or German lines, its stop at Cannes had been cancelled. Maugham instead took the *Queen Mary*, and arrived in Cherbourg on 16 March after a calm and restful voyage. Stopping in Paris for several days, where they were disconcerted by the assumption that war was imminent, the travellers headed back to the quiet of Cap Ferrat.

The peace of the Villa Mauresque was only relative since its pool was being rebuilt on the money received from its rental, but the greater disquiet came from the growing murmurs of war. Hitler's occupation of Czechoslovakia in the middle of March had signalled the end of appeasement, and when Mussolini took Albania in April rumours of an impending Italian raid spread along the Riviera, causing Maugham's footman Francesco to return to Italy to protect his small property. By May the countryside of southern France was full of soldiers, all the bridges were guarded, and machine guns were mounted on the coast. The Duke and Duchess of Windsor, frequent visitors to the Villa Mauresque, were advised to forgo a planned trip to Morocco, and Jacques Raindre brought depressing reports from Paris.

In the face of such unsettled conditions Maugham and Haxton abandoned plans to sail the *Sara* along the Dalmatian coast to Constantinople. Instead they joined friends Piet Polovtzov and Lou Burton at the beginning of June for a cure at Montecatini – Haxton for his liver and Maugham for the rheumatism that had plagued him since his accident and for a recurrence of his malaria. In the spa, amidst a Tuscan countryside fresh and green after the May rains, the days were spent leisurely doing the cure – drinking the waters, taking the mud baths, eating sparingly, eschewing alcohol, going on short excursions to Florence, Lucca, and Pistoia, and playing bridge in the evenings with Polovtzov and Burton. Here the threat of war seemed remote, and Maugham believed that only some German outrage would threaten the peace.

In the middle of June Haxton took the *Sara* for a cruise, while Maugham went to London for a month to visit family and friends and to find out what those in power really thought of the chances of war. At dinner the Lord Chancellor assured him that nothing would happen until September at the earliest, and that though Hitler might bluster, he would not force the issue. Conditions in Germany, added Frederic, were nevertheless such that war would be inevitable within a year, though by that time Britain and America would be sufficiently strongly armed to triumph in any confrontation. For his part Willie was reassured by this analysis, believing that before then Hitler and Mussolini might be overthrown.

By the time that Maugham returned to Cap Ferrat in the middle of July the soldiers had been removed, and the summer at the Villa Mauresque seemed much like any other. Robin arrived in late July, and in early August Vincent and Liza came for a fortnight. As well, there were Peter Stern, David Horner, and Karl Pfeiffer, a young American academic and journalist whom Maugham had met in Washington in the twenties. Paul Dottin, whose two book-length studies of Maugham's works were the first serious treatments of his writing, came from Toulouse for a day. Jacques Raindre, in close touch with French business circles, brought the news from Paris that, since German businessmen were opposed to war, peace was nearly certain.

The weather was idyllic, and Maugham and his guests spent the days sailing, bathing, dining, and dancing in Monte Carlo. The host himself did not ignore his work, and wrote a short novel, *Up at the Villa*, for which he had a contract with an American women's magazine. While in London he had attended the trial of a 'Mayfair man' at the Old Bailey in order to collect material for other work. If Frederic were right about the prospects for continued peace Maugham intended to return to India in the winter to do more research for his novel of mysticism.

Any such plans were, however, made irrelevant by the announcement on 22 August of the Nazi–Soviet Pact, which would divide Poland and certainly lead to war. Within hours the mayor of St Jean called the Villa Mauresque to warn that mobilization orders would be posted the next day, and most of Maugham's staff departed for military service in Italy or France. Black Senegalese troops appeared overnight and were stationed by the railway bridge across the entrance to Cap Ferrat. Vincent, who had been playing in a tennis tournament in Monte Carlo, hastily returned to say that the tourists were frantically getting out, the Blue Train was packed, and the roads were choked with cars crammed with baggage.

It was agreed that Liza and Vincent should return to England immediately, and when Haxton came back from Villefranche with the news that all private yachts were to leave the port within twenty-four hours, they decided to take the *Sara* to Cassis, a sheltered port near Marseilles. After stocking up on whatever tinned foods were left in the depleted shops, and leaving the villa in the hands of the cook, the one remaining maid, and the gardeners, they took the boat and its crew of three westward along the coast.

The American flag, to which the *Sara* was entitled by Haxton's citizenship, was a sort of guarantee of safe passage, though no protection against the mines along the Iles d'Hyères and around Toulon. After a day's sailing in gentle breezes and bright sunlight, they stopped at Ste Maxime, where they spent the final evening they would ever have with Horace de Carbuccia, who railed against the folly of Britain and France going to war to defend Poland. Leaving in the morning, Maugham and his crew faced fierce winds for two days, and after twice tying up for the night finally reached Bandol, a small but attractive port just west of Toulon.

Maugham and Haxton remained in Bandol, shopping in the market, anxiously scanning the five-day-old English papers, and maintaining a slim hope that the crisis would pass. After nearly a week, however, a shaken Haxton returned to the *Sara* from a shore errand with the news that the German armies had marched into Poland. It would, he observed, mean war. 'Good,' replied Maugham.

8

THE OLD PARTY AT WAR:
1939–1946

MAUGHAM GREETED THE outbreak of war with a mixture of relief and a strange sense of exhilaration. There had been at least three years of increasingly ominous signs, and during the previous twelve months the French Army had mobilized three times. Maugham had much to lose – his planned visit to India, the completion of his novel of mysticism, and of course the Villa Mauresque, but the declaration of war at least removed the frustrating uncertainty for a man who always liked to map out his life well in advance. Besides, he believed, the Germans could hardly last more than three years, and the French Army and British Navy would ensure an ultimate Allied victory.

Maugham's response to the end of the ambiguity of diplomatic skirmishing is understandable; the intensity of his wish to get into the struggle, so forcefully revealed in his correspondence of that period, is more surprising. He had, after all, written a powerful play attacking jingoists and war profiteers only seven years earlier, and he shared Churchill's contempt for those who had complacently allowed Hitler's power to grow. Moreover, he was nearly sixty-six years old, bothered by rheumatism and malaria, and could justifiably have retreated to the relative safety of Britain or the distant security of America.

Little had happened in the twenty-five years since the beginning of the first great war, however, to alter Maugham's attitude toward serving one's country in time of national crisis. A civilized man, he could describe the ravages of war when peacetime gave him the freedom to do so. When that freedom was threatened, he could nevertheless join any struggle to preserve it. Though essentially shaped by his Victorian and Edwardian background to believe in service to one's country in time of need, Maugham's attitude was more aptly expressed by Shakespeare's warrior-king Henry V: 'In peace there's nothing so becomes a man / As modest stillness and humility / But when the blast of war blows in our ears / Then imitate the action of the tiger.'

Maugham had anticipated the inevitable blast, and during his visit to London in July he had made discreet enquiries first at British Intelligence about the possibility of doing espionage work and then at the Ministry of Information, to whom he offered his pen. His intention had always been to leave for England as soon as war broke out, but on 3 September he and Haxton were stranded in Bandol. Telegrams were subject to censorship, people were forbidden to leave the department of Var, and authority to travel took weeks to secure. For more than a fortnight Maugham and his companion passed the days aboard the *Sara*, dining below deck with the portholes painted over to satisfy blackout requirements.

On about 21 September the pair discovered that the travel restrictions were more illusory than real, and they returned to the Villa Mauresque with surprising ease. Leaving the yacht in the care of a local sailor one day, they simply told a taxi-driver that they wished to go to Cap Ferrat, and to their amazement they made the trip along the coast with no interference. Awaiting Maugham at home was a letter from the Ministry of Information requesting that he keep himself available for assignment. The promise of useful work was pleasing, but he was disappointed by the absence of any news of Liza and Vincent, of whom he had heard nothing since their departure nearly a month earlier.

Maugham was also, as he indicated in a letter to Nellie Maugham on 23 September, anxious to hear about Robin, who he knew would be seeing active service if the war lasted very long. At the same time he was concerned about the long-term future of his nephew, who would inherit his father's title but, with three sisters, only a modest capital. It would not be much with which to pursue his dream of a political career. Willie therefore arranged for Alanson to establish a trust fund of $25,000 for Robin, the money to come from one of the author's American accounts.

For a month after his return from Bandol Maugham heard nothing from the Ministry of Information, and both he and his companion found the inactivity tedious. Haxton wrote to Robin that they were 'feeling very aged and on the shelf' because no one seemed to want their services and that Maugham was 'very low and gloomy about it'.[1]

Preoccupied by the various possibilities of the early months of the war, Maugham was unable to concentrate on writing fiction, and so he busied himself putting together *Books and You*, a short collection of pieces on literature which was published the following year.

By late October the Ministry had asked Maugham to write a series of articles for British consumption about wartime France and the French war effort. Though he would have much preferred a more interesting intelligence job, he seized the opportunity with alacrity and left for Paris where a friend in the Bureau of Information could provide the necessary information. He had barely settled into the Hôtel Vendôme when he was off to Nancy, from which for a strenuous week he visited Strasbourg (where he experienced his first air raid) and the Maginot Line. Along the front, he toured a sugar factory, a textile mill, and a foundry. On his return to Paris on 5 November he spent a week visiting a number of industries in central France: factories for the manufacture of armoured cars, artillery shells, airplane guns, explosives, and other war materials.

After a fortnight Maugham went to Charente, in the south-west part of the country, to interview the evacuees from the threatened area of Alsace-Lorraine. Though for propaganda purposes Maugham underplayed their suffering in his article for the Ministry of Information, he was appalled by the insensitive handling of the problem by the French Government. As he later revealed in *Strictly Personal*, the refugees were transported by cattle trucks, housed in appalling conditions, and barely clothed. As if this were not enough, they soon learned that in their absence their homes had been looted by the soldiers left to guard them.

In addition to his investigation of specific situations, Maugham was asked to write more generally about the parts played by organized religion and women in the war effort. For the former, the life-long agnostic went first to the church of Notre Dame des Victoires in Paris and then to the country to interview rural parish priests. For the latter, the reputed misogynist relied on his observations of the refugee women of Alsace-Lorraine and of those he had seen working in the factories. His account of their contributions is warmly admiring, though he could not resist ending with a suggestion that, with the shortage of cosmetics, the number of blondes was rapidly diminishing.

Maugham's last task for the Ministry of Information was a late November tour of the French fleet at Toulon. Given his choice of travelling in a minesweeper, submarine, or battleship, he immediately chose the largest battleship, though he eventually found himself viewing exercises from both a heavy cruiser and a torpedo boat. The Ministry was especially anxious that Maugham go to Toulon because the French Navy felt ignored and slighted, and it was necessary to demonstrate that the British were properly appreciative. Though the resulting article was laudatory, Maugham could not help noting that the French officers seemed more emotionally attached to their homes than to their professions, that a democratic impulse had led to a more casual relationship between officers and men than in the British Navy, and that there was a more relaxed attitude towards dress in the French Navy. Though in Maugham's eyes these were admirable traits, they were interpreted by the French as insults and only added to their disquiet.

When Maugham returned to Paris in early December he was exhausted, and he soon left for the Villa Mauresque to regain his strength and to write his articles. They were published in book form as *France at War* in April 1940 at the instigation of the Ministry of Information. In February of that year, a Ministry official, J. N. Parrish, wrote to Alexander Frere of Heinemann to assign the copyright, to describe the format, and to establish the price. Moreover, the Ministry agreed to purchase 4000 copies for free distribution and insisted on being involved in publicity and disposal of review copies.[2] The book immediately sold in large numbers on both sides of the Atlantic, and until France fell it was an effective bridge between the two countries. Maugham's faith in the French forces, more sanguine in his propaganda pieces than in private, proved to be misplaced, and in June 1940 distribution of the book ceased.

As useful as Maugham's work for the Ministry of Information was, it may well be that he was as valuable to the British effort in a clandestine way. In a letter written to Alanson from England on 24 October Alan Searle said: 'W. wired to say that he was doing some of his old work (Ashenden) and has disappeared for the time being.'[3] On 14 November Maugham wrote to Eddie Marsh to say that he had been given several tasks, one to write a series of articles and another somewhat more delicate.[4] If these remarks are merely an exaggeration of his propaganda role, they are uncharacteristic acts of immodesty in a man who never puffed himself up to his friends.

It is possible that Maugham did some field work for British Intelligence in the autumn of 1939, though there is presently no available proof of such activity, but it is more likely that his 'delicate' task was to provide the British authorities with an assessment of the morale of the French and especially their attitude towards Britain. His detailed observation of the Russian political atmosphere in late 1917 had been very useful to the Foreign Office, and the novelist's keen eye could still provide a sensitive reading of a fragile situation. In *Looking Back* he reveals that he was asked to comment on the French opinion of their allies across the Channel, and that his observations were necessarily of southern France. This suggests that he sent his first report in October before leaving for Paris, which is confirmed by his letter to Frederic of 7 November in which he is grateful that his brother found his memorandum useful.

Attached to this letter was a second report, which, like the first, described French cynicism about the British war effort. Having been led to believe that there were at least 300,000 British troops in their country, the French were shocked to hear Hore-Belisha, the Secretary of State for War, admit that the number was in fact half of that total. Maugham's tour of the Maginot Line confirmed that the British were perceived as taking the war too lightly, and that German propaganda was effectively persuading the French that their friends would fight to the last drop of French blood. One of Maugham's suggestions was that British anti-aircraft batteries be placed among the French forces so as to make the British more visible, but French military officials concluded that it would be too difficult to accommodate their allies. Though the contents of Maugham's memoranda to London are unknown, it is clear that he suggested a number of measures to counteract German propaganda, one of which he commended to Frederic by saying that such a gesture would arouse immense enthusiasm in the whole of France.[5]

Maugham spent the Christmas of 1939 with Haxton at the Villa Mauresque, and in January he did a small, unidentified job for the French Government. His own Ministry of Information wanted him to follow up his articles on France with similar ones on Great Britain, to be translated and distributed in France, and so he left for England in early February. On the way he spent several days in Paris gathering more information, and while there he was invited to serve on a committee which would attempt to devise terms for a future peace treaty. This came to nothing when the Foreign Office rightly decided that such efforts were premature.

The hazards of a wartime Channel crossing persuaded Maugham to fly for the first time in his sixty-six years, but he could hardly have chosen a less reassuring initiation. Heavy rains had flooded most landing fields in England, and poor weather grounded all planes in central France for five days. Maugham twice made futile trips to the airport at

Le Bourget, once spending half an hour in the plane before the pilot abandoned the flight. On the third occasion, the RAF plane carrying embassy bags chanced the elements and, after flying a circuitous route at about one hundred feet above the water, it landed at a military airport in Sussex. Arriving in London on a Sunday, cold, tired, and hungry, the Phineas Finn in Maugham urged him to a late dinner at the Café Royal.

Maugham remained in England for three uncertain months, once again frustrated by a feeling of being less than fully used. Bruce Lockhart saw the novelist several times during this period and later remembered his eagerness to help France, his belief in the necessity of an immediate declaration of war aims, and his bitterness about bureaucratic barriers to potential contributors to the war effort.[6] Much of his time was spent collecting material for articles which never appeared. A plan for him to write about the 'little fleet' – minesweepers, trawlers, and other small craft doing dangerous work off the English shores – was scuttled by the German invasion of Norway. Similarly, historical events overtook a scheme to have him write a series of pieces on the Home Front, for which he had visited the Paddington district of London and had solicited a diary of one of the organization's members. More successful was an article called 'The French in England', which appeared in a number of English newspapers and was a plea for sympathetic and generous treatment of the French forces which were evacuated to Britain along with the British troops at Dunkirk.

Maugham's most important contribution at this time, however, was two BBC radio talks on the work of the French Navy. The first was a five-minute broadcast on the 'Vive la France' programme on 15 March, the second a thirteen-minute piece for the Empire and Overseas Service on 15 April. Though these were recorded before transmission, they were an ordeal that Maugham had always avoided. Self-conscious of his stutter, he had always refused to make speeches, and through the late thirties had remained adamant in the face of repeated invitations to read his stories on the BBC. In the spring of 1940, however, Maugham had advised Sir John Reith, the new Minister of Information, that the French regarded British radio with a respect not given the broadcasting of their own country. As former director of the BBC, Reith needed no persuasion, and he undoubtedly in turn pointed out that few English voices were as convincing in France as that of an admired man of letters born Paris and resident of the country for a dozen years. Faced with this appeal, Maugham overcame his fear of the microphone, believing, as he observed to William Lyon Phelps on the day of the second broadcast, that nothing mattered but winning the war for freedom.[7]

While in London Maugham offered the manuscript of *Cosmopolitans* to Hugh Walpole, who, as Chairman of the Books and Manuscripts Committee of the Red Cross, was soliciting items for a fundraising sale. As well, he wrote warmly to Walpole to congratulate him on the publication of *Roman Fountain*. He refused Cyril Connolly's request to publish the introduction to *The Mixture As Before* in *Horizon* because he considered it inseparable from the stories it prefaced. He saw Alan Searle a number of times, as well as Robin, and he made the usual rounds of cocktail parties and luncheons. At an April dinner with Harold Nicolson, Kenneth Clark, Clementine Churchill, and Leslie Howard, the talk was of the resentment caused by Aldous Huxley, Christopher Isherwood, and Wystan Auden remaining in the United States during the war.

Maugham's own eyes were on Paris. Since the autumn he had hoped for some sort of interesting liaison job similar to that of Noël Coward, who was set up in an office in the Place de la Madeleine to work closely with the French Commissariat d'Information. Given this, he would settle in a comfortable flat and spend the duration of the war in the French capital. In late April the Ministry of Information agreed that the novelist would be most useful in France and gave him a dual assignment. As before his public role would be to write a series of articles for an illustrated paper; in private his knowledge of a number of influential people in the French political and social world would enable him to send assessments of the French situation.

Maugham flew to Paris on 6 May and left for Cap Ferrat for a week's holiday, but before he could take up his new post Holland and Belgium were invaded. The rapidly advancing German armies made it risky for Britons to remain in Paris and this, together with the change of Ministership of Information from Sir John Reith to Duff Cooper, meant the cancellation of Maugham's assignment.

Maugham stayed at the Villa Mauresque through May and much of June, restlessly awaiting instructions and unable to concentrate on his own writing. It was beginning to look as if his services were no longer needed, but, with the Italians poised to move into southern France at any time, he found it difficult to begin a novel. Mail again became sporadic and, receiving no letters from England for three weeks, Maugham spent his days listening to the radio and scanning those British newspapers which got through.

The news was increasingly bleak and setback followed setback with dizzying rapidity. The Germans broke through the Maginot Line at Sedan, the Belgian Army surrendered, and the British Expeditionary Force was pushed out of Europe at Dunkirk. The French Government moved first to Tours and, when the Germans marched into an undefended Paris on 13 June, to Bordeaux. By 16 June Marshal Pétain had formed a new government determined to sue for peace, a position soon made public by French radio.

Maugham was not surprised by the decision but he listened to Pétain's address with a mixture of sadness for France and apprehension about his own safety. All Britons were at risk in the country, and he had more to fear than most. In *Strictly Personal* he refers to Goebbels speaking on German radio about the discreditable forms of British espionage revealed in *Ashenden*, and even if one discounts this as a propaganda statement Maugham would have been identified as someone who might continue to provide information to the British. Moreover, German intelligence would certainly be aware of Maugham's propaganda work in the first nine months of the war, and it probably knew about his more secretive role. With former friends like Carbuccia working for the new Vichy Government the novelist would not go unnoticed.

Not wanting to risk even internment by the Italians and rejecting the idea of suicide (which he considered), Maugham drove to the British consulate at Nice later on 16 June and at 6 p.m. was ordered to be at the quay at Cannes early the next morning with a blanket, one suitcase, and food for three days. There he and 1300 other refugees would be evacuated in two requisitioned colliers which quickly became known as 'the Hell Ships'. Mistakenly believing that Haxton's American citizenship would protect him and his property, Maugham left his companion to save as many of the valuables of the Villa Mauresque as possible. More important were two typescript volumes of comments distilled from fifty-six years of notes and the Indian observations which would form the background to much of his novel of mysticism. For the journey Maugham chose three books from his library: Plato's *Trial and Death of Socrates*, Thackeray's *Henry Esmond*, and Charlotte Brontë's *Villette*. With considerable difficulty he left instructions that his beloved dachshund Erda should be destroyed if the house had to be abandoned, and he left the villa for what he reasonably believed to be the last time.

Maugham has provided a vivid account of the hazardous and tedious journey to England in *Strictly Personal*: the hastily and carelessly assembled provisions, the strange assortment of wealthy vacationers, retired soldiers and civilians, butlers and governesses, and the pathos and comedy enacted along the way. Maugham's ship, the *Saltersgate*, had coal dust in every corner, and within a few days the daily ration of a pint of water could not prevent the passengers from becoming blackened. Maugham slept on an iron deck in a hold with seventy-eight others, and lived on bully beef, sweet biscuits, and tea. The lavatories, designed for a crew of thirty-eight, had to serve more than five hundred. Before the voyage was over, five passengers had died from the conditions.

So harrowing was the experience that several years later, when Maugham was comfortably settled in New York's Ritz-Carlton Hotel, visitors were often intrigued by an old cracked cup sitting on top of a chest of drawers. It was the vessel that had held his daily ration of water aboard the *Saltersgate* and, said Maugham, 'it serves to remind me that the best things in life are the simplest – and the least appreciated, because we take them for granted.'[8]

The two colliers left Cannes on 17 June for Marseilles where they joined a French convoy for Oran. When they reached the Algerian port on the morning of 23 June, however, they were prevented from disembarking by the French surrender the day before, and the *Saltersgate* was sent back across the Mediterranean with another French convoy. After another forty-eight hours at sea, they docked at Gibraltar for three days, though most of the travellers were allowed off the ship for only a brief period. Finally, with fewer passengers and more room, the collier left for Lisbon and then England in a flotilla escorted by a destroyer. Acutely conscious of the ever-present threat of Axis submarines, Maugham found Plato's description of the trial and death of Socrates more moving than ever before.

When the *Saltersgate* arrived at Liverpool in the evening of 8 July, it had been twenty days since its passengers had embarked at Cannes, and for much of that time the outside world knew nothing of the whereabouts of one of its most famous passengers. Moreover, since communication with southern France had been poor for several weeks before the evacuation, Maugham had been essentially incommunicado for a month. As a result, the *New York Times* had claimed on 23 June that friends of his believed he was in Paris shortly before the German occupation and they feared for his safety. Not until the 29th was the paper able to report that the novelist had reached Lisbon. So uncertain was the atmosphere that earlier on 8 July Maugham's old friend Walter Payne assumed the power of attorney on the writer's behalf, to conduct his affairs until Maugham's return.[9]

Maugham's arrival in Britain naturally created a great deal of interest in the press, and on 9 July he told reporters that he was convalescing in seclusion following three weeks of hardship. 'When we reached this country', he said, 'I was half starved and desperately in need of sleep. I will require peace and quiet.'[10] The exhaustion of a sixty-six-year-old man following such a journey was undoubtedly oppressive, but Maugham was a little disingenuous in pleading for peace and quiet. In reality, on disembarking he had taken the first train to London, where, as the following BBC interoffice memo (dated 6.40 p.m., 8 July) indicates, he immediately offered his services to radio:

> Somerset Maugham asked me to give you this message:
> He has just arrived in London from the Riviera with 500 refugees who travelled on a tramp ship. He wonders whether the BBC would like him to do a broadcast. He is holding off all the newspaper interviews meantime. He may be found at the Dorchester Hotel.
> I think I should refresh your memory about his stutter: it was very evident during his telephone conversation.[11]

The Ministry of Information and the BBC wasted no time in using Maugham. Early in the afternoon of 10 July, he was on the Home Service telling of his journey in a talk entitled 'Escape From the Riviera', an anecdotal account of the harrowing voyage emphasizing the courageous determination of the passengers and the dedication of the crew. A few hours later he recorded a four-minute item for overseas transmission during the night. Far more significant were two broadcasts he made the following day: a commentary on the fall of France for the English public and a French-language broadcast aimed at listeners across the Channel.

The first transmission, 'Talk on France' broadcast on 'Radio News Reel', was intended to soften the British reaction to the collapse of the French war effort and to separate the collaboration of the Vichy Government from the actions of the average French citizen. Arguing that millions of Frenchmen were grieved by the surrender, Maugham implored his listeners to pity their allies rather than blame them: 'I ask you to have patience until this madness that has swept the country has run its course, and to trust, as I trust, that after this bitter trial France will regain her freedom, and with the old watchwords "Liberty, Equality, Fraternity" resume her rightful place in the vanguard of democracy.'[12]

The purpose of Maugham's commentary was clearly propagandistic, but behind the words lay a deeply-felt and sincere emotion. Beginning in his early childhood he had developed a special affection for France, and now he had no way of knowing whether he would ever see it or the Villa Mauresque again. He had, moreover, studied the French defences himself, maintaining adamantly that they would hold, and now he had to admit his misjudgement. This mixture of feelings undoubtedly prompted his strange outburst to his sister-in-law Beldy, when she visited him at the Dorchester. Expressing her unhappiness over the fall of France, she watched in astonishment as Maugham became angry with her, losing his temper so completely that she was forced to leave. As Frederic Raphael suggests, Maugham had likely bottled up his own feelings so much that this lamentation struck too closely to his own heart. 'It requires no great intuition', he writes, 'to guess that it was fear of his own tears which led him to so reprobate those of others.'[13]

Having spoken to the English about the French, Maugham turned to the more delicate task of explaining the British position to the French, and it is here that he made his greatest contribution to the propaganda war being waged over the European airwaves. The British attack on the French fleet at anchor in Algeria on 3 July had given the German and Vichy Governments excellent material with which to fan latent Anglophobia in France, and it was essential to launch a counter-attack.

The Ministry of Information's guidelines for the subject matter of the talk were relayed to Maugham by BBC officials, but so important was the broadcast that he was personally briefed by Duff Cooper the evening before. He was instructed to emphasize to the French that the British still regarded them as allies – that the only animosity was towards the Vichy Government as traitors to their country. He was to make it clear that the British aims remained unchanged by recent setbacks, and that not only would they defend the British Isles but they would soon take the offensive. The British, he should explain, were distressed by the spectacle of the Vichy regime obeying German orders, thus creating a situation where the British had to fire on the French fleet when its government refused to surrender it.

Guided by these points, Maugham spoke for five minutes on the 'French News Talks' programme at ten o'clock on the evening of 11 July. On 22 July he broadcast an expanded account of his escape from France for Empire and overseas transmission, attempting to counter potential Anglophobia by stressing that the refugees were not merely rich holidaymakers or Britons who had opted out of the war effort. Five days later he spoke briefly on 'Radio News Reel' about the new

Free French Navy, pointing out that it would now be fighting along-side British forces. Finally, on 30 August, Maugham discussed 'War-Time Reading' for fifteen minutes on the overseas network.

Given Maugham's apprehension about his speech impediment, none of these talks could have been less than an ordeal, though they demonstrated to him that he could indeed be articulate before a microphone. He had been persuaded to undertake them because his reputation and recent experiences made him an especially persuasive commentator. That he was paid around five to ten guineas for each broadcast should not suggest that he was anything less than sincere. Just as he had believed it naïve to serve as an unpaid agent in the First World War, he saw no reason to forgo modest fees at a time when access to his own accounts might be restricted.

Once he had completed the initial flurry of broadcasts, Maugham eagerly sought out his closest friends. He made several visits to Alan Searle, then in charge of a YMCA branch in York, and he drove to Northamptonshire to see Robin and Vincent Paravicini, who were stationed at Kettering. Vincent had become a British subject in order to enlist, and Liza, then pregnant, had gone to America.

Like the Duff Coopers and Emerald Cunard, Maugham had taken rooms at the Dorchester Hotel, from where as the summer wore on he tried to maintain the semblance of a normal life in the shadow of the expected German invasion and the bombing raids on London. Vincent Sheean recalled several gatherings at Sibyl Colefax's Westminster home, once observing Maugham leaning his head wearily against his hand as the company listened to Mozart and Schubert trios being bravely performed to the sounds of bombs exploding. On another occasion he joined a luncheon party of Maugham, Moura Budberg, Diana Cooper, and Bruce Lockhart in sitting under electric lights at midday, with the windows blocked by wooden frames, because H. G. Wells refused to be driven by the German raid into going to the shelter.[14]

It may well have been after one of these evenings that Maugham witnessed the extraordinarily destructive effect of the bombing on the sensibilities of Virginia Woolf, who was soon to take her own life. In the midst of a raid, Woolf insisted on walking home alone, and fearing for her safety Maugham and a friend followed at a distance in a taxi. When the attack intensified, said Maugham, 'we shouted to her to take cover but in the noise she couldn't hear us. She made no attempt to take cover but stood in the middle of the road and threw her arms into the air. She appeared to be worshipping the flashing sky. It was a most weird sight to watch her there, lit up now and then by the flashes from the guns. Then the planes passed by and she moved on, with us still behind.'[15]

The German air onslaught against Britain had begun in mid-July, but it did not reach its peak until 7 September, when for the next two months London was attacked by an average of 200 bombers a night. On the 8th, Maugham dined with Mrs Lionel Guest, Lord and Lady Willingdon, and General Raymond Lee, head of American intelligence in Britain. While the group toasted with champagne the commencement of the 'real' war, Victoria Station and the Battersea power plant were being knocked out by enemy bombs. By the time that they walked home through the taxi-less streets, 400 Londoners had been killed and 1000 injured.

On 16 September government officials warned the press to expect a German invasion, and the *Times*'s Robin Barrington-Ward later recalled spending that evening with Canadian High Commissioner Vincent Massey and his wife at the Dorchester. After bombs had struck Park Lane and Berkeley Square the trio moved to the ground floor with the usual odd assortment of cosmopolitans. 'Somerset Maugham', Barrington-Ward's diary notes, 'was striding up and down with his jaw stuck out. It was exactly his milieu and he looked as if he was mentally recording the scene.'[16]

Well before the September raids the Ministry of Information had concluded that Maugham was more valuable elsewhere, and as early as 19 August he was telling friends that he would be going to the United States. It was essential to counteract German fifth column activity and the strong isolationist movement in America, and Henry Melchett suggested using prominent men of letters such as H. G. Wells, Noël Coward, and Maugham to explain the British position. 'Carefully selected Britishers', he argued, 'of outstanding ability and reputation could form a British mission under the leadership of the British Ambassador.'[17]

Since the American Neutrality Bill made it illegal for paid foreign agents to conduct propaganda in the United States, it was necessary to send those who were able to support themselves financially. Maugham's popularity in the country made him an ideal voice for British interests, and in October 1940 he joined such writers as Cecil Roberts and Vera Brittain as an 'unofficial' representative. If he ran into difficulties, he would receive no overt assistance from London, but it is clear that he was sent by the British Government and he had instructions to consult with the British Ambassador, Lord Lothian, as soon as possible after his arrival in America.

An assignment in the United States appealed to Maugham for several reasons. First, Liza was there alone awaiting the birth of her child, and this would be a chance to see her and be of help. As well, he could be reunited with Haxton, then still at Cap Ferrat. He had twice cabled to indicate that the villa had not yet been occupied, but the Italians were sure to move in before long. Despite the strains which had developed in their relationship during the thirties, Maugham retained a love of his companion, who was still prohibited from entering Britain. Moreover, if Haxton joined Maugham in the United States, he could bring the typescripts of the notebooks and the Indian material left behind in Maugham's hasty departure.

Maugham left England on 2 October, flying from Bristol to Lisbon in six hours, and a week later he took the *Atlantic Clipper* to New York. In 1940 this entailed a sixteen-hour flight, and after one unnerving bout of turbulence during the night Maugham took a sleeping tablet. H. Montgomery Hyde, a security officer in Bermuda, vividly remembers the novelist arriving at the stopover pale and shaken.[18] Stepping off the plane at La Guardia airport in New York, Maugham told the waiting press that he was absolutely certain of an Allied victory, though the war would probably last two years. Then with his last three dollars he ordered a cocktail.

Maugham's apparently straitened financial circumstances resulted from the freezing of his continental assets and the strict British currency regulations. He had been allowed to take only twenty pounds out of England, most of which had been spent during his week in Lisbon, and on excess luggage charges and the head tax. The British Treasury seized all of his dollar assets in the United States and required him to turn over all future income, in return for which he would be given an allowance. This sum has been estimated to be $2500 a month, though in a letter to Alanson Maugham mentions the more likely figure of $1000.[19] In any case, there were always the securities held in Alanson's name, which therefore would not be frozen.

Out of this income came not only Maugham's own expenses but also some of Liza's, to whom, according to Karl Pfeiffer,[20] he gave $300 a month. Then, too, there was the matter of alimony for Syrie, who had arrived in the United States as a resident alien, with her bond being posted by Nelson Doubleday. She soon learned, however, that the currency restrictions blocked her from receiving her settlement of £2400 per annum in sterling, and that the British Treasury would not let her substitute American royalty dollars. The Doubledays arranged for her to live at the River Club, where, charging everything (including cash withdrawals) to her hosts, she soon ran up horrendous bills. When Ellen Doubleday finally gave her an ultimatum to leave in two months, Syrie calmly pointed out the embarrassing scandal that would be created if such news hit the papers.[21]

It appears that in the end Syrie was rescued by one of Maugham's acquaintances, the well-known American lawyer Fanny Holtzmann. According to her biographer, Edward Berkman,[22] Holtzmann dared to do the unthinkable: discuss with Maugham a matter of his personal affairs. Using the argument that he would not want to do anything which might make his daughter unhappy, she persuaded him to arrange for some provision of funds from his allowance. Syrie then moved into the Dakota, from which she sold furniture.

Maugham's diminished income, meanwhile, still permitted him to move into the Ritz-Carlton Hotel in New York, though he found his room dark, gloomy, and cramped. On his arrival in America he had been taken by the Nelson Doubledays to their Oyster Bay estate for a fortnight's rest which he badly needed after his escape from France, the bombing of London, and the transatlantic flight. There Maugham was able to see a good deal of Liza and Nicholas, who were living nearby in a house for refugee children and their mothers provided by the Doubledays. Several weeks later he confided to Alanson his wish that his daughter would be able to live with him in New York,[23] but whether because of Liza, Maugham, or the arrival of Syrie, this hope was never fulfilled. Nevertheless, even after he moved into the Ritz-Carlton, he continued to spend his weekends at Oyster Bay.

Maugham's brief holiday had not ended before he was put to work. He helped to sell books for the British War Relief bookshop, and he gave at least three speeches, the first of which was to 3000 delegates at the *New York Herald-Tribune*'s Forum on Current Problems held at the Waldorf-Astoria. In a session entitled 'Resources of the Creative Arts', Maugham stressed the intimate connection between the literatures of Britain and the United States and pointed out that the defence of British culture was also a preservation of American culture. On 31 October he joined Dorothy Thompson, Thomas Mann, and Franz Werfel at an Emergency Rescue Committee dinner for 1500 at the Hotel Commodore. There he guaranteed that Britain would survive with American help, and he looked to the day when both countries would be under one flag.

Maugham reiterated the idea of unification much more dramatically on 26 November when he spoke to 3000 people at a meeting to support a federal union of all democratic countries, along lines proposed in Clarence Streit's book *Union Now*. Sharing the platform with such notable figures as playwrights Robert Sherwood and Henri Bernstein, and actors Raymond Massey and Constance Collier, Maugham announced his conversion to a form of world government. Whether he was totally convinced of the value of a world-wide union of democracies, the movement's emphasis on the common goals of the English-speaking countries and the attacks on American isolationists usefully served British propaganda interests.

Maugham had not been in the United States long before he was persuaded to do radio broadcasts, the first of which was an interview with Edward Weeks on NBC, which revealed both the difficulties created by his stutter and Maugham's quick wit in the face of them. When he rehearsed the material which the network writers had extracted from *The Summing Up* he stumbled over the words, stuttering and perspiring. At the pre-broadcast dinner, Weeks discovered that Maugham had rewritten the dialogue, removing all the difficult words, and the resulting delivery over the air was free of any stuttering or hesitation. When a three-minute hiatus necessitated an impromptu question about the source of the next great war novel, Maugham began to struggle: 'Well, Mr Weeks, every novelist would rather write about defeat than victory. And j-j-just as the b-b-best novel about the First World War, *All Quiet on the Western Front*, came out of Germany's defeat, so I hope and b-b-believe that the best book about this war will come from the same source, and f-f-for the same reason!' It was, says Weeks, a bold answer in 1940 and it elicited an outburst of applause from the studio audience.[24]

In addition to his public appearances Maugham was kept busy writing articles. His April radio talk on the French Navy had been published in *The Listener* and then in *Living Age*, and in September *Redbook* had carried 'The Refugee Ship', an account of the *Saltersgate*. Now asked for more such pieces, he wrote 'The Inside Story of the Collapse of France', 'The Lion at Bay', 'What Tomorrow Holds', and 'They Are Strange People, the Germans' for the October to February issues of *Redbook*. Believing that a common culture was one of the strongest links between his country and the United States, he produced 'Reading Under a Bombing' for *Living Age* and 'Give Me a Murder' for the *Saturday Evening Post*. As the war stretched on, he would follow these literary pieces with 'The Culture That is to Come', in August 1941, 'Painting I Have Liked' in December of that year, 'Reading and Writing and You' in August 1943, and 'Write About What You Know' in November 1943. Over the winter of 1940–1, he wrote four more articles on his wartime experiences for serialization in the *Saturday Evening Post*, and on 3 September 1941, an amplified version of these accounts was published in book form as *Strictly Personal*.

Maugham contributed more than twenty such propaganda articles before the end of the war but he hated writing them. Unaccustomed to dealing with detailed factual material, he missed the creative flow of his imaginative work. When he arrived on the *Clipper* he told reporters that he intended to write four more novels but these would have to await a less demanding time. *Up at the Villa* had been serialized in *Redbook* in the spring of 1940, and another collection of stories, *The Mixture As Before*, had been published in early June when Maugham was isolated in southern France. He would not publish another important piece of fiction until *The Razor's Edge* at the beginning of 1944.

As the autumn of 1940 wore on it was decided to send Maugham to Chicago and then California where British publicity was poor and isolationist convictions deeply-rooted. A few months earlier Vera Brittain had been forcibly struck by the mid-western antipathy to European affairs. 'What people remember', she noted, 'are the secret treaties, the vindictiveness of Versailles, the defaulted war debts and the post-war blindness of England and France. There is also a deep-seated suspicion of British and French motives: people here feel they are up against something they don't understand – the European system.'[25] The hard centre of the antagonism was Chicago, where the *Tribune*'s owner, Colonel McCormick – called 'one of the finest minds of the fourteenth century' – persuaded millions of readers to oppose intervention. British lecturers could expect to receive a welcome as chilling and harsh as the winter winds blowing off Lake Michigan.

Maugham's foray into politically unsympathetic territory was made much easier by the presence of Haxton, who, after waiting for five weeks in Lisbon for the *Clipper*, had sailed on the *Excambion*. He had stored the best of Maugham's paintings with their neighbour Lady Kenmare, but everything else in the villa was at the mercy of whoever chose to occupy it.

The pair left for Chicago on 20 December, later than planned because a lingering fatigue had finally driven Maugham to see a New York doctor. Once in Chicago he developed a kind of influenza which so sapped his energy that he was forced to cut short his planned four-week stay to recuperate with the Alansons in San Francisco. Before leaving Chicago, however, he called on a fellow resident of the Hotel Ambassador, the actress Ruth Gordon, whom he had met years earlier in Europe. After he had attended her play and a post-performance party, Gordon summoned the nerve to ask him to join Alfred Lunt, Lynn Fontanne, and herself for a quiet New Year's Eve supper. Whether because of his health or his natural preference for small dinner parties, Maugham was so delighted by the invitation that he cancelled an opera seat and party in order to accept. From this point until the writer's death he enjoyed a fond, teasing friendship with the vivacious actress and her husband, Garson Kanin.

Maugham remained with the Alansons until the end of January, avoiding the cocktail parties but speaking at the San Francisco Press Club. From there he and his companion drove to Beverly Hills, where he visited Rex Evans, Edmund Gwenn, and John Van Druten, and attended a glamorous Hollywood party along with such cinema stars as Charlie Chaplin, Ronald Coleman, Rosalind Russell, Loretta Young, and Hedy Lamarr. At the same time, he met with various studio executives to discuss the feasibility of writing a screenplay for a propaganda film which would dramatize life in wartime Britain. If the Ministry of Information approved and Maugham was able to write a satisfactory screenplay, David Selznick was prepared to spend two and a half million dollars. Maugham would be paid $15,000 on delivery of the manuscript, $5000 a week for twelve weeks, and $4000 for another four.

Leaving a busy Hollywood for three days of relaxation at Santa Barbara, Maugham and Haxton then returned to Chicago in early March to complete the work interrupted by illness. There he gave four speeches, one of which was a University of Chicago lecture chaired by David Daiches. 'I remember', said Daiches, 'being very disappointed with his lecture, which consisted in explaining the fall of France on the grounds of the corruption of French officials exemplified by the fact that they very often short-changed you in French post offices. I thought that as a contribution to the political and military events of 1940 this was somewhat minimal.'[26]

Daiches is doubtlessly right that Maugham's analysis was overly simplistic, especially for a university audience. His observations, however, had always been primarily those of a novelist: the states of mind and behaviour of people, rather than the larger political and military background. His focus had led to a misreading of the French vulnerability to German tanks and their own ambivalent attitudes, and now he was attempting to explain their surrender in moral terms.

Similarly, while Vera Brittain could determine the complex historical reasons for American isolationism, Maugham tended to see the problem in terms of Anglophobia, much of it caused by the English themselves. Writing to Robin in May 1941, he observed that the manners of some Britons were so disgraceful that they seemed to be trying deliberately to offend Americans.[27] The solution, he believed, was to undercut the British stereotype both by one's own conduct and by writing about it. Thus in April 1942 he wrote a piece for the *Saturday Evening Post* called 'Why D'You Dislike Us?' in which he attempted to dispel the idea of the English as being complacent, supercilious, stingy, ill-mannered, inhospitable, snobbish, and humourless. As if Maugham's list was not long enough, more than 300 Americans wrote to him to add their own complaints, but it did not stop his publishing another article, 'To Know About England and the English', two months later, and 'We Have a Common Heritage' in 1943.

Whether or not he was guilty of simplifying the isolationist impulse, Maugham's sensitivity to American attitudes led him shrewdly to look beyond the immediate problem of wartime exigency. In 1943, when an eventual Allied victory seemed assured, he asked Eddie Marsh to tell Churchill that there was considerable resentment in the United States about the tax money going to Lend Lease. Much more was required to make Americans recognize the extent of the British war effort, or else they would think at the end of the war that they alone were responsible for the victory. The future of Britain and the Empire, he realized, would depend heavily on the United States, and it was therefore essential that its citizens be sympathetic to the British.[28]

Maugham continued to work toward this goal, returning to New York in the middle of March to give lectures along the east coast. On 21 March he was a guest at the Centennial Banquet of the New York University College of Medicine, and a week later he spoke in Philadelphia. At the end of April he spent several days with William Lyon Phelps in New Haven and addressed a group of students at Yale. He had insisted on meeting the undergraduates without the intimidating presence of distinguished faculty members, and except for one lapse of memory he enjoyed the vigorous questions of his young audience.

Maugham suffered another attack of influenza at the beginning of April, and the heat of the city was becoming oppressive. He relished the company there of friends such as Sam Behrman, Carl Van Vechten, and Clare Booth Luce. Then, too, there were other exiles: Victor Cazalet, Emerald Cunard, Elsie Mendl, H. G. Wells, and Lou Burton and Charlotte Boissevain from the Riviera. On the weekends, however, he managed to escape to various friends' homes in New Jersey, Long Island, and Connecticut. One such especially attractive retreat was Georgetown, where he was frequently the guest of the sculptor

Sally Ryan at her High Perch Farm. Nearby was Edna Ferber, in the words of Ralph Gustafson, 'the princess lointaine in her *Better Homes and Gardens* residence on a Connecticut ridge. Hear and see them together, and they were two professionals of abiding affection.' Or there was American playwright Sam Behrman. 'The conversation', recalls Gustafson, 'should have been heard the afternoon I listened to Maugham and Sam Behrman. There were three hours of wit in the Connecticut sun if ever there was wit.'[29]

Gustafson, now one of Canada's most distinguished poets, was then working at the British Information Service in New York and beginning his writing career. '[Maugham's] kindness to me, a far from publicly-proven writer, was continual,' he recalls. 'He judged my poems in generous terms even though he discounted himself as unqualified to assess poetry. On prose grounds, we talked and exchanged freely, as though I were as good and knowledgeable as he was, which was far from the case ... These and other stories shown to Maugham brought forth a spontaneously generous praise without stammer: "Still waters run deep with you".' In Gustafson's copy of *Theatre*, its author wrote: 'For Ralph, a poet. W. Somerset Maugham, who can only write prose,' It was an attitude, suggests Gustafson, that was both humble and respectful.[30]

By the last week in May plans for Maugham's propaganda film had been settled and, with Haxton at the wheel, he drove across the continent to Beverly Hills. Within days they found a comfortable house on South Beverly Glen Boulevard, employed two Chinese servants, and invited the Alansons to visit them. As he had hoped Liza and her children arrived in July and stayed for much of the summer. She had been delivered of a daughter, Camilla, and was, said the proud grandfather, prettier than ever.[31]

Soon after his arrival in California Maugham plunged into his British war story and by the end of July he had completed a prose fiction version entitled *The Hour Before the Dawn*. The project was complicated because *Redbook* had commissioned a four-part serialization to begin in December, and from that Paramount studio writers would produce a screenplay. This was eventually done by Lesser Samuels, with Christopher Isherwood contributing a tribunal scene because of his familiarity with the experiences of conscientious objectors. Even before the film was finally released in 1944, by which time it was hardly needed, Paramount had persuaded Maugham to expand the serial version into a novel published in June 1942.

In all of its forms *The Hour Before the Dawn* was mediocre. Intended to illustrate the effects of the war on a typical British family, it was instead an outdated picture of the landed gentry, whose adventures were scarcely representative of the ordinary person. Though a scattering of reviews were complimentary, most hammered its cardboard characters and contrived plot. Well aware that it was a poor piece of work, Maugham refused to allow it to be published in Britain, and years later even intimate friends like Gerald Kelly had never heard of it.[32]

The truth is that *The Hour Before the Dawn* was written without enthusiasm by an author already jaded by his propaganda duties. He was becoming exhausted by the unrelenting need to be original and interesting, and the handshaking and small conversation required in the inevitable receptions had worn the nerves of an essentially shy man. Moreover, and perhaps more importantly, he was gravely distressed over his inability to work on any of the fiction with which he planned to round out his career. In *The Summing Up* he had spoken forcefully of the inner compulsion of the artist, yet for the first time in more than four decades he had gone for two years without producing a piece of imaginative writing.

Neither was the Hollywood environment intellectually satisfying. As usual Maugham was invited to innumerable cocktail and dinner parties, and he lunched with such film stars as John Barrymore and Bette Davis, the Mildred of the 1934 version of *Of Human Bondage* who had just played Leslie Crosbie in an adaptation of *The Letter*. And he enjoyed the company of Ruth Gordon, who, as always, made him laugh. Maugham was grateful for the warm hospitality, but his boredom with the Hollywood milieu was apparent when he attended a large party in his honour given by Cedric Hardwicke. Many of the most famous screen beauties were in the room, which caused one of Maugham's dinner companions to observe: 'The women here are so lovely that they have the bloom of peaches.' 'Oh,' murmured the writer, 'how I long for an apple!'[33]

What Maugham missed was the clever conversation of London, New York, and the Villa Mauresque, and he cherished the company of a few Hollywood intellectuals with the enthusiasm of a long denied addict. John Van Druten was interesting, but, as Maugham said to Eddie Marsh, Aldous Huxley and Gerald Heard were 'godsends'.[34] Huxley had joined Heard in Los Angeles in 1937, and with the arrival of Christopher Isherwood two years later they became the leading figures of the California Vedanta movement. Though always remaining an observer rather than a convert, Maugham undoubtedly learned much from them about the Indian religious beliefs which he was to use in *The Razor's Edge*. In February Maugham had reminded Isherwood of 'an old Gladstone bag covered with labels' and only God knew what was inside,[35] but now, as he described his planned novel of mysticism, he seemed 'much mellowed and gentler though tired'.[36]

Maugham and Haxton remained in Beverly Hills until the end of September, visiting the Alansons in San Francisco and having Karl Pfeiffer, then teaching at Washington State University, as a house guest for a week. After completing *The Hour Before the Dawn*, Maugham began reading a number of history books as background material for an article he planned on the discrepancies between English and American versions of the American Revolution and the War of 1812. An accurate and objective presentation of the historical facts, he believed, would teach the young of both countries not to grow up with the dislike of each other he found so common.

In the first week of October Maugham and his companion drove 2900 miles from Los Angeles to Charleston, South Carolina, on their way to New York. This route was chosen so that they could inspect a house that Nelson Doubleday was building on his plantation near Yemassee. There Maugham would spend the winters away from the strenuous pace of his life in New York. The white clapboard bungalow, known as 'Parker's Ferry', had three bedrooms, a large dining-room, a living-room, entrance hall, and kitchen. Nearby were two small cottages: one for the servants and another to serve as a writing-room. It was hardly the Villa Mauresque, but Maugham was pleased with its comforts and enchanted by the view of the Combahee river in front and the magnificent pines behind.

Since the house was not yet furnished, Maugham and Haxton went to New York to buy furniture. Another, and much more interesting reason for being in the city, was an invitation Maugham had received from William Lyon Phelps to serve on the Drama section of the Pulitzer Prize Committee. It was a flattering suggestion, though he was afraid that he would miss some of the plays, and whenever he was in New York that winter he attended as many productions as possible. Unfortunately he saw nothing that captivated his interest.

Maugham returned to South Carolina at the end of November, and he stayed with the Doubledays until he was able to move into Parker's Ferry at Christmas. With the Japanese attack on Pearl Harbor, he heaved a sigh of relief, believing that it meant the end of his propaganda duties. To his dismay he was asked to write the novel version of *The Hour Before the Dawn* and to compile an anthology of English and

American literature of the previous fifty years. The latter project was much less onerous because he recognized its value not only as a useful introduction for a beginning serious reader but also as an illustration of the common cultures of Britain and the United States.

Maugham and Haxton had not been settled into Parker's Ferry for a month before both became ill. In January Maugham suffered one of his recurring attacks of malaria and another, undetermined ailment. When the local doctor was unable to diagnose the problem, he went to New York for X-rays and tests. At first, it seemed as if he had a duodenal ulcer, but this was later rejected, and he was told that there was nothing substantially wrong with him. Haxton's health, however, had more seriously deteriorated from the years of drinking, though since his arrival in America he had tried to limit himself to two cocktails a day. After three weeks in a New York hospital, he went to recuperate at the Key Largo Angler's Club, in Florida, where for a month and a half he fished in the Gulf Stream and lounged in the sun. He was able to rejoin Maugham in South Carolina in the middle of March, but he remained weak.

After Maugham's own recovery life at Parker's Ferry began to fall into a pattern it would have until the end of the war. He had a coloured cook named Norah, who under his tutelage soon could prepare his favourite French dishes, a parlour-maid, and a gardener. Situated two miles from the Doubleday house, thirteen from the nearest village, and fifty from Charleston, the bungalow had a solitude that Maugham found attractive. On the other hand, the distances made shopping for provisions inconvenient, and severe rationing of tyres and gasoline would make it impossible to remain there.

Maugham's working day at Parker's Ferry differed little from those of the previous forty-four years. After breakfast at eight, he would walk to the writing-room, where he would remain until noon. Following luncheon he would often ride through the estate with a young negro guide employed by the Doubledays to see that their eminent author came to no harm. On other occasions he would stroll in the woods behind the house, finding the silence of the massive oaks shrouded in grey Spanish moss more intense than any silence he had ever known. 'There is a strangeness about these bedraggled, abandoned woods,' he wrote with uncharacteristic romanticism, 'and though you walk alone you do not feel alone, for you have an eerie feeling that unseen beings, neither human nor inhuman, flutter about you. A shadowy something seems to slink from behind a tree and watch you silently as you pass.'[37]

As much as Maugham relished the solitude, he was hardly a hermit. While Haxton eventually found Parker's Ferry too quiet, other house guests came from time to time. Karl Pfeiffer made the trip at least once, as did Monroe Wheeler, but a much more frequent and welcome visitor was the American writer Glenway Wescott, whom Maugham had first met in 1928 and came to know better in New York in 1941. Maugham admired the younger man's work, giving him advice and encouragement, and he was pleased to share his house with another hard-working author. Wescott enjoyed the quiet hospitality, but the ambience was clearly not for every taste. In March Dorothy Parker and Alan Campbell arrived for what Parker called the longest three weeks of her life. 'That old lady', she said of her host, 'is a crashing bore.' She had gone there hoping to find a gathering of bright people, but there was only Maugham and 'various handsome young men who were not interested in ladies but who were interested in Mr Maugham. And for three long, long, long weeks Mr Maugham had wanted to do nothing other than play bridge.'[38] Parker, one assumes, found Maugham much less boring two years later when he generously wrote an admiring introduction to the Viking Portable Library edition of her stories and poems.

Parker's Ferry gave Maugham a retreat denied him since the beginning of the war, a necessary escape from the intensity of New York, and he was grateful. He wrote happily to Eddie Marsh in 1941 that he had some very delightful friends in the United States. Their affection and thoughtfulness were touching, and it seemed that they could not do enough to make him contented.[39] Only the inability to do his own work – he was then writing and speaking for the USO and preparing to broadcast on behalf of the sale of Defence Bonds – made him dissatisfied.

Much of April was spent answering the 300 letters sparked by his article about American attitudes towards the British, and when the South Carolina heat came in early May he went to New York to work on his British-American anthology at the Public Library. At the end of June he joined Franz Werfel and Countess Renée Maeterlinck in autographing books for the purchasers of War Stamps and the Lane Bryant store and then left for the Massachusetts coast.

Maugham had been looking for a relatively quiet resort where Haxton could sail and they both could play bridge or gin rummy, his latest enthusiasm. Haxton had meanwhile found a job with the OSS which kept him in Washington, but the Colonial Inn at Edgartown, on Martha's Vineyard, was ideal for Maugham. In this first summer he took only one room, but in succeeding years the management insisted that he have a sitting-room at no extra charge, and he was able to follow his customary pattern: breakfast and reading in bed, work until noon, and relaxation for the remainder of the day. Taking the ferry to the beach at Chappaquidick, he would sunbathe and then swim at the end of the afternoon. Returning to the hotel, he would play bridge until dinner at the Edgartown Yacht Club, after which he often went to the local cinema.

Maugham enjoyed the relative tranquillity of his life at Edgartown, though he could not escape his celebrity. 'Admirers', commented *Life* magazine, 'invariably surround him, sometimes girls, more often elderly ladies who try unsuccessfully to corral him for dinner or cocktails.'[40] Maugham occasionally obliged the local lion-hunters, but he was much more comfortable with such neighbours as the Missouri painter Thomas Hart Benton, or poet and critic Max Eastman, whom he considered a wonderfully engaging companion.

After a few weeks in the sun and sea, Maugham felt his strength returning, and over the summer he completed his anthology. On 5 September, three days before he left Edgartown, he attended the world première of the film version of *The Moon and Sixpence*. With the exception of *The Letter* in 1940, he had declined to be at the opening of any of the previous twenty-two film adaptations of his works, but *The Moon and Sixpence* was different. From as early as 1921 at least eight companies had taken options on it, but no one had found a way to adapt the first-person narration to the screen. Not merely a technical problem, the difficulty lay in the narrator's expressions of admiration for the amoral, socially destructive Gauguin figure.

Albert Lewin and David Loew bought the rights to *The Moon and Sixpence* in the late thirties, and Lewin directed George Sanders in a version that pleased its author so much that he not only made personal appearances but made a speech at the première, all for no fee. The American Legion of Decency, however, were much less enthusiastic, believing that the film had no compensating moral value, and required that the opening and closing credits carry a statement saying in effect: 'We don't want you to have the impression that this character we are telling the story about is an admirable character. He is not.' Maugham, according to Lewin,[41] hated the rubric, and before long it was lost on most prints.

From the placidity of Edgartown Maugham went to New York for two hectic months of meetings, social gatherings, and public appearances. He spoke in Boston and New Jersey, and on 9 November he gave the Francis Bergen Memorial Lecture at Yale, to which he had just donated the manuscript of *Strictly Personal*. At the invitation of William Lyon Phelps, he agreed to speak about freedom and the responsibility of the citizen, and in preparation he borrowed Sir Frederick Pollock's *Political Obligation*. Intending to conclude with a statement about the price of liberty, he suffered another of his blackouts and never did finish the speech.

Maugham's two months in New York in the autumn of 1942 were strenuous, but they marked the end of his heavy involvement in propaganda. He would continue to write an occasional article, but being relieved of making public appearances gave him more freedom than he had enjoyed for three years. When he returned to South Carolina in November he was committed to writing several articles and a short story, but after that he could at long last begin the novel that he had said would 'round off my life's work'.[42]

Haxton, who was still in Washington, did not accompany Maugham to Parker's Ferry, and over the winter the novelist came to see that their relationship had undergone a significant change. With the cooling of his ardour in the thirties and his growing frustration with Haxton's alcoholic, often scandalous, misbehaviour, he had been on the verge of pensioning him off. When Maugham was unable to take that painful final step, the two men continued living affectionately at the Villa Mauresque, with Haxton remaining useful as a secretary and each for the most part going his own way. Since the outbreak of war, however, they were apart much of the time, and Maugham gradually realized that he could live without the younger man. He had developed other relationships since coming to America, and more importantly he already planned to ask Alan Searle to join him after the war.

Haxton's job with the OSS was thus fortunate, and it was with relief that Maugham concluded in January 1943 that Haxton had permanently left his service. He no longer needed to feel responsible for his companion – financially or emotionally. Later in the year Maugham instructed Alanson to supplement Haxton's $300-a-month income with the interest – about $2500 – from a trust fund of $35,000 he had established for him years earlier. This would continue until Haxton's death, when the funds would go to Nicholas and Camilla.

As important as Haxton's financial independence, in Maugham's view, was the sense of self-worth provided by his employment. Over the year his job underwent several changes, but it was the first time since his youth that he had worked at anything except being Maugham's secretary-companion. When his Washington assignment ended in

April he was hired by Nelson Doubleday to manage a commissary selling fruits and vegetables at a plant in Garden City. Having forty-seven employees under him, he was able to exert the authority he had been denied through the years of subordination. Maugham offered to furnish a small nearby house for him, and Haxton cheerfully left for work at six-thirty in the morning and remained there until eight in the evening.

In late October Haxton accepted a permanent position with the OSS in Washington, a job that promised to keep him busy even after the end of the war. He had a small apartment and though he occupied a minor position it gave him a satisfaction he had not felt in his years in what he considered a subservient position as a writer's secretary. For his part, Maugham was delighted by Haxton's new independence since it freed him (Maugham) from responsibility, an arrangement he hoped would continue after the war.

Without Haxton, life at Parker's Ferry was more difficult for Maugham, especially since he had lost several of his servants from the previous winter. The problem of securing provisions had worsened with increased rationing, but there was always the Doubledays' vegetable garden and the canned goods shipped down from New York. To offset his loneliness he began to dine with the Doubledays two or three times a week and on the other days to go to their house for an hour or so of bridge.

Some time in December Maugham began the long postponed *The Razor's Edge*, and by the beginning of March he was able to describe the characters and setting to Pfeiffer. Unsure of the accuracy of his portrayal of Americans and Chicago, he asked Pfeiffer to serve as a kind of editor-adviser, reading his typescript chapter by chapter for obvious British idioms he might unwittingly have put into the mouths of his American characters. A month later Maugham sought help from another source, the French writer André David, whose book *La Retraite aux hommes chez les Dominicains* he had admired the previous summer. He borrowed a copy again in order to find authentic background material for his picture of his young protagonist's monastic retreat. His eagerness was barely hidden in his reply to David a fortnight later: 'I could only wish you had made your book longer and had given a more detailed account of your life from hour to hour in the monasteries you stayed at.'[43]

Maugham had already discussed various aspects of Indian mysticism with Heard, Huxley, and Isherwood in Beverly Hills two years earlier, and in July 1943 he again consulted Isherwood. He wrote to ask the precise translation of a verse in the *Katha Upanishad*, part of which he proposed to use as a title for the novel: 'The Razor's Edge' or 'The Edge of a Razor'. Isherwood and his guru, Swami Prabhavananda, replied that in the comparison of enlightenment to the edge of a razor, the image of the razor symbolizes a path that is both painful and narrow. Many translations falsely suggest that the path is difficult to cross, when the real difficulty is to tread the razor's edge, the path to enlightenment. In the end, the novel's epigraph stated that 'the sharp edge of a razor is difficult to pass over', which Isherwood found almost as inaccurate as 'cross'.[44]

It has been said that Maugham's research for *The Razor's Edge* amounted to at least forty volumes, and the portion of his library which he gave to King's School contains a number of heavily annotated books about Indian and Chinese religion. If he were more than usually concerned about authenticity, it was because he saw the novel, the culmination of years of thought, as his final exposition of a serious and profound theme. Garson Kanin, observing Maugham's commitment to producing an acceptable screenplay for *The Razor's Edge* in 1945, noted that 'this work means a great deal to him, more than any of us suspected. He thinks of it as being, perhaps, his last major work. No matter what the critics or the public thought of its philosophical content, it is profound and meaningful to him.'[45]

At the core of *The Razor's Edge* lies Maugham's lifelong preoccupation with freedom. Like *Of Human Bondage* it is concerned with the ageless question of 'how to be?' and Larry Darrell is the Philip of a new generation. While Philip's search for self-awareness was so credibly played out against a turn-of-the-century background, Larry's quest is that of the young of the mid-twentieth century. Perhaps because of his years in exile Maugham recognized that the United States had become the most powerful, wealthy, and influential nation in the world, and so the background and central characters are American. The American ethos, which would dominate much of the post-war world, was that of a developing country and necessarily materialistic. The New World offered unlimited scope for ambition, energy, and dedication, but the concomitants were competition and pressure to contribute to the accumulation of wealth. Any search of the modern young for spiritual and physical independence would be enacted against those forces.

The novel begins in Chicago, and Maugham creates a number of characters who epitomize the values of American materialism. Gray Maturin, though good-natured and likeable, sees only concrete, easily-recognizable goals: property, family, and wealth. Larry's fiancée, Isabel, is a marvellous character, a wicked picture of American womanhood seen through the eyes of a European. Though charming and vivacious, she shares Gray's pursuit of the American Dream, to which with relentless tenacity she attempts to hold Larry.

The most memorable character in the novel, however, is Elliott Templeton, who has rejected his American background and its values for a materialism of a different sort: the European social structure. With all the intensity of a convert, he embraces all the superficial aspects of gentility: clothes, jewellery, appearances, aristocracy and 'the season'. Maugham modelled Templeton on 'Chips' Channon and a Riviera neighbour Henry May, but he succeeded in a brilliant portrayal of a certain type of expatriate American man of the world.

After a number of picaresque experiences, Larry finds his freedom from the restrictiveness of the American Dream in mysticism. This, Maugham is saying, is the new means of escape. The time when one could preserve one's independence through artistic isolation or distant travel is past; the world no longer allows solitude and anonymity. The new movement is spiritual; while physically bound to the common existence, one can escape inwards into the depths of self. Thus Larry is capable of submerging himself into the life of New York, the epitome of American materialism and industry, without surrendering his essential liberty. At the novel's end, when Larry gives up his income and leaves for New York, perhaps to become a taxi driver, it is with the conviction that he has never been happier or more independent in his life.

Throughout *The Razor's Edge* Maugham treats his protagonist with admiration for his sincere goodness and with sympathetic understanding of his belief that happiness ultimately lies in a life of the spirit. For a writer in his seventieth year, it is a remarkable leap of the imagination. There is, however, never any doubt that Larry's quest is that of a new generation and that his pattern is one which leaves Maugham only a sensitive observer. As he says, 'I am of the earth, earthy; I can only admire the radiance of such a rare creature, I cannot step into his shoes and enter into his inmost heart as I sometimes think I can do with persons more nearly allied to the common run of men.'[46] In a sense, this dichotomy between narrator and protagonist repeats the structure of *The Moon and Sixpence*; in both cases, Maugham uses the device to dramatize a character and a way of life which he admires but cannot share.

The Razor's Edge is Maugham's last major work written in the first person singular, and it is more personal than anything he had written since *The Narrow Corner*. Once asked how long it took him to write it, he replied: 'Sixty years.'[47] In many ways, it is a summing-up of his life, with references to his early career, his experiences among the Bohemians in Paris, and his subsequent literary eminence. As well, many of his comments are distillations of those he had expressed over the decades in drama and prose.

Maugham had, of course, used the first person singular in *The Moon and Sixpence*, *Cakes and Ale*, and many of his short stories. In *The Razor's Edge*, however, the narrative persona is more candidly and transparently Maugham than that of any other work, and for the first time in his fiction he calls himself 'Mr Maugham'. He had developed a confidence and self-assuredness that allowed him to risk such exposure, and this narrative voice is Maugham at his most attractive. Though there are qualities of caution, restraint, and guardedness, he is mellower and warmer than in any other piece with the possible exception of *Cakes and Ale*. Detached in an avuncular way from the central conflicts of the story but sensitive to the difficulties of the characters, he is able to be compassionate and generous.

The Razor's Edge is not Maugham's best novel, and with the passage of time its flaws have become more obvious. The most serious weakness lies in the character of the protagonist himself, who remains largely an abstract symbol while the worldly Elliott Templeton is vividly realized. Despite this, the novel became an immediate bestseller in 1944, with three and a half million copies being sold in the next twenty years. Critical reaction was mixed, but the novel's presentation of Indian mysticism earned the praise of many of its advocates. Though Isherwood regretted a lack of exploration of the intellectual stumbling blocks which lie along the path to salvation, he found much to admire, and Paramhansa Yogananda inscribed a copy of his *The Autobiography of a Yogi* to the 'author of *The Razor's Edge*, which has done so much good in the world by spreading the seed of India's teachings'.

Much of 1943 was devoted to writing *The Razor's Edge*, and Maugham finished a first draft on 8 May and the final typescript on 15 August. Except for several jaunts to Washington and New York, he remained in South Carolina until the middle of May, his solitude there broken only by visits from Pfeiffer, Wheeler, Wescott, and Haxton. The late spring was again spent at the Ritz-Carlton in New York, and the summer at Edgartown.

With Gerald happily settled in his job, Maugham's pleasure in writing his novel was marred only by an increasing concern about Liza. In late 1942 he had begun to express the wish that Vincent would take the children and her back to England because, he claimed, the Americans were sick of the British refugees and if his daughter remained away from her own country much longer she would find it difficult to return there permanently. Behind these reasons, however, lay a fear that if Liza and Vincent continued to live apart the marriage would collapse. In late February he wrote to Dr Rudolf Kommer, who had been seeing Liza, to express his apprehension,[48] and by September Barbara Back was writing to ask if the rumours of an impending divorce were true. Maugham replied that Liza had promised not to do anything until the end of the war, and he believed that when the three-year separation was over they would be reconciled.[49]

Maugham had always been fond of Vincent and he intended to do anything he could to save the marriage. As his correspondence indicates, he felt a strong affection for his grandchildren and, though marriage had not suited him, he hoped for the sake of them and their parents that the family would remain whole. Thus he was gratified in November when the young man suddenly arrived from New Guinea, where he had contracted malaria, dysentery, and shattered nerves. He was delighted to see his children – Camilla for the first time – and they adored him. Observing this, Maugham hoped that Vincent and Liza would settle down as happily as do most married couples after the first flush of passion dies away.

Maugham spent two months in New York in the autumn of 1943, during which he was kept busy correcting proofs of *The Razor's Edge*, negotiating serial and film rights to the novel, speaking on radio, and sitting for a bust for Sally Ryan. As well, there were conferences about the casting of *Sheppey*, which was to be mounted the following April in a form which he had rewritten to eliminate some of the ambiguity which had weakened the original production. It was an exhausted Maugham who returned to South Carolina in mid-November, grateful for the calm of Parker's Ferry and the chance to begin work on the revision of his notebooks.

Over the winter Maugham produced a 500 page typescript of notes, which he left in the safe at the Doubleday house to be published at the end of his writing career or after his death. The editing process in the seclusion of his bungalow caused him to reflect on his life, and on his seventieth birthday he composed a meditative piece as a postscript to the notebooks, though it is just as much an addendum to *The Summing Up*.

Like the earlier autobiographical book, the tone of this fragment is serene. Maugham is forced to admit that at seventy he is 'just an old man', but 'the greatest compensation of old age is its freedom of spirit'.[50] Liberated from envy, hatred, and malice, he is no longer vulnerable to the opinions of others and is content with his professional reputation. Though convinced that life would have been different had he been four or five inches taller and had not had a prognathous jaw, he is gratified to be free of many of the afflictions which beset others. Ten years closer to death than when he began *The Summing Up*, he can view his extinguishing with equanimity.

This postscript is one of a series of valedictions, beginning with *The Summing Up*, and including an appendix he added to his notebooks when they were published five years later. All of these pieces are marked by a sense that the author is in complete control of his material, that he has come to terms with the traumas and triumphs of his life. In the birthday reflection Maugham confesses that, though he has always lived more in the future than in the present, he has become more preoccupied with the past. There are regrets for unconsummated sexual adventures and injuries done others, but, he says, he tells himself that it was a different Maugham who made these mistakes. If there is a hint of unresolved tension lying beneath the surface of this calm it might be found in his comment that 'I have done various things I regret, but I *make an effort* not to let them fret me'[51] (my italics).

The sense of the summation of a life that came with the editing of the notebooks and his seventieth birthday spurred Maugham to begin to make arrangements for the disposition of his estate on his death. He wrote to Alanson in January to enquire about the residue of the trust fund following the settlement of the annuity on Haxton. At the same time, he revived his dream of founding a scholarship for writers, and he announced his intention to donate a sum of money to King's School to provide an education for working-class boys. It would, he told Alanson, be at least a step towards mitigating, if not abolishing, the class consciousness which he saw as an unfortunate feature of English life.[52] This intention was in fact realized in October 1944 by a gift of £10,000.

Maugham hoped that a successful run of *Sheppey* would help him found his scholarship, but once again the play failed to capture an audience. The pre-publication sales of *The Razor's Edge*, however, had reached 50,000 and Twentieth Century-Fox were making a generous offer for the screen rights. As well, *The W. Somerset Maugham Sampler*, an anthology of his works edited by Jerome Weidman and published the previous year, was selling in large numbers. People were buying more books than ever, and few authors benefited from this more than Maugham.

Even on his allowance Maugham was affluent, but in July he claimed to Alanson that at seventy money did not seem important any more.[53] If Maugham had begun to develop a disinterest in accumulating wealth, it may have been a reaction to several events which were profoundly disturbing. The first of these was a cancer scare which he had in April, following several months of poor health. The initial diagnosis suggested a malignancy, but a fortnight of X-rays and tests proved otherwise, and he was told simply to rest.

The other, and much more distressing, development was the sudden collapse of Haxton's health. In April, following a lengthy bout of pleurisy, it was discovered that both lungs were affected by tuberculosis, and that he also had Addison's Disease – an illness causing muscular weakness, weight loss, vomiting, and diarrhoea. The tuberculosis could be cured but the Addison's Disease was inoperable. If it were arrested, Haxton might live for years but always under doctor's care; if the disease suddenly worsened, he could die within days.

Maugham was stunned by Haxton's condition, and he immediately moved to ensure that his friend would suffer as little as possible. He wrote to Alanson to make arrangements for Haxton's financial security in the event that Maugham predeceased him, because he could not bear the thought of his not having everything that could make the end of his life as easy and comfortable as possible.[54] Moreover, as soon as Haxton was able to leave his New York hospital, Maugham planned to fly him to a sanatorium in Colorado Springs for six months.

Haxton, however, never regained the strength for the trip west. He remained in Doctor's Hospital, the best and most expensive nursing home in New York, for eleven weeks, during which Maugham daily endured the agony of hearing him racked with painful coughs that seemed almost to tear him to pieces. By the middle of May he weighed only 112 pounds and, suffering from perilously low blood pressure, he had his lungs collapsed and was given blood transfusions. By late June it appeared that he would not last a week, and twice it seemed that the end had come.

In the last days of June, however, Haxton improved slightly, and the specialists told Maugham that his friend would have a fifty-fifty chance of recovery if he could survive the next few weeks. He would remain an invalid for the rest of his life but it was better than nothing and Maugham decided to take him to a sanatorium at Saranac in upstate New York. He was now too weak for the flight to Colorado, and the fresh country air might bring some improvement. He was now constantly given morphine for the pain, but Maugham was gratified to see that, unaware of the Addison's Disease, he remained calm, patient, and cheerful.

Maugham spent a month with Haxton at Saranac, and when there was some improvement at the end of July he left for Edgartown. If things continued to go well he intended to take his companion to Johns Hopkins in Baltimore for an operation and then to Tucson, Arizona, for the winter. When Haxton began to deteriorate again, he was moved to a hospital in Boston where his condition could be studied by the Leahy Institute. The specialists there were no more successful at arresting his decline, and so at the end of August he was transferred to New York, carried to and from the train on a stretcher.

Throughout September and October Maugham kept his vigil over Haxton, sharing his distress in letters to Alanson, Robin, and Barbara Back, but guarding his emotions with those immediately around him. Ralph Gustafson, who saw him often during this period, remembers 'how he got out of the car we were both in as if [Haxton's illness] meant nothing. "I have to see Gerald," he spoke and was gone. Consequently he undercut anything romantic – and always, possessed deep feeling – hidden lest he lose control and the feeling be expressed in sentimentality.'[55]

No one who has seen Maugham's correspondence can doubt that he was in agony. Writing to Back in September, he pointed out that she was the only person who had said anything truly consoling, which was that he should remember that the sick man is always so busy being sick that the situation is never as hard for him as for the onlookers. He tried to think of that when he saw Haxton lying on his back looking into space, with death on his face.[56] To Edward Knoblock, he observed that it is untrue that one feels less as one grows older.[57]

Though Maugham had a number of acquaintances – he had recently seen Cecil Beaton and Chips Channon – in the eastern United States, he began to feel desperately alone. Liza and the children sailed back to England in September, and Bert Alanson was a continent away, and he longed for someone with whom he could unburden himself. Alan Searle was in Britain and unable to leave the country, and so in late June Maugham had sounded out Nellie Maugham about the possibility of his nephew coming to the United States. Robin had been wounded in a tank battle in North Africa in May 1942 and invalided back to England with a disability pension. Behaving with a courage that amazed and delighted his uncle, he had been hit with shrapnel in the arm, chest, and head, and he was left with a fragment lodged in his brain. Back home he continued to suffer from severe headaches, fits of vomiting, and periods of amnesia.

By the summer of 1944 Robin required further surgery, and Maugham suggested to Nellie and him that it be done in the United States. Afterwards he could spend the winter in South Carolina, where the isolation, riding and shooting, would help calm his excitable nerves. The suggestion appealed to Robin, and Maugham was delighted to hear in the middle of August that his nephew would soon join him. To his disappointment, however, there were difficulties with the exit permit and the young man did not arrive at Parker's Ferry until mid-December.

By that time, Haxton was dead. An operation had disclosed a large ulcer in the stomach but, since Haxton's frail constitution could not withstand its removal, it was closed off. Haxton then seemed to improve, but on 6 November he had an attack of oedema, or swelling of the lung, lost consciousness, and died early next morning.

Though Maugham had often wished that death would quietly end Haxton's suffering, he was devastated by the actual event. Not since the death of his mother sixty-two years earlier had he lost anyone whom he loved so deeply, and he collapsed in grief. Isolating himself in his hotel room, he told a solicitous Cecil Roberts: 'I don't want to see you! I don't want to see anyone! I want to die!' 'I went at once to the Ritz-Carlton Hotel,' said Roberts, 'and went up to his room. He opened the door, very haggard in appearance. I walked in and talked to him firmly, quelling his hysteria . . . When I left he was in a more normal mood. He astonished me by embracing me. I felt he was terribly lonely.'[58]

Haxton was buried on 9 November following a funeral service at the Episcopal Church of St James on Madison Avenue. A number of Maugham's friends – notably the Doubledays, Glenway Wescott, and Monroe Wheeler – attended, and for Maugham, who almost never went to funerals, it was understandably an ordeal. In the middle of the service, he was overcome with emotion and broke down sobbing. Afterwards an American friend, Eleanor Stone Perenyi, remarked to him, 'I can't abide your weeping over that man,' arguing that it was a blessing that Haxton had been spared a miserable old age. Without replying, Maugham walked away from her and never saw her again.[59]

Perenyi's comment may have reflected the attitude of some of Maugham's friends, however it was not only insensitive but short-sighted. For a number of reasons, his tears were justified, and Haxton deserved them. Maugham was weeping for the past, for the loss of a part of his life which had perhaps been the richest. Haxton had been with him through all the best years of his life, travelling into the farthest corners

31. Maugham leaving the Dorchester Hotel to receive the Companion of Honour at Buckingham Palace in 1954. (*Humanities Research Center Library, The University of Texas at Austin*)

32. Receiving an honorary degree from the University of Toulouse. (*Humanities Research Center Library, The University of Texas at Austin*)

33. Maugham at the entrance to the Villa Mauresque, guarded by the sign against the Evil Eye brought by his father from North Africa.
(*Syndication International*)

34. The Moorish sign could be found on many of Maugham's possessions – making them valued collectors' items for light-fingered house guests.
(*Humanities Research Center Library, The University of Texas at Austin*)

35. Maugham in the grounds of the Villa Mauresque with several of his beloved dogs. (*Humanities Research Center Library, The University of Texas at Austin*)

36. Though eighty years of age, Maugham strolls vigorously through the terraced grounds of the villa. (*Syndication International*)

37. The consummate storyteller making a dramatic point to Frederick Prince-White in 1955.
(*Humanities Research Center Library, The University of Texas at Austin*)

38. Maugham at his beloved bridge with Godfrey Winn and others, 1961.
(*Humanities Research Center Library, The University of Texas at Austin*)

39. 'The Very Old Party' makes a point.
(*Humanities Research Center Library, The University of Texas at Austin*)

40. Maugham and Alan Searle dining on the patio around which the Villa Mauresque was built.
(*Syndication International*)

41. Surrounded by some of
the fruits of imagination and
discipline, Maugham has
reason to smile.
(*Syndication International*)

42. Examining the
manuscript of *Ten Novelists
and their Novels* in his study
atop the Villa Mauresque.
(*Syndication International*)

43. Maugham consults with Annette, whose cooking was legendary along the Riviera, about the menu for the day.
(*Syndication International*)

44. Maugham's day always began with breakfast in bed and the morning paper.
(*Syndication International*)

45. The mellow Willie Maugham who entertained Noël Coward before the attack on Syrie in 'Looking Back' strained their friendship.
(*Syndication International*)

46. Maugham on his last visit to London in November, 1962, when he felt the chill of disapproval over 'Looking Back'.
(*Syndication International*)

of the world, and with him almost all Maugham's happiest recollections would die. Moreover, almost everything he had written for the previous thirty years had Haxton's mark on it, if only as a typist. Until only recently Maugham had always expected his companion to outlive him, and now he was left with the special pain of seeing a much younger loved one die. Not only did part of the pattern of his own life seem extinguished, the pattern itself had gone awry.

Then, too, there was the guilt. Maugham's mind must have gone back to the emotions he had felt a year and a half earlier when Haxton had achieved a measure of independence. Did his sense of relief now seem like an abandonment and did he wonder if perhaps he had subconsciously willed Haxton's end? This is speculation, but there is no doubt that Maugham blamed himself for not having done more to save his friend. The death was a futile waste, he believed, because Haxton both wanted to live and knew that he was killing himself, but did not have the self-discipline to prevent his death. Perhaps if he had been firmer with him when it all started, he began to think, and perhaps later if he had forced him into some institution, he might have been saved. Haxton was always weak, and Maugham came to believe that he should have been strong for them both.

These feelings of nostalgia and regret understandably contributed to Maugham's grief, but its real source was quite simply love. There never had been, nor ever would be, anyone for whom he had felt such passion, nor was there anyone with whom he had shared so much of his life. In their early years he had experienced the kind of requited love that he had come to believe would never exist for him. Later, as the passion was gradually replaced by an affectionate companionship, there were the stresses caused by Haxton's drinking and licentious behaviour, as well as the tension caused by the inequity of their positions. But, until the last two years, they had remained together, bound by something that must be considered love.

In one way or another, the relationship between Haxton and Maugham lasted for twenty-nine years, longer than many marriages. And how many marriages do not suffer a transmutation of passion to affection, or undergo the strains inevitably created when two lives and personalities are intertwined? Maugham's and Haxton's union was far from perfect, but it was better than that of many others – with its moments of shared achievement, laughter, and adventure, as well as jealousy, anger, and conflict. If unconventional, it was a love born of shared experiences and grounded in a fundamental loyalty, a commitment that kept them together and brought Maugham so quickly to his dying friend's side. It should surely be unnecessary to argue that two men – or two women – can have a deeply committed, sensitive, and enduring love for each other. Those who were disdainful of Maugham's tears, however, little understood that he was mourning the loss of his own, albeit imperfect, experience of it.

In the months following Haxton's death Maugham was consumed by a sense of loss. A few days after the funeral, he left for South Carolina, and in the isolation before Robin's arrival he could not escape the memories. Half a dozen times a day, something would remind him of Haxton and he would be swept with misery. Even in late February he could hardly bear to discuss his grief even with his most intimate friends. At the end of April he wrote to Margot Hill that she was wrong to believe that Haxton's death must have come as a relief. Even after six months his grief and loneliness were so intense that if he did not have several things he wanted to do he would contemplate suicide.[60] It is hardly surprising that from time to time over the following years, friends would notice that Maugham would mistakenly call Alan Searle 'Gerald'.

Throughout this period of mourning Maugham found some consolation in the company of Robin, who stayed first for a month and then intermittently between trips to New York and Washington. New Year's Eve was spent at the Doubleday house, where Maugham continued to play the occasional game of bridge or gin rummy. Though distracted, he adhered to his work schedule, beginning a new novel set in Renaissance Italy, for which he had done some background reading in the summer. At the end of April he left for his spring visit to New York.

Maugham had not been long at the Ritz-Carlton when he got a call from his friend the director George Cukor, who made him a fascinating proposition. Darryl Zanuck had bought the screen rights to *The Razor's Edge* for Twentieth Century-Fox and had assigned the veteran Hollywood screenwriter Lamar Trotti to produce a screenplay. Attracted to the novel but disdainful of Trotti's work, Cukor had offered to direct the film if Maugham could be persuaded to do the script. Zanuck doubted that he could afford the eminent author, but Maugham told Cukor that he would do it for nothing. It was a chance finally to conquer the cinema by creating a film that accurately recreated a novel which he considered important. Besides, it was different from his usual work, and he leaped at the opportunity to break out of a pattern that had too many associations with Haxton.

Maugham went to California in early June and stayed with Cukor at his home on Cordell Drive in West Hollywood. Provided with a comfortable study, he began to write in the morning and read proofs or go to films with Ethel Barrymore in the afternoon. The evenings were often filled with the customary parties where, though usually bored by cinema stars, he was delighted to find a kind of soul-mate in Greta Garbo. As well, there was a week's visit with the Alansons in San Francisco, followed by another week spent at Lake Tahoe, where he found the scenery attractive but the hotel uncomfortable and the food vile.

When Maugham agreed to go to Hollywood he thought that he was expected only to offer some advice and perhaps make a few revisions. On his arrival, however, he learned that he was to create an entirely new screenplay, and so he set about writing a script that would convey the novel's philosophical elements. In sketching the Paris background, he sought the advice of André David, and he took pains to ensure the authenticity of the presentation of Indian mysticism. Together with Cukor, he met several times with Isherwood and Swami Prabhavananda so that the guru could tell him precisely what instructions his fictional holy man would give to Larry. At the novelist's urging, the swami carefully wrote out a concise rendering of the directive.[61]

The result of Maugham's work was, in Cukor's words, 'the kind of script [which] told the audience from the opening sequence, "This is the kind of picture it's going to be, you'd better listen, you listen here!" A taxi drives up to a house, a man gets out, he goes inside and immediately starts a long conversation with someone in the house . . . The original script, you see, had what the studio called entertainment, which means dancing and country clubs and all that crap. Nothing to indicate you were supposed to sit down and listen to what was being said. Whatever important things this script retained were sandwiched between all kinds of nonsense.'[62]

According to Cukor, the studio was delighted with the script, but decided to postpone shooting until the end of the war, when Tyrone Power would become available to play the lead. By that time Cukor was committed to another film, and Edmund Goulding directed *The Razor's Edge* using the original screenplay. 'Maugham behaved very well about it,' recalled Cukor, 'considering he couldn't bear that script . . . I'm sure that he was deeply disappointed, more than he let on.'[63] He did, however, come away with a $15,000 Pissarro, a gift from Zanuck for his work on a script that was never used.

Maugham left Hollywood at the beginning of September and, after spending ten days with the Alansons in San Francisco, took the train to

New York. He carried with him the typescript of his Italian Renaissance novel, *Then and Now*, which he had revised in the late summer. Conscious of the difficulty of writing a persuasive historical novel – which he had last attempted in 1898 – he had it read by Thomas B. Costain, who enjoyed great success in the historical fiction genre.

Then and Now was published in May 1946 and, whatever advice the author may have received, it made for dull reading. Like *The Making of a Saint* it relies too much on historical detail, and Maugham is rarely able to breathe vitality into his scholarly reading of the period. He explained that he tried to imagine the events which provided the material for Machiavelli's comedy *Mandragola*, but the story is really a lesson on the political realities of the twentieth century.

In 1941 Maugham had observed in his notebook that history shows that if citizens are not prepared to provide money for armaments and to fight they will lose their liberty. 'No one', he argued, 'can enjoy freedom unless he is willing to surrender some part of it.'[64] To dramatize this dictum, he turned to the world of Niccolò Machiavelli and Cesare Borgia, finding its duplicity, machinations, and diplomatic intrigue an excellent parallel to the events in Europe in the thirties and forties. The novel begins with the axiom, 'Plus ça change, plus c'est la même chose', and ends with an uncharacteristically didactic address to the present:

> You say that Caesar Borgia suffered the just punishment of his crimes. He was destroyed not by his misdeeds, but by circumstances over which he had no control. His wickedness was an irrelevant accident. In this world of sin and sorrow if virtue triumphs over vice, it is not because it is virtuous, but because it has better and bigger guns; if honesty prevails over double-dealing, it is not because it is honest, but because it has a stronger army more ably led; and if good overcomes evil, it is not because it is good, but because it has a well-lined purse. It is well to have right on our side, but it is madness to forget that unless we have might as well it will avail us nothing. We must believe that God loves men of good will, but there is no evidence to show that he will save fools from the result of their folly.[65]

While in New York Maugham encountered a vivid and moving reminder of the price of liberty. Writing to G. B. Stern in October he was forced to pause because he was interrupted by a visit from a young one-armed British officer who was unable to strike a match and would not let anyone do it for him. The sight of the young man's tortured attempts so upset Maugham that he found it difficult to return to the letter he was writing.[66] It was as if a character had walked out of *For Services Rendered*, which he had written to save the young from such wreckage, but he was no more immune to the pathos of the soldier's loss.

Maugham remained in New York doing various minor tasks until late November, staying at the Plaza Hotel because the Ritz-Carlton was full. With fewer obligations than he had had for some time, he was able to see more of his friends, and he was delighted to make the acquaintance of the English theatrical producer Peter Daubenay, whom he found charming and congenial. With the Japanese surrender in August, his thoughts had increasingly turned to Europe and what form his remaining years might take in the post-war world. In California he had begun to feel terribly far removed from his own milieu, and now he wanted to return to France or England. The Villa Mauresque was in a dilapidated condition, without a window left in it, but he wanted to see it before deciding whether to restore it or return to Britain.

Though Maugham was resigned to delaying his departure for Europe until at least the spring of 1946, he was impatient to have Alan Searle join him as soon as possible. Even before the European war had ended Maugham had begun the process and by early June Searle had been released from his duties. Securing a travel permit, however, was more difficult than expected, and as the matter dragged on during the summer Maugham decided to donate the manuscript of *Of Human Bondage* to the Library of Congress with the suggestion that it should be transported from Britain by his friend. Negotiations with the American Embassy in London continued through the autumn, but finally in early December Searle was permitted to sail on a cargo boat. Delayed by storms in the mid-Atlantic which washed all the lifeboats overboard and then put them out of touch with the land for three days, he landed in the United States on Christmas Day and went straight down to Parker's Ferry.

For several years Maugham had planned to have Searle become his companion-secretary, and after Haxton's death his intention became a longing. Searle could hardly have been more unlike his predecessor, but Maugham was now past seventy and his needs were understandably different. As he explained to Pfeiffer (who had suggested himself for the job), he wanted someone who was kind, considerate, and unselfish, who would look after him until his death. Searle was not as vital and energetic as Haxton, but he was sober, modest, affectionate, and gentle.

Searle had not been at Parker's Ferry long before he proved to be everything that Maugham had hoped. Moving into his work with ease, he relieved the novelist of many of the minor time-consuming chores, handling his correspondence, and typing his manuscripts. The young man's happiness at being there delighted Maugham and by May he reported to Back that Searle was taking on more and more with energy and efficiency, and doing it well.[67]

This happy arrangement resulted, among other things, in one of the most productive periods of Maugham's years in the United States. He corrected the proofs of *Then and Now*, and wrote three short stories which, added to those brought in typescript from the Villa Mauresque, would make up a collection published as *Creatures of Circumstance* in 1947. In addition, he completed the first draft of what he now considered would be his last novel: *Catalina*.

Maugham left Parker's Ferry for the last time on 31 March, and after nearly three weeks in New York he went to Washington to present the manuscript of *Of Human Bondage* to the Library of Congress. In a ceremony on the evening of 20 April at the Coolidge Auditorium, Maugham spoke to an audience of dignitaries and a newsreel camera. He repeated his familiar point that he was merely a story-teller, and he announced that he was making the gift out of appreciation for the country that had so generously treated him and his family in the previous six years. Several weeks later, the State Department asked that he make a record of the address to be used as propaganda.

Maugham's plans to leave the United States in late May had become widely known, and on his return to New York he was deluged with gifts and invitations to farewell parties. The Alansons' pilgrimage to say goodbye several weeks earlier had been especially important. 'I cannot tell you how we missed you when you left,' Searle wrote, 'it did Willie all the good in the world to be with you – you don't need me to tell you that he idolizes you.'[68] Now there was a succession of interviews, photographing sessions, meetings with tax officials, and a multitude of other demands. 'Willie', said Searle, 'is more social than Mr Truman – I try to protect him all I can, but you would never believe the wiles people indulge in to get at him.'[69]

When they sailed for Marseilles on the French ship the *Colombie* on 29 May Maugham was exhausted and apprehensive about what awaited him at Cap Ferrat, but he was thrilled to feel a ship's deck below his feet again. Not since he was eight years old had he remained in one country so long, and even the vast spaces of the North American continent had failed to satisfy his wanderlust.

9

GRAND OLD MAN:
1946–1958

THOUGH THE WAR had not come unexpectedly to Maugham, it had been deeply disruptive. At the age of sixty-five he had been forced from his home to a peripatetic existence, from the Maginot Line to London under the Blitz, and across the breadth of America. The careful design of the final stages of his career had been shattered by three years of intensive war work, so that the long-delayed *The Razor's Edge* appeared finally in the year he was to have finished writing fiction. The war had also spelled the end of his relationship with Haxton – first through prolonged separation and finally through death.

When Maugham returned to Europe in the summer of 1946 he was seventy-two and now calling himself a 'Very Old Party'. He knew that the actuarial tables did not promise many more years, but he began what Cyril Connolly later called a 'leisurely process of winding up'[1] his writing career. In the end, it was sixteen years before Maugham published his final work, and for fourteen of those years he enjoyed an adulation and sense of satisfaction beyond anything he had previously known.

Aboard the *Colombie* on that return voyage were 250 Jewish exiles returning to their native countries, and at Marseilles, where there was only one customs official, it took seven hours of waiting on the quay before anyone was cleared to disembark. Maugham's irritation with this inefficiency, however, did not prevent his feeling that landing again on French soil was one of the happiest days of his life.[2] His anger with the French collapse had dissipated over the years in the United

States, and now he was touched by the inescapable signs of the Axis occupation. It was, after all, the land of his birth, the only place where he ever felt spiritually at home, and it did not take him long to decide that he would rebuild his life there.

Until the Villa Mauresque could be made habitable again, Maugham and Searle stayed at a small hotel, Le Voile d'Or, overlooking the harbour at the nearby village of St Jean, Cap Ferrat. The first sight of the villa was shocking. Dilapidated and neglected, it had no windows, the roof leaked, and the walls were pock-marked from the British fleet's attempted shelling of a nearby signal post. The garden had become a wilderness, many of the 100-foot trees had been killed by shellfire, and the swimming-pool was disfigured. The Germans, who had used the house during the Occupation, had drunk the best wines in the cellar and slashed the furniture as a parting gesture. Since then, moths and rust had attacked the remaining furnishings. As disheartening as this destruction was, nothing gave Maugham such a wrench as the first time he revisited the room occupied for so many years by Haxton.[3]

Before long Maugham had employed five stonemasons to repair the holes in the walls and pool, and with a new coat of paint the damage to the exterior of the villa was barely noticeable. By late July the good furniture had been returned from storage and the paintings brought back from Lady Kenmare's home where they had been kept during the war. Maugham was delighted that his prized cook, Annette, would again rule his kitchen, and when the garden had been replanted in the autumn the Villa Mauresque was once more a comfortable and gracious retreat.

While living at Le Voile d'Or, and amidst the restoration of the villa, Maugham maintained his pattern of writing in the morning. Firth Shepherd, wishing to mount a revival of *Lady Frederick* set in the 1880s, asked its author to adapt the script to this earlier period, a task for which Maugham sought the assistance of Eddie Marsh. Opening at London's Savoy Theatre in November with Coral Browne and Phyllis Dare, the play proved remarkably durable and carried on for 144 performances.

There were also the finishing touches to be made to *Creatures of Circumstance*, published in July 1947. An amalgam of old and new stories, it contains some of Maugham's best work in that genre: 'The Colonel's Lady', 'A Woman of Fifty', 'Flotsam and Jetsam', 'Winter Cruise', 'Episode', and 'The Kite', The latter two tales, like 'The Round Dozen' before them, came to Maugham from Searle's experience as a prison visitor, and the 'Ned Preston' referred to in them is very loosely based on Searle. 'The Unconquered' is a story of a French girl who kills her new-born child as an act of revenge against the German soldier who has fallen in love after raping her. Written in 1943, it is a powerful allegory of the tragedy of both France and Germany, and more generally of the political rape of Europe.

Creatures of Circumstance marked the end of Maugham's career as a short-story writer. Showing the same resolution with which he had retired as a dramatist in 1933, he never published another short story. What remained for him as a creative writer was the novel form, and here he uncharacteristically abandoned the pattern he had envisaged a decade earlier. With a sense of symmetry, he had hoped to finish first with an historical novel to balance his second book, *The Making of a Saint*, and then a story of London slum life to bring him full circle to the world of *Liza of Lambeth* with which he had begun his career. According to Searle,[4] some time in the late thirties he and Maugham lived for three weeks with a family in Bermondsey known to Searle in order to collect material. It may seem extraordinary that the writer would forgo his usual comfortable flat for a working-class home in south London, but Searle's claim is given credence by the fact that Maugham was in London from 15 June to 14 July 1939, a month during which there are now, strangely, no known letters from him. As well, the Bermondsey anecdotes attributed to 1939 in *A Writer's Notebook* suggest a fairly intimate contact with the area.

Searle said that Maugham amassed useful background and had blocked out his story and characters, but when he learned that many of the people had been killed in German raids he no longer had the heart to write his novel. Maugham's own public explanation was that the war had transformed life in the slums so dramatically that the world he had hoped to portray had been rendered anachronistic. The joyful vivacity amidst the hardship – which he had captured in Liza forty-nine years earlier – had been replaced by envy and bitterness, and he was no longer interested.

Maugham's last novel thus became *Catalina*, a romantic celebration of Spain, promised much earlier in *Don Fernando* and published in 1948. Though much of it is an historical comedy, the influence of twentieth-century political events is unmistakable in the sections dealing with the Inquisition. When the Bishop, as Inquisitor, is compelled to torture his old intellectual companion for holding heretical opinions, readers are offered a parallel to the dehumanizing state censorship common to much of contemporary Europe. It is, in Laurence Brander's words, 'a study of power stresses, of the absolute and insolent exertion of power by people who had no enlightened conception of human values or human dignity. It is a picture of an Establishment twisted and deformed by an excess of zeal and power. In terms of Maugham's own ethic, it is simple goodness at the mercy of a human organization.'[5]

Maugham considered the publication of *Catalina* to be the end of his career as a professional writer. Thereafter, he frequently told reporters that he no longer thought in terms of fiction, just as he long ago had stopped thinking in terms of plays, and a decade later he claimed that he had not had an idea for a story in ten years.[6] Finding plots for short stories, however, had become deeply ingrained in him and from his brief observation of people in any situation – aboard ship, in a hotel lobby, or at a dinner party – he could spin a Maugham tale. As Peter Quennell has noted, he would explain a mother's efforts to please her adult children by speculating that one of them was probably black-mailing her for her involvement in some earlier slightly scandalous lawsuit.[7]

Breaking this habit of nearly sixty years was not, however, so simple, and Maugham did continue in a manner to fabricate an imaginative world. As late as 1959, for example, when he was invited to a dinner party in Singapore, he was still uncovering the material which at another time he would have turned to fiction. 'We all took cushions and sat on the patio,' recalled Dr Charles Wilson of the Raffles Hotel, 'and Somerset Maugham said, "I would love to hear some Singapore tales". And out they flowed! From people you would never have realized had very extraordinary things happen to them. It was when I was driving him back to the hotel that Maugham said that if I didn't write some of the stories down, he would!'[8]

Ceasing to write fiction was probably more difficult than Maugham had anticipated because it denied him one of the most satisfying ways of expressing his interest in people. 'Not being a creative writer any-more', he once confessed to George Cukor, 'is very lonely. Your characters don't exist with you anymore.' Cukor believed that this immersion in a fictional world partially explains Maugham's seeming distraction at times, and cited an incident in a Venice restaurant where the author began describing a couple of elderly diners to Searle and himself. When his listeners' attention was diverted by a funeral proces-sion on the Grand Canal, Maugham was furious. 'You fools,' he ex-claimed, 'I'm giving you a *story*! And you're not *listening*!' 'You could see', observed Cukor, 'how the creative process was starving.'[9]

As if to underline that his days as a writer of fiction were definitely over, Maugham published *A Writer's Notebook* in 1949. It had actually been completed several years earlier, but he seems to have preferred to wait until he had published his last novel before exposing the raw material of his art to the public. Even then he instructed his agent to inform Heinemann that he reserved the right to make any use of the contents of the book – to fashion them into stories, play, or novels.[10] To his seventieth birthday summation he appended several pages of commentary on the succeeding five years, concluding with the observation that his age made him like a passenger ready to embark but not knowing when the ship will leave. 'I am on the wing,' he wrote, echoing the lines of *The Rubáiyát of Omar Khayyám* – 'The Bird of Time has but a little way / To flutter – and the Bird is on the Wing' – which he had thrilled to hear John Ellingham Brooks recite fifty-eight years earlier.

For Maugham writing was more than merely the expression of a creative imagination; it was a habit, an essential part of each day, and this he did not abandon until the last, senile years. Though *Catalina* was his last work as a 'professional' author – that is, he explained, one who writes to satisfy public tastes – he continued to fashion essays and retrospective pieces. In late 1947 he had already written a series of biographical and critical articles for the *Atlantic Monthly* on what he considered the ten greatest novels: *Tom Jones, David Copperfield, Madame Bovary, Old Man Goriot, Wuthering Heights, The Brothers Karamazov, The Red and the Black, Pride and Prejudice, Moby Dick,* and *War and Peace*. In 1948 the American publisher John C. Winston published them in book form as *Great Novelists and Their Novels* and the following year they served as introductions to separate editions of each work. Having long believed that even the best novels contained dead wood, Maugham abridged each one, an act which many critics considered impertinent. In 1954 a revised version of the biographies was nevertheless published in an enormously successful series by the *Sunday Times*, and the subsequent Heinemann book, *Ten Novels and Their Authors*, drew advance sales of 50,000 copies.

It has been pointed out that Maugham's compulsion at the age of eighty to undertake the lengthy task of reworking the ten essays is vivid proof of his respect for literature. Curiously, he performed a similar task of amendment when *Don Fernando* was published in the Heinemann Collected Edition in 1950. Not only did he omit a number of observations that he had developed more fully in *The Summing Up*; he also deleted an entire chapter and entirely rewrote and amplified another.

As Maugham's interest shifted from fiction to criticism he began to write essays on a variety of subjects which he knew would appeal to only a minority of readers. In 1948 the *Cornhill* carried his article on his old friend Augustus Hare, and this was followed the next year by pieces on the Spanish painter Zurbarán and the style of Edmund Burke. In 1952 he added three more essays on Kant, detective fiction, and novelists whom he had known such as H. G. Wells, Arnold Bennett, and Henry James, and the collection was published as *The Vagrant Mood*.

In the early fifties Maugham also wrote a number of prefaces to books by friends such as Gladys Cooper and Violet Hammersley, introductions to catalogues of the theatrical paintings he had donated to the National Theatre and of an exhibition of portraits by Gerald Kelly, and contributions to a tribute to Eddie Marsh and to the Transactions of the Royal Society of Literature.

Maugham would not accept any payment for the prefaces done for his friends, but when the Aga Khan, for whose memoirs Maugham wrote an introduction, attempted to pay him the author's reaction was curious but characteristically professional. He bridled at what he considered to be an insultingly low fee, arguing that, while he had expected nothing except perhaps a token gift, if he were going to be paid it should be at a proper rate. This, he said, was $2500 and if the Aga Khan baulked at it, he could have the introduction for nothing.

Another of Maugham's essays of the fifties, his introduction to *A Choice of Kipling's Prose* (1952), was also potentially troublesome. In an address to the Royal Society of Literature in November 1947 he had described Kipling as the only short-story writer in England who could compare with the great European masters of the genre. Word of this praise reached Kipling's daughter, Elsie Bambridge, who decided that a collection of his stories prefaced by an encomium by Maugham might revive an interest in her father's writing. Maugham's admiration was genuine at a period when Kipling's reputation was low, and his interest in the project was keen. He was nevertheless aware that Frederick Birkenhead had written an admirable biography of the writer only to have Bambridge block publication. If she were to veto the new collection, Maugham was prepared to publish his introduction in his next book of essays, but his comments were sufficiently complimentary that there were no objections.

Maugham continued to write essays through much of the fifties, but by the time that his last collection, *Points of View*, was published in 1958 he was pretty much a spent force. It comprised five pieces – on

Goethe, Tillotson, a swami he had met in India, the short story, and three French journalists – written over six years, and he found the last one exhausting. For some time he had suffered from writer's cramp, and by the age of eighty-four his hand was so crippled that it required the support of a surgical glove in order for him to be able to write for even an hour a day. The loss of inventive power was even more frustrating and in July 1958 he was so sick even of correcting the typescript of *Points of View* that he told Ann Fleming that he was tempted to tear it into pieces.[11]

Maugham was determined that after *Points of View* he would, in his words, 'put up the shutters and close up shop'. 'I am looking forward to being free,' he claimed in January 1958. 'In the autumn when this book of essays is finished, then I shall be liberated from work.'[12] A year later, however, he described the void in his mornings by referring to the story of the Frenchman who, after years of meeting his mistress for evening assignations, was freed by the death of his wife to marry the girl. 'But where', the man asked, 'will I spend my evenings?' 'That is my position,' Maugham told John Beavan. 'Where shall I spend my mornings? How shall I spend my mornings?'[13]

While the post-war years were a period of calculated winding down of Maugham the author, they also saw the emergence of the Very Old Party as performer. The exigencies of the war had pushed him to the radio microphone where he discovered that he was not only articulate but surprisingly effective. Shrewdly sensing the possibilities of taking his work to a wider audience than the reading public, he began to appear on radio, television, and film, and he became a star. Noël Coward might turn to the cabaret stage in his final years; Maugham became a broadcasting celebrity.

The BBC was the first to entice Maugham to read his work by arguing in November 1947 that it was anxious to record eminent authors of the older generation for its archives. It was not until the writer had given it a half-hour reading, which was broadcast the following January, that the corporation decided that it was worthwhile to draw up a list of other men of letters to be approached. In the autumn of 1949 Maugham returned to the British airwaves to discuss Rodney Ackland's dramatization of his short story 'Before the Party' and to read excerpts from *A Writer's Notebook* for the Overseas Service.

In November 1950 Maugham went further and recorded five stories for the BBC, first intended for its 'Morning Story' series and then given a more auspicious place in its schedule. Pleased by the response to these programmes, Maugham intimated to Julian Hall that he would like to do more, especially to read some of his more serious stories such as 'The End of the Flight' or 'The Happy Couple'. Surprisingly, the BBC rejected this offer, likely concerned about the perceived amorality of many of his tales. Maugham nevertheless appeared on British radio again in 1954 to give an eightieth birthday address, and on trips to Spain in 1948 and 1949 he spoke over the air in Spanish. In 1949 he also recorded four short stories for Columbia records.

The film world had long known Maugham's writings as a rich source of material, and by the mid-forties it had translated at least thirty of them to the screen. In 1948, however, the author himself went before the cameras. Sydney Box, of the Gainsborough studios in England, conceived of the idea of presenting five short stories in an omnibus picture, and when one was dropped it became *Quartet*. Maugham was persuaded to appear on screen as a narrator and to provide a parting comment. He was amused at being considered a film figure at the age of seventy-four and pleased to find that the public responded favourably to the experiment. Thus, when Gainsborourgh produced another collection, *Trio*, in 1950, he not only advised R. C. Sherriff about adapting 'Sanatorium' but he wrote the screenplay for 'The Verger' himself. Once again Maugham introduced his work, this time from a reproduction of the writing-room at the Villa Mauresque, and in October 1950 he attended a gala première in New York. The final omnibus film, *Encore*, was produced the next year by Two Cities, and for that Maugham not only appeared on screen but also at two trade and press showings, a London premiere, and an all-night party at Ciro's. He had not been satisfied with the alterations to his stories which the studio's fear of the censor had required, but this did not prevent his enjoying the celebrity which accompanied his film appearances.

The newest form of popular entertainment, television, found Maugham in 1950, when the Columbia Broadcasting System in the United States presented nearly forty of his stories in a series entitled 'The Somerset Maugham Theatre'. The producer/director was the highly respected Martin Ritt, and the network signed the author at a lavish press reception at the Sherry Netherland Hotel. As in the omnibus films, Maugham opened and closed each episode, the first three of which were live performances while the remainder were taped. Though never having seen television before, he was intrigued to watch himself on the monitor to see 'whether or not I'm making a fool of myself', but he declined to watch anything else, saying: 'I am familiar with the story.'[14]

Many of Maugham's stories were ideally suited to adaptation for television – as the excellent BBC series in 1969–70 demonstrated – and in the spring of 1951 Maugham taped more such introductions in London. In 1957 he appeared on both American and British television to discuss the reissue of *The Magician*, and he could be seen on British screens from time to time in the fifties talking about such subjects as Graham Sutherland's portrait of him.

Maugham's popularity as a public personality was grounded on a post-war perception of him as a Grand Old Man of English Letters. In the years before the Second World War he was generally respected, but the widespread success of *The Razor's Edge*, greater in its first two years of publication than anything else he had written, propelled him into eminence. As well, there was simply the matter of his age. He had outlived many of his contemporaries like Wells and Bennett, and ironically, like Edward Driffield in *Cakes and Ale*, he was acclaimed partly because of his longevity. 'Who but the English', wrote Maugham, 'would fill Covent Garden to listen to an aged prima donna without a voice?' And with each passing year, as he slipped into his eighties and then his nineties, the British awe for this Edwardian relic grew.

There were, of course, the detractors, those who interpreted the popular interest in Maugham as a sign of declining literary taste. No one could have had more contempt for his work than the respected American critic Edmund Wilson, who used a *New Yorker* article in June 1946 to launch a withering assault. Ignoring *The Razor's Edge* and any of Maugham's best work, Wilson focused on *Then and Now*, calling its author 'second-rate'. He is, in Wilson's terms, 'a half-trashy novelist, who writes badly, but is patronized by half-serious readers who do not care much about writing'.[15]

Maugham seems to have been an obsession for Wilson, Garson Kanin and John Lehmann being only two of many who heard him launch vigorous attacks. Though Maugham was always stung by adverse criticism more than he would admit, his response was much more generous. When, for example, Nelson Doubleday sent him the manuscript of Wilson's *Hecate County* for advice, Maugham urged his publisher to accept it.[16] Moreover, more than one friend heard Maugham refer to Wilson as the most brilliant critic in America and deplore a culture that would not reward such a figure with some sort of financial security.[17]

Wilson was not alone in his disdain for Maugham's writing, but the reputation and honours continued to grow. More comfortable addressing large gatherings than he had ever been before the war, he became a witty and sometimes provocative speaker. In 1947 he gave his Kipling lecture to the Royal Society of Literature, and in 1950 he gave three talks in the United States: at the National Society of Arts and Letters reception at which he was made an associate member, at the Library of Congress when he donated the manuscript of 'The Artistic Temperament of Stephen Carey', and at the Pierpont Morgan Library at a dinner in his honour. The following May the relatively new President of the Royal Academy, Gerald Kelly, persuaded him to respond to the toast to literature before 200 people at the Academy's annual banquet. Though his fellow speakers included Churchill, Attlee, Lord Samuel, and Lord Cork and Orrery, Maugham's speech was the best of the evening, and the next year Kelly complained of being unable to find anyone as witty. After his performance Maugham was besieged by invitations to speak, and he turned down several requests to do lecture tours of the United States because he remembered how fatiguing his wartime talks had been. In October 1951, however, he addressed the National Book League on 'The Writer's Point of View' at London's Kingsway Hall, and this talk was later published by Cambridge University Press. In 1956 he spoke about authors who had been involved with the graphic arts, as part of the opening of an exhibition of Authors as Artists at the Army and Navy Stores in London.

Maugham's reputation had grown to the point that, even if he were not speaking, his presence enhanced the glitter of many occasions. In 1953 Gerald Kelly placed him next to Queen Elizabeth at a Royal Academy dinner at Burlington House to mark the closing of the Dutch Exhibition. When Kelly told the Queen that the author had come from the South of France in order to sit next to her, she replied that it was the prettiest compliment she had ever received.[18] The following year Maugham was at the head table between the Cardinal Archbishop of Winchester and the Duke of Wellington at the annual banquet of the Royal Society of Literature. In 1957 he occupied a similar position of honour at the centenary dinner of London's Savage Club, founded for professional men of literature and art who claimed to be free from convention.

In 1956 Maugham was one of the Riviera set who attended the social event of the year: the wedding of Grace Kelly to Prince Rainier. When the hundreds of reporters discovered that the royal couple was inaccessible, they besieged the eminent author for copy. Two years earlier his fame had proved more useful when he travelled through Spain as the guest of the Spanish State Tourist Department, which insisted that he stay at its Paradores and Wayside Inns at its expense.

Maugham received numerous distinctions during the post-war

period, some informal and others more official. There was 'An Evening With Somerset Maugham' at the St Pancras Town Hall in London, during which Constance Cummings read a story, the Tavistock Repertory Company performed a play, and Lionel Hale, G. B. Stern, and Val Gielgud discussed his writing. A few months later he was voted the author people most wanted to meet by listeners to the BBC radio series 'A Man I Would Like to Meet'. In 1956 following the 500th performance of L'Adorable Julia (a French dramatization of Theatre) in Paris, he was given a party on the stage of the theatre. Later that year he was honoured at a private dinner at the Authors' Club in London, and in 1958 he was elected Vice-President of the Royal Society of Literature along with Churchill, Edith Sitwell, and Cecil Day-Lewis. Three years later the Royal Society of Literature awarded him – along with Churchill, E. M. Forster, John Masefield, and G. M. Trevelyan – its new Companionship of Literature. This honour, limited to a maximum of ten holders, is given to authors who have brought exceptional distinction to English letters, and they must be elected unanimously by the council.

There were also honorary degrees, first a Doctor of Letters from the Université de Toulouse, then one from Oxford in 1952, and finally from his old university of Heidelberg in 1957. In the fifties, several American universities offered similar honours, but Maugham declined on the grounds that he was no longer able to stand up to the rigours of a journey to the United States.

In the British adulation of ageing artists, decades ending in a zero are special milestones, and no public recognition of Maugham matched the celebration of his eightieth birthday. The BBC produced a miniseries of five of his plays and dramatizations of five short stories. The Times Literary Supplement carried an appreciation and an assessment of his career, John O'London's Weekly published essays in his honour by G. B. Stern and Frank Swinnerton, and admiring friends such as Gerald Kelly, Alec Waugh, Harold Nicolson, Cyril Ray, and L. A. G. Strong wrote birthday tributes.

On the eve of his eightieth birthday, Maugham was honoured by a dinner at the Garrick Club, which he had loved for five decades. Only three writers before him – Dickens, Thackeray, and Trollope – had been given such a distinction, but it became the occasion of one of his most potentially humiliating experiences. It has been described in a variety of ways by a number of those who were present (and some who were not), but none captures the moment better than St John Ervine's letter to Richard Church:

I wish you . . . could have heard that superb speech – not mine, but Willie's in reply: a most impressive performance, full of wit, humour, well-turned phrases, and, surprisingly to some people, but not to me, full of feeling. He gave one of the most remarkable displays of moral courage and self-control that I have ever seen. He had obviously learnt his speech by heart, and, as often happens when a man does that, he suddenly dries up, as actors say, towards the end of his speech. Anybody else would have sat down in confusion. I would have howled piteously for my wife. But Maugham stood perfectly still, though his fingers were trembling. After a few moments he said, 'I'm just thinking of what I shall say next!' then he lapsed into silence again. A little later he said, 'I'm sorry to keep you waiting!' and he became silent once more. Then, suddenly, the machine of his mind moved again, and he finished his speech finely . . . he remained imperturbable throughout what must have been a dreadful ordeal . . . It was an amazing performance and, I think, highly characteristic of him.[19]

When the dinner was over, Maugham went upstairs to the card room, where he played bridge until the club shut down at one o'clock in the morning.

On the day following his birthday, Maugham, together with Frederic, Liza, and John Hope, attended the *Times* bookshop exhibition of his manuscripts, first editions, theatre programmes, and cinema stills. Author T. S. Strachan observed that, surrounded by such evidence of his fame, 'he achieved self-effacement. A great capacity to put up with bores. Polite to the overdressed women who grimaced at him . . . Distinction all over him . . . I thought the whole evening extraordinarily revealing of Maugham's modesty, his achievement, and his kindness to young authors.'[20]

Before the month of January was out Maugham had received over 1200 congratulatory letters and telegrams, and, since he was always scrupulous about replies, Searle was kept busy for weeks typing acknowledgements. As an interim measure, the author placed an advertisement in the personal column of *The Times* to explain to well-wishers that his responses would be coming in due course and that his writer's cramp prevented handwritten letters.

In the whirl of publicity surrounding Maugham's eightieth birthday, the British Government seems to have realized that almost the only distinction he lacked was some sort of official recognition from his own country. In the Queen's Birthday Honours List several months later, he was therefore made a Companion of Honour, an order founded in 1917 and limited to sixty-five members, among whom were Churchill and Attlee. Maugham received his insignia from the Queen in July in a simple ceremony in Buckingham Palace, after which he talked congenially with her for a quarter of an hour.

The announcement sparked another 500 letters of congratulations and Maugham was genuinely gratified that it met with public approval. One thing that pleased him immensely, he commented to Alanson, was the warm response of the press and the public.[21] Behind this remark, repeated to numerous of his friends, must lie his chronic insecurity, a fear that such a distinction might evoke derision.

Maugham's pleasure with the Companion of Honour was, however, far from unqualified. Shortly after the Palace ceremony, he dined with George Rylands and Arthur Marshall, who offered their congratulations. 'But don't you see what the CH means for somebody like me?' he replied. 'It means very well done . . . but!'[22] Marshall suggests that his friend believed that he deserved the Order of Merit, a view confirmed by Canon Shirley, the Headmaster of King's School. On a visit to Canterbury in October 1952 Maugham took Shirley aside, saying: 'I will tell you my two secret wishes – I have never revealed them to any other living person. I think I ought to have the OM. I don't want anything else – I would refuse anything like a knighthood. But they gave Hardy the OM and I think I am the greatest living writer of English, and they ought to give it me. The other secret is that I should like my ashes buried somewhere in the Precincts – I don't mind where, as long as it is within the Precincts.'[23]

According to Robin Maugham, his uncle once claimed that he had refused the offer of a knighthood many years earlier because 'I didn't want to look a fool. I felt I'd look so silly if I went to a literary party and they announced "*Mr* Arnold Bennett, *Mr* H. G. Wells, *Mr* Bernard Shaw – and Sir-Sir Somerset Maugham".'[24] Frederic Prokosch claims, however, that the aged Maugham once confessed that one of the three disappointments of his life was the lack of a knighthood. 'I knew in my heart of hearts that I'd n–never receive a knighthood but I kept hoping against hope for the possibility of a knighthood.'[25] There is no way of knowing whether Maugham was ever offered such an honour, but his clever flippancy in Robin's story may well hide a lingering wound. He would hardly have been the only author to carry the title, and it is hard to believe that a man who so liked to associate with the aristocracy would turn it down.

The more plausible explanation for the absence of any official recognition from the Crown is Maugham's homosexuality. Hugh Walpole, awarded the CBE as early as 1917, was given a knighthood in 1937, but his lengthy affair with the policeman Harold Cheevers had been discreet. Maugham's relationship with Haxton, intertwined as it was with the divorce of Syrie, was public, obvious, and well-known in British political and social circles, if not to the general public. 'There can be no other reason', writes H. Montgomery Hyde in *The Other Love*, 'why William Somerset Maugham had to wait until the occasion of his eightieth birthday to receive his first and only such award, Companion of Honour, an Order of comparatively recent foundation, which carries with it no title, ranks below that of knighthood, and is usually given to retired politicians and generals.'[26]

Whether Maugham deserved the Order of Merit is a matter of debate, but there can be little doubt that he had been systematically excluded from the Honours List for nearly forty years. If the nature of his service in the First World War was too delicate to permit public recognition, his achievements in fiction and drama were grounds enough. His work on behalf of the British cause during the Second World War would have earned many others some sort of distinction, but it seems to have required nearly a decade of Haxton-less old age to prove to the British authorities that Maugham was now acceptable. The French, not surprisingly, had much earlier made him a Commander of the Légion d'Honneur.

That Maugham should be denied honours because of his homosexuality is ironic because of his care in keeping his sexual orientation from the general public. Robin Maugham was emphatically reminded of his uncle's attitude toward the subject when he wrote *The Wrong People* in the fifties. After reading the typescript of this novel about homosexuals, Maugham gave his verdict: 'I must tell you that I began reading your book last night in bed and I simply couldn't put it down. It's easily the best work you've ever done and I think it's perfectly excellent. Having told you that, I must tell you that if you publish it, it will kill you as a writer stone dead. The public will be disgusted by it and you'll be panned by all the critics and you'll lose such little public as you've got.'[27]

In the fifties, when England was rocked by a series of homosexual scandals and when a number of respected public figures began to call for more liberal laws regarding homosexual conduct, Maugham remained silent. When Terence Rattigan was gathering signatures for a petition, Maugham refused his; even when non-homosexuals were among the signators to a letter to *The Times*, he would not lend his name. According to Beverley Nichols a homosexual friend, Arthur Jeffress, once pleaded with Maugham to make some sort of public gesture.[28] He refused, and in 1961 Jeffress himself became both a victim of punitive homophobia and an example of the risks of defying conventional standards. Deported from his home in Venice for homosexual behaviour, he killed himself in Paris.

Though the harsh British laws regarding homosexual conduct remained in effect to the end of Maugham's life, his reluctance to make his sexual orientation generally known came primarily from an old-fashioned view of respectability. If, from the perspective of the nineteen-eighties, this suggests a lack of moral courage, it should be remembered that Maugham's response was identical to that of nearly everyone of his generation. E. M. Forster, for example, was famous for his credo that, if he were forced to choose between betraying his country and betraying his friends, he hoped that he would have the courage to betray his country. Though respected as one of Britain's most sensitive and liberal men of letters, he chose never to acknowledge his homosexuality to the public, and to publish his homosexual novel *Maurice* only posthumously, when much of its moral and social significance had become meaningless.

Younger writers such as Noël Coward, who had not lived through the trauma of the Wilde trial and its aftermath, also kept silent. Even Rattigan, in 1953, had closed the door of his London flat when a defendant in a much publicized case of homosexual conduct sought refuge from a plague of reporters. He would not risk being connected with anyone involved in the case or with homosexuality.[29] As late as 1966 Cecil Beaton, born thirty years after Maugham, vividly described the psychological damage inflicted on generations of homosexuals by legal and social sanctions:

Of recent years the tolerance toward the subject has made a nonsense of many of the prejudices from which I myself suffered acutely as a young man. Even now I can only vaguely realize that it was only comparatively late in life that I would go into a room full of people without a feeling of guilt. To go into a room full of men, or to a lavatory in the Savoy, needed quite an effort. With success in my work this situation became easier. But when one realizes what damage, what tragedy has been brought on by this lack of sympathy to a very delicate and difficult subject, this should be a great time of celebration ... For myself I am grateful. Selfishly I wish that this marvellous step forward [acceptance of the Wolfenden Report] could have been taken at an earlier age. It is not that I would have wished to avail myself of further licence, but to feel that one was not a felon and an outcast could have helped enormously during the difficult young years.[30]

If Beaton, who travelled in highly sophisticated circles, was gripped by this insecurity, it is not hard to imagine its effect on Maugham, by nature a much more reticent person. Arthur Marshall recalls that Maugham brought a kind of chill with him when he entered a room, partly because of his self-consciousness and partly because of his physical appearance. On many occasions he was living a life in translation, watching his language, appearance, and gestures to avoid betraying his homosexuality. This inevitably contributed to that sense of rigid control so graphically expressed in the Sutherland portrait, of a smile not relaxed and easy and a manner not warmly open.

Hector Bolitho believed that the deepest source of Maugham's unhappiness 'was that he did not accept, generously and calmly, the fact that he was at least partly homosexual . . . Maugham grew up in a social world that knew nothing of the possible integrity, manners, and unselfishness, apart from all the moral issues, in which homosexuals learn to live.'[31] The horrible truth may be that he remained haunted by the self-condemnation of one who truly believed in the narrow sexual morality of an earlier age.

In any case, to the end of his life Maugham feared public exposure of his sexual orientation and this must account for the vigour with which he attempted to manipulate what would be known of him after his death. Beginning in the thirties, he discouraged biographers, and he left instructions in his will that his executor should not co-operate with anyone wishing to write his life. In the fifties, he conducted 'bonfire nights' when he and Searle burned unpublished manuscripts and letters to him from a host of notable writers of the time: H. G. Wells, T. S. Eliot, Rebecca West, Violet Hunt, Ada Leverson, Arnold Bennett, Carl Van Vechten, Sam Behrman, Raymond Mortimer, Desmond MacCarthy, Alec Waugh, and many others. Finally, in November 1957, Maugham addressed his friends and acquaintances through the pages of the British press to request that they destroy any letters from him in their possession. 'Don't please think me ungracious,' he said, 'but I hate having my letters published. I regard my letters as my personal affair and I cannot see that their publication after my death will be any useful contribution.'[32]

As the several thousand Maugham letters held in various archives throughout the world indicate, few of his friends heeded this request. Moreover, he was unable to prevent the inevitable posthumous revelations in various memoirs and autobiographies, portraits which ranged from Beverley Nichols's angry denunciation to Garson Kanin's flattering anecdotes. It is arguable that, as with so many attempts to suppress biographies of public figures, his strictures simply led to incomplete, frequently inaccurate, and often unsympathetic accounts of his life.

While Maugham did not lend his name to the fight for more liberal laws regarding homosexual conduct, he was active in other causes in the latter stages of his life. In 1957, for example, he joined T. S. Eliot, C. P. Snow, E. M. Forster, Rebecca West and others in writing to *The Times* to protest at the imprisonment and trial of four distinguished Hungarian writers. In 1948 he contributed money to a British Theatre Conference organized by J. B. Priestley, and he donated his theatrical pictures to the Trustees of the National Theatre, to be mounted at such time as the long-awaited theatre was constructed. Second only to that of the Garrick Club, the collection of eighty oils and watercolours included a number of works by Zoffany, de Wilde, Beechey, and Reynolds. In 1960 he donated the manuscript of *Up at the Villa* to a sale to raise money for the London Library. It earned £1100 out of the total proceeds of £25,600.

Before the Second World War Maugham had donated a dozen eighteenth-century mezzotints to King's School to decorate the Masters' Common Room, as well as £200 for three tennis courts. Writing from South Carolina in 1945, he asked that the Common Room be provided with a new dining table, sideboard, and set of chairs at his expense. After the war, in part because of the shrewd soliciting of Canon Shirley, he became even more generous. He gave money for a new boathouse, and he established a £10,000 scholarship fund for a working-class boy as a tribute to the working classes for the way in which they had stood up to German bombs during the Blitz.[33] Moreover, he believed, bringing such boys into contact with those of the middle and upper classes would be enlightening for all of them. He overestimated the ambitions of working-class boys to attend King's, however, and only one such Scholar was ever named. When the scheme was abandoned, the author agreed to the funds being used to complete a new Science Building, which he formally opened in June 1958.

Three years after the construction of the Science Building, a new room was added to house Maugham's library, which he proposed to donate to the school in stages. Wanting it to be the finest such library in the country, he sent 1670 volumes, many of them highly valuable autographed books by such writers as Edith Sitwell, H. G. Wells, Rudyard Kipling, and Jean Cocteau. Together with the manuscripts of his first and last novels, *Liza of Lambeth* and *Catalina*, which he had given in 1948, they did indeed comprise the best collection in any such library.

For readers of *Of Human Bondage*, this generosity to a school at which Maugham had been so miserable is astonishing, and it has been argued that it was intended merely to overshadow the gifts of another former student, Hugh Walpole. Maugham's support, however, continued for more than two decades after Walpole's death in 1941, and if he had been jealous of the latter he would hardly have consented to have the manuscripts of *Liza of Lambeth* and *Catalina* housed in the Walpole Collection.

The truth is that Maugham developed a genuine affection for King's School late in his life. With the passage of time, the pain of his childhood in Whitstable and his school days in Canterbury had been replaced by a kind of wistful nostalgia as his thoughts increasingly turned to the past. According to Canon Shirley, the compelling reason for the writer's periodic returns to Kent was to see for himself that the graves of his aunt and once-despised uncle in Whitstable were being properly kept. Furthermore, in 1948 and 1951 he made sentimental journeys back to the vicarage.

Behind Maugham's return trips to King's School lay a similar nostalgia, though here his emotions may have been more complex. He had little regard for the public school system, but he was interested in the human element of King's: the masters and the boys. His gifts were intended to improve conditions for both groups, and he insisted on seeing the results for himself. Sometimes he would talk with a dozen or so boys in someone's room, and from time to time he would dine with them in hall. His concern was not limited to the students, as the Revd J. P. P. Newell, Canon Shirley's successor as Headmaster, soon learned. On what was to be his last trip to England in the autumn of 1962, Maugham arrived in Canterbury and said: 'I have j-j-just c-c-come down to ask you: Are you h-h-happy here?' He was concerned that Newell might be finding his position difficult with his formidable predecessor still being at King's and, Newell says, 'at least one of my misconceptions was removed -- there was no doubt whatever about his humanity or human sympathy.'[34]

Maugham's commitment to the people at King's School rather than to the institution itself suggests a desire to be part of its life. Canon Shirley argued that 'in a real sense he belonged, he still had a security here,'[35] but this had not always been so. It had been not only the scene of some of his greatest humiliations but also the place where he had spent his most formative years. It was here that he had decided that he would carve out his own future, even if it meant leaving the conventional path represented by the school and striking out on his own. When he returned in old age, it was as an old boy who had made good, in fact one of the most illustrious of all the students who had passed through its halls. He had shown the school bullies, the teachers who had ridiculed his stammer, and those who opposed his leaving, that he was right; he had done it, and done it with distinction. Now he could believe that he truly belonged at King's School.

The best-known of Maugham's post-war benefactions was, of course, his establishment in 1947 of the Somerset Maugham Award. Administered by the Society of Authors, Playwrights and Composers, it is given annually to a British author under thirty-five of outstanding promise, Maugham's intention being to mitigate the provincialism and insularity from which he believed so many young writers suffered. Candidates are required to spend at least three months outside Great Britain, and Maugham urged the panel of judges to select those with originality and promise and not merely play for safety in their choices. To carry out their travel, winners received £500, though in later years when the British pound fell in value Maugham increased his contribution. He believed that if only one young writer was so stimulated and strengthened by the experience that he produced one superior book, his prize would have been successful. Though it would be impossible to assess its effect on literary work, those who benefited from it are among the most distinguished of contemporary British authors: Doris Lessing, V. S. Naipaul, Kingsley Amis, Thom Gunn, Ted Hughes, John le Carré, and John Wain. In any case, those who subscribe to a view of Maugham as mean-spirited might consider how many other writers have founded any such fellowships to encourage young authors.

Maugham had conceived of his prize in the twenties, when his wanderings in the South Pacific and Far East had uncovered such rich material. Though the effects of age precluded such lengthy journeys after the Second World War, he continued to travel extensively and compulsively. In 1948 he went to Spain to research his essay on Zurbarán, and he found himself facing an exhausting series of interviews, autographings, photography sessions, luncheons, and visitors. In

Guadalupe, he and Searle stayed in a monastery where they attended Mass at seven in the morning in an icy church and then returned to an equally icy room to shave with nearly freezing water. Maugham had never lost his deep love of the Spanish and their culture, and he returned the following year and finally in 1954. In the 1949 trip he went to Portugal for the first time, and went to the Douro to see the vintage.

In December 1948 Maugham and Searle sailed to the United States, where they stayed with the Doubledays at Oyster Bay, an especially grim visit because Nelson Doubleday was dying and wanted to see the author one more time. Maugham was shocked by the look of death on the face of his friend and publisher and by the fear of death in his eyes, and he was pleased to be able to help settle a company dispute between the Doubledays, Douglas Black, and Dorothy Doubleday before Nelson's death in January.

The real purpose of this American trip was to fulfil a promise made to Bert Alanson in 1924 that Maugham would spend his seventy-fifth birthday in San Francisco. When Alanson wired 'Dear Willie: We expect you on the twenty-fifth,' the author happily accepted. George Cukor came from Beverly Hills for the celebration, and Maugham was feted at a luncheon at the Stock Exchange Club attended by the President of the University of California and the British and American Consuls General. Back in New York, he was given another luncheon party by the Overseas Press Club, at which he spoke wittily to the 250 guests of his attitude to journalism.

Maugham returned to the United States in September 1950 to attend the première of *Trio*, to be honoured by the National Institute of Arts and Letters and the Pierpont Morgan Library, and to tape his television introductions. In addition to these formal occasions, he dined with a dozen members of the Columbia University Faculty at the Coffee House Club. It was to be Maugham's last visit to the country in which so much of his reputation as playwright and fiction writer had been created, and in which he had gratefully spent the war years. Though Alanson begged him to return, and invitations to receive various honours were extended, he no longer believed that he could make the long trip across the Atlantic.

As Maugham neared eighty, his journeys increasingly took on the nature of one last look at what he had known and thrilled at decades earlier. Having long lost the urge to explore new territory, he was nevertheless drawn to return to the places he associated with his happiest days, and with each such trip came a sense of completion, of a part of the pattern fulfilled. He would tell friends and reporters that he was glad to have made the journey because, though he enjoyed it, he knew that he would never want to make it again.

Maugham's pleasure in travel was enhanced by the presence of his companion. Searle had never been able to travel widely, and the younger man's excitement with each new discovery reminded Maugham of the enthusiasms of his own youth. The trips to Spain were such revisitings, as were journeys to Morocco in 1950, Capri and Sicily in 1951, Turkey and Greece in 1953, and Egypt in 1956. It had been thirty years since he had been to Capri, the sunny and carefree oasis of his youth, and it was in Sicily four decades earlier that he received word that *Lady Frederick* was to be produced.

On his tour of Greece and Turkey Maugham was treated with the kind of awe usually accorded film stars, and he found it both flattering and exhausting. In Athens the King and Queen asked him to a private lunch with the Princess Nicolas, the mother of the Duchess of Kent. On disembarking at Istanbul, he was greeted by a battery of reporters, photographers, and radio microphones at which he made an impromptu speech. Maugham endured this attention patiently, but asked that the authorities remove the plainclothes policemen who had been assigned to follow him everywhere to ensure that he come to no harm. Though Maugham's writing was well-known throughout the country, Turkey had not subscribed to the International Copyright Agreement and so the author had never received any royalties. At a dinner in his honour, the government therefore decided that the presence of publishers and translators would be in poor taste and so deleted their names from the guest list.

The trip to Egypt in January and February 1956 was initiated by the Aga Khan, whose friendship with the author had not diminished over the matter of payment for Maugham's preface. Once again Maugham was astonished by his following in the country, and his days in Cairo were filled with interviews and receptions. The trip up the Nile, punctuated by visits to temples, was nevertheless exciting, and at Aswan the Aga Khan provided him with a spacious suite with a terrace and a stunning view of the Nile. From Aswan Maugham took a boat further upriver to Wadi Halfa in the Sudan to view the second cataract, and then back to Luxor. There the rigours of the journey caught up with him, and he spent a week confined to his hotel room with bronchitis.

In May 1957 Maugham paid another farewell visit when he accepted an invitation to be honoured by Heidelberg University, where, though his links had been tenuous, he was treated as a distinguished alumnus. He was given a plaque at a formal dinner, and he performed the ceremonial opening kick-off at the football match between the Press and the Theatre. Before the match he sent cameramen ducking for safety with the vigour of his foot, and afterwards he was so mobbed by autograph seekers that he had to be rescued by Searle. He was nevertheless patiently indulgent with the colourfully dressed members of the Alemania Society who politely abducted and carried him off to their clubhouse. It had been sixty-eight years since he had come there as an inexperienced but eager young man, and though he now felt like an anachronism he was gratified by this gesture of acceptance.

In addition to these sentimental revisitings, Maugham continued to make frequent motor trips through western Europe. In the immediate post-war years, he and Searle spent several weeks each year at the spa at Vichy doing the cure. In the mid-fifties they went to Abano Terme in Italy, where Maugham felt that the hot black mud plasters and mineral baths eased the ache of his rheumatism. There were also annual trips to Bayreuth for the Wagner festival and to Munich for more opera, and there were occasional tours of Belgium and Holland to view the paintings. Almost every excursion included stops at Salzburg, Vienna, Florence, and especially Venice, perhaps Maugham's favourite city.

One of the pleasures of such jaunts was familiarity, of returning to long-known concert halls and to paintings which came to seem like old friends. A creature of habit, Maugham usually stayed in the same hotels, almost always in the same rooms, where he was known and respected. Noël Coward once claimed that Maugham planned his trips gastronomically. 'If Alan Searle proposes that they stay three days at the Gritti in Venice,' he remarked, 'Maugham is likely to say that two is enough. One day for the *risotto con pesce* at Burano and the second for the scampi at Harry's Bar. What he has in mind for dinner I don't know. Perhaps they eat at the hotel. If you mention some out-of-the-way place in France, Maugham searches his memory . . . and comes up nodding with the name of some dish characteristic of the region.'[36]

If Maugham did indeed plan his journeys gastronomically, he always began his motor trips with a ritual stop at one of Europe's finest restaurants, La Mortola, just across the border on the Italian Riviera. Set in the famous garden created in 1867 by Sir Thomas Hanbury, La Mortola struck Maugham's friend Augustus Hare as the most important private garden on the Continent and 'more beautiful than anything out of the *Arabian Nights*'.[37] Even in the fifties, the restaurant retained a turn-of-the-century atmosphere, and Maugham and Searle always looked forward to lunch at La Mortola to begin a new jaunt.

There were also, of course, the visits to London – the occasional special trip to receive an honorary degree or to attend Liza's wedding, and always a late autumn extended stay. Maugham and Searle would annually arrive in England at the beginning of October and customarily remain until the middle of December, often returning to the South of France on Christmas Day when there were few other travellers. Before the war the author had stayed in flats in Portland Place, but in 1946 he took a suite in the Dorchester Hotel and kept it until his final visit in 1962. Before his arrival his eighteenth-century drawings and Henry Moore bronze would be brought out of storage and hung, giving the rooms a touch of individuality. Since Maugham preferred to entertain his friends at intimate luncheons or dinners in his suite, he was thus able to offer them some of the grace they would find at the Villa Mauresque.

The autumn visits to London were always hectic, beginning with great anticipation by Maugham and Searle and ending with exhaustion and relief for both. The arrival of the famous writer would launch a flood of requests for interviews and photograph sessions, and invitations to speak on radio and at various public events. Eager journalists sought his opinions on such matters as current literature, his own work, the political scene, and, most often, what it was like to be seventy-five, eighty, or eighty-five. Maugham and Searle would enter the Dorchester suite to be met by a variety of flowers, chocolates, and other gifts from loyal friends, and there was always a pile of invitations to luncheons and dinner parties.

Maugham and his companion could be seen at glittering occasions: the first nights of revivals of his own works such as *Lady Frederick* and *Our Betters* in 1946 and the première of *Quartet* in 1948. In 1957 they attended the opening of the operatic adaptation of *The Moon and Sixpence* at Sadler's Wells, sharing with the Kenneth Clarks the box usually reserved for royalty. Maugham's presence was sought for the launchings of the works of others, such as Terence Rattigan's *The Sleeping Prince*, and he was the guest of film producer Alexander Korda at the Royal première of the Olivier film version of *Richard III*.

Since Maugham's attendance could enhance an opening night, his reactions were closely watched by the press. Aware that a sign of seeming disapproval would damage the chances of a good run, he became careful about his behaviour. Producer Peter Daubenay has recounted how he invited Maugham to his revival of Coward's *Fallen Angels* in 1949, and was afterwards met by his grim-faced guest in the foyer of the Savoy Grill. 'After the insult you've subjected me to this evening,' Maugham hissed, 'I never want to see or speak to you

331

again.'[38] Though Daubenay reported that they did dine together that evening and had a kind of reconciliation years later, his account is typical of many which have painted Maugham as a malicious old tyrant.

Like many such anecdotes it tells only part of the story and thus misrepresents the man. In this case, Maugham and Searle had been given tickets far back in the Dress Circle, and at the age of seventy-five the author's eyesight and hearing made appreciating the play an ordeal from such a distance. He none the less remained for the entire performance and then privately expressed his anger, going to dinner only at Searle's urging.[39]

London theatre manager Richard Shulman once witnessed an example of Maugham's patience and sensitivity to the harm he could cause to his fellows in the theatre. During the first act of an avant-garde play at the New Arts Theatre Club, his hearing-aid stopped working, and he could follow none of the succeeding dialogue. Knowing that his leaving the theatre early would undoubtedly be seen as dissatisfaction with the production, he sat through the entire performance though he could understand little of what he saw.[40]

Maugham's London visits were also liberally sprinkled with parties among many of the notable figure of the literary and social world. He could be found at one of Chips Channon's lavish soirées along with Noël Coward, Sacheverell Sitwell, and the Queens of Spain and Rumania; or at Hans Juda's with Graham Sutherland, Eddie Marsh, Herbert Read, and Sir Philip Hendy. On election night in 1950 he joined Greta Garbo, Cecil Beaton, and others at Lord Camrose's party at the Savoy Hotel. Never at ease in large groups, Maugham was usually the first to arrive and first to leave such gatherings. One of the advantages of old age, he had discovered, was the freedom to plead that his health demanded that he go home to bed.

Much more to Maugham's taste were the small dinner parties where the conversation sparkled. The most witty and intelligent talkers, he claimed in 1956, were Pamela Berry, Diana Cooper, Lady Moore, Lord Beaverbrook, Lord Woolton, Churchill, Oliver Lyttelton, and Lord Hore-Belisha. Others whose intellectual company he appreciated were Noël Coward, the Kenneth Clarks, the Graham Sutherlands, the David Nivens, Laurence Olivier and Vivien Leigh, Victor Gollancz, Cyril Joad, Frank Swinnerton, L. A. G. Strong, Yvonne and Jamie Hamilton and J. B. Priestley. On his annual weekend jaunt to Bulbridge House, his old friend Juliet Duff's home in Wiltshire, he would meet a variety of creative figures such as Cecil Beaton, Frederick Ashton, Paul Bowles, or the Russian painter Tchelitchew.

Occasionally the conversation would crackle in unexpected ways. When Maugham was the guest of honour at a dinner party given by Ann Fleming, for example, Angus Wilson inadvertently suggested that Evelyn Waugh was easily the greatest living writer. As Maugham's face grew darker, the hostess kicked Wilson under the table until he nearly shouted the qualifier, 'the best novelist under sixty, UNDER SIXTY'.[41]

As busy as Maugham's London schedule might be, there was always time to see his oldest and closest friends: Gerald and Jane Kelly, Ivor and Barbara Back, Robert and Elsie Tritton, G. B. Stern, Christabel Lady Aberconway, Arthur Marshall, Raymond Mortimer, and others. As well, he would entertain younger and less prominent acquaintances such as the aspiring author Daniel Farson, and George Bullock, then in the advanced stages of tuberculosis. And always there would be bridge for half a crown a point at Crockford's with the masters Kenneth Konstam and Guy Ramsay, and occasionally the visiting Charles Goren.

From time to time in the final years of his life, Maugham contemplated moving to London permanently, but he considered himself too old to be uprooted again. Moreover, he loved the Villa Mauresque too much to give it up, and he had long wanted to die in his bedroom overlooking the Mediterranean. He would increasingly complain about the cost of maintaining the house and garden, but under Searle's discreet management they offered both a quiet retreat and a gracious milieu in which to meet the world.

For the first decade after the Second World War, there were few times when the Villa Mauresque was empty of guests. Those who returned year after year were Barbara Back, the Kellys, the Clarks, his publisher Alexander Frere and his wife, and an American friend Thyrza Fowler. None, however, were as eagerly anticipated or missed as Bert Alanson. Others who came less regularly included the Sutherlands, Cyril Connolly, Monroe Wheeler, Sam Behrman, Desmond Mac-Carthy, Harold Nicolson, Cecil Beaton, Peter Daubenay, Beverley Nichols, Alec Waugh, George Cukor, Noël Coward, Duff and Diana Cooper, Ellen Doubleday, Douglas Black and Ken McCormick of Doubledays, and Peter Quennell. Irwin Edman, the Columbia University philosophy professor, and George Rylands from Cambridge, were especially welcome for their brilliant conversation. Jerome Zipkin, a young American, was an occasional guest, as was the American scholar Richard Cordell and the young Daniel Farson. In 1952 Evelyn Waugh and Diana Cooper arrived together, and Lady Diana was immediately offended when her companion was given the better room. Waugh proceeded to call his host 'Doctor' for the rest of the visit and to read his latest novel aloud for more than two hours after dinner.[42]

In addition to offering his house to his friends, Maugham enjoyed entertaining both neighbours and tourists at luncheon or dinner. At his table might be found the Duke and Duchess of Windsor, the Prince of Monaco, Nadia Boulanger, T. S. Eliot, Alan Pryce-Jones, Julien Green, Arthur Rubinstein, Robert Boothby, Herbert Morrison, or Lord Beaverbrook. Whenever Churchill came to the Riviera, he lunched with Maugham, and when magazines offered very large sums of money for an account of the reunion of two very old friends, Maugham replied: 'NOTHING DOING.'

Like much about Maugham's life, his circle of Riviera friends was a' paradoxical mixture. On the one hand, there were the titled, rich, and in some cases superficial; on the other, there were the artists and the intellectuals. Among his immediate neighbours were Lord and Lady Bearsted, whose villa La Serena was very near the Mauresque, and at La Fiorentina was Lady Kenmare. As well, there were the Kingsley Macombers, Daisy Fellowes, and perhaps the most surprising of all, Lady Bateman, whose friendship with Maugham baffled his friends. A very rich and attractive widow who lived in Monte Carlo, Lady Bateman was snobbish and shallow. Maugham, however, insisted to friends such as Raymond Mortimer and Cecil Beaton that she had read and appreciated their work, and he often included her in his parties. For her part, Lady Bateman lavished gifts on the author, and he in turn faithfully wrote to her when travelling and brought her presents. Even in later years, when she began to become senile, Maugham remained loyal to her.

As much as his intellectual guests might be appalled by some of his Riviera circle, there were those with the best of credentials. One was Henri Matisse, who, though in his eighties and bedridden, continued to paint with a long brush on canvases attached to the ceiling above his bed. Though Maugham found him brusque and contemptuous of his desire to buy his paintings to decorate the Villa Mauresque, he was touched when Matisse gave him a volume of his drawings with a flattering and warm dedication. Maugham, too, was probably one of the few people to own a bathmat designed for him by Matisse.

Another artist whom Maugham knew in the fifties was Marc Chagall, then living nearby with his young and beautiful wife. A closer friend, however, was Jean Cocteau, whose affectionately inscribed books could be found in Maugham's library. Maugham delighted in

Cocteau's company, though it usually meant being talked at continually by one of France's most voluble conversationalists. According to Searle, Cocteau tried unsuccessfully to persuade Maugham to use opium late in his life.[43]

Maugham's oldest friend on the Riviera, however, was Romaine Brooks, the painter who had once been briefly married to John Ellingham Brooks. In the twenties, she began to go to the South of France with her lover Natalie Barney, eventually settling permanently in Nice, and she developed a friendship with Maugham which lasted until his death. Born the same year, he was not only her oldest acquaintance but by the late fifties one of the few left to her. She was genuinely fond of Maugham, who would address her as 'romantic Romaine' or 'dearest Romaine' and write to Barney and her as 'dear glamorous girls'. His praise for her art was always generous, and he once delighted her with the gallant remark that Cocteau would be remembered only because of her portrait of him. They would meet for lunch at a favourite restaurant on the quay at Nice, or Romaine would be driven up to the villa to dine and reminisce about the distant past.[44] When Maugham was struck by the beauty of her Vuillard painting of several white roses, she lent it to him with the provision that on his death it should be given to Searle.

At the Villa Mauresque, neither house guests nor local parties were allowed to disrupt the clockwork schedule which Maugham had followed for all of his adult life. There was breakfast in bed at eight, reading the newspapers until nine, and then his bath. This would be followed by a walk around the garden with Searle and then – except in his final years – several hours of writing. After lunch Maugham always took a half-hour nap, and, depending on the weather, he would swim or take a three-mile walk. Tea at five would be followed by reading until seven, when he would dress for cocktails at seven-thirty and dinner at seven-forty-five. When there were guests the evening would be spent in conversation or bridge; otherwise the game was patience. In either case Maugham retired to bed never later than ten-thirty.

Maugham had never lost the joy in reading he had discovered in his youth, and in old age it remained his greatest pleasure – whether he opened a classic or a detective novel by Raymond Chandler. At the other extreme he went to the boxing matches in Nice whenever possible, not so much because of the fights themselves as for the atmosphere of the crowd. If Maugham and Searle were alone they often dined out at one of the fine restaurants along the coast or in the hills overlooking the Mediterranean. It might be a modest seafood bar in Nice or the grand Hôtel de Paris in Monte Carlo, but their favourite was the elegant La Réserve, founded in 1894 in nearby Beaulieu and for decades one of the Riviera's best-known restaurants. So frequent a patron that he was provided with special wine glasses, set only at his table, Maugham would rub his hands with glee when preparing for an evening at La Réserve.

In part because of the disciplined moderation of his life, Maugham remained in surprisingly good health until his mid-eighties. Though he had announced as early as 1938 that he could face death with equanimity, he took almost any step which might ensure his longevity. His medical training had given him a fundamental understanding of the human body, and his interest in medicine was such that he continued to subscribe to *The Lancet*, the British medical journal. He carefully watched his own condition, and was not reluctant occasionally to write a prescription for himself.[45] He had, as well, the wealth which enabled him to take cures at the fashionable spas and to be treated by some of Europe's finest doctors.

Maugham had always feared a return of the tuberculosis which had killed so many of his relatives, but he stayed free of it after his months in the sanatorium at the end of the First World War. He continued none the less to succumb to the occasional recurrence of the malaria he had contracted in the Far East. There were also the minor mishaps and indispositions to which the old are vulnerable: a broken toe on his trip to Greece in 1953, which left him hobbling in pain for months, and another fall the succeeding year which created lingering chest pains first suspected to be lung cancer. In the spring of 1949 he spent some time in the Alpes Maritimes regaining his strength after a long period of listlessness, and in 1952 a severe case of nervous exhaustion forced the postponement of the trip to Greece and Turkey. The Egyptian visit in early 1956 was curtailed by bronchitis and Maugham was unwell for most of that autumn's London jaunt and then again two years later, when he contracted food poisoning. In his mid-seventies, he began to suffer from writer's cramp, for which his London osteopath gave him a special writing harness. When his hearing began seriously to fail in his mid-eighties, he ordered a hearing-aid from the United States, though he resented using it so much that he once threw it into the sea.

These ailments were hardly unusual in a person of Maugham's age, but in 1952 he nearly died. After a spring marked by exhaustion and vague pains in his groin, Maugham was diagnosed in early July as having a strangulated hernia. Before he could be operated on, he developed an acute intestinal infection which gave him an alarmingly high fever, double vision, and an inability to retain any food. One day, as he recalled two years later, he felt that he was dying and muttered to himself: 'Well if death is like this I am all for it.'[46]

When the fever abated in a few days, the physicians in Nice were prepared to operate. Searle, however, persuaded Maugham to wait until he had regained his strength and to fly to Lausanne where there was the best medical treatment on the Continent. 'I shall be glad to get him away from these local doctors,' he reported to an anxious Bert Alanson. 'I took the responsibility and refused to allow them to operate on him in the condition that he was – they would have killed him.'[47]

In the absence of any of the author's family and with Maugham himself too delirious to care about anything, Searle did indeed make all the critical decisions, and as Maugham himself acknowledged to Alanson, he had looked after him as no trained nurse would or could have done, and was now exhausted.[48] It was this 'kind nursery', as Shakespeare calls it, that enabled Maugham to remain at the Villa Mauresque long after he could no longer care for himself.

At the end of July Searle took Maugham to Lausanne where, after a thorough examination, it was decided that the operation should be postponed until the author was much stronger. Finally on 18 September, the hernia was corrected by Dr Pierre Decker at the Cantonal Clinic, and within six hours Maugham was walking about his room. After ten days at the clinic, Maugham spent a fortnight recuperating at the nearby Hôtel Beau-Rivage, and by the middle of October he and his companion were again on their way to London.

Within a year of his hernia operation, Maugham took the first of his three cellular therapy treatments at Dr Paul Niehans's Clinique La Prairie in Vevey, Switzerland. Developed in 1931 and based on the ancient medical theory that the organs of young animals possessed strengthening and curative powers, the Niehans process involved the transplantation of cells from the foetuses of sheep. Though widely believed to rejuvenate or to revive a dormant sex life, its real purpose was to replace and revitalize the cells of deficient organs. Thus, for example, a patient would be injected with foetal heart muscle cells for heart and circulatory problems, liver cells for anaemia and cirrhosis, and kidney cells for nephritis. The foetuses came from a nearby abattoir where the uteruses were removed from pregnant ewes and rushed to the Niehans laboratory.

By the fifties the Niehans process had become the most famous 'rejuvenation' treatment, and could count Konrad Adenauer, Charlie Chaplin, Bernard Baruch, Charles de Gaulle, Gloria Swanson, Marlene

Dietrich, and Pope Pius XII among its clientele. Maugham joined this group on the advice of Dr Max Wolf, a Viennese physician who had known Niehans in the early days of cellular therapy in the thirties. By the Second World War Wolf had moved to the United States where he carried on a lucrative practice among the very rich from his five-storey office-home in Manhattan. He successfully treated Maugham there several times in the forties, but when the writer enquired about some sort of revitalization treatment, he recommended the Niehans clinic.

Despite Wolf's advice Maugham was sceptical about cellular therapy. After a preliminary meeting with Niehans in London he decided that he and Searle would go to Vevey. There they were courted by the publicity-conscious Niehans, who entertained them at luncheon and dinner in his luxurious home in Burier-La-Tour-de-Peilz. After inspecting the laboratory and clinic Maugham decided that Searle should undergo the treatment first because the injections were known to cause severe shock in some patients, and he would stand up much better to such a reaction than the seventy-nine-year-old author. When his companion suffered no ill effects – Searle later quipped that he was prepared to climb trees with anyone and that 'when I see little girls in the street, I want to go and play with them (don't get me wrong)'[49] – Maugham underwent the process himself. It cost them each £1000, and according to Searle 'Maugham told me it was my Christmas present for the next three years.'[50]

Maugham had two further treatments at the Niehans clinic – in 1958 and 1960 – and their effect on him has become a matter of conjecture. He was undoubtedly a vigorous octogenarian, and always proud of his fitness. Walking on one occasion along Cap Ferrat with Rebecca West, he triumphantly pointed to a height of land and crowed: 'Rebecca, after my treatment I can scale that cliff over there.' Pointedly referring to the myth of sexual regeneration associated with the Niehans therapy, West replied: 'But, Willie, that wasn't what I understood you took the treatments for.'[51] Ann Fleming, however, recalled that Maugham always walked very quickly, with almost a spring in his step, and often revealed an almost alarming energy.[52] In 1954 a visitor found him practising with an underwater breathing apparatus so that he could explore the sea bottom, and at the age of eighty-five he still dived into the Mediterranean.

The Niehans treatments may indeed have given the ageing Maugham a renewed vigour – though it needs to be remembered that from middle age onward he had always appeared younger than his years. In retrospect, however, Searle and a number of Maugham's friends became convinced that his body had been given a vitality that his mind could no longer match. This would be particularly true of the final two treatments, taken in the author's mid-eighties, but there is evidence that the first one in 1953 may also have been harmful.

Maugham's personal physician for the last fourteen or so years of his life was Dr Georges Rosanoff, whose practice in Nice included many of the most noted residents and visitors to the Côte d'Azur: among them, Graham Greene, King Ibn Saud, King Faisal, Churchill, Beaverbrook, and Caloust Gulbenkian. Maugham came to him in the early fifties after having severed his connections with his previous physician for having in some way attempted to interfere with the author's private affairs. Typically, Rosanoff was tested on Searle, examining him in his office in the Boulevard Victor Hugo while Maugham watched quietly from a corner. Having met with approval, the doctor was invited to the Villa Mauresque to become Maugham's own physician.

According to Rosanoff, it was after the first Niehans treatment that he especially gained Maugham's confidence. The author and his companion, maintains Rosanoff, returned from Vevey in a state of severe reaction to the foetal cell injections, and it required considerable care to restore their equilibrium. After some weeks they returned to normal health and, though Maugham returned to Niehans twice more, Rosanoff remained convinced that such therapy was harmful.

Rosanoff treated Maugham until the end of his life, and over the years the road to Cap Ferrat became very familiar. He would not normally see his patient for a fortnight, but there were many times when he would be at the Villa Mauresque three times a week or even three times a day. Most often he was required to deal with the exhaustion brought on by one of Maugham's lengthy journeys or his visits to London. Once, in April 1957, however, he was called in the middle of the night to treat a severe attack of nephritis which had Maugham convulsed in pain. Given a double injection of morphine, the author slept for twenty-four hours, and when the doctor confidently arrived next day he was greeted by a furious patient. 'Go to the Devil,' cursed Maugham. 'You nearly killed me with your damned medicines.' Within minutes, however, Maugham's anger had subsided, and he was almost apologetic for losing his temper.[53] Except for this one episode Rosanoff always found the writer courteous and considerate. If Maugham were even half a minute late for an appointment, he would apologize, saying: 'I'm angry to have kept you waiting, doctor, your time is so much more precious than that of an old man like me.'[54] Though he never paid his physician a single centime more than the sum on the bill, Maugham frequently brought him gifts from his travels – from Thailand, Japan, Egypt, and England. When he learned that the doctor collected autographs, Maugham took considerable pains to pass on the signatures of many of his famous acquaintances, and he invited Rosanoff and his wife to lunch with one of their idols, Churchill. When Rosanoff, already awarded the Croix de Guerre and the Medal of the Resistance for his wartime service, was being considered for the OBE, Maugham wrote a generous letter of recommendation.

Rosanoff is adamant that Maugham remained in good health throughout the fifties and that he was not clinically senile until his last two or three years. Then his decline was rapid and shocking in a man he had found 'impressive' both physically and mentally.[55]

With advanced age Maugham's once handsome features gradually took on a severe cast. The prognathous jaw became more pronounced, and the downturned mouth increasingly suggested dissatisfaction or resentment. It is this image of Maugham that is most remembered today, not the handsome young Edwardian or the distinguished middle-aged writer, and since his death he has been described in various colourful adjectives such as 'reptilian', 'hawk-like', 'Mephistophelian', 'gila-monsterish', and 'toad-like'.

Maugham had always believed that he was unattractive, but in old age he came to view his looks more dispassionately. When the fashionable West End photographer Dorothy Wilding asked if she could remove some facial lines when retouching her pictures of him in 1957, he replied: 'Certainly not. It's taken me eighty years to get these lines. Why should I allow you to remove them in two minutes?'[56]

Maugham had not, however, been able to be as nonchalant when viewing the most revealing portrait of his final years, the famous Graham Sutherland portrait done in 1949. Not previously a portrait painter, Sutherland had lunched at the Villa Mauresque the year before, and had suggested to a mutual friend that if he ever took up portraiture he would like to tackle Maugham's face and personality. On learning of this interest, Maugham pursued the matter, and Sutherland did the picture which became a significant turning point in his career, one which led to portraits of Churchill, Beaverbrook, Daisy Fellowes, and others.

Maugham had given the artist absolute freedom, and when after a glass of champagne it was unveiled at the studio in May 1949, Sutherland was prepared for his subject's reaction. 'Only those', he once observed, 'totally without physical vanity, educated in painting, or with exceptionally good manners, can disguise their feelings of shock or even revulsion when they are confronted for the first time with a reasonably truthful image of themselves.'[57] The picture was, in Roger Berthoud's words, 'a telling likeness yet far from flattering, bold, if a trifle coarse, in treatment and with a trace of caricature. The somewhat skeletal right hand and the legs were perhaps not completely convincing. But the power was terrific and the originality undeniable.' Maugham was portrayed as 'the sardonic, aloof and quietly amused observer of human frailty, perched on the café stool with arms and legs crossed, mouth turned-down, face lined and generous bags under his eyes, against a plain background unusually thickly painted (for Graham) in shades ranging from apricot to yellow-green, with a few palm fronds suggesting a hint of the orient at the top.'[58]

Though his response was more controlled than Churchill's violent antipathy to Sutherland's later portrait of him, Maugham visibly blanched at the first sight of such an unforgiving representation.[59] He soon recovered, however, and the artist in him came to respect the truths revealed in the picture, aspects of his character of which he had been unaware. He bought the painting (and the copyright, which brought him handsome royalties on postcard and other reproductions), and he eventually donated it to the Tate Gallery in his daughter's name. So pleased had he become with it, that for some time he tried to dissuade Sutherland from painting other portraits, though he later suggested that Beaverbrook and Churchill would make splendid subjects.

Gerald Kelly once commented to Sutherland that 'you and I both know how extraordinarily paintable Maugham is',[60] but none of Kelly's eighteen canvases ever captured the disillusionment and cynicism so transparent in the Sutherland picture. Kelly and Sutherland were, of course, radically different painters, but it can be argued that both kinds of interpretation are revelatory. The former's work shows the public Maugham – from the self-satisfied Edwardian dandy to the distinguished Old Party, the W. Somerset Maugham who faced life with calm acceptance. The latter's portrait exposes the interior, the often bleak and disillusioned landscape of the mind behind the carefully controlled façade. It is little wonder that Maugham found it shocking, while none of Kelly's pictures had ever surprised him.

As revealing as these portraits are, it must be remembered that they represent only part of the truth, and that a physical likeness frozen at a moment cannot entirely stand for the living, moving, acting being. Here the observations of two other artists – the sculptor Jacob Epstein and the photographer Yousuf Karsh – who studied Maugham in the fifties are interesting. To Epstein, he seemed like an old Roman patrician, but 'in spite of his fastidious and aloof expression he proved a model sitter, was most genial whilst posing and discoursed on contemporary letters most entertainingly.'[61] Karsh found Maugham's face arresting, like the carved wooden image of a South Seas tribal god, with penetrating and almost hypnotic eyes. 'That well-known expression of starkness (often taken for cynicism)', he said, 'broke frequently into the most engaging smile. To my surprise Maugham, the realist, the hard-boiled sceptic, possessed an irresistible warmth.'[62]

Most of the world has taken the exterior image of aloof severity for the man, but to those who knew him well he was something different. Journalist Nancy Spain's encounter with him in the Dorchester Hotel in 1961 is typical of those which broke through the exterior. Seeing the dapper old author buying a paper in the lobby, Spain flung her arms around his neck and kissed him warmly. 'He drew back like a cobra about to strike,' she recalled, 'recognized me and his marvellous old face suddenly split into its macabre grin of cheerful acceptance and defeat, and he stuttered a typical greeting, both witty and devastating.'[63]

If Maugham's appearance masked a warm interior, his reputation as miserly and unsympathetic belies the many acts of private kindness and generosity of his old age. Just after settling back into the Villa Mauresque in 1946, for example, he sent parcels of his books to stock the American Library at Heidelberg. He agreed to lend his name to Daniel Farson's application to Cambridge, and he wrote a letter of recommendation for Klaus Jonas in support of an MA tuition grant at Columbia University. In 1950 he offered to lend his friends Robert and Elsie Tritton the Villa Mauresque for the month of October, pay all expenses, and provide a car. In 1955 he lent the villa to Rab Butler when he learned that the British politician was exhausted by various personal and political strains.[64]

On his trip to Greece in 1953 Maugham and Searle went on a picnic with a couple to whom they had been introduced by Francis King. At one point the woman accidentally broke a thermos on a rock and exclaimed: 'Oh, what a shame! Now we won't be able to have the martinis.' A few days later, a parcel arrived containing a new thermos, a gift of the author.[65]

Georges Rosanoff recalled another thoughtful act when he was once treating Maugham for exhaustion. Seeing his patient dressed for an evening out, Rosanoff chided him: 'I'm trying to keep you alive and you're trying to kill yourself!' Like a penitent child, the author replied that he could not avoid going against his doctor's orders. A Russian prince who had been at the Villa Mauresque many times had asked him to dinner, and he was afraid of hurting his feelings by declining the invitation. 'You will destroy your health,' Rosanoff reproached, but Maugham none the less went to dinner.[66]

This kind of sensitivity to the feelings of others was also revealed when Maugham came to the defence of Graham Sutherland over his highly controversial portrait of Churchill. On the day that Lady Churchill previewed the picture, the painter invited Maugham and Searle to be present to reduce the inevitable tension. Maugham agreed to accompany Lady Churchill to the studio to spare Sutherland the embarrassment of being present for her first reaction. When she seemed pleased by the work Maugham discreetly signalled to the painter that all was well.

Churchill himself, however, reacted with distaste for the portrait, so much so that Lady Churchill eventually destroyed it. In the swirl of adverse criticism surrounding the official unveiling, Sutherland found Maugham 'extraordinarily understanding'.[67] At a party at 10 Downing Street, he came to the painter's defence and in a subsequent letter he urged Sutherland not to let the attacks affect him:

> You have had an immense deal of praise, and justly, for your work in the past, and now that you are a public figure, which means that you attract the attention of masses of ill-instructed people, you must be prepared to suffer from their ignorant reaction . . . I know that criticism is wounding, but believe me, it is very soon forgotten, and the work remains. I am convinced that posterity will receive your portrait as a convincing and powerful representation of the man who will have become a great historical figure.[68]

Maugham was, however, capable of offering more than just sympathy and encouragement. Robin Maugham's claim that his uncle could be 'almost ridiculously extravagant'[69] in response to appeals for money is an overstatement, but he could be generous to those in genuine need. In 1954, for example, he donated £100 to a friend of Patrick Kinross that he had met only once, and when Ivor Back's death in 1951 left his widow short of funds Maugham sent her a cheque. He later suggested that she raise money by selling all her signed copies of his books, and until late in his life he continued to pay for all her visits to Cap Ferrat. Back was, moreover, only one of several widows for whom Maugham provided financial assistance in the fifties.

Maugham's sympathies were always most strongly touched by the young and powerless, and his generosity toward the English writer George Bullock is characteristic. Though angered by the pacifism of Bullock and his friend Raymond Marriott at the beginning of the Second World War, Maugham continued to see Bullock and to send letters and gifts from the United States. When the younger man's tuberculosis worsened following the war, and neither he nor his working-class parents could afford treatments, Maugham provided money so that he could go to clinics in Switzerland and stay for months in sanatoria.

Over a decade Maugham gave Bullock more than £500 ($2500) but, according to Marriott, at a certain point the author decided that Bullock had had enough from him and that there would be no more. Searle, however, continued to give the young man something in the form of gifts – for example, a kind of blender since by then he could eat only soft foods – but this had to be kept secret from Maugham.[70] This decision to stop providing funds is undoubtedly one of the results of Maugham's obsessive fear of not having enough money which gripped him in the last ten years of his life. This does not, of course, absolve him, and Marriott is right to find it mean-spirited to cut off support at a time when Bullock was dying. Against it, however, must be set the two decades of encouragement and assistance to a young man to whom Maugham owed nothing and from whom he had little to gain.

Derek Patmore wrote in 1960 that 'whenever I have met [Maugham] in later years, I have been surprised by his unexpected sympathy and kindly, if detached, interest in the changing world around him.'[71] At the same time, Ethel Barrymore wrote in her autobiography that 'he has become a warmer person than when I first knew him.[72] These perceptions of Maugham in old age are hardly isolated, as a number of his friends saw a new mellowness in him in the fourteen years following the war. In the autumn of 1949 Noël Coward found him 'enchanting',[73] and in the following summer Chips Channon noted that his 'mandarin manner remains but he was friendly and witty'.[74] At Bulbridge House several months later Channon observed: 'Willy Maugham . . . as he approaches eighty, is growing gentler and more mellow and is, in fact, sweetness himself.'[75] Michael Davidson, dining with Robin Maugham at the Villa Mauresque in 1951, found the host 'unusually good-humoured, in his dry way',[76] and a year later another visitor, Julien Green, wrote: 'I think that I could have confided in him, a thing I could never have done with Gide. There is something indomitable and honest about him.'[77]

When Coward lunched with Maugham in December 1953 he commented: 'I only hope that when I am eighty I shall be as bright and charming,'[78] and shortly afterwards Nancy Mitford wrote to Harold Acton from Paris: 'I've seen something of Willie while he's here – I've never known him so agreeable.'[79] That year journalist Noel Barber devoted an article to 'The New Somerset Maugham', arguing that there was 'a new, changed, a more contented "Willie" Maugham . . . In the last few years,' he continued, 'he has mellowed, has become more companionable . . . Even though it is tiring meeting strangers, Maugham enjoys it. He has become more approachable as he has mellowed with age, and anybody who is sincere is sure of getting past the front door.'[80]

Even as late as June 1958 Coward spent 'a lovely four days' with an 'enchanting' Maugham,[81] and when he had found him 'really extraordinary' a year earlier he speculated about this amiability. After a day at the Villa Mauresque, Coward 'drove home to Biot in the evening sunlight happy and stimulated and deeply impressed by the charm of old age when it is allied to health and intelligence'.[82]

The Indian summer serenity of this period of Maugham's life may owe much to health and intelligence, but a much more fundamental element was the emotional stability of a loving companionship. 'Undeservedly', he wrote in 1962, 'I have a friend . . . of thirty years' standing, who has been willing to give up his life to ease my loneliness, to care for me in sickness, to protect me from the intruders on my solitude which my increasing fame – or notoriety if you like better – has brought me, to answer the innumerable letters I receive and to enable me to pass my few remaining years in happiness and comfort.'[83] Meant to be fulsome praise from a man characteristically reticent about public expressions of emotion, this comment none the less falls far short of describing the importance of Alan Searle in the final two decades of Maugham's life.

When Searle joined Maugham in the United States in 1945 it was ostensibly as his secretary, a role that he performed admirably over the years – more capably, in fact, than Haxton ever did. This meant typing all of the author's manuscripts and correspondence, which became a staggering load as Maugham's fame grew. Each birthday would bring hundreds of telegrams and letters to be acknowledged, and on any occasion of public honour they would reach a flood. The job also required making all the travel arrangements for a man who spent almost half of each year away from home. As well, Searle gradually began to assume more and more of the management of the Villa

Mauresque: dealing with the staff, arranging meals, settling accounts, and generally overseeing the smooth running of a large estate.

As Maugham increasingly became a public figure in the years following the war, part of Searle's role was as a buffer between the writer and the larger, inquisitive world. Though essentially quiet and unassuming, he adopted a number of strategies to protect his friend from those who were demanding and exploitative – often drawing their wrath onto himself. 'I rather enjoy the reflected glory,' he once observed, 'but, oh dear! I do get some nasty snubs sometimes. A lot of people pursue Willie that he doesn't want to be mixed up with, so I take them on, and behave like a disagreeable old spinster, and I *do* protect him, but, my God! they do give me hell, and I don't like it very much.'[84]

Even among friends Searle's protectiveness could cause resentment. He was rarely from Maugham's side when they had company, and they developed the practice of the younger man providing a word when Maugham's stutter became particularly troublesome. On at least one occasion, even this assistance was greeted with hostility when such an interjection caused Lady Churchill to snap: 'I was talking to *Mr Maugham!*'[85]

Beyond any of his formal duties, Searle was the source of much of the liveliness and laughter in the Villa Mauresque, filling the silences surrounding the shy and taciturn Maugham. By nature gentle, sensitive, and fun-loving, he orchestrated much of the life of the house to alleviate the old man's periods of boredom and gloom. His particular kind of playful wit is familiar to anyone who knew him and is apparent in many of his letters. There is, for example, his invitation in 1957 to Kitty Black, then a member of the Curtis Brown literary agency. 'It's wonderful here just now,' he wrote. 'Hot and sunny, and the air smells of mimosa and we are sunbathing and eating ice-cream, and everybody is jolly good-looking, and longing for love, and why don't you come over.'[86] In 1963 he whimsically asked Maugham's agent at A. P. Watt if he could have a part in a musical adaptation of a Maugham play being produced in Budapest. 'I sing like a bird,' he said, 'dance like a fairy (please don't misunderstand me) and can act anyone off the stage – so Mr Maugham says, but then he also says I am the best nagger since his wife died.'[87]

Like his predecessor Searle enjoyed trying to shock the author in front of his friends, though his teasing lacked the knife edge of Haxton's. At other times he subtly played the fool, drawing Maugham out before his company by deliberately making himself the butt of his friend's wit. Searle could nevertheless quietly contradict Maugham, in the later years especially undercutting the author's bouts of self-pity by pointing out, for example, that the stutter had not really been such a handicap or that his life had not really been full of mistakes. Compliments, on the other hand, always embarrassed Maugham, causing him to reply to any emotional remark: 'Stop being such a silly ass!'[88]

Maugham and Searle had begun as lovers in the late twenties, and like any sustained relationship their union underwent an evolution over its thirty-seven years. Even before the war the sexual attraction had begun to be replaced by a deeper and more durable affection, and in the last two decades of Maugham's life the relationship became more that of father and son. Searle, after all, was forty and Maugham seventy-one in 1945 and, though Searle later claimed that his friend was a good and energetic lover until very late in his life, it is more likely that the sexual element had become secondary. Searle would strike up brief sexual liaisons with others – often sailors on leave in Nice – and Maugham tolerated them so long as he was sure that they did not threaten their relationship.

To the end of his life, Searle spoke of thirty-seven wonderful years with Maugham, a man for whom he not only felt a deep love but also an unqualified admiration as a writer. Maugham, moreover, offered him protection, not only the shelter afforded by wealth but in the early years a kind of paternal caring. Searle had been employed as an excellent prison visitor and was capable of taking care of himself, but his sensitive, fairly passive and almost timid character drew him to Maugham's more dominant and authoritarian personality. The author had power, position, and wealth, and Searle felt secure in the world which his friend had worked so diligently to master. Ironically, of course, time would eventually reverse the roles and make Searle the protector of a frail and vulnerable old man.

Through Maugham, Searle experienced a cosmopolitan life he would never have known as a social worker in England. He got to see the world from Bangkok to Istanbul, and to meet many of the memorable figures of the time – Churchill and Beaverbrook, O'Neill and Wells, Cukor and Katharine Hepburn. His days were spent in the Mediterranean sun, at the Gritti Palace in Venice, the Dorchester in London, or the Raffles Hotel in Singapore; and his evenings passed at the opera in Bayreuth, the theatre in London, or fashionable restaurants in Paris.

As attractive as this kind of life may have been, it was not without its costs. Even before the senility of the final years, Maugham could be a difficult companion, and Searle often bore the brunt of his anger or jealousy. Maugham was, for example, so annoyed that Bernard Berenson wrote in his autobiography that Searle had a greater understanding of art than did the author that he refused to let the younger man read the book or to see Berenson again. Maugham would never forgive those who spoke ill of his friend, but neither would he forgive those who spoke too well of him. Then, too, there was Maugham's temper, which he once admitted was occasionally so violent that he could almost imagine killing someone. Cecil Beaton has recounted an episode in the late forties when Maugham was irritated by Searle's tossing a stone at a snail in the garden at the villa. When he ignored Maugham's demand to stop, Searle found himself 'lying with an unrecognizable face in a nearby hospital'.[89] Though Searle later pointed out that Beaton's story exaggerates the violence of the altercation, he admitted its essential truth.[90]

No matter how blinding, Maugham's rage was always fleeting and followed by regret. Georges Rosanoff was present one day when Maugham launched such a tirade that a flushed and humiliated Searle fled into the garden. Within minutes, his anger having subsided, a concerned Maugham begged his butler and the doctor to bring back his friend. When Searle returned and sat on the sofa on the verge of tears, Maugham 'with great dignity and gentleness ... found, stuttering throughout, the words that were needed to assure a reconciliation'.[91]

The most exacting cost of Searle's life with Maugham was the surrender of his freedom. Being a secretary, a nurse, and a lover – especially to an octogenarian – meant being with Maugham most of the waking hours of every day. When he once asked for a holiday, Maugham replied: 'A holiday? What do you think your life is?' Searle did manage to spend a week with his relatives on one of the trips to England in the fifties, but that was the only time he had on his own until he went alone to London for the sale of the paintings in April 1962. The holidays were apparently supposed to be the trips to Italy, Germany, Spain, or Greece, but they always meant a flurry of travel arrangements and the exhausting task of dealing with the author's demands without the comforts and convenience of the Villa Mauresque. And though he was young enough to enjoy the night life of the cities they visited, Searle was rarely allowed to leave his friend for the evening. Francis King recalled an occasion in Japan in 1959 when Searle concluded a busy day by saying: 'I'll put the old boy to bed and then we can do the town.' Maugham became suspicious, however, and by asking where his companion was going effectively forbade him to leave.[92]

One of the strongest holds that Maugham had over Searle was, of course, financial. Since almost all of his necessities were provided, the younger man received only a modest salary for any personal expenses. From time to time Maugham would give him spending money, but usually in such small amounts as to be useless. 'Go and see if you can amuse yourself on that,' Maugham would say. A number of Maugham's friends believed that he deliberately underpaid his companion in order to prevent his leaving him. Whether by intention, or simply by circumstances, Searle certainly became more and more financially dependent on the old man. Each passing year made it harder than ever to return to his career as a social worker, and by the age of fifty the only alternative to life at the Villa Mauresque was a similar position elsewhere – if there was an opening and if his departure from Cap Ferrat were amicable. Then, too, there was the distinct possibility of Maugham's death at any time, with no guarantee that he would have provided adequately for his friend. In the absence of a clearly stated will, the law does not favour companions in a disputed settlement.

Maugham himself recognized his friend's vulnerability, and as early as 1947 took steps to ensure his security. In March of that year he instructed Alanson to invest $3000 a year, with the interest to go to Searle for the rest of his life and the capital thereafter to the Author's Society. Six years later the amount was increased to $2000 annually in addition to the interest from the trust fund and an English annuity of £500. Maugham made such payments conditional on Searle being in his service at the time of his death, a provision that reportedly stung the younger man.

Even allowing for the higher value of these sums in the fifties, they are not generous when one considers the gulf between the style of Searle's life at the villa and what it would have become had Maugham died in, say, 1954, when he was eighty. Whether a result of Maugham's innate parsimony or design, the modest pension was for many years all that Searle could anticipate for the period following Maugham's death. He might continue living with Maugham for the comforts of the famous writer's world, but he was guaranteed little else.

In the end Searle remained at Maugham's side, and he was treated generously and unconditionally in his friend's will. He stayed, however, not for the promise of what he might inherit but simply for love. Edith Sitwell, Ann Fleming, Roderick Cameron, and Beverley Nichols have all called him a 'saint', Rebecca West used the term 'a strange sort of semi-saint',[93] and Kenneth Clark wrote that Maugham 'was looked after like an angel by Alan'.[94] Raymond Marriott remembered his 'extraordinary kindness, sensitivity and compassion' and that 'amazingly he had infinite consideration for practically everyone without in the least being a prig or a goody-goody.'[95] In Lord Boothby's words, 'far from being grasping and "on the make", he was one of the nicest, kindest and most generous men I have ever known. From start to finish he served Maugham with selfless devotion, and certainly prolonged his life.'[96]

Boothby was not alone in believing that Searle extended the author's life. Robin Maugham observed that in Maugham's senility almost anything could happen and 'it was Alan – untiring, loyal, patient Alan – who had to cope. I honestly believe that had it not been for Alan's unceasing care and devotion during the last years of Willie's life my uncle would have gone mad or killed himself . . . If ever the overused words "loyalty and devotion" meant anything, Alan Searle exemplified them.'[97] 'Without Alan', wrote Nichols, 'the long last decades of the Master's progress through the world would have degenerated into a shambles, if he had gone on living at all . . . Alan was an influence for sanity, for dignity and for moderation.'[98]

Maugham himself was not oblivious to these qualities in his companion. While his love for Searle never matched the intensity of his passion for Gerald Haxton, he none the less came to realize that he had at last found someone who was genuinely loving, who genuinely loved him. Long ago he had divided love into sexual passion, which was usually painful and imprisoning, and loving-kindness, a less intense but more compassionate and generous emotion. In Haxton, Maugham experienced the former – at times joyous, but often frustrating and humiliating. Searle offered the latter: a sensitive and tender caring which, while less exciting, was unqualified and unfailing.

While the relationship between Maugham and Searle deepened in the two decades following the war, each year brought the deaths of friends, many of whom were sincerely mourned. Cyril Connolly's claim that Maugham was deeply upset by the passing of Emerald Cunard in 1948[99] is confirmed by his comment to Lady Bateman that she was a very old and irreplaceable friend without whom London would seem dull and empty.[100] He missed Desmond MacCarthy and his Riviera friend Frieda von Seidlitz, and Robert Tritton, who died in January 1957, had been the one who first introduced him to Searle.

In May 1955 Mabel Alanson died after a prolonged and painful illness, but it was Bert Alanson's death in the summer of 1958 which caused the most intense grief. Alanson was one of Maugham's few remaining friends of his own age, and the unlikely relationship between the famous English writer and the San Franciscan stockbroker had lasted undiminished for four decades. In 1950 Searle reported to Alanson: 'You are the only person in the world that Willie has any deep feelings about. He is starved for affection, he gets none of it from his own family – they've only one idea.'[101] About the American's stay at the Villa Mauresque a few months later, Searle commented: 'You have no idea how much your visit bucked him up.'[102] After Alanson departed from Cap Ferrat in 1955 Searle wrote: 'He's a shy bird, and could not bring himself to tell you just how much it meant, but he talked freely of it to me. I wish you could have heard him, it would have pleased you and warmed your heart.'[103]

The relationship between Maugham and Alanson was – with the exception of the latter's visits – necessarily conducted at a great distance. Maugham nevertheless found Alanson a loyal confidant, someone whom he trusted entirely both with his money and his personal life. As they grew older Maugham feared losing his friend and became frantic when he did not hear from him for a length of time. Searle would have to send a telegram and Maugham would not be satisfied until he had received a reassuring letter from Alanson.

Alanson never forgot Maugham's birthday, and his gifts always touched Maugham more deeply than the many others he received. In 1953, for example, he was nearly overcome when he was greeted by dozens of roses sent by Alanson. 'I have rarely seen him so pleased,' said Searle, 'and when in the evening, to his great surprise the champagne glasses were suddenly put in front of him, and the champagne poured in, he said, "Where did this come from?" and I again said Bert, he sat quite silent for a moment or two and then the tears rolled down his cheeks. You have no notion what it meant to him.'[104] In 1958 Alanson sent the last of his gifts – beginning with five huge bowls of dark red carnations. 'Willie asked where they all came from,' recounted Searle, 'and when I said, "Bert sent them," he burst into tears. And then in the evening, after dinner, he asked for a cigar, and I handed him a box – with your card, again he was overwhelmed with emotion.'[105] By the time that Alanson had arranged for these presents he had contracted cancer of the throat, and when he died, on 26 May 1958, at the age of eighty-one, Maugham was devastated.

Two months earlier Frederic Maugham had died in London. Willie expected the death of his ninety-one-year-old brother after a lengthy illness, but he was none the less moved by a sense of loss. Their relationship had never been especially warm – though closer than Robin Maugham has claimed – but there was a kind of blood loyalty between them. A sense of competition, and the clash of two taciturn temperaments, might give their meetings a frigid tone, but there was a begrudging mutual admiration which they characteristically were better able to reveal to outsiders than to each other. Willie's pleasure in his brother's rise to the Lord Chancellorship had been genuine, and Frederic took pride in being related to a famous writer. Alexander Frere remembered lunching with Frederic at the House of Lords when Evelyn Waugh was loudly boasting at the next table that *Brideshead Revisited* had become a bestseller. Frederic listened for a while, and then turned to Waugh and said: 'Young man, you say you're a bestseller! I have a brother who's just written a book [*The Razor's Edge*] which has sold seven million copies.'[106]

The other brothers, Henry and Charles, had died in 1904 and 1935, and Frederic's wife Nellie, of whom Willie was very fond, succumbed after a long illness in 1950. In the following eight years Frederic stayed at the Villa Mauresque a number of times, and though the brothers always parted with relief they continued to see each other in France or in London. Frederic's passing, though not as troubling as Alanson's, was nevertheless another break with the past and a reminder of Maugham's own mortality. A month after Frederic's death, Maugham attempted to console Bert Alanson over the loss of his brother by pointing out that the death of a close relative one has known since childhood robs one of part of one's youth[107] – comments that surely come from Maugham's own experience.

The deaths of Nellie and Frederic and many of his friends left Maugham increasingly isolated as he approached his nineties. Added to this was a distancing from his other relatives – Liza and her children and Robin and his sisters. Maugham had always liked his niece Kate Mary, who was a talented novelist and playwright, and he considered her sister Diana a clever writer. In 1953 he expressed delight that Diana was having her first play produced, and in 1957 when Robin had a play produced in Germany while another of Diana's was being done by the Repertory Company, he exclaimed: 'My word, the literary works that my family produces!'[108]

Maugham was never particularly close to his nieces, but Robin was more like a son than a nephew. By the time that he had reached his mid-twenties, however, the young man had begun to disappoint his uncle, who saw him living an undisciplined life and thereby squandering his talents. During the war Maugham had written to chastise him for his drinking and loose-living, and he would periodically repeat the criticism. In 1952, when reminding Alanson that the trust fund he had established for his nephew was now worth $75,000, Maugham confessed that Robin had been a great disappointment to Frederic and him. Never having grown up, he remained frivolous, mixing with questionable people and spending money recklessly. Unable to stick to any occupation, he had begun to write movie scripts and drink heavily.[109] Three years later Maugham added gloomily that he could not see how Robin could avoid coming to a shabby end and he hoped that it would not occur until after Frederic's death. Though congenial and high-spirited, he had become too smug and too fond of drinking.[110]

Maugham's disillusionment with his nephew did not cause him to cancel his trust fund nor did he cease to see him often. It did, however, create a tension between them which could not help being a barrier to a close relationship. Interestingly, though Maugham did not live to see it, his prognosis was borne out over the remainder of Robin's life. His first novel, *The Servant* (1948), became his best-known work, largely because of Joseph Losey's hypnotic film of Harold Pinter's screenplay adaptation. Though the rest of his books were competently written and dealt somewhat daringly with homosexual themes, none ever fulfilled the promise of the early years. Never able to escape from the literary shadow of W. Somerset Maugham, he tried to recreate his uncle's cosmopolitan life – but always at a lower level. Willie had a luxurious villa at Cap Ferrat; Robin bought a modest one on Ibiza. Willie had the best chef along the Riviera; Robin had a good one on Ibiza. Willie had an impeccable staff; Robin had several competent servants. Willie had a secretary-companion; Robin once told a friend: 'You will be Gerald Haxton to my Willie Maugham.'[111] Uncannily, as in some melodramatic science fiction story, Robin even began physically to resemble his uncle.

As Maugham had foreseen, his nephew became an alcoholic and lost most of whatever talent he had possessed. In *Parallel Lives*,[112] his friend Peter Burton describes how he (Burton) wrote many of the articles and parts of books which appeared in the seventies under Robin's name. By the end, he was barely capable of completing any writing task, and when he died in 1981 he was only sixty-five.

For at least a decade after the Second World War, Maugham's relationship with Liza and her children seems to have been as amiable as could be expected given Maugham's advanced age and the history of his life with Syrie. He had seen his former wife only occasionally since the divorce, and when he learned of her death in July 1955, he could not feign grief, even for the shared past. It would be hypocrisy, he told friends, to pretend that he regretted her death.

The problems in Liza's marriage had deepened at the end of the war, and in the spring of 1947 she was granted a divorce. Maugham was disappointed and hoped that he would like her next husband as much as he had been fond of Paravicini. On 21 July 1948 Liza married Lord John Hope, the son of Lord Linlithgow, who in 1938 had irritated Maugham by snubbing Haxton on the Indian tour. Maugham flew to London for the wedding, paid for a lavish reception at Claridge's, and gave a toast to the couple. As well, he agreed to settle £20,000 on Liza in addition to various trust funds he had established which made his grandchildren and her self-supporting.

For nearly ten years Liza, her husband, and their children spent several weeks each summer at the Villa Mauresque, and on some occasions the parents would leave the children for an extra few days while they went to Scotland for the grouse shooting. In addition to Liza's offspring by Paravicini, there were two sons by Hope: Julian, born in 1950, and Jonathan, born in 1952. If one small boy had intruded upon the solitude of the vicarage in Whitstable sixty years earlier, four energetic children could not help but disrupt the orderly world of the Villa Mauresque. As well, Maugham did not share Hope's sense of humour. Once, to amuse the children, Hope approached him on the patio wearing a false beard and greeted him warmly. Maugham, deceived, replied icily, '*Allez-vous-en, monsieur, je ne vous connais pas.*'

Never having played the part of father or grandfather with any natural ease, Maugham now found the family visits exhausting, though as he admitted it was Searle who bore the brunt of the extra work. By 1957, at the age of eighty-three, Maugham decided that he could not face the disruption any more, and for the first time since he bought the Villa Mauresque there were no houseguests for the summer. From that point on there were few visits from his immediate family.

Maugham had liked the idea of Liza marrying into the aristocracy but he remained wary of John Hope. It has been suggested that Maugham had not forgotten Lord Linlithgow's action in India, but the offence is much more likely to have occurred later. In 1949 Lord Linlithgow suggested that the author form a company in the Channel Islands, thereby saving his heirs from paying inheritance tax. Maugham always resented what he perceived to be interference in his personal affairs – he once refused to speak to a friend for two days because she expressed the hope that he had provided for Searle in his will. The Channel Island idea, moreover, assumed that he would automatically bequeath the bulk of his estate to the Hopes, and his lawyers advised him that it would take the control of his capital out of his hands.[114] Whether justified or not, Maugham became convinced that his daughter and son-in-law were interested only in his wealth, and he even went so far as to tell friends that he had caught Hope 'counting the silver'. When Liza became pregnant in 1949 he bridled at what he interpreted as their assumption that he would automatically settle money on this newest grandchild. On one occasion he is reported to have deliberately paused beneath the open window of the Hopes' room and commented loudly: 'He married her for my money and she married him for his title.'[115]

By 1956 the question of the disposition of Maugham's estate was causing tension, as Ann Fleming reported in a letter to Evelyn Waugh: 'I did have a jolly time at the Villa Mauresque, a beautiful slice of human comedy, Alan Searle persuading me that Willie's stutter always became worse before his daughter came to stay, tremendous undercurrents about "The Will", and all three parties taking me for walks along those carefully raked gravel terraces and swearing me to secrecy. Alan incites Willie against Liza, Willie loathes Lord John Hope, and poor Liza ill at ease but a cautious, discreet, ambitious girl.'[116]

Maugham baulked at the idea of turning over the management of his financial affairs to anyone else for a number of reasons. Most distasteful was the implication of senility, that he was no longer competent to control his own life. As well, he had an irrational but none the less real fear of not having enough money to live on comfortably. Finally, he wanted to be able to decide for himself what would become of the estate he had worked for more than five decades to accumulate.

Though the relationship between Maugham and Liza and her husband grew strained in the fifties, he continued to settle sums of money on her offspring. Years earlier he had set up trust funds for the Paravicini children, and in 1953 he instructed Alanson to do the same for Julian and Jonathan. As late as 1957 he lent Liza £15,000 to buy a house in London, and in May 1959, when he came to London to be the guest of honour at Camilla's coming out ball at the Savoy, he gave her a ball gown. This was surprising, she said, because 'usually when he wants to give me a present he sends me a cheque'.[117]

The growing estrangement between Maugham and his family in the late fifties was only one aspect of the general isolation which was enveloping him. Raymond Chandler had called him 'a lonely old eagle'[118] in 1950, but it was not really a fitting description until 1959. By then he had lost many of his friends through death or distance. The inevitable ravages of advanced age – loss of hearing, memory, and stamina – meant few houseguests and such exhaustion on his London visits that they began to end in irritable convalescence. Finally, in November 1958, he published the last book in his pattern, *Points of View*, and pronounced himself an unemployed writer. Urged to continue to work by critic John Beavan at the end of that year, Maugham declined. A writer, he argued, 'must mingle with life, be immersed in life – and I am a stranger in the world today.'[119]

10

THE BURDEN OF
ONE'S MEMORIES: 1959–1965

FOR ALL OF his adult years Maugham had believed in imposing a pattern on life. The famous Persian carpet episode of *Of Human Bondage* was a metaphor for his belief that the only meaning in human existence came from the pattern each individual worked out over his lifetime. His own career had been largely a triumph of determination and will, the success in three genres of a man not naturally gifted as a writer. As early as the nineteen-twenties, he had settled on the number and progression of his works which would take him to retirement, and though the war was disruptive it did not alter the essential plan. With deliberation, he ceased first to write plays and then fiction, and finally in 1958 he published what he repeatedly called his last work of non-fiction.

In 1957 Maugham replied to a question about what life had taught him by saying: 'Chiefly, I think to take things as they come.'[1] He may indeed have learned in old age to adjust to the vagaries and flux of the world, but for eight decades he had attempted to control and impose a pattern on his life – not merely his professional career but also his emotional and spiritual being. Feelings, because they threatened to overwhelm judgement and to cause pain, were thus feared and reason preferred. Spontaneity, because it exposed a person to humiliation, was kept in check by a vigilant self-discipline, and if a relationship failed or a person disappointed, the suffering was submerged beneath a façade of cynical resignation. Or it became grist to the mill, good copy for a professional writer. Above all, life's chances and mischances were kept from disrupting the pattern.

Had Maugham died peacefully in 1958 he would have been largely successful in persuading the world that a long, distinguished career had ended in the calm acceptance of a man who had come to terms with himself and his life. The careful design did not, however, take into account the unpredictability of the human life span and the vulnerability of senescence. While Maugham's body functioned remarkably for another seven years, the sharply disciplined mind collapsed, revealing a hidden turmoil and destroying his carefully crafted façade.

In 1959 Maugham broke the pattern in two astonishing ways: he began to write his memoirs and he travelled to the Far East. In a lengthy interview published in the *New York Times* in January of that year, he stated that he would write nothing more, but in May at least two articles announced that he was working on a book of reminiscences to be published posthumously as *The Ragbag*.[2] By September he was writing to Barbara Back to get details about Syrie's decorating career, and in November the press reported that he had written a book to be held for publication after his death and that three Japanese publishers were bidding for the rights.[3]

Besides the difficulty of breaking a life-long habit of writing, Maugham likely began this extensive autobiographical piece so soon after announcing his retirement because of something he read at the beginning of 1959. In January he received an advance copy of the American Karl Pfeiffer's *Somerset Maugham*, published in the United States by Norton and in Great Britain by Gollancz. There had been earlier books about him – Paul Dottin's *W. Somerset Maugham et ses Romans* (1928) and *Le Théâtre de W. Somerset Maugham* (1937), Suzanne Guery's *La Philosophie de Somerset Maugham* (1933), and Richard Cordell's *Somerset Maugham* (1937) – but they were all primarily works of literary criticism. Even so, Maugham found reading about himself uncomfortable and he could rarely bring himself to open their covers.

Pfeiffer's book was different from anything that had come before. It was the first straightforward biography, and Maugham was aghast. He had not paid much attention to Pfeiffer's request to do the book and he had given no assistance, and the result was a portrait that was at times shrewdly accurate but at others far off the mark. The biographer drew on his own acquaintance with his subject in the thirties and especially in the United States during the war, and he paraphrased much of Maugham's correspondence with him.

For several decades Maugham had discouraged would-be biographers, conducted 'bonfire nights', and requested the burning of his letters. Pfeiffer, however, had slipped through the net, and Maugham was horrified to see himself and those close to him exposed so graphically to the public gaze. He attacked the book in letters to various friends, and refused to allow Searle to mention it or talk about it to anyone. In April Maugham publicly condemned Pfeiffer in a lengthy and unusually candid interview with Robert Pitman, calling his biography 'a very vulgar book – full of inaccuracies'.[4]

Maugham was at work on his reminiscences a month later, perhaps as a result of some remark by Pitman, whose *Sunday Express* ultimately published them, or perhaps because his dissatisfaction with the Pfeiffer book compelled him to record his version of some troublesome episodes in his personal life. If Pfeiffer could portray him surrounded by liveried servants, sailing his yacht, and remaining aloof from his family, how might future biographers describe Syrie, the marriage, and Gerald Haxton? He had told his side of the story to various close friends over the years, but what might the general public be given in the years to come? It would be hard to control the public perception of him after his death, but a posthumous time-bomb might blow away all other accounts.

No less surprising than this decision to write his memoirs was his trip to the Far East, first announced in his interview with John Beavan in December 1958. Since 1950 he had firmly turned down many invitations – even those of Bert Alanson – to go to the United States because the voyage would be too rigorous, and the trip to Egypt in 1956 had ended in illness. Now at the age of eighty-five, however, he proposed to sail thousands of miles to a part of the world where the crowds, the conditions, and the problems of language could only be exhausting.

Maugham and Searle left Marseilles on 5 October aboard the French liner *Laos*, and after a thirty-four-day voyage through the Suez Canal to Aden, Bombay, Colombo, Singapore, Saigon, and Manila, they arrived in Yokohama. At each port reporters and photographers clamoured to see the famous author, and the trip began to resemble the triumphal farewell tour of some film star. The American scholar Klaus Jonas had put Maugham in touch with a University of Tokyo professor, Matsuo Tanaka, who was the head of the Japanese Maugham Society, a vigorous organization that reflected the high regard for the author in the Orient. Maugham was grateful to have a knowledgeable guide to Japan, but Searle became alarmed by the intensive round of public functions planned by Tanaka and Mr Kabawata, the President of the Japanese PEN society. He wrote to Tanaka to remind him of Maugham's age and frailty and to urge him not to meet the ship in Yokohama.

Tanaka may not have met the *Laos*, but several thousand other admirers did, and for the remainder of Maugham's Japanese visit he was besieged by autograph seekers and interviewers. When 300 people were invited to see him open an exhibition of his books and manuscripts on loan from Stanford University, 5000 people showed up. Considering him the greatest living English writer and second only to Shakespeare, students and faculty members of the university lined up with copies of his books. Rather liking the adulation, Maugham dutifully signed his name to everything thrust in front of him.

Francis King, then working for the British Council in Kyoto, saw a good deal of Maugham in Japan and found him very courteous and considerate. Appreciative of the trouble he was causing for the people showing him around, he was always afraid that he was imposing on their generosity. King took him to a Noh play, which his European guests usually found boring and wanted to leave after half an hour. To King's surprise, Maugham sat there for two or three hours, a small, frail figure absorbed by a highly stylized drama in a language he did not understand.[5] On another occasion, Maugham accompanied Ian Fleming and writer Richard Hughes to a judo academy where he was fascinated by the disciplined drills.

By the middle of December Maugham and Searle had moved on to Saigon, from where they flew to Angkor Wat. Thirty-seven years earlier, he and Haxton had made the tortuous boat trip through the jungle to reach the monumental ruins, and now he recalled that time as 'probably the happiest of my life'.[6] This was indeed a farewell tour, but much of it was spent in hotel rooms reading mysteries, though he was pleased to be able to show a bartender in Siemreap, Cambodia, how to mix a proper whisky on the rocks.

Maugham and Searle reached Bangkok near the end of December and remained there for a month. Maugham's birthday was celebrated at a party given by students of Chulalongkorn University, who honoured him with a Siamese birthday ceremony. Buddhist priests poured lustral water on his hands and he was offered a traditional gift of cloth.

From Bangkok Maugham and Searle flew to Rangoon and on 10 February they went south to Singapore, where they stayed at the Raffles Hotel because, Maugham told reporters, the management had written such warm letters that it would hurt their feelings if he refused. What he did not say, however, was that he was being given free accommodation. In 1954 the manager of the Raffles, Frans Schutzman, invited the author to stay as his guest, but Maugham declined because he did not want to travel such a great distance. Five years later, Mr Schutzman was surprised to receive a letter from Maugham saying that he would be pleased to accept his generous offer. When the hotel now refused to honour the obligation, the manager was forced to pay the bill himself.[7]

That Maugham could remember such an invitation among the several thousand letters he received over five years is only one symptom of his growing concern with finances. He had always been careful not to waste money, but in the last decade of his life he became obsessed with the idea that he would become bankrupt. In Japan Francis King had been astonished by Maugham's parsimony, revealed first when a press conference was delayed while he checked every item on his bar bill. Seeing an entry for three drinks, he complained: 'I have never had three drinks in a day in my life.' At a subsequent dinner with a friend who was a wine connoisseur, Maugham interrupted their study of a particularly interesting wine list to enquire if they would like to have another Japanese whisky or beer. He clearly was not prepared to pay for an expensive wine.[8]

While in Malaya, Maugham travelled to Johore Bahru, where he was a guest at the coronation of the eighteenth Sultan of Johore in the throne room of the royal palace. Maugham was fascinated by the four-hundred-year-old ceremony, which after thirteen hours culminated in a crown of rubies, emeralds and diamonds being placed on the ruler's head. Back at the luxurious Tanglin Club in Singapore, however, he showed that he had not lost his disdain for the pretensions of British colonials. Having been initially refused entry because he and his host, Frans Schutzman, were not wearing jackets and ties in the oppressive heat and humidity, Maugham eventually gained admission and proceeded to talk in an uncharacteristically loud voice. 'Observing these people,' he said as he gazed around the room, 'I am no longer surprised that there is such a scarcity of domestic servants back home.' His remark led to his being asked to leave the club and Schutzman was subsequently declared *persona non grata*.[9] It was unusual of Maugham to draw attention to himself and to embarrass a companion, and the difference in behaviour in the Tanglin Club and the courtesy King observed in Japan is perhaps an indication of the fatigue gripping him at the end of his tour. Running into him in the Raffles, the English writer James Pope-Hennessy found Maugham 'deadbeat'.[10]

Behind the outburst might also have lain a recognition that the past can never be recaptured. On leaving Singapore on the *Laos* on 16 February, Maugham wistfully remarked: 'The East is a very different world from the one I knew. The people are different. The planters, the government officers and the businessmen who stayed very long stretches here and who, except for infrequent trips, lived the rest of their lives in the East, have all gone. Today, I feel very much a stranger here.'[11]

When Maugham arrived in Marseilles on 5 March he had not only been on the road for five months but had been the focus of intense public attention for most of the time. It was a journey that would have fatigued a man half his age; in Maugham's case, it did irreparable damage to his health and hastened his mental deterioration. Dr Rosanoff, who had advised against the trip and had declined an invitation to accompany the author, began immediately to treat him for extreme exhaustion. In May Maugham went to Badgastein where he thought the cure might revitalize him, but in early August Rosanoff ordered him to rest and to avoid any work. By September it became clear that Maugham would never fully recover the vigour that he had lost, and Searle wrote sadly to Klaus Jonas that 'Mr Maugham is fairly well, there is nothing wrong with him physically, it is just the frailty and fatigue of old age. I am afraid that he is failing fast. It makes me very unhappy because I love him so much, and after more than thirty years together, I cannot imagine life without him.'[12]

Maugham made a concession to old age by flying to London for his autumn visit at the beginning of October; he remained there for two months. Though he continued to make his round of social engagements, dining with Robin and friends such as Barbara Back and Ann Fleming, his activities were limited as never before by his diminishing energy and stamina. Increasingly he declined requests for interviews and other tasks on the grounds of indifferent health and from 1960 on his letters – even to friends – became briefer and briefer. His correspondence of the last three years of his life, in fact, appears to have been almost entirely written by Searle, who worked diligently to maintain the author's lifelong practice of replying to every letter he received.

Maugham was in poor health again in February 1961, but in May he went to London to receive his companionship from the Royal Society of Literature and then to Heidelberg to be given an honorary senatorship by the university. From there Maugham and Searle went to Venice and Milan, but by then Maugham was overcome by fatigue. 'I was very anxious about him,' wrote Searle from the Villa Mauresque. 'It is horrible to be ill in hotels and to be away from home. However, I finally got him here. He is, I am sorry to say, very poorly indeed, and is failing fast.'[13] In July Searle reported that his friend was 'terribly frail and exhausted'.[14]

A month later Searle was quoted in *Time* magazine as saying that Maugham was 'not at all well', but was working on his autobiography. Astonishingly, Searle added that Maugham had abandoned his plans to publish posthumously because, finding himself 'bloodying so many of his colleagues . . . he has gamely decided to hustle it out as soon as possible. If the autobiography is published after his death, they might well pull him out of his grave.'[15] This intended flippancy proved to be prophetic, though the only one bloodied in the published version was Syrie. That she was the main target of the memoirs is confirmed by the comment of Felix Marti-Ibanez, a Spanish psychiatrist who had known Maugham for fifteen years. Following a visit to Cap Ferrat in the summer of 1961 he wrote to Jonas: 'I am looking forward very much to the publication of his latest book, *Looking Back*, if and when his family will allow it.'[16]

The decision to publish 'Looking Back' in the author's lifetime – or even that of his daughter – was a monumental blunder, and there are a number of theories about how Maugham's customary shrewd judgement could have gone so awry. Ted Morgan's explanation, founded largely on his conversation with Lord and Lady Glendevon, is that Maugham had assigned the copyright and serialization rights to Searle, who then became an enthusiastic promoter of its sale and immediate publication. Searle leaped at Lord Beaverbrook's offer of £75,000 for British Empire rights, though he eventually settled for less than half that amount. Maugham, argues Morgan, became uneasy but his companion argued that it was then too late to back out.[17]

Searle's version, told to the present writer, is that Beaverbrook came to the Villa Mauresque one day when Searle was away on an errand and persuaded Maugham to loan him the typescript. Arriving back, Searle protested, but Beaverbrook none the less took the memoirs, had them photocopied, and offered Maugham a huge sum for their rights. No longer fully in control of himself, the old man agreed and Searle could do nothing to prevent what he knew was a grave mistake.

The suggestion that Beaverbrook played a major role in the decision to publish is supported by a number of those who knew Maugham and Searle well. Rebecca West, for example, argued that the press baron had a strong vein of misogyny and might well have enjoyed the attack on Syrie.[18] Others have maintained that it was not so much malice that impelled Beaverbrook as his shrewd publishing instinct. Any kind of final memoirs from a writer of Maugham's popularity were guaranteed to sell huge numbers of papers.

The most persuasive account of the publishing of 'Looking Back' is that given by John Sutro, who lived along the Riviera and knew Maugham for many years. Writing in *London Magazine* in 1967, Sutro claimed that Maugham wrote a draft of the memoirs, which he then burned along with a good deal of other personal material. Recovering from an illness, Maugham ran into Beaverbrook, who answered Maugham's complaints about Syrie by urging: 'Write it down again and get it out of your system. It will do you good.' When the new version was complete, Beaverbrook offered a fabulous sum. 'Maugham,' says Sutro, 'childishly proud at being offered "a larger sum per word than any other writer in history", gave way and accepted Lord Beaverbrook's offer, against the violent opposition of his secretary, Alan Searle.'[19]

Sutro's account is convincing for a number of reasons. First, Maugham had begun his reminiscences in 1959, and in September 1960 Searle told Klaus Jonas that Maugham had made him a gift of the typescript.[20] This suggests that the work had been completed, yet on 20 December of that year Searle reported that Maugham was working on his autobiography.[21] Maugham was either amplifying his material or, as Sutro indicates, rewriting it entirely.

Second, Alexander Frere, Chairman of Heinemann and one of Maugham's closest remaining friends in 1961, has stated that 'it was Beaverbrook who persuaded him to let it appear ... He was there, living at his villa in Cap d'Ail, and he bore down on Maugham very hard. He told him he'd offer more money than any other writer had ever been paid per word, and that tickled Willie to death. You see, he and Arnold Bennett always had this thing, they each wanted to be able to boast that they were the world's highest paid writer. That was what really got him in the end ... He was over-persuaded by Beaverbrook.'[22] The intensity of this pressure is reflected in the comments of the *Sunday Express* editor John Junor: 'We simply saw a damn good story and went for it ... I had to go down to see [Maugham] at the Villa Mauresque and personally persuade him to let us publish. The old boy didn't want to let it go, but in the end he accepted our offer.'[23]

Maugham's pride in his earning power was well known to friends over his long career, but there is another facet of his professionalism which almost certainly influenced his decision. In *The Summing Up* he describes how the first, unpublished draft of what was later to be rewritten as *Of Human Bondage* did not provide the catharsis of the later version. 'If the writing of this first novel did not finally repress into my unconscious the unhappy memories with which it was concerned it is because the writer is not finally disembarrassed of his subject till his work is published. When it is delivered to the public, however heedless the public be, it is his no longer and he is free from the burden that oppressed him.'[24]

'Looking Back' was born of the same desire to rid himself of disquieting memories. There can be no other reason for Maugham's sudden change of direction in the spring of 1959 or, if Sutro is right, for Beaverbrook to persuade him to tackle a second version. The writing process, moreover, was obviously a deeply disturbing personal struggle, as he fought to uncover and deal with old wounds and resentments which had lain repressed and unresolved for decades. 'It has been very tough for Willie turning over the past,' reported Searle in 1962, 'especially the memories of his marriage troubles. He hasn't been able to sleep.'[25] Maugham would have nightmares and wake up screaming, but this stopped after he completed 'Looking Back'.[26]

Given Maugham's belief in the cathartic effect of publication, it is understandable that he could not wait to see his memoirs in print. That he, and not Searle, was making the decision – however foolish it may have been – is clear in a letter from Frere to Maugham in January 1962. Maugham's literary agent, Spencer Curtis Brown, had broached the subject of the memoirs and the author himself had written to ask when Heinemann would bring them out in book form. Surprisingly, this was the first that the firm had heard of them, and Frere told Maugham that if he could provide a typescript the book would be released as soon as the *Sunday Express* serialization was completed. Believing that the newspaper would publish in May, Heinemann rushed to get the book out and the 3 February issue of *The Bookseller* announced it for June. Moreover, when *Purely For My Pleasure* appeared on 9 April the dust jacket of the Heinemann edition carried an advertisement for *Looking Back*.

The memoirs, however, never appeared in book form. Some time in the spring of 1962 Frere finally received a typescript and was horrified by what he read. Knowing that it would cause great pain to Liza and immeasurable damage to Maugham's own reputation, he refused to publish it. Maugham thus found himself rejected by a publisher with whom he had had a fruitful fifty-eight-year relationship.

Serial publication none the less went ahead, despite the pleas of Maugham's daughter. Hearing of the nature of the revelations, she telephoned from Edinburgh, but was told by Searle that Maugham was refusing to speak to her. He wished her to know that what he published was his own business.[27] He continued to rework his material, writing to Beaverbrook on 8 February to note that the release of *Purely*

For My Pleasure in April would allow him to complete his auto-biography to his own satisfaction.

The writing of 'Looking Back' was not the only sign of confusion and disintegration in the autumn of 1961. On 14 September Searle informed Klaus Jonas that Maugham had arranged to sell his extensive and valuable collection of paintings, though this was not announced publicly for several months. There had been a startling increase of major art thefts along the Riviera and Maugham had grown weary of shipping his collection to Marseilles, where they were stored in a bank vault during his English visits. As well, insurance was costly, and so, Maugham said, he was reluctantly selling the paintings so as to remove the anxiety.

The matter, however, was almost certainly more complex. A number of the author's friends – notably Ian Fleming[28] – were convinced that the sale of the paintings, like the sale of the memoirs, was a matter of ego. Maugham wanted to see how much his paintings would bring, to prove that his buying had been shrewd. Somewhere in his muddled brain was the thought that a successful sale would prove that he indeed had the artistic temperament, that he was in fact a sensitive judge of art.

Bernard Berenson's conclusion that Maugham lacked much taste for visual art has been echoed by many qualified observers. George Cukor once stated that Searle had told him that Maugham, despite his knowledge of art, never really cared for his pictures, that it was Searle's pleasure in them that he enjoyed.[29] Beverley Nichols argued that Maugham thought of art only in terms of money, that he once said that he had bought a painting because 'it was a better investment than Standard Oil'.[30] Cecil Beaton felt that Maugham 'has no real understanding or love for [art]', that he collected investments and status symbols,[31] and Peter Quennell saw 'a rich man's shrewd collection rather than the lively and variegated record of his private tastes and feelings'.[32]

Against these judgements must be set the authoritative voice of Kenneth Clark, who recalled that Maugham was 'remarkably perceptive of excellence in all the arts'. After describing Maugham's 'sublime' reading of a Dylan Thomas poem, Clark argued that 'the same was true of painting. In the big sitting-room were pictures by Renoir and Monet in richly carved frames; on the staircase pictures by Matisse; but if one showed him reproductions of work by a painter unknown to him, like Paul Klee, his response was surprisingly quick and just. I once tried him to the limit with a Mondrian. To my astonishment he said, "Yes it is very fine."'[33]

Even if one accepts Clark's more generous minority opinion, it cannot be denied that Maugham strongly identified his paintings with their monetary value. As *Purely For My Pleasure* indicates, he knew how much he had paid for them, and it is not hard to believe that before he died he wanted to know – and the world to know – how good his eye had been.

There is also a likelihood that Maugham decided to sell his paintings in order to simplify his assets and to forestall a battle over his estate. Dr Rosanoff remembered telling Maugham that he hoped that he was not disposing of his collection because Rosanoff had earlier warned him of the dangers of theft. Maugham replied that, on the contrary, he had had the idea in mind for some time, suggesting to the doctor that he was attempting to resolve a family problem.[34] Like King Lear, of course, Maugham's attempt to prevent future strife ironically led to conflict more intense than he ever could have imagined.

Maugham's will and the disposition of his estate were clearly preoccupying him at the time he decided to sell his paintings. In October, Rupert Hart-Davis observed to George Lyttelton that 'it is generally believed that, apart from diverting his huge fortune from his daughter and her children, his one ambition is to outlive Winston [Churchill].'[35] On 9 October he announced that, except for certain bequests, he intended to give all his estate to a special fund administered by the Society of Authors, Playwrights and Composers. This would provide money to rescue ageing authors who were ill or in economic difficulties. It would relieve others, he said, from the drudgery of hack work while they were attempting to establish a career. That he intended the funds from the sale of the paintings to provide much of this special fund is clear from his later comments that if Liza's claim to own many of them was upheld it would be the Society which would ultimately lose.

Behind Maugham's desire to leave his money to needy authors was his belief that he knew better than anyone else how best to use his money. Thus he had established his travel award, contributed to King's School, and selectively helped certain individuals. He became convinced, according to Gerald Kelly, that Liza would 'play' with his money, that what he had accumulated over a lifetime of disciplined work, would be wasted.[36] He began to claim that his offspring had done nothing to deserve his money but to have been born, and besides he had already provided for them through various gifts and trust funds. Nicky and Camilla had been given £60,000 each and Julian and Jonathan £10,000. Liza had bought the house in Chelsea and the bulk of the shares in a company he had created to hold the Villa Mauresque.

Having made these provisions, Maugham wanted to use the remainder of his estate as a means to an end: first, to provide for Searle and then to give practical assistance to his fellow writers who had been less successful than him. His mistake, of course, was forgetting that over the years he had given a number of his paintings to his daughter.

According to Hope, Maugham told him about the sale during their stay at the Villa Mauresque in August, pointing out that the proceeds from her pictures would be hers. She did not broach the matter directly with her father, but later wrote to suggest that they go to the sale together during his autumn visit to London. Shortly after his arrival, however, she learned from Searle that Maugham was enraged by her letter, inferring from it that she was questioning his judgement and demanding a share of the proceeds. When he refused to see her, Lady Glendevon wrote again, only to receive a letter from her father's solicitors suggesting that she and her husband meet with them to deal with the matter. She returned the letter to Maugham, and a few days later was invited to tea with him in his Dorchester suite. On the advice of Searle, she says, she once again did not raise the issue directly with her father, and made no more attempts to do so in the months before the sale.[37]

In the face of Maugham's determination, Liza and her husband turned to Ann Fleming to act as an intermediary. 'Yesterday', she wrote to Evelyn Waugh on 25 October, 'Lord John Hope telephoned and said could he see me, that he and Liza depended on my *wisdom* and *kindness* to heal the breach with Willie. I was frightfully excited and enjoyed it all immensely, it was far from disappointing, after three whiskies and soda all the nonsense of "that poor little love, Liza" sobbing on the bed because Father wouldn't speak to her was forgotten, and instead it was revealed that if Willie can move to Lausanne and rid himself of French law, he may prevent Liza inheriting the paintings. I pointed out that the sale of the villa would be quite something, and if the grandchildren were already subsidized things might be worse.'[38]

Throughout the summer and autumn of 1961, the Glendevons had observed violent mood swings in Maugham. Though he could frequently be gracious and warm he was capable of explosive and seemingly inexplicable rages. On one such occasion Maugham retired without a word to his room after dinner, then began shouting: 'I will show them. I'll put them back into the gutter where they belong. I'll get even with them! Sons of bitches!' Searle, according to Lady Glendevon, confided that these acts of paranoia had begun a year earlier and were becoming more frequent and intense. Later in London Searle reported that Maugham alternated between calm moods when he was willing to give her half of the proceeds from the paintings and bouts of hysteria when he would swear that she would not get a penny. The attacks of screaming and throwing water and furniture now came almost nightly.[39]

Another symptom of confusion and deteriorating mental capacity in the autumn of 1961 was a sudden decision to leave the Villa Mauresque for good and take up residence elsewhere. First, there was a strange episode with the press on Maugham's arrival in London on 1 October, where Searle commented that 'you can take it from me that Mr Maugham is staying here for good this time.' When Maugham contradicted his companion by saying that they would return to Cap Ferrat in two months, Searle continued; 'That's true, but it will be to clean up his affairs.'[40] This apparent indecision is confirmed by Maugham's departure from England after only five weeks rather than his customary two months. On 20 October Searle wrote to Klaus Jonas to say that in a few days they were going to live in Switzerland and that they might never return to the Villa Mauresque.

There are several theories to account for this uncharacteristically impulsive behaviour. Lady Glendevon's explanation, shared by some others, is that Maugham developed a paranoid delusion that she and her husband intended to sell the Villa Mauresque, having been given its controlling shares. When she protested that he should remain there for the rest of his life, her father replied that a rich neighbour intended to buy the villa in order to return it to him.

If Maugham did indeed make such a bizarre claim, it surely came from a suspicious and befuddled mind. Knowing that he was embarking on a struggle with his daughter and son-in-law about the paintings, he might naturally believe that their response would be to claim any other assets he had given to them. This fear is suggested by his letter to Lord Beaverbrook in November 1961, in which he stated that he had recently learned from his lawyers that the Villa Mauresque would remain his until his death, at which time it would then belong to his daughter.[41]

That letter, however, also points to another explanation: that Maugham had been persuaded to be domiciled in Switzerland in order to escape inheritance taxes. Corroboration for this can be found in a letter to Ann Fleming in which he says that he had been advised that by living there six months of each year he would pay fewer taxes during his lifetime and practically nothing after his death.[42] Given his obsession with money in old age, his growing fear of becoming destitute, it is not hard to believe that such a proposition could be seductive. Moreover, it would be even more compelling if he was convinced that he was soon to be evicted from the Villa Mauresque.

Maugham and Searle did travel to Lausanne at the end of October, but within a fortnight Maugham became restless and returned to the South of France, reconciled to ending his days at Cap Ferrat. He arrived home suffering from influenza, requiring a visit from Dr Rosanoff on 16 December. The next day the physician assured an inquisitive press that the aged author was recuperating and, moreover, working on some writing (almost certainly 'Looking Back'). Maugham's health, however, was deteriorating quickly and by 23 February he reported to Robin that he had been under doctor's care for a number of weeks. The severity of his illness is reflected in his comment to his nephew that 'dying is a very dull, dreary affair and my advice to you is to have nothing whatever to do with it'.[43] On 31 March Searle informed Jonas that 'Mr Maugham has been very ill indeed. He is recovering slowly now but is terribly frail . . . I have had a very unhappy time of it. It is terrible to watch someone you love slowly fading away, and to be able to do nothing about it. After thirty-three years of perfect companionship and happiness, I cannot imagine life without him.'[44] A week later Maugham wrote to Ann Fleming about the sale of his paintings in five days' time, adding 'then I have half a mind to get on a ship and go somewhere – where is no matter'.[45]

This note of desperation, the reaching for the old panacea for irksome obligations, suggests that Maugham realized that he was about to unleash a storm. The thirty-five paintings were sold on 10 April before 2500 people, the largest number ever to witness a sale at Sotheby's. Picasso's *Death of a Harlequin* brought £80,000, at that time the most ever paid for a single work by a living artist. Monet's *Zaandam* went for £40,000, and Matisse's *The Yellow Chair* sold for £38,000. The total proceeds for the collection were £523,880 ($1,466,864).

One month after the sale the Maugham family quarrel became litigious and public when Lady Glendevon sued for the proceeds ($648,900) of nine of the paintings, having assigned them in trust to her lawyers on 2 April. The money, which Maugham had instructed Sotheby's to send to his New York bank to escape sterling devaluation and loss of exchange control permission, was placed in a joint account pending the hearing of the action. Lady Glendevon was legally entitled to it, she later told Ted Morgan, because she possessed receipts for the pictures as well as letters from her father and others indicating that they belonged to her. This claim is supported by the fact that the paintings – by Bonnard, Toulouse-Lautrec, Monet, Matisse, Renoir, Rouault, Sisley, and Utrillo – were all acquired late in Maugham's life, when he might well have been thinking of leaving them to his daughter.

Maugham's public response, reported by Searle, was that he was 'distressed and shocked' by the writ and that he had been advised not to make any further statement. Privately he told friends that he had thought that the Glendevons were bluffing about fighting for a share and that any loss would be to the Royal Literary Fund, to which he intended the funds ultimately to go. Legally, in July he lost an appeal against the retention in Britain of the disputed money.

By this time, however, Maugham had already played what seemed to be a very strong card: two days after the sale he had signed papers to adopt Searle, and they had been approved by the court in Nice on 7 June. In one way this was a device to enable Maugham to rescind all gifts he had made to his daughter and make them over to his newly legitimized son, who of course would not receive them until after the author's death.

In another way the adoption was undertaken to prevent the possibility that Lady Glendevon might attempt to have him certified incompetent to conduct his own affairs, a step not uncommon in such family disputes. Searle, recognized as a legal offspring, could block any move to have Maugham committed to an institution, thus preserving the old man's control of his own life.

Through all of this Maugham's health continued to decline. Searle took him to Switzerland at the end of April, hoping that the change of air and scenery would invigorate him. Catching him there on one of his better days, Noël Coward observed: 'Willie looks wonderful, bright as a button,'[46] but beneath the surface lay a deeply disordered mind. During a miserable trip to Venice in June Searle confided to George Cukor that Maugham's body clock had become reversed, so that he was drowsy during the day and wide awake all night. Maugham, he said, 'often wakes at 2 or 3 a.m., comes into his room, and paces about, smoking and talking until morning. The talk is of wild, impractical schemes and plans: writing projects; legal devices to protect elements of his estate; money-making ideas; and vindictive, vengeful pranks.'[47]

Back at the Villa Mauresque, Searle reported that Maugham was in a 'very frail condition',[48] and when his niece Diana Marr-Johnson and her husband visited him during the summer, she concluded that he was suffering from senile dementia – alternating between words of affection and outbursts of profanity, and frequently mistaking even Searle for a threatening stranger. On a good day, he could be so touched by a violinist reduced to playing for a restaurant crowd that he tipped him extravagantly, but on others he was 'like Lear raving on the heath'.[49]

Coincidental with, but not inseparable from, the litigation about the paintings was the publication of 'Looking Back'. Though most British readers did not see the pieces until the *Sunday Express* serialization in September and October, many of the author's friends heard of them when they were published in the United States in the glossy magazine *Show* from June through August. Some, like Rebecca West, were enraged; some, like Garson Kanin, were perplexed; and for many, like Noël Coward, they destroyed an old friendship. Only three months after his warm visit in Switzerland, Coward could remark: 'I don't think I want to see him again.'[50]

'Looking Back' is a wide-ranging autobiographical fragment touching on a number of familiar elements: Maugham's parents and childhood, King's School and Heidelberg, medical school, 'Rosie', war work, attitudes to religion and death, and sketches of such figures as Edward Caroway and Winston Churchill. Surprisingly well-written, these observations are interesting both historically and autobiographically, and there is nothing offensive in them.

What angered so many of those who knew the story of Maugham's life was the section describing Syrie and their marriage. Simply making public the explicit details of their illicit affair, the birth of their daughter before their marriage, and their growing estrangement and divorce was considered bad form. But Maugham went far beyond this to vilify the character of a dead woman who could not defend herself. He accused her of having no taste or regard for literature and art, of making his domestic life a misery through her shrewish nagging, and of spending money wantonly. Her career as a decorator had been built on the plagiarized style of all-white interiors, and her financial dealings were frequently unscrupulous and occasionally criminal. An ambitious social climber, he suggested, she had a number of lovers before she met him, and several during their marriage.

Maugham's treatment of Syrie is indefensible. Beyond the questions of propriety and accuracy lies the essential sexual dishonesty. Though the affairs with 'Rosie' and Syrie are described at length and in detail, a veil is drawn over the relationship with Gerald Haxton. Maugham recalls his own intense grief over Haxton's death, but nowhere is he referred to as anything but a secretary, travelling companion, and friend. Alan Searle is briefly cited as 'a friend of thirty years' standing'.

As a number of people have observed, if Maugham was prepared to bare his soul about his sexual life and marriage, he was obliged to discuss his sexual orientation candidly and honestly. He needed to admit his own part in the failure of the marriage and the very large part played by his love of Haxton. Instead the blame is placed almost entirely on Syrie, and Maugham is portrayed as the hurt and imprisoned husband in what he calls a copy of a letter to her. Since it is highly unlikely that he would have kept such a copy for three decades – especially through the upheaval of the Second World War – this is almost certainly a fabrication, one last piece of fiction.

Ironically, Maugham's attempt to convince the world of his version of Syrie and their marriage created the opposite effect. Though there had been little public comment at her death in 1955, many of her friends now voiced their admiration for her and their contempt for Maugham. Oliver Messel wrote to the press to praise her creative flair, resourcefulness, and sympathy, and Rebecca West organized a fund which paid for a bust of Catherine the Great, by Shubin, to be presented to the Victoria and Albert Museum in her memory in 1964. Among those who attended the reception held at Cecil Beaton's home were Lady Aberconway, Diana Cooper, John Pope-Hennessy, Noël Coward, Beverley Nichols, Victor Gollancz, and Elizabeth von Hofmannsthal. A more delayed reaction was Nichols's book *A Case of Human Bondage*, published only after Maugham himself was safely dead.

Maugham learned of this scorn most forcefully during his autumn visit to London. Though he was made an honorary member of the New Arts Theatre Club and attended such social occasions as dinner with Evelyn Waugh, Diana Cooper, and others at Ann Fleming's home before the première of *Dr No*, there was an unmistakable chill in his meetings with many old friends. When he walked into the Garrick Club, it has been said, many members signalled their disapproval in the traditional manner of leaving the room. In the face of this response, Maugham spent only a month in London, and when he left in early November it was for the last time. The city which had so shaped his early life, to which he had always returned with fondness, no longer offered any pleasure, and he refused to set foot in England again.

While the attack on Syrie in 'Looking Back' is offensive for its vindictiveness, it is equally shocking for what it reveals about its author. Maugham, after all, had written about the unfortunate marriage calmly and dispassionately twenty-four years earlier in *The Summing Up* as if it were nothing more than a minor disturbance. Though he had then been only a decade away from the relationship, the brief and casual treatment – the 'trouble that harassed me' – suggested that he had dealt with and accepted its failure.

The outpourings in 'Looking Back', however, reveal that this serene equilibrium was a façade, an illusion woven by a man capable of willing his emotional trauma into the recesses of his mind. For over three decades his intellect buried this distress, but with the advance of senility came a loss of such control. As a result, the unresolved and festering issues came flooding back to the surface, revealing wounds received forty years before.

As Maugham's obsession deepened, it seems that the distant past began to become confused with the present. On one occasion, for example, he mistook his daughter for his long-dead wife, shouting: 'Syrie, you bitch. You've ruined my whole life. How dare you come into my house? Get out of it at once.'[51] It has been suggested that Maugham, having been (or believing that he had been) blackmailed by Syrie over Gerald Haxton, became convinced that his daughter was prepared to do the same over his relationship with Alan Searle. Thus, it seems, his battle with the ghosts of the past became enmeshed with his fight to retain control of his present.

This merging of then and now became dramatically public on 27 December 1962 when Maugham's lawyers revealed that he was suing to deny legal recognition of his daughter. 'I always considered her as my daughter,' his declaration stated, 'but legally she is the daughter of Henry Wellcome. She was born in 1915 . . . Wellcome never denied paternity.'[52] He would have continued to regard her as his daughter, he said, but since she was not his legitimate child he could legally revoke all his gifts to her – in particular her shares in the Villa Mauresque. Citing Article 950 of the French Civil Code, which states that such gifts can be revoked if the beneficiary shows ingratitude, the suit contended that Liza never took care of Maugham and that her claim to the paintings constituted ingratitude. 'My daughter', added Maugham, 'never cared a rap about me.'[53]

Instantly the centre of a sensational story, Liza told reporters that she was 'shocked, surprised and absolutely mystified' by the action, that the kindest thing she could say was that 'when people get very old they become a little strange sometimes'.[54] She and her father had been on very good terms, until last year, she claimed, corresponding regularly and visiting each summer and autumn.

Adding to the drama of the Maugham suit was the revelation for the first time that he had adopted Searle, who could therefore become the author's chief beneficiary. Searle was pleased by the adoption, but not surprised since he had been with Maugham for thirty-five years. He felt very awkward about the matter, he claimed, because Liza had always been a friend. For her part, she was reported to be astonished because she had always looked upon Searle 'only as an employee'.[55]

Advised by her lawyers that Searle, as a legal son, could inherit all of Maugham's estate, Liza decided in February 1963 to appeal against the adoption. 'I did not do it for financial reasons,' she later told Ted Morgan. 'You just cannot take being disowned sitting down. It's not a question of our dignity and standing, but of our children.'[56]

The appeal was heard *in camera* in the civil court in Nice on 12 June, with each side represented by leading Paris lawyers. Liza argued that Maugham had failed to reveal that he had a daughter when he filed the adoption papers, that this omission prejudiced the right of inheritance of her children, and that her paternity was proven by correspondence, entries in various *Who's Who* books, and by the fact that she was named after the title of his first novel. The court agreed with her, ruling in July that she was Maugham's legitimate daughter and that the adoption must therefore be annulled. Since all the principals were British, the case was decided on the British law that a child born out of wedlock becomes legitimized if the parents subsequently marry. Ironically, the author's description of these events in 'Looking Back' significantly persuaded the court that Liza was indeed his daughter.

Word of the judgment was conveyed by telephone to Searle, who told reporters that he was deeply disappointed. Maugham was in bed when Searle broke the news to him, and at first he did not seem to comprehend. As its significance began to sink in, Maugham became quiet and despondent, and Searle told reporters that they were not discussing the matter. 'It's really shaken him terribly. He's very old, you know.'[57]

Privately, Searle admitted to friends that he was having a very difficult time with Maugham and he hoped that he would be able to cope until the end. Maugham had been unwell for much of the winter, and in April a planned excursion through Italy to Greece had to be curtailed. Writing to Jonas, Searle observed that he would find the old man very much changed and that it would be better for him to remember Maugham in happier times. In Searle's view, Liza's appeal had appreciably accelerated Maugham's decline, and increasingly he complained to friends that she was making her father's final years a misery.

Unfortunately the quarrel had not ended in the Nice court. In August Maugham appealed against the annulment, but at the hearing on 22 January 1964, it was revealed through lawyers that an out-of-court settlement had been reached. It gave Liza $250,000 of the $648,900 she had claimed as her share of the proceeds from the paintings, almost all the shares in the Villa Mauresque, and all her court costs. She agreed to renounce any further claims on the estate, and Maugham dropped his appeal over the adoption of Searle.

The ending of this lengthy and painful quarrel was announced with the terse statement that 'Mr W. Somerset Maugham and Lady John Hope are happy to state that all differences between them have been settled.' The latter confessed realistically to reporters, however, that the agreement was a matter of relief, not happiness, and when asked if she would attend her father's ninetieth birthday she replied: 'It is too soon to talk about reconciliation.'[58] In fact, Liza saw her father only one more time, the following August, when he mistook her for her mother.

By the time of the settlement Maugham had declined to the point where he was lucid for only short intervals. For the first time since 1946 he did not spend the autumn in London, travelling instead to Munich, where he quickly became depressed and wanted to leave. 'Mr Maugham is in a strange condition,' Searle wrote to Jonas. 'It is terribly sad to see him. I am very, very unhappy.'[59] When Sam Behrman spent what he called 'four macabre days' at the Villa Mauresque, he came away feeling 'very sorry for Alan. He is on the verge of a nervous breakdown.'[60] Searle had described how he had slipped away from the villa for several hours to have dinner in Nice and returned to find that Maugham had disappeared. After much uproar he was found wandering along the winding Cap Ferrat roads, muttering: 'Alan's left me.'[61] On other occasions, Maugham would emulate the mad Lear on the cliffs of Dover by running for a short distance like a child, then stop and start off running again.[62]

In the last two years of Maugham's life Searle became a virtual prisoner in the Villa Mauresque, leaving it on his own no more than a dozen times. When Lionel Hale arrived to do an interview in January 1964, Searle came to his hotel in Beaulieu for short visits but always left soon with the exclamation: 'I must get back!'[63] Though Maugham's spells of paranoia and irrationality were more and more frequent, he was still master of his house, and, mindful of their jobs, his servants still carried out his orders. Only Searle could gently talk him out of some foolish action.

With the collapse of Maugham's faculties, Searle had become increasingly protective. He maintained the habit of responding to the hundreds of letters sent to the villa each week, often providing a short reply in the Maugham style. Throughout the battles over the paintings and the adoption, he had kept Maugham away from the persistent interrogations of the press, though he did arrange for interviews to be conducted just before the author's ninetieth birthday.

On that occasion Searle told reporters that Maugham tired easily and that his days had increasingly become those of the very aged. After breakfast Maugham would wander through the gardens, and after a quiet lunch he would have a siesta which grew longer with each month. In the late afternoon he would take his two Pekinese and his dachshund for a short walk along the road, and occasionally he and Searle would go for a drive. Dinner, for which he still dressed, was now moved ahead, and, following a short game of patience with Searle, Maugham retired early.

The morning writing period, a habit of six decades, had now become a time for a nap or for listening to music, though growing deafness made this difficult. From his youth in Whitstable, reading had been one of his greatest pleasures and consolations, but now his eyes were clouded by cataracts. His memory had begun to fade so that he could not recall writing *Cakes and Ale* or *The Razor's Edge*, though he could recollect his little house in South Carolina. Bridge, one of his passions for fifty years, was now impossible.

When Maugham himself appeared, reporters saw a small frail figure walking with shuffling hesitant steps. He was casually dressed in a collarless shirt, a scarf around his thick neck, flannel trousers, brown tweed sports jacket, and grey suede slippers. His white hair, faintly tinged with blue, was thin, but his eyes looked out brightly from his ancient oriental face.

Those who had made the pilgrimage from New York and London were both touched by his fragility and impressed by his flashes of insight. From time to time, the storyteller wove the old spell, hypnotically evoked in his stammering delivery, and the Edwardian courtesy was still evident. 'Even at ninety', observed Stephen Coulter, 'Maugham gives the impression of a sensitive man. He makes enormous efforts not to disappoint people who come to see him. When one Parisian left him after a recent visit – Maugham had sat mostly slumped but groping to remember some amusing story and saying, "But you have come all this way!" – his friend and companion Alan Searle said as he walked the visitor through the garden to the car, "I know I shall go back and find him collapsed on the sofa, absolutely out."' Recalling his travels, Maugham said, 'I have been all over the world, and all over the world people have done everything they could to make life pleasant for me.' 'There was a catch in his voice,' wrote Coulter. 'It was moving.'[64]

It was surely such a moment of nostalgia that had led Maugham a year before to write a short note to Grace Morse, friend of agent Elizabeth Marbury, simply to remind her of his existence.[65] And it must have been such a performance that led Kenneth Allsop to call him 'as beakily trim and comfortably alert as an eagle settled upon its nesting-crag'. 'I am enjoying', Maugham told him, 'a new state that I did not know for almost all my life: a calm of spirit,' and Allsop came away believing that 'illusionless, Godless, and tranquilly unperturbed by the aspect of the void, he stands in silence for a few moments, if not precisely at peace with himself, content with the expedient truce.'[66]

Momentarily frozen in these still photographs, Maugham is an old man with a grip, albeit not firm, on his world. To those who observed him at length, however, there was another, pathetic side. When Lionel Hale attempted to interview him for the BBC, he found Maugham lucid for only ten-minute intervals. Searle was always present to smooth over difficulties and to translate for him, and Maugham frequently forgot what was being done. Once believing he was imprisoned, he whispered: 'They're plotting to keep me here in Venice,' and Searle confided that he actually had to hold him down to get him to go to bed at night. 'I wished to God', recalled Hale, 'that I'd never gone.'[67]

Robin Maugham flew to the South of France for his uncle's birthday, with a large-print Bible as a gift. Waking up to a room filled with flowers and gifts, Maugham commented: 'One would think I was in a graveyard.'[68] Ignoring the advice of Dr Rosanoff, he lunched with his old friends Lady Doverdale and Lady Bateman and nine others at the Château de Madrid, but by the afternoon he was so exhausted that he had to cancel a birthday dinner with Lord Beaverbrook. 'There is no reason', he told reporters, 'to be happy at ninety.'[69]

A few days earlier Maugham had confessed to Stephen Coulter: 'I love the East. I'm only comforted and happy when I'm in the East. There are places where I *long* to go, and I know that if I do go to them I shall die. I want to go to Capri because I started life there; and from there I would like to go to Angkor Wat. My doctor says if you want to go, go, but you won't come back.'[70]

Denied so many of his other pleasures – reading, music, bridge – Maugham retained the impulse to travel, to be on the move, to put a distance between himself and his troubles. The boy who had watched the ships glide past Whitstable Bay to distant ports had become a man whose pulse quickened when he stepped up the gangplank of a P & O liner or walked into the lounge of an oriental hotel. No other major writer had ever taken to the road as often. Travel had provided material for his writing and the freedom of life on the move. It had perhaps been too much of an addiction, a convenient means by which to escape obligations and remain the detached observer in a series of fleeting encounters. Graham Greene, another peripatetic author, may have echoed Maugham's situation when he said: 'I seem to have been to too many places and travelled too much and had, in a way, too many experiences. I think probably for a happy life one should have fewer and perhaps deeper experiences.'[71]

Maugham made his last trip on 7 April, when Searle took him to Venice. Though it was, as he had told John Cruesemann a few months earlier, 'a city I love above all others',[72] and while he had always delighted in the Gritti Palace Hotel, the magic now failed. On his return to Cap Ferrat, he wrote – or Searle wrote for him – to Ian Fleming to say that he had been sick and miserable, returning from Venice with the realization that he would never travel again.[73] On the same day, Searle commented to Jonas that 'it was a disaster. I am having a terrible time.'[74]

The remaining year and a half of Maugham's life was spent at Cap Ferrat, and it can only be described as a nightmare. Always fastidious, he now became incontinent. Never at ease with the physical contact of strangers, he refused to be put into the hands of private nurses. It was Searle, by then sleeping in Maugham's room so as to be immediately available during the night, who took over the task of washing and shaving him, and thus preserving some semblance of dignity in the degrading senility.

More difficult for Searle was Maugham's mental condition. A decade earlier, he had written: 'What makes old age hard to bear is not the failing of one's faculties, mental and physical, but the burden of one's memories.'[75] Now these memories came flooding uncontrollably back, and the burden often became intolerable. His dreams haunted by figures long dead and supposedly forgotten, he would wake up screaming: 'Free me from all these people.'[76]

In his last two years the conviction that Syrie had ruined his life became replaced by a deeper, but no more accurate, belief that everything he had ever touched had turned to ashes. 'I've been a failure,' he told his nephew. 'The whole way through my life I've made mistake after mistake. I've had a wretched life. And I've made a hash of everything ... Every single one of the few people who have ever got to know me well has ended up by hating me.'[77]

This sense of guilt, justified or not, affected Maugham's attitude toward death and the afterlife. To the end Searle looked hopefully for signs of developing religious faith in his friend, who had always been interested in spiritual matters and envious of those who had retained some form of belief. In fact, Maugham not only remained a sceptic, he was relieved that there was not an afterlife. On his ninetieth birthday, he calmly told Ewan MacNaughton: 'I look forward to death with no apprehension for I do not believe in a hereafter and so, if I have sinned in men's eyes and have not been punished, I have no fear of punitive treatment when I cease to remain on this planet.'[78] Among his close friends, however, his need for assurance of his own coming oblivion, and its escape from some kind of retribution, was almost compulsive.[79]

The most painful burden of Maugham's memory may have been his oldest wound. As he confessed to MacNaughton, 'perhaps the most vivid memory left to me is the one which has tortured me for more than 80 years – the death of my mother. I was eight when she died and even today the pain of her passing is as keen as when it happened in our home in Paris.'[80] Neither the intended catharsis of *Of Human Bondage* nor the dispassionate references in *The Summing Up* had after all healed the wound, and so Searle would awaken in the middle of the night to find Maugham sitting in a chair holding a picture of his mother, with tears streaming down his face.

Searle and those friends who still came to the Villa Mauresque attempted to mitigate the old man's distress, but by December 1964 he had for the most part become isolated in his senility. To Patrick Kinross, Searle wrote: 'Your Christmas card touched me deeply and gave me much happiness. My life here for the past three years has been HELL. A period of sadness and unreality. Poor old Willie is in a pretty poor state. His memory has gone completely and his mind wanders. He lives in some terrifying world of his own which must be grim if his screams and terror are anything to go by. It is a tragic end.'[81]

Even on his best days Maugham could only cause his friends to wish that death would soon give him peace. In January 1965 Alec Waugh met Maugham and Searle walking along the Promenade des Anglais in Nice and Maugham commented to Waugh's female companion: 'The wind in your cape makes you look like a bird.' 'He was smiling,' wrote Waugh, 'he looked brisk and cheerful. It was one of his good days. As I watched him walk away, I said, "I wonder if that's the last time we'll see him." I hoped for his sake it was.'[82]

Maugham himself frequently told friends and reporters that he longed for death, that each night he went to bed with the hope that he would never wake up. At other times his desire for release was more anguished. Walking out to his terrace one day after luncheon, he suddenly leaned his head against a wall, burst into tears, and exclaimed to Robin: 'I'm so miserable. Why can't they let me die?'[83]

Maugham, however, was a survivor. The death of his mother, the loss of his home, and his bleak emotional life in the vicarage and at King's School had toughened his will and given him a fierce determination to be his own master. This strength of character had carried him through his medical training and his lengthy and discouraging apprenticeship as a writer. In the decades that followed he had in every possible way sought to control his life, even at the expense of his relationships with others. Though he had announced as early as 1938 that he faced death calmly, he had embraced any medical means of prolonging his life. Though small and tubercular, he had always been remarkably resilient, and now, perhaps because of the Niehans treatments, his body continued to function while the mind collapsed. Thus, even if his brain were sending unambiguous signals, the body seemed unable to wind down. It would fight on and carry the mind, now broken and dysfunctional, with it.

Maugham woke up to his ninety-first, and last, birthday with the comment, 'Oh Hell, another birthday.' He was greeted by the usual flood of letters, telegrams, and gifts, and he posed for press photographers. Such was his condition, however, that for the first time in many years there were no celebratory luncheons or dinners.

Some time in the winter he had suffered a slight heart attack and on 3 March he contracted influenza, which led to serious pulmonary congestion. Searle reported that the prostrate Maugham was not speaking. Two days later he was carried into the Anglo-American Hospital near Nice on a stretcher, and the world at large prepared itself to hear that he was dead. On 8 March, however, Maugham walked out of the hospital on his companion's arm and returned to Cap Ferrat with the hope that he would be able to travel to Germany in a month's time.

The recovery was remarkable, and in May Maugham was able to entertain Robin and his friend Derek Peel at dinner, though they stayed at a nearby hotel rather than the villa. He greeted their arrival by exclaiming: 'Alan! Two charming young gentlemen have arrived,' and during dinner was very attentive to Peel, making sure than he was being looked after. It was obvious that Maugham's memory was nearly gone and that he was very deaf. At one point, he insisted that Searle bring his Heidelberg medallion and, recounted Peel, 'he stood smiling, a very old child with a prize . . . I had arrived at the villa for the first time, feeling very nervous – those awful stories of his senile tantrums.

The nervousness soon disappeared when I saw him as a very small shuffling old man – rather sentimental, with mere snatches of his memory, enjoying the ribbon and the medallion.'

When Maugham sat down and withdrew into silence for a while, Searle implored Peel to go over and talk with him because he hated to feel left out. 'I went over to him,' said Peel, 'and not being able to think of a question that would break his strange silence, I asked, after I sat down next to him, "Tell me, sir, what is the happiest recollection of your life?" He stammered, "I ca–can't think of anything."' When Peel praised the garden, Maugham replied that he could no longer see it. As Peel and Robin left, Maugham shook their hands and said: 'It was good of you to come. Enjoy yourself – if one can in these days.'

The account of this visit, recorded by Peel's friend Hector Bolitho, is interesting for several reasons beyond merely providing a picture of Maugham's last year. First, even in his senility there is the kindness to those who approached him sincerely and without pretensions. As Bolitho explained it, 'Derek is a person of guileless honesty, of mind, heart and behaviour and, during his visit, he enjoyed [this] aspect of Maugham: that he cast aside all bitterness and was kind – when he came on these virtues in someone else.'[84]

Second, the episode reveals how Maugham's utterances have often been refashioned to create more sensational and misleading impressions. Peel's version of the old man's response to the question of his happiest recollection – 'I ca–can't think of anything' – emphasizes the inability of the aged mind to recall. In *Conversations With Willie*, however, Robin Maugham writes that his uncle responded to *his* question by saying: 'I can't think of a single one.'[85] The effect of this rewording is to give Maugham a seemingly rational and certainly bleak summing up of his entire life – which was in fact far from totally unhappy.

In December 1964 Searle had commented to Patrick Kinross: 'Our life is monastic. We see few people and rarely go out. The last time that I had an evening to myself was more than two years ago. I must confess that I long for freedom.'[86] He none the less continued to care for Maugham loyally in the increasingly difficult months that followed, but by September he was willing to admit publicly that a death watch now lay over the Villa Mauresque. Since Maugham could no longer read, Searle could safely confide to journalist Michael Moynihan: 'He wants to go. The doctor comes every day – but there is nothing organically wrong with him. He's as strong as a horse and relishes his food . . . [The Niehans treatments] have kept his body alive but not his mind.'

On 12 September Moynihan gave the readers of the *Sunday Times* a touching portrait of what he called 'a consummate story-teller who cannot in his life as in his writings appropriately bring down the curtain':

> He wears an open-neck shirt, crisp blue-and-white striped jacket and newly pressed dark grey flannel trousers, an inch too short, as though they had belonged to his boyhood . . . Searle, sunburned, in red sleeveless shirt and shorts, fills in the long silences as we stroll round part of the exotic, tree-shaded gardens conjured from rock and shrub over the past forty years. Maugham's constant companion since the war, his manner is a mixture of the paternal and fraternal, always attentive, sometimes a little teasing . . . The photographer . . . tries to get both Maugham and his dachshund, George, into his lens. Maugham becomes aware of what is wanted and beckons: 'Viens, George, viens. Non?' Searle gently takes his arm: 'George will not come to Willie. Willie must come to George.' . . . Beside a cageful of canaries, fluttering in the sunlight, [Maugham] puts in his hand and withdraws it with a look almost of pain: 'They don't want me to touch them!' . . . Once the spark catches a trail of the old sardonic self. He is walking up a path ahead of us when he stops and looks back. The words come over his shoulder, wryly, challengingly: 'Are you amused at us?'

Searle explained to Moynihan that three or four hundred letters still arrived each week, which he now answered with five stock replies, and that concerned friends frequently telephoned. Visits, however, had become painful: 'Recently Noël Coward and David Niven called – Noël is a very old friend. But there was no real communication. And last week three sixth-formers from King's, holidaying at Beaulieu-sur-Mer, came to pay their respects. They just shook hands.'[87]

Coward, whose anger over 'Looking Back' had subsided, recorded in his diary that he was glad that he had called on Maugham because 'he was wretchedly, pathetically grateful. He is living out his last days in a desperate nightmare, poor beast. He barely makes sense and, of course, he knows his mind has gone. I managed to cheer him a bit and certainly helped poor Alan who is going through hell.'[88] When George Rylands came to the villa, he found Maugham frightened that someone was standing behind him preparing to stab him in the back, and that Alan was about to leave him. Though Maugham was incoherent, Rylands sat patiently pretending that they were having another of the intellectual conversations they had enjoyed over the years.

Another old friend, Raymond Mortimer, came to stay with Roder-ick Cameron, at the nearby Villa Fiorentina, and he invited Searle to luncheon one day. To everyone's astonishment, Maugham decided to join them. He did not recognize Mortimer, and at the table said very little, but kept trying to pick up imitation peas and peapods on an ornamental china dish. At one point, he commented: 'I hear that the King is coming down,' presumably referring to the Duke of Windsor.[89]

By late November Maugham's condition had deteriorated to the point that power of attorney was given to Searle. Then, on 10 Decem-ber, Maugham tripped on a carpet and fell, cutting the side of his face on the corner of a table. Dr Rosanoff was summoned to apply a bandage, but when he left Maugham childishly tore it off and made the injury worse. In the middle of the night, he got up, tripped again and hit his head on the corner of a mantelpiece. This second blow seemed to snap him back to a sense of reality, and, as if returning from some long, dark, and confused journey, he exclaimed to Searle: 'I've been looking for you for two years and we have much to talk about. I want to thank you and say goodbye.'[90]

Shortly after uttering these words Maugham lapsed into a coma, and he was rushed to the Anglo-American Hospital, where it was determined that he had suffered a stroke. Dr Rosanoff called in a heart specialist and a neurologist, who concluded that the arteries in his brain had weakened so much that circulation was blocked in many places. He was put in an oxygen tent, and Dr Rosanoff reported that his strength 'is slowly failing him, but his body is fighting back with energy'.

On 14 December Maugham's condition improved, with his tempera-ture returning to normal and the congestion in his lungs clearing up. Nevertheless, Rosanoff, now besieged almost hourly by reporters, ob-served that only a miracle could save him. Faced with this inevitability, Searle told the press that he wished to take his friend back to the Villa Mauresque because he had always wanted to die in his own house. Rosanoff, however, was adamant that his patient should remain in hospital until his condition was absolutely desperate.

By the next day, the coma had deepened, his temperature had begun to rise markedly, and it was clear that death was imminent. In the early hours of 16 December Rosanoff and Searle summoned an ambulance, and for the last time Maugham made the winding journey along Cap Ferrat to the villa. Though he could not have been aware of it, he was home among the possessions collected in a lifetime, in sight of the sea that had called him from his boyhood in Whitstable. At 3.30 a.m., an hour after he arrived, he died in his room, surrounded by three pictures of his mother and by Alan Searle. The pattern, with all its imperfections, was complete.

'A doctor', observed Rosanoff, 'is used to death. But it was for me also the death of a friend.'[91] As a sign of respect for the man they had often called 'Cher Maître', a number of French people placed flowers beneath the Moorish sign at the gates of the Villa Mauresque. On Maugham's own instructions, however, there was no memorial service. Instead, he was cremated in Marseilles on 20 December and his ashes flown to England to be interred at King's School.

Maugham had first indicated his desire to be buried at King's School during a visit there in 1952. He and the Headmaster, Canon Shirley, surveyed the Precincts for a suitable location, but it took more than a year to obtain the Chapter's consent. At one point, Maugham wrote: 'I really did not want you to go to so much trouble over my burial place. Since I saw the marble sarcophagus for a Queen of Aragon in the Museum at Barcelona and saw that they could not even put a name to her and reflected that in her day she might have been highly respected, powerful, loved perhaps and mourned, I felt that it didn't matter a damn where one was buried; and so, if it is convenient and the Chapter agree let me be buried where you say, and if not my ashes can be put in the Cemetery at St Jean among the bones of the inhabitants of the village.'[92]

Maugham wanted to be interred in the cloisters of Canterbury Cathedral, but since there was no possibility of his remains lying where only Archbishops and Deans were buried, a compromise was reached. His ashes, identified by a simple plaque, were placed in the wall of the Maugham Library within the Precincts of the Cathedral, within sight of his various contributions and where he had returned to speak in his later years.

King's, however, was also the site of the many humiliations and wounds so graphically described in *Of Human Bondage*. It seems astonishing that Maugham, born in Paris and resident of Cap Ferrat for nearly four decades, who had fallen in love with the Mediterranean on his first visit to Capri seventy-five years before and who always felt most spiritually at home in the Far East, should choose to lie in Canterbury. The explanation is surely that he was a man without roots, whose life had been fundamentally itinerant and detached, and so King's School came to represent, not pain, but some link to the past and to a society to which he had never fully belonged. For all his cosmopolitanism,

Maugham was an Englishman and King's was quintessentially English. For all his supposed cynicism, Miss King's dying word in *Ashenden* – 'England' – may have come more deeply from within Maugham than anyone realized.

Maugham's ashes were interred on 22 December in a private ceremony attended by Liza (who had not gone to the South of France when her father was dying), other members of his family, and forty schoolboys who returned from their holidays for the occasion. The committal service was conducted by the Dean of Canterbury, the very Revd Ian White-Thompson, and the Headmaster of King's School, the Revd J. P. Newell, who called it 'a ceremony such as Maugham himself might well have approved – with its mixture of a simple homecoming, a touch of the bizarre – but no more, and the interlocking strands of human emotion, interest and understanding.'[93]

As the service concluded, a black cat cautiously made its way along the medieval stone wall facing the square. It paused for a moment to observe the group of mourners ringing the lawn, and then, its curiosity satisfied, it ambled on its way. It was a touch that would have amused the master storyteller.

Maugham's will, signed on 9 July 1964, provided $5600 each to his cook, Annette, and his valet, Jean, and $1400 for all other servants who had been with him for at least five years. Liza received the Villa Mauresque, in addition to two trust funds that had been established for her in 1929 and 1948. In 1968 she successfully applied to have half the funds given to her absolutely and half held in trust for her children. A year later the villa was sold for $730,000 to an American developer who gutted and remodelled it, opening up the third-floor writing-room's seaward wall that had kept Maugham from being distracted. The grounds were divided into a number of lots for luxury villas.

Alan Searle was given the contents of the villa, most of which were sold at Sotheby's in 1967 for $76,000; a lump sum of $140,000; and all the royalties from Maugham's works for his lifetime. Thereafter the income went to the Royal Literary Fund, to provide assistance to authors and their dependants who are in financial difficulty. In 1987 the Fund received £133,237 from the Maugham bequest.

Walking through the garden of the Villa Mauresque in the final months of Maugham's dying, Searle had commented to Michael Moynihan: 'I am a prisoner here.'[94] Maugham's death, however, did not free him. Early in 1966 he suffered a nervous breakdown and later he developed a series of medical problems, the most serious being Parkinson's disease. In his grief he took to eating as a kind of substitute, his weight ballooned, and he began to spend money recklessly.

Having devoted most of his life to Maugham, Searle had few friends of his own, and he soon discovered that many of those who had come to the Villa Mauresque had been interested in the famous author, not his companion. He tried relationships with both males and females, but nothing lasted.

Before Maugham had invited him to join him in America, Searle had been a skilled social worker who, in Raymond Marriott's words, 'from the most altruistic of motives helped many a prisoner when freed from jail. He helped many other people too, specially the sick and crushed, though few knew of this.'[95] At Maugham's death, though, Searle was sixty, and it was too late to return to his profession. He might have been wise to have moved back to London, where he could have begun life again, but he found it difficult to contemplate leaving the Riviera and his memories. Thus he settled in a comfortable flat in the Avenue de Grand Bretagne in Monte Carlo.

If Maugham had resembled a modern-day King Lear, Searle was not so much his Fool as his loyal servant Kent, who is prepared to sacrifice his own life to protect his master from his self-destructive madness. At the end of Shakespeare's play this servant *par excellence* is about to follow his king into death, and in many ways it would have been fitting if Searle could have joined his friend on this last voyage out.

The twenty years following Maugham's death were spent trying to recapture the past. Searle retraced paths: to the Dorchester, to Paris, to Hollywood and the still loyal George Cukor, and even to the same room in the Gritti Palace in Venice in which he and Maugham had always stayed. When he dined at La Réserve de Beaulieu, the table was set with the pair of distinctive wine glasses which they had used. To those who visited him – old friends or new acquaintances – he was extraordinarily generous, delighting in taking his guests to places where 'Willie' had taken him – La Réserve, La Mortola across the Italian border, or L'Hôtel de Paris in Monte Carlo. He returned to the Villa Mauresque only once, and wept in the courtyard at the changes to it and the magnificent garden.

At the time of Maugham's death Hector Bolitho wrote admiringly of his relationship with Searle, 'of how he kept Alan Searle's friendship and unselfish devotion, when both of them had long passed the hazards of anything physical in their life together.'[96] It was, when everything is considered, a deeply committed, loving, and durable relationship, and Bolitho's view was shared by almost everyone who had known them well. Searle was nevertheless deeply wounded late in his life when he was portrayed as a grasping, self-seeking sycophant who manipulated a senile old man in order to gain his estate. For all his loyalty to Maugham's memory, his refusal to write about their life together, he found himself pilloried. He died at his home in Monte Carlo on 25 August 1985, at the age of eighty.

Notes

Preface
1 Peter Burton, *Parallel Lives* (London, GMP Publishers, 1985), p. 89.
2 As quoted by Hugo Vickers, *Cecil Beaton* (London, Weidenfeld and Nicolson, 1985), p. 567.

1 Orphan: 1874–1889
1 W. Somerset Maugham, *The Summing Up* (London, Heinemann, 1938), p. 15.
2 Ibid., p. 16
3 As quoted by Robin Maugham, *Somerset and All the Maughams* (New York, Signet Books, 1966), p. 54.
4 As quoted by Maurice Zolotow, *Stagestruck* (New York, Harcourt, Brace and World, 1964), p. 255.
5 Violet Hammersley, 'A Childhood in Paris', *Orpheus II*, ed. John Lehmann (London, Lehmann, 1949), p. 186.
6 Robin Maugham, p. 116.
7 *The Summing Up*, p. 17.
8 Hammersley, p. 186.
9 Francis Oppenheimer, *Stranger Within* (London, Faber and Faber, 1960), p. 132.
10 Robin Maugham, p. 113.
11 Frederic Raphael, *Somerset Maugham and His World* (London, Thames and Hudson, 1976), p. 7.
12 Robin Maugham, p. 179.
13 W. Somerset Maugham, 'Looking Back', *Show* (June 1962), p. 63.
14 Robin Maugham, p. 118.
15 Hammersley, p. 185.
16 Ibid., p. 187.
17 Robin Maugham, p. 115.
18 Anthony Curtis, *Somerset Maugham* (London, Weidenfeld and Nicolson, 1977), p. 22.
19 W. Somerset Maugham, *Of Human Bondage* (London, Heinemann, 1937), p. 4.
20 Ibid., p. 15.
21 Ibid., p. 1.
22 Ibid., p. 9.
23 *The Summing Up*, p. 18.
24 Robin Maugham, p. 131.
25 'Woman's Hour', BBC Radio 2, 17 September 1969.
26 Lionel Hale to R. L. Calder.
27 Graham Payn and Sheridan Morley (eds), *The Noël Coward Diaries* (London, Macmillan, 1982), p. 240.
28 W. Somerset Maugham, *A Writer's Notebook* (London, Heinemann, 1949), p. 27.
29 Robin Maugham, p. 117.
30 Arthur Marshall, 'In Gratitude', *New Statesman* (25 February 1977), p. 251.
31 Ralph Gustafson to R. L. Calder, 21 March 1982.
32 Lord Boothby to R. L. Calder, 6 March 1982.
33 Frederic Prokosch, *Voices: A Memoir* (New York, Farrar, Straus, Giroux, 1983), p. 258.
34 Sigmund Freud, *Three Essays on the Theory of Sexuality*. Trans. J. Strachey (London, Imago, 1949), p. 23 n.

35 John Money, 'Sin, Sickness, or Status: Homosexual Gender Identity and Psychoneuroendocrinology', *American Psychologist* (April 1987), p. 384.
36 Daniel Cappon, *Toward an Understanding of Homosexuality* (New Jersey, Prentice-Hall, 1965), p. 56.
37 Kenneth Jones, Louis Shainberg and Curtis Byer, *Sex* (New York: Harper and Row, 1969), p. 30.
38 D. J. West, *Homosexuality* (Harmondsworth, Penguin, 1960), p. 120.
39 Leon Edel, 'Of Willie's Bondage', *Saturday Review* (15 March 1980), p. 36.
40 Godfrey Winn, 'Maugham: The Summing Up', *Evening News* (16 December 1965), p. 4.
41 *The Summing Up*, p. 19.
42 Robin Maugham, p. 135.
43 Rebecca West, 'W. Somerset Maugham', *Nash's* (October 1935), p. 97.
44 *A Traveller's Library* (New York, Doubleday, Doran, 1933), p. 6.
45 Robin Maugham, p. 130.
46 Ibid., p. 129.
47 Hamilton Basso, 'Very Old Party – II', *New Yorker* (6 January 1945), p. 29.
48 *Of Human Bondage*, p. 24.
49 *Whitstable Times* (30 July 1887), p. 8.
50 *Whitstable Times* (31 March 1888), p. 8.
51 *Whitstable Times* (13 October 1888), p. 8.
52 *A Writer's Notebook*, p. 261.
53 *Of Human Bondage*, p. 11.
54 Alan Searle to R. L. Calder.
55 *Whitstable Times* (22 May 1886), p. 8.
56 Robert Goodsall, 'Two Kent Authors', *A Fourth Kentish Patchwork* (Harrietsham, Kent, Stedehill Publications, 1974), p. 88.
57 Robin Maugham, p. 132.
58 W. Somerset Maugham, *Cakes and Ale* (London, Heinemann, 1930), p. 41.
59 Robin Maugham, p. 162.
60 Ibid., p. 163.
61 Ibid., p. 133.
62 *The Summing Up*, p. 48.
63 Ibid., p. 66.
64 W. Somerset Maugham, Introduction to *Mrs Craddock* (New York, Arno, 1977), p. 10.
65 *Of Human Bondage*, p. 32.
66 *The Summing Up*, p. 67.
67 As quoted by Jeffrey Meyers, *Homosexuality and Literature: 1890–1930* (London, Athlone Press, 1977), p. 12.
68 *Of Human Bondage*, p. 94.
69 Ibid., pp. 71–2.
70 Robin Maugham, pp. 162–3.
71 F. J. Shirley, 'William Somerset Maugham', *Cantuarian* (December 1965), p. 18.
72 'Looking Back,' *Show* (June 1962), p. 64.
73 *Of Human Bondage*, p. 64.
74 'Looking Back', *Show* (June 1962), p. 64.
75 *Of Human Bondage*, p. 81.
76 Ibid., p. 89.
77 Ibid., p. 71.
78 As quoted by Leslie Rees, 'Remembrance of Things Past: A Meeting With Somerset Maugham', *Meanjin Quarterly* (Summer 1967), p. 493.
79 *Of Human Bondage*, pp. 85–6.

80 Ibid., p. 88.
81 Ibid., p. 91.

2 **Apprentice: 1889–1897**

1 'The Traitor', *The Complete Short Stories of W. Somerset Maugham* (New York, Doubleday, 1952), p. 545.
2 *Of Human Bondage*, p. 124.
3 Alan Searle to R. L. Calder.
4 *The Summing Up*, p. 255.
5 *Of Human Bondage*, p. 121.
6 'Looking Back', *Show* (August 1962), p. 72.
7 Ted Morgan, *Maugham* (New York, Simon and Schuster, 1980), p. 24.
8 *The Summing Up*, p. 62.
9 Ibid., p. 63.
10 Joseph Lurie, 'William Somerset Maugham: An Appreciation and a Probe', *St Thomas's Hospital Gazette* (Autumn 1966), p. 112.
11 *The Times* (3 November 1949), p. 7.
12 Marie Lohr interview with Sir Julian Hall, 18 August 1969, Theatre Museum transcript, p. 9.
13 Preface to F. T. Bason (ed.), *A Bibliography of the Writings of William Somerset Maugham* (London, Unicorn Press, 1931), p. 9.
14 *The Summing Up*, p. 76.
15 Maugham to Wentworth Huyshe, 30 August 1897. Texas mss.
16 W. Somerset Maugham, 'The Ionian Sea', *A Traveller in Romance: Uncollected Writings, 1901–1964*, ed. John Whitehead (New York, Potter, 1984), p. 117.
17 Stephen Coulter, 'Maugham at Ninety', *Sunday Times* (19 January 1964), p. 30.
18 A. L. Rowse, *Homosexuals in History* (New York, Dorset Press, 1977), p. 169.
19 Lurie, p. 110.
20 Frederic Raphael, 'Fiction and the Medical Mode', *The Listener* (3 April 1975), p. 452.
21 Louise Morgan, 'Somerset Maugham', *Writers at Work* (London, Chatto and Windus, 1931), p. 94.
22 As quoted by Derek Patmore, *Private History* (London, Jonathan Cape, 1960), p. 185.
23 Patrick Back to R. L. Calder, 26 December 1976.
24 Michael Wardell, 'A Visit to Somerset Maugham', *Atlantic Advocate* (April 1962), p. 26.
25 Raphael, 'Fiction and the Medical Mode', p. 452.
26 'Looking Back on Eighty Years', *A Traveller in Romance*, p. 259.
27 'Daisy', *Seventeen Lost Short Stories by W. Somerset Maugham*, ed. Craig V. Showalter (New York, Doubleday, 1969), p. 136.
28 Ibid., p. 136.
29 Ibid., p. 137.
30 Unwin Reader Reports, Berg mss.
31 W. Somerset Maugham, *Liza of Lambeth* (London, Heinemann, 1934), pp. vii–viii.
32 Unwin Reader Reports, Berg mss.
33 Maugham to Frank Swinnerton, 25 January 1938. Arkansas mss.
34 Raymond Toole Stott, *A Bibliography of the Works of W. Somerset Maugham* (London, Kaye and Ward, 1973), p. 18.
35 *Spectator* (13 November 1897), p. 692.
36 *The Academy* (11 September 1897), p. 65.
37 *Bookman* (October 1897), p. 23.

38 *Athenaeum* (11 September 1897), p. 347.
39 Robin Maugham, *Somerset and All the Maughams* (New York, Signet Books, 1966), p. 154.
40 *Liza of Lambeth*, p. ix.
41 *The Academy*, p. 65.
42 Morgan, p. 58.
43 Mrs Belloc Lowndes, *A Passing World* (London, Macmillan, 1948), p. 262.
44 W. Somerset Maugham, *The Making of a Saint* (New York, World Publishing Company, 1944), p. 9.
45 Maugham to J. B. Pinker, 22 September 1909. Texas mss.
46 *The Summing Up*, p. 293.
47 'On His Ninetieth Birthday', *A Traveller in Romance*, p. 263.
48 W. Somerset Maugham, *Don Fernando* (London, Heinemann, 1935), p. 50.

3 Struggles: 1897–1907

1 W. Somerset Maugham, *Andalusia: Sketches and Impressions* (New York, Knopf, 1920), p. 58.
2 *Don Fernando*, p. 50.
3 Maugham to Ada Leverson, 23 April 1909, and 27 February 1910. Yale mss.
4 Alan Searle to R. L. Calder.
5 Leopold Bellak, 'Somerset Maugham: A Thematic Analysis of Ten Short Stories', *The Study of Lives*, ed. Robert W. White (New York, Atherton Press, 1963), pp. 142–3. Reprinted as 'The Application of Thematic Analysis to Literary Products', in *The Thematic Apperception Test, The Children's Apperception Test and the Senior Apperception Technique in Clinical Use* (New York, Grune and Stratton, 1975), pp. 163–72.
6 Ibid., pp. 153–4.
7 W. Somerset Maugham, *The Complete Short Stories*, Vol. I, pp. 768–9.
8 *Don Fernando*, p. 51.
9 *Andalusia*, p. 12.
10 *Don Fernando*, pp. 76–7.
11 *Andalusia*, p. 11.
12 Ibid., p. 59.
13 'By the Ionian Sea', *A Traveller in Romance*, p.119.
14 D. H. Lawrence, *Letters*, ed. A. Huxley (London, Heinemann, 1932), p. 620.
15 *Andalusia*, p. 233.
16 'By the Ionian Sea', p. 118.
17 Maugham to Colles, 10 November 1898. Berg mss.
18 H. V. Philips to Joseph Dobrinsky, 16 September 1966. I am grateful to Professor Dobrinsky for the use of Mr Philips's letters to him.
19 *The Making of a Saint*, pp. 86–7.
20 Frank Scully, 'Somerset Maugham At Home', *The World Today* (August 1928), p. 238.
21 Kenneth Allsop, 'Grand Old Maugham', *Scan* (London, Hodder and Stoughton, 1965), pp. 93–4.
22 Dwight Taylor, 'Maugham and the Young Idiot', *Vogue* (1 September 1953), p. 172.
23 Eugene Goossens, *Overtures and Beginners* (London, Methuen, 1951), p. 211.
24 Allsop, p. 94.
25 'Looking Back', *Show* (June 1962), p. 62.
26 Ted Morgan, *Maugham* (New York, Simon and Schuster, 1980), p. 33.
27 Robin Maugham, *Somerset and All the Maughams* (New York, Signet Books, 1966), p. 212.

28 Francis King, 'Timon of Antibes', *Sunday Telegraph* (20 February 1977), p. 16.
29 John Whitehead, *Maugham: A Reappraisal* (London, Vision, 1987), p. 77.
30 Rebecca West to R. L. Calder.
31 Morgan, p. 95.
32 Raymond Mortimer to R. L. Calder.
33 Gerald Kelly to R. L. Calder.
34 Douglas Goldring, *Odd Man Out* (London, Chapman and Hall, 1935), p. 5.
35 Ibid., p. 54.
36 Ibid., pp. 56–7.
37 Ibid., p. 57.
38 Louis Wilkinson, 'William Somerset Maugham', *Seven Friends* (London, Richards, 1953), p. 142.
39 Robin Maugham, pp. 121–2.
40 *Mrs Craddock* (London, Heinemann, 1955), p. 338.
41 Douglas Goldring, *South Lodge* (London, Constable, 1944), p. 42.
42 BBC memo from Lance Sieveking, 19 March 1948. BBC Written Archives Centre, Caversham Park, Reading.
43 Ian Fleming, *Thrilling Cities* (London, Jonathan Cape, 1963), p. 52.
44 Anthony Curtis, *The Pattern of Maugham* (London, Hamish Hamilton, 1974), p. 116.
45 Robin Maugham, p. 208.
46 Ibid., p. 176.
47 Ray Mander and Joe Mitchenson, *Theatrical Companion to Maugham* (London, Rockcliff, 1955), p. 20.
48 Maugham to Colles, December 1904. Lilly mss.
49 Preface to *Liza of Lambeth*, p. xxiii.
50 W. Somerset Maugham, *The Merry-Go-Round* (London, Heinemann, 1904), p. 92.
51 Ibid., p. 388.
52 Ibid., p. 388.
53 Ibid., pp. 34–5.
54 Ibid., p. 35.
55 Ibid., p. 146.
56 *A Writer's Notebook*, pp. 32–3.
57 *The Merry-Go-Round*, p. 150.
58 'Looking Back', *Show* (June 1962), p. 67.
59 Dorothy Peel, *Life's Enchanted Cup* (London, John Lane, 1933), p. 105.
60 Mrs Belloc Lowndes, *The Merry Wives of Westminster* (London, Macmillan, 1946), p. 66.
61 Morgan, p. 95.
62 Maugham to Edward Marsh, 1 April 1942. Berg mss.
63 Alec Waugh, 'W.S.M.: R.I.P.', *My Brother Evelyn and Other Profiles* (London, Cassell, 1967), pp. 272–3.
64 *The Times* (18 December 1943), p. 6.
65 Netta Syrett, *The Sheltering Tree* (London, Geoffrey Bles, 1939), p. 193.
66 Ibid., p. 243.
67 Robert Ross, 'The Literary Log', *The Bystander* (1 March 1911), p. 450.
68 Syrett, p. 177.
69 Ibid., p. 243.
70 Robin Maugham, p. 177.
71 'Old Friends', *The Times* (24 January 1954), p. 6.
72 Ibid., p. 6.
73 Derek Hudson, *For Love of Painting* (London, Peter Davies, 1975), p. 28.
74 'Sir Gerald at 90', *The Times* (18 March 1969), p. 10.

75 *The Merry-Go-Round*, p. 249.
76 H. V. Philips to Joseph Dobrinsky, 16 September 1966.
77 W. Somerset Maugham, *The Magician* (London, Heinemann, 1908), p. 30.
78 Aleister Crowley, *The Spirit of Solitude: An Autohagiography, vol. II* (London, Mandrake Press, 1929), p. 243.
79 Edward Marsh, *A Number of People: A Book of Reminiscences* (London, Heinemann, 1939), p. 328.
80 Arnold Bennett, *Journals: Volume I: 1896–1910* (London, Cassell, 1932), p. 208.
81 James Hepburn (ed.), *Letters to J. B. Pinker* (London, Oxford University Press, 1966), p. 63.
82 As quoted by R. T. Stott, *A Bibliography of the Works of W. Somerset Maugham* (London, Kaye and Ward, 1973), p. 42.
83 Ibid., p. 30.
84 Maugham to Violet Hunt, 22 January 1906. Berg mss.
85 *A Writer's Notebook*, p. 80.
86 Max Beerbohm, *Lost Theatres* (London, Hart Davis, 1970), p. 440.
87 Doris Arthur Jones, *What a Life* (London, Jarrolds, 1932), p. 224.
88 Gerald Kelly to R. L. Calder, 4 February 1970.
89 *Cakes and Ale*, pp. 189–90.
90 Preface to *Liza of Lambeth*, p. xv.
91 Stott, p. 51.
92 John Symonds and Kenneth Grant (eds), *The Confessions of Aleister Crowley: An Autohagiography* (London, Cape, 1969), p. 572.
93 Preface to *Liza of Lambeth*, p. xxv.
94 *The Magician*, p. 8.
95 Ibid., p. 23.
96 Ibid., p. 26.
97 Maugham to Golding Bright, 16 September 1907. Texas mss.

4 Syrie and Gerald: 1908–1918

1 *A Writer's Notebook*, pp. 84–5.
2 'Somerset Maugham', *Stage* (November 1940), p. 49.
3 'Angry Young Men? – I Admire Them', *Sunday Times* (6 October 1957), p. 26.
4 Frederic Raphael, *Somerset Maugham and His World* (London, Thames and Hudson, 1976), p. 29.
5 *The Summing Up*, p. 177.
6 As quoted by Klaus Jonas, 'The Gentleman from Cap Ferrat', *The World of Somerset Maugham* (Connecticut, Greenwood Press, 1959), p. 34.
7 George Doran, *Chronicles of Barabbas – 1884–1934* (Toronto, George MacLeod, 1935), p. 153.
8 Preface to *Collected Plays*, vol. I, p. xv.
9 Malcolm Muggeridge, 'Maugham: Compassionate Cynic', *Sunday Times* (19 December 1965), p. 35.
10 Louis Wilkinson, *Two Made Their Bed* (London, Gollancz, 1929), p. 9.
11 Preface to *Collected Plays*, vol. I, p. xv.
12 'The Tragedy of Mr Maugham's Dramatic Success', *Current Literature* (August 1908), p. 203.
13 Ibid., p. 202.
14 Maugham to St John Adcock, 14 May 1908. Lilly mss.
15 'The Bad Habit of Mr Maugham', *Saturday Review* (22 October 1910), p. 517.
16 Maugham to Robin Maugham, 9 February 1935. Texas mss.
17 Margery Ross (ed.), *Robert Ross: Friend of Friends* (London, Cape, 1952), p. 157.

18 W. Somerset Maugham, *The Vagrant Mood*, p. 218.
19 Ibid., p. 219.
20 Louis Wilkinson, 'William Somerset Maugham', *Seven Friends* (London, Richards, 1953), pp. 144–5.
21 *Sotheby's Catalogue of the Contents of the Villa Mauresque*, 20 November 1967, p. 18.
22 Maugham to Ada Leverson, 31 December 1908. Yale mss.
23 Maugham to Ada Leverson, 21 February 1910. Yale mss.
24 Ada Leverson, *The Limit* (London, Grant Richards, 1911), pp. 51–2.
25 Francis Toye, *For What We Have Received* (London, Heinemann, 1950), p. 77.
26 Elsa Maxwell, *The Celebrity Circus* (London, Allen, 1964), p. 20.
27 Marie Lohr interview with Sir Julian Hall, 18 August 1969. Theatre Museum transcript, p. 8.
28 Irene Vanbrugh, *To Tell My Story* (London, Hutchinson, 1948), p. 78.
29 Billie Burke, *With A Feather On My Nose* (New York: Appleton-Century-Crofts, 1949), p. 107.
30 Gerald Kelly to R. L. Calder.
31 Derek Hudson, *For Love of Painting* (London, Peter Davies, 1975), p. 37.
32 Hugh Walpole, 'William Somerset Maugham: A Pen Portrait By a Friendly Hand', *Vanity Fair: A Cavalcade of the 1920s and 1930s*, ed. Cleveland Amory and Frederic Bradlee (New York, Viking Press, 1960), p. 40.
33 Isaac Marcossan and Daniel Frohman, *Charles Frohman: Manager and Man* (New York, Harper, 1916), p. 271.
34 *The Summing Up*, pp. 194–5.
35 Van Wyck Brooks, *An Autobiography* (New York, Dutton, 1965), p. 568.
36 Eric Barnes, *The High Room: A Biography of Edward Sheldon* (London, W. H. Allen, 1957), p. 64.
37 Maugham to C. F. Cazenove, 25 July 1911. Lilly mss.
38 Maugham to C. F. Frohman, 28 February 1912. Texas mss.
39 William Heinemann archives.
40 Ibid.
41 Edmonton *Daily Bulletin* (10 April 1914), p. 2. As quoted in Robert G. Lawrence, 'The Land of Promise: Canada, As Maugham Saw It in 1914', *Theatre History in Canada* (Spring 1983), p. 22.
42 J. T. Grein, *Sunday Times and Special* (10 January 1909), p. 9.
43 *The Summing Up*, pp. 197–8.
44 *Of Human Bondage*, p. 647.
45 Garson Kanin, *Remembering Mr Maugham* (New York, Atheneum, 1966), pp. 131–3.
46 Rebecca West to R. L. Calder.
47 Gerald McKnight, *The Scandal of Syrie Maugham* (London, W. H. Allen, 1980).
48 Rebecca West to R. L. Calder.
49 'A Case of Ill-Nature', *Daily Telegraph* (19 May 1966), p. 22.
50 McKnight, p. 53.
51 As quoted by McKnight, p. 65.
52 Ibid., pp. 56–7.
53 'Looking Back', *Show* (July 1962), p. 42.
54 As quoted by Beverley Nichols, *A Case of Human Bondage* (London, Secker and Warburg, 1966), p. 133.
55 Rebecca West to R. L. Calder.
56 Hamilton Basso, 'Very Old Party – I', *New Yorker* (30 December 1940), p. 33.
57 'A Visit With Somerset Maugham', *Look* (5 January 1960), p. 50.
58 W. Somerset Maugham, *Ashenden*, p. 46.
59 Nichols, *A Case of Human Bondage*, p. 22.
60 *The Summing Up*, p. 197.

61 Peter Quennell to R. L. Calder.

62 Harold Acton, *Memoirs of an Aesthete* (London, Methuen, 1948), p. 188.

63 Alec Waugh, 'W.S.M.: R.I.P.', *My Brother Evelyn and Other Profiles* (London, Cassell, 1967), p. 280.

64 Alan Searle to R. L. Calder.

65 George Rylands to R. L. Calder.

66 As quoted by Ted Morgan, *Maugham* (New York, Simon and Schuster, 1980), p. 192.

67 Raphael, p. 46.

68 Rhodri Jeffreys-Jones, *American Espionage: From Secret Service to CIA* (London, Collier Macmillan, 1978), p. 86.

69 Faith Mackenzie, *As Much As I Dare* (London, Collins, 1938), p. 269.

70 'Looking Back', *Show* (July 1962), p. 44.

71 General Sir Walter Kirke, Diary, 26 October 1915, Imperial War Museum.

72 Christopher Andrew, *Secret Service: The Making of the British Intelligence Community* (London, Sceptre, 1986), pp. 227–8.

73 Ted Berkman, *The Lady and the Law* (Toronto, Little, Brown, 1976), pp. 229–30.

74 Kirke Diary, 8 February 1916.

75 *The Summing Up*, p. 201.

76 Ibid., pp. 200–1.

77 Morgan, p. 203.

78 Wilmon Menard, *The Two Worlds of Somerset Maugham* (Los Angeles, Sherbourne Press, 1965), p. 321.

79 *A Writer's Notebook*, p. 105.

80 Ibid., p. 108.

81 As quoted by Morgan, p. 217.

82 *A Writer's Notebook*, pp. 138–9.

83 Morgan, p. 220.

84 Cathleen Nesbitt, *A Little Love and Good Company* (London, Faber and Faber, 1975), p. 141.

85 'Maugham-By-the-Sea', *Saturday Review* (14 October 1961), p. 74.

86 Nesbitt, p. 141.

87 As quoted by Morgan, p. 221.

88 Raphael, pp. 44–5.

89 Alan Searle to R. L. Calder.

90 As quoted by Morgan, p. 221.

91 Alan Searle to R. L. Calder.

92 As quoted by McKnight, p. 123.

93 W. H. Auden, *Forewords and Afterwords* (New York, Random House, 1973), pp. 307–8.

94 Wiseman mss. File 90–42, E. M. House Collection, Yale University Library.

95 Maugham to William Wiseman, 7 July 1917. Yale mss.

96 Walpole, 'William Somerset Maugham', p. 41.

97 *A Writer's Notebook*, p. 166.

98 Barbara Gelb, *So Short a Time* (New York, Norton, 1973), p. 142.

99 Jeffreys-Jones, p. 96.

100 Private Secretary Archives, 1917–24, A. J. Balfour, FO 800/205, Public Record Office.

101 Jeffreys-Jones, p. 100.

5   Wanderer: 1918–1929

1 *The Summing Up*, p. 206.

2 W. S. Maugham, 'Love in a Cottage', Act IV, p. 24. Library of Congress mss.

3 W. S. Maugham, *Home and Beauty, Collected Plays*, II, p. 288.

4 W. S. Maugham, *Caesar's Wife, Collected Plays*, III, pp. 66–7.

5 Introduction to *Collected Plays*, III, p. vii.

6 W. S. Maugham, *Yesterday* (London, Cassell, 1947), p. 256.

7 *The Summing Up*, p. 51.

8 W. S. Maugham, *The Moon and Sixpence* (London, Heinemann, 1935), p. 72.

9 Ibid., p. 200.

10 'The Development of William Somerset Maugham', Columbia University Doctoral Dissertation, 1953.

11 *Times Literary Supplement* (12 August 1915), p. 269.

12 Published in *A Comprehensive Exhibition of the Writings of W. Somerset Maugham* (Stanford, Stanford University Press, 1958).

13 Burton Rascoe 'A Gossip on Miss West and Mr Maugham', *Arts and Decoration* (December 1923), p. 72.

14 Maugham to Edward Marsh, 5 July 1919. Berg mss.

15 W. S. Maugham, *The Circle, Collected Plays*, II, p. 78.

16 *Complete Short Stories*, I, p. 65.

17 Ibid., II, p. 279.

18 Ted Morgan, *Maugham* (New York, Simon and Schuster, 1980), pp. 202–3.

19 Fanny Butcher, *Many Lives – One Love* (New York, Harper and Row, 1972), pp. 234–5.

20 Maugham to Knoblock, 17 August 1921. Berg mss.

21 Maugham to Alanson, 8 March 1923. Stanford mss.

22 Alan Searle to R. L. Calder.

23 For a full account of the origins of 'The Letter' see Norman Sherry, 'How Murder on the Veranda Inspired Somerset Maugham', *Observer Magazine* (22 February 1976), pp. 12–16.

24 Letter to *The Times* (1 August 1955), p. 9.

25 'The Faces of Maugham: A Portrait For His Centenary', *The Listener* (7 February 1974), p. 169.

26 *A Writer's Notebook*, pp.186–7.

27 Basil Dean, *Seven Ages* (London, Hutchinson, 1970), p. 177.

28 Irene Vanbrugh, *To Tell My Story* (London, Hutchinson, 1948) p. 108.

29 'The Faces of Maugham', p. 169.

30 Gladys Cooper, *Gladys Cooper* (London, Hutchinson, 1931), p. 245.

31 Maugham to Alanson, 25 July 1922. Stanford mss.

32 W. S. Maugham, *The Gentleman in the Parlour* (New York, Doubleday, Doran, 1970), p. 245.

33 Ibid., pp. 220–1.

34 W. S. Maugham, *On a Chinese Screen*, p. 60.

35 *The Gentleman in the Parlour*, p. 64.

36 *On a Chinese Screen*, pp. 152–3.

37 Ibid., pp. vii–viii.

38 *The Gentleman in the Parlour*, p. 6.

39 Beverley Nichols, *Twenty-Five* (London, Cape, 1926), p. 238.

40 'Mr Maugham on Desk and in the Sitting Room', *New York Times Book Review* (17 June 1923), p. 7.

41 'What I Think of Your Theatre', *Theatre Magazine* (August 1923), p. 27.

42 Carl Bode, *Mencken* (Carbondale and Edwardsville, Southern Illinois University Press, 1969), p. 156.

43 Dwight Taylor, 'Maugham and the Young Idiot', *Vogue* (1 September 1953), pp. 214, 216.

44 *Letters to His Nephew* (London, Heinemann, 1936), p. 141.

45 Julian Hall, 'Somerset Maugham in the Theatre', BBC Radio 3 (2 October 1969).
46 Frances Donaldson, *Freddy Lonsdale* (London, Heinemann, 1957), pp. 84–5.
47 Maugham to Alanson, 24 January 1924. Stanford mss.
48 Eugene Goossens, *Overtures and Beginners* (London, Methuen, 1951) p. 266.
49 Dean, p. 234.
50 *New York Times Book Review* (27 May 1923), p. 1.
51 Bruce Kellner, *Carl Van Vechten and the Irreverent Decades* (Norman, University of Oklahoma Press, 1968), p. 220.
52 Edward Nehls (ed.), *D. H. Lawrence: A Composite Biography, II: 1919–1925* (Madison, University of Wisconsin Press, 1958), p. 366.
53 Frieda Lawrence, *Not I, But the Wind* (New York, Viking, 1934), pp. 147–8.
54 'Making a Voice in the World', *The New Yorker* (7 October 1972), p. 96.
55 As quoted by Sara Mayfield, *The Constant Circle* (New York, Putnam's, 1972), p. 104.
56 Lee Israel, *Miss Tallulah Bankhead* (New York, Putnam's, 1972), p. 104.
57 Maugham to Paul Dottin, 1928. Texas mss.
58 W. S. Maugham, *The Painted Veil* (London, Heinemann, 1925), p. 156.
59 Ibid., p. 192.
60 Ibid., p. 47.
61 Ibid., p. 28.
62 Beverley Nichols, *A Case of Human Bondage* (London, Secker and Warburg, 1966), p. 75.
63 *The Painted Veil*, pp. 78–9.
64 Ibid., p. 24.
65 Ibid., pp. 288–9.
66 Raymond Mortimer to R. L. Calder.
67 Cathleen Nesbitt to R. L. Calder, September 1976.
68 As quoted by McKnight, *The Scandal of Syrie Maugham* (London, W. H. Allen, 1980), p. 103.
69 Bruce Lockhart, *Diaries, Vol. I: 1915–1978*, ed. Kenneth Young (London, Macmillan, 1973), pp. 312–13.
70 Beverley Nichols, *The Sweet and Twenties* (London, Weidenfeld and Nicolson, 1958), pp. 38–9.
71 Maugham to Knoblock, October 1925. Berg mss.
72 Maugham to C. H. Towne, 25 September 1925. Yale mss.
73 Maugham to Towne, 1925. Yale mss.
74 George Doran Company to W. S. Maugham, 16 July 1926. Indiana mss.
75 Burton Rascoe, 'A Chat With Somerset Maugham', *A Bookman's Daybook* (New York, Liveright, 1929), pp. 151–2.
76 Maugham to Paul Dottin, 23 October 1927. Texas mss.
77 Maugham to Knoblock, 27 March 1926. Berg mss.
78 *Letters to His Nephew*, p. 188.
79 As quoted by Michael Holroyd, *Lytton Strachey: A Critical Biography, II: The Years of Achievement (1910–1932)* (London, Heinemann, 1968), p. 533.
80 *The Journals of Arnold Bennett* (London, Cassell, 1932), p. 874.
81 Sir Ronald Howe to R. L. Calder.
82 Alan Searle to R. L. Calder.
83 Jerome Weidman, *Praying for Rain* (New York, Harper and Row, 1986), p. 255.
84 Dean, p. 322.
85 As quoted by Hollis Alpert, *The Barrymores* (New York, Sun Dial Press, 1964), p. 277.
86 *Collected Plays*, II, p. 160.
87 Ibid., p. 181.

88 As quoted by the *New York Times* (5 December 1927), p. 26.
89 'Collected Plays of England's Most Civilized Dramatists', *New York Times Book Review* (27 May 1927), p. 7.
90 Maugham to Knoblock, 1 February 1925. Berg mss.
91 Messmore Kendall, *Never Let the Weather Interfere* (New York, Farrar, Straus, 1946), p. 306.
92 Maugham to Messmore Kendall, 15 February 1928. Texas mss.
93 Maugham to Back, 22 April 1929. Texas mss.
94 Alan Searle to R. L. Calder.
95 Anita Loos, *Kiss Hollywood Goodbye* (New York, Viking, 1974), p. 72.
96 David Herbert, *Second Son* (London, Peter Owen, 1972), p. 134.
97 As quoted by McKnight, p. 118.
98 Kanin, *Remembering Mr Maugham* (New York, Atheneum, 1966), p. 193.
99 Beverley Nichols, 'Exhuming Maugham', *Books and Bookmen* (May 1980), p. 13.
100 Arthur Marshall to R. L. Calder.
101 Frank Swinnerton to R. L. Calder, 28 September 1976.

6   The Gentleman in the Villa: 1929–1932

1 Roderick Cameron, *The Golden Riviera* (London, Weidenfeld and Nicolson, 1975), p. 27.
2 Ibid., p. 44.
3 Rebecca West to R. L. Calder.
4 Patrick Back to R. L. Calder, 26 December 1976.
5 Cecil Beaton, *The Strenuous Years* (London, Weidenfeld and Nicolson, 1973), p. 28.
6 Peter Quennell to R. L. Calder.
7 Ann Fleming to R. L. Calder.
8 Mark Amory (ed.), *The Letters of Evelyn Waugh* (London, Weidenfeld and Nicolson, 1980), pp. 371–2.
9 Garson Kanin, *Remembering Mr Maugham* (New York, Atheneum, 1966), p. 33.
10 Cameron, p. 42.
11 G. B. Stern, 'Somerset Maugham Comes of Age', *John O'London's Weekly* (22 January 1954), p. 2.
12 Fay Compton interview with Sir Julian Hall, 17 July 1969, Theatre Museum transcript.
13 Ralph G. Martin, *Cissy: The Extraordinary Life of Eleanor Medill Patterson* (New York, Simon and Schuster, 1979), p. 216.
14 Beverley Nichols, *A Case of Human Bondage* (London, Secker and Warburg, 1966), p. 100.
15 Rebecca West to R. L. Calder.
16 Kenneth Clark, *Other Half: A Self Portrait* (Toronto, Longmans, 1977), p. 117.
17 Letter to the Editor, *Spectator* (17 May 1980), p. 16.
18 Beverley Nichols, 'Exhuming Maugham', *Books and Bookmen* (May 1980), p. 15.
19 Arthur Marshall, 'In Gratitude', *New Statesman* (25 February 1977), p. 251.
20 W. S. Maugham, *Strictly Personal* (New York, Doubleday, Doran, 1941), p. 96.
21 *A Writer's Notebook*, pp. 230–1.
22 Arthur Marshall to R. L. Calder.
23 Vane Ivanovic, *LX: Memoirs of a Yugoslav* (New York, Harcourt, Brace, Jovanovich, 1977), p. 363.
24 Maugham to Paul Dottin, 1 January 1931. Texas mss.
25 Robert Gittings and Jo Manton, *The Second Mrs Hardy* (Heinemann, 1979), p. 132.
26 As quoted by Rupert Hart-Davis, *Hugh Walpole: A Biography* (London, Macmillan, 1952), p. 316.

27 Nigel Nicolson and Joanne Trautmann (eds), *A Reflection of the Other Person: The Letters of Virginia Woolf* (London, Hogarth Press, 1978), pp. 250–1.
28 As quoted by Elizabeth Steele, *Hugh Walpole* (New York: Twayne, 1972), p. 126.
29 Ibid., p. 159.
30 Derek Hudson, *For Love of Painting* (London, Peter Davies, 1975), p. 43.
31 Hector Bolitho, 'The Other Somerset Maugham', unpublished ms. Texas mss.
32 As quoted by Gittings and Manson, p. 5.
33 Frank Swinnerton, *Figures in the Foreground* (London, Hutchinson, 1963), p. 92.
34 Jack Hawkins, *Anything For a Quiet Life* (London, Hamish Hamilton, 1973), p. 43.
35 G. B. Stern, 'Somerset Maugham Comes of Age', p. 68.
36 Cathleen Nesbitt to R. L. Calder, September 1976.
37 Frederic Raphael, 'A Visit to the Villa Mauresque', *Saturday Review/World* (5 October 1974), p. 23.
38 Ludovic Kennedy to R. L. Calder, 2 January 1977.
39 Alec Waugh, 'W.S.M.: R.I.P.', *My Brother Evelyn and Other Profiles* (London, Cassell, 1967), p. 283.
40 Beverley Nichols, 'W. Somerset Maugham, or Dark and Difficult', *Are They the Same at Home?* (New York, Doran, 1927), p. 209.
41 Rebecca West, 'W. Somerset Maugham', *Nash's Magazine*, p. 97.
42 John Sutro, 'Le Grincheux', *London Magazine* (January 1967), p. 105.
43 George Rylands to R. L. Calder, and quoted in 'The Faces of Maugham', p. 169.
44 Raphael, 'A Visit to the Villa Mauresque', p. 22.
45 *Strictly Personal*, p. 162.
46 Robin Maugham, *Conversations With Willie* (London, W. H. Allen, 1978), pp. 113–14.
47 Karl G. Pfeiffer, *Somerset Maugham: A Candid Portrait* (London, Victor Gollancz, 1959), p. 178.
48 Hector Bolitho, 'The Other Somerset Maugham', *Medical News* (21 January 1966), p. 20.
49 Letter to the Editor, *Daily Telegraph* (26 May 1966), p. 28.
50 F. T. Bason, *A Bibliography of the Writings of William Somerset Maugham* (London, Unicorn, 1931), p. 16.
51 F. T. Bason, 'My Who's Who', *The Saturday Book*, Seventh Issue (London, Hutchinson, 1947), p. 42.
52 As quoted by Robert Rhodes James, *Victor Cazalet: A Portrait* (London, Hamish Hamilton, 1976), p. 144.
53 As quoted by George Bishop, *Barry Jackson and the London Theatre* (London, Arthur Barker, 1973), p. 146.
54 'Why Mr Maugham Wrote It', *Daily Express* (3 November 1932), p. 11.
55 *For Services Rendered, The Collected Plays of W. Somerset Maugham*, III, p. 164.
56 *Sunday Times* (6 November 1932), p. 6.
57 'Theatre', *Saturday Review* (12 November 1932), p. 503.
58 *Daily Express* (17 November 1932), p. 10.
59 *Daily Express* (19 November 1932), p. 8.
60 *Guardian Weekly* (13 May 1979), p. 22.
61 *The Narrow Corner* (New York, Doubleday, Doran, 1932), p. 314.
62 Ibid., p. 206.
63 Frederic Raphael, *Somerset Maugham and His World* (London, Thames and Hudson, 1975), p. 78.
64 Robin Maugham to Kevin Byrne, in an interview commissioned by R. L. Calder for the Canadian Broadcasting Corporation 'Ideas' programme.
65 W. S. Maugham, *The Narrow Corner*, p. 129.
66 Ibid., pp. 253–4.

67 Raphael, pp. 78–9.
68 Harold Acton, *Memoirs of an Aesthete* (London, Methuen, 1948), pp. 189–90.
69 Frederic Prokosch, *Voices: A Memoir* (New York, Farrar, Straus, Giroux, 1983), p. 259.
70 Anthony Curtis, *The Pattern of Maugham* (London, Hamish Hamilton, 1974), p. 226.
71 Peter Burton, 'W. Somerset Maugham: The Man, the Mask, and the Writer', *Gay News* (31 January–13 February 1974), p. 11.
72 *New Yorker* (3 March 1986), p. 85.
73 Peter Burton to R. L. Calder.
74 *College English* (November 1974), p. 285.
75 *Complete Short Stories*, I, pp. 112–13.
76 Ibid., pp. 917–18.
77 Ibid., p. 936.
78 Ibid., p. 949.
79 *Complete Short Stories*, II, p. 548.
80 *Complete Short Stories*, I, p. 793.
81 Ibid., p. 794.
82 Leopold Bellak, 'Somerset Maugham: A Thematic Analysis of Ten Short Stories', p. 171.
83 Bellak to R. L. Calder, 21 December 1981.
84 Robin Maugham to Kevin Byrne.

7 Curtain Calls: 1932–1939

1 As quoted by Zolotow, *Stagestruck* (New York, Harcourt, Brace and World, 1964), p. 196.
2 Maugham to Back, 1932. Texas mss.
3 Jean Rhys, *Letters*, ed. Francis Wyndham and Diana Melly (New York, Viking, 1984), p. 29.
4 Richard B. Fisher, *Syrie Maugham* (London, Duckworth, 1978), p. 19.
5 Maugham to Back, 24 February 1937. Texas mss.
6 Maugham to Alanson, 15 March 1938. Stanford mss.
7 As quoted by Hamilton Basso, 'Very Old Party – II', *New Yorker* (6 January 1945), p. 30.
8 Peter Burton, 'An Interview With Robin Maugham', *Gay Sunshine* (Summer/Fall, 1977), p. 24.
9 Robin Maugham, *Somerset and All the Maughams* (New York, Signet Books, 1966), p. 201.
10 *The Summing Up*, p. 8.
11 Ibid., p. 317.
12 Ibid., p. 10.
13 V. S. Pritchett, 'Living and Writing', *Fortnightly Review* (March 1938), pp. 369–70.
14 Bruce Lockhart, *Diaries, Vol. I: 1915–1938*, ed. Kenneth Young (London, Macmillan, 1973), p. 379.
15 Jane S. Smith, *Elsie de Wolfe* (New York, Atheneum, 1982), p. 276.
16 *A Writer's Notebook*, pp. 272–3.
17 Ted Morgan, *Maugham* (New York, Simon and Schuster, 1980), p. 413.
18 *A Writer's Notebook*, pp. 289–90.
19 Ibid., p. 276.
20 Virginia Woolf, *Leave the Letters Till We're Dead*. ed. Nigel Nicolson and Joanne Trautmann (London, Hogarth Press, 1980), p. 112.
21 Geoffrey West, 'The Artist and the World Today', *The Bookman* (May 1934), p. 92.

22 André David to R. L. Calder.
23 Glenway Wescott, *Images of Truth* (London, Hamish Hamilton, 1963), pp. 71–2.
24 G. B. Stern, *And Did He Stop and Speak to You* (London, Coram, 1957), p 32.
25 Virginia Woolf, *Diaries*, V, ed. Anne Olivier Bell (London, Hogarth Press, 1984, pp. 184–85.
26 Christopher Isherwood, *Christopher and His Kind: 1929–1939* (New York, Farrar, Straus, Giroux, 1976), pp. 325–7.
27 Cole Lesley, *The Life of Noël Coward* (Harmondsworth, Penguin, 1978), p. 224.
28 Maugham to Robin Maugham, 11 February 1939. Texas mss.
29 Maugham to Alanson, 25 February 1939. Stanford mss.

8   The Old Party at War: 1939–1946

1 Gerald Haxton to Robin Maugham, 28 September 1939. Texas mss.
2 J. N. Parrish to Alexander Frere, 1 February 1940, Heinemann archives.
3 Alan Searle to Alanson, 24 October 1939. Stanford mss.
4 Maugham to Marsh, 14 November 1939. Berg mss.
5 Maugham to Frederic Maugham, 7 November 1939. Texas mss.
6 Bruce Lockhart, *Comes the Reckoning* (London, Putnam, 1947), p. 76.
7 Maugham to William Lyon Phelps, 15 April 1940. Yale mss.
8 As quoted by Jacques Chambrun, 'Mr Maugham's Magic Cup', *Reader's Digest* (December 1954), p. 10.
9 Payne to Golding Bright, 8 July 1940. Indiana mss.
10 'Author Tells of Flight', *New York Times* (10 July 1940), p. 8.
11 W. S. Maugham files, BBC Written Archives Centre, Caversham Park.
12 'Talk on France', 'Radio News Reel', BBC mss.
13 Frederic Raphael, *Somerset Maugham and His World* (London, Thames and Hudson, 1975), pp. 87–8.
14 Vincent Sheean, *Between the Thunder and the Sun* (London, Macmillan, 1943), p. 194.
15 As quoted by Michael Swan, *Ilex and Olive* (London, Home and Van Thal, 1949), p. 75.
16 As quoted by Donald McLachlan, *In the Chair: Barrington-Ward of the Times: 1927–1948* (London, Weidenfeld and Nicolson, 1971), pp. 234–5.
17 Jean Goodman, *The Mond Legacy* (London, Weidenfeld and Nicolson, 1982), p. 183.
18 H. Montgomery Hyde to R. L. Calder.
19 Maugham to Alanson, 13 October 1940. Stanford mss.
20 Karl G. Pfeiffer, *Somerset Maugham: A Candid Portrait* (London, Victor Gollancz, 1959), p. 169.
21 Ted Morgan, *Maugham* (New York, Simon and Schuster, 1980), p. 447.
22 Ted Berkman, *The Lady and the Law* (Boston, Little, Brown, 1981), pp. 215–17.
23 Maugham to Alanson, 13 October 1940. Stanford mss.
24 Edward Weeks, *Writers and Friends* (Boston, Little, Brown, 1981), pp. 21–2.
25 Vera Brittain, *Testament of Experience* (London, Gollancz, 1957), p. 235.
26 David Daiches to R. L. Calder, 27 September 1976.
27 Maugham to Robin Maugham, 23 May 1941. Texas mss.
28 Maugham to Marsh, 1 March 1943. Berg mss.
29 Ralph Gustafson to R. L. Calder, 21 March 1982.
30 Ibid.
31 Maugham to Margot Hill, 24 April 1941. Fales mss.
32 Gerald Kelly to R. L. Calder.
33 Sir Cedric Hardwicke, *A Victorian in Orbit* (New York, Doubleday, 1961), p. 237.

34 Edward Marsh, *Ambrosia and Small Beer*, p. 163.
35 As quoted by Brian Finney, *Christopher Isherwood* (New York, Oxford University Press, 1979), p. 180.
36 Christopher Isherwood to Sybille Bedford, quoted in Sybille Bedford, *Aldous Huxley: A Biography*, Vol. II (London: Chatto and Windus, 1974), p. 23.
37 *A Writer's Notebook*, p. 353.
38 As quoted by John Keats, *You Might as Well Live* (New York, Simon and Schuster, 1970), pp. 237–8.
39 Maugham to Marsh, 1 April 1942. Berg mss.
40 '*Life* Calls on Somerset Maugham', *Life* (18 September 1944), p. 123.
41 Bernard Rosenberg and Harry Silverstein (eds), *The Real Tinsel* (New York, Macmillan, 1978), p. 120.
42 Unidentified newspaper cutting. Stanford mss.
43 As quoted by André David, *Pleins Feux sur Hollywood* (Paris, André Bonne, 1956), p. 123.
44 Christopher Isherwood, *My Guru and His Disciple* (London, Eyre Methuen, 1980), pp. 183–4.
45 Garson Kanin, *Remembering Mr Maugham* (New York, Atheneum, 1966), p. 113.
46 W. S. Maugham, *The Razor's Edge* (New York, Doubleday, 1944), p. 343.
47 As quoted by Kanin, p. 107.
48 Maugham to Rudolf Kommer, 24 February 1943. Lilly mss.
49 Maugham to Back, 10 September 1943. Texas mss.
50 *A Writer's Notebook*, pp. 352–3.
51 Ibid., p. 357.
52 Maugham to Alanson, 23 January 1944. Stanford mss.
53 Maugham to Alanson, 1 July 1944. Stanford mss.
54 Maugham to Alanson, 29 April 1944. Stanford mss.
55 Gustafson to R. L. Calder, 21 March 1982.
56 Maugham to Back, 9 September 1944. Texas mss.
57 Maugham to Knoblock, 2 October 1944. Berg mss.
58 Cecil Roberts, 'Memories of Maugham', *Books and Bookmen* (July 1974), p. 21.
59 Glenway Wescott, as quoted by Morgan, p. 489.
60 Maugham to Margot Hill, 25 April 1945. Fales mss.
61 Isherwood, p. 185.
62 As quoted by Gavin Lambert, *On Cukor* (New York, Putnam's, 1972), p. 229.
63 Ibid., pp. 232, 235.
64 *A Writer's Notebook*, p. 345.
65 W. S. Maugham, *Then and Now* (New York, Doubleday, 1946), pp. 277–8.
66 Maugham to Stern, 7 October 1945. Texas mss.
67 Maugham to Back, 7 May 1946. Texas mss.
68 Searle to Alanson, 22 April 1946. Stanford mss.
69 Searle to Alanson, 9 May 1946. Stanford mss.

9 Grand Old Man: 1946–1958

1 Cyril Connolly, 'Maugham: Compassionate Cynic', p. 35.
2 Reported by Michael Swan, 'Conversations With Maugham', p. 70, and S. H. Vilette. 'Retour de Somerset Maugham', *Les Nouvelles Littéraires* (11 July 1946), p. 1.
3 Searle to R. L. Calder.
4 Ibid.
5 Laurence Brander, *Somerset Maugham: A Guide* (London, Oliver and Boyd, 1965), p. 195.

6 As quoted by William Hickey, 'Somerset Maugham Sums Up', *Daily Express* (20 January 1958), p. 3.

7 Peter Quennell, *The Wanton Chase* (London, Collins, 1980), p. 163.

8 As quoted by Ilsa Sharp, *There is Only One Raffles* (London, Souvenir Press, 1981), p. 108.

9 As quoted by Gavin Lambert, *On Cukor* (New York, Putnam's, 1972), pp. 233–4.

10 A. P. Watt Ltd to Louise Callender, 17 December 1948, Heinemann archives.

11 Maugham to Ann Fleming, 3 July 1958. Fleming mss.

12 As quoted by William Hickey, p. 3.

13 John Beavan, 'Maugham: A "Free Man" at 85', *New York Times* (25 January 1959), p. 37.

14 As quoted by Val Adams, 'A Minute-and-a-Half Work Week', *New York Times* (11 November 1950), p. 13.

15 Edmund Wilson, 'The Apotheosis of Somerset Maugham', in *Classical and Commercials* (New York, Farrar and Straus, 1958), p. 326.

16 S. N. Behrman, *People in a Diary* (Boston, Little, Brown, 1972), p. 284.

17 *New Yorker* (25 December 1965), p. 17.

18 Kelly to Alanson, 3 March 1953. Stanford mss.

19 St John Irvine to Richard Church, 19 February 1954. Texas mss. Published by permission of the Society of Authors © the Estate of St John Irvine.

20 T. S. Strachan typescript. Texas mss.

21 Maugham to Alanson, 27 June 1954. Stanford mss.

22 Arthur Marshall to R. L. Calder.

23 F. J. Shirley, 'William Somerset Maugham', *The Cantuarian* (December 1965), p. 21.

24 Robin Maugham, *Somerset and All the Maughams* (New York, Signet Books, 1967), p. 147.

25 Frederic Prokosch, *Voices: A Memoir* (New York, Farrar, Straus, Giroux, 1983), pp. 257–8.

26 H. Montgomery Hyde, *The Other Love* (London, Heinemann, 1970), p. 190.

27 As quoted by Peter Burton, 'Robin Maugham', p. 27.

28 Beverley Nichols, *A Case of Human Bondage* (London, Secker and Warburg, 1966), p. 13.

29 Michael Darlow and Gillian Hodson, *Terence Rattigan* (London, Quartet Books, 1979), p. 228.

30 As quoted by Hugo Vickers, *Cecil Beaton* (London Weidenfeld and Nicolson, 1985), p. 41.

31 Hector Bolitho, 'The Other Somerset Maugham', *Medical News* (21 January 1966), p. 20.

32 'Somerset Maugham Makes a Very Odd Request', *Daily Mail* (12 November 1957), p. 12.

33 Shirley, p. 19.

34 J. P. P. Newell to R. L. Calder, 25 June 1976.

35 Shirley, p. 21.

36 As quoted by William Merchant, *The Privilege of His Company* (New York, Bobbs-Merrill, 1975), p. 66.

37 As quoted by Roderick Cameron, *The Golden Riviera* (London, Weidenfeld and Nicolson, 1975), p. 233.

38 'A Visit to Maugham, and a Visit from Coward', *The Times* (10 April 1971), p. 15.

39 Alan Searle to R. L. Calder.

40 Richard Shulman to R. L. Calder.

41 As quoted by Alistair Forbes, 'All About Evelyn', *Times Literary Supplement* (3 September 1976), p. 1074.

42 Philip Ziegler, *Diana Cooper* (London, Penguin, 1983), p. 306.
43 Alan Searle to R. L. Calder.
44 Meryle Secrest, *Between Me and Life* (New York, Doubleday, 1974), pp. 366–7.
45 Georges Rosanoff to R. L. Calder.
46 As quoted by Thomas F. Brady, 'The Eighty Years of Mr Maugham', *New York Times* (24 January 1954), p. 53.
47 Searle to Alanson, 18 July 1952. Stanford mss.
48 Maugham to Alanson, 23 July 1952. Stanford mss.
49 Searle to Kitty Black, 13 June 1958. Indiana mss.
50 As quoted by Patrick McGrady, *The Youth Doctors* (New York, Coward-McCann, 1968), p. 119.
51 Rebecca West to R. L. Calder.
52 Ann Fleming to R. L. Calder.
53 Georges Rosanoff to R. L. Calder.
54 As quoted by Leonard Mosley, 'Matters of Mink, Matisse and Malady', *Daily Telegraph Magazine* (14 November 1975), p. 32.
55 Georges Rosanoff to R. L. Calder.
56 'Lines Please', *Daily Express* (12 December 1957), p. 10.
57 As quoted by Leon Edel, 'The Figure Under the Carpet', *Telling Lives: The Biographer's Art*, ed. Marc Pachter (Washington, New Republic Books, 1979), p. 34.
58 Roger Berthoud, *Graham Sutherland: A Biography* (London, Faber, 1982), pp. 141, 142.
59 Graham Sutherland to R. L. Calder.
60 As quoted by Derek Hudson, *For Love of Painting* (London, Peter Davies, 1975), p. 107.
61 Jacob Epstein, *Epstein: An Autobiography* (London, Vista Books, 1955), p. 235.
62 Yousuf Karsh, *Karsh Portfolio* (Toronto, University of Toronto Press, 1967), p 167.
63 'My Friend Willy', *News of the World* (26 January 1964), p. 15.
64 Lord Butler, *The Art of the Possible* (London, Hamish Hamilton, 1971), p. 183.
65 Francis King to R. L. Calder.
66 Georges Rosanoff to R. L. Calder.
67 As quoted by Fleur Cowles, *Friends and Memories* (London, Cape, 1975), p. 86.
68 As quoted by Berthoud, p. 199.
69 Robin Maugham, *Conversations With Willie* (London, W. H. Allen, 1978), p. 116.
70 Raymond Marriott to R. L. Calder.
71 Derek Patmore, *Private History* (London, Jonathan Cape, 1960), p. 186.
72 Ethel Barrymore, p. 291.
73 Graham Payn and Sheridan Morley (eds), *The Noël Coward Diaries* (London, Macmillan, 1982), p. 135.
74 Channon, p. 448.
75 Ibid., p. 450.
76 Michael Davidson, *The World, the Flesh, and Myself* (London, Arthur Barker, 1962), p. 287.
77 Julien Green, *Diary 1928–1957*. Selected by Kurt Wolff, translated by Anne Green (London, Collins and Harvill, 1964), p. 251.
78 *Coward Diaries*, p. 223.
79 Harold Acton, *Nancy Mitford* (London, Hamish Hamilton, 1975), p. 97.
80 'The New Somerset Maugham', *Holiday* (February 1954), pp. 16, 18.
81 *Coward Diaries*, p. 381.
82 Ibid., p. 359.
83 'Looking Back', *Show* (August 1962), p. 100.
84 Searle to Alanson, 4 December 1952. Stanford mss.
85 Searle to R. L. Calder.

86 Searle to Kitty Black, 16 February 1957. Indiana mss.
87 Searle to John Barber, 18 October 1963. Indiana mss.
88 Searle to R. L. Calder.
89 Cecil Beaton, *The Strenuous Years* (London, Weidenfeld and Nicolson, 1973), p. 28.
90 Searle to R. L. Calder.
91 Georges Rosanoff, *Racontez . . . Docteur!* (Paris, Guy le Prat, 1977), p. 141.
92 Francis King to R. L. Calder.
93 Rebecca West to R. L. Calder.
94 Kenneth Clark to R. L. Calder, 29 December 1981.
95 Letter to *The Times*, 14 September 1985, p. 10.
96 Lord Boothby to R. L. Calder, 6 March 1982.
97 Robin Maugham, *Somerset and All the Maughams*, pp. 206, 214.
98 Beverley Nichols, *A Case of Human Bondage*, pp. 148, 149.
99 Cyril Connolly, 'When the Loving Kindness Stopped', *Sunday Times* (3 April 1966), p. 34.
100 Maugham to Bateman, 10 September 1948. Yale mss.
101 Searle to Alanson, 12 January 1950. Stanford mss.
102 Searle to Alanson, 4 March 1950. Stanford mss.
103 Searle to Alanson, 8 February 1955. Stanford mss.
104 Searle to Alanson, 29 January 1953, Stanford mss.
105 Searle to Alanson, 28 January 1958. Stanford mss.
106 As quoted by Anthony Curtis, *Somerset Maugham* (London Weidenfeld and Nicolson, 1977), p. 175.
107 Maugham to Alanson, 25 April 1958. Stanford mss.
108 Maugham to Back, 14 January 1957. Texas mss.
109 Maugham to Alanson, 13 October 1952. Stanford mss.
110 Maugham to Alanson, 28 July 1955. Stanford mss.
111 As quoted by Peter Burton, *Parallel Lives* (London, GMP Publishers, 1985), p. 89.
112 Ibid., p. 76.
113 Lord Glendevon, 1 November 1988.
114 Maugham to Alanson, 10 April 1949. Stanford mss.
115 Ann Fleming to R. L. Calder.
116 Mark Amory (ed.), *The Letters of Ann Fleming* (London, Collins Harvill, 1985), p. 184.
117 As quoted by William Hickey, *Daily Express* (7 May 1959), p. 15.
118 Dorothy Gardiner and Kathrine Sorley Walker (eds), *Raymond Chandler Speaking* (London, Hamish Hamilton, 1962), p. 86.
119 Beavan, p. 14.

10 The Burden of One's Memories: 1959–1965

1 As quoted by Gordon Young, 'The Scum and I', *Sunday Dispatch* (6 October 1957), p. 8.
2 William Hickey, *Daily Express* (7 May 1959), p. 15 and Paul Tanfield, 'It's Against Doctor's Orders, But Maugham (at 85) Still Dives', *Daily Mail* (18 May 1959), p. 10.
3 'Maugham Keeps Book Secret', *New York Times* (10 November 1959), p. 9 and Richard Hughes, 'Tokyo En Fête for Maugham', *Sunday Times* (15 November 1959).
4 'Yachts? Caviar? Not For Me, Says Mr Maugham', *Sunday Express* (19 April 1959), p. 6.
5 Francis King to R. L. Calder.

6 As quoted in 'Maugham Predicts World Use of English Within 3 Centuries', *New York Times* (26 January 1960), p. 29.

7 Ilsa Sharp, *There is Only One Raffles* (London, Souvenir Press, 1981), p. 83.

8 Francis King to R. L. Calder.

9 Sharp, p. 108.

10 Peter Quennell (ed.), *A Lonely Business: a Self Portrait of James Pope-Hennessy* (London, Weidenfeld and Nicolson, 1981), p. 110.

11 Sharp, p. 106.

12 Searle to Jonas, 6 October 1960. Texas mss.

13 Searle to Jonas, 18 June 1961. Texas mss.

14 Searle to Jonas, 7 July 1961. Texas mss.

15 'People', *Time* (11 August 1961), p. 28.

16 Felix Marti-Ibanez to Klaus Jonas, 26 September 1961. Texas mss.

17 Ted Morgan, *Maughan* (New York, Simon and Schuster, 1980), p. 599.

18 Rebecca West to R. L. Calder.

19. John Sutro, 'Le Grincheux', *London Magazine* (January 1967), p. 105, p. 102.

20 Searle to Jonas, 6 September 1960. Texas mss.

21 Searle to Jonas, 20 December 1960. Texas mss.

22 Gerald McKnight, *The Scandal of Syrie Maugham* (London, W. H. Allen, 1980), p. 213.

23 As quoted by McKnight, pp. 213, 211.

24 *The Summing Up*, pp. 195–6.

25 As quoted by Michael Wardell, 'A Visit to Somerset Maugham', *Atlantic Advocate* (April 1962), p. 28.

26 Searle to R. L. Calder.

27 Lord Glendevon, as quoted by McKnight, p. 211.

28 Ann Fleming to R. L. Calder.

29 As quoted by Gavin Lambert, *On Cukor* (New York, Putnam's, 1972), p. 235.

30 Beverley Nichols, 'Exhuming Maugham', *Books and Bookmen* (May 1980), p. 14.

31 Cecil Beaton, *The Strenuous Years* (London, Weidenfeld and Nicolson, 1973), p. 27.

32 Peter Quennell, *The Wanton Chase* (London, Collins, 1980), p. 164.

33 Kenneth Clark, *The Other Half: a Self Portrait* (Toronto, Longmans, 1977), p. 116.

34 Georges Rosanoff to R. L. Calder.

35 Rupert Hart-Davis (ed.), *The Lyttelton Hart-Davis Letters*, vol. VI (London, John Murray, 1978), p. 119.

36 Gerald Kelly to R. L. Calder.

37 Morgan, pp. 594–7.

38 Mark Amory (ed.), *The Letters of Ann Fleming* (London, Collins Harvill, 1985), p. 184.

39 Morgan, pp. 595–6.

40 *New York Times* (2 October 1961), p. 28.

41 Morgan, p. 598.

42 Maugham to Ann Fleming, undated. Fleming mss.

43 Robin Maugham, *Somerset and All the Maughams* (New York, Signet Books, 1967), p. 223.

44 Searle to Jonas, 31 March 1962. Texas mss.

45 Maugham to Ann Fleming, 5 April 1962. Fleming mss.

46 Graham Payn and Sheridan Morley (eds), *The Noël Coward Diaries* (London, Macmillan, 1982), p 504.

47 Garson Kanin, *Remembering Mr Maugham* (New York, Atheneum, 1966), p. 17.

48 Searle to Jonas, 13 July 1962. Texas mss.

49 Morgan, pp. 603–4.

50 *Coward Diaries*, p. 511.
51 Alec Waugh, 'W.S.M: R.I.P', *My Brother Evelyn and Other Profiles* (London, Cassell, 1967), p. 292.
52 'Maugham Suit Against Lady John Hope', *Daily Telegraph* (28 December 1962), p. 1.
53 'Ruling Against 89-Year-Old Writer Touches Dispute on Sale of Paintings', *New York Times* (4 July 1963), p. 2.
54 'Maugham Suit Puzzles Lady John Hope', *Daily Telegraph* (29 December 1962), p. 9.
55 'Author's Daughter "Loves Him Dearly"', *Pittsburgh Press* (29 December 1962).
56 Morgan, p. 608.
57 'Ruling Against 89-Year-Old Writer', p. 2.
58 'Maugham Family Settles Dispute', *New York Times* (23 January 1964), p. 33.
59 Searle to Jonas, 15 November 1963. Texas mss.
60 Sam Behrman to Richard Cordell, 29 November 1963. Lilly mss.
61 Arthur Marshall to R. L. Calder.
62 Graham Sutherland to R. L. Calder.
63 Lionel Hale to R. L. Calder.
64 Stephen Coulter, 'Maugham at Ninety', *Sunday Times* (19 January 1964), p. 30.
65 Maugham to Grace Morse, 28 January 1963. Lilly mss.
66 Kenneth Allsop, 'Grand Old Maugham', pp. 96–7.
67 Lionel Hale to R. L. Calder.
68 'Maugham at 90 Defies Doctors and Celebrates', *New York Times* (25 January 1964), p. 28.
69 *The Times* (27 January 1964), p. 12.
70 Coulter, p. 30.
71 *Toronto Globe and Mail* (20 September 1984), p. 13.
72 'Maugham Talks', *Daily Express* (23 January 1964), p. 6.
73 Maugham to Ian Fleming, 7 May 1964. Lilly mss.
74 Searle to Jonas, 7 May 1964. Texas mss.
75 W. S. Maugham, *Points of View*, p. 55.
76 Searle to R. L. Calder.
77 Robin Maugham, *Somerset and All the Maughams*, pp. 207, 219.
78 'On His Ninetieth Birthday', *A Traveller in Romance*, p. 263.
79 Ann Fleming to R. L. Calder.
80 'On His Ninetieth Birthday', p. 263.
81 Searle to Patrick Kinross, 28 December 1964. Huntington mss.
82 Waugh, p. 271
83 Robin Maugham, *Somerset and All the Maughams*, p. 220.
84 Hector Bolitho, 'The Other Somerset Maugham', unpublished ms. Texas mss.
85 Robin Maugham, *Conversations with Willie* (London, W. H. Allen, 1978), p. 178.
86 Searle to Kinross, 28 December 1964. Huntington mss.
87 'At the Villa Mauresque', *Sunday Times* (12 September 1965), p. 48.
88 *Coward Diaries*, p. 607.
89 Raymond Mortimer to R. L. Calder.
90 Searle to R. L. Calder.
91 Leonard Mosley, 'Matters of Mink, Matisse and Malady', *Daily Telegraph Magazine* (14 November 1975), p. 32.
92 F. J. Shirley, 'William Somerset Maugham', *The Cantuarian* (December 1965), p. 22.
93 J. P. Newell to R. L. Calder, 26 June 1976.
94 'At the Villa Mauresque', p. 48.
95 Raymond Marriott.
96 Hector Bolitho, 'The Other Somerset Maugham'.

INDEX